Key Buildings from Prehistory to the Present

Plans, Sections and Elevations

Andrew Ballantyne

Published in 2012
by Laurence King Publishing Ltd
361–373 City Road
London EC1V 1LR
Tel +44 (0)20 7841 6900
Fax +44 (0)20 7841 6910
E enquiries@laurenceking.com
www.laurenceking.com

A catalogue record for this book is available from the British Library

ISBN 978 185669 837 5
Project managed and edited by Henrietta Heald
Designed by The Urban Ant Ltd.
Picture research by Claire Gouldstone
Printed in Hong Kong

Key Buildings from Prehistory to the Present

Plans, Sections and Elevations

Andrew Ballantyne

Laurence King Publishing

Contents

Introduction

Great Temple of Amon-Ra

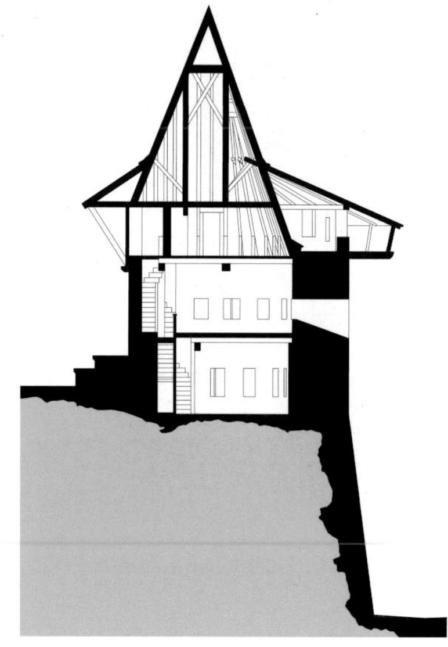

Carcassonne

Architecture does many things, and ***Key Buildings from Prehistory to the Present*** explores a range of them. Each chapter covers an aspect of architecture through a number of buildings from around the world. The buildings are illustrated in plan, section and elevation, as well as photographically, and appear in chronological order in each category.

In many cases, a building could be put in more than one category. The **Great Pyramid of Khufu** (pages 14–15) is a memorial and the **Empire State Building** (pages 38–39) is an office building, for example, but they are both included in chapter 1 in order to highlight how some buildings come to designate a culture. There is an international shorthand that can evoke the idea of a complex and varied country in an image of a single building. France is signified by the **Eiffel Tower** (pages 36–37), China by the **Twin Pagodas** at Suzhou (pages 30–31).

The choice of representative buildings poses a dilemma. While the best buildings are remarkable, ordinary buildings can tell us far more about the culture, climate and technology of the society that made them. This tension is clearest in chapter 2, whose subject is dwellings. It includes traditional houses from different parts of the world alongside some acknowledged masterpieces and royal retreats. One of the **Karo Batak Houses** in Sumatra (pages 58–59) is different in every way from Andrea Palladio's **Villa Capra** (pages 70–71) or the castle of **Neuschwanstein** (pages 84–85), for example, except that all three were dwellings that met the needs of their occupants.

Places of worship, covered in chapter 3, always call for special efforts from the community that builds them, and they usually have pride of place in a settlement. Sometimes – as in the case of the **Great Temple of Amon-Ra** (pages 100–101) – they are associated with the state and can be colossal. Other examples, such as the **Lingaraj Temple** (pages 122–23) and the **Basilica of the Madeleine** at Vézelay (pages 130–31), have been sustained by popular support from pilgrims.

At the heart of chapter 4 are historical defences, but those that are still in use can be impossible to document in plan, section and elevation. (For example, Britain's signals-monitoring station at Menwith Hill in Yorkshire could not be represented, despite its eerie beauty.) The Athenian **Acropolis** (pages 168–69) had a military use in the seventeenth century, when a Venetian shell hit a store of Turkish explosives and blew up the Parthenon. It was a celebrated place, but difficult to visit. In the nineteenth century, when they were judged to be militarily redundant, the ramparts of **Carcassonne** (pages 184–85) were transformed into a potent vision of a medieval city.

Villa Capra

Chapter 5 covers buildings where people work, study or pass through on their travels. Such edifices often have to be built economically, but even then their scale and the pride taken in their design can make them internationally significant. Titus Salt's worsted mill at **Saltaire** (pages 208–209) and the **AEG Turbine Factory** in Berlin (pages 220–21) are buildings designed for a firmly utilitarian purpose that have nevertheless had a profound cultural influence.

Chapter 6 is concerned with government buildings ranging from the grandiose **Residenz at Würzburg** (pages 252–53) to Alvar Aalto's little **Säynatsälo Town Hall** in Finland (pages 260–61), while chapter 7 is devoted to buildings designed to enhance the quality of people's lives. The **Theatre at Epidauros** (pages 266–67), a sanctuary and health resort, transformed the slope of a hillside into a powerful geometric form that, even now, commands the surrounding landscape.

The memorials described in chapter 8 are reminders of great lives and great deeds. No one now remembers much about the Persian satrap Mausolus, but the **Tomb of Mausolus** (pages 288–89) proved the model for the many mausoleums that followed. The **Lincoln Memorial** (pages 300–301) is not one, since it is not a burial place, but it serves to commemorate a life and to remind a mighty nation of its values.

The public spaces in chapter 9 are reminders of how cities work, illustrating the fact that urban vigour and vitality depend on chance or casual meetings in the street and in public, as well as on formal meetings in more private places.

In short, this book presents a wide range of structural achievements. It is incomplete, of course, but all the examples chosen are interesting and intended to open your eyes to other things that are equally interesting and may be closer to home.

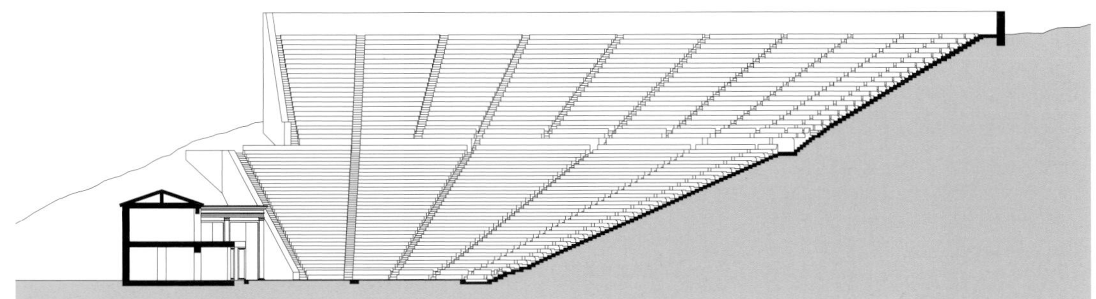

Theatre at Epidauros

Culture-defining monuments

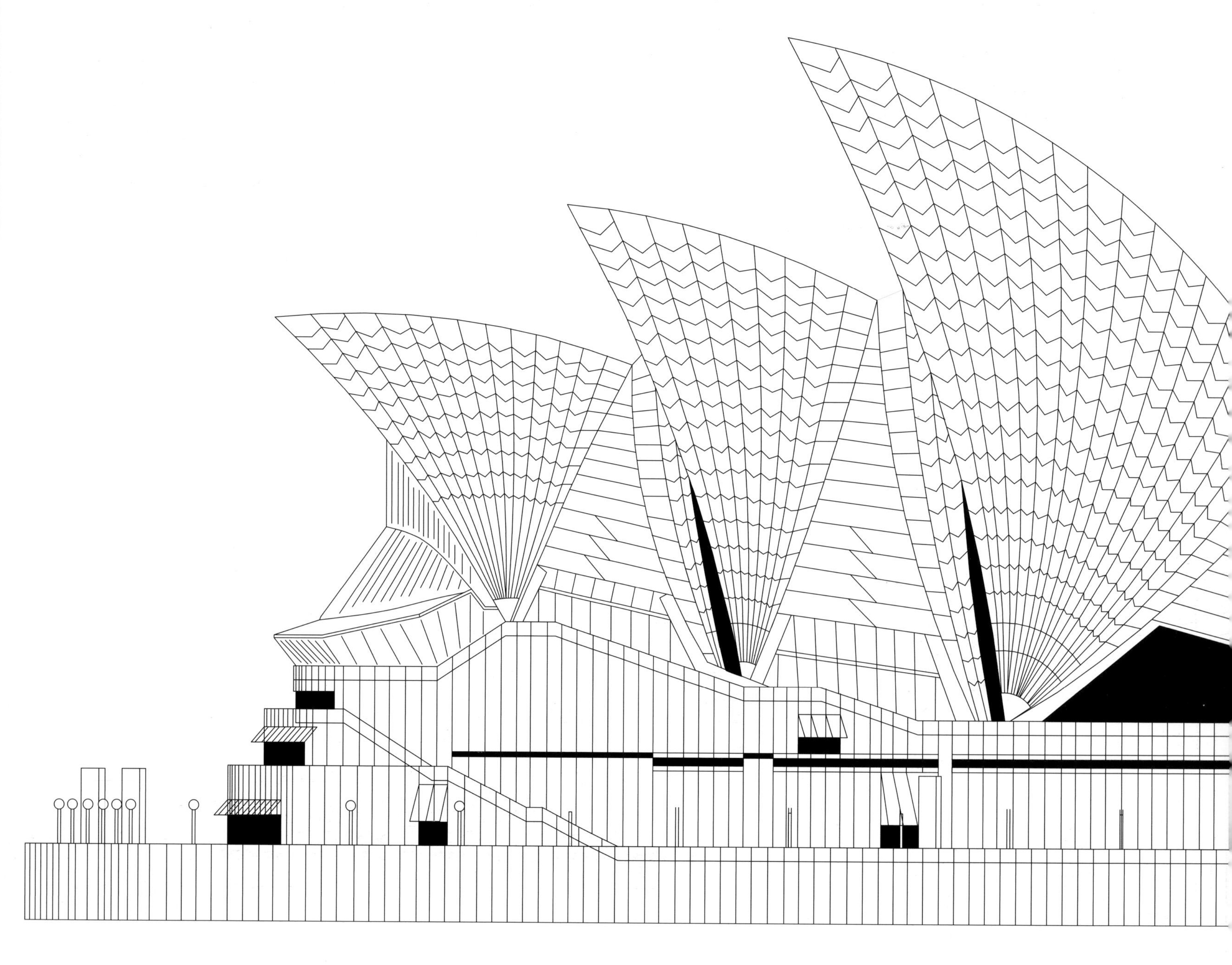

Many cultures produce no monuments. The Mongols were one of the great dynamic civilizations and their culture revolved around horsemanship rather than building. Architectural history hardly notices people such as the Mongols, giving pride of place to sedentary cultures that walled themselves in with blocks of stone – Egyptians, Romans, Chinese.

Uluru is a striking landscape formation that was adopted by the nomadic Aboriginal population in Australia and made to do all the things that monuments do, so it is included in this chapter as landscape architecture that has a monumental role for a culture that grew up around it.

The temples at Tik'al in Guatemala – man-made mountains – are much smaller. The platform at the top of them is tiny compared with the plateau on top of Uluru, but people who make the ascent are touched by a change in feeling about their place in the world that is no less dramatic. At the bottom, there is endless forest, where paths are easily obscured by the quick-growing vegetation and a sense of direction is easily confounded. At the top, the distant horizon can be seen over the tops of the trees. It is like being taken into another world with a completely different conception of space. These structures were plainly important for the civilization that built them – they consumed a huge proportion of the society's resources – and they have come to define the civilization for later ages. How did these people conduct their lives? We hardly know. But we do know that they sacrificed people there – and, for us, this became the civilization's distinguishing characteristic.

There are other places where a raised plateau takes on overtones of divinity, such as the Acropolis at Athens, where the Parthenon was built, and Machu Picchu, where a whole government took on semi-divine status, living as it did among mountain peaks. Perhaps this quality lingers in very tall buildings from the modern world, which invite us to step outside our normal, street-level experience of the city. From the top of the Eiffel Tower or the Empire State Building, the city becomes a landscape, and people who have attained those summits can see their own position in relation to other peaks – the Tour Montparnasse and the Sacré-Coeur, or the Chrysler Building and the Rockefeller Center – just as the rulers at Machu Picchu did. As far as the experience is concerned, it makes little difference whether the landscape is natural or man-made, intended or accidental.

Los Angeles is one of the world's great cities, and it has some fine buildings, many of them shut away from public view, but they do not seem particularly characteristic of the place. Its defining monuments are the freeway interchanges, which work at the scale of a grand landscape. In the modern world, travel is the expression of freedom, and the interchanges are the great monuments to that freedom. Imagine them redundant, a thousand years in the future, when our successors have learned to be content to stay where they are. How metaphysical and monumental those buildings will seem to be.

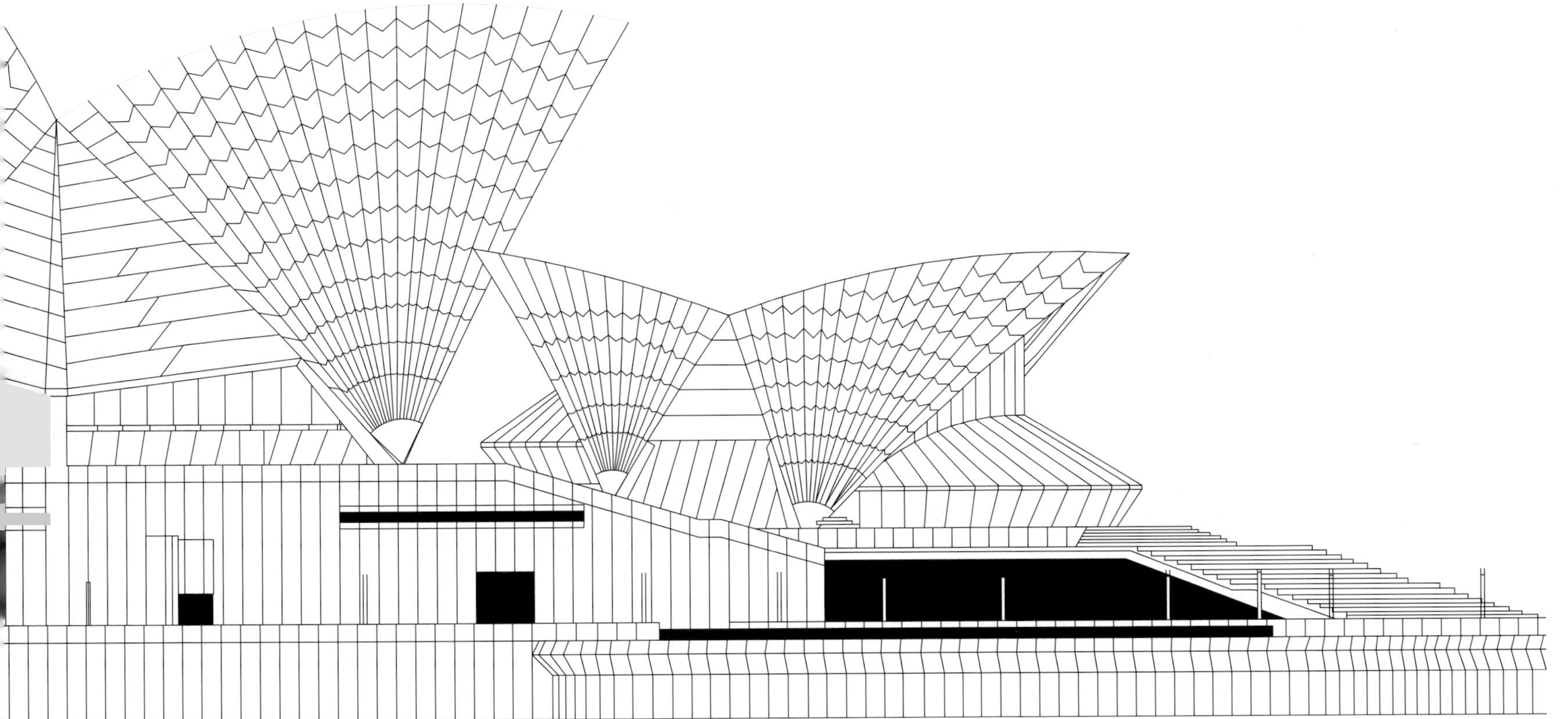

Uluru

Pitjandara tribe

Northern Territory, Australia; Dreamtime

The great rock shown here, which is 345 metres (1,130 feet) high, has two names: Uluru and Ayers Rock. This is because the site has significance for two cultures that both have a hold on it.

The modern administrators of the Australian continent are of European descent, and their history goes back to the nineteenth century, when the name Australia was adopted – derived from the Latin word *australis*, meaning 'of the south'. In this era the rock was named after Sir Henry Ayers, who was governor of Australia in 1873, when the rock was 'discovered' by William Gosse. In 1987 it was designated a UNESCO World Heritage Site.

Seen through European eyes, Ayers Rock is not an architectural object at all, but a striking geological formation that has been left standing above an enormous plain while the surrounding rock has eroded away. At some point in the distant past, the rock's strata must have been deposited horizontally, but upheavals have left it with strata that are now almost vertical.

The visible part is a small proportion of the whole, which penetrates deep underground. The rock's prominence in the landscape means that it can be seen from huge distances, and in different atmospheric conditions, especially when the sun is low in the sky, it seems to change colour and to be responsive and alive. It is a natural wonder, a source of fascination, a place that people want to visit.

The name Uluru has been in use for much longer – maybe for 10,000 years. Aboriginal culture developed separately from that of the continent's incomers, and when the two cultures came into contact it was clear that the Aboriginal people had a fundamentally different way of interpreting the world. In Aboriginal culture there is no linear history or book-learning, and there are no houses. There is strong attachment to place, through a profoundly ingrained nomadic habit of moving along traditional tribal journeys. Many of those journeys converge at Uluru.

There are various accounts in Aboriginal tradition of how the Earth's features took shape. In the time of the ancestors, the Dreamtime, the world was featureless until the rocks were given form by singing or by other means – and the songs that conjured the rocks and streams are sung on the traditional journeys, or Songlines, which maintain the creation.

Far from being unique to the Aboriginal people, the recognition of resonance between place and music is one of the few cultural insights that are very widely shared. In western tradition it was Orpheus who civilized by his song and Amphion who charmed the stones of Thebes into place by music. Joshua at Jericho played music that caused the city walls to fall. German Romantics said that architecture was frozen music. Birdsong establishes territories, and human beings share a surprising amount of DNA with nest-building birds, so perhaps in music and building we awaken our 'inner bird', calling forth ancient primitive instincts.

The various caves and fissures at Uluru are interpreted as incarnations of events that took place there. There is a mouth that silently screams in anguish, a scar that runs with water when a word is shouted, and bodies everywhere. However it came to be as it is, Uluru is experienced in Aboriginal culture as a memorial.

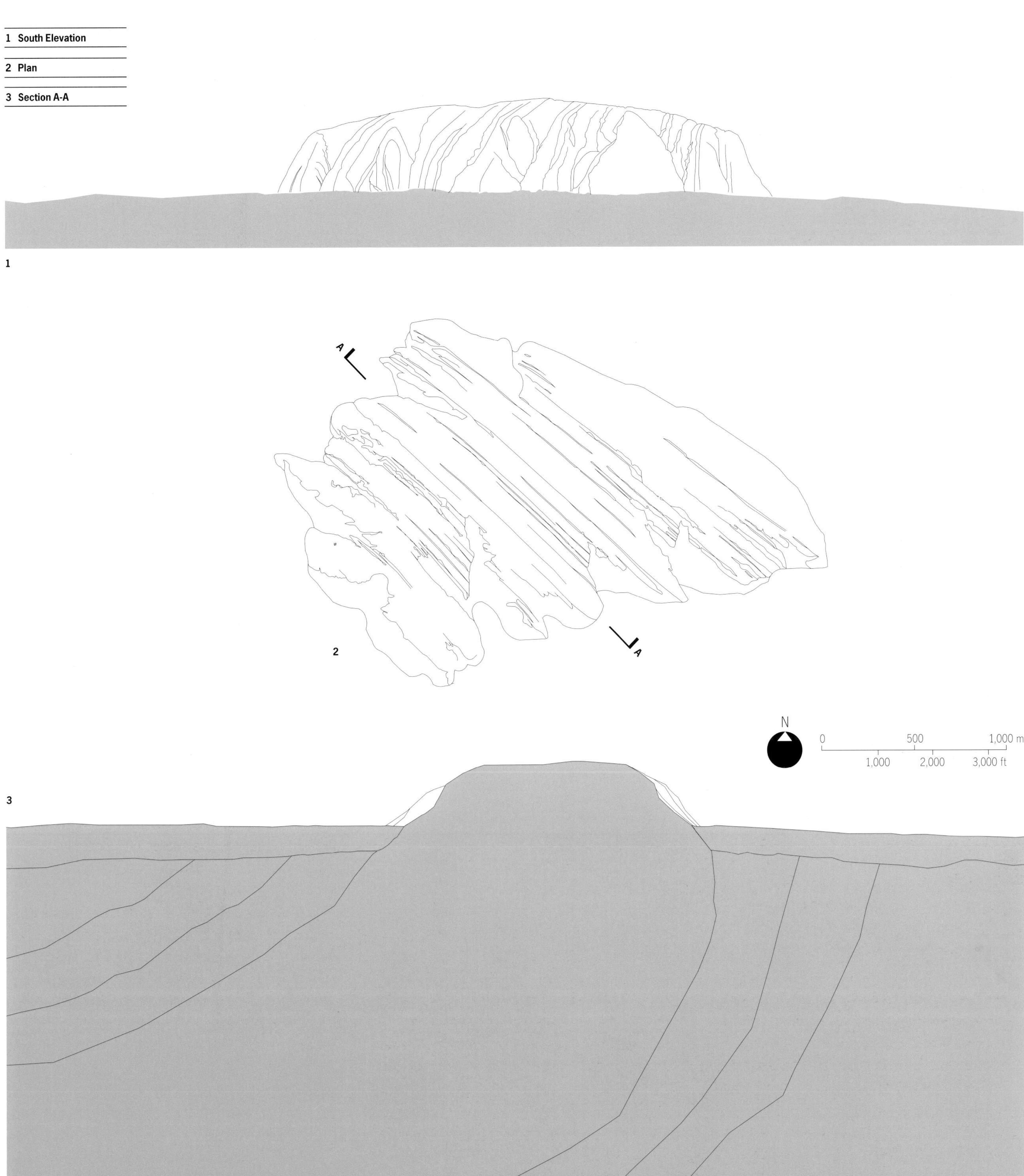
1 South Elevation
2 Plan
3 Section A-A
1
A
A
2
N
0
500
1,000 m
1,000
2,000
3,000 ft
3

Great Pyramid of Khufu

Giza, Egypt; c.2500 BCE

The Great Pyramid at Giza was built to honour a god-king, the pharaoh Khufu, who was called Cheops by the Greeks. It stood 146 metres (480 feet) high and was the tallest man-made structure in the world for 4,000 years, until it was overtopped by the spires of the most ambitious medieval cathedrals.

Khufu's memorial was not the first of its kind, but the last and largest in a 200-year-old tradition that began when Imhotep organized the building of the pyramid at Saqqara (2667 BCE) as a monument to the pharaoh Zoser. Imhotep's pyramid did not have the neat geometrical lines of the later pyramids, but it drew on an already ancient tradition of mud-brick memorials that were low and rectangular in shape, about the size of a single-storey house; the burial was in the earth beneath. These structures recall the mud-brick benches (*mastabas*) that were built outside dwellings.

Zoser's monument resembles a stack of *mastabas*, arranged to make a series of steps. For the first time the *mastabas* were built not in brick but in much more durable stone, as were the other buildings in the complex, some of which are like tents with timber poles and hanging fabrics modelled in stone.

The great pyramids were colossally expensive to construct, and by the time Khufu's pyramid was needed the entire society was structured around the idea of building them. The workforce was available seasonally, when the Nile flooding made it impossible to work the land. The pyramids and the other temples and tombs were built on higher ground, away from the flood plain, on land that could not be cultivated. Egyptian society was centralized in a way that few other ancient societies could be. This was made possible by the Nile, which acted as a thoroughfare and the means of communication that linked the separate parts of the society. Desert land formed a defensive barrier against neighbours to east and west.

The pyramid was the place where the pharaoh was buried, along with treasures and images of everything that he might need to look after his people in the afterlife. Almost all the pyramids were robbed of their treasures in ancient times. The only tomb to have survived for modern investigation was a small set of underground chambers where a relatively insignificant monarch called Tutankhamen was buried. Tutankhamen died young, but the hoard found with him evokes the staggering grandiosity that must have been involved in the burial ceremonies.

All the pyramids date from the third and fourth dynasties of the Old Kingdom of Egypt, which eventually collapsed as the result of drought. But pyramid-building had ended much earlier than that, having apparently been found unsustainable. One factor may have been that the pyramids too blatantly advertised the whereabouts of the royal treasures.

Elaborate rituals were involved in embalming the bodies of pharaohs to prepare them for the afterlife. Internal organs were removed and embalmed separately. This was done in the 'valley building', from where the mummified body was taken along a covered causeway for burial in the pyramid. The valley building's solidity allowed its interior to remain cool, while narrow slot windows admitted just enough light.

A wall was built around the edge of the pyramid to keep people away from it. A temple for tributes was attached to the wall, but after the pyramid had been sealed it became an inviolate sacred zone. Various interior passageways gave access to the burial place, which in the case of the Great Pyramid of Khufu was well above ground – although this seems to have resulted from a change of mind on the part of the builders, as there was also an unused underground chamber.

In later times the pyramids came to be seen as very mysterious, and all sorts of interpretations of their function were projected on to them, many involving magic and superstition.

1 Plan

1 Western *mastaba* field
2 Pyramid of Khufu
3 Pyramid of Khephren
4 Pyramid of Menkaure
5 Eastern *mastaba* field
6 Valley temple
7 Great Sphinx
8 Valley temple

2 Section A-A

3 South Elevation

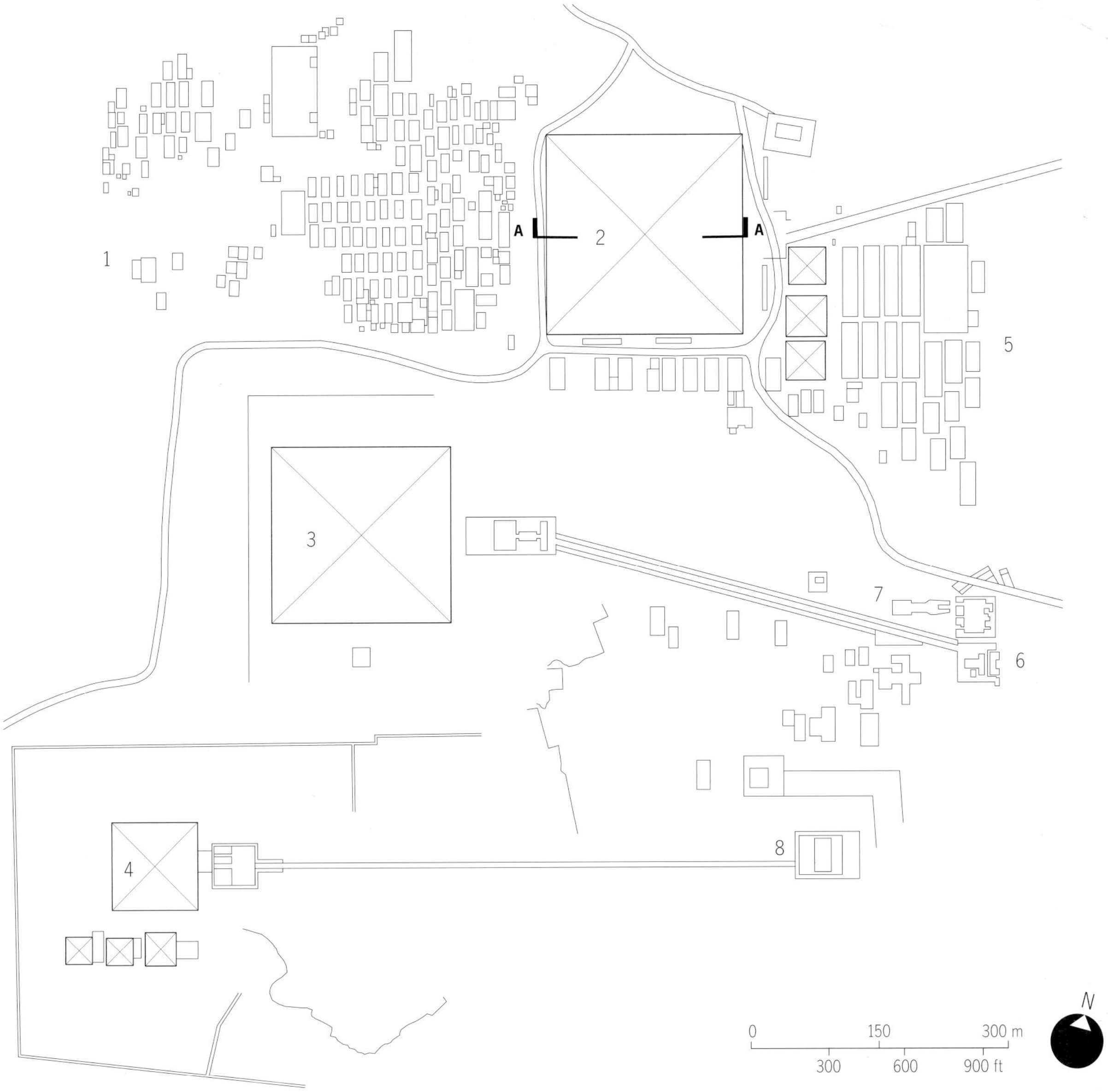

0 150 300 m
300 600 900 ft
N

1

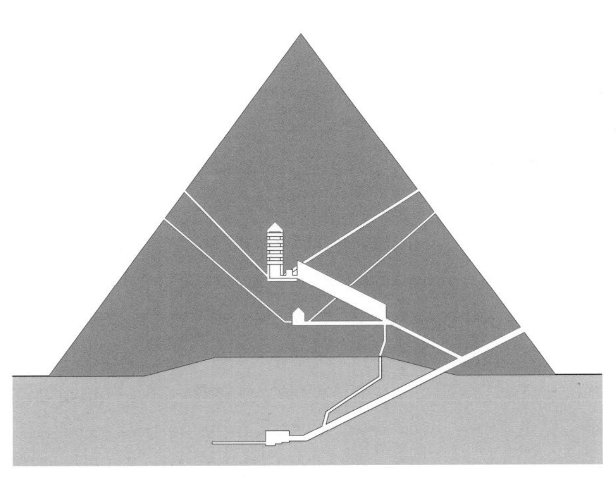

2

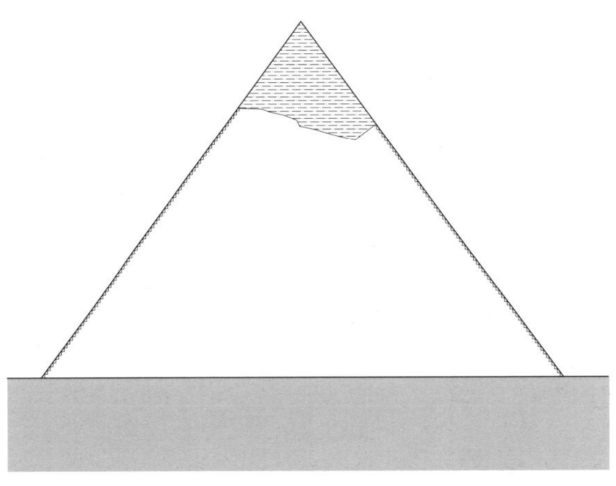

3

0 75 150 m
150 300 450 ft

Parthenon

Iktinos

Athens, Greece; 447–432 BCE

Revered as one of the world's outstanding artistic accomplishments, the Parthenon is an international symbol of Greece. It was both an extravagance and a complex achievement that drew on the knowledge of earlier structures, but it is more refined and sophisticated than its predecessors.

The Parthenon was a temple dedicated to Athena, who gave her name to the city of Athens. It was built on a rocky outcrop that had once been a fortified citadel but by the fifth century BCE had become a sacred precinct – the Acropolis – with several important buildings on it, including the Erechtheion, where religious relics were kept.

The principal function of a temple such as the Parthenon was to house the cult statue of a god. Worship involved making sacrifices at an altar in the open air in sight of the statue, so that the god could witness the proceedings. The slaughtered animals – typically, cattle – would be cooked at the sanctuary and eaten there by men. (Women were involved in some ceremonies, but respectable women always ate separately from the men.) Very little meat would be eaten by any citizens except on these occasions. Sanctuaries would have had stoas with a row of dining rooms leading off a colonnade, but at the Acropolis of Athens none of these survives.

Incorporating many features of a typical Greek temple, the Parthenon has steps on all sides, making a plinth (stylobate) on which stands the run of columns that surrounds the building (the peristyle). They are Doric columns, which means that they have shallow-fluted shafts and fairly simple-looking, disc-like capitals at the top. Above the columns is a frieze of the type to be expected in a Doric temple: alternating square and rectangular panels. The rectangular panels are known as triglyphs and the square panels as metopes. The metopes are finely sculpted and show scenes of conflict between heroic Greeks and various mythical adversaries.

The Parthenon is the largest Doric temple of its age, with eight huge columns across each end instead of the usual six. It is made of glittering marble from Mount Pentelicon, which could be carved with great precision. It was normal to paint Greek temples, sometimes with intricate patterns, but here the quality of the materials and workmanship is so impressive that it is difficult to believe that the structure was covered up, except in the sculpted elements, where traces of underpainting remain.

Iktinos, the architect of the Parthenon, is also credited with the design of the temple of Apollo at Bassae (pages 104–105), the most original of the Doric temples. In both instances, he used column-types inside the building that were different from those outside. There were two great rooms inside the Parthenon. One of them housed a famous sculpture of Athena by Phidias, who had also made the statue of Zeus at Olympia and was among the most celebrated sculptors of antiquity. The other had four Ionic columns in it, and was used as a treasury, where the city's taxes and other assets were stored.

The Ionic capitals, each with a distinctive spiral curl (volute), are associated with a frieze that runs continuously round the building. The Parthenon is unusual in having not only the Doric frieze round the outside of the building above the columns, but also a second frieze on the Ionic model, which was built into the wall behind the columns, very high up. It is sculpted in low relief and would have been painted, but it would always have been in shadow and seen intermittently between the columns.

The Parthenon survived substantially intact until 1687, when the Turkish authorities were using it as a weapons store and it came under Venetian attack. Even in ruins, the quality and size of Athens's monuments made the city seem more important than it strictly merited, and in 1834 resulted in its being adopted as the capital city of modern Greece.

1 East Elevation

2 Section A-A

3 Site Plan

4 Doric Capital

5 Ionic Capital

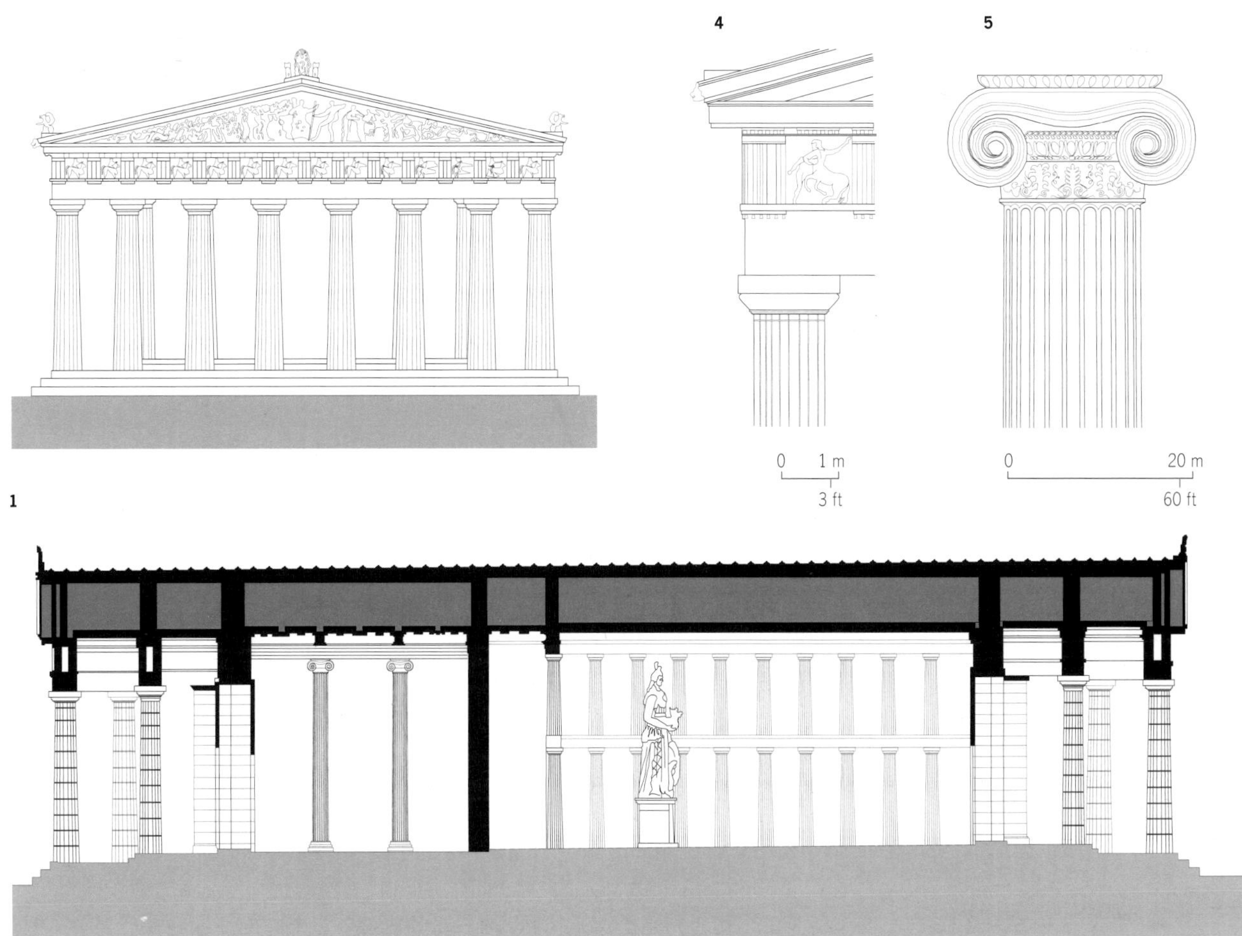

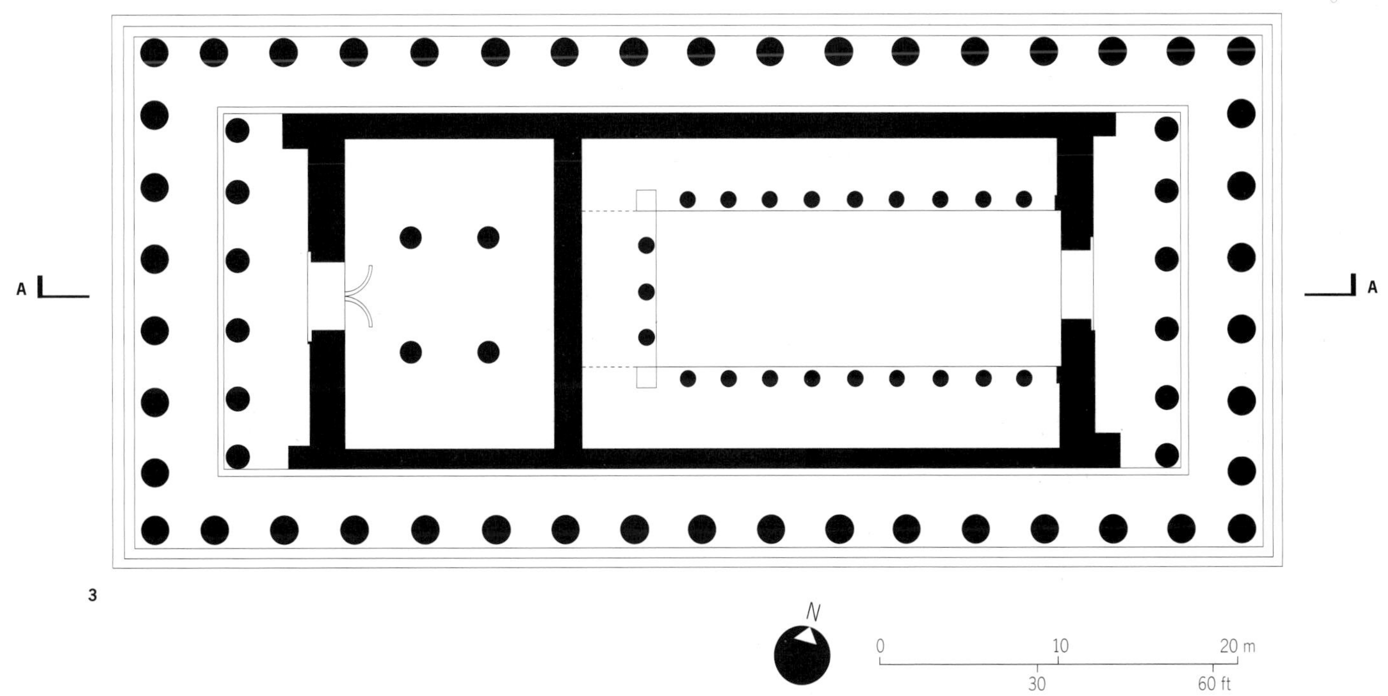

Colosseum

Rome, Italy; 70–82

Rome was the capital of a great empire, which annexed Greece in 146 BCE and adapted Greek architecture. The empire spread across Europe, northern Africa and western Asia – all the lands bordering the Mediterranean and much more besides. By the time the Colosseum was built, Rome was by far the largest and most powerful city on Earth, and it had problems that had rarely been faced before, including the threat of popular revolt. The rulers' formula was to offer 'bread and circuses' – sustenance and entertainment – to divert the masses from protesting about their poor living conditions.

A surprising amount of the space in Imperial Rome was given over to monumental structures that glorified the emperors and provided venues for public spectacle. Most ordinary Roman citizens inhabited the spaces in between the monuments, in dwellings that have since collapsed, even if they did not fall down in their own day.

The Colosseum was built on the site of a lake in the garden of the emperor Nero, the last of the Caesars who ruled Rome from 49 BCE to 68 CE. An unsympathetic history of the Caesars by the Roman author Suetonius has made the names of some of them, including Nero, bywords for depravity and corruption. Nero annexed for himself land that had been cleared of buildings by fire, apparently intending to build a palace on it. His immediate successor, Titus Flavius Vespasianus, or Vespasian, was therefore making a populist move when he commissioned the Flavian amphitheatre, which came to be known as the Colosseum because of its colossal size.

The building could seat up to 80,000 spectators, who came to see events such as gladiatorial combats and prisoners being torn apart by wild animals. Brought from the farthest reaches of the empire, the animals could be introduced into the arena through trapdoors, to take combatants by surprise. The arena could also be flooded for naval displays.

Spectators were separated by rank into four tiers, and entry was controlled by regulating access to passages underneath the raked seating; the poorest people were assigned to the highest tier, the farthest from the arena. The amphitheatre was built on fairly flat ground, so the whole of the vast rake of the seating could be supported on concrete vaults, which the Romans were adept at constructing. What looks like a fairly continuous slope on the inside of the building is resolved on the outside into a series of four tiers that are adorned with repetitions of versions of the Greek styles of column: Doric, Ionic and Corinthian – but these structures are simply decorative, connoting some cultural sophistication and magnificence. They are simplified columns, done without fluting the shafts, and they are incomplete since the back of them is incorporated in the wall that actually supports the building. The arched openings in the wall allow some illumination and air to penetrate, as well as lightening the mass of the masonry that has to be carried. The top tier, which has no openings, is decorated with flat pilasters. Above that were once masts used to secure an awning roof that helped to shade the spectators.

The Colosseum represents a type of architecture that springs from populist politics. It gave the people what they wanted and enabled the Flavian dynasty to establish itself. It is the largest surviving monumental structure in Rome.

1 Plan

2 Elevation

3 Section A-A

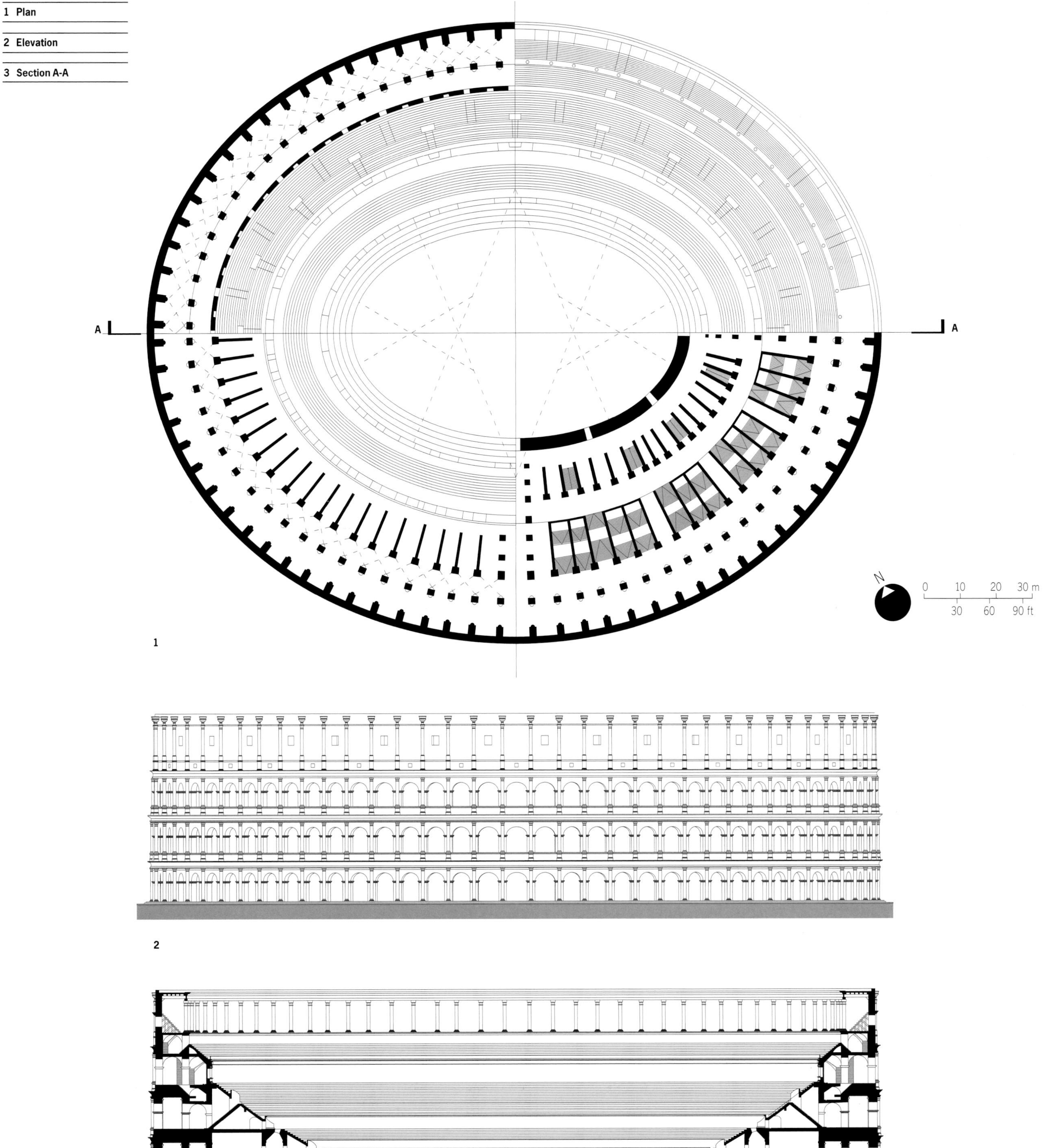

Temple 1, Tik'al

Guatemala; 695 CE

Tik'al is the very image of a lost city. Even its name is lost. 'Tik'al' – the place of voices – has been attached to it in modern times, to suggest that it is haunted by its past. Deserted since the tenth century, the city is surrounded by jungle. There are the remnants of six great temples and thousands of houses that remain unexcavated beneath mounds of luxuriant vegetation. The tallest of the temples, Temple IV, is 64 metres (210 feet) high.

The city of Tik'al was produced by the Mayan civilization, which flourished in the area that is now the southern tip of Mexico and Guatemala – the land between the two American continents, known as Mesoamerica. Tik'al had been founded by the fourth century BCE, and monumental structures show it to have been a seat of power, but there was a hiatus, during which the city was subjected to rule from outside, and the imposing temples date from the late seventh century CE, when internal control was restored. They were monuments built to celebrate the idea that glory had returned to the site, under Ha Sawa Chaan K'awil, who founded the new order in 682 CE – and sacrificial ceremonies took place there.

The enormous height of the temples at Tik'al established a separation from the everyday life down below and took the participants above the forest canopy, so that a much wider horizon opened up to them as they reached the top of their ascent. Ha Sawa Chaan K'awil is known to the archaeologists as Ruler A, and was buried, by his successor, in the base of Temple 1.

Temple 1 is known more evocatively as the Great Jaguar Temple, from the sculptural carving of a jaguar on its lintel. (The tomb, with its precious goods, was sealed before the construction above it began.) The temple's interior space is small, consisting of a chamber with a corbelled stone vault supporting a massive stone superstructure.

It was here that the business of sacrifice was carried out. The victim was held down while the priest made an incision and ripped out the still-beating heart, before emerging from the door to hold up the heart to the sun and the crowd assembled below.

Most of the construction work was devoted to creating the substructure that gives this high stone chamber its commanding position. The pyramidal form is not an allusion to anything in Egypt. Rather, it is a way to make the tall structure as stable as possible. The temple was given nine striations, which suggest the nine levels of the underworld, and the ascent to the chamber takes the form of an unforgiving staircase with large steps and an unrelentingly steep rake.

Temple 1 faces another, similar structure – Temple 2, the Temple of Masks – built a little later on the other side of the Great Plaza, where games were played with a rubber ball in order to select the sacrificial victims. The stakes were high, but it is not clear that 'winning' would always have been the aim.

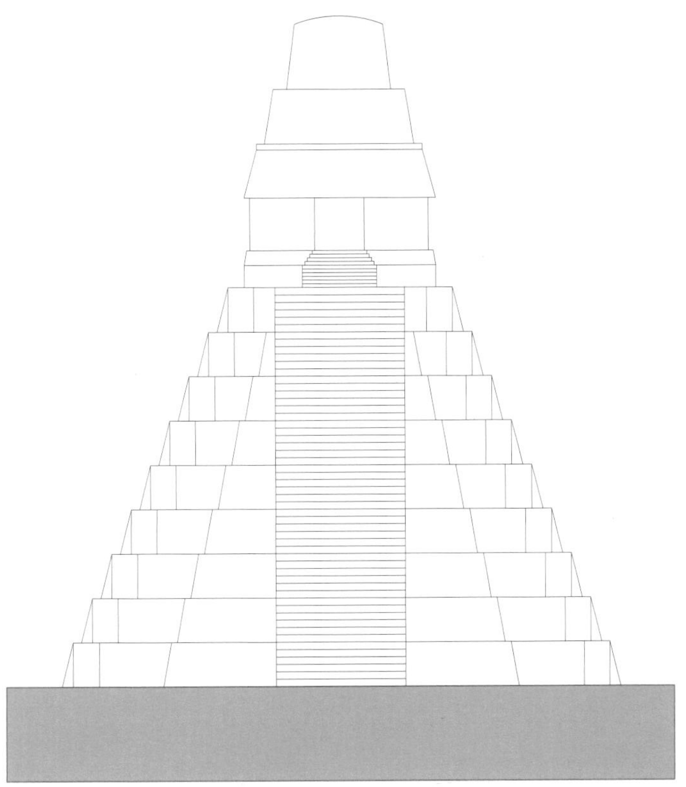

1

2

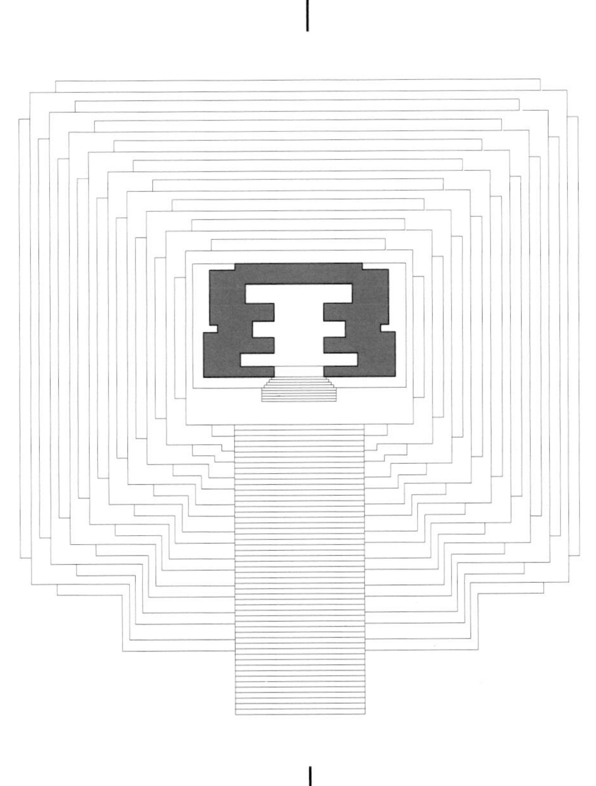

3

1 Elevation

2 Section A-A

3 Plan

Great Stupa of Sanchi

Bhopal, India; 300 BCE

A stupa is a mound commemorating the place where a significant event took place or where holy relics were kept. The impulse behind the creation of a stupa was the same as the inspiration for the building of cairns of unworked stones, as related in the Hebrew bible, or prehistoric tumuli, or the Egyptian pyramids. Stupas are associated with Buddhism, and the Great Stupa of Sanchi, a small village 46 km (29 miles) from Bhopal, is one of the oldest, largest and most authoritative. The site, which includes other stupas, and the remains of palaces, is the oldest Buddhist sanctuary. It fell out of use in the thirteenth century, but was rediscovered and excavated in the nineteenth.

The Great Stupa of Sanchi was built by the emperor Ashoka (304–262 BCE), who took the reputed relics of Buddha there and established a monastic settlement around them. The mound is resolved into a mighty dome (*anda*) of sandstone blocks, supporting a symbolic orthogonal relic-chamber (*harmika*), and has again become a major place of pilgrimage. Its embellishments include four ornate gateways at the cardinal points and finely carved pillars, including one with the forequarters of four Indian lions, which was adopted as India's national symbol when the country became independent in 1947. After Ashoka's time, during the second century BCE, the shrine was vandalized, but it was then remodelled, enlarged and elaborated.

The great mound itself has a fairly simple shape, and impresses with its size and austerity. The stone finial above the *harmika* is in the form of a parasol, which signals the building's high status. In later examples of stupas, this was sometimes elaborated as a diminishing series of parasols, and eventually as a cone. But here the mass of the mound is pre-eminent, lifting the relics to prominence, while the focus for artistic elaboration is around the gateways (*toranas*), which date from the first century CE. They depict scenes from the life of the Buddha: plants, animals and humans involved in a variety of complex narratives.

The stone gateways mimic the appearance of timber, but timber made permanent – a transition that is regularly found in monumental architecture, where something relatively mundane is petrified, or turned into a statue of its ordinary self.

Devotional ceremonies follow a processional route round the base of the mound, stopping at the gateways. These now have statues of the Buddha by them, which were placed against the sides of the mound in the fifth century CE. There is no accessible interior to the building, but the building itself gives structure to the space around it and acts as a symbolic focus: the egg-shaped dome represents the cosmos, the square platform represents the Earth, and the parasol indicates the connection between them.

This site was chosen for the stupa because it is far away from the noise of cities but within easy reach of a major route from Vidisha, where there were many religiously inclined citizens. The monks were mendicant, meaning that they had to subsist by begging, which was possible because the lack of traffic did not compromise the serenity of the otherwise isolated place.

1 Elevation

2 Plan

3 Section A-A

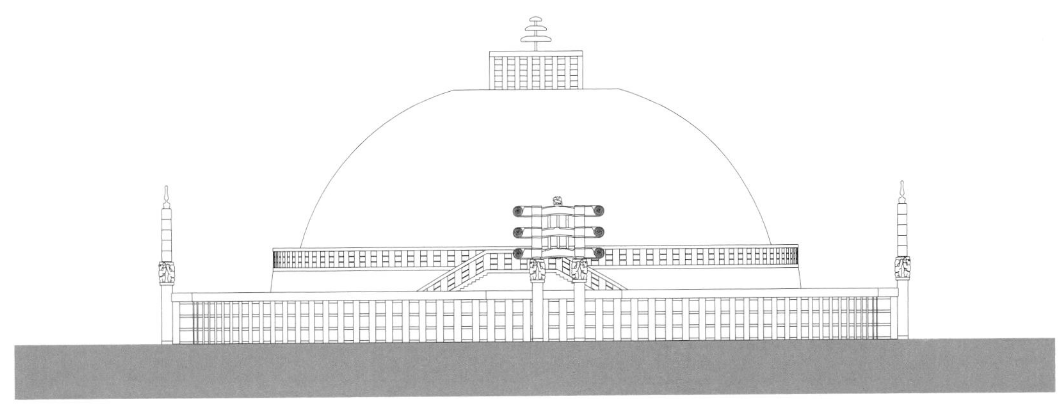

1

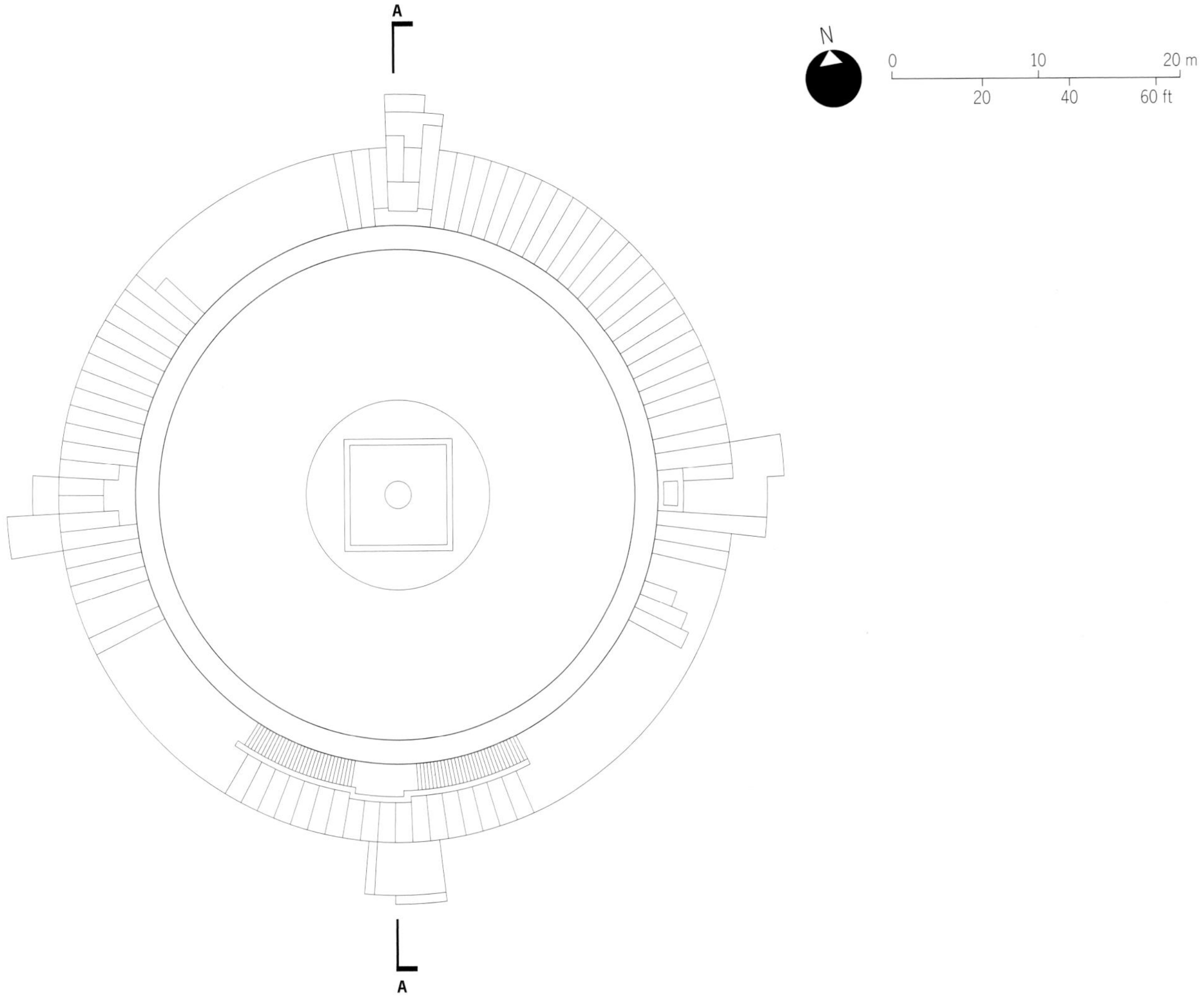

A

N

0 10 20 m

20 40 60 ft

2

A

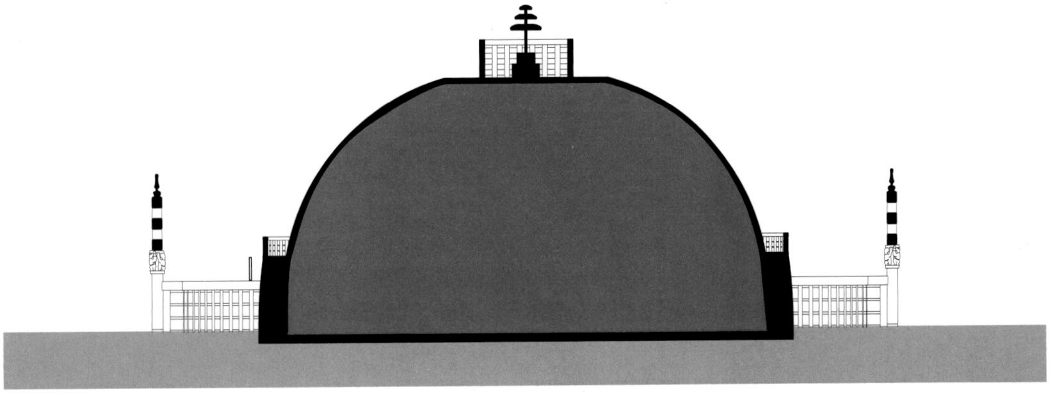

3

Hagia Sophia

Isidoros, 442–539, and Anthemios, 469–539

Istanbul, Turkey; 532–58

When Hagia Sophia was constructed in the first half of the sixth century, it was the greatest Christian church, with a commanding position in the city of Constantinople. It was part of the complex of buildings that made up the imperial palace of Justinian, a Roman emperor. Various names have changed. The city is called Istanbul, the empire of Justinian and his successors is called Byzantine, and the church is now a museum, having been used for some time as a mosque, after the defeat of the Greeks in 1453.

The Greek name for the city, Constantinople, comes from the Roman emperor Constantine, who established an administration there in the fourth century, after Rome had become unmanageable. The new capital, based on an older port called Byzantium, stood at a great crossroads between Europe and Asia, where the land-routes from east to west crossed the shipping lanes that ran, at that point, north to south, connecting the Black Sea with the eastern Mediterranean. Constantine built a church there dedicated to Hagia Sophia (a Greek phrase meaning 'holy wisdom'), but Justinian replaced it with something much more splendid.

From the outside its domes and half-domes are visible, mounding up to a central high-point, but it was the breathtaking interior that astonished visitors. The huge vaulted space still has its bronze doors, finely carved marble columns and intricate capitals, but it has lost some of its opulent furnishings and the imagery that once filled the walls and vaults. There were mosaic images of biblical figures, saints and emperors against a glittering gold background.

Most of the light that comes into the building enters through windows on the upper storey, where there is a gallery. These windows are not visible from below, and when the light was reflected by the gold mosaics, it seemed to be generated and mysteriously held within the building. A ring of windows around the base of the central dome, exposing its structure of radiating ribs, also contributed to the effect of bravura in throwing this vault across the heavens.

In the early days it was a struggle to make Hagia Sophia stand. Its construction is a triumph of engineering, based on expertise in balancing opposing forces that had been developed over many generations of ambitious works in Rome and around the empire. The principal structural material is concrete, but the concrete disappears behind the rich surfaces. Four huge masses of masonry support the central dome, but they are placed in such a way that the lines of the internal geometry mask them. When the original dome began to collapse, it was replaced by one with a slightly steeper slope, which made the structure more stable.

Hagia Sophia remained without equal until the revival of interest in vaults in the medieval cathedrals hundreds of years later. It has had particular influence in the tradition of mosque design, especially in Turkey after 1550 – a thousand years after the original church was built – when the architect Sinan at last worked out how to imitate and surpass this model.

1 Elevation

2 Section A-A

3 Plan

1 Courtyard
2 Narthex
3 Nave
4 Apse
5 South gallery (above)
6 Baptistery

1

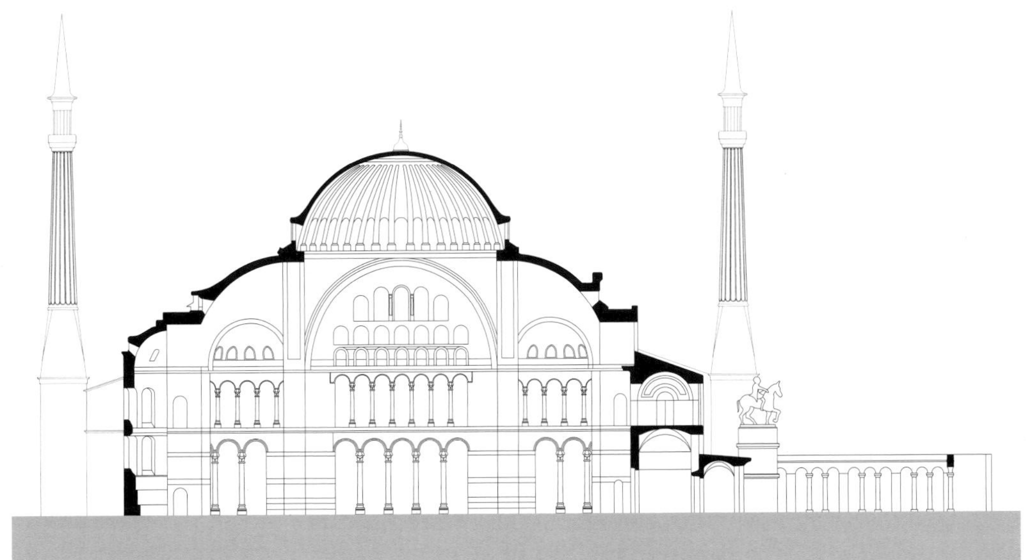

2

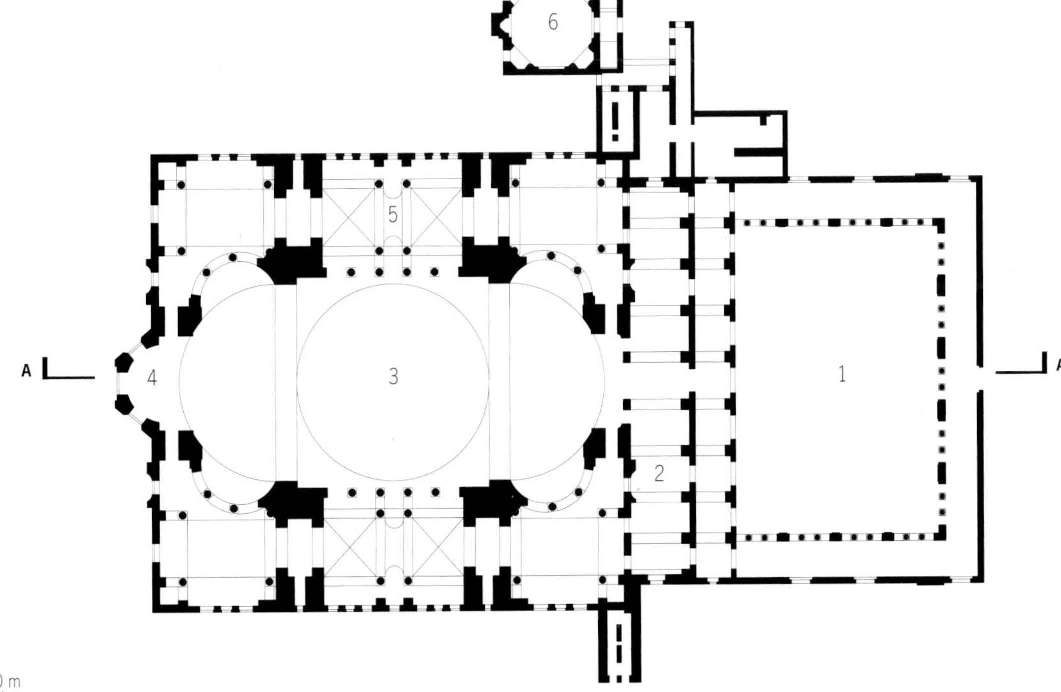

3

N

0 25 50 m
50 100 150 ft

Ise Grand Shrine

Ise in Mie, Kansai, Honshu, Japan; eighth century, repeatedly rebuilt

Ise is the holiest shrine in Japan, dedicated to the Shinto sun goddess, Amaterasu-Omikami, a distant ancestor of the Japanese emperor's family. The high priest at Ise is always a member of the imperial family, and the general public is kept away from the innermost parts.

The shrine is located in an extensive cypress forest called Ise Jingu. Walking through the forest and encountering fast-flowing streams is an important part of a pilgrim's meditative worship. At the sanctuary there are many small shrines – more than 100 – but the principal one, in white Japanese cypress with a thatched roof, is best known for being rebuilt every 20 years to exactly the same design.

There are two sites for the temple, and at any given moment only one of them is in use. Meanwhile, the other one is being renewed according to a well-established procedure.

After the demolition of the previous building, the site is covered with large white pebbles. A post is then erected at the centre of the site, with a small hut around it, waiting for rebuilding to begin. This process began as a formal institution in the eighth century, but something less systematic may have been going on even earlier, for the post surrounded by a field of pebbles is said to evoke much more ancient Shinto shrines. The design of the building must not be copied elsewhere.

According to the Shinto religion, the Ise shrine has been in place for centuries without a break – rather than having been rebuilt on the site every 20 years. It is one building that is repeatedly being renewed – just as a forest is continually renewed through the life-cycles of growth and decay of individual trees. The office of emperor is also regarded as continuous, even though the post has been occupied by different people.

This idea of systematic renewal – tearing the building down completely when it has reached the end of its designated cycle, even though it is in a perfectly good state – means that the Ise shrine appears to be quite different from the other monuments covered in this book so far, where the fabric of the building is expected to have been in place from its inception. In fact, that is often far from the case. Even stone buildings decay over time, and the effects of earth tremors, erosion and pollution have led to many efforts to strengthen, repair and re-carve both structure and decoration. Very solid buildings may remain standing despite centuries of neglect, but most survive only because they have been maintained. The Ise shrine represents a radical idea of maintenance: 100 per cent renewal on a nearby site. The continuity is in the design of the building, not in its fabric. There is no question of appreciating the cultural continuity through patination or decayed timbers. It is always fresh and new, despite being ancient.

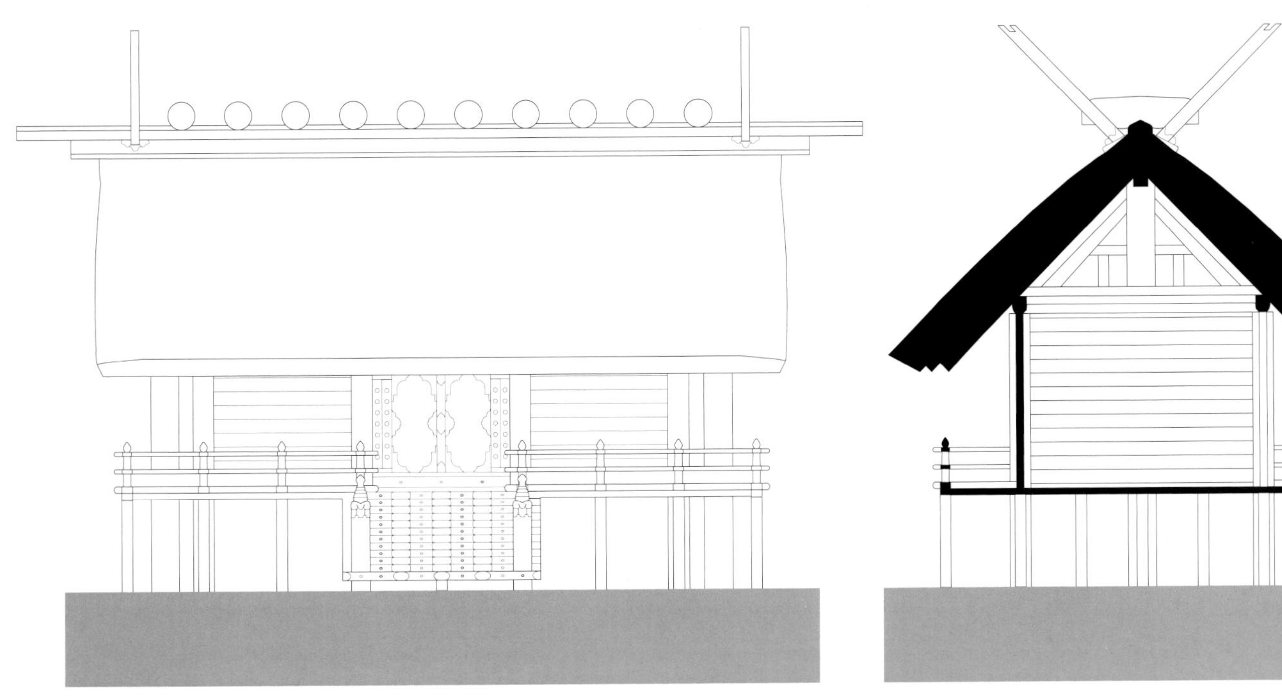

1

2

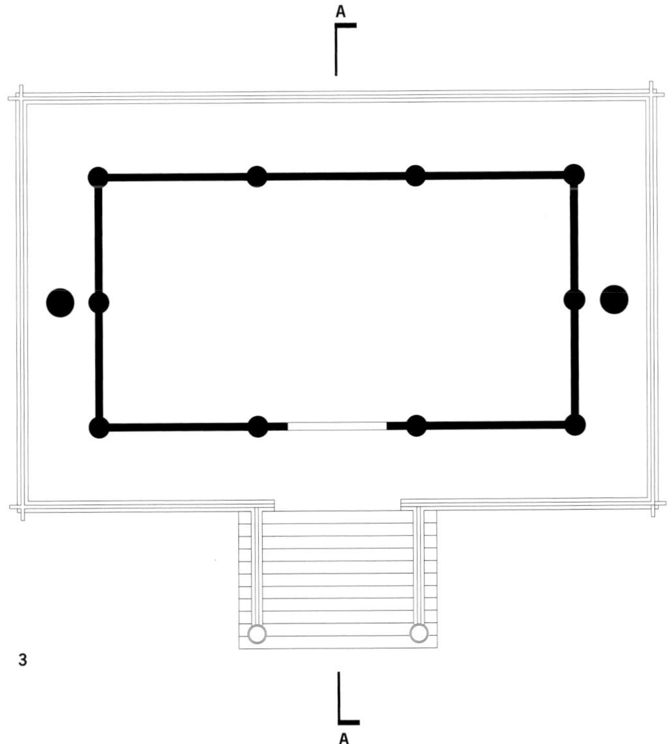

3

1 Elevation
2 Section A-A
3 Plan

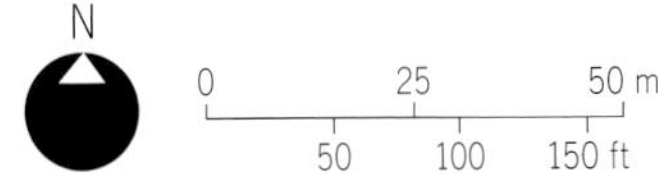

Great Enclosure, Great Zimbabwe

Zimbabwe; eleventh to fifteenth centuries

Great Zimbabwe, the seat of power of the Shona people, was for a time the largest and most prosperous city in Africa south of the Sahara. Its ruins are extensive and impressive; they gave their name to the modern nation of Zimbabwe, and a stone carving of a bird found at the site appears on the country's flag.

The name Zimbabwe, which clearly post-dates the settlement, means 'stone houses', and there were enough of them to shelter up to 10,000 people, maybe more, which would have made it a significant city anywhere in the pre-modern world. It grew until it overstretched its resources and was unable to bring in enough food from the surrounding land to feed its citizens – so it was abandoned, rather than conquered.

The supposition that there was nothing like Great Zimbabwe in this region of Africa has led to speculation that it was a foreign import, the most persistent myth being that it was built for the Queen of Sheba, but this is nonsense. For a start, there are hundreds of other stone settlements, built using similar techniques, that are peculiar to the region, and which seem to replicate in stone the spaces that were made earlier by earth walls. Finds at the site indicate that it was settled from the fifth century, but the stone houses seem to have been built at a later date. The particular monumental quality of Great Zimbabwe is a matter of degree rather than of kind. It is larger and more imposing than the other stone settlements, but not altogether different. It was probably the result of generations of competition with other settlements; there was a need to defend against rivals, but also a desire to make a fine display.

The Great Enclosure – the most architecturally striking part of the city – consists of an elliptical space enclosed by a cut-stone wall that is 5.5 metres (18 feet) thick at the base and 7 metres (23 feet) high. Made of granite, which in this area splits into layers (like slate), the stones were painstakingly shaped to fit together without mortar. The enclosure is well protected by this immense solidity, and the activities that took place in it must have been highly valued. A frieze of two rows of chevrons carved along the top of the wall makes it clear that this is not simply a utilitarian structure but one that was invested with care and a sense of decorum. There are two towers, the larger 10 metres (33 feet) high, but their purpose is not understood.

People of high standing in the community would have inhabited the few houses in the enclosure, but the royal household and seat of government for the city and the region is believed to have been in the acropolis – another walled enclosure on higher ground. It dates from the fourteenth century, when the site was at its apogee. It is possible that the two enclosures had the same function but that they accommodated the ruling family at different times in the settlement's long history.

A high degree of specialized knowledge and a great deal of time would have been needed to construct the walls of the Great Enclosure. It is the work of a large workforce over a relatively short time or of a small workforce over many years, but either way it is work that an ordinary peasant community could not afford to undertake. There was gold in the surrounding land, and probably a more stratified society than was typical in the area, with a powerful elite able to take strategic decisions involving the diversion of resources into building works. Part of the cost of monumental architecture is the development of a society with specialist skills and inequalities, and that is a price that some cultures have found themselves disinclined to pay.

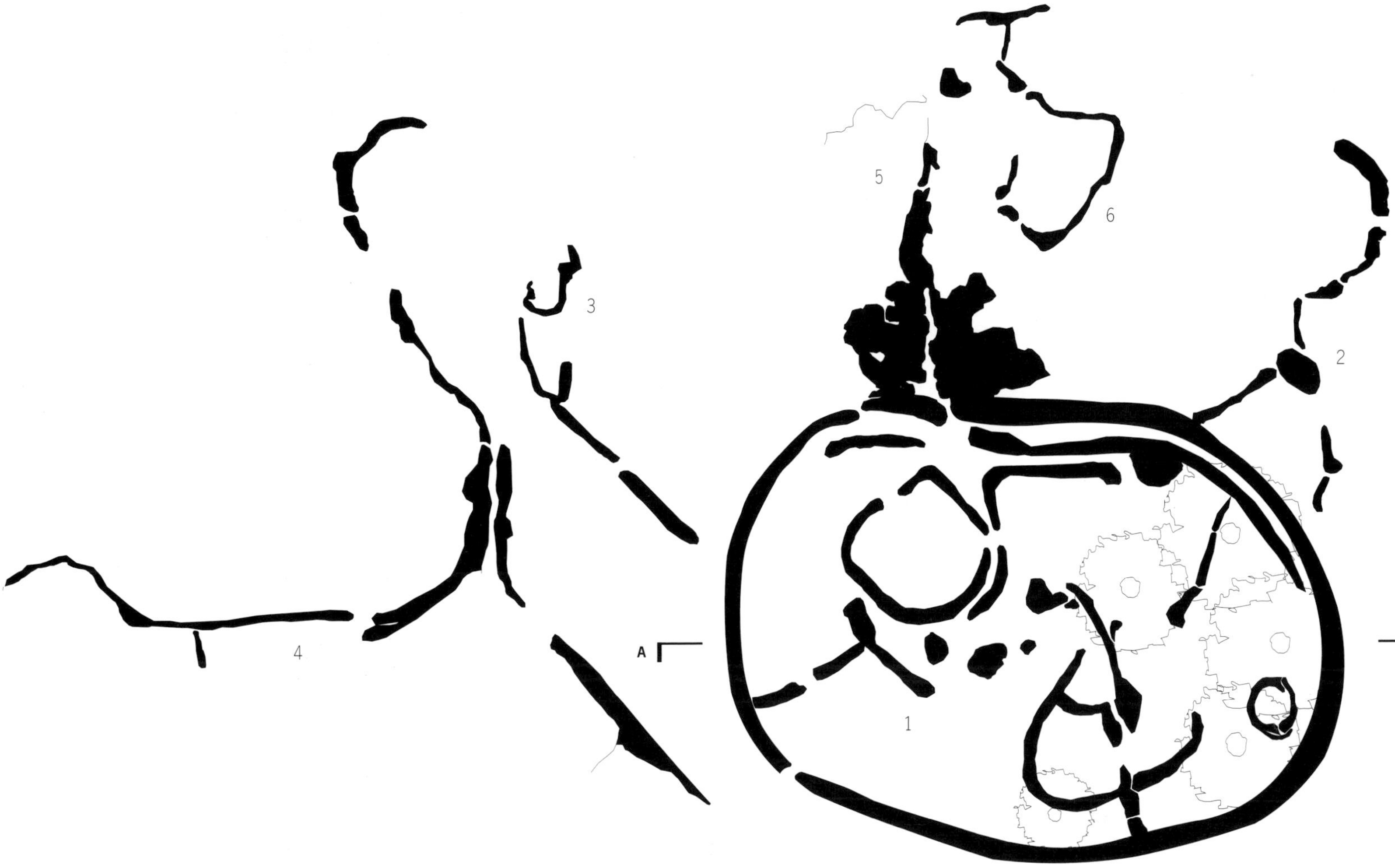

1

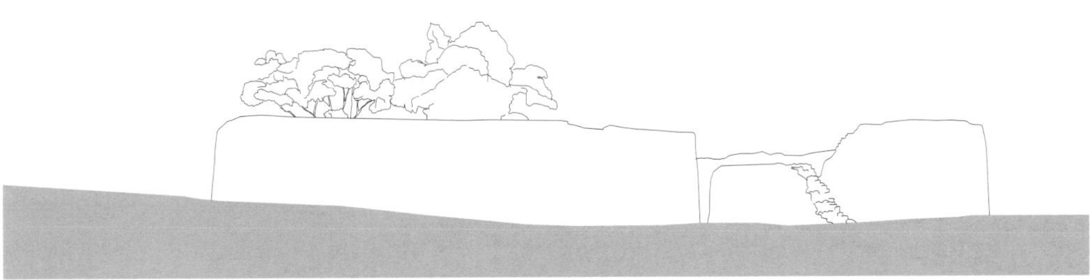

2

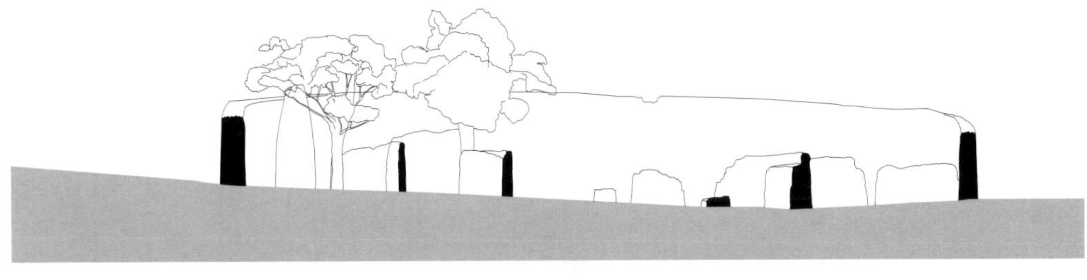

3

N

0 15 25 m

25 50 75 ft

1 Site Plan

1 Great Enclosure
2 Mauch ruin
3 Ruin no. 1
4 Ridge ruins
5 Posselt ruin
6 Philips ruin

2 North Elevation of Great Enclosure

3 Section A-A

Twin Pagodas, Luohanyuan Temple

Wang Wenhan and Wang Wehua

Suzhou, Jiangsu, China; 982

The pagoda is the building type that above all others signifies Chinese culture to the outside world, so it has become emblematic of China itself, even though it was built only by Buddhists. A development of the Indian stupa, the pagoda might be used to mark an important site or to house relics of the Buddha's disciples. The parasol forms seen in the stupa were reinterpreted as a series of projecting roofs that get smaller as the building tapers in its ascent.

Unlike the stupa, the pagoda had some usable interior space, but its arrangement in small rooms one above the other was hardly convenient, and in many cases the upper floors were inaccessible except by ladder. The rooms could be used for storing texts and for contemplation, but the building's form was not shaped by functional considerations.

The main purpose of a pagoda was as an honorific marker. It would always be associated with a temple, sometimes as part of a group. Pagodas had a similar role to that of church spires, so they were not generally found as autonomous buildings. During the Cultural Revolution many temples were destroyed but, as subsidiary structures, pagodas were not targeted in the same way, so they do now sometimes stand as independent towers, decoratively calling attention to a place that was once sacred.

Suzhou in southern China is famous for its natural scenery and for its gardens, which developed in a sophisticated way. Arranged in a relatively small compass for variety, entertainment and contemplation, and achieving an extraordinary density of evocative effects, are the Master Fisherman's Garden, the Humble Administrator's Garden, the Beautiful Lion's Garden – more than 150 of them in all. From ancient times, Suzhou has been regarded as an earthly paradise. State officials have maintained retreats there and its cultural buildings have been highly valued.

Many pagodas survive in Suzhou, all towering, though their former prominence has been diminished by the towers of the modern city. The tallest of them, at 75 metres (236 feet), is the North Temple Pagoda, which was once taller than it is now.

There has been a pagoda on this spot since the third century, but the current building's design dates from the twelfth, when it stood eleven storeys high. It was damaged by fire and rebuilt or repaired in the late sixteenth century under the Ming Dynasty as a nine-storey structure. It is an octagonal brick tower of immense solidity. Some stone pagodas are even more solid than this brick version and have virtually no internal space. Other pagodas are made with a timber structure and yet others, miniature ones, in cast iron.

The pagodas shown are a matching pair in Suzhou, some 30 metres (98 feet) high, built mostly in masonry but with the upper part tapering into a cast-iron spire. Among the oldest surviving pagodas, they are traditionally supposed to have been designed by two brothers, Wang Wenhan and Wang Wehua – but perhaps the attribution derived from the two towers' fraternal appearance.

Each of the twin buildings has an octagonal base with thick masonry walls, and the internal space on the ground floor is small, with four doors leading into it. The upper floors are accessible through trap doors by means of very steep movable stairs. Above the octagonal first floor, the upper floors are all square, but each is set at an angle of 45 degrees to the floor below, and each is progressively smaller than its predecessor. Projecting roofs define the towers' seven storeys, covering the balustraded walkways that encircle the structures at each level. The roofs tip up to sharp points at the corners, making a lively silhouette. Each wall face has, alternately, a blind window or a real door. Their delicacy of form makes the pagodas seem light and fragile, but their longevity confirms that they are very robust indeed.

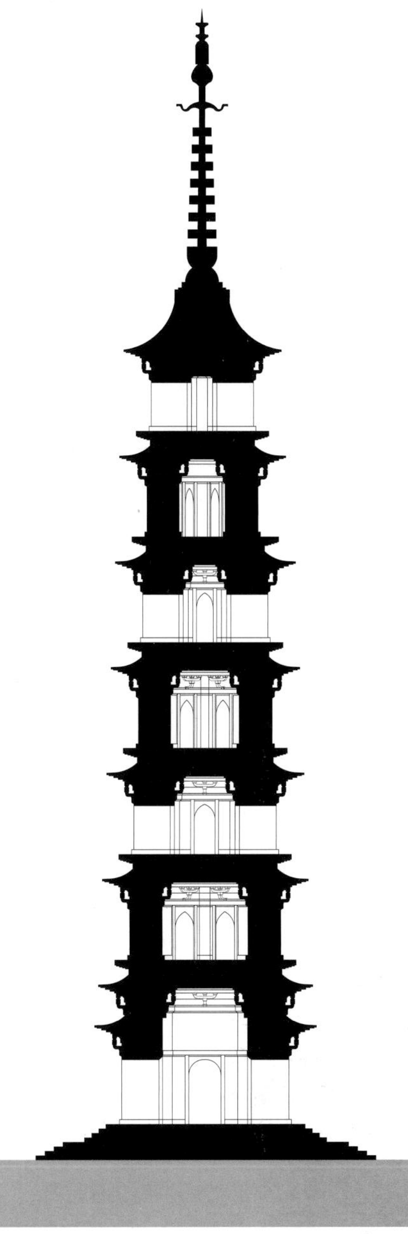

1

2

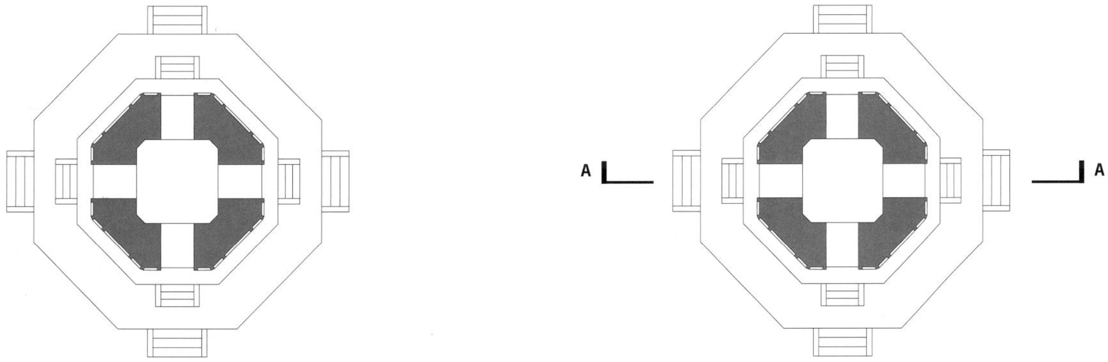

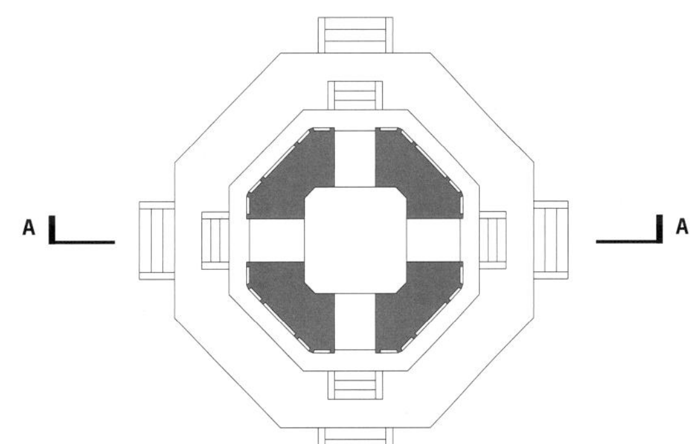

1 Elevation

2 Section A-A

3 Plan

3

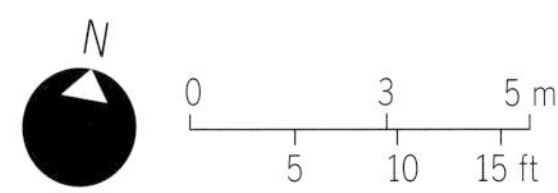

St Peter's Basilica

Donato Bramante, 1444–1514, Michelangelo Buonarotti, 1475–1564, Carlo Maderno, 1556–1629, and others

Rome, Italy; 1506–1626

The Roman emperor Constantine built the earliest church on this site in Rome, the traditional burial place of Jesus Christ's disciple Peter. However, Constantine and his successors also moved the administration of the empire away from Rome to Constantinople and Ravenna, and the churches there grew in splendour, while Rome remained something of a backwater.

Divisions between the eastern and western Church were formalized as a schism in the eleventh century, and the leaders of the western Church later moved to Avignon. When they returned to Rome at the end of the fourteenth century, Constantine's venerable basilica was still standing, and it was not until after the great vault of Hagia Sophia (pages 24–25) had been turned into a mosque that the decision was taken to replace the basilica with the greatest church in Christendom.

The initial design fell to Donato Bramante, who was in thrall to the ruins of imperial Rome, and who sought to create a rival to the Pantheon (pages 108–109), the vast domed temple that by then was in use as a church.

In 1506 work began on a centralized domed building based on Bramante's grand concept, but it would be left to later architects to develop and enhance the design. Raffaello Sanzio (Raphael, 1484–1520) was appointed on Bramante's death, and continued until he died, at which point Antonio da Sangallo (1484–1546) working with Baldassare Peruzzi took over.

In 1539 Sangallo proposed something much bigger and more elaborate than the original plan, but even this would have had less impact from a distance than the design that Michelangelo eventually resolved when he took over in 1546. Scathing about Sangallo's concept, Michelangelo revised the dome to the design that was actually built. He also pulled the whole composition of the building together with the addition of a giant cornice – an idea that was retained by his successors.

The dome is positioned directly above the tomb of St Peter and the drum beneath it incorporates the ornate columns that formerly ran across Constantine's church, raptured up halfway to heaven. Down below, over the tomb, is a very ornate baldacchino – a canopy supported on four great bronze pillars, designed by Giovanni Bernini (1598–1680) and echoing the twisted form of the columns from the old church, which in turn were meant to evoke the columns of Solomon's Temple in Jerusalem.

Drawing on the ideas of his predecessors, Carlo Maderno designed the entrance façade, which overlooks Bernini's grand piazza with its two curving colonnades. Crowds can assemble here, and regularly do so, especially at Easter, to hear the Pope's address from the window centrally placed in the portico. St Peter's is next to the Vatican City, from where the Roman Catholic church is administered, and which houses wonderful collections of artistic and historical treasures from antiquity onwards.

When the piazza was built, Rome retained its medieval character. To emerge from its narrow irregular streets into this huge open space would have been to be presented with a stunning vision of rational order. In the twentieth century the west side of the piazza was opened up by Mussolini to allow a processional approach along a grand avenue.

1

2

3

1 Section A-A

2 Elevation

3 Plan

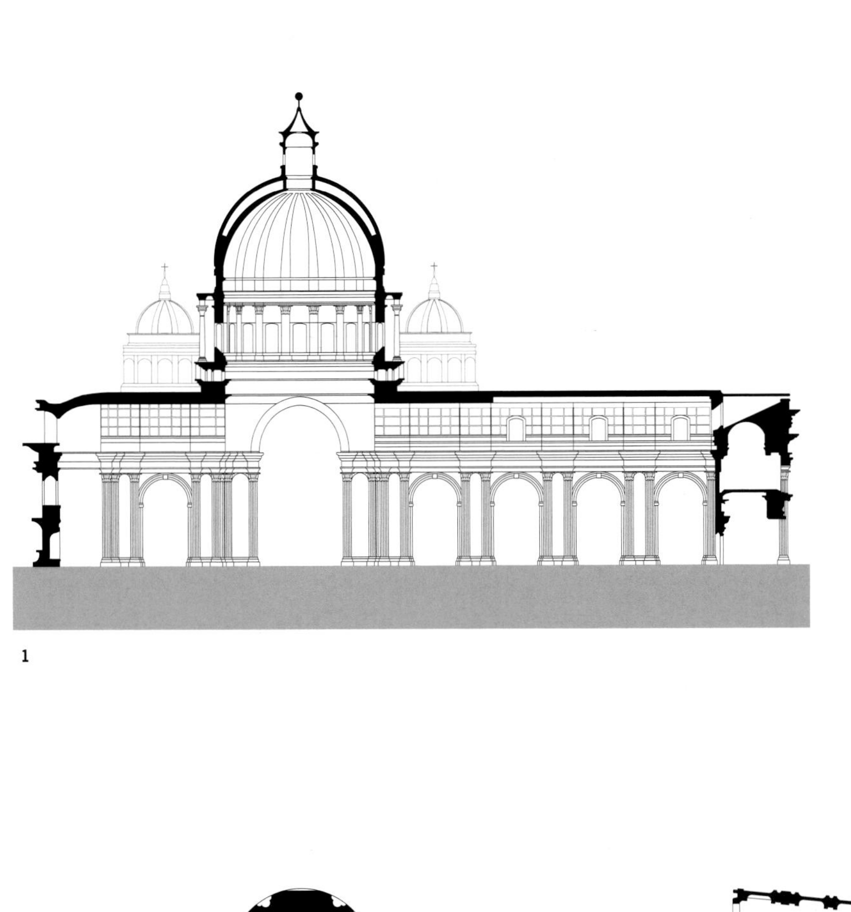

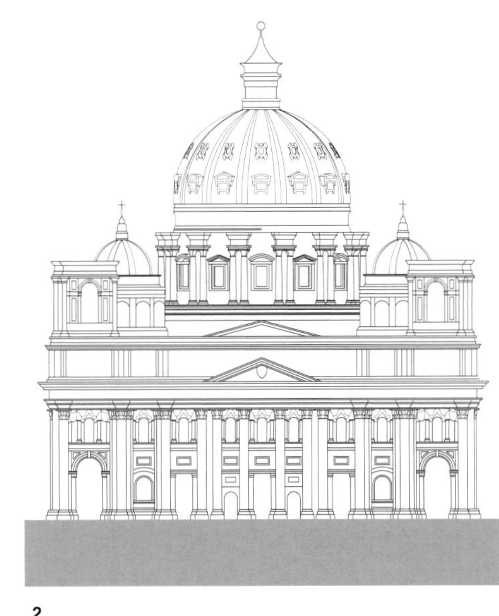

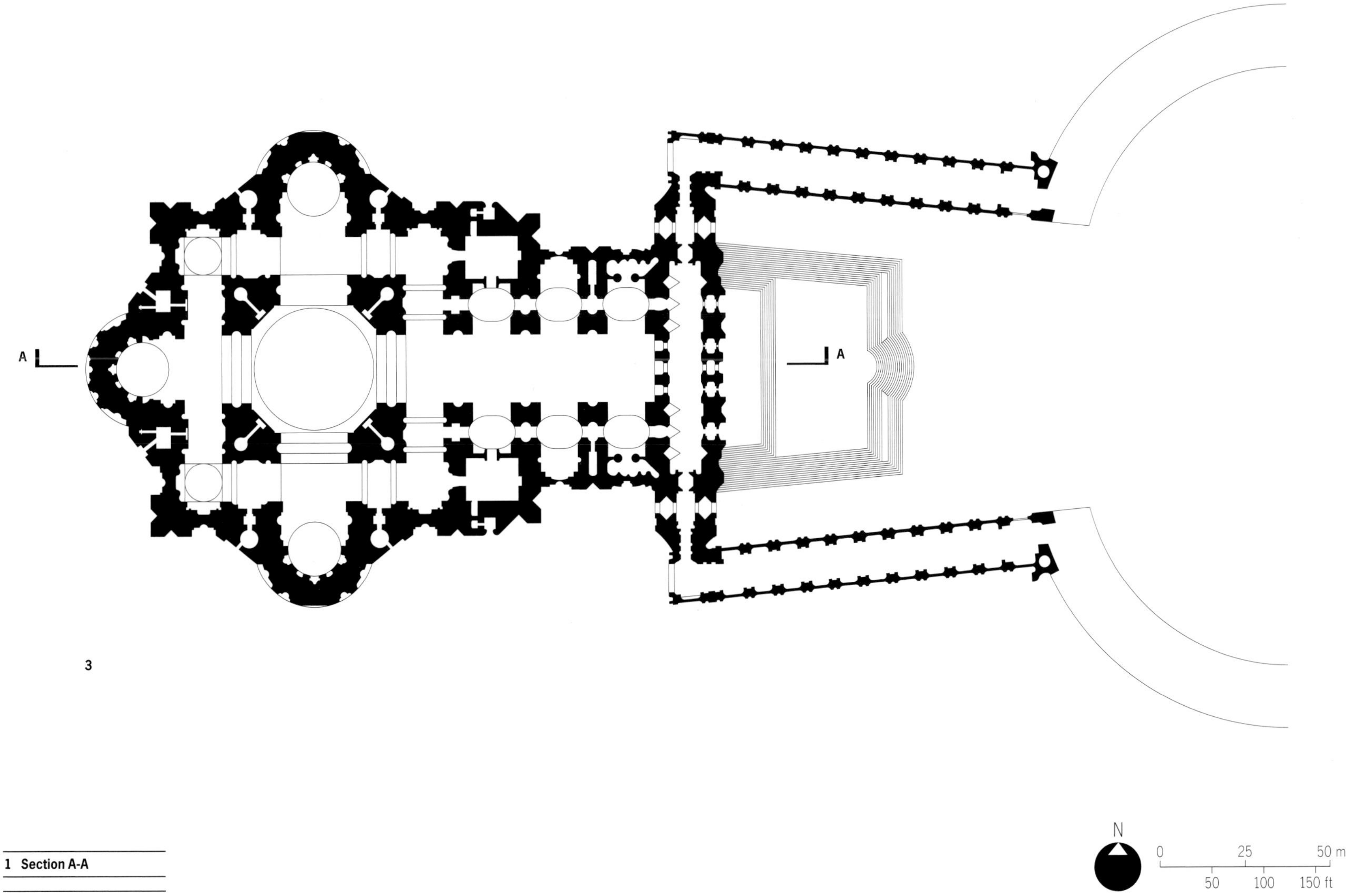

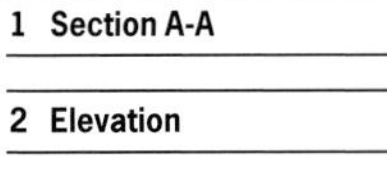

Taj Mahal

Agra, Uttar Pradesh, India; 1632–53

The Taj Mahal is one of the world's most recognized buildings. Famous for its beauty and for the fact that it was created by a grieving widower in memory of his wife, it is a sublimely romantic gesture of a building. Internationally, the Taj Mahal is emblematic of India, in the same way that the pyramids are emblematic of Egypt.

Shah Jehan, who commissioned the monument, ruled India as part of the Mughal Empire, which stretched from Persia across the subcontinent. Mahal was his wife's name, and a *taj* is an honorific hat, sometimes translated as a crown. They were married for 18 years and she died immediately after giving birth to her 14th child. The building's whiteness – it is completely covered in marble – reflects light, even moonlight, and in certain conditions gives the building a dematerialized quality that enhances its allure. Although the architect is uncertain, the names of Ustad Isa and, more recently, Ustad Ahmad Lahauri have been associated with the building.

There is a chapter in Herman Melville's *Moby-Dick* called 'The Whiteness of the Whale' which makes the creature mysterious and intensifies the sailors' obsession with it. The white whale is a blank canvas on to which the readers can project their own feelings and have them reflected back. There is something of that quality about the Taj Mahal, where the story about love and death stirs strong emotions in visitors – emotions that the building somehow reflects back, etherealizing them and making them seem noble and dignified.

The building's surfaces are intricately decorated with lettering, abstract patterns and plant motifs, but representations of the human form have been avoided. The plan has a strongly geometric character and high levels of symmetry. The mass of the construction is pierced by narrow passageways and chambers, grouped around a central chamber where the tombs of both Mahal and her husband are surrounded by exquisitely worked pierced marble screens called *jalis*, framed by marble inlaid with coloured stones in the shape of flowers. Further marble screens in the walls allow a soft light to filter through.

The form of the mausoleum belongs to a tradition of Islamic domed monuments, and the adornment also draws on a long line of sophisticated decorative development. Within a complex of buildings, the balance of different elements is carefully judged for aesthetic effect – unusually, the red-sandstone mosques that are part of the composition are given subsidiary status, so that the mausoleum takes pride of place, dominating the gardens laid out symmetrically around reflecting pools.

The extravagance of the project was extraordinary. The claim that 20,000 craftsmen worked on the Taj Mahal for 22 years is not easily substantiated, but it is absolutely clear that the value of the work that went into the building was prodigious, and it is hard to find words to give an impression of the sense of perfection, accomplishment and fine judgement that it instils.

1 Elevation

2 Section A-A

3 Plan

1

2

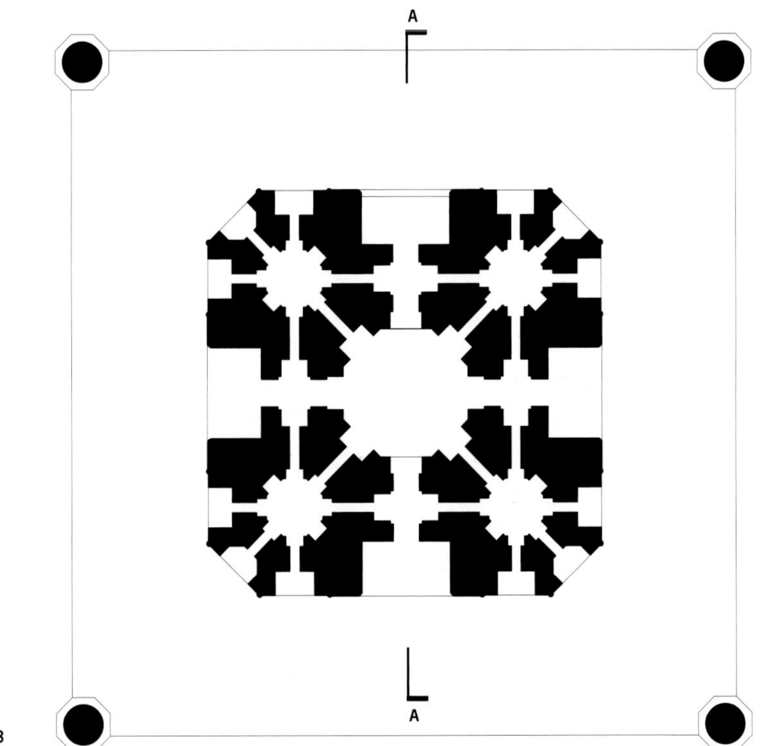

3

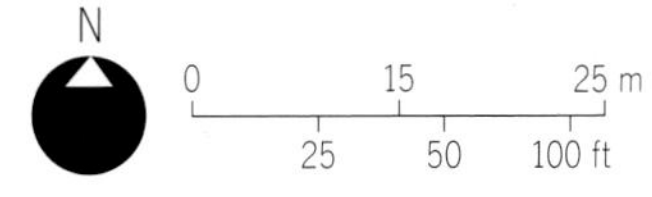

Eiffel Tower

Gustave Eiffel, 1832–1923

Paris, France; 1889

The Eiffel Tower was the tallest building in the world when it was constructed in Paris for the Universal Exposition of 1889. Although it was originally envisaged as only a temporary structure, it has remained in place ever since.

Gustave Eiffel was an experienced engineer of bridges by the time he made the design, and the shape that he came up with is the result of a threefold concern: for rigidity, for stability in the face of winds, and for minimizing the mass of the tower itself.

No building is less hidebound by tradition. A modern material – iron – was used without reference to architectural convention, except in the detail of the arches around the base, which are unnecessary from an engineering standpoint, but which give the building a monumental air when seen from below.

Yet this is a project of the most traditional type, with antecedents as old as the biblical Tower of Babel – a reflection of the human instinct to attract glory by reaching for the stars.

The siting of the Eiffel Tower is impressive, positioned as it is on a grand axis between the École Militaire and the Palais de Chaillot across the river, and the views from the top are spectacular. Since the topography of central Paris is generally flat, except for the hills of Montmartre in the north and the Buttes-Chaumont to the east, the monumental architecture of the city is surprisingly easy to identify.

The tower's function has always been to astonish with its height, and to give a novel view of familiar places, the promise of which attracts millions of visitors every year. It is also used for the transmission of radio signals. It was its indispensability as a radio transmitter that, in 1909, gave the building its first reprieve from being dismantled.

The Eiffel Tower has become such an instantly recognizable symbol of France that few people stop to ask how such a situation came about, when other places seem more often to adopt their most venerable buildings as national emblems. It has been used in effect to promote the idea of Paris as the capital of modernity, and indeed to suggest that modernity is more or less a French invention.

The philosopher and critic Walter Benjamin called Paris the capital of the nineteenth century. What is undoubtedly modernist about the Eiffel Tower is the way in which it projects a sense of new possibilities. There had been nothing like it before. Rather than being built to last, it had an anticipated lifespan of 20 years – and, if it were not maintained, it would rust and collapse. No one is buried in it. It does not commemorate an imperial victory or a centenary. It is simply a building that got over-excited about what iron could do and carried the world along in its enthusiasm.

1 Elevation

2 Plan

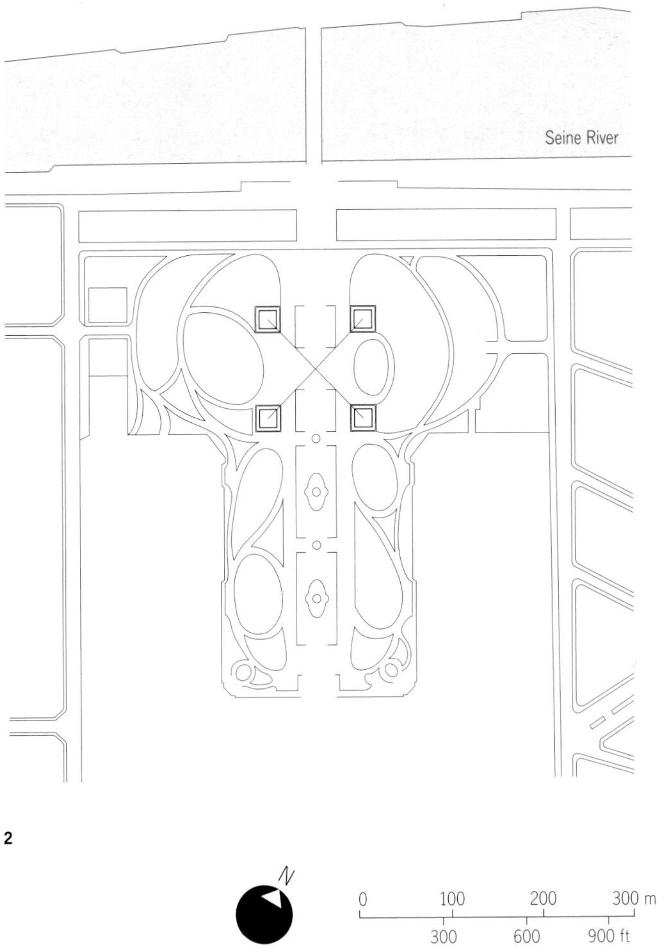

Seine River

2

N

0 100 200 300 m
300 600 900 ft

1

0 10 20 30 m
30 60 90 ft

Empire State Building

William F. Lamb, 1883–1952

New York City, New York, USA; 1931

The Eiffel Tower was overtaken as the world's tallest structure in 1930, on the completion of the Chrysler Building in New York City, but the Chrysler Building ceded precedence the following year to the Empire State Building, which had been steadily rising at the same time only a few blocks away. The Empire State held the title until 1972, the year that saw the opening of the twin towers of the World Trade Center. Since then, the tallest structures have had relatively brief reigns.

The Empire State Building's status as a symbol of New York and the USA in general is secure. Its early use in the final scenes of the film *King Kong* (1933) perhaps helped to root it in the popular imagination, but its prominent position on Manhattan Island has ensured its continuing visibility, and its name makes it seem like the very embodiment of New York State.

In this instance, the word 'empire' suggests the idea of 'commanding' or 'wealthy' rather than an ambition to rule other countries. At the core of the financial centre of the USA, the Empire State Building stands as a mighty emblem of commerce – a towering monument in a city of towers. The building has become a landmark, but it was produced as a speculative venture, designed to make money, rather than as a way of consuming money that had already been made – as had been the case for all the other monuments covered in this book so far, from the Egyptian pyramids to St Peter's in Rome.

In the event, the building's value as an asset was not immediate, because it opened during the Great Depression and its office space was initially impossible to let, but it became an address with great prestige.

The Empire State is America's most popular building and tourists visit its observation deck in vast numbers, perhaps more in the spirit of pilgrimage to the heart of American civilization than for the sake of the views, which nevertheless are extensive and magnificent. For its first 20 years the building's owners could not make a profit from it, but they were always able to sell tickets to visitors.

The building's syringe-like silhouette has a broad base that not only provides stability but also integrates the structure into the pattern of Manhattan streets. The upper reaches of the tower are set back, and the spike at the top was originally designed as a place where airships could be tethered – an idea that was never practicable because of the building's updraughts. Some of the photographs taken during the construction process show surprisingly straightforward building practices going on at breathtakingly high altitude, and it is remarkable that only five workers lost their lives in the works, according to official figures.

The Empire State Building's symbolic charge has a far wider significance than its financial value, but it was produced in a culture of intense commercial competition and marks the culmination of that rivalry in the 1930s, when the developers overreached themselves – not catastrophically, but in doing so they established that a limit had been reached.

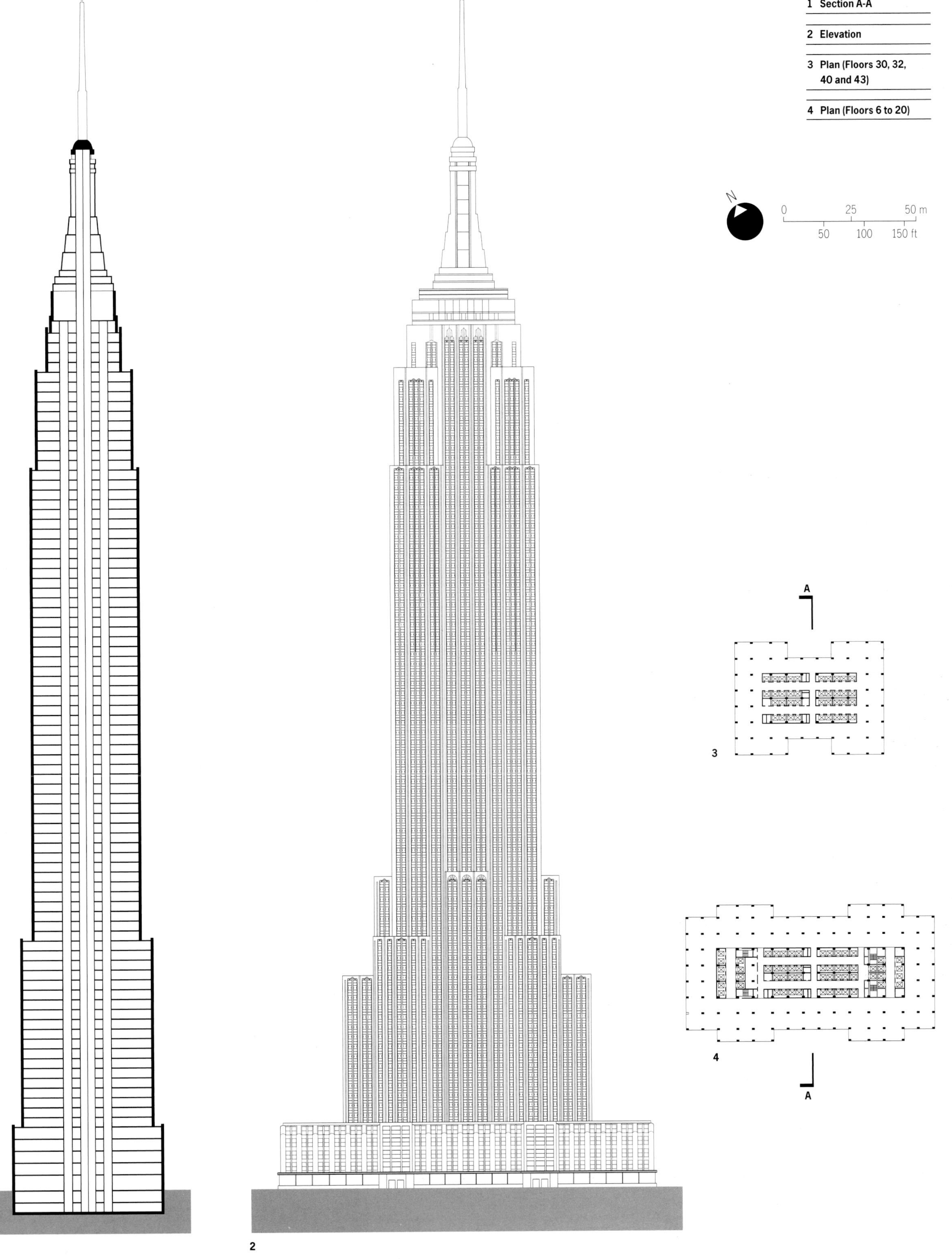

1 Section A-A

2 Elevation

3 Plan (Floors 30, 32, 40 and 43)

4 Plan (Floors 6 to 20)

Cathedral of Light

Albert Speer, 1905–81

Nuremberg, Germany; 1937

The Nazis, who took control of Germany in the 1930s, are now regarded as the epitome of an evil government. During the Nazi era, the state turned against many of its citizens and sought programmatically to exterminate Jews, the nomadic Roma people, homosexuals, Jehovah's Witnesses, and others who were seen to be anti-Nazi.

Their leader, Adolf Hitler, took a strong interest in art and architecture, and his main architect, Albert Speer, was one of his most trusted aides. Speer planned grandiose schemes for the centre of Berlin, the most excessive of which never came to fruition, since the regime was foreclosed by the concerted international military action of World War II.

One of Speer's most brilliant achievements was the design for the staging of the Rally of Labour at Nuremberg in 1937. This annual rally had become a vast spectacle, designed to galvanize the resolve of faithful Nazi party members.

Leni Riefenstahl's film of the 1934 event, called *Triumph of the Will*, gives the most vivid idea of the rally's character: regimented crowds, stirring traditional music, and amplified speeches that now look like mad demagoguery, but which were evidently effective as oratory at the time. The enormous parade ground was known as the Zeppelin Field. Across one end of it was an area of raked seating with the speakers' podium in the centre, modelled on the configuration of the finely sculpted altar from Pergamon, an ancient Greek city in modern-day Turkey. (The altar is now in the Pergamon Museum in Berlin.)

Speer gathered together 134 anti-aircraft searchlights and arranged them at intervals of 13 metres (43 feet) around the parade ground, pointing vertically into the air. After dark the searchlights were illuminated and their beams gave onlookers the impression of being in a staggeringly large cathedral with a ceiling that soared towards the heavens. The lights exerted their effect inside the parade ground, where everyone felt that they were in a single unified space, and also outside, where even from a great distance it was obvious that something of global importance was occurring.

In plan, section and elevation this effect is not obvious. The Cathedral of Light could exist only at night, and needed a certain amount of mist or smoke for it to be visible at all. Its ephemerality is part of its magic. The fact that the magic was put to work for supremely evil ends means that it is unlikely ever to be repeated in an authoritative way. No regime hoping to inspire popular support would do anything to invite comparison with the Nazis. The places where light-beam-defined spaces are to be found in modern culture are discotheques, fields and stadiums where loud throbbing music and lasers encourage patterns of behaviour that would have been inimical to the Nazis.

1 Elevation

2 Plan

3 Section A-A

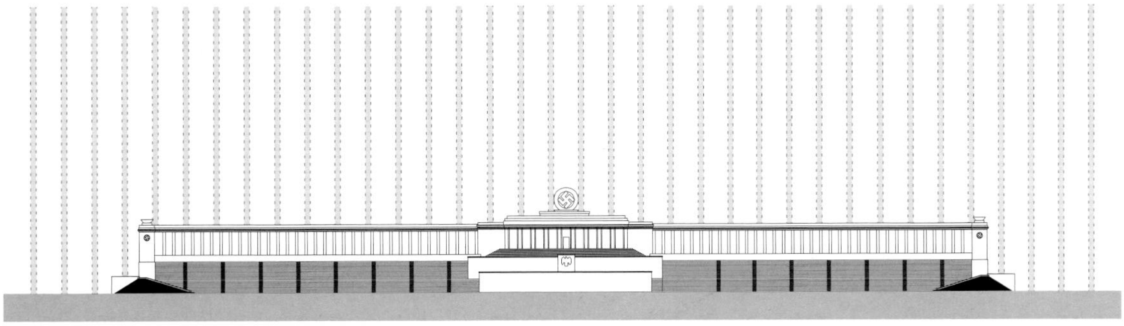

1

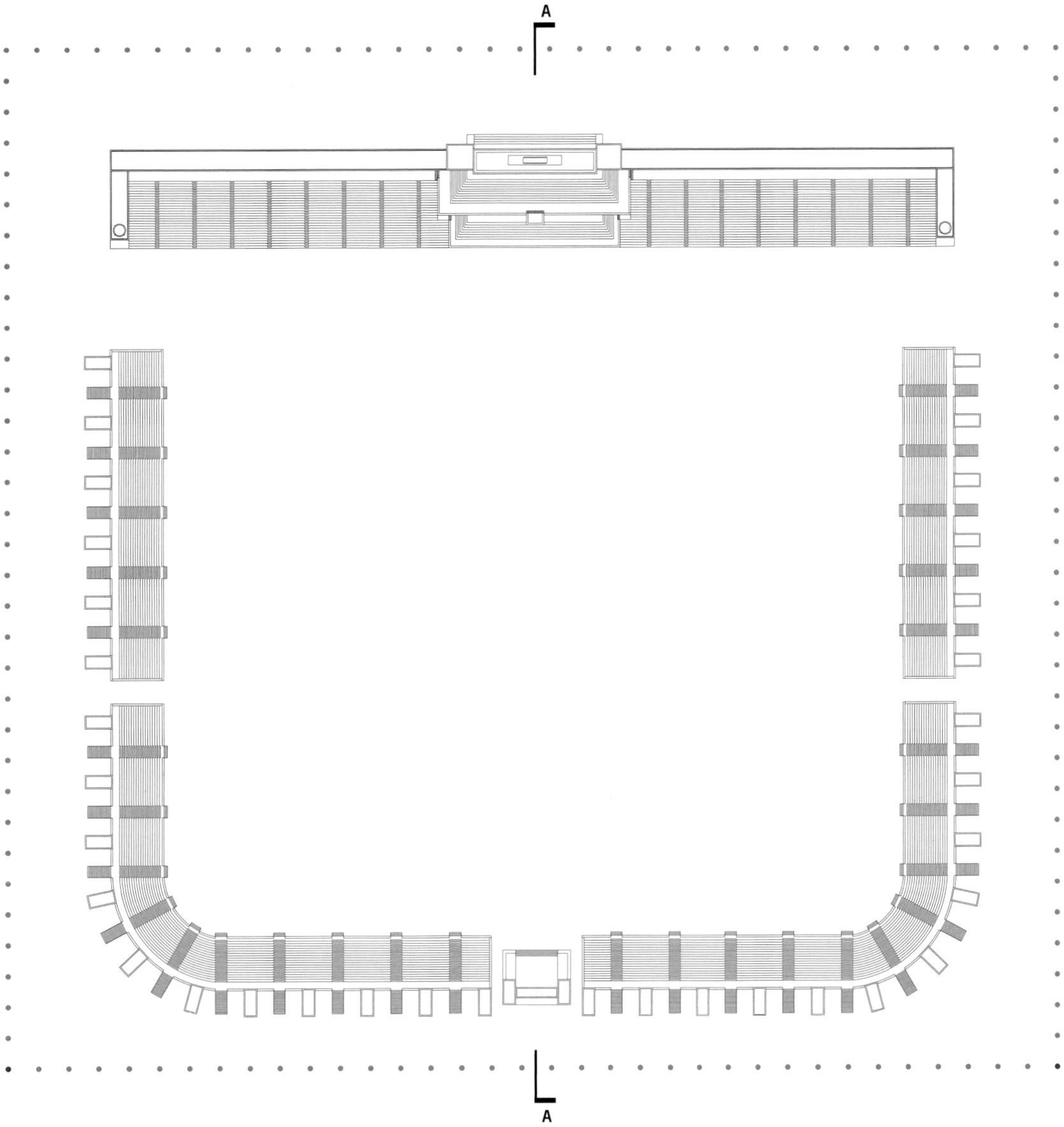

A

A

2

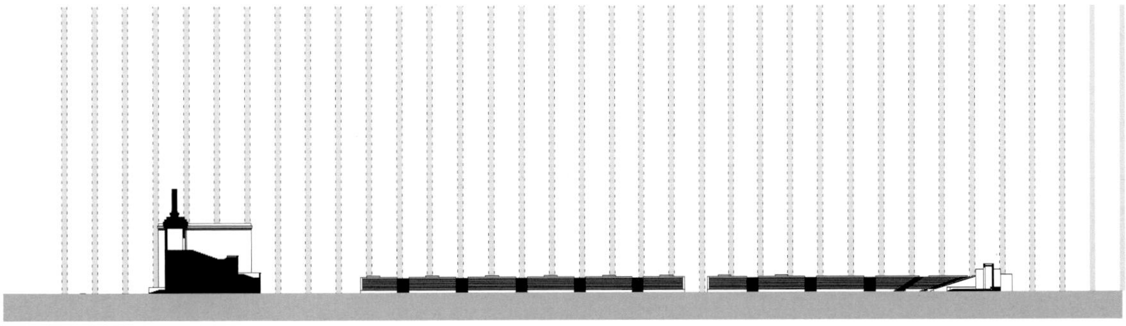

3

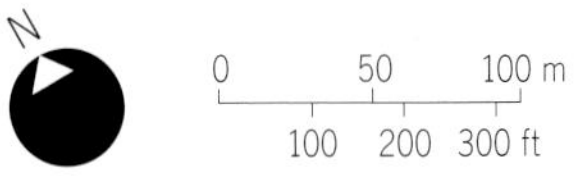

Sydney Opera House

Jørn Utzon, 1918–2008

Sydney, NSW, Australia; 1958–73

It may not be immediately obvious what impelled an Australian city to make an opera house its most prominent feature, but the idea can be traced back to Dame Nellie Melba (1861–1931) from Melbourne, a diva of the first order, who was one of the first Australians to become an international star. With a prominence comparable to today's Australian film stars, Nellie Melba gave the nation a presence in high culture that bolstered its self-confidence in its dealings with Europe.

Dame Joan Sutherland from Sydney achieved similar prominence in the twentieth century. Bearing in mind that Australian opera stars have made a global impact – and given the established rivalry between Melbourne and Sydney – the decision to build an opera house on this spectacular site does make sense.

An international competition was organized to find the best designer for the opera house, and the Danish architect Jørn Utzon was selected on the basis of some highly innovative proposals. Turning those ideas into reality turned out to be a much more complex and expensive process than anyone had anticipated, and the many problems – technical, financial and political – became overwhelming for the architect, who resigned from the project long before it was finished. The building was eventually completed with funding from a popular lottery established for the purpose.

The trials involved in creating Sydney Opera House were extraordinary, but the achievement is unarguable. While there are reservations about the building's suitability as a place to stage operas, it has been stupendously successful in asserting Sydney's presence on the world stage. From the moment its gleaming white shell roofs were visible, images of them circulated as symbols of Australia. Internationally the misconception that Sydney is Australia's capital is perpetuated by the continuing existence of the opera house. (The capital of Australia is Canberra.)

The audience for this building is much greater than the audience for opera. It is even greater than the number of visitors to Sydney – or Australia, for that matter. For this wider audience, the internal organization of the space is not an issue. What matters is the compelling and distinctive silhouette – the curved concrete shells covered with iridescent tiles that preside authoritatively over Sydney Harbour. The bulk of the building consists of a self-effacing plinth, a continuation of the land-mass on a natural promontory. A great flight of steps on the landward side brings visitors up the outside of the building, as though they are walking up a hill. The shells sit on top, looking delicate and poised, and housing the upper reaches of the main auditoriums.

To some eyes, Sydney Opera House is a highly sculptural edifice that owes more to the traditions of twentieth-century abstract sculpture than to traditional architectural form. However, the shells are a small part of the whole, and the general idea of making a relatively light canopy seem to float above a dense mass of building has many precedents. Symbolizing Australia's current prominence in world culture, Sydney Opera House is a counterpart to Uluru's continuing and no less iconic presence in the outback (pages 12–13).

1 Elevation

2 Section

3 North Elevation

4 Foyer Level Plan

1 Major hall
2 Minor hall

5 Podium Level Plan

1 Entrance foyer
2 Stage
3 Auditorium
4 Lounge
5 Orchestra
6 Restaurant

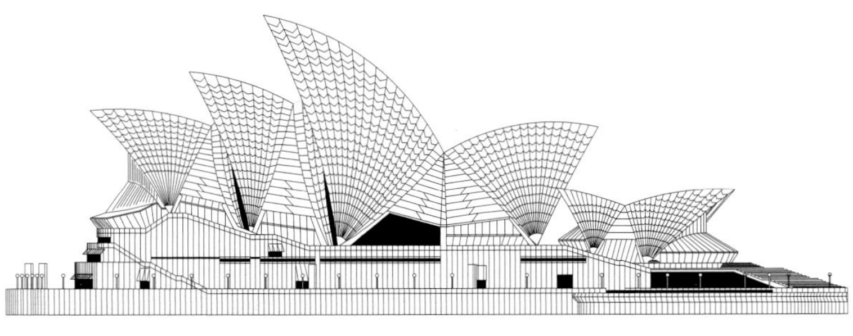

1

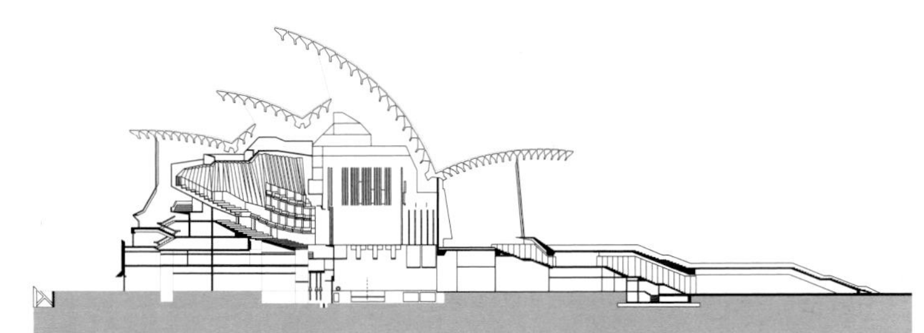

2

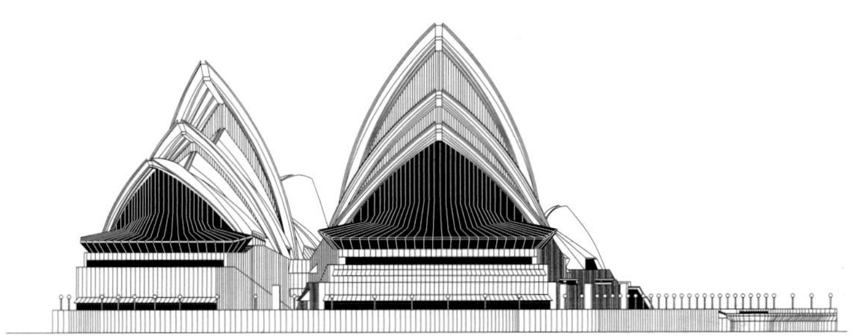

3

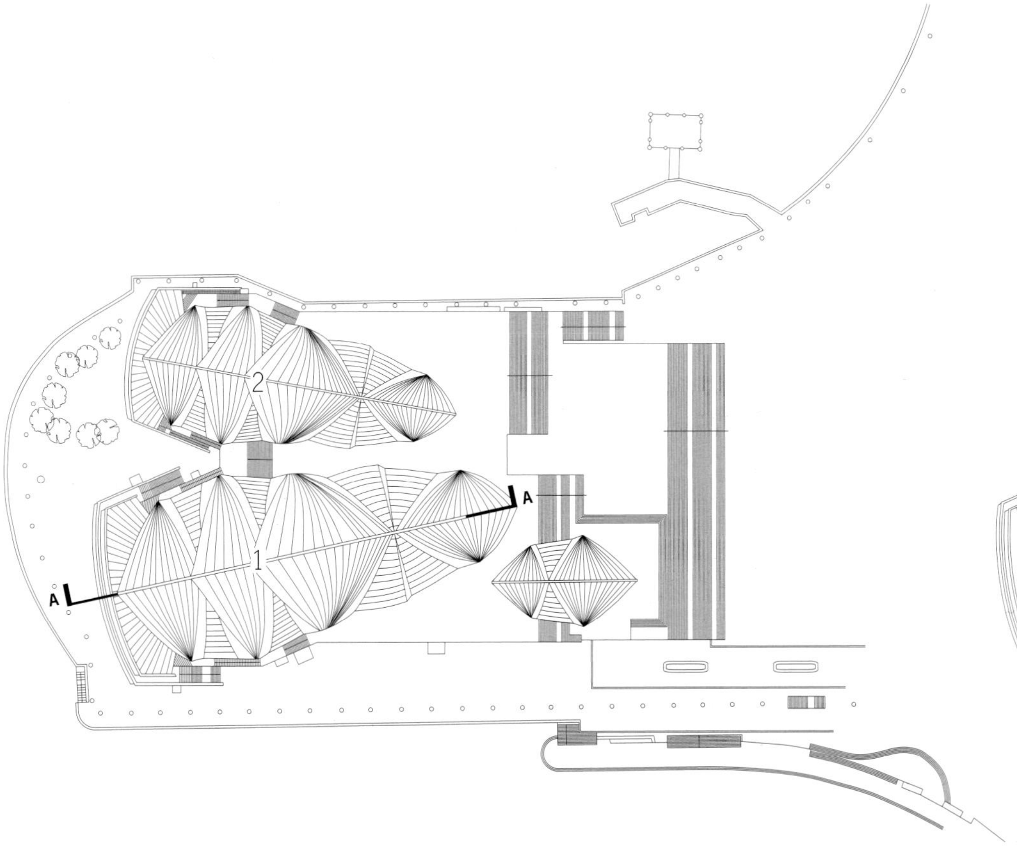

4

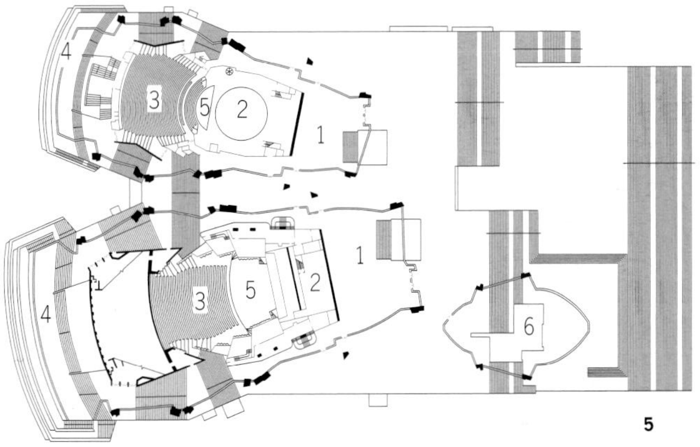

5

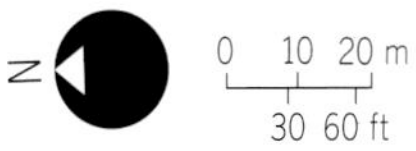

0 10 20 m
30 60 ft

Judge Harry Pregerson Interchange

Los Angeles, California, USA; 1993

The freeways of Los Angeles are the largest building works in one of the world's largest cities. They serve the automobile, which is the dominant mode of transport there. Most major cities work by bringing people together in places where they can form crowds and develop a sense of collective identity – whether the place is the Agora of ancient Athens (pages 306–307) or Fifth Avenue in New York. Los Angeles does not work in that way, and its citizens rarely meet one another by chance in the street.

The city's public realm is less splendid than the homes of some of its wealthier citizens, and the road network that enables travel from one destination to the next is the greatest of the public buildings. There is no doubt about the network's utility, nor its cultural impact. There may be doubt about its architectural credentials, but in the interchanges, such as the one where freeways 110 and 105 meet and cross, there is an aesthetic pleasure to be had from driving under, over and through the swooping forms.

It is the cultural value of this interchange that makes architecture of it. Los Angeles has traditionally lacked conventional monuments, though it is acquiring them. The road system has been its identifier but, in contrast to Manhattan's uptight grid, it is made of relaxed spaghetti curves. The ancient Athenians came to the conclusion that it was the people who constituted a city, not its buildings, but they made monuments nonetheless. Their word for a city, *polis*, is the root of our word 'politics', meaning the relations between people.

In Los Angeles the connections between people are sometimes invisible and electronic, but in the freeways the links become monuments in their own right. The monumental quality of this interchange is confirmed by the fact that it was named after Judge Harry Pregerson, who oversaw a legal case against the Century Freeway that, had its outcome been different, would have prevented its construction.

Freeway 105 runs east and west, while 110 runs north and south; they intersect on the edge of a district called Athens. Also known as the Century Freeway, 105 is relatively short, but usually busy because it leads to the main airport. Even before it opened in 1993, it was used as the set for a Hollywood film called *Speed*. Freeway 110 is the oldest of the freeways, parts of it dating back to the 1940s. It is known as the Harbor Freeway at the interchange, but further north it becomes the Pasadena Freeway.

The place where the roads intersect on five levels is made even more complex by the presence of a metro station and car-pool lanes that connect with the Harbor Transitway. Curving gracefully through space are the various lines of the vehicles' trajectories. While the plan of the intersection gives a good idea of its layout, the horizontal dimensions are so much longer than those of a conventionally inhabited building that the whole interchange drawn in section looks merely flat.

Not far from the Judge Harry Pregerson Interchange are the so-called Watts Towers, built over a 33-year period by the construction worker Simon Rodia in his back yard, and the two structures can be seen as polar opposites in the spectrum of Los Angeles' monument-building culture. One is an official construction, evidently for the public good, costing millions of dollars; the other is born of a personal obsession, built with salvaged materials – and doing nothing recognizably useful except inspiring us to notice the resilience with which human creativity finds means of expression.

1 Interstate 110

2 Interstate 105

Dwellings

Was there a time when no one lived in buildings? If so, humans would have been able to inhabit only those places where the climate made survival possible. Our buildings allow us to modify the effects of climate, so that we can warm or cool ourselves as desired, and inhabit places that are naturally less hospitable. Speculating about the ancient past, we have come up with the idea of the 'cave man', as though all our ancestors lived in caves, which is unlikely – mainly because there were not enough caves to go round. Certainly there were caves that acted as dwellings, and because they are solid they have preserved the relics of their occupants, but most people would have lived in light temporary structures that have vanished without trace.

Evolutionary theory can offer clues about what primitive structures were like, especially through observation of animals who build. Birds' nests offer a model of scavenging and arranging that might well be ingrained in humans as an instinct that impels us to make purchases to furnish our homes – and bower birds are spectacular builders with a strongly developed aesthetic sense. Beavers and badgers burrow and build, and we share DNA with them. Our distant ancestors were probably already builders before they were altogether recognizable as humans. Some traditions of minimal dwelling may stretch back many thousands of years, but we have no way of checking, because the shelters – be they grass-roofed domes made by Australian Aborigines or the ice domes of the Inuit – do not make such an impact on their terrain as stone buildings whose foundations leave a longer-lasting trace.

For most humans in most parts of the world, finding shelter is the first priority. Once that need has been met, other issues, such as status, come into play – and there seems to be no upper limit in this respect to the human imagination. Dwellings become sites for the kind of ostentation that establishes social standing, whether through extravagant displays of towering stone and large areas of glass, or by serving sumptuous food on fine dishes. Dwellings such as the Palazzo Medici were also places of business, while the palaces of some heads of state were so much more than dwellings that they have been included in chapter 6 (pages 232–61) as administrative buildings. Ludwig II's Neuschwanstein might one day have functioned as a palace, had he lived longer – it has a throne room, after all. However, it was never an official building, remaining a private realm that went far beyond the usual ways of establishing status. It was visited by hardly anyone during Ludwig's tenure. It is now a very popular building that invites visitors to share the dream of dwelling in a mythical world of magic and chivalry. It was the evocation of that dream that was the cause of the building's ruinous expense, not the need for shelter, nor the desire for status.

On a much more modest budget, the Schröder House established itself as an extrovert private dwelling that had absorbed cultural value because of its obvious connection with the art world. It is the smallest of UNESCO's World Heritage Sites – recognized by the committee as a masterpiece of human creative genius.

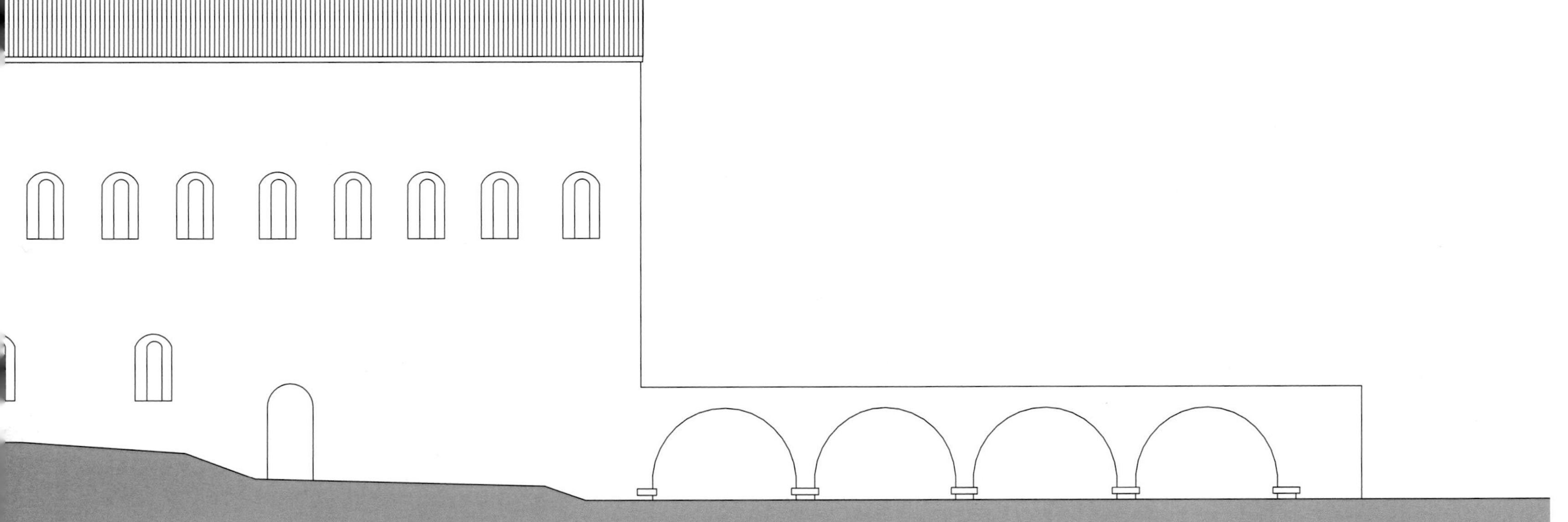

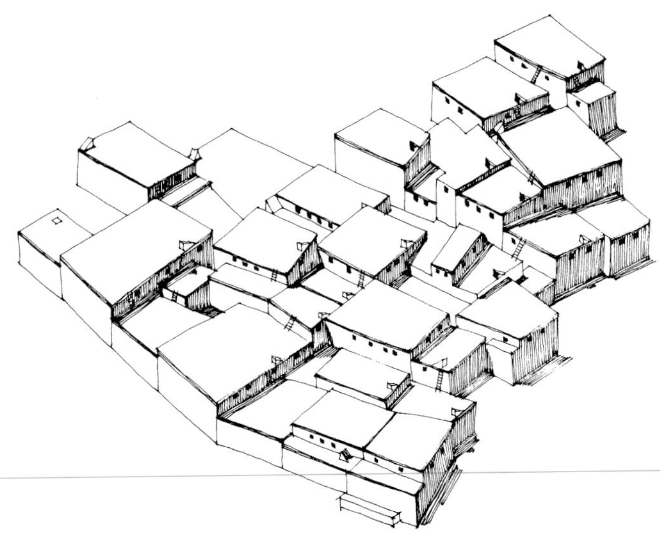

Houses at Catal Huyuk and Troy

Turkey; c.6000 BCE and c.1250 BCE

One of the earliest known settlements is Catal Huyuk, which developed in Neolithic times on the landmass that used to be called Anatolia. The dwellings were made of mud bricks, which needed periodic renewal, and during the centuries when the place was occupied the earth from demolished houses built up into the mounds that gave Catal Huyuk its modern name (meaning 'forked mound'). It is thought that about 10,000 people lived there, making it probably the largest settlement in the world at the time. (See photograph above left and drawings opposite, above.)

Conditions for farming did not arise until the global warming of the Holocene, the geological age that began about 11,000 years ago and continues to the present. The climate change made possible a shift from hunting and scavenging to cultivating food – the most fundamental step in establishing a sedentary culture, which would lead eventually to a tradition of high-status monuments and sophisticated artistic developments.

The first moves towards growing crops and domesticating animals seem to have been made in Mesopotamia – the region between the Tigris and the Euphrates – on land that is now part of Iraq, and in Jericho on the west bank of the Jordan.

The flat-roofed houses at Catal Huyuk were better than minimal dwellings, having several small chambers. They were packed closely together and entered through the roof – so the circulation around the settlement would have involved walking across roofs of neighbouring homes. Burials took place in the houses, which suggests a strong rapport between a house and its occupants. Walls finished with multiple layers of plaster suggest that the houses were occupied for long stretches of time.

Catal Huyuk's individual dwellings are less remarkable than their agglomeration, which produced what may have been the first urban environment – though what that meant at that time is an open question. In later settlements, social stratification would be expected – with some relatively rich people, some relatively poor, some engaged directly in food production, others with more specialized skills such as potters or toolmakers – but at Catal Huyuk, all that may have lain in the future.

The city of Troy was on the same landmass as Catal Huyuk but developed much later and belonged to a different civilization. (See illustration above right and drawings opposite, below.) The first settlement at Troy dates from c.3000 BCE, but culturally its most important period came later since it was the setting for the events in Homer's *Iliad*. Homer lived in the late ninth or early eighth century BCE, but the events he described are thought to be broadly historical and to have occurred in the twelfth century BCE. Paris, a Trojan prince, abducted Helen, the wife of the king of Sparta, causing all the Greek states to gather together and lay siege to Troy to avenge the wrong. The Trojans were famous warriors, but the Greeks defeated them by a mixture of valour and trickery. The leaders of the Trojan War had dealings with gods and were seen as heroes in later ages. Citadels from this era sometimes became the sites of temples.

At Troy itself the archaeology is disappointing because it was excavated in the nineteenth century by the Prussian archaeologist Heinrich Schliemann. Schliemann correctly identified the site but became over-excited in his quest for Homeric treasures, and dug right through the archaeological layers that he sought, destroying them in the process. So the evidence that can be salvaged today is actually of an earlier era – an era that was already ancient history in the age of Achilles.

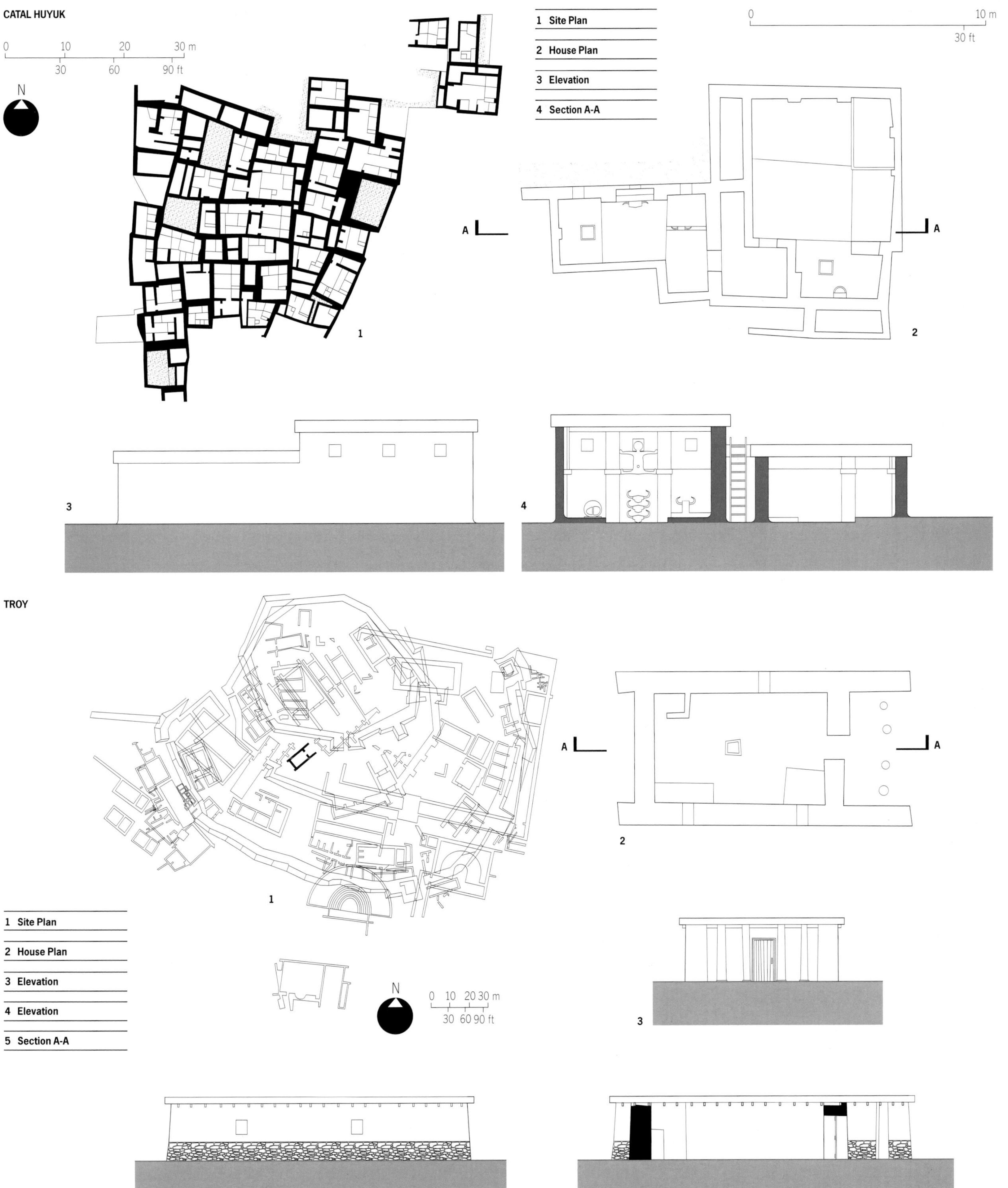
CATAL HUYUK
0 10 20 30 m
30 60 90 ft
N
1
1 Site Plan
2 House Plan
3 Elevation
4 Section A-A
0 10 m
30 ft
A
A
2
3
4
TROY
A
A
2
1
1 Site Plan
2 House Plan
3 Elevation
4 Elevation
5 Section A-A
N
0 10 20 30 m
30 60 90 ft
3
4
5

Houses at Nagano and Skara Brae

Nagano, Koshin'etsu, Japan; 5000–2500 BCE | Skara Brae, Orkney, UK; c.2500 BCE

The Jomon people occupied the archipelago of islands that make up Japan. From prehistoric times they dwelled in villages, including some large settlements. The pit houses they developed were circular and hollowed into the ground to a depth of about a metre, then covered with a roof that was probably thatched, as in the houses reconstructed at Nagano in the Koshin'etsu region (see photograph above left and drawings opposite, above) – but all direct evidence of them has long since perished. The houses were typically 3 or 4 metres (10 or 13 feet) in diameter.

The earliest known culture to have produced pottery, Jomon takes its name from its distinctive pots, which were decorated with a rope that had been coiled round a stick. Significantly, these village communities emerged quite independently from Mesopotamian influence – Mesopotamia was the site of the very first settlements – and the early developments in Japan were not associated with agriculture, but they must have had abundant supplies of fish and fruit near at hand to provide sustenance for the inhabitants.

The little group of houses at Skara Brae in the Orkney Islands, off the north coast of mainland Scotland, is remarkable for different reasons (see photograph above right and drawings opposite, below). These houses were built entirely in stone and must have been exceptional in their day or there would have been other survivals.

At this site, stone was plentiful, and it was used not only for the walls but also for the furniture inside the dwellings. There is something that resembles a dresser or credenza and other arrangements that look like beds. Perhaps heather was used to create a soft sleeping surface. It would have been kept in place by the stone kerb and covered with animal skins.

There is much scope for conjecture about what life would have been like at Skara Brae and it is perhaps unwise to draw modern inferences from the ambiguous stones. If an arrangement of stones recalls a dresser, then it might be imagined that the inhabitants had crockery to display in it – whereas the stone container might in fact have been designed as a place to stow fishing tackle or to venerate the household gods.

The houses were once surrounded by debris discarded by their occupants, which built up into a surrounding hillock. Even when they were in use, the original dwellings would have been almost lost to view among surrounding sand dunes. When they fell out of use, the sands drifted across them, preserving them. Then the settlement was rediscovered and re-used at a later period – but the second occupiers had no knowledge of the Neolithic furniture that by that time was buried by the sand beneath their feet.

NAGANO

1 Front Elevation

2 Side Elevation

3 Section A-A

4 House Plan

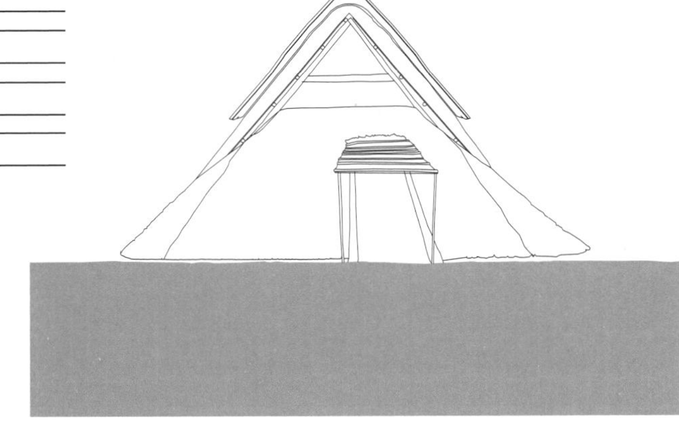

1

2

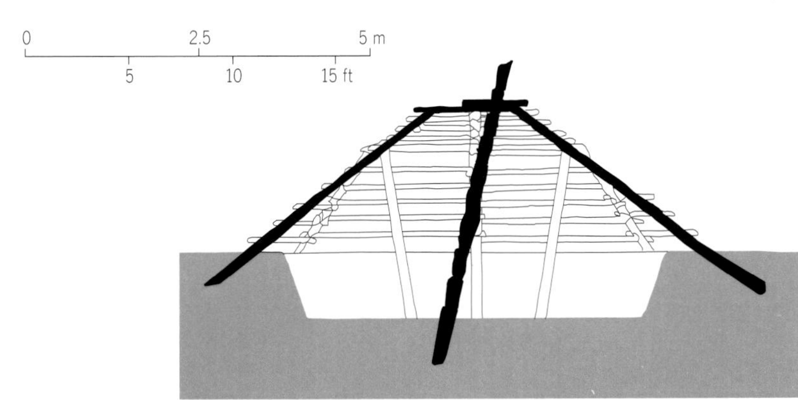

3

A

A

4

SKARA BRAE

Site Plan

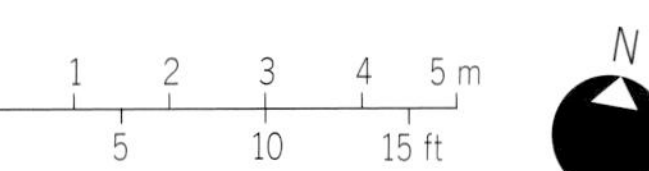

N

Igloo, Tipi and Bedouin Tent

Central Inuit, North America and Greenland | Lakota Nation, North America | Northern Africa

There is a perfection about the igloo that sets it apart from all other dwellings. It is made from building material that falls from the sky. There are no old igloos, no authoritative examples. Igloos are made to order and, when the need for them has passed, they melt away into the landscape.

'Igloo' is used by the Inuit people to mean any sort of house, including the timber and earth huts that are part of their repertoire. When used by anyone else, the word means the snow-dome that has been constructed by Inuits for as long as the rest of the world has known about them. The igloo is made by building up blocks of compressed snow in a circle, one ring after another, until the dome is complete. It can be refined by introducing a block of ice to act as a window and let in some light, and by building a tunnel from the entrance so that it is less exposed to freezing winds.

As long as the temperature is low enough, the structure remains sound. The air trapped in the snow gives it excellent insulating properties, allowing comfortable temperatures to be maintained within. The inside surface can melt away with the internal heat, but the blocks of snow tend to weld together. There is no need for a fire: the heat generated by bodies and oil lamps is enough if the draughts of icy air are excluded. Stones warmed in a camp fire can be brought inside and animal skins are used to line the space so that occupants do not touch the wet walls.

Snow igloos are unlikely to last longer than a season. Small ones are made as shelters on hunting trips and may be occupied for only a night or two. They can be made quickly – in under an hour – and the igloo is perhaps better understood as an activity of making than it is as a drawing in plan and section.

The tipi is a tent developed by the Lakota people who lived nomadically on the great plains of north America before the creation of the United States. Its distinctive conical form was produced by a structure of tall, straight pine trunks leaning from the perimeter to support one another at the apex, thereby avoiding the need for a central post. The pine supports were covered in buffalo hides joined together and cut into a semi-circle, which was wrapped over the structure. It gave effective protection from rain but had much less insulation than an igloo. Tipis were made large enough to allow the lighting of a fire inside, and flaps in the covering made it possible to adjust to wind direction and ensure a decent chimney effect – so that smoke was drawn up and out rather than just filling the tent. Tipis are still in use, but modern ones have canvas coverings.

A different form of tent that answered similar purposes was developed by the Bedouin people who herded livestock nomadically in the Middle East. This traditional way of life has been largely given up, as the imposition of national borders and new ways of making a living have influenced the old patterns.

Bedouin tents (shown above) are made of heavy woven fabrics that give some insulation from the heat. Propped in place with posts, the fabrics in turn keep the upper ends of the posts in position. At the edges, the posts are tethered with guy-ropes, which are pegged into the ground. Sometimes the hanging-fabric walls are shaded by awnings and sometimes the tents are joined together to create an extensive interior space – but it is never high, so the larger spaces bring with them a sense of pronounced horizontality. A tent would be the defining unit of a Bedouin family, and it would always have at least two major compartments so that the women could be separate from the men.

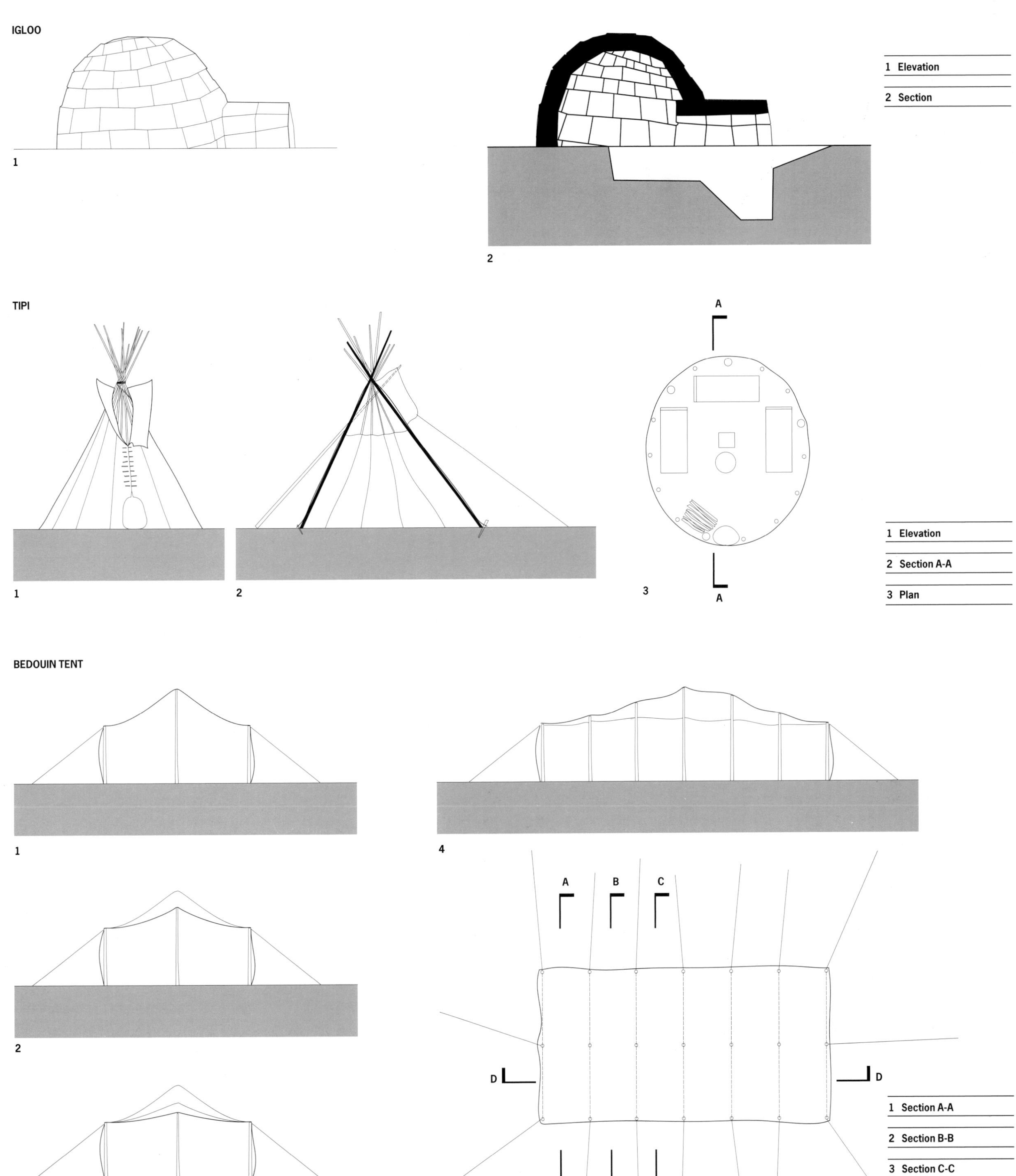
IGLOO
1
2
1 Elevation
2 Section
TIPI
1
2
A
A
3
1 Elevation
2 Section A-A
3 Plan
BEDOUIN TENT
1
4
A
B
C
D
D
A
B
C
2
3
5
1 Section A-A
2 Section B-B
3 Section C-C
4 Section D-D
5 Plan
0
5
10 m
15
30 ft

Villa of the Mysteries

Pompeii, Italy; before 79

In the year 79 the town of Pompeii near modern Naples was obliterated by an eruption of the neighbouring volcano, Vesuvius, which buried the place in ash. Pompeii was a resort town, inhabited by prosperous Romans when the Roman Empire was at its height.

Pompeii's buildings and their contents are remarkably well preserved because they were buried suddenly in dry volcanic ash, from which they have been excavated in modern times. The Roman inhabitants of the place perished, leaving voids in the ashy earth, which have been filled with plaster to recover the forms of the bodies and even their horrified expressions.

Much more is known about Pompeii than about any other Roman settlement – or, indeed, anywhere else in the ancient world. Its houses therefore dominate the study of Roman domestic life in a way that they would not if there were a wider range of material. It is not known whether the settlement was typical or very unusual, but the level of affluence on display there cannot have been widespread.

The finer houses had rooms decorated with frescoes, and the houses' modern names mostly come from the objects and activities depicted in these paintings. The 'mysteries' in the Villa of the Mysteries form part of a religious ritual, maybe a marriage, that is shown in one of the rooms – a dining room that seems to have been part of an extension to an older house.

Dining rooms were important places for entertaining and display, and this one is given prominence by being placed on axis. A visitor would arrive at an inconspicuous entrance, which was surrounded by and guarded by the servants' quarters and the kitchens. The passageway from the entrance led into a courtyard, which gave access to some important rooms, notably a room with an apse and another containing a wine press.

Doors in the covered peristyle that ran round the courtyard opened on to another peristyle in a much smaller courtyard, the atrium, a more private and exclusive space. The dining room was on the far side of the atrium, and beyond that was a secluded garden.

This is the scene of glamorous living. The status represented by the different parts of the villa would have been indicated not only by their furnishings but also by the activities engaged in by the servants (slaves), overwhelming the largest element of the household. Around the outer courtyard the servants would have been engaged in productive occupations. In other parts they would have attended to the needs of the resident family members and their guests.

The servants' attendance would have been most conspicuous and intense when the dining room was in use for a feast. The diners would recline on daybeds round the edge of the room, propped up on the left elbow, leaving the right hand free to pick up food and drink. Each new course would arrive with a flourish and would be distributed by the servants, while the diners remained in place, talking, eating and drinking.

1 Plan

1 Entrance
2 Peristyle
3 Crypt
4 Atrium
5 Tablinum
6 Exedra
7 Torcularium
8 South colonnades

2 West Elevation

3 Section A-A

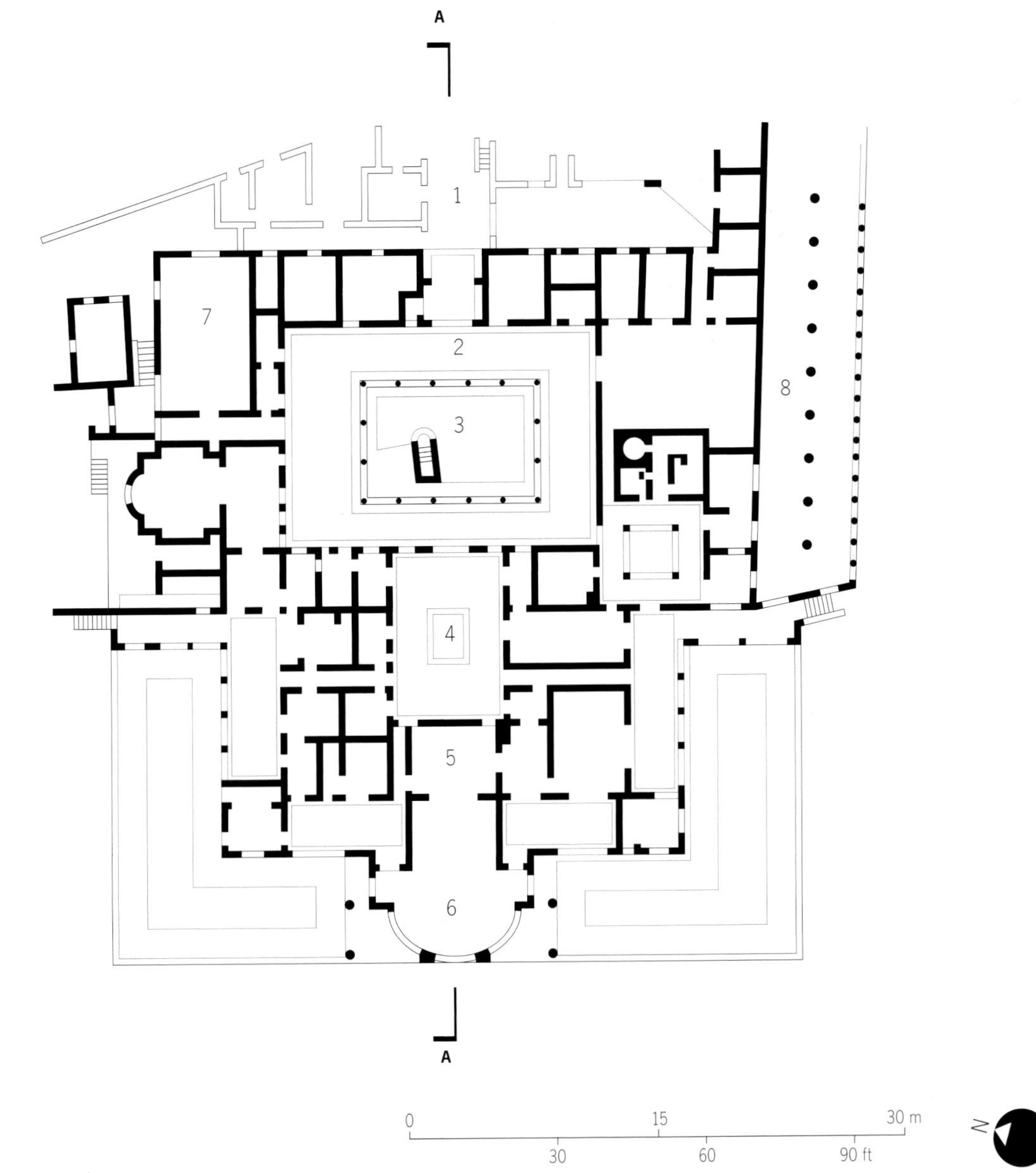

1

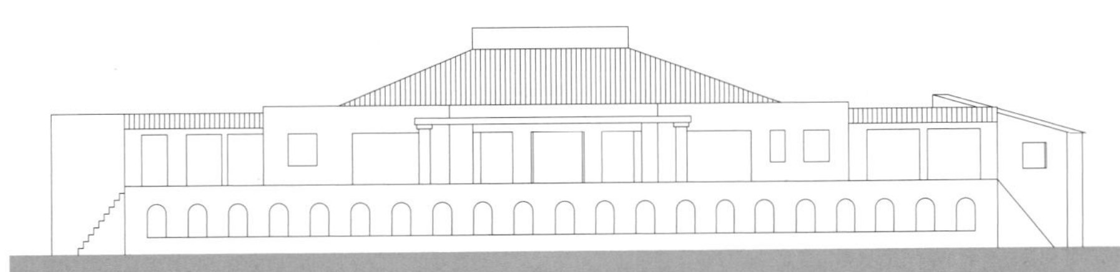

2

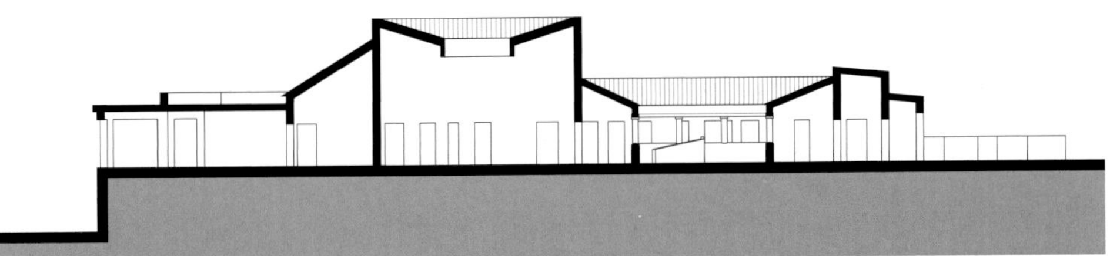

3

Houses in Burkina Faso and Kythera

Nankani village, Burkina Faso, West Africa | Paliochora, Kythera, Greece, c.1450

Adobe is basically mud. It is strengthened and stabilized by being mixed with sand and straw or animal dung. It is not as strong as fired ceramic bricks or concrete, but in the right conditions it can be very durable. In a hot dry climate, adobe bakes hard and takes on the texture of terracotta. In damper places, its surface needs to be protected to stop it deteriorating.

Regional names for much the same thing as adobe in Europe include cobb and pisé. A mixture of clay and dung makes a surprisingly waterproof coating, whether for walls or a flat roof, but it needs renewing when cracks appear.

The boundaries of modern African states often cut through traditional tribal areas. For example, most of the Nankani people live in Ghana, but the compound shown above left (and the drawings opposite, above) is just north of the border with Burkina Faso, within reach of Ziou, where there is a weekly market that acts as the main point of contact with the wider world.

Consisting of an assembly of small adobe cells grouped around an open communal area, the Nankani compound is organized almost like a household, but with the population of a hamlet. There is space to corral cattle, goats and sheep, and an outdoor cooking place (used on special occasions when the capacity of the ordinary roofed cooking space is inadequate). Also within the compound is an area of cultivated ground where the women grow food.

The adobe cells have various designated functions, including a shrine, and some of them have bands of geometric decoration that heighten the buildings' resemblance to huge ceramic vessels.

When someone dies in one of the sleeping rooms, the corpse is removed not by the normal ways of access, but by breaking a hole in the compound's exterior wall, which is repaired afterwards. This is done to prevent death from entering the living realm.

The foundation of Paliochora on Kythera in the mid-fifteenth century was predicated on a fear of what turned out to be its eventual fate. It was built inconveniently on a highly defensive site, to ward off the depredations of Turkish pirates.

Paliochora has 26 churches, built by successive generations of the two elite families that ran the place. The ordinary peasants lived in a state close to serfdom, which was unusual in Greece at the time. Their houses were built solidly with unshaped stones gathered from the surrounding fields and held together with an abundance of strong mortar. Facilities were not good. Individual houses consisted of a single room, lit principally from the doorway, and the lack of fireplaces suggests that the notoriously poor food of the field-labourers was cooked in a communal pot.

The defensive wall that protected the dwellings was a massive stone structure designed to resist arrows. When the Turkish fleet came with gunpowder, the defences were breached and the inhabitants taken and sold into slavery. The site was never resettled, so the old buildings were never replaced. They survive only where they have not collapsed.

BURKINA FASO

1 Section A-A

2 Elevation

3 Site Plan

1 Packed-earth court
2 Shrine
3 Exterior cooking space
4 Interior cooking space
5 A woman's space
6 A man's space
7 Thatched-roofed pens for goats and sheep
8 Entrance to compound (low wall)

1

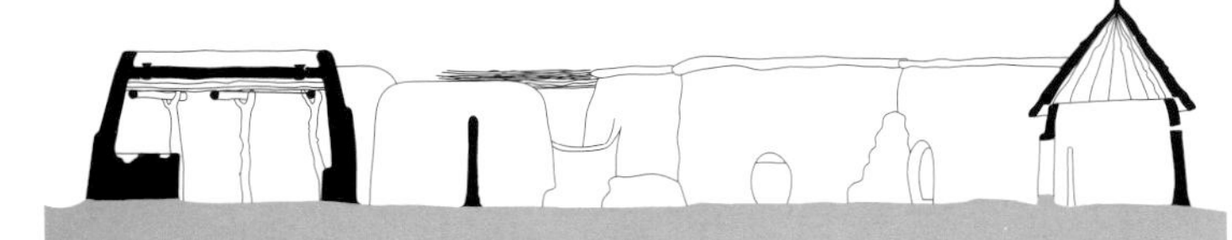

2

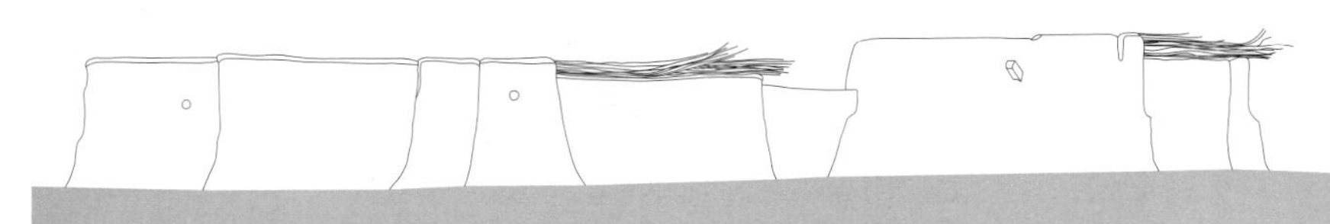

3

KYTHERA

1 Section A-A

2 Section B-B

3 House Plan

1

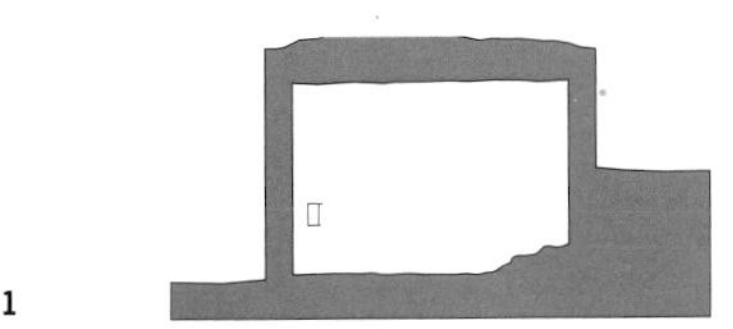

2

3

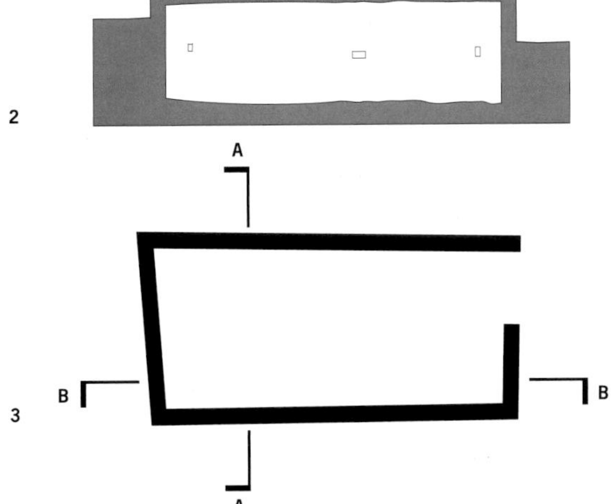

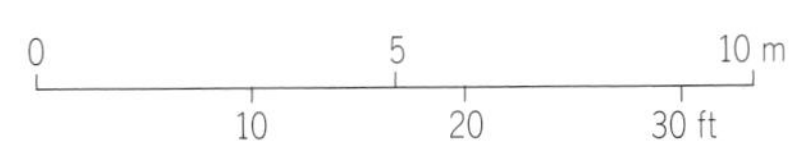

Karo Batak Houses

Northern Sumatra, Indonesia

Nobody has been able accurately to count the number of islands that make up Indonesia's landmass. There are about 18,000 – significantly more if the counting is done at low tide – some 900 of which are inhabited. Around 238 million people live in Indonesia, making it the world's fourth most populous country. The climate is tropical, with heavy rainfall and vigorous forest growth.

Indonesia's traditional buildings have timber structures and thatched or shingled roofs. There is tremendous diversity, and in the last few hundred years the styles of house-building have been influenced by the fusion of many cultures, not least those deriving from Chinese and Dutch colonial interests.

Traditional ways of building make use of locally plentiful materials to deal with the extremes of climate, and the house in various forms has been the focus of architectural expression. The established religion, which involved the veneration of ancestors at domestic shrines, did not produce monumental buildings. The dwelling was the main focus of activity in building.

In Bali the traditional house was distributed among several pavilions in a compound, but in Sumatra the dwellings could take on a monumental role, and were imposing in scale. Sumatra is more than 1,600 km (1,000 miles) long, with the Equator running across its mid-point.

Karo Batak was the name that the Malaysians gave to the indigenous people of Sumatra when the island came under Malaysian control in the seventh century. (The name was dropped when the people converted to Islam – which, over the centuries, most of them did.) Their houses developed a variety of characteristic roof forms, including those illustrated here. The roofs project well beyond the walls of the building and are steeply sloped, ensuring that rainwater is shed effectively. The roof is the most substantial part of the house, sailing high over an internal space that could house about eight families. Its height helps to keep the interior reasonably cool – the warm air rises up into the tall space, and the roof's overhangs shade the walls – while thick thatch provides insulation and useful protection against the heat of the sun. By contrast, the walls and floors are insubstantial.

In this hot and humid climate, the circulation of air keeps people comfortable, and it helps that the houses are typically raised off the ground. There are no windows in the walls, and any light that comes in finds its way through gaps between the boards or hurdles woven from plant material. Inside there are hearths for cooking – one for each family – and a central gulley for waste. Nineteenth-century Dutch settlers were shocked by the interiors of these dwellings, which looked impressive from the outside and were decorated with intricate timber carvings on boards that followed the gables or were attached at the ends of the roof ridge. Inside there was no furniture and little privacy – it was all smoke, darkness and wandering hens. The interiors seemed primitive and insanitary, but the Karo Batak were accustomed to them and found them unproblematic.

Their way of life meant that little time was spent in the house, except when they were sleeping or cooking. The surrounding forest produced an abundance of food, and each village had a shelter that acted as the focus for social life, such as a rice barn on stilts above the community space. The status of individual domestic buildings was established not by the hoarding of private goods within, but by the public display of ornament on the exterior.

KARO BATAK HOUSE 1

1 South Elevation

2 Section A-A

3 Plan

1 Entrance
2 Main room

1

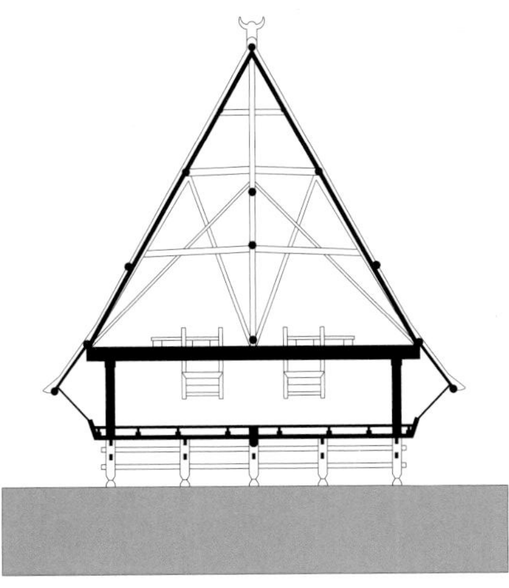

2

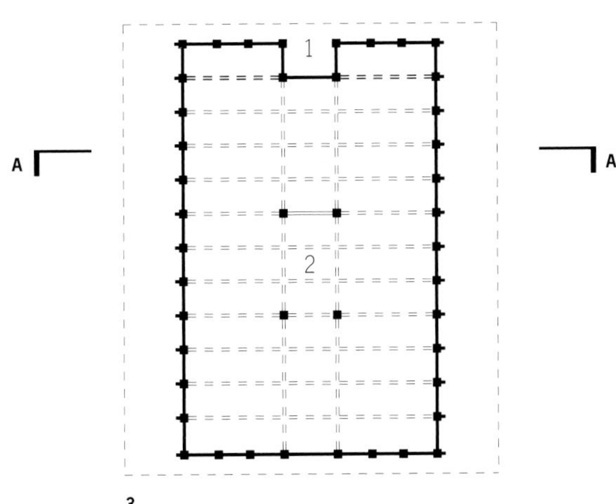

3

KARO BATAK HOUSE 2

1 South Elevation

2 Section A-A

3 Plan

1 Entrance
2 Main room
3 External walkway

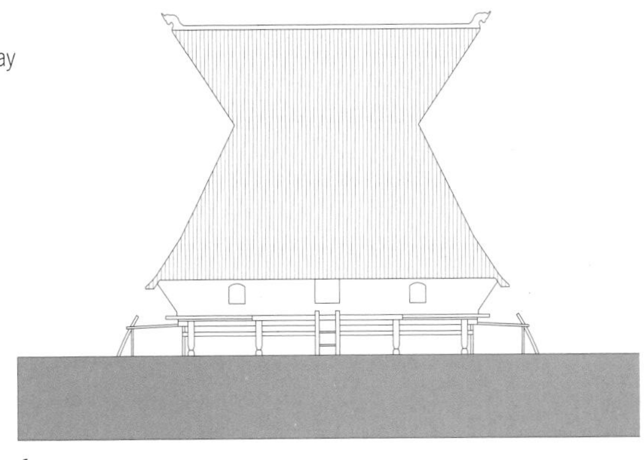

1

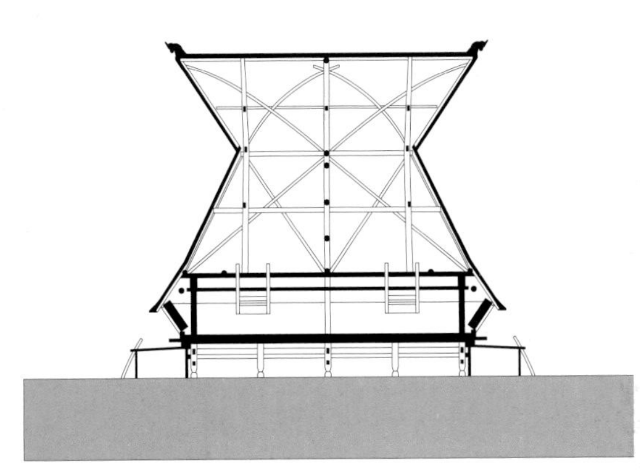

2

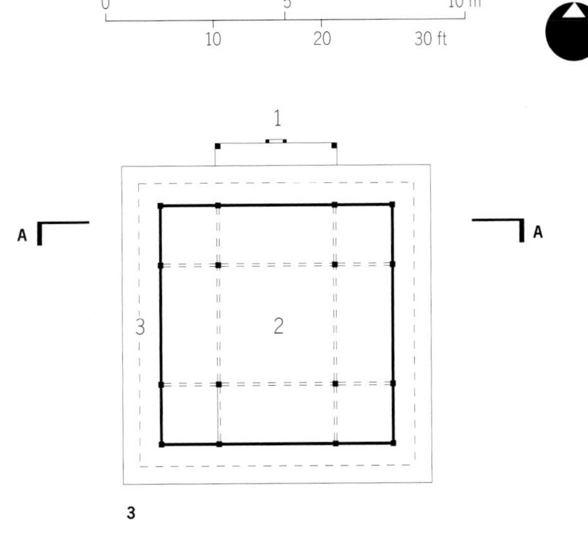

3

Le Thoronet Abbey

Le Thoronet, Provence, France, 1170–1200

The word monk derives from the Greek *monachos*, meaning solitary, and the earliest monks lived alone as hermits in the desert. The first monastic community is thought to have formed in Egypt in the fourth century around St Anthony; the monks were drawn to him as a father figure (*abba* in Hebrew). By the sixth century, the monastic practice was established and St Benedict wrote his Rule, a set of principles that codified how monks in a community should behave in relation to one another and to their father-like abbot. Women could also live in religious communities, as nuns, with an abbess.

By the time Le Thoronet Abbey was built in the late twelfth century, there were many monastic communities throughout Christendom. Individual monks owned no property but devoted their lives to work and prayer. The religious institutions to which they belonged attracted gifts from benefactors, but the monks also worked to make books or, with help from lay members of the community, farmed the lands attached to the monastery, which could be extensive. Some monasteries, such as the abbey at Cluny in southern Burgundy, grew to be very rich.

Le Thoronet was set up as part of a reform movement in the monastic world. Building began in 1098, when an abbey was founded at Cisteaux (later spelt Cîteaux) with the idea of following more vigorously the austere Rule of St Benedict. Adherence to the Rule spread particularly under the influence of St Bernard in the twelfth century, and by the beginning of the thirteenth century there were 500 Cistercian communities. In contrast to the monasteries that continued under the influence of Cluny, which could be richly decorated, Cistercian abbeys were plain and severe. Le Thoronet was typical in this respect, but unusual in being built entirely of stone. Not only the church but also the cloister and the subsidiary buildings all had stone vaults, so there is a remarkable uniformity about the spaces, especially now that the furnishings have been removed. Also, it was built in a single 30-year period, which makes it stylistically coherent.

There is no figurative carving at Le Thoronet. Most of the stone blocks are carved into stern geometric shapes with crisp corners. The capitals of columns are sometimes softened into a curve or a scrolled leaf, but window and door openings are very plain, with semi-circular arches above them in Romanesque tradition. In northern France by this time the arches would have been pointed, and the church given much larger windows, which would have introduced light into the upper parts of the vaults, but Le Thoronet was unfashionable. The solidity of its masonry and the firmly closed vaults gave it an exceptionally resonant acoustic.

Bearing in mind the intensity of the Provençal sun, the shade of the vaults is very welcome at Le Thoronet. At its peak in the thirteenth century, about 24 monks lived there. They decided how the place was run, meeting in the chapter house to do so. The chapter house opened off the cloister, which was not only a circulation space but also a place for contemplation. The monks' dormitory could be reached from the cloister and also directly from the church, so they could visit the church during the day and night to keep up the daily routine of prayers.

Le Thoronet declined during the fifteenth century and had been all but abandoned when it was put up for sale in 1791. It was taken into state ownership by the revolutionary government and preserved as a national treasure. Its fate was in marked contrast to what happened to Cluny, which was deliberately humiliated. Cluny Abbey was sacked and its few standing remains were turned into a stud farm.

1 Ground Floor Plan

1 Church
2 Sacristy
3 Library
4 Chapter house
5 Audience room
6 Parlour
7 Warming house
8 Cloister
9 Refectory site
10 Provision room
11 Lay brothers' building

2 Section A-A

3 East Elevation

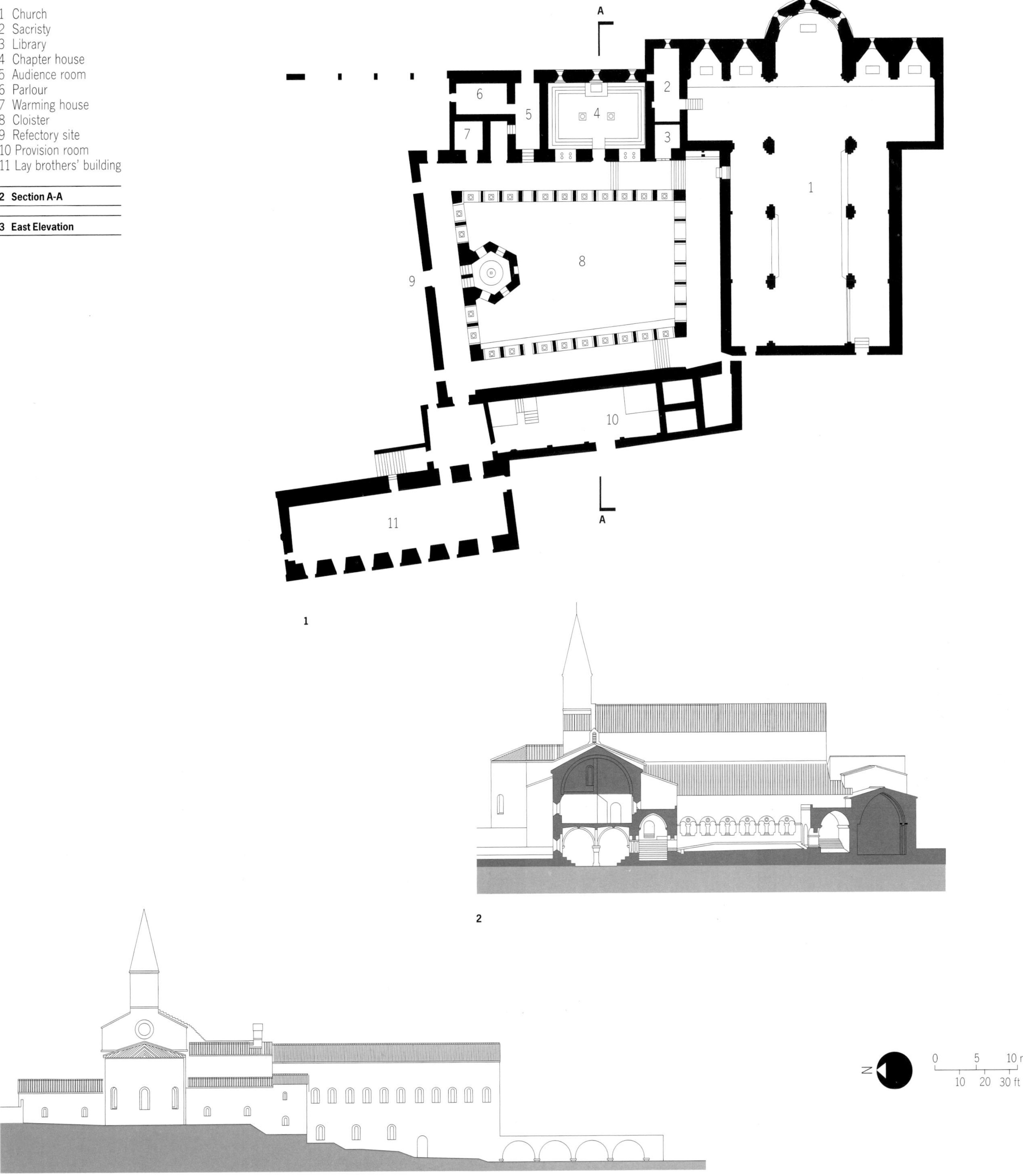

Dürer House

Nuremberg, Germany; c.1420

In places where there were forests nearby, houses were often built in timber. The smaller cottages of the peasantry would be built of earth, but the more substantial houses had timber frameworks with earth-based material filling in the spaces to make walls. Timber-frame construction was found in fortified towns across Europe during the Middle Ages, from northern Spain to Poland and Britain.

The example shown here, which was bought in 1509 by the German Renaissance painter Albrecht Dürer (1471–1528), is an unusually large city-centre house that was adapted to Dürer's particular needs but was not built for him. Its previous occupant had been an astronomer.

The house's large structural timbers had withstood centuries of neglect when the building was rediscovered in the nineteenth century and restored as a museum. A modern annexe has been added, to make the building work better as a museum, but the main body of the house dates from the fifteenth century and represents the continuation of a much older tradition.

Within the fortifications of a medieval town there was protected space, where people and livestock would muster if the region were under attack. Even when life was running normally, there would have been many more animals in the town than would be expected today, especially horses, but also hens, goats and pigs, which would live in the 'undeveloped' parts, reached by a network of narrow alleys and lanes that ran back from the main thoroughfares. Houses with lower status would be found in these areas, some of them no more than hovels. The principal routes, linking the city gates, castle, market and churches, were lined with the best buildings, such as Dürer's house.

Dürer was the most successful German artist of his time and he had a flourishing business producing paintings and prints. He bought the timber-framed house in Nuremberg when he was at the height of his fame and used it as the base for his operations, which extended internationally.

The lower two storeys are built in stone with a fine finish, which supports the timber-framed upper storeys. There is an imposing arched front door and a grand entrance hall, which was used as a place for routine business transactions.

Dürer's wife, Agnes, ran the business side of the household, so the hall and the first-floor domestic rooms were her territory. She prepared pictures for delivery and travelled away from Nuremberg to sell Dürer's prints. There were no children of the marriage, so the couple had plenty of space. The details of domestic life are not known, beyond the marked independence of husband and wife, but Agnes's maid would have lived there and presumably some of Dürer's studio assistants. They would have had rooms in the attic space.

The use of a timber frame for the upper storeys would have made it possible to introduce larger areas of window, had the studio use been anticipated – though glass was still very expensive. The broad open spaces in the upper floors are not characteristic of ordinary domestic interiors, but their orientation means that they are filled with diffuse north-easterly light, which is useful in a studio, and must have been influential in Dürer's decision to buy the house.

1 Ground Floor Plan

1 Entrance hall
2 Office
3 Store
4 Stairs up to domestic accommodation and studio
5 Modern annexe

2 South Elevation

3 Section A-A

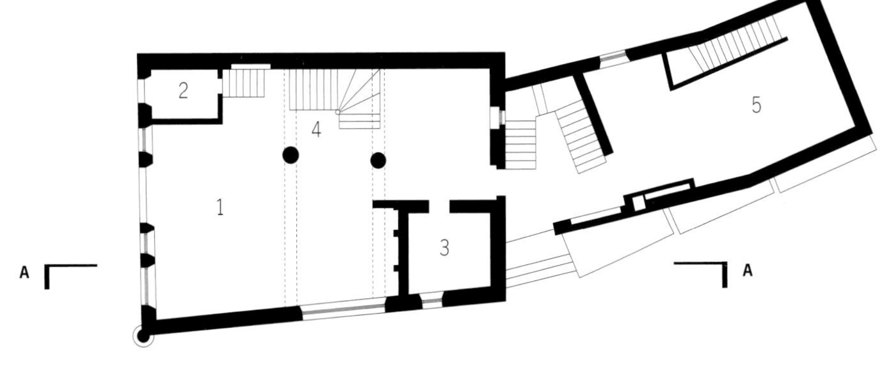

1

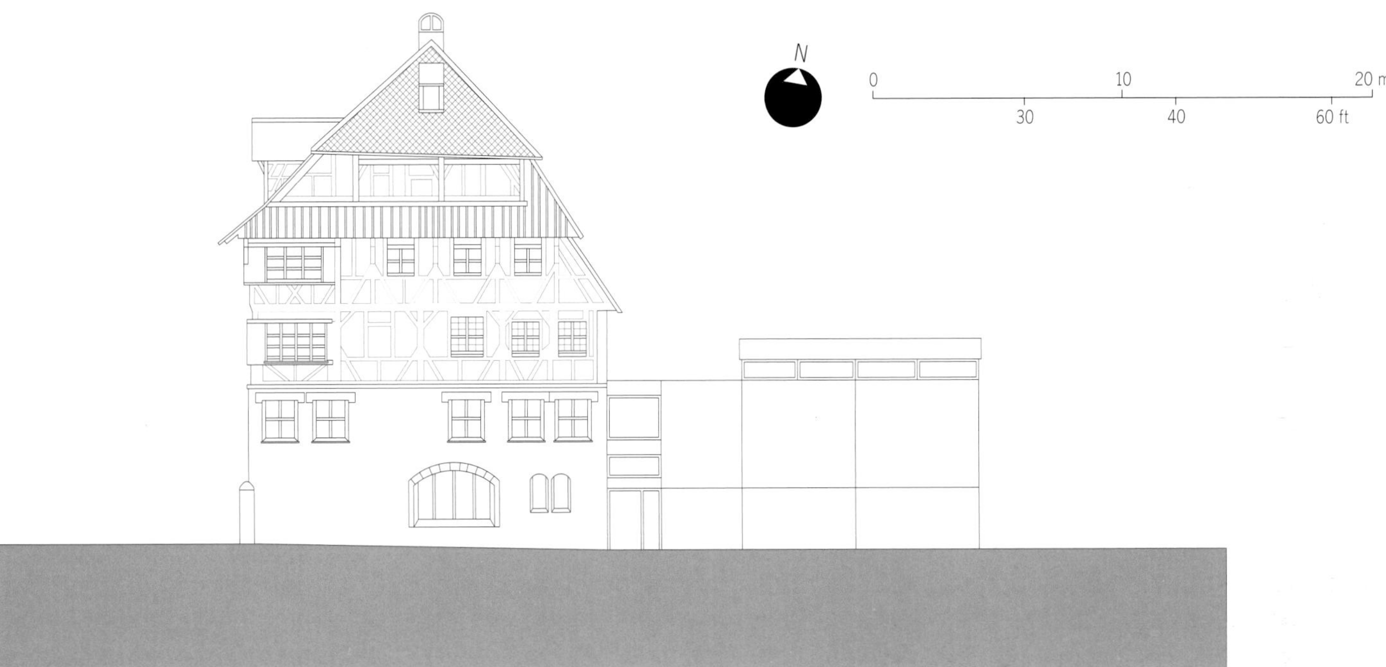

2

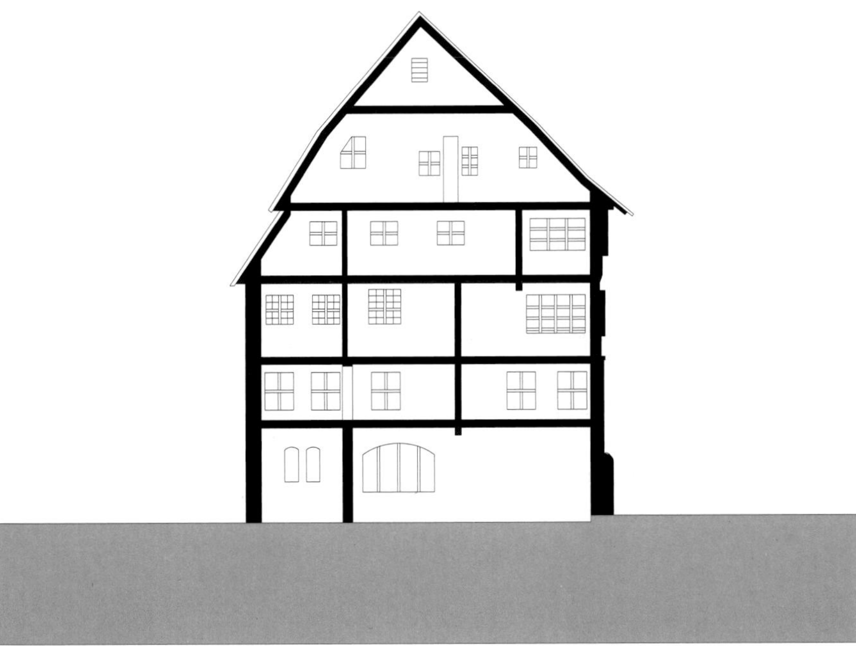

3

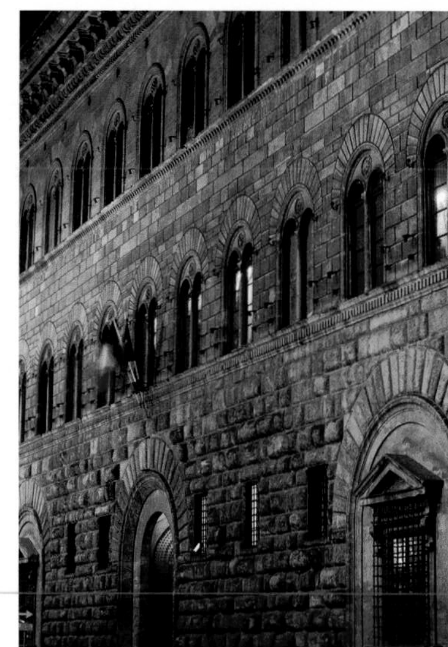

Palazzo Medici

Michelozzo di Bartolomeo, 1396–1472

Florence, Italy, 1444

The Medici bank made the Medicis one of the richest families in Europe. Cosimo de' Medici, who commissioned the Palazzo Medici in Florence, never held political office but exercised immense power behind the scenes. He had the wealth and influence of a ruler and lived at a time when fortunes such as his – made by commercial activity rather than by annexing lands through military strength – were a novelty.

The Renaissance, which the Medici family did so much to support with its commissions, represented more than a change in artistic style; it also marked a great social upheaval: the end of the feudalism of the Middle Ages and the advent of the modern commercial world.

When other powerful factions in Florence thought that Cosimo was too powerful for the city's good, he was banished, but he took his bank with him, and the city was impoverished until he was welcomed back.

On his return, Cosimo commissioned a palace from his friend Michelozzo di Bartolomeo, who had followed him into exile in Venice. (For Michelozzo, to be separated from his patron Cosimo would have been a more serious problem than leaving Florence.)

Occuping an entire city block, the palace is immensely solid and imposing in a reticent and dignified way. If it looks more like a corporate headquarters than a dwelling, that is entirely apt. It is not quite fortified like a feudal castle, but it would have been secure against riots. The outer wall at ground level is built of bulging rusticated stones that convey an air of gigantic robustness. Up above, the stone is smoother and more refined, and the block is topped off with an enormous overhanging cornice that makes the edifice even more imposing.

However the building is not ostentatious on the outside. Cosimo knew the effects of envy. Originally there were shops at the corners, which would have made the building seem more open to the outside, but in fact the entrances were limited and brought the visitor into an atrium space, reminiscent of a Roman villa. The principal apartments, including a magnificently decorated chapel, are on the first floor (the *piano nobile*), reached by a grand staircase.

Except for the chapel, the rooms would have been used in various ways, rather than having one particular purpose assigned to them. The business that went on there demanded a level of privacy and discretion. Cosimo's apartment was his office as well as his living area. It had anterooms, where clients would have waited, maybe without knowing who else was present. There would have been a steady traffic of servants, providing a form of security, but the place would have had the character of a private domain. The city of Florence was run from here, despite the fact that Cosimo rarely occupied a political position. He selected the people who would hold office, and saw to it that they were elected. The artworks and fine furnishings gave the palace an atmosphere of probity and stability.

The most sumptuous rooms are from the seventeenth century, lavishly decorated after the palace had been sold to the Riccardi family. Starting from the street, it makes a compelling sequence to step behind the somewhat forbidding façade, to enter the serene and harmonious world of the courtyard with its sober order, and then to ascend the staircase and find something altogether more unbridled: tumbling gold baroque ornament under a sky full of drapery, fleshy limbs and rather substantial cushiony clouds.

1 Second Floor Plan

1 Ballroom
2 Service room

2 First Floor Plan

1 Semi-public room
2 Chapel

3 Ground Floor Plan

1 Michelozzo's Courtyard
2 Apartment
3 Garden
4 Large salon
5 Courtyard of the Mules or Wells
6 Former public loggia
7 Stables
8 Tack room and grooms' space

4 Section A-A

5 East Elevation

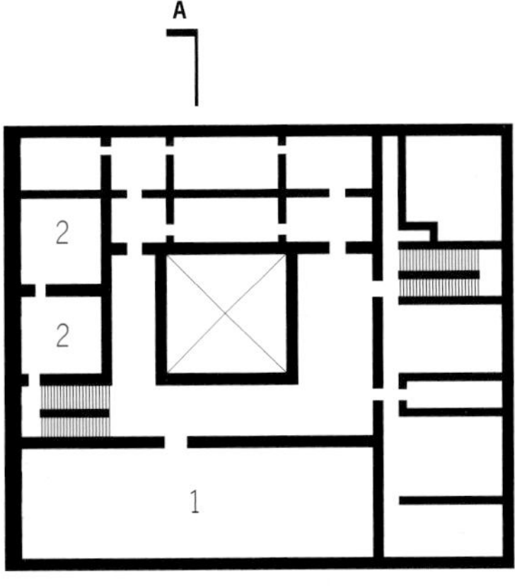

1

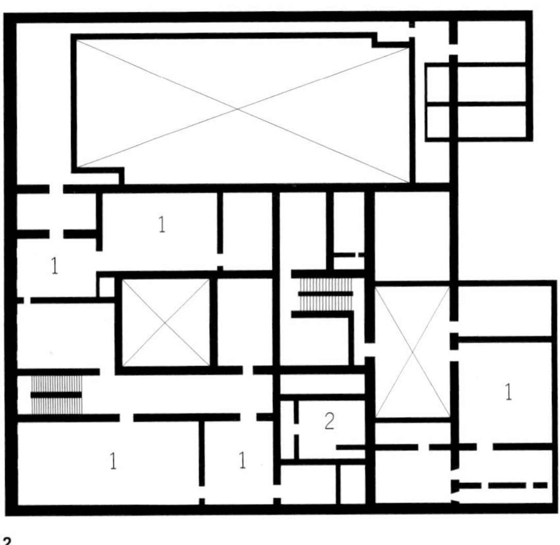

2

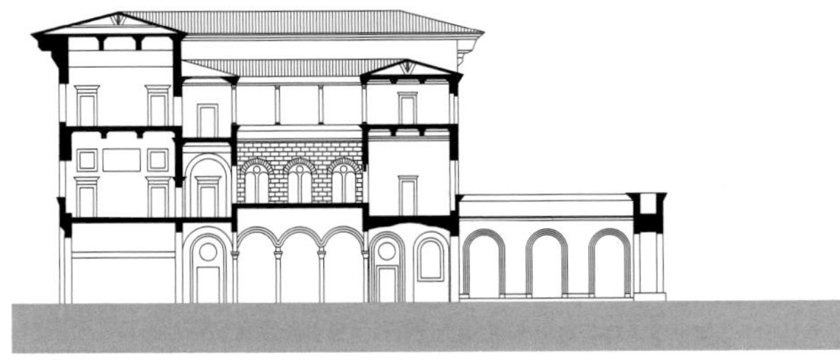

4

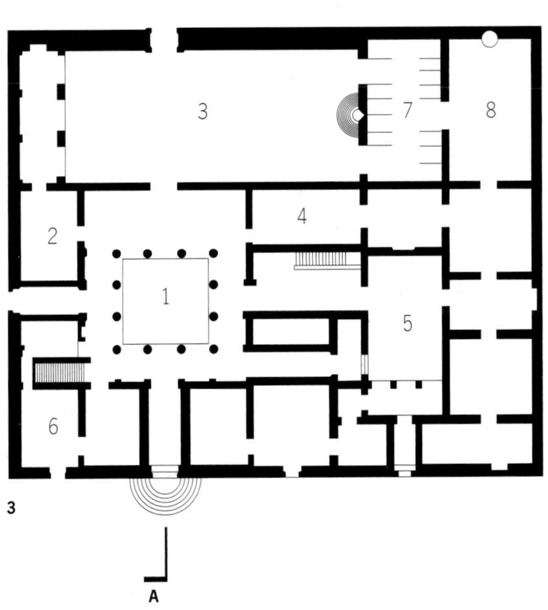

3

5

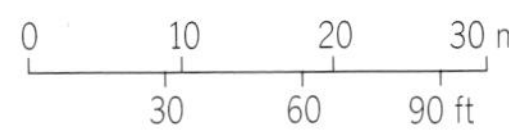

Chateau of Chambord

Domenico da Cortona or Pierre Nepveu

Chambord, Centre (central region), France; 1519–47

Chambord is the largest of the chateaux of the Loire, built by François I of France as a hunting lodge. The ground plan looks like the plan of a fortification, with its round towers at the corners, but it is the work above the cornice-line that gives the building its special character. The steeply sloping roofs, chimneys, lanterns, turrets and pinnacles proliferate in a way that seems scarcely possible, and the building appears as a mirage of vanished magnificence.

To call the place a hunting lodge is to mask the building's more important function as a display of splendour. It is a good place for hunting, being surrounded by forest. The flat ground meant that the building could spread out and its geometry was not compromised by the site. In that respect, Chambord is different from the fortified medieval chateaux, which were typically located on outcrops of high ground.

France was governed from this region, and François had inherited chateaux at Blois and Amboise from earlier French kings. The powerful noble families had establishments in the Loire valley, and the purpose of the building at Chambord was to outshine them all. A famous early visitor, in 1535, was the Duke of Burgundy – also known as Charles V, a Holy Roman Emperor, and Carlos I of Spain – who was significantly wealthier than François and sporadically at war with him (and with François's ally Suleyman the Magnificent). This was the kind of person that François was out to impress.

The construction work at Chambord was overseen by Pierre Nepveu, but the architect is most often taken to be Domenico da Cortona, who had been brought from Italy by François's predecessor, Charles VIII. François persuaded Leonardo da Vinci to move from Italy to Amboise, where he spent his last years and died shortly before the building of Chambord began.

Leonardo's influence can be inferred most convincingly in the double-helix stair that winds up through the heart of the building, from the ground to the roof – there is a sketch of such a stair in Leonardo's notebooks, but it is not known whether he suggested it be used here.

The vast interior spaces of the chateau would have been impossible to heat, and the place was used seasonally. It is estimated that François spent about 72 nights there altogether. The place was not furnished with its own permanent accoutrements, since visiting entourages (including the king's) would bring their own furniture with them.

Artistically, Chambord is important for its fusion of the Italian Renaissance style of decoration with French Gothic tradition – from a distance the building's silhouette looks gloriously medieval, but the details are all classical in their origin. The windows are square-headed and take up much more of the wall area than would have seemed wise in an earlier building. Most of the accommodation is in three grand storeys. Above these, at cornice-level, is a roof terrace reached by means of the two intertwining helical stairs. The terrace includes a network of connecting paths that give views across the surrounding countryside and across the roofs, along geometric vistas with classical pilasters, cones and miniature buildings with doors and windows. The composite effect is something like a premonition of a Renaissance cityscape, at a time when all existing towns were medieval with twisting streets.

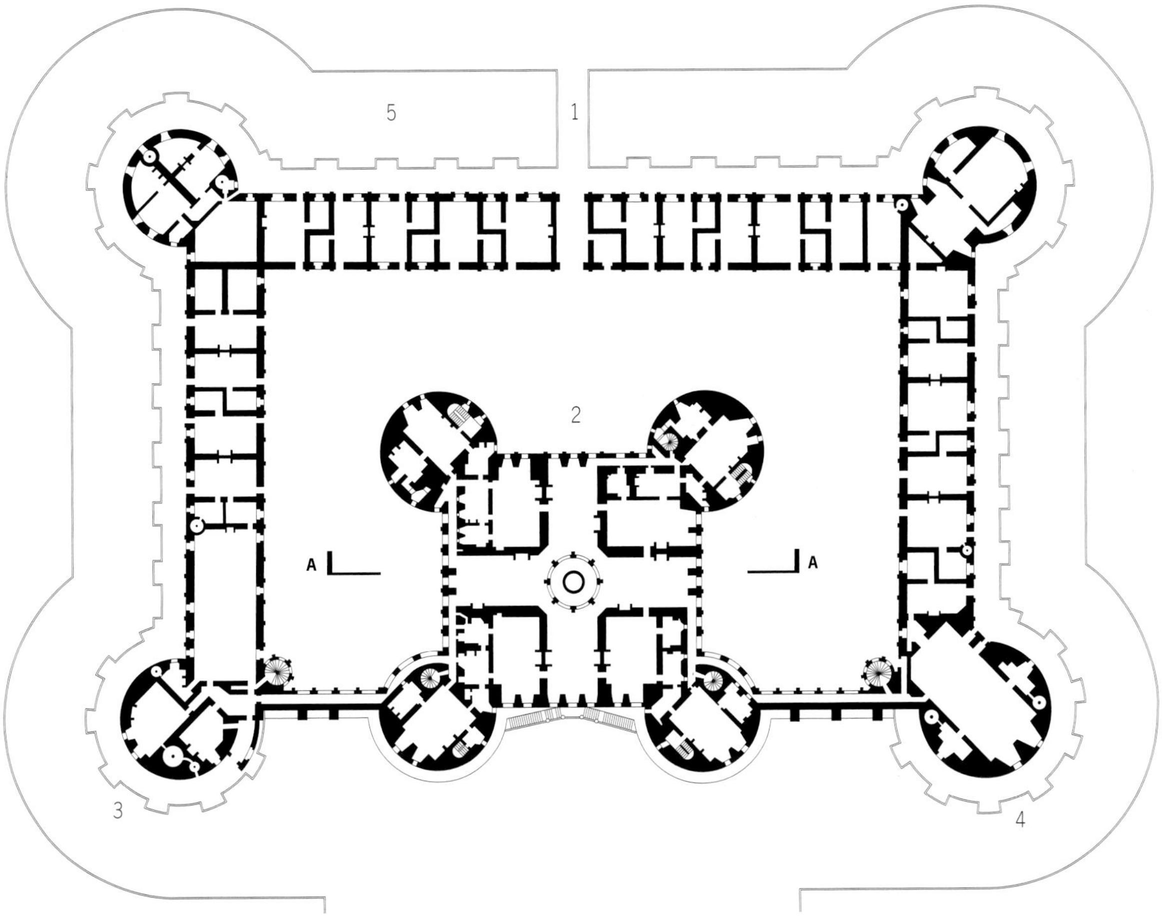

5 1 2 A A 3 4

1

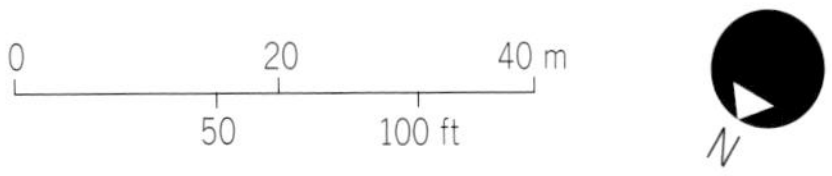

0 20 40 m
50 100 ft
N

2

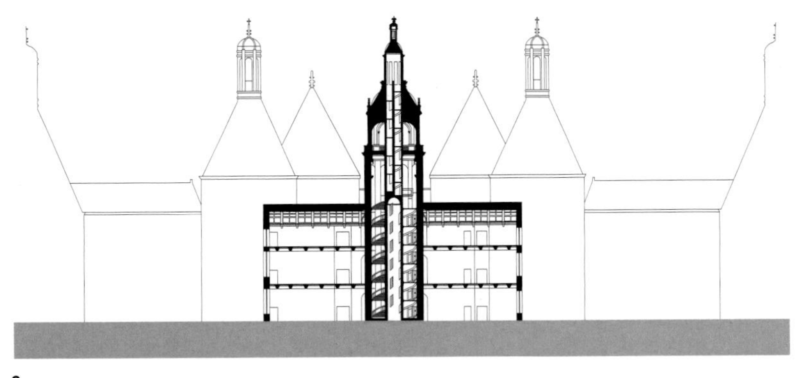

3

1 Plan

1 Royal porch entrance
2 Dungeon
3 Royal wing
4 Chapel wing
5 Moat

2 North Elevation

3 Section A-A

Chateau of Ancy-le-Franc

Sebastiano Serlio, 1475–1554

Tonnerre, Burgundy, France; 1546

The Italian architect Sebastiano Serlio wrote a series of books about architecture, authoritatively explaining how to deploy the classical orders. The earliest illustrated books about architecture to be printed, they were credited with introducing the Renaissance style to northern Europe.

François I brought Serlio to France and employed him at Fontainebleau, where the king had established his principal palace. It is a fine building, but it has been extended and adapted over several centuries, so Serlio's vision for architecture is seen more clearly in a smaller but nevertheless substantial chateau, Ancy-le-Franc, which Serlio designed for one of François's courtiers, Antoine de Clermont, comte de Tonnerre.

The formal geometries of Ancy-le-Franc extend out from the building, making its mastery over the surrounding territory clear for all to see. The chateau sits uncompromisingly foursquare, organized around a square courtyard, with two tall storeys running between square towers that step forward and rise up an extra storey on the outside corners of the building.

The external elevations are restrained, decorated only with carved Doric pilasters and cornices that imply a structure of columns and beams. This is done for decorative effect, in imitation of the way the ancient Romans decorated the concrete structures of their theatres and amphitheatres. Wall surfaces are fairly plain, except for an outbreak of high-relief carving around the entrance – an arched doorway, raised up from the ground so that it is approached by a flight of steps. This raising of the building makes the massing of the whole more imposing and also allows the introduction of some low-level windows that light the servants' quarters in the basement. The whole building seems to sit on a solid rustic plinth.

In the courtyard, which is raised to the level of the ground floor, the decoration is much more intense, with hardly any plain wall surface. The walls are divided up by pilasters and cornices, as on the outside, but here the pilasters' capitals are more ornate (Corinthian) and raised on pedestals; again, these are implied pedestals, sculpted in low relief – in reality, the wall is doing the work of support. Between the pilasters, windows alternate with niches, and their rhythm is maintained around the courtyard, even at the corners, where the niches are oddly 'folded'. The effect is a little relentless but refined and controlled, and more enveloping than any of the exterior spaces at Fontainebleau.

The sumptuous main interiors, organized over two floors, were decorated with Italian tiled floors and wall paintings that were unrivalled outside the royal palaces, including scenes of animals being sacrificed, and Judith and Holofernes – a biblical story, in which Judith beguiles the enemy general Holofernes, and then cuts off his head when he falls asleep. In the painting the general was given the king's face, while Judith was given the face of his son's mistress, Diane de Poitiers. She was Antoine de Clermont's sister-in-law, so the symbolism seems pointed.

This is architecture designed to impress with its sophistication. François I did not visit the chateau, which is probably just as well, but three later French kings did, including Louis XIV.

1 Ground Floor Plan

1 Old kitchen
2 Assembly hall
3 Archives hall
4 Yellow lounge
5 Hall of Diane
de Poitiers

2 North Elevation

3 Section A-A

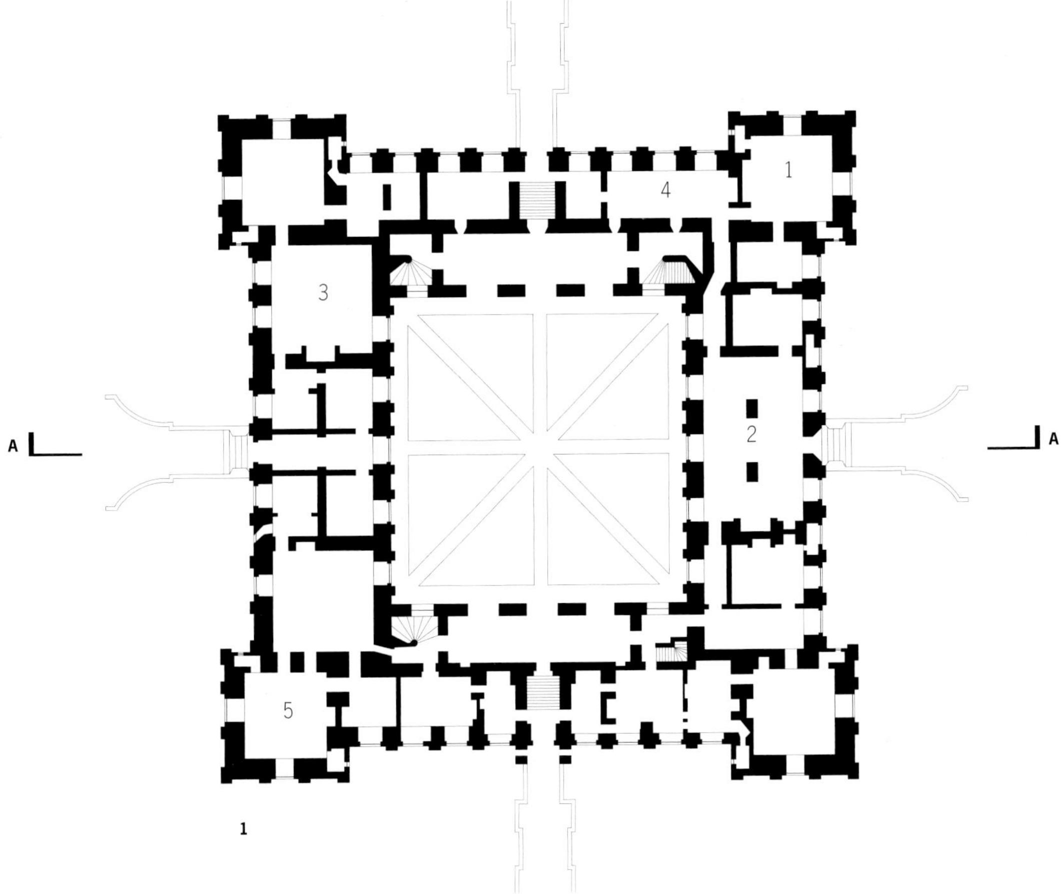

A A

1

2

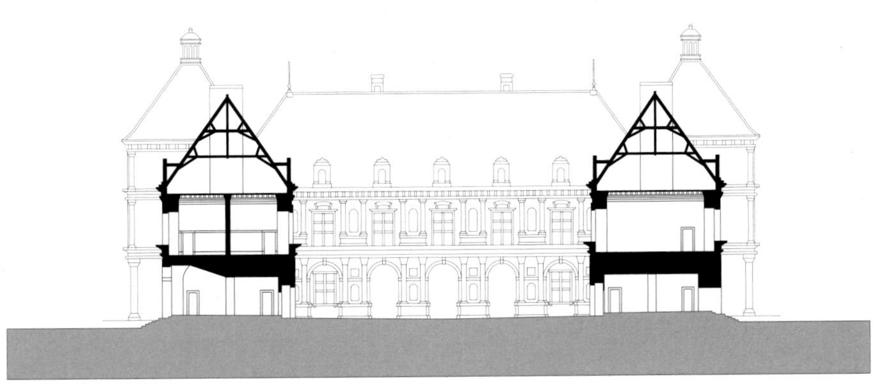

3

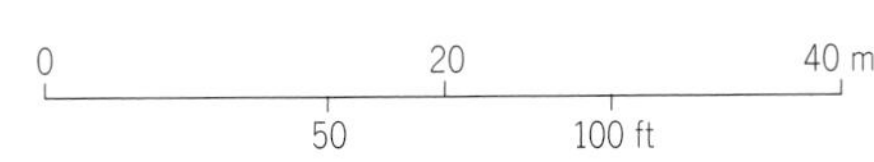

Villa Capra

Andrea Palladio, 1508–80

Vicenza, Italy; 1566–91

The Italian architect Andrea di Pietro della Gondola came to be known as Palladio (after Pallas Athene, the goddess of wisdom) because of his aptitude for study. Although his career overlapped with that of Sebastiano Serlio, the architect of Ancy-le-Franc (page 68), he was a generation younger than Serlio.

Palladio was taken up by the nobility in Vicenza and Venice, and in 1570 published a famous treatise on architecture, *I Quattro Libri dell'Architettura* (*The Four Books of Architecture*), which included plans, sections and elevations of his own buildings set alongside some of the great monuments of antiquity and the work of admired modern architects such as Donato Bramante. The villas designed by Palladio have been imitated more widely than the buildings of any other architect.

The noble families with palaces along Venice's Grand Canal also owned farms on the Italian mainland – the Veneto, which was then part of the Venetian Republic – producing food for the capital. These landowners, for whom Palladio designed country houses, would visit their estates at harvest time but would be absent for most of the rest of the year. The ingenuity that characterizes Palladio's villa designs is a matter of putting on a good show. Farm buildings are arranged in symmetrical masses to create a sense of a sizeable construction, while the grand rooms that make a fine impression are few in number and arranged for maximum effect – a loggia with expansive views, an impressive hallway, reception room and dining room, perhaps with painted murals – but, beyond that, simplicity is the guiding theme. The buildings rely on fine proportions, rather than fine materials, to achieve their effects.

The Villa Capra is not a typical Palladian villa. Palladio himself called it a palazzo, reflecting the fact that it was closer to being a town house than a farm. Outside but not far from Vicenza, it was designed for Paolo Almerico, who retired there when he left his employment at the Vatican. The building was habitable from 1569, but the money must have run out because it remained incomplete until it came into the hands of Odorico and Marco Capra in 1591, after Almerico's and Palladio's deaths, when it was finished under the guidance of Vincenzo Scamozzi.

The house sits on top of a hill, with varied views in all directions, and has four virtually identical façades, each with a flight of steps leading up to a loggia on the principal floor. It is the building's four-way symmetry that gives the impression of its being an uncompromised 'ideal'. Its distinguishing feature is the central rotunda, running the whole height of the building, inspired by the Pantheon (pages 108–109) in Rome. From the villa's central space one can look out to all the loggias, and during the lifetime of the original occupant it remained open to the sky. The dome remained incomplete, with an open oculus like the Pantheon's. The building is sometimes called the Villa Rotonda because of this distinctive central space. Palladio's published version of the design showed it with a cupola, more pronounced than the one added by Scamozzi, but the space would have been more striking without it and the building's 'incompleteness' over such a long time was surely because Almerico came to love it the way it was.

All the main rooms are on one floor, so there is no grandiose stair in the interior leading up to guest bedrooms. The house was close enough to Vicenza for visitors from the town to return home in the evening without needing to stay overnight.

The experience of visiting Canon Almerico in his incomplete house on a summer afternoon, taking in views of the countryside, wandering from the garden into the rotunda, must have been like encountering an enchanting ancient ruin.

1 Section A-A

2 Elevation

3 Plan

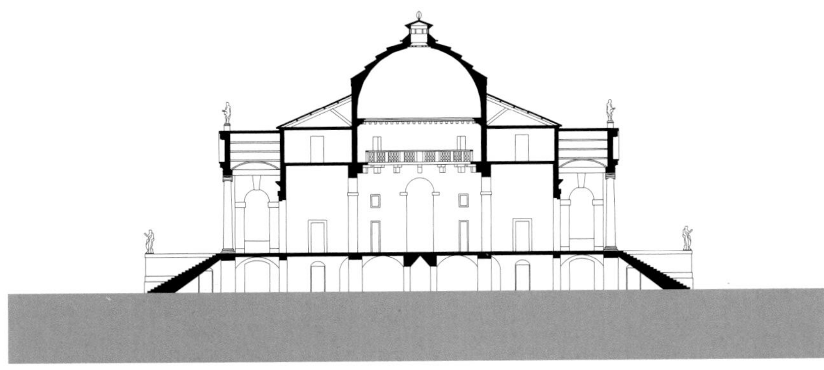

1

2

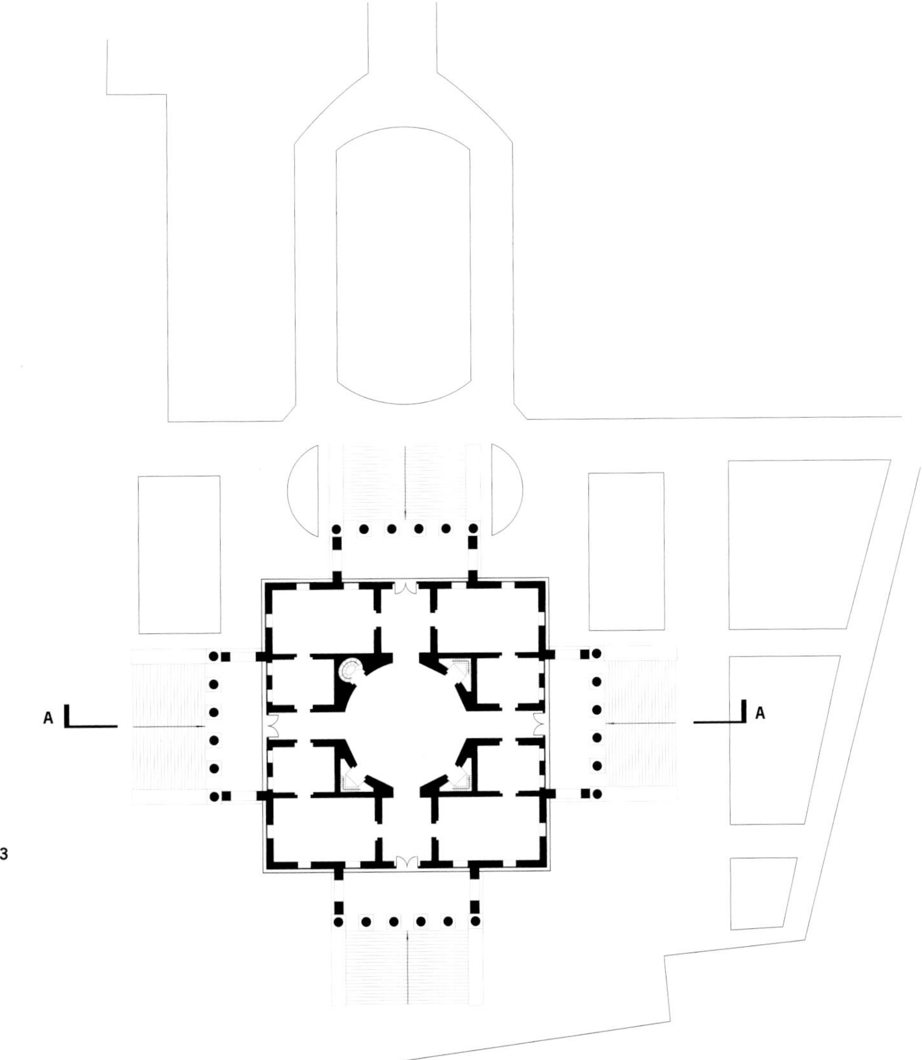

3

N

0 5 10 m
20 30 ft

Hardwick Hall

Robert Smythson, 1535–1614

Derbyshire, UK; 1590–97

Hardwick Hall, which still makes a powerful impression today, escaped the normal financial and practical constraints of house design. It was built for Bess of Hardwick, who was born at the old hall, a conventional manor house, which remains standing in ruins close to its replacement. Bess married well four times, outlived her husbands and inherited from them. As Countess of Shrewsbury, she moved the family seat to Chatsworth, further west in Derbyshire, and commissioned the first house there, but it was replaced at the end of the eighteenth century.

Her house at Hardwick survives substantially intact. It was never her principal residence, and would have been impossible to heat in winter. Glass was very expensive at the time, and its use here was sensational, giving rise to the saying: 'Hardwick Hall, more glass than wall.' If the silhouette retains an idea of a turreted castle, the fabric of the building was made newly delicate; even the walls of Chambord (pages 66–67) look more solid than those of Hardwick.

Robert Smythson was a mason who had worked at Longleat in Wiltshire, which followed a similar pattern for the walls, but at Hardwick this approach was pushed as far as anyone would have dared. Smythson had a craftsman's sense of the limits of his materials. He had been reading the work of Sebastiano Serlio and incorporated Renaissance motifs in the work, including the square-headed windows. However, he was steeped in the medieval English traditions of masonry, and at Hardwick the tracery of the windows is so powerful that it seems to form a network across the whole façade, so that even from an external view the house becomes as diaphanous as the great Gothic churches aspired to be.

The structural ingenuity of Hardwick lies in the way in which its mass is concentrated in a long central spine wall, with the shorter walls coming off the central wall at right angles, which serve to buttress it. This means that the building's outer walls simply have to hold themselves up, along with the floors, and do not need to resist the tendency to fall sideways. It is an architectural strategy that would be impossible in a church, where the central area has to consist of open space, so the outside becomes a mass of buttressing of one sort or another. At Hardwick, the buttressing happens within, and the building's outer layer is given over to a surprising amount of glass, with just enough stone reticulation to hold it in place.

The most spatially arresting parts of Hardwick are linked by a long stair that ascends through two storeys along the spine, twisting at the end to lead into a stupendous high gallery that runs the entire length of the building, lit by the largest windows in the house. The walls are hung with tapestries. Then at roof level there is a terrace connecting the topmost storey of each of the six towers. The towers are imposing when seen from below, but from up above they form glassy summer-houses, playful little pavilions with elaborate parapets boldly holding Bess's initials (ES, for Elizabeth Shrewsbury) and visible for many miles across the rolling Derbyshire countryside.

1 Ground Floor Plan

1 Entrance
2 Entrance hall
3 Chapel
4 Kitchen
5 Buttery
6 Pantry
7 Nursery
8 Nursemaid's room
9 Stairs up to principal floors

2 West Elevation

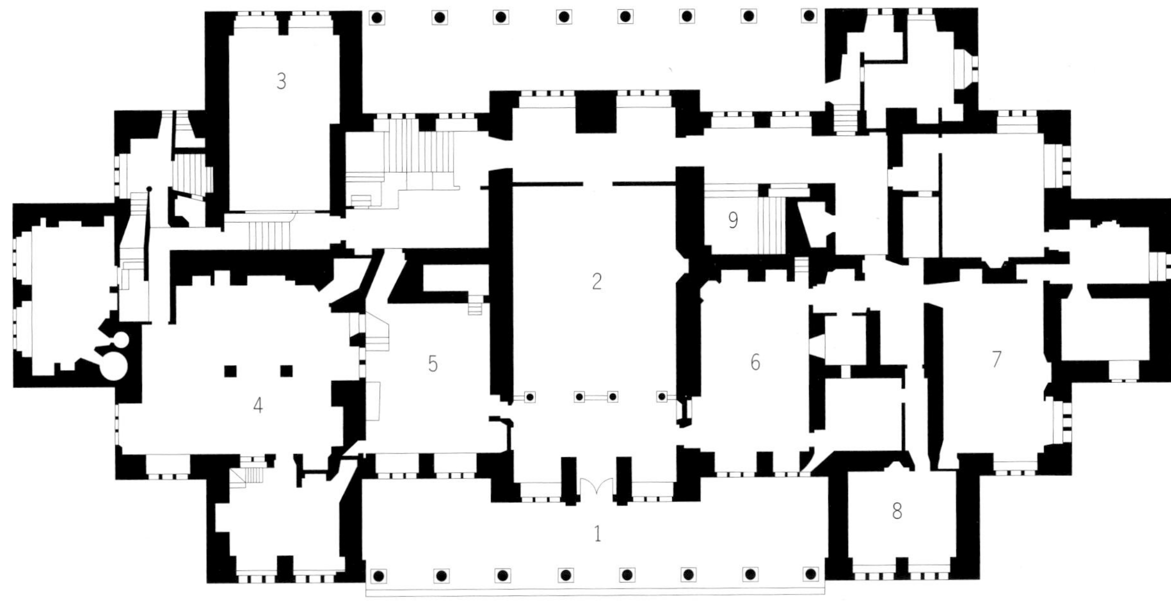

1

2

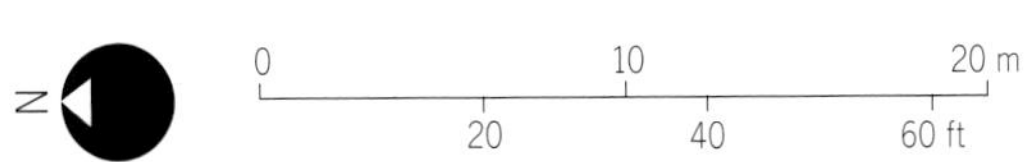

Tea Houses, Katsura Imperial Villa

Prince Hachijo Toshihito, 1579–1629, and Kobori Enshu, 1579–1647

Kyoto, Japan; 1630–62

The Imperial Villa at Katsura dates from the Edo period, considered to be a time when the Japanese arts were particularly highly developed. Structurally, the buildings that make up the villa are traditional for the region – timber posts support the floors and heavy overhanging tiled roofs, while the walls are very light. There is no glass but the walls consist of sliding screens of translucent paper. The internal partitions are also sliding screens, but in this case the paper is stretched on both sides of the timber frames, so as to make the walls more opaque.

This is a building of exquisite refinement, designed as a retreat for Prince Toshihito, the emperor's younger brother, his family and their guests. The prince's means were limited and the project took shape quietly and gradually over the years. In the process, traditional construction techniques were honed to perfection, and the buildings' openness made the garden an important part of the ensemble.

The Tale of Genji, written in the eleventh century by Murasaki Shikibu, gives a good impression of the ambience of the place – not because it is the palace depicted in the story, but because the Katsura Imperial Villa was designed to evoke the palace depicted in the story. The village of Katsura is mentioned in the book in connection with an image of the moon reflected in water. 'Katsura' was the name of a species of tree that was traditionally supposed to grow on the moon, and the contemplation of the moon was one of the privileged activities that took place at the villa. There was a moon-viewing deck, from which, if the timing were managed to perfection, guests could be shown the image of the moon reflected in the pool. Reading was a regular activity, and so was the writing and reading aloud of renga poetry. There was a culture of enhanced sensitivity to nature and atmosphere, and the buildings' minimalist aesthetic gave prominence to the smallest nuances.

In such an environment the tea houses in the garden take on a particular charge, a potent reminder of the tea ceremony devised by Zen Buddhist monks in the fifteenth century as a social and meditative practice. At the Imperial Villa the tea-house roofs are thatched with reeds and the floors are of beaten earth, so they have a more rustic ambience than the main buildings, conducive to the sense of serene simplicity that the ceremony inculcated.

Kobori Enshu was an aristocrat who was best known in his day as a master of the tea ceremony, and he is usually credited with the layout of the Katsura villa and its extensive garden. He designed many other tea houses, in domestic surroundings and at temple sites. However, there is no doubt that Prince Toshihito took charge of decisions, including the orientation of the principal dwelling so that it faced the rising moon.

When the German architect Bruno Taut visited the palace in the 1933, he found it a revelation – an example of modern architecture that had been built unaccountably early. Taut misunderstood the seventeenth-century fascination with plain surfaces and austere aesthetic discipline, but the refinement of this style is now appreciated, and its considered artistry of judgment and placement outshines the bombast of much larger and more ostentatious works.

1 Plan

1 Running water for handwashing
2 Entrance
3 Tea room
4 First room
5 Second room
6 Pantry
7 Kitchen
8 Hearth
9 Cabinet

2 North Elevation

3 Section A-A

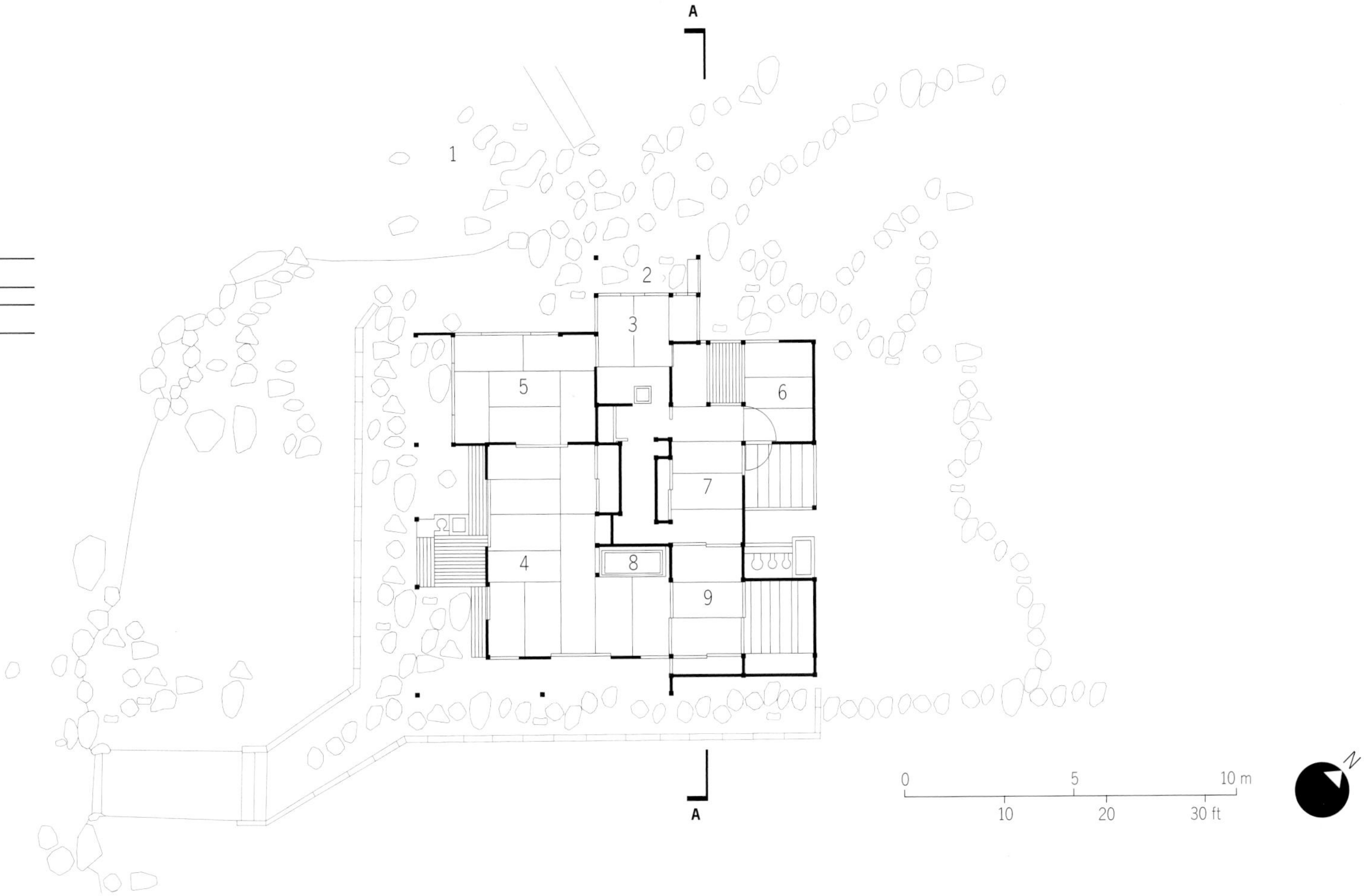

1

2

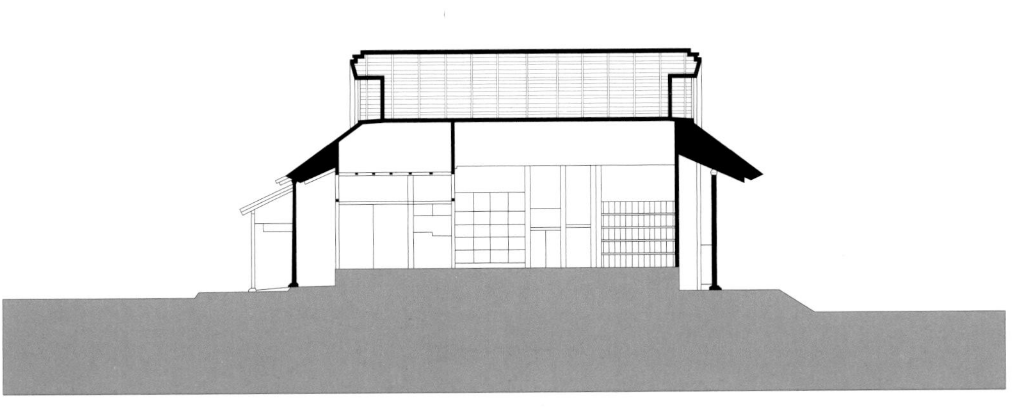

3

Chateau of Maisons-Laffitte

François Mansart, 1598–1666

Maisons-Laffitte, Île de France, France; 1642–51

Built at the top of a slope, the chateau at Maisons dominates the view from the south-east, from Paris. Its location is now suburban, but when it was built the chateau was in the countryside – near Paris, but definitely outside the city. It is no longer on the edge of a forest, and its park has gone, but it presides over an impressive formal garden, laid out on the same axis as the house. The 'Laffitte' was added when the chateau was bought by a banker of that name in 1818, having changed hands several times over the previous century.

Maisons-Laffitte is a spectacular example of French classicism, its imposing symmetry handled with great refinement of detail and exemplary use of the orders, which made it a place of study for architecture students at the Ecole des Beaux-Arts.

The architect, François Mansart, was notorious for reconsidering his designs while they were under construction, making it necessary to take work down and rebuild. His buildings were therefore hugely expensive but beautifully resolved. The Chateau of Maisons-Laffitte is his best-preserved creation. It was originally approached along straight avenues, which would have made its claim on the landscape still more impressive. The entrance front is two storeys high, with another three storeys in the slope of the roof. On the garden front, which looks towards Paris, the slope of the ground means that there are three storeys below the parapet. A monumental white marble staircase with an ingratiatingly gentle slope leads up to the grandest rooms on the upper floor. Their doorways line up with one another to make a great processional enfilade that runs the whole length of the building.

Maisons-Laffitte feels more like a display than a home. It makes a powerful impression, but, since it is only one room deep, the house seems to have fewer rooms inside it than the imposing façades would suggest. The décor is consistently fine and very carefully modulated.

The garden façade is quite flat, running in a straight line, but its modelling implies three 'pavilions', one central and one at each end – an impression strongly signalled by the roof forms. The walls break forward a little to define each of these three masses, and there is a regular rhythm of columns running along the building, but they are not all identical. The different masses are articulated by the use of flat pilasters and fully round columns, which sometimes have flutes and sometimes do not. There is variety within the order, as the different column-types have slightly different visual weights despite the consistency of their size and proportion. The design of the Chateau of Maisons-Laffitte is an object-lesson in how to discipline a large façade: its dignity remains intact but it has an unaffected vitality.

1 Ground Floor Plan

2 North West Elevation

3 Section A-A

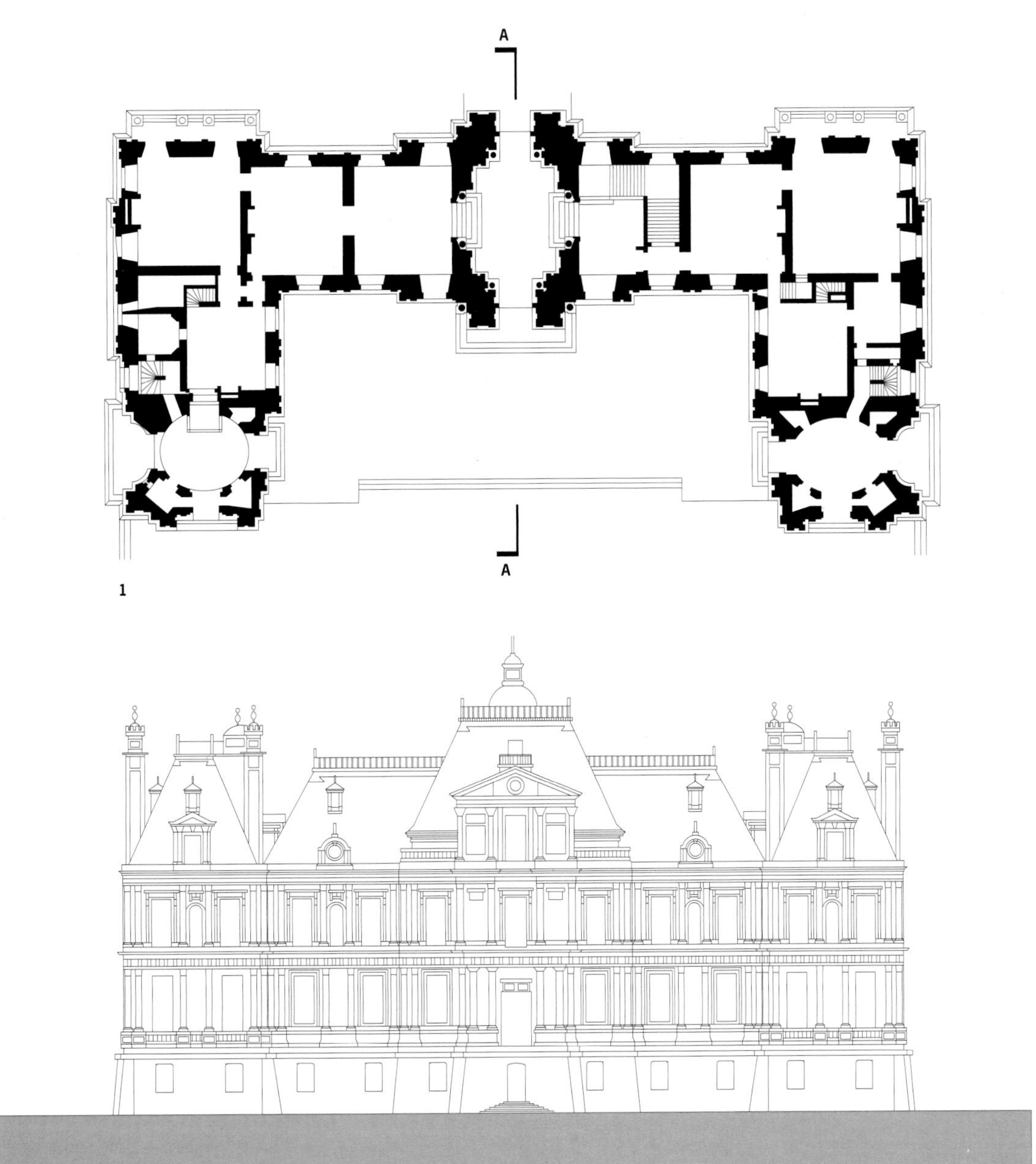

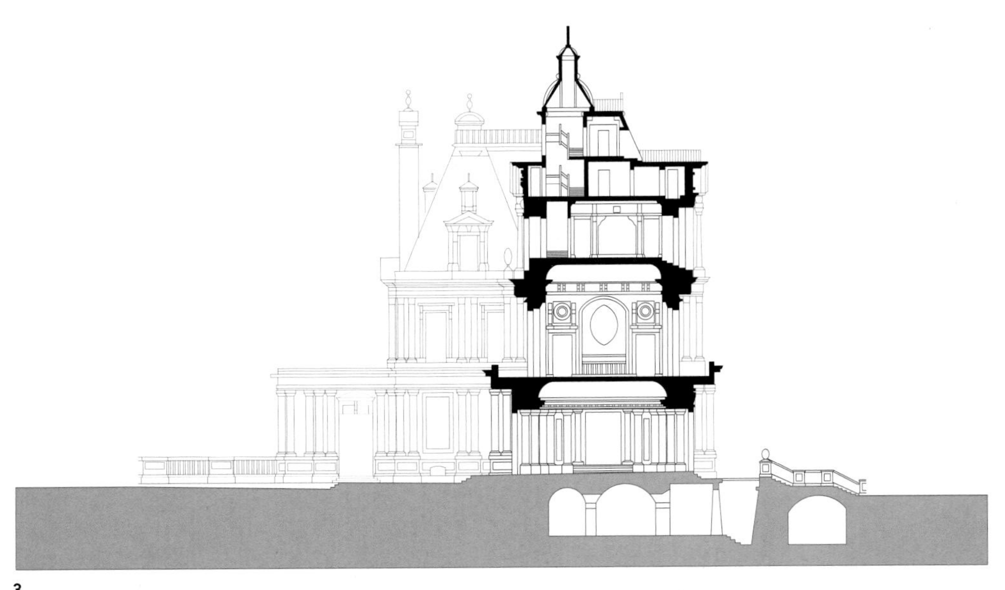

0 20 40 m

50 100 ft

Berrington Hall

Henry Holland, 1745–1806

Herefordshire, UK; 1778–81

Berrington Hall is the very image of an eighteenth-century aristocratic English country house. Its rectangular main block has a projecting portico with four Ionic columns and it looks perfectly Palladian.

The hall's naturalistic setting is by Lancelot 'Capability' Brown, England's most celebrated landscape gardener. It follows his usual formula of opening up views of rolling farmland and bringing them uninterruptedly right up to the house. People unfamiliar with this style wonder if the landscape has been designed at all, imagining the house to have been placed in a naturally idyllic spot. Brown's subtle contrivances at Berrington include the damming of a stream to make a lake for the middle distance, a ha-ha (a sunken wall and ditch, invisible from the house) to keep the grazing animals at a respectful distance, and a forest of trees that screens views and opens them up as people and vehicles move through the grounds along winding carriage drives.

Behind the house is a service courtyard, part of an arrangement that continues the symmetry of the main block in lower buildings – kitchens, bakery, laundry, a finely decorated dairy, clearly intended for display, and the servants' hall. This is an unusual configuration; the service buildings would more often be put to one side of the house, maybe hidden behind trees. In this case, rather than having an entrance front and a garden front, the house has only one main door, which is both the principal entrance and the means by which the house opens up to the landscape.

The grand reception rooms are at the front of the house, with views of parkland, while the smaller rooms are tucked away, some of them looking out on to the service court, which is in sandstone like the main house, and surprisingly formal.

In the middle of the house, a glass dome in the roof illuminates a magnificent staircase leading up to a floor of more personal spaces – bedrooms and sitting rooms – for family and guests. A smaller service stair runs from the cellars through to the attic.

The symmetry of the façades is maintained by the use of fake windows. These are fully modelled real windows with glass in them, but the glass is painted black on the reverse and the window frames are set in niches in solid walls. There was a tax on windows in the nineteenth century, which is often blamed for the blocking-up of windows; but more often, as in this case, blind windows were introduced for compositional reasons. Internally the rooms are perfectly well lit, and had they had windows along their two external walls they would have been even more difficult to heat.

Thomas Harley, who commissioned the house, was the younger brother of the Earl of Oxford, who inherited the family seat at Eywood. Thomas independently made a fortune in banking and commerce and set himself up at Berrington Hall. His architect, Henry Holland, had developed parts of Kensington and Chelsea, including Sloane Square, and Holland's next commission after Berrington was to design Carlton House for the Prince of Wales – later demolished when Trafalgar Square was formed.

1 Ground Floor Plan

1 Portico
2 Marble hall
3 Inner hall
4 Courtyard
5 Drawing room
6 Billiard room
7 Dining room
8 Smoking room
9 Kitchen
10 Servants' hall
11 Pantry
12 Laundry
13 Bakery
14 Larder

2 South West Elevation

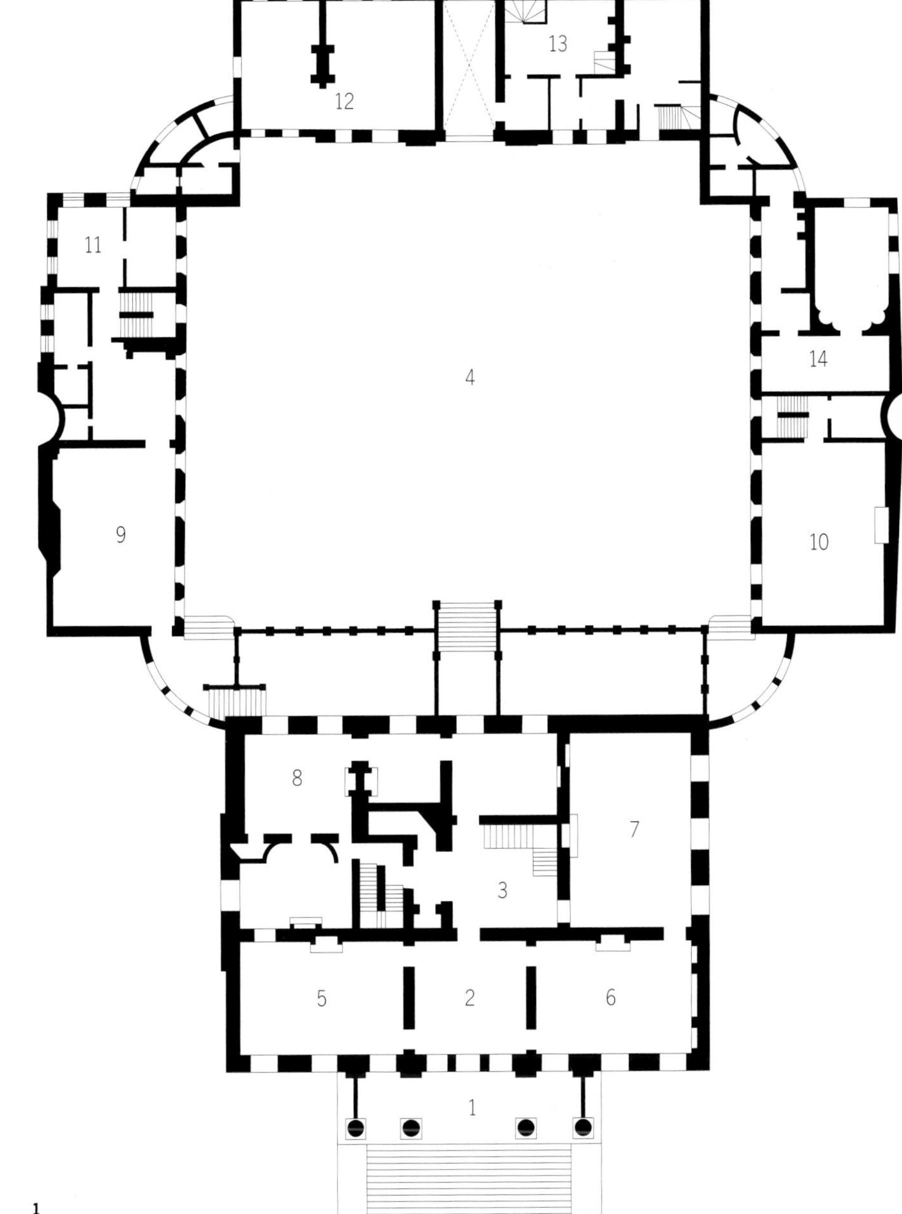

1

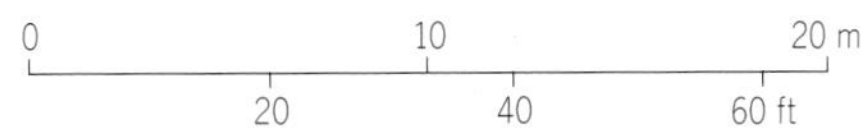

2

Queen's Hamlet, Versailles

Richard Mique, 1728–94

Versailles, Île de France, France; 1774–85

The vast Palace of Versailles (pages 250–51) was established under Louis XIV of France in the mid-seventeenth century. It was Louis who bought a nearby village called Trianon as the site for a second palace, known as the Trianon, which was rebuilt several times. The Trianon is far enough away from the monumental pageantry of the main palace of Versailles to seem lost in the park, and it became a more personal place – though still extremely grand by normal standards.

A smaller palace was built a little further away by Louis XV (Louis XIV's great-grandson), originally for his mistress Madame de Pompadour, who died before it was finished, so her successor, Madame du Barry, was installed there.

From the start, therefore, the Petit Trianon was a woman's place and a private domain. When Louis XVI came to the throne, he gave it to his wife, Marie Antoinette, who used it as a refuge from what she regarded as the stifling ritual of the court. Only close friends were allowed there, never anyone on official business. The little hamlet that she commissioned for the garden is the expression of her yearning for a simpler life – while also illustrating how far removed she was from being able to have such a life.

The hamlet consists of a dozen cottage-scale buildings, most of which resemble cottages. Grouped around a pool, they look simple and rustic and appear to have been repaired. However, rather than housing agricultural labourers, they contain the facilities for a more comfortable way of life

What looks on the outside like a two-storey thatched cottage turns out to be a well-appointed kitchen for reheating plain meals – a welcome alternative to elaborate court banquets – built in stone with a high ceiling and clerestory lighting. Another little house is designed as the queen's boudoir; another is a billiard room.

Organizationally, the hamlet is a single house, with its facilities dispersed among various buildings. In fact, it is less than a single house: it was used in connection with the Petit Trianon, so there was no need for sleeping spaces. Its finest room is the dairy, with a fountain splashing in a wall niche and a centrally placed white marble table. The walls are painted in trompe l'oeil marble, and there is a finely painted ceiling with an effect of coffering. It is more like a sacristy than a dairy.

Jean-Jacques Rousseau (1712–78) is generally credited with the initiation of Romanticism and the promotion of simplicity in eighteenth-century France, but there is a long tradition in poetry and storytelling of seeing the unsophisticated peasant life as offering greater access to true feelings than the constrained lives of people who had to be seen as respectable.

Many a young man in literature has fallen for the charms of a milkmaid or a shepherdess. In life, of course, the fact of poverty would tend to undermine the feeling of freedom, but Marie Antoinette was trying through her arrangements of buildings to put herself and her friends in touch with unfettered emotion in a highly artificial world.

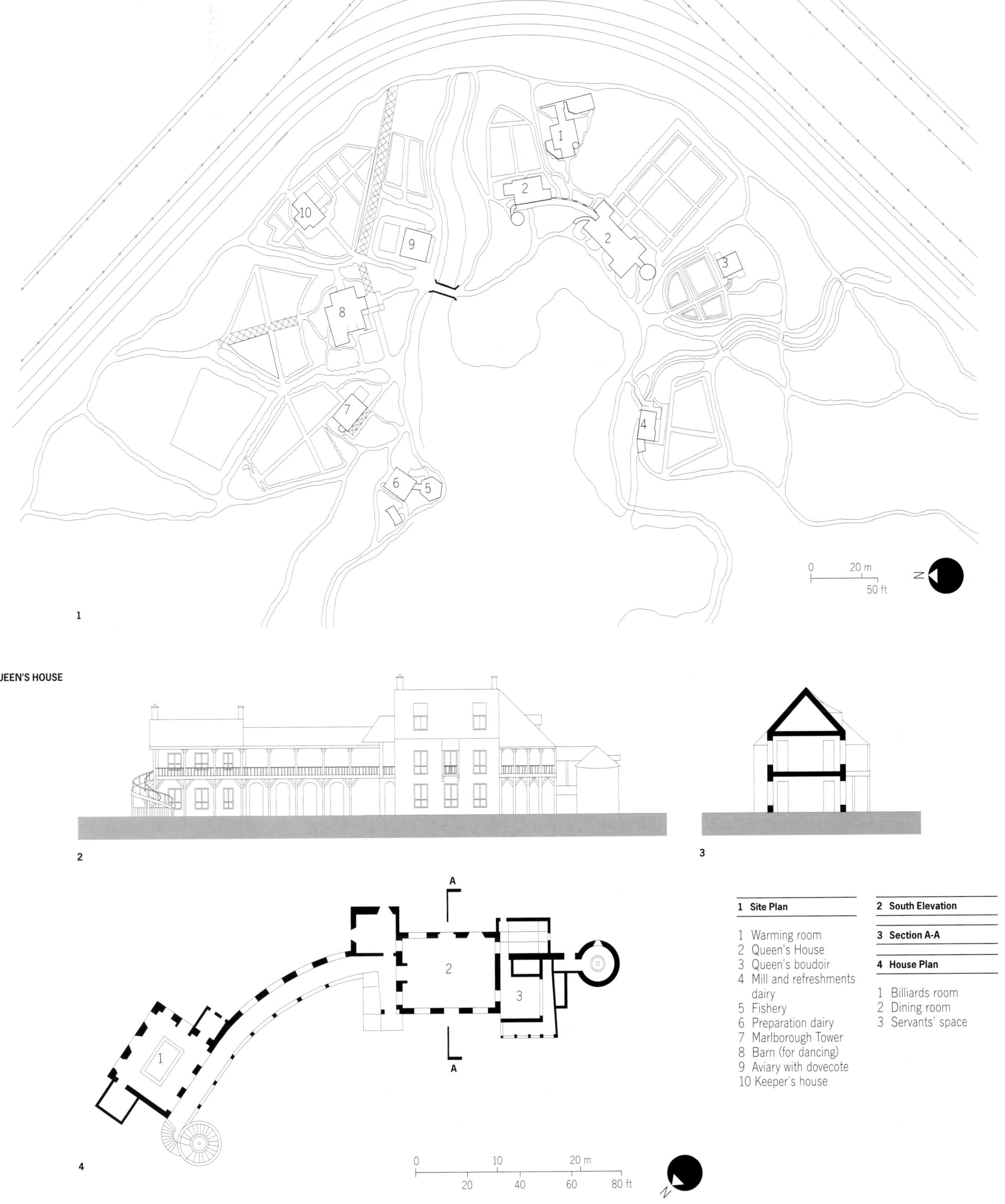

1 Site Plan

1 Warming room
2 Queen's House
3 Queen's boudoir
4 Mill and refreshments dairy
5 Fishery
6 Preparation dairy
7 Marlborough Tower
8 Barn (for dancing)
9 Aviary with dovecote
10 Keeper's house

2 South Elevation

3 Section A-A

4 House Plan

1 Billiards room
2 Dining room
3 Servants' space

Monticello

Thomas Jefferson, 1743–1826

Charlottesville, Virginia, USA; 1794–1809

Monticello was the base from which Thomas Jefferson ran the plantations that were the source of his wealth. The principal author of the American Declaration of Independence, a founding father and third president of the USA, who doubled the size of the nation with the Louisiana Purchase, Jefferson is a revered and inspirational figure.

As a house, Monticello is an oddity. It began life in 1768 as a farmhouse. Had it remained no more than that, it would have seemed today an ingenious curiosity, idiosyncratically adapted to meet Jefferson's needs. But Jefferson worked and travelled in Europe, especially in Paris, and returned with a sense of aristocratic style and a fondness for the style of Andrea Palladio. His remodelling of Monticello continued through his presidency and gave the house a level of dignity and polish that had not been seen before in this part of the world. He also chose to be buried there, and Monticello has become as much a national shrine as a work of art.

The house is a more remarkable achievement in Virginia than it would have been in Vicenza, where Palladio had a local tradition of craftsmanship to draw upon. In Virginia, the craftsmen had to be educated from Palladio's published books, which they followed with some precision. The bricks for the house were fired on site at Monticello, and the structural timbers came from Jefferson's estates. The glass for the windows was imported from Europe.

The model for Monticello is Palladio's Villa Capra (pages 70–71), but Jefferson's house is a free adaptation. It has a porch on each of its four sides, but the porches are not identical, and one is glazed as a greenhouse. The symmetry has been relaxed. Monticello's dome covers not a central rotunda but a curiously out-of-the-way room with no clearly defined purpose. As at Villa Capra, the main rooms are all on one floor and the building has no grand staircase.

At Monticello, Jefferson's bedroom was on the ground floor, as were the grander guest rooms, but the family rooms were on the upper floor, reached by way of stairs that are more like the service stairs of a stately home. Jefferson's wife died in 1782, and his daughters married in 1790 and 1797, so for a time, while the house was remodelled, he lived there alone except for the household's slaves.

Jefferson's younger daughter died at Monticello in 1804, but his elder daughter, Martha, outlived him. She acted as First Lady when Jefferson was President (1801–08), and when he retired she came and joined him at Monticello with her eleven children, leaving her husband, Thomas Mann Randolph, Governor of Virginia, in Richmond to run the state.

Jefferson's personal suite of rooms comprised his bedroom and a small study (with the bed in an alcove between them), his library and the south-porch greenhouse. The house was a place for business as well as for study and domestic life, and the capacious entrance hall was used as a waiting room for the numerous visitors. The guests who stayed there would have been comfortable but, in contrast with a contemporary European aristocrat's house of this scale, the layout of the rooms is designed for convenience rather than display. There is no scope for a grand procession into dinner from the drawing room. The lofty ambitions here are underpinned by practical simplicity.

1 Plan

1 North-east portico
2 Entrance hall
3 Parlour
4 South-west portico
5 Dining room
6 Jefferson's bedroom
7 Library
8 Piazza

2 Elevation

3 Section A-A

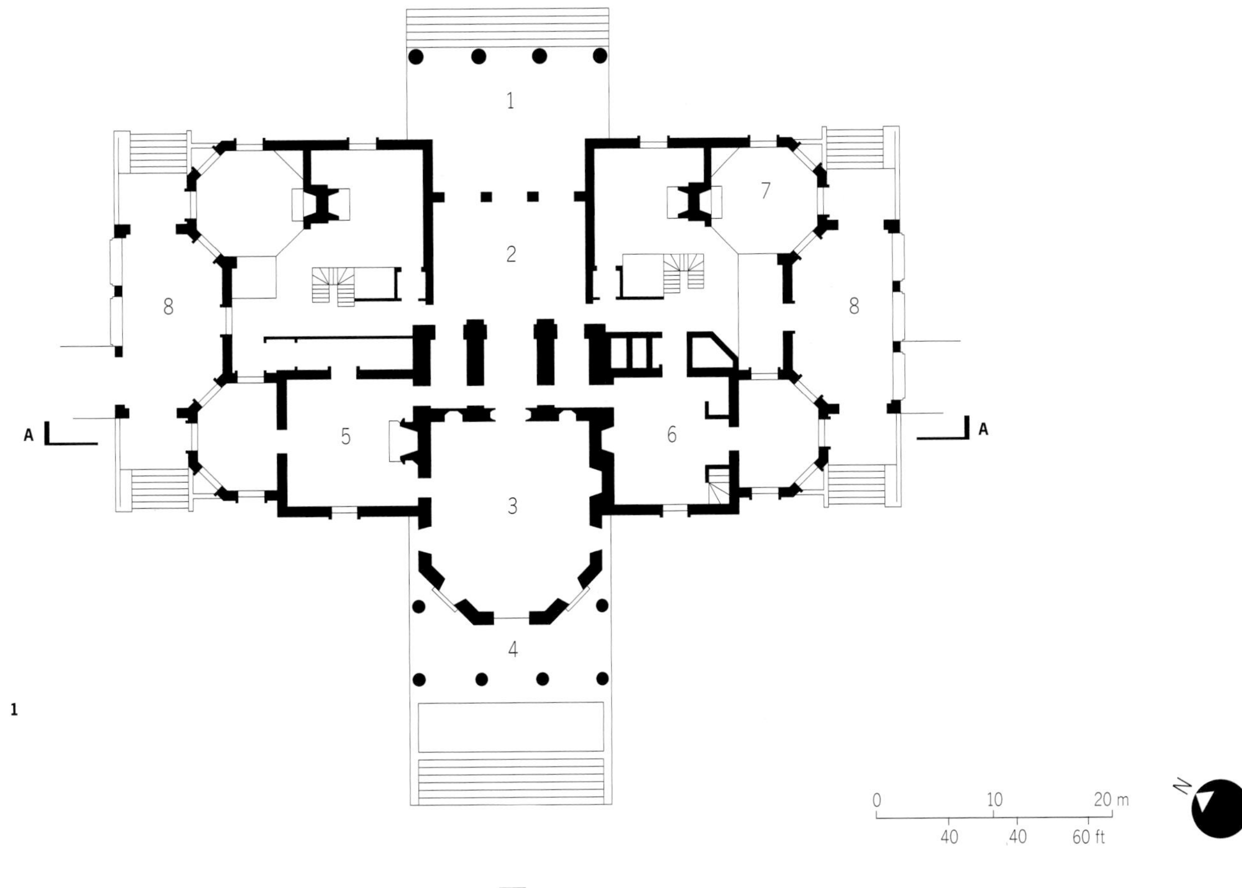

1

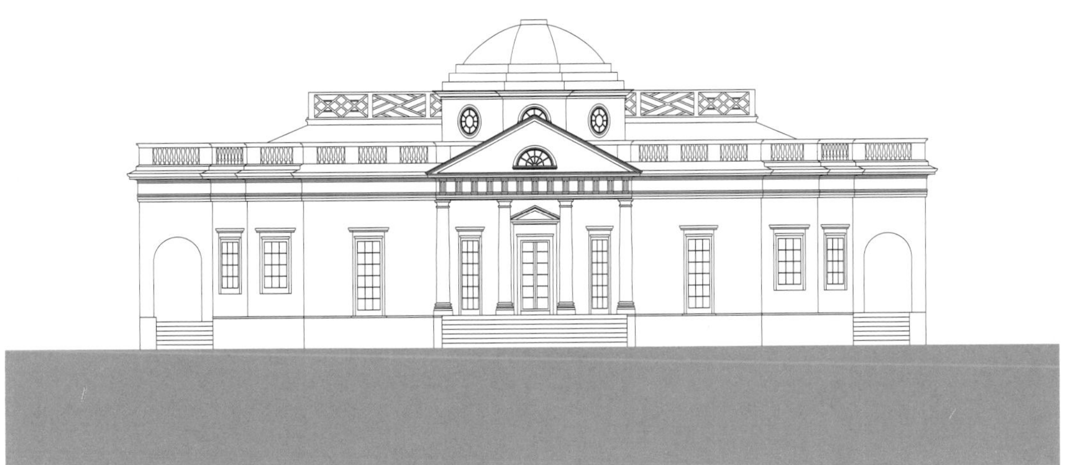

2

3

Neuschwanstein

Christian Jank, 1833–88, Eduard Riedel, 1813–85, and Georg von Dollmann, 1830–95

Hohenschwangau, Bavaria, Germany; 1869–86

To be more interested in architecture and opera than in running a country is not necessarily evidence of insanity; but when the enthusiast is a king, and there is no other way to remove him from the throne than establishing that he is mad, it can be portrayed in that way.

Ludwig II of Bavaria was crowned at 18, remained politically naïve, and allowed himself to be too much in the thrall of the composer Richard Wagner. He funded the building of Wagner's theatre at Bayreuth in northern Bavaria before embarking on a series of extravagant building projects of his own, which left him with enormous personal debts – but Bavaria with its most potent tourist attractions.

If Ludwig had lived in the era of recorded music, his desire to hear repeatedly the works of Wagner might have been less ruinous, but the music was only the beginning. Ludwig seems to have wanted to live in the heightened emotional state associated with opera. His infatuations with actors and singers exhausted them because he wanted them to remain in character. His houses demand the soundtrack that Luchino Visconti's 1972 film about him, entitled simply *Ludwig*, obligingly supplies.

Neuschwanstein could hardly be more romantically sited. It is at the edge of the Alps, on a small mountain with much larger ones beyond it. The foundation is a medieval ruin, and the building was meant to be much larger, but the castle that materialized before the money ran out is breathtaking. The approach road – up which all the building materials had to come – is narrow and steep, with the castle towers looming over it.

The interiors are intensely realized evocations of medievalism, with fine carving, coloured glass in the windows and painted murals depicting scenes from Wagner's medieval operas about chivalry. At Neuschwanstein, Ludwig identified particularly with Wagner's Lohengrin, the swan prince.

The two largest rooms are the throne room and a singers' hall. The Byzantine-style throne room has a strongly religious atmosphere. There is a great deal of gold, lapis lazuli and porphyry in evidence, along with depictions of Christ in a semi-dome above the throne, with six kings who were also saints just beneath him and the twelve apostles flanking the throne. Designed for medieval-style song competitions, as depicted in Wagner's opera *Die Meistersinger von Nürnberg*, the singers' hall runs right across the top storey of the main block, reached by a spiral stair with a stone dragon at its top. It was never used during Ludwig's lifetime.

The most intensely evocative space is the king's bedchamber. The intricately carved canopy over the bed has dozens of delicate spires. The washstand delivers water through the neck of a silver swan. An oratory is dedicated to St Louis – whose name translates into German as 'Ludwig', and who was king of France. The wall paintings show scenes from *Tristan und Isolde*; and a door leads out on to a small balcony with a vertiginous view of a waterfall, which plunges so far down into a mountain gorge that it seems to vaporize before it crashes to the ground.

1 Site Plan

1 Entrance hall
2 Upper courtyard
3 Lower courtyard
4 Hall
5 Bower
6 Gateway building

2 South Elevation

1
2
3
4
5
6

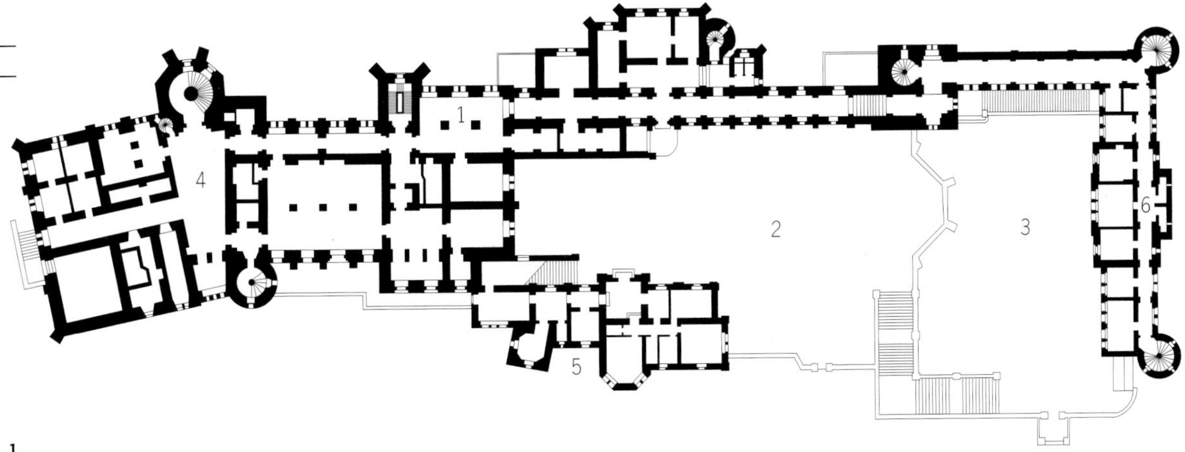

1

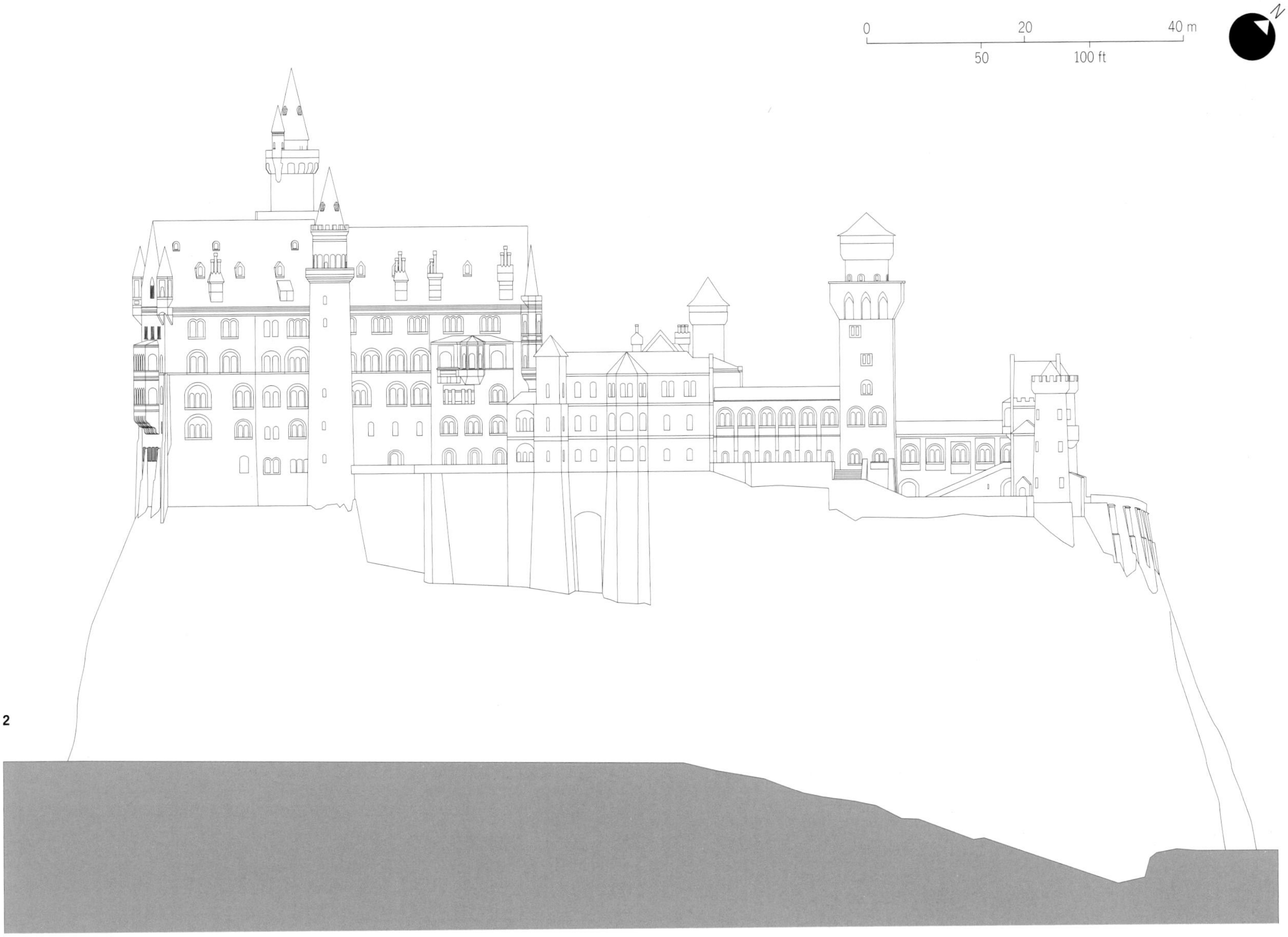

0
20
40 m
50
100 ft
N

2

Horta House

Victor Horta, 1861–1947

Brussels, Belgium; 1898

During the nineteenth century there was an increase in European knowledge about the architecture of earlier times and far-flung places, and buildings were made to evoke all sorts of things. Roman classical architecture continued to be an inspiration for buildings that needed to establish their importance, but with advances in archaeological knowledge the purity of older classical Greek architecture came to have greater cultural prestige for an educated elite. Alongside classical buildings of various types there were revivals of medievalism, nationalist styles and exoticisms.

The architectural theorist Eugène Viollet-le-Duc, whose particular expertise was in rescuing medieval monuments, came to understand the rationality of the vaulting systems used in the great cathedrals, and argued that modern architecture should have a distinct style of its own based on the characteristics of modern building materials – that it should escape from simply mimicking building forms of the past.

This idea was in circulation from the 1860s, but it did not immediately produce convincing results. It did, however, inspire a flowering of creativity in the 1890s, in a movement that came to be known as Art Nouveau. The label is applied to the work of various people in different countries who had little in common except that they were all trying to reinvent architecture from first principles without reference to historical styles.

Victor Horta's early work is in this category. It is elaborate, serious-minded and finely executed. His own house and studio were showcases for his innovative use of materials such as structural iron and large sheets of glass to create an all-embracing work of art. Richard Wagner coined the term *Gesamtkunstwerk* to describe the synthesis of the arts that he wanted to achieve in his operas, but the term was also adopted in discussions about architecture when a designer sought to control every aspect of a building's furnishing.

Horta's Art Nouveau style involves sinuous lines – stonework seems to soften, balusters feel their way like plant tendrils, fireplaces droop. The curves of wrought iron are taken up in painted decoration, ceramic tiles and pieces of furniture. Since it was impossible to convey the intricacies of the detail by using architectural drawings, Horta and his assistants made plaster models to explain to craftsmen what they were required to execute in timber or stone. Compared with traditional design, this process was expensive and, for a harmonious effect, every significant item of furniture had to be specially commissioned to fit with the others.

As a result, only Belgium's richest citizens could afford Horta's Art Nouveau houses. The country had been independent from the Netherlands since 1830 and there was a sense that Art Nouveau might become a national style, but the need for so much one-off design tended to rule out that idea. Horta's later work moved towards more geometric forms, achieving a particularly appealing synthesis in the Wacquant department store in central Brussels (now a cartoon museum), where the geometry of the heavier lower part of the building is offset by the lightness and freedom of the ironwork of the balustrades and the roof.

The Art Nouveau work in Horta's houses is intense and inventive and makes a little world of its own. In pictures it looks woozily soporific, as if the houses' inhabitants have supremely serene lives in which aesthetic values are very much to the fore. In reality the effect can be rather more bracing, as in Horta's own dining room, with its walls and floor covered in ceramic tiles and a shallow curving iron-and-masonry vault.

1 Ground Floor Plan

1 Kitchen
2 Servants' staircase
3 Main staircase
4 Parlour

2 Section A-A

3 North West Elevation

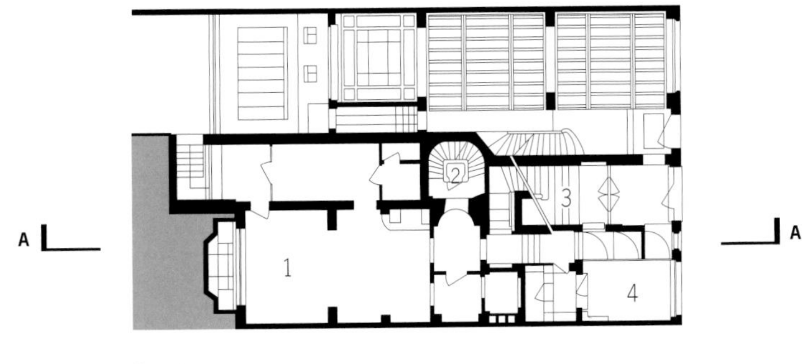

1

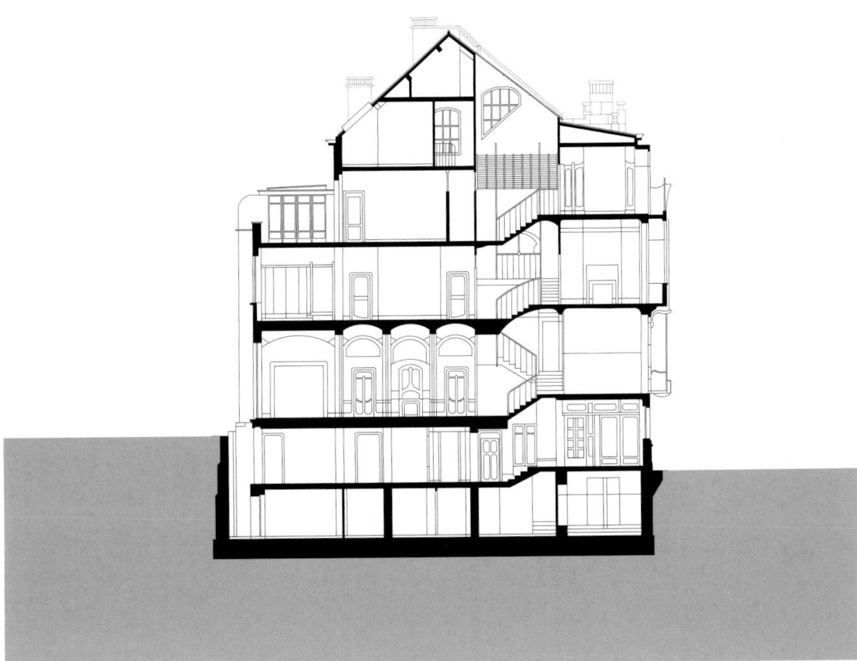

2

3

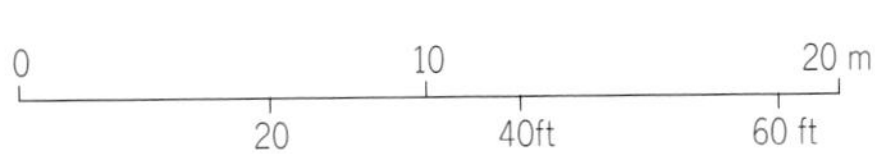

Unité d'Habitation

Le Corbusier (Charles-Edouard Jeanneret), 1887–1965

Marseilles, France; 1947–52

Charles-Edouard Jeanneret grew up in Switzerland but left to work in Auguste Perret's office in Paris, where he learnt about the potential of reinforced concrete before it was widely used. During the 1920s, under the pseudonym Le Corbusier, he made his reputation as an avant-garde architect with concrete houses. He was interested in the redesign of cities to meet modern needs, accepting the presence of the motor car and embracing non-traditional construction methods.

Le Corbusier's model for the individual house involved raising it up off the ground, making available external space under the house and more space in a garden on the flat roof. He proposed a structural system of flat concrete slabs supported by concrete posts. This made it possible to open up the internal space, which could then be freely subdivided by non-structural walls. It also allowed the external walls to be freed from their traditional load-bearing function, so windows could run right round the building as a continuous strip.

Most of these projects were glamorous homes for art-lovers, but the aim was to make such houses widely available at low cost. Le Corbusier designed an exhibition pavilion in 1925 that showed a modest apartment furnished with industrially produced furniture. This theme was continued in 1929 in a settlement of workers' housing at Pessac in the suburbs of Bordeaux.

The Marseilles block called Unité d'Habitation was Le Corbusier's first large-scale apartment building, and he treated it as a prototype for the reconstruction of cities after World War II, when the need for new dwellings was acute. Hugely influential, the design was replicated in various forms around the world with varying levels of success. Apartments were cast in concrete at ground level and then hoisted up into position and lodged in a concrete frame. Le Corbusier had himself photographed with a rack of wine bottles to explain the principle to potential tenants. Each apartment rested on lead blocks, to stop sound transmission from one unit to another. Some early tenants complained about the silence, which they found eerie after the companionable noises of their previous neighbourhoods.

The apartments themselves are on two levels, with a double-height main living room. Each apartment runs right through the block, giving views in both directions and allowing for good natural ventilation. Access is by an internal corridor that has no natural light. The apartments are designed in pairs that wrap around the corridor. In one type, a tenant enters on the lower floor and goes upstairs in the apartment to cross the block and look out the other end. A neighbour on the other side of the corridor enters on the upper floor and descends to go into the living room and to cross the block.

To make this ingenuity work, the apartments are long and thin, with the bathrooms and circulation tightly planned around the corridor, but the outer surface is as open as possible, with large windows and balconies. Some of the rooms are awkwardly narrow, but everyone has a view of the Mediterranean.

The whole block is lifted up on expressively rough concrete legs. There is a roof garden with play spaces and sculptural chimneys, and halfway up the block is a well-lit street of shops. The idea was that everyone's day-to-day needs could be met in the single building, as on an ocean liner. In fact, though, people had to leave the building to do their paid jobs and the shops did not attract enough custom to survive. Some of them were converted into a hotel, which is now popular with architectural pilgrims.

1 Typical Floor Plan

2 Section

3 Typical Unit Section

4 Typical Unit Plans

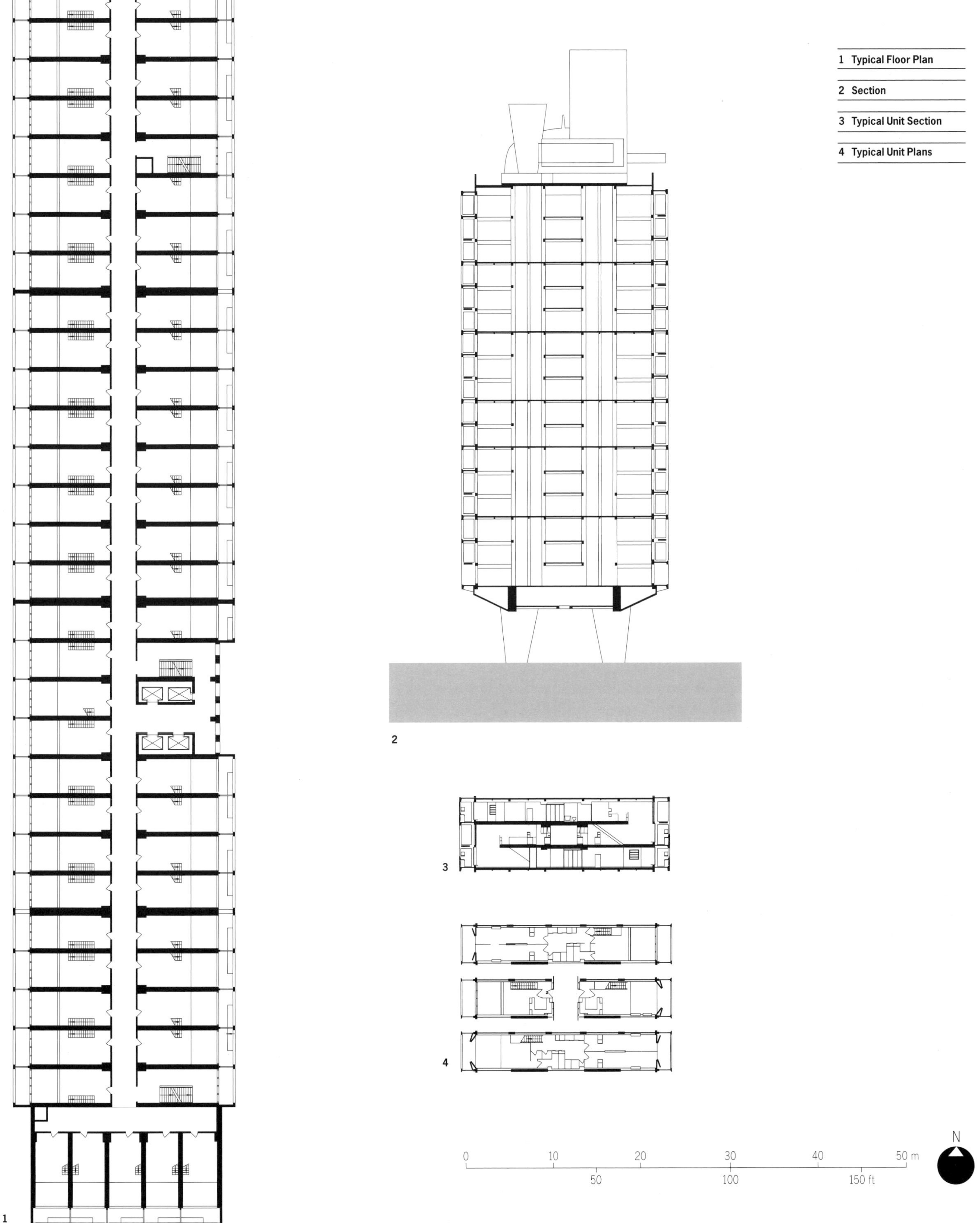

Lake Shore Drive Apartments

Ludwig Mies van der Rohe, 1886–1969

Chicago, Illinois, USA; 1949–51

When Mies van der Rohe arrived in the USA in 1937, he was already a famous architect. He had designed the German national pavilion for the international exposition in Barcelona in 1929, and had been the third and final director of the Bauhaus, before its state funding was withdrawn. In 1927 he had organized a celebrated exhibition of design for workers' housing at the Weissenhof Estate in Stuttgart and three years later he had designed the fabulously glamorous Tugendhat House in Brno, now in the Czech Republic.

Mies settled in Chicago. He established a studio in the downtown area, and taught out of the institution that would become the Illinois Institute of Technology, whose campus he designed.

His lasting preoccupation was a minimalist aesthetic, which in the earlier works used radically simplified forms and sometimes very precious materials, such as onyx walls in the German Pavilion and the Tugendhat House. In his American work, it is the expression of steel-frame structure that comes to the fore. Drawing on the structural rationalism described by Eugène Viollet-le-Duc, this architectural element is based on industrially produced steel girders, which Mies invested with cultural authority. His designs were carefully scaled and refined in their detail, giving them a presence and quality that would not be anticipated in routine industrial or commercial production.

The Lake Shore Drive apartments were important not so much for their technical innovation, but because they were the first tall residential buildings to make use of such a clearly expressed steel frame. Rather than the steel being hidden behind brick or stone, it is put on display, with only glass between the steel frame-members.

The two towers of the original development were very prominent, being on the road that runs along the shore of Lake Michigan, and their appearance was absolutely uncompromising. They were joined in 1953–56 by two more matching towers by Mies and established the model for more recent developments in the area, so they now look quite at home there, and would look at home in many cities round the world that have felt the influence of their example.

Achieving this simplicity of appearance is more complicated than it seems. When masonry covers a steel frame, it makes the building look more traditional, but it also protects the steel from fire damage. Mies's building needed such fire-protection, and it is there as a concrete casing for the steel, but the concrete is then covered over with steel to make the appearance match the original intention. So there is more than expedient pragmatism involved. There is ingenuity and deviousness involved along the way, but the final expression has the authority of truth.

The apartments were modest in size (with either one or three bedrooms). The circulation and plumbing were in the core of the building, so that the external walls were unencumbered, and every habitable room's external face was floor-to-ceiling glass. The walls could be covered by white roller-blinds, which had a mechanism that allowed them to be fully open, fully closed, or open part way, so that the blind's lower edge aligned with the sill-level transom.

Individually aberrant decisions about home furnishings are lost behind this disciplined façade, which now has the appearance of a corporate headquarters, but when it was new it was a daring experiment in modern living. Mies lived here for a while, but felt that the other residents were treating him like the maintenance man, so he moved to a larger apartment in a nearby Italianate building.

1 Site Plan

1 North building
2 South building

2 North Building Typical Floor Plan

1 Access corridor, stairs and lifts
2 Entrance/hall
3 Kitchen
4 Dining area
5 Living room
6 Bedroom
7 Bathroom

3 South Building Typical Floor Plan

1 Access corridor, stairs and lifts
2 Entrance/hall
3 Kitchen
4 Dining area
5 Living room
6 Bedroom
7 Bathroom
8 Service hall

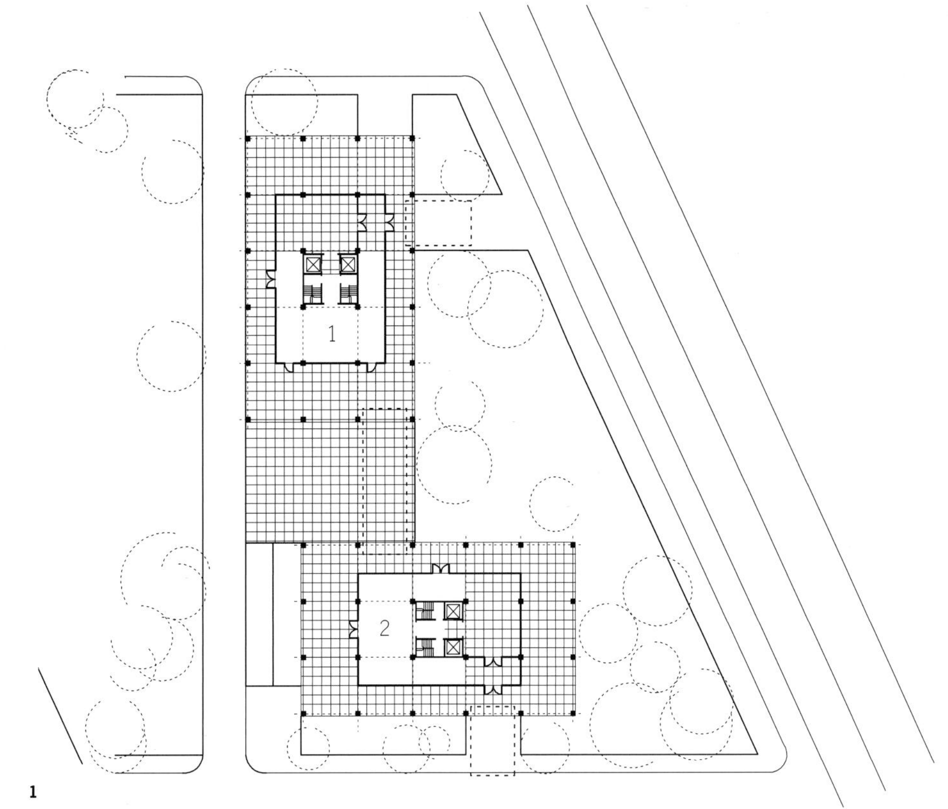

1

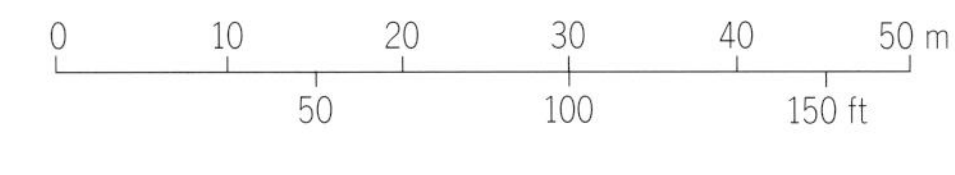

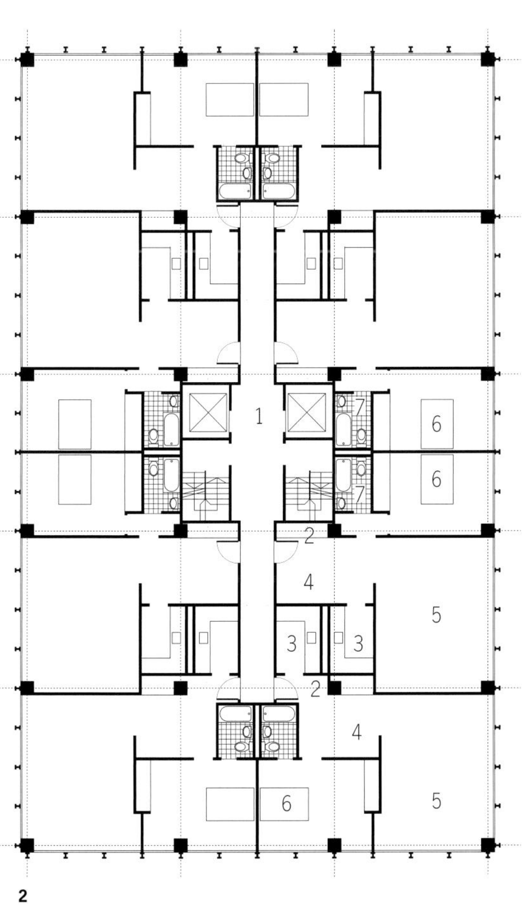

2

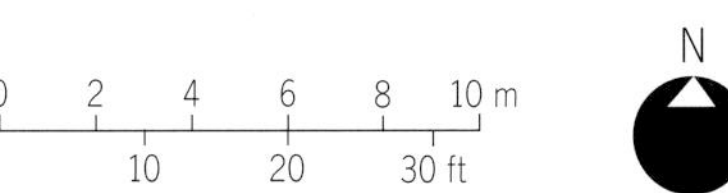

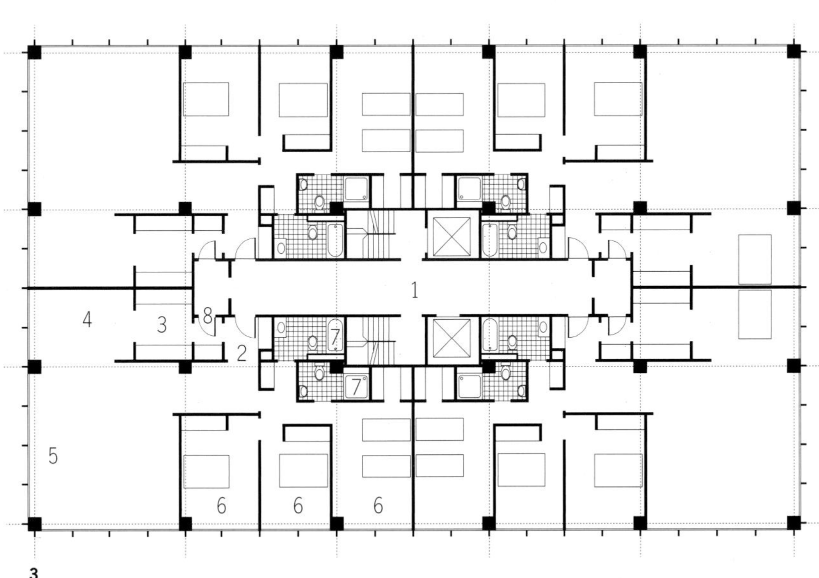

3

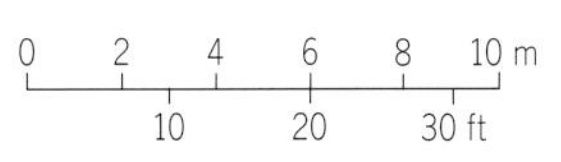

Schröder House

Gerrit Rietveld, 1888–1964, and Truus Schröder-Schräder, 1889–1985

Utrecht, Netherlands; 1924

This modestly sized house in Utrecht is a UNESCO World Heritage Site and one of the best-known buildings of the 1920s. It was designed by Gerrit Rietveld, a joiner and furniture designer, working closely with Truus Schröder-Schräder, who in her early thirties found herself widowed with three children but financially well off. She had previously engaged Rietveld to reorganize part of her apartment, and after her husband's death she decided to set up a household that would suit her life as an independent woman.

The house was located on the edge of town, looking out across flat fields. In this position, its striking composition of white planes and coloured linear elements gave it the status of a landmark; it was like a gatepost to the town for people returning from their Sunday promenades.

The building adhered to the rules of the De Stijl group of artists that formed around Theo van Doesburg (1883–1931), the most famous member of which was the painter Piet Mondrian. Rather than working through imagery, the work of the De Stijl group was designed to influence the state of the soul directly by its arrangement of geometric shapes in primary colours. The group ceased to cohere after van Doesburg's death, and although Rietveld produced furniture designs that continued in this manner, his architectural practice became more conventionally modernist, as a modernist orthodoxy took shape, and the Schröder house remained unique in his output.

Its arresting appearance explains why the house became memorable as an image that circulated in the art world, but it was also very successful as a home. Mrs Schröder lived in it until she died at the age of 95. After the children had grown up and left, Rietveld moved in with her.

The arrangement of the house was ingenious and flexible. The lower storey was laid out with compartmented rooms, and in the original request for building permission this was presented as the principal floor, while upstairs was shown an undifferentiated attic space.

In fact, it was the upper floor that was remarkable. It had large windows that opened outwards and flexible internal partitions that allowed different combinations of spaciousness and privacy for the inhabitants. For example, the bathroom was configured so that it took up very little space when the bath was not in use. Each of the bedrooms created when the screens were folded into position had its own washbasin and its own door to an outside balcony, so the children could be fairly autonomous and have their own independent domain. The screens offered little acoustic separation, however, and there was a piano in one of the rooms, so the spatial autonomy was offset by the intimacy of being able to hear the activities of the other occupants.

The flexible space in the Schröder House was a radical adventure in contemporary living. The building's construction was surprisingly traditional, with brick walls covered by white and grey stucco to create a purely abstract appearance.

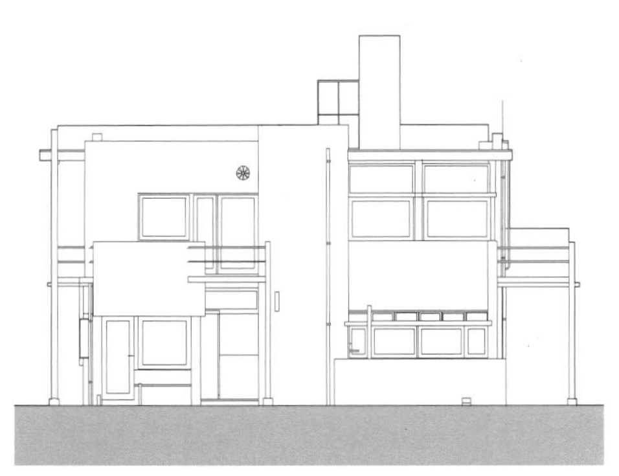

1

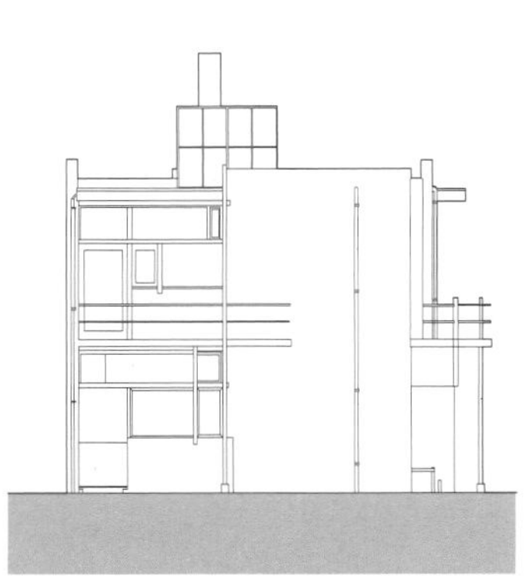

2

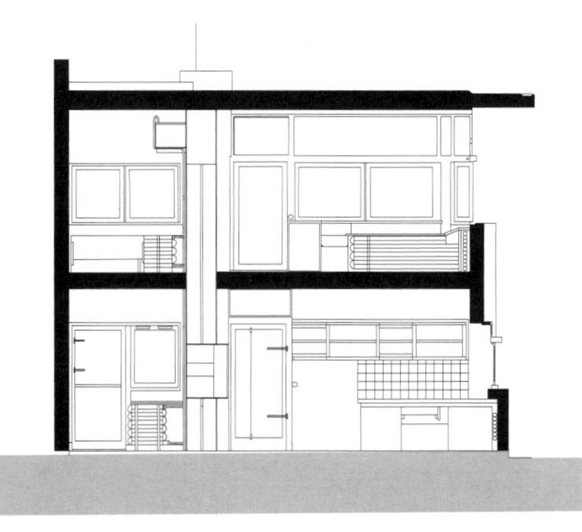

3

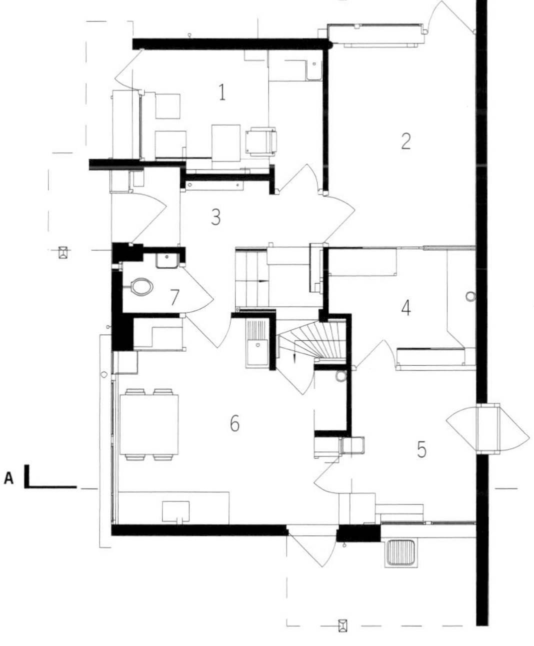

4

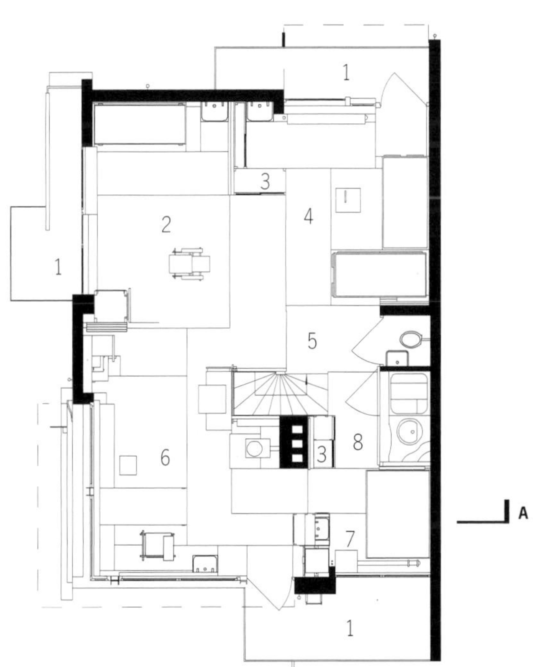

5

1 West Elevation

2 South Elevation

3 Section A-A

4 Ground Floor Plan

1 Reading room
2 Studio
3 Hall
4 Work room
5 Bedroom
6 Kitchen/dining/ living room
7 WC

5 First Floor Plan

1 Balcony
2 Work room/bedroom
3 Storage
4 Work room/bedroom
5 Hall
6 Living/dining room
7 Bedroom
8 Bathroom

N

0 5 10 m

10 20 30 ft

Places of Worship

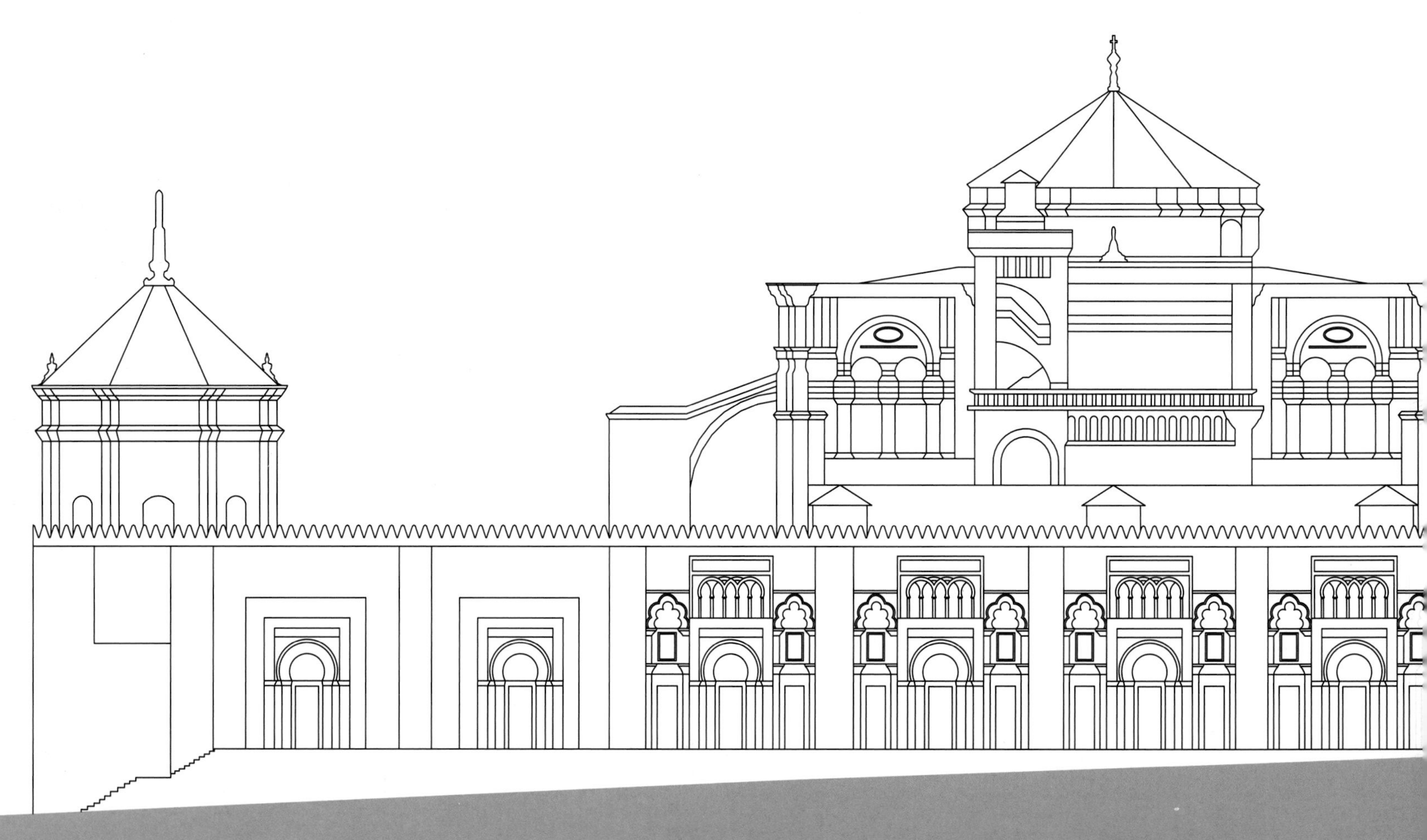

Anywhere can evolve into a place of worship, but the places that become architecturally interesting are those invested with special meaning, especially those that embody the values that their builders hold to be most important. When these places attract the devotions of thousands or millions of devotees, all determined to give as much as they can to sustain the place and make it as special as possible, then the results can be astounding. The driving force in such a case is not economy but the aspiration to show how much the god or the principles are valued.

The results are varied across the world, but they show what groups of people can do when they set themselves the task of going beyond what they would do in their everyday working lives. These are buildings of devotion, though in some cases the patron's magnificent vision might have been realized through the work of ordinary slaves.

Religious buildings have a way of surviving long after the collapse and disappearance of the homes of the people who built them. They are often constructed to much higher standards than dwellings, from much more solid materials, with the expectation that they would stand for ever – so, for some ancient civilizations, the places of worship are all the evidence remaining of what their life was like. When they were built, these buildings were exceptional. Their presence is proportionate to their value in the society that created them, so they deserve attention for what they can tell us, as well as for their aesthetic and other qualities.

The most imposing monuments often have a strong connection with the head of state, in which case promoting the piety of religion can also be a means of maintaining political order. This was true of the great temples on the Nile, and in Rome, also at Hagia Sophia in Constantinople, and the Suleyman Mosque. However, there are also popular shrines that grew rich and splendid not because they had especially powerful patrons, but because they had so many of them. These include the Basilica of the Madeleine in France (where the pilgrims included kings), Vierzehnheiligen in Germany, the Djenné Mosque in Mali – which is kept intact by a fresh coat of mud, applied by thousands of hands each year – and the Crystal Cathedral in California, which reaches out to its congregation through television and accepts sustenance by way of credit cards.

The forms of worship vary. In some places, there are sacrifices; in some, crowds participate in mass declarations of faith and thanks; in others, the experience is essentially solitary and meditative. But the adherents all bear witness to the importance of their institution by making the place of worship as good as it can be – maybe by making it the largest building in the region, or by adding ornate carving or gilding; maybe by covering the building in marble, or making it seem to melt into the air in a glow of coloured glass.

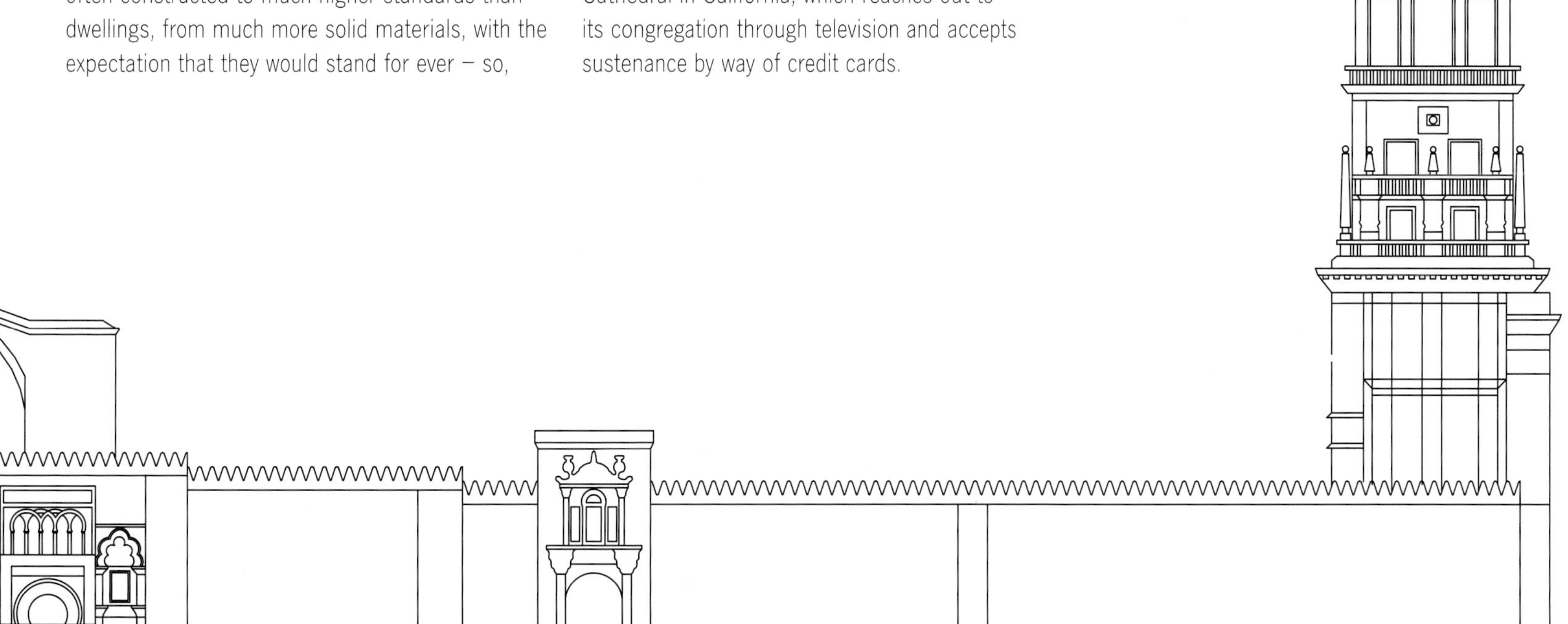

Megalithic Temples of Malta

Malta; 2500 BCE

Enormous stones called megaliths were used in the construction of temples on Gozo, one of the islands of Malta, which are among the oldest buildings known anywhere (above left). Ggantija, meaning 'giantess', was the name given to this pair of temples in a later age, on account of the stones' size. Clearly the result of great effort on the part of the communities that built them, whose identity and character remain obscure, the temples were used as burial places and the bones of dozens of people accumulated in them.

Relying as they do on the analysis of carbon samples, estimates of the buildings' date vary, but there is no doubt that they are very old indeed. The two temples were not built at the same time. Presumably the smaller one was constructed first and had acquired an air of venerable sanctity by the time it was felt necessary to build the larger one.

Each temple has its own concave façade, but a perimeter 'retaining wall' encloses them both. The layout of the internal spaces is strikingly like the bulbous forms of the carved sleeping female figurines that were found at another temple – and it is easy to see the shape of a person in the plan, with the head at the top and two limbs either side.

The burials seem to have involved covering the bodies with red ochre while they decomposed, perhaps preparing them for an afterlife. Ochre is a yellow earth, which can be ground to a powder and is still used as a pigment. It turns red when heated and has been used to represent the colour of blood. The space between the interiors and the perimeter wall was filled with rubble and earth, and there was probably once a roof, though that is long gone. The interiors seem to be modelled on caves.

In a street in Valletta, Malta's capital, there is a modest and unremarkable house that gives access to a series of underground chambers that were excavated in the same era as the Ggantija temples. The network of caves, known as the Hypogeum (above right), was discovered in 1902, having been made long before there was a city on this spot, or indeed anywhere, and then forgotten. The caves are like an image of the unconscious, dealing with life and death in an instinctual way beneath the rational business of the modern city.

Many people were buried there. The interiors are painted with red ochre, sometimes in spirals, and some of the doorways coming off the major space are carved so as to resemble the portals of a megalithic temple like Ggantija: vertical stones at the sides seem to support a horizontal lintel, but they are carved from the solid rock of the cave wall.

So here is a space that seems to be intact with its roof – an underground cave system arranged over three storeys. The Ggantija temples seem to be setting up spaces that modelled caves, but the Hypogeum is a cave of the same era that seems to be modelling megalithic construction. It is not clear which type of temple came first.

Floor Plan of South and North Temples at Ggantija

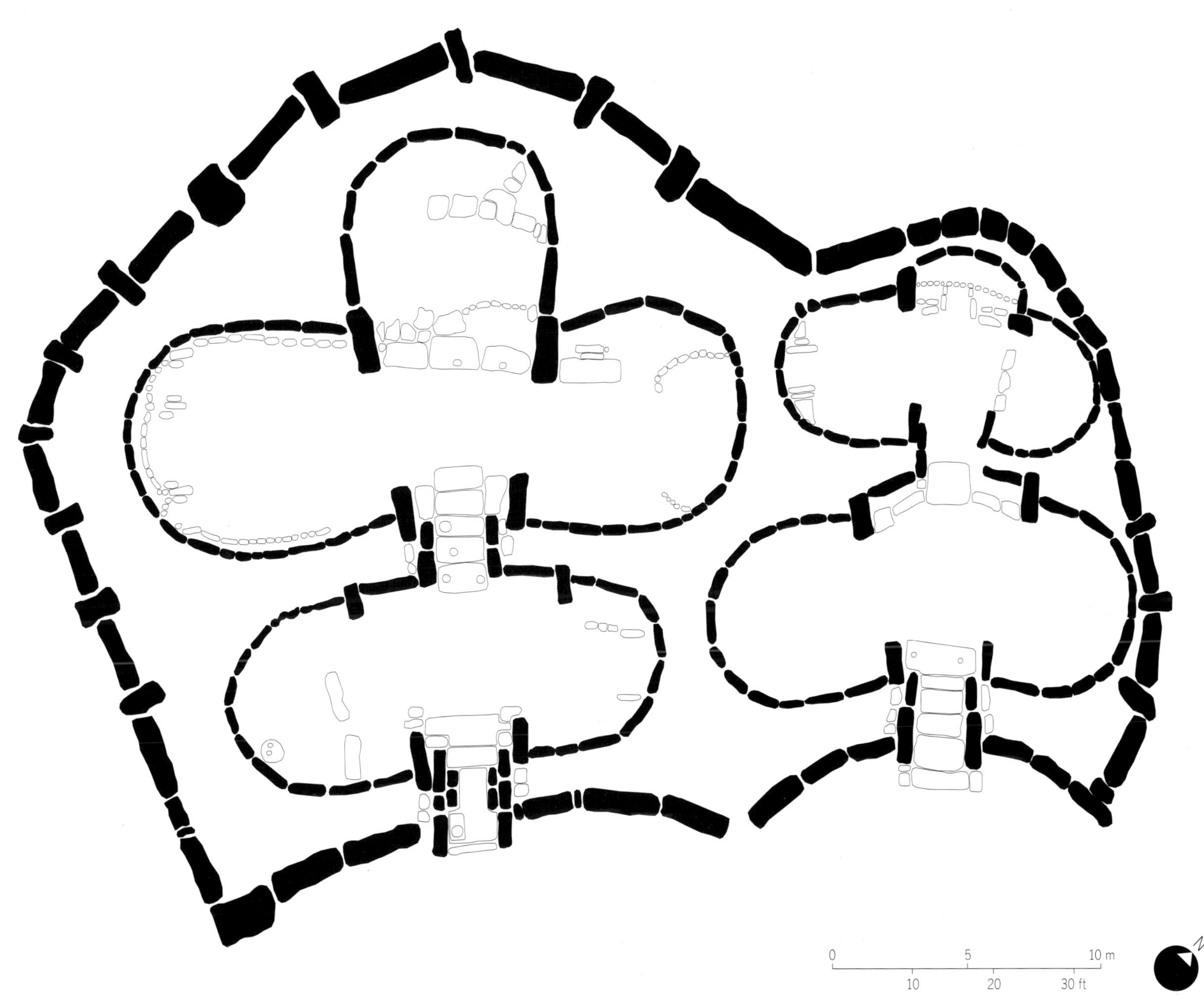

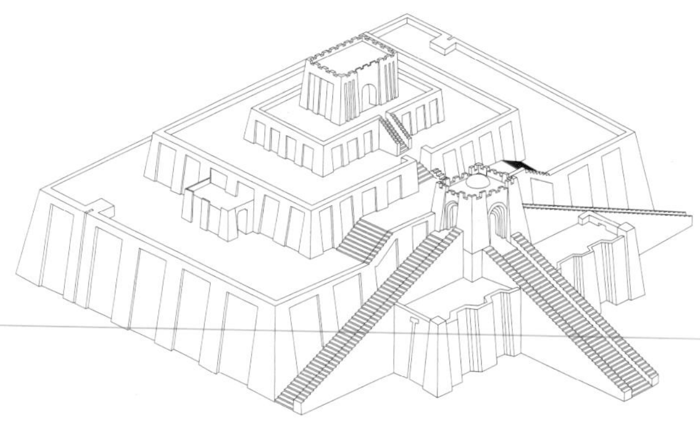

Great Ziggurat of Ur

Nasiriyah, Dhi Qar Province, Iraq; 2000 BCE, rebuilt 600 BCE

The idea of agriculture first took root in a land between two rivers which the Greeks called Mesopotamia. Crop cultivation seems to have been invented independently in various places, including China, but it was in the regions defined by the Tigris and Euphrates rivers – part of modern Iraq – and then in the areas bordering the Nile, that the ancient hydraulic civilizations irrigated the land, planted crops, and established a way of life that started to produce cities.

Ur was the largest city in the world, with an estimated population of 65,000, when work on the Great Ziggurat began. A temple dedicated to the moon goddess, Nanna, the ziggurat took the form of a raised platform made of sun-dried bricks and encased in a layer of fired bricks bonded together with bitumen. It is an artificial sacred mountain, built close to the mouth of the Euphrates on flat terrain with no natural mountains in sight. The shoreline has moved and the ziggurat is no longer by the sea, but the terrain is as flat as ever.

There is an idea that the people who settled this land had moved here from mountainous country in the north, and that they built the ziggurat as an ancestral memory from their homeland. Divine presence and mountains are associated in many religions – for example, the Greek gods on Olympus and Moses' encounter on Sinai that produced the Tablets of Law. At Ur there was no natural high place, so one was built.

The ziggurat was part of a complex of buildings, including the royal palace, that functioned as the city's administrative headquarters. The land was owned by the goddess and managed by those in contact with her. This was a prosperous and much-fought-over spot, so the administration repeatedly changed. Moses' patriarch Abraham came from Ur, which is described in the Bible as 'Ur of the Chaldees'. The Chaldeans settled here from the ninth century BCE, by when the city was a place of great antiquity and the ziggurat was crumbling. It was restored and enhanced in the sixth century BCE by Nabonidus, a Babylonian king who supplanted the Chaldeans. He was the father of Belshazzar, who lost the kingdom to the Medes and Persians.

Nabonidus was a devotee of the moon. He enhanced the ziggurat at Ur and rededicated it to the moon goddess, whom the Babylonians called Sîn. Three huge processional staircases on the same side of the building led up by way of several plateaux to the shrine at the top, which was covered in blue-glazed bricks and seemed to belong more to the sky than the earth. It is not clear what rites were enacted here, but they would have been in a realm apart, and would not have been witnessed by ordinary citizens. There was another temple in the city, on low ground, that would have received less exalted devotions.

The site was stabilized and restored in the 1980s, and a military base built alongside it, calling on the ziggurat for protection. This represented no metaphysical appeal to the moon but a more pragmatic calculation that the site's cultural value would be recognized by those who might seek to attack the modern state.

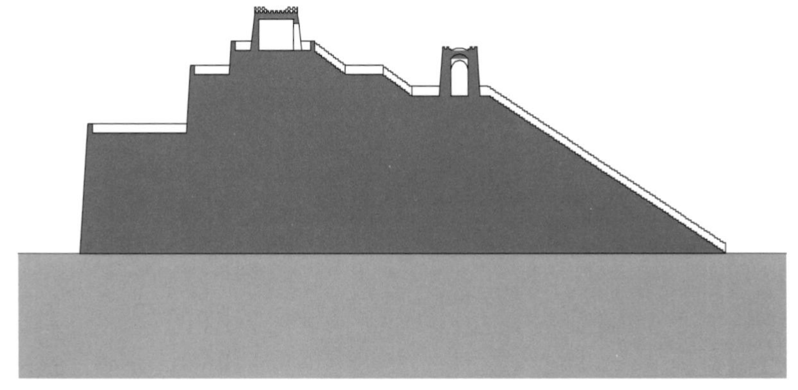

1

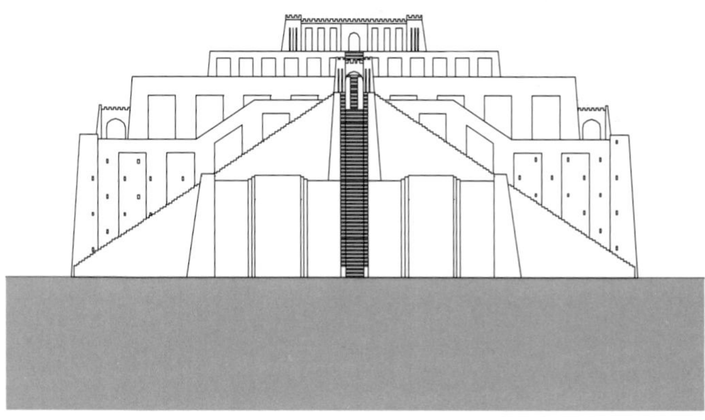

2

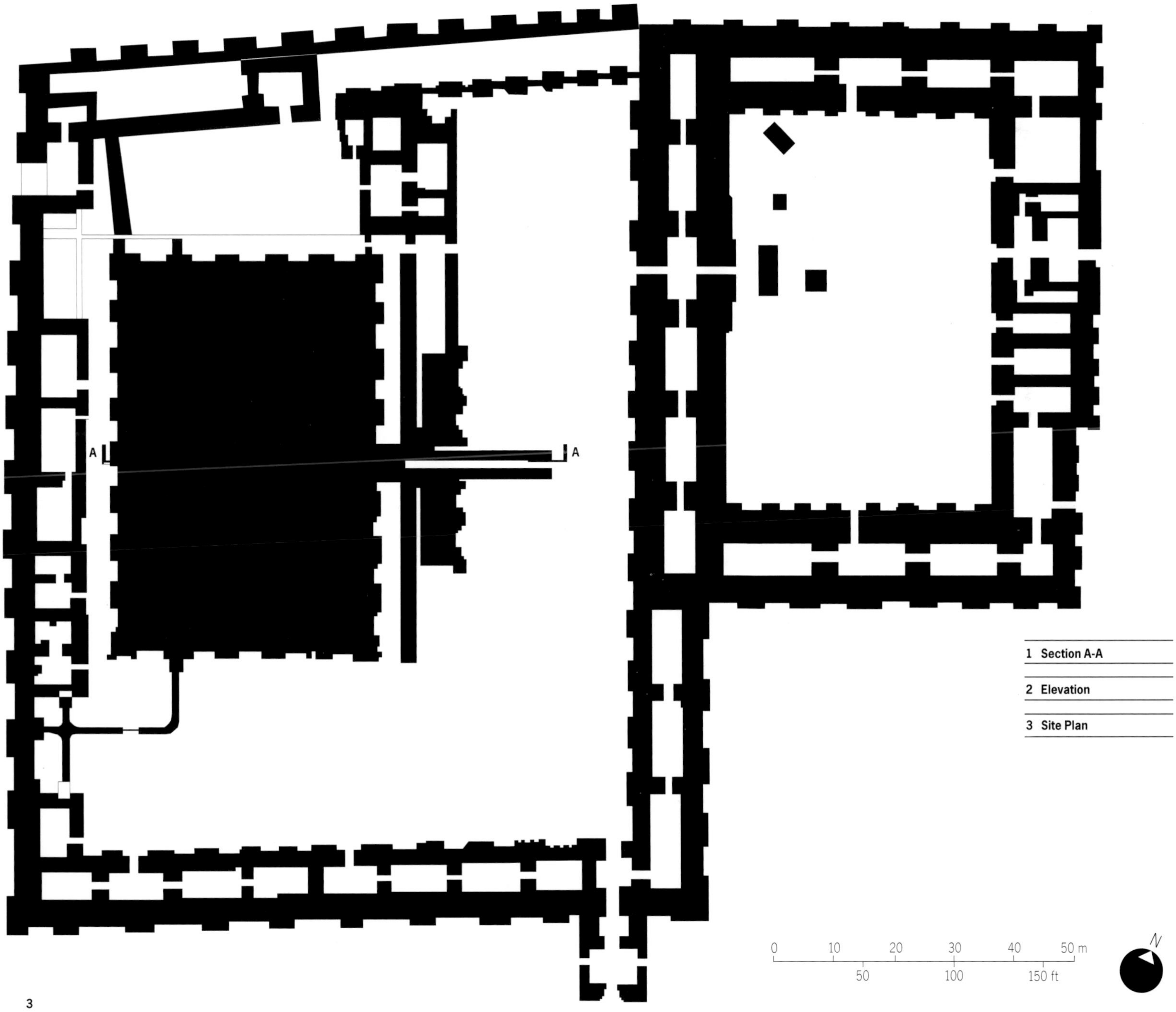

A A

0 10 20 30 40 50 m
50 100 150 ft

N

3

1 Section A-A

2 Elevation

3 Site Plan

Great Temple of Amon-Ra

Karnak, Thebes (Luxor), Egypt; c.2000 BCE

The foundation of the Amon-Ra temple complex dates from the Middle Kingdom period of Egyptian history, when the building of great pyramids had come to an end. The centre of government had moved away from the Nile delta to Thebes, now known as Luxor, about 700 km (400 miles) to the south. A concentration of great monuments developed nearby, at Karnak, including the spectacular funeral temple of Queen Hatshepsut and the later tombs with their treasures hidden away in the Valley of the Kings.

The sacred precinct is bounded by walls set out almost as a rectangle but with sides that are not quite parallel. Unlike the pyramids, the temples at Karnak are not aligned with the cardinal points, but a great avenue leads from the main temple across the Nile to align with Hatshepsut's temple.

Entry to the precinct is by a huge gateway – a pylon – which was the tallest part of the complex. There are three major pylons facing the outside world, each linked with a processional route to a different temple inside it. They tower like billboards inscribed with huge images of the gods, which now show up in low relief but were once painted and flanked by banners on timber masts. They were designed to make an impact from a great distance.

A monumental version of the ancient Egyptian noble's house, the temple complex is approached from the street through a courtyard. The courtyards there are vast and lined with rows of columns, and there is a succession of pylons – one entrance after another – on the way to the inner sanctum, which would have been inaccessible to almost everyone. The innermost place was also the oldest, with the courtyards and pylons being added as a way to frame and aggrandize what had begun as a simple shrine.

There were later accretions, with shrines to newer gods being added as long as the complex continued to be used for devotions, but the most significant project of monumentalization dates from the reigns of Thutmose I (1530 BCE) and Rameses II (c.1300 BCE), with the outermost pylon dating from the Ptolemaic period (c.330 BCE) but imitating the form of pylons a thousand years older.

The most architecturally arresting part of the building is the hypostyle hall – an interior space on the processional route to the shrine of the great Amon-Ra, completed in Rameses II's time. The hall was roofed with colossal stone slabs, which could span only a limited distance between the columns. The tallest columns flank the axis across the centre, and the roof they supported was higher than that over most of the space. Between the two roof levels was a stone grille letting in light, so the central axis – the processional route – was the most brightly lit part of the room, while the multitude of columns to the sides were lost to view in darkness. Everything is covered in hieroglyphs attesting to Amon-Ra's power.

The great girth of the columns – the largest are 3.6 metres (12 feet) in diameter – and the limited space between them (not much greater than their diameter) means that there are no diagonal views, and the space, despite being unlimitedly vast, does not seem to offer room to do anything. The puny human presence is crowded out by the unrelenting masonry.

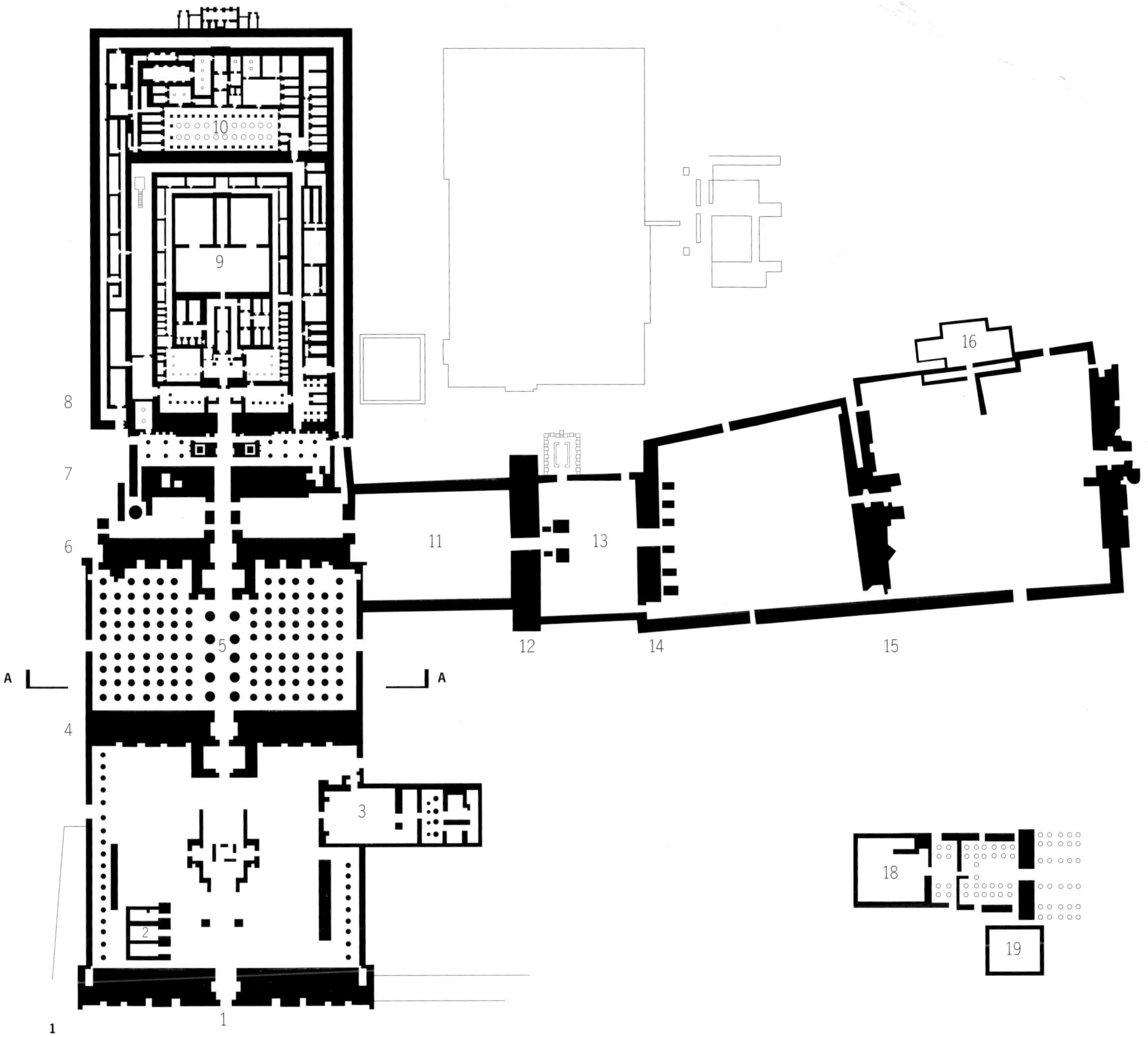

1

1 Ground Floor Plan

1 First Pylon
2 Triple Shrine of Sety II
3 Temple of Rameses
4 Second Pylon
5 Great Hypostyle Hall
6 Third Pylon
7 Fourth Pylon
8 Fifth and Six Pylon
9 Middle Kingdom Court
10 Festival Hall of Thutmose III
11 First Court
12 Seventh Pylon
13 Second Court
14 Eighth Pylon
15 Ninth Pylon
16 Sed-Festival Temple of Amenhotep II
17 Tenth Pylon
18 Temple of Khonsu
19 Temple of Oper

2 West Elevation

3 Section A-A

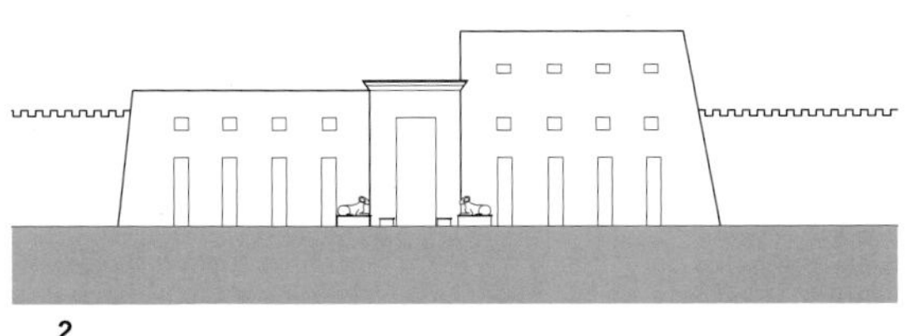

2

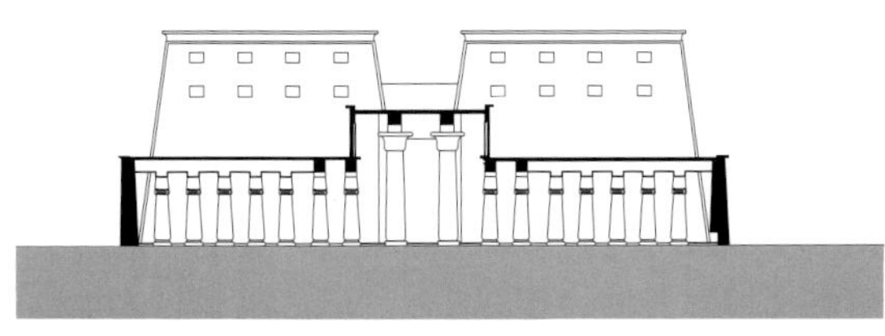

3

0 50 100 m
120 140 ft

Temple of Apollo at Delphi

Delphi, Greece; prehistoric origins, main temple rebuilt 373 BCE

The sanctuary at Delphi, on the lower slopes of Mount Parnassus – where Apollo and the muses had their home – was among the most important ancient Greek shrines. Calliope, the muse of epic poetry, was the mother of the half-mortal Orpheus. Orpheus lived here, charmed the wild beats with his singing, visited the underworld and was torn limb from limb by a mob of women.

Parnassus is emblematic of artistic inspiration and accomplishment, and the so-called Orphic hymns – very ancient texts – give some insight into archaic Greek religion. It was also supposed to be the place where the Earth's umbilical cord had connected, before the world was born.

Delphi offered a potent fusion of chthonic mysteries and worldly sophistication. The Delphic oracle could be consulted, with due preparation and at great expense, and was consulted by representatives of heads of state. The route that ascends to the principal temple, dedicated to Apollo, is lined with buildings that displayed treasures, sometimes trophies of war, brought here as offerings to the sanctuary's gods. The Treasury of the Athenians was built in thanksgiving for the Athenian victory against the Persians at Salamis. The Spartans erected a stoa to house a statue-group commemorating their victory over the Athenians at Aegospotamoi. Delphi was a place outside the principal city-states, where inter-state rivalries could be felt and might on occasion be resolved. It was not a large city, but it was possible to imagine that it was the centre of the world.

People visited Delphi from across the Greek-speaking world, with the result that the priests there developed an unusually good impression of what was going on. There was no systematic news service, and the network for relaying information was by today's standards limited, but it was more extensive than any other, so the oracle's gnomic and often ambiguous utterances were surprisingly well informed. Engraved in the pavement in front of the temple was the injunction to 'know thyself' – a command that may be heard in a moment but which can absorb the attention of a lifetime.

There are fine artistic works at the sanctuary. The most famous is a pre-classical statue of a charioteer, composed and poised – in control of his emotions, even in the moment of triumph. There were competitive performances of plays, with dancing and music in the theatre let into the slope of the ground, and there were athletic events at the stadium beyond – the Pythian games. These competitions suggest intellectual, technical and highly disciplined accomplishment, but they took place in the presence of an extraordinary object called an *omphalos* – a stone in the form of a navel sculpted to look as if it were tied up with knotted bandages. The *omphalos* is probably a replacement for a older stone whose bandages were real, and over which libations of olive oil or blood would have been poured. Delphi was also in touch with life's primitive and instinctual side.

The buildings reflect a world of decorum and propriety. Apollo's temple was correctly Doric, rebuilt over decades in the middle of the fourth century BCE, after an earlier one had been destroyed by earthquake, so it came later than the classic Doric temples. It was itself destroyed in 390 CE on the order of a Roman emperor, Theodosius, in the interests of Christianity. At some other places, such as the Parthenon (pages 16–17), the old temples were turned into churches, but at Delphi the power of the underworld seemed too strong to be reappropriated. The sanctuary disappeared beneath landslips until excavations began in the 1890s and it was brought back to the light.

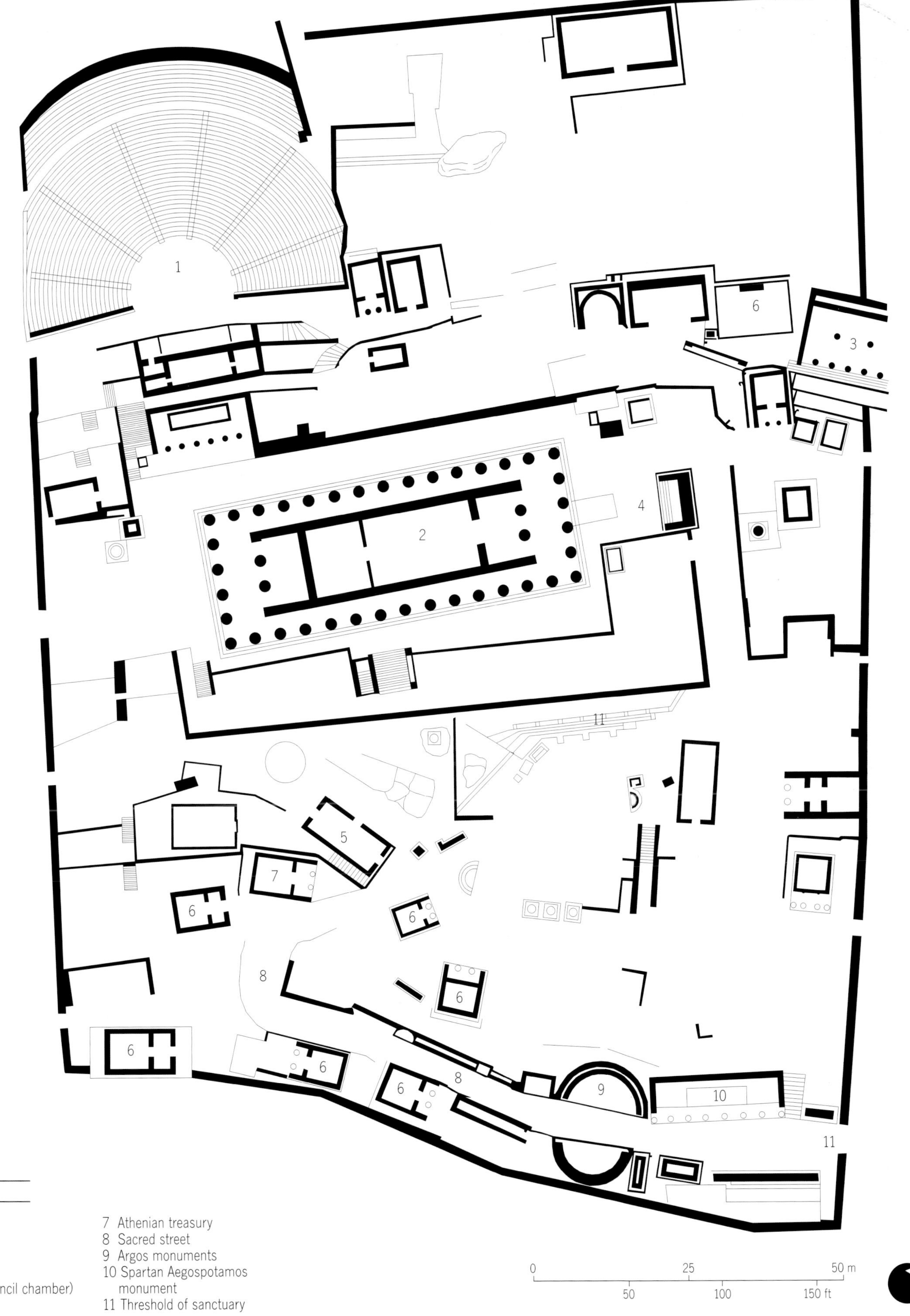

Site Plan

1 Theatre
2 Temple
3 Stoa
4 Altar
5 Bouleterion (council chamber)
6 Treasury
7 Athenian treasury
8 Sacred street
9 Argos monuments
10 Spartan Aegospotamos monument
11 Threshold of sanctuary

Temple of Apollo Epikourios

Bassae, Greece; 450–425 BCE

Apollo Epikourios was Apollo the saviour, credited (on the hearsay evidence of an ancient traveller) with having helped the local population through a plague. It is unclear who the local people were, as the temple is not close to a city but in the remote mountainous region of Arcadia.

It seems amazing that the inhabitants were able to commission a building of such high quality – a structure that was unknown to the wider world until it was rediscovered in the early nineteenth century. Once it had been found, the finely carved marble parts were soon dispersed. The frieze went to the British Museum and some other blocks to Copenhagen, leaving the walls and columns of local limestone on the site. Old earthquake damage and continuing erosion and weathering endanger the building, which is now housed in a protective tent.

The traveller from whom we know about the temple was Pausanias, who visited long after it was completed, by which time Greece was a Roman province. He was impressed by the building and thought he had seen only one that was more perfect, at Tegea. The Tegea site is flat and today seems unremarkable, encroached upon by modern houses. As at Bassae, there was a door in one of the temple's long walls, and it too was an unusually long, narrow building, so the proportions may have reflected an established Arcadian tradition rather than having been dictated by the lie of the land at Bassae.

In its decorative detail the building was remarkable. The Doric columns outside were not continued within; instead, the ends of piers there were carved into half-columns with unusual Ionic capitals – perhaps in anticipation of their being seen from below, as would be the case in the confined interior. The frieze of fighting figures ran round the room and would have been all but lost to view in the shadows beneath the ceiling.

The sectional drawing on the opposite page shows C. R. Cockerell's implausible 'reconstruction' of a rooflight, which would have made sense in nineteenth-century England. Cockerell also shows the cult statue placed off-centre, beyond the last semi-columns and the central freestanding column. This makes sense of the layout but is probably a misinterpretation. The statue is oriented to look out of the side door, which faces east, so that Apollo can greet the dawn. It is unlikely that the ancient builders had this intention. The room's decoration stops with the columns, so the statue, if placed there, would have been outside the honorific space defined by the columns and the frieze. Modern scholarship suggests that the statue would have been put in the normal orientation, facing the main door and standing in front of the central column.

This column is the most noteworthy detail of the building. It has the earliest known example of the Corinthian capital – the most decorative of the Greek capitals, and the one that the Romans took up with the greatest enthusiasm and used on their most impressive buildings. This might not be where it was invented, but no earlier use of it is known. The masons were specialists who probably came from Athens, and the locals evidently liked to think that Iktinos, the architect of the Parthenon (pages 16–17), had been involved, but there is no evidence of this.

The one thing that Pausanias tells us about the building's interior is that by his day the heroic bronze statue of Apollo was not in it. It is not that he mentions its absence – but he does tell us that he saw it at Megalopolis.

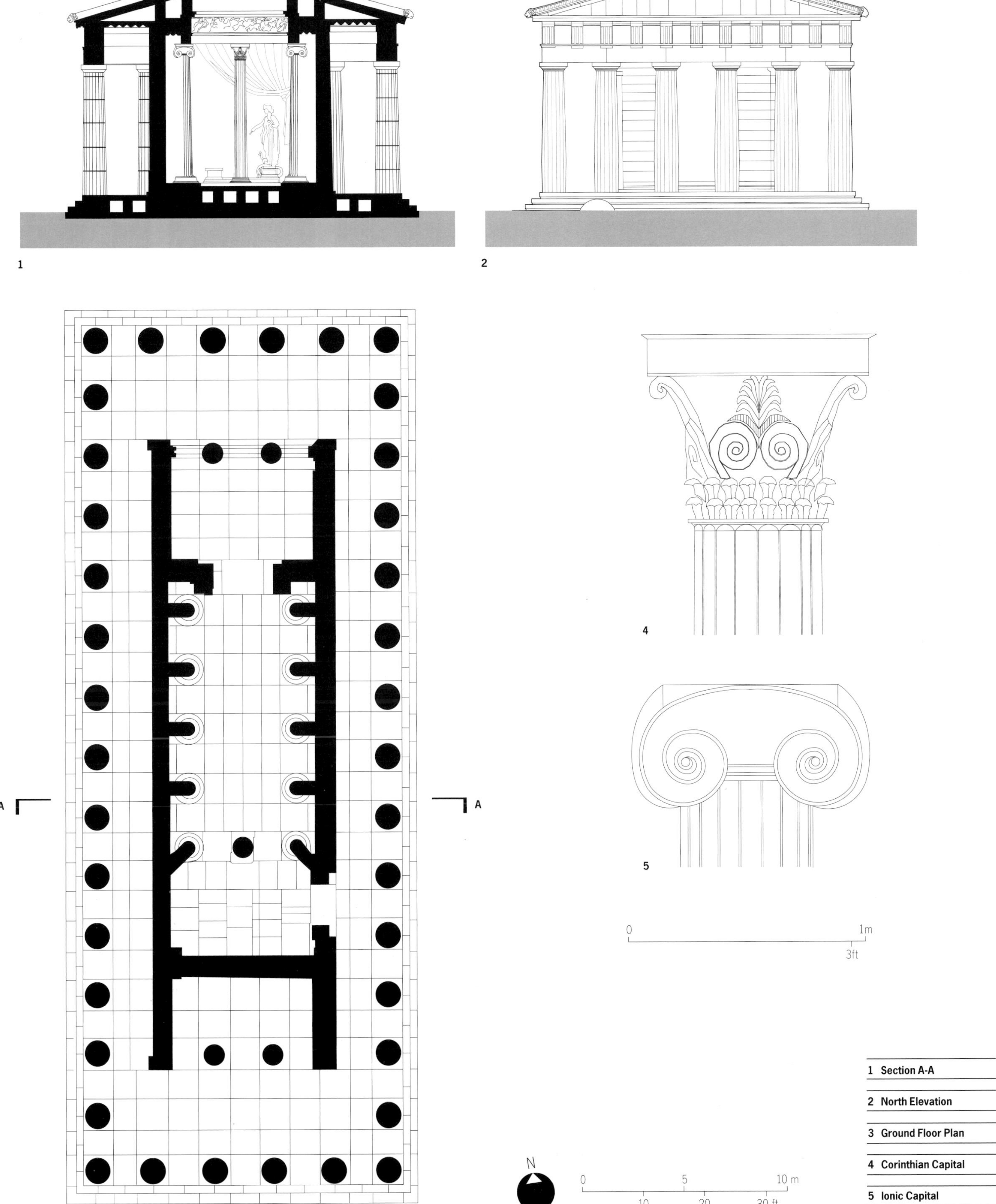

1 Section A-A

2 North Elevation

3 Ground Floor Plan

4 Corinthian Capital

5 Ionic Capital

Maison Carrée

Nîmes, France; 20 BCE

The Maison Carrée in Nîmes is the best-preserved typical Roman temple. Greek temples were usually built in special places, such as the sites of Bronze Age settlements (like the Acropolis at Athens) or in remote situations (like Delphi). The Romans conquered mainland Greece at Corinth in 146 BCE, but they had already been impressed by Greek culture, which they saw as more sophisticated and civilized than their own. They regarded Sparta as a precursor of Rome's military culture, and Virgil imitated Homer's epic poetry. The Romans imitated Greek sculpture and architecture, but in their enthusiasm for grandiose monuments their model was Athens rather than Sparta.

The most spectacular and idiosyncratic Roman monuments were in Rome itself, whereas in a city like Nîmes – an important but provincial administrative centre – buildings were used to impose a Roman character on a place that was established in occupied territory. The southern part of Gaul, conquered in 121 BCE, had strategic importance because it connected Italy with Spain. The important Roman road to Spain went through Nîmes, which seems to have been founded as a city soon after Julius Caesar's Gallic wars, which ended in 51 BCE, bringing the rest of Gaul under Roman control.

Nîmes became one of the five important cities in Gaul. It had fortified walls, an imposing basilica for official business (now disappeared), an amphitheatre for entertainment – much smaller than the Colosseum (pages 18–19), but along the same lines – and some places of worship. The building that is now often called the Temple of Diana was in fact a nymphaeum that provided a high-status setting for a water source. The Maison Carrée occupied a prominent site, dominating the forum. One of the city's foundational monuments, the original structure was replaced by the current temple. On the instigation of Marcus Agrippa, it was dedicated to his sons (the emperor Augustus's grandsons) Gaius and Lucius Caesar, who had died young. Its institutional importance is unambiguous: Rome has jurisdiction here.

Greek temples had typically been freestanding entities with a row of columns – the peristyle – running all the way round, making a 'peripteral' temple. The early Roman temples, called Etruscan after the province where Rome was situated, were similar in many ways, but were typically a row of three enclosed rooms placed on a stone platform. In front of these rooms was a covered space, made by continuing the roof and supporting it with columns, and a flight of steps at the front coming up to the plinth. This arrangement is different from that of a Greek temple, which would normally have three steps running right round the plinth – small steps for a small temple, and large steps for a large one, supplemented by a stone ramp at the entrance, if the size of the steps made it undignified to walk up them. By contrast, the Roman civic temple would have a longer flight of steps that were always conveniently sized.

The Maison Carrée is finely modelled and follows the pattern of the Roman temple, but it has a closer resemblance to a Greek temple than might be expected, in that the rhythm of the columns is continued right round the building. The type is called pseudoperipteral. The columns are fully formed and structural at the front, where they support the portico, but decorative when they are modelled on the surface of the load-bearing wall that concealed the cult statues from open view.

When Christianity became an official religion in the Roman Empire in the fourth century and the temple was transformed into a church, the statues were taken away. The building's new form of sanctity saw it safely through the Middle Ages.

1

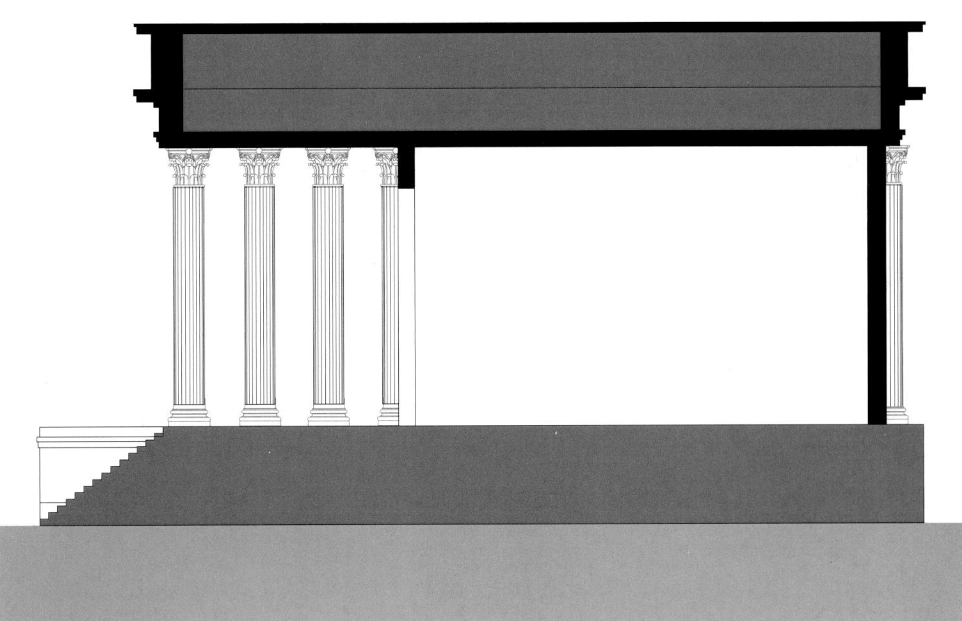

2

3

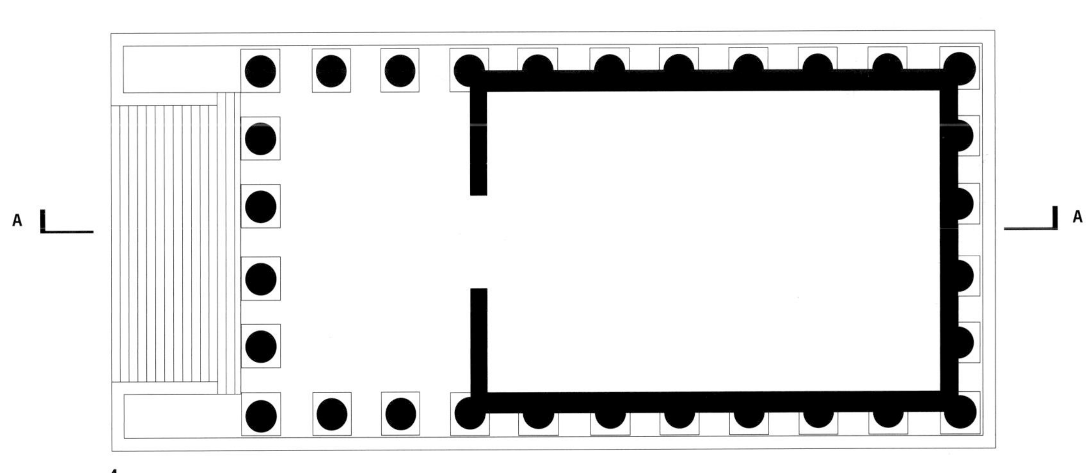

4

1 Elevation

2 Section A-A

3 Detail

4 Plan

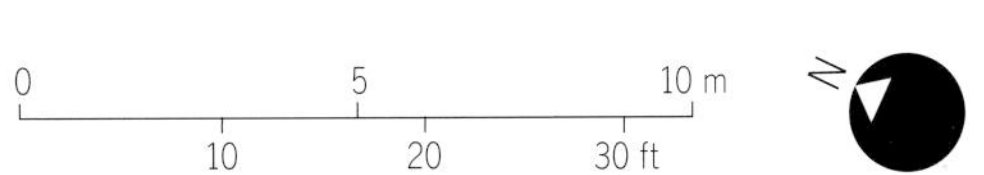

Pantheon

Rome, Italy; 120–24

The Pantheon in Rome was another temple that became an early church. It is even better preserved than the Maison Carrée (pages 106–107), but it was not a typical temple: it was always unique. However, it has some recognizable characteristics of the Etruscan temple. The columns divide the Pantheon's portico into three, as if remembering the three-celled arrangement of the Etruscan temple – but, instead of there being three doors, there is only one, and what would have been the side rooms are reduced to niches that once held statues, while the central room has inflated to become the most magnificent religious interior in a city that came to be congested with grand monuments.

The exterior of the Pantheon looks traditional to a misleading degree. The portico reused not only the columns but also the dedicatory inscription from an earlier structure, which says that the builder was Marcus Agrippa (who had built the Maison Carrée) rather than – as was in fact the case – the emperor Hadrian, an unusually ardent philhellene.

Originally the approach to the Pantheon was through a rectangular forum, which would have dominated the immediate area in the usual way, hiding from view the enormous dome that makes up the bulk of the building.

The dome was the largest to have been built, wider even than that of Hagia Sophia (pages 24–25), which through the addition of semi-domes has a larger volume of space in its interior. The next dome to surpass its diameter was the one at the Duomo in Florence, built from 1420 (1,300 years later). The dome of the Pantheon is remarkable for its confidence and finesse. It is made of concrete, which is given extra structural depth (but not excessive extra weight) by the use of coffering: recessed panels in the ceiling. Each recess once held a gilded bronze rosette, so the dome seemed to be picked out with a regular geometric array of stars.

Concrete is made by cementing together pieces of rock that do not need to be carefully shaped. The Romans knew about the special properties of a volcanic ash, pozzolana, that made a very strong cement. At the top of the dome the concrete is made as light as possible by using pumice – aerated volcanic lava that floats in water – as the rock. The apex is omitted, replaced by a bronze ring 8 metres (26 feet) in diameter but open to the sky. This is the great room's major source of light; a little comes in through the doorway when its huge bronze doors are open (the original doors are still in place). When the sun shines, a disc of intense light makes its way round the vault, which the coffers divide into 28 radial sectors – one for each day of the lunar month.

Theories about the occult meaning of the space include a supposed association with the skies and the planets. The seven niches around the perimeter of the circular space are believed by some to represent the days of the week, which were named after the Roman planets (sun-day, moon-day, mars-day, mercury-day, etc.).

The Pantheon is distinguished from other temples by the importance of its interior. A temple's interior was usually the place for housing the cult statue, while the sacrificial ceremonies took place in the god's line of sight, but at a distance, outside the building. At the Pantheon, the interior is so large and elaborate that it is impossible to doubt that something of significance went on there, which suggests an unusual form of worship, maybe a mystery cult such that at Eleusis in Greece.

Initiates of the Eleusis cult were put to death if they revealed its secrets, so it is surrounded by more speculation than certain knowledge, but similarly there was a temple – now long perished – that could let in light from above at key moments during religious observances.

1 Front Elevation

2 Section A-A

3 Ground Floor Plan

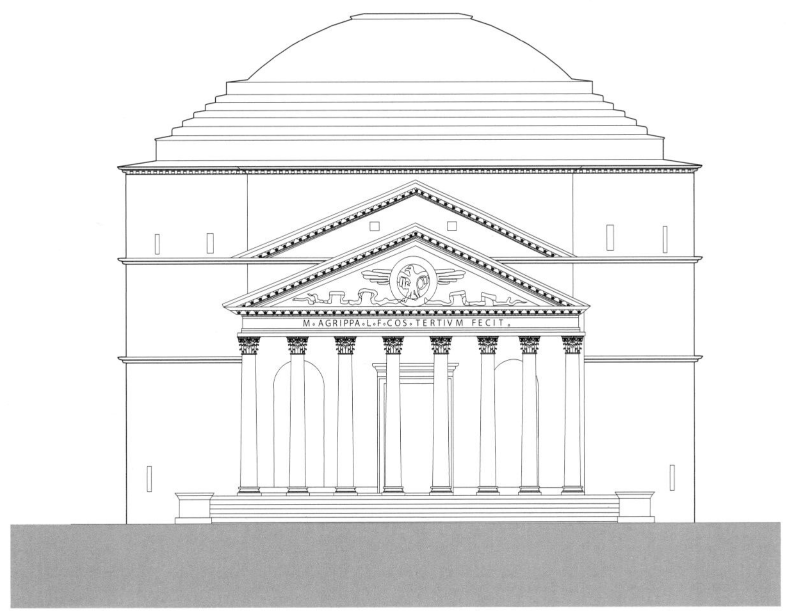

1

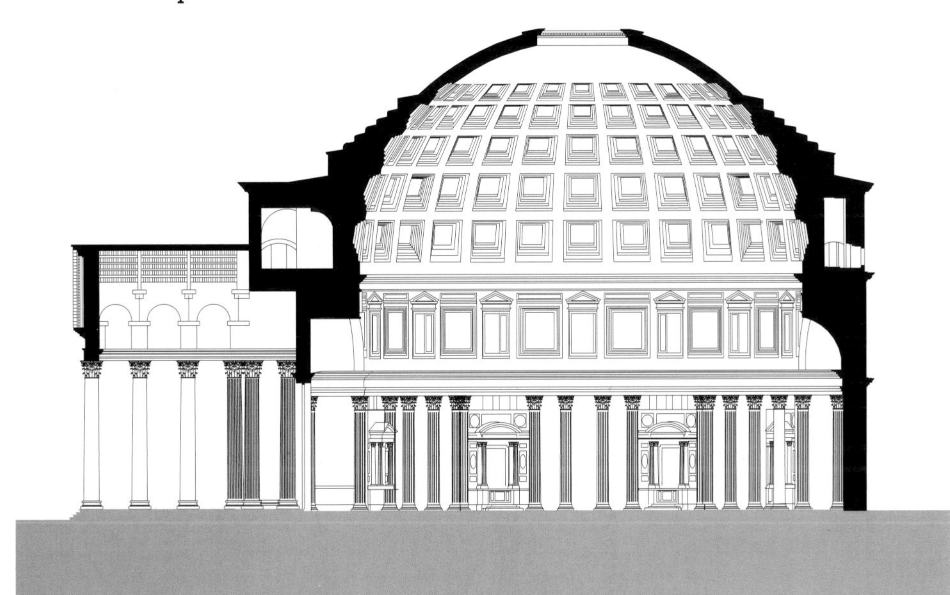

2

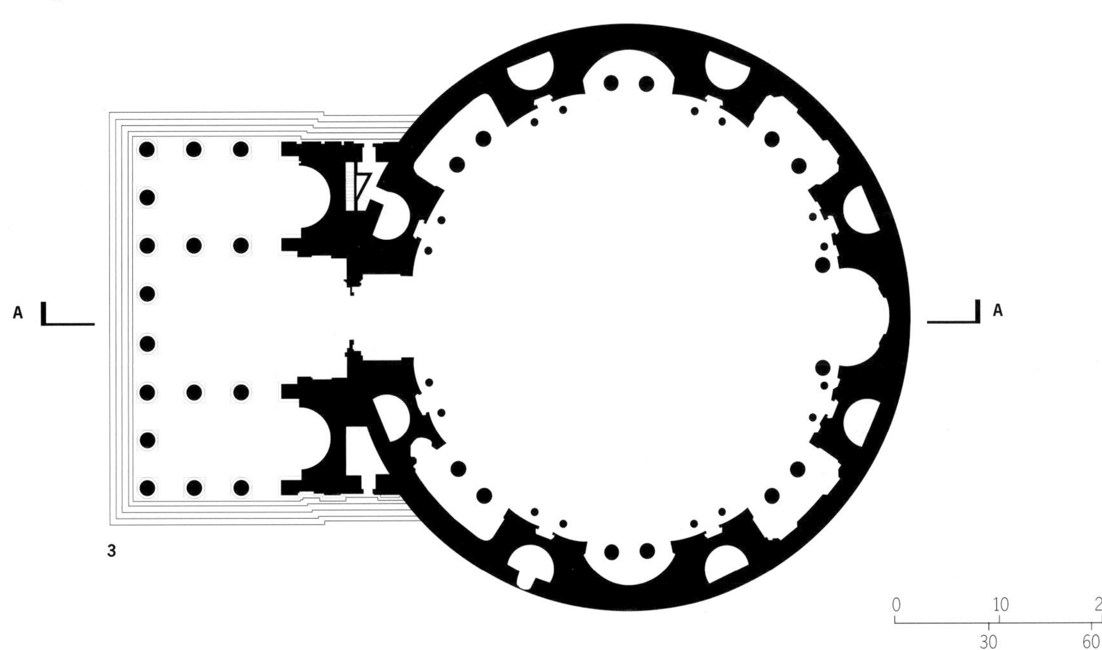

3

Mahabodhi Temple

Bodh Gaya, Bihar, India; fifth and sixth centuries CE

Prince Siddhartha Gautama was born in the sixth century BCE in the region now known as Nepal. He lived a life of privilege, but at the age of 29 he left his palace, wife and son, and set out into the world in search of enlightenment. He studied meditation with monks and adopted their ascetic practices, but one day, while meditating in the shade of a fig tree, he realized that the path to liberation came from moderation rather than extreme asceticism. His reputation spread as the Buddha – the enlightened one. The tree beneath which he achieved enlightenment was venerated in his lifetime and its direct descendant is in the sanctuary of the Mahabodhi Temple – the Temple of the Great Awakening.

The Indian emperor Ashoka, who lived in the third century BCE, played a key role in turning Buddhism into something more than a local cult. He was responsible for the earliest temple at Bodh Gaya, but the temple's present state is based on subsequent rebuilding that made the structure taller and more elaborate. Its UNESCO World Heritage Site listing describes Mahabodhi Temple as one of the earliest and most impressive brick structures of the Gupta period (320–550 CE) but it was heavily restored in the late nineteenth century. The shrine includes the remains of an older temple dedicated to the Buddha (the Diamond Throne), now in ruins, and it is surrounded by monastic buildings of various ages and traditions that attest to the diversity of its religious visitors.

The most important part of the shrine is the Bodhi Tree – the Awakening Tree – which is surrounded by a carved stone fence that sets the tree apart and protects it. A fence in this position marked out the whole extent of Ashoka's temple. It has been replaced, but the surviving stone is the oldest in the sanctuary. The tree's branches spread well beyond the little enclosure, and it is possible to sit meditatively under its spreading branches.

The site's dominant structure is a 55-metre-(180-foot)-high stupa in the form of a tower with sloping sides. The intricately carved stone blocks suggest an assembly of thousands of smaller stupas piled up on one another, making a small square platform at the top, on which sits a circular finial that was presumably once a reliquary. There are smaller stupas around, including one at each corner of the tower's square base, and about 100 more distributed through the garden.

The shrine has an interior that houses a golden sculpted image of the Buddha at the moment of his inspiration, touching the ground with one hand, and wrapped in a saffron robe. The statue does not look out at the tree as might be anticipated, but is in a tomb-like vaulted space, some 5 metres (16 feet) below ground.

In comparison with the space of the garden around it, however, the interior is insignificant. The Bodhi Tree is the main focus for contemplation, but the whole garden is used as a place of spiritual discipline, sometimes by organized groups of people, but often by solitary individuals meditating in the manner devised by Siddhartha Gautama, using the body's movement to help the mental state: walking slowly, deliberately, with extreme self-awareness, clockwise, always clockwise, round the tower as part of a crowd, or more privately around a lesser monument.

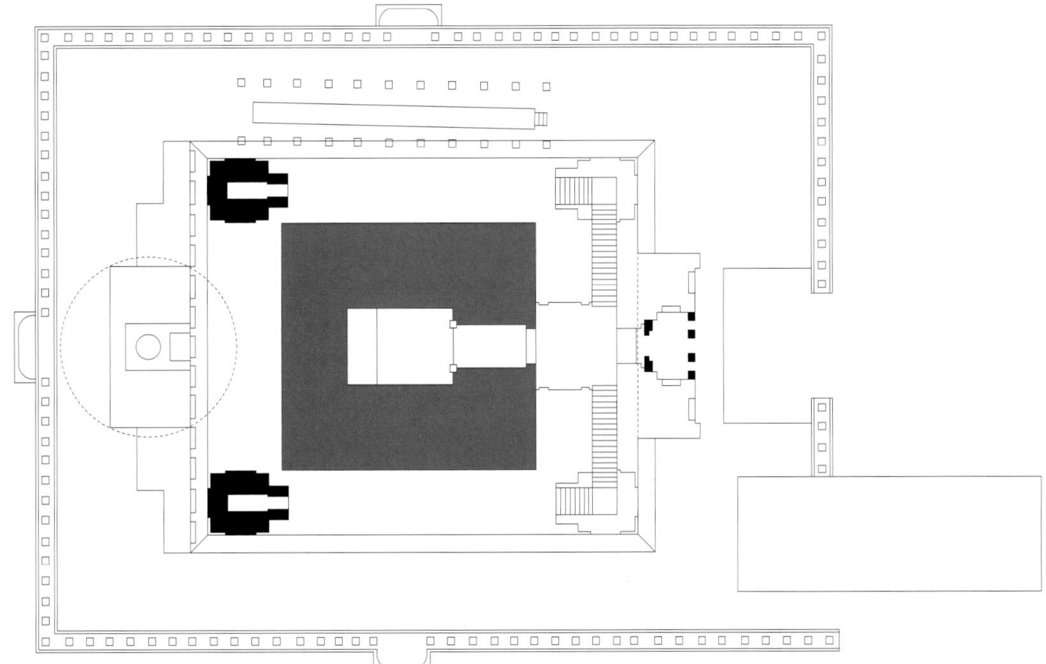

1

2

1 Plan

2 East Elevation

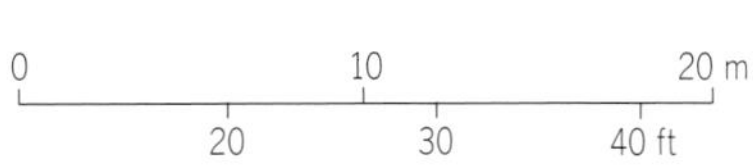

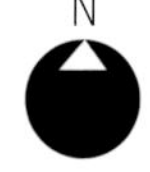

Dome of the Rock

Jerusalem, Israel; 687–91 CE

Tradition has it that the Ark of the Covenant, in which Moses' Tablets of Law were carried during his 40 years of wandering, eventually found a home in the temple that Solomon built in Jerusalem. That temple was ransacked and destroyed in 568 BCE by Babylonians. It was replaced by a second temple, larger in size but less preciously ornamented, which was sacked by the Romans in 70 BCE.)

Some of the second temple's substructure remains. It was located on a natural rocky outcrop, the Temple Mount, which was built up artificially to make a level platform for the building. The rock around which the Dome of the Rock was built is the highest point of the natural mount. Beneath it is a hollow cavern, known as the Well of Souls, which is visible through a hole in the rock and accessible by stairs at the side. There is a tradition that this was the location of the Holy of Holies in the old temple, where the Ark was kept. The archaeological evidence is inconclusive, but the tradition is firm. It is from this rock also that Mohammed is said to have ascended to heaven on his Night Journey.

The building therefore marks a special place, a destination for pilgrims. There is a mosque in the same sanctuary that is a much larger building, used for congregational worship. The dome, which was established soon after Mohammed's death in 632, enshrines the natural rock in a setting of great magnificence. The dome itself is timber, and has been repaired and replaced over the years. Originally it was covered in lead, but in the 1960s it was sheathed in gold-anodized aluminium, and was further enhanced in 1993 when it was re-covered with a more substantial layer of gold. The Dome of the Rock is one of Jerusalem's most conspicuous sights, and has become an emblem of the city.

The form of the building ultimately derives from the Roman mausoleum-type, such as the Mausoleum of Augustus – a monumental building with a circular plan. In early Christian Rome, this was adapted in buildings such as Santa Costanza (c.370) – a mausoleum for a daughter of the imperial family that has since been turned into a church. The most typical manifestation of the form is as a martyrium, commemorating the spot where a saint was slain or is buried. In Jerusalem, the Church of the Holy Sepulchre (c.330) made use of such a centralized arrangement around the supposed tomb of Jesus Christ, but attached a basilican church, so the building is spatially rather confusing. On the Temple Mount the two buildings – one the shrine, the other for the congregation – are kept separate, and the dome's form is therefore unencumbered and makes its impact with much greater clarity.

Jerusalem has long been contested terrain. In 1099 Crusaders took the city and turned the dome (briefly) into a church. The Knights Templar, who in principle helped medieval travellers to reach Jerusalem, founded various circular churches during the twelfth century, including the Temple Church in the City of London. By the sixteenth century, the Dome of the Rock was in Ottoman hands, and Suleyman the Magnificent had the building covered in fine tiles from Iznik in Turkey.

The interior is defined by two rings of Corinthian columns, interspersed with piers, supporting arches that are not quite pointed but are a little taller than semi-circles. The interior surfaces are covered in richly veined marble and coloured glass mosaics with much gold among them, following the pattern of Byzantine work but avoiding any figurative representations. It is the richest of martyriums – without a martyr, but enshrining a spot that is as intensely invested with meaning as Uluru (pages 12–13).

1 Plan

2 Section A-A

3 South Elevation

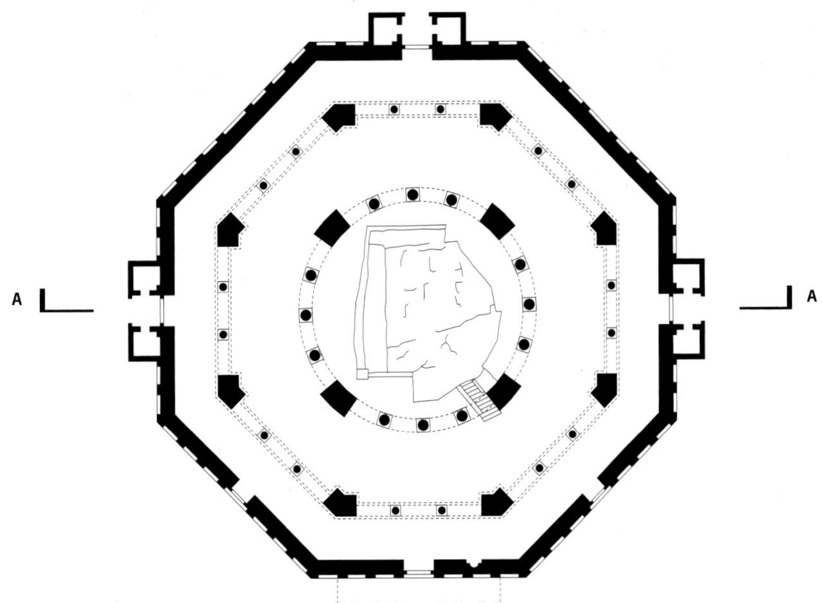

1

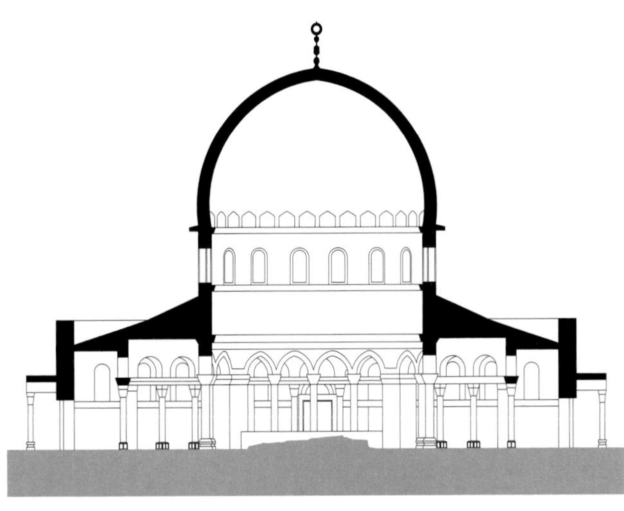

2

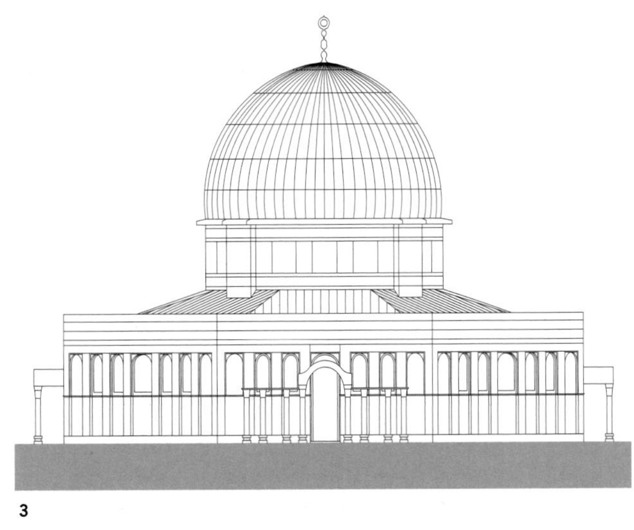

3

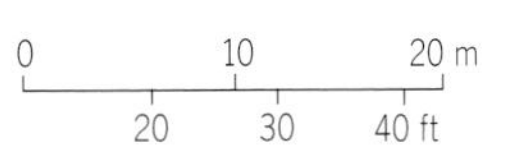

Great Mosque of Damascus

Damascus, Syria; 706–15

The earliest mosques, like the earliest churches, were domestic buildings where believers met to pray. With the adoption of Christianity as an official religion of the Roman Empire in 313, it became possible and desirable to have monumental churches with a civic presence.

Roman temples would typically be set up as places for the cult statue to dwell, looking out towards the altar where sacrifices would be made. The crowd of participants would gather outside, around the altar. Churches were different because they demanded people to assemble in a space, and the model that was adopted was the 'royal presence chamber', or basilica – actually a civic administration building, where a king would be unlikely to appear in person, but where a statue of the emperor stood at one end of the nave.

Islam first established itself as an official religion in lands around the eastern Mediterranean that had earlier been part of the Byzantine Empire, the Greek-speaking eastern Roman Empire run from Constantinople. Where a city surrendered peacefully, a new mosque would be constructed on a prominent site. When a city resisted and was conquered by force, its most important church would be requisitioned and turned into a mosque. A mosque could also be a space open to the sky, based on the idea of the courtyard in the Prophet Mohammed's house.

At Damascus the story is complicated by the fact that one part of the city resisted the advent of Islam while another acquiesced. The Muslims conquered in 635, very soon after the Prophet's death. A cohabitation around the church and its courtyard was resolved in 705 by displacing the Christians, and the mosque was built. It is still recognizably a basilica, and looks much the same as a church of the same date might have done, with its ranks of stilted arches supported by Corinthian columns. The most striking difference is in the orientation.

Churches of the time were constructed to reflect the orientation of the Roman temples, with their principal door on the west side and the congregation looking east towards the altar. In the Great Mosque the congregation is oriented towards Mecca, almost due south of Damascus, so worshippers look across the width of the building, rather than along its length, and the tall transept that crosses the nave is the location not of an important entrance but of the *minbar*, from which the imam leads the prayers.

The corner towers of the Great Mosque, introduced to help to call the faithful to prayer, represent an important innovation. A singing voice carries further than a speaking voice, and the sound reaches further if it emanates from the higher reaches of a tower. The towers, originally built for defence, have been remodelled and embellished, but they are believed to be the first minarets, which would later become a standard component of a mosque.

The site has been sacred for as long as Damascus has been a city – and Damascus is the oldest city known to have been continuously inhabited. The site had already had a temple on it for a thousand years before the Romans conquered and established a temple of Jupiter there. In the fourth century it was rededicated as a church of St John the Baptist, who is respected in Islam as a prophet, and whose head is still kept there.

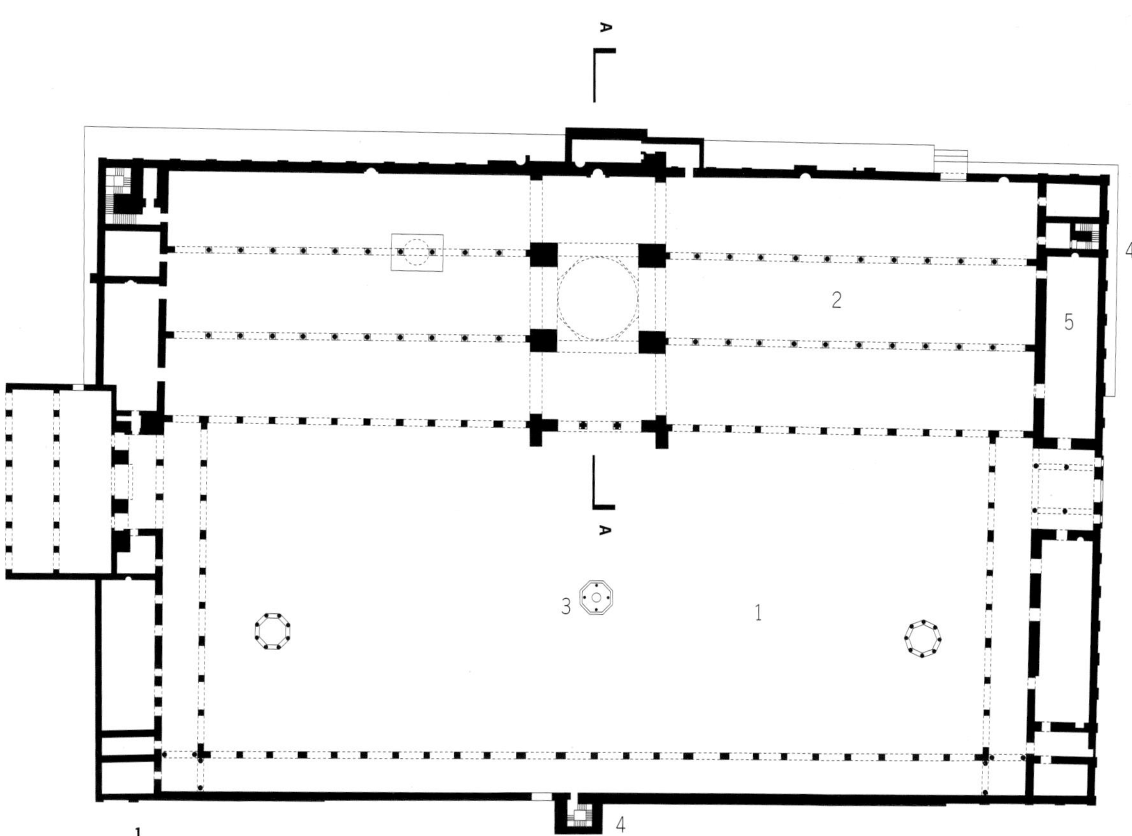

1

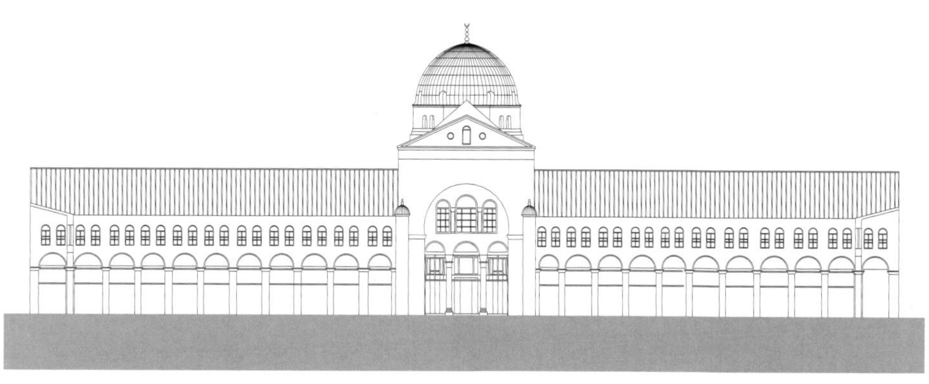

2

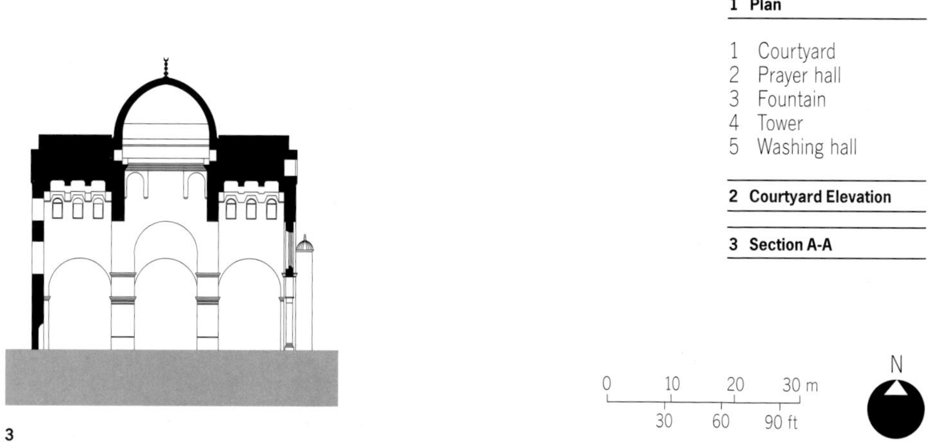

3

1 Plan

1 Courtyard
2 Prayer hall
3 Fountain
4 Tower
5 Washing hall

2 Courtyard Elevation

3 Section A-A

0 10 20 30 m
30 60 90 ft

N

Shore Temple

Mamallapuram, Tamil Nadu, India; 700–28

The old temples of southern India were sculpted in situ from 'living' rock such as the walls of a cave or a rocky outcrop. They could be sculpted from a lump of basalt the size of a building that had been left exposed when the softer sandstone around it had been eroded away. It was the same process, on a much smaller scale, as that which left Uluru (pages 12–13) to preside over the Australian outback. But it was evident that these rocks were 'placed' as special things, and there was a cultural will to respond to them, or appropriate them, and to sacralize them.

Standing on a headland at Mamallapuram, overlooking the Bay of Bengal, the Shore Temple (or Temple du Rivage) is the oldest surviving temple in southern India to have been built from blocks of stone. It is part of a group of temples commissioned by the kings of the region (the Pallava kings) at a time when Mamallapuram was an important and prosperous port. The other shrines in the group, dispersed over several kilometres, were carved from deposited rock.

The Shore Temple is made up of three shrines set in a square sanctuary. Two of the shrines are dedicated to Shiva; the third, in between, is dedicated to Vishnu. The interior spaces are small and were designed to accommodate cult statues that would be venerated, bathed and dressed by priests, and taken in procession around the town. The two Shiva shrines have elaborate pyramidal roofs, the taller of which is 20 metres (66 feet) high.

Although the shrines are made of granite, their exposed location has resulted in the erosion of the carvings' detail, but comparison with the other rock-cut temples nearby shows how fine they would have been. The pyramidal roofs once teemed with images of Shiva in action. His name means 'the auspicious one', but he is known also as 'the destroyer' or 'the transformer' who sets things in motion.

Worship would take the form of bringing offerings of fruit, wrapped in banana leaves, and leaving them at the sanctuary, making a circuit (clockwise) and praying at each of the sanctuary's four walls. A worshipper would not ordinarily visit the inner parts of the shrines, and in any case the bigger of Shiva's shrines is difficult for large numbers to reach because the passageway to it is very narrow. The individual and meditative form of worship was transformed into something very different on the major feast days, when large swarms of people would be performing such a routine at the same time.

The shrines at Mamallapuram reproduce in stone a form that would have been recognizable from earlier structures made in more perishable materials, most notably the 'chariots' in which the cult statues were taken in procession on their feast days. The largest and most elaborate of these wheeled chariots with pyramidal superstructures were those associated with Lord Jaganatha, a version of Krishna, who has found his way into the English language as 'juggernaut'.

1 Plan

1 Shrine of Shiva
2 Shrine of Vishnu
3 Shrine of Shiva

2 Courtyard Elevation

3 Section A-A

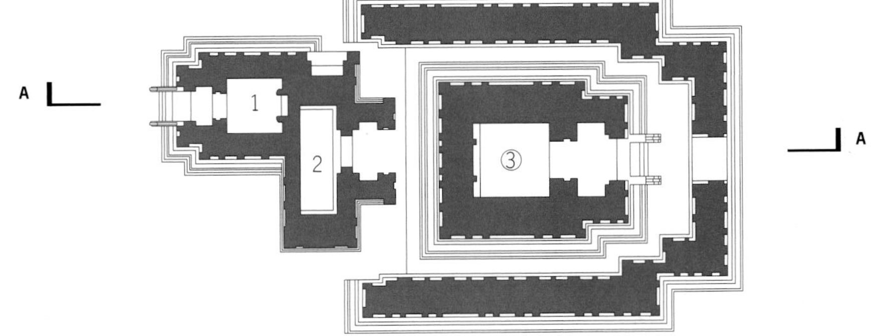

1

2

3

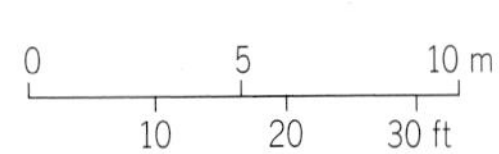

Mosque Cathedral of Córdoba

Córdoba, Andalusia, Spain; mosque begun 786, cathedral begun 1523

Córdoba has been a provincial capital since Roman times, and for some stretches of its history the province it headed was an important one. In the tenth century Córdoba was the largest city in the world, and at that time it oversaw the independent Islamic state of al-Andalus, or Andalusia. The city's mosque was built on a site formerly occupied by the principal Roman temple and, later, when the country was ruled by the Visigoths, by a church. The church was commandeered as a mosque after the Islamic conquest of 711, when the city was answerable to Damascus, and then rebuilt shortly after the formation of the Emirate of Córdoba (in 750) as a mosque commensurate with the city's new status, confidence and growing prosperity.

A multitude of modestly sized columns, of marble and semi-precious stones salvaged from Roman sources, was arranged on a grid supporting a superstructure of horseshoe arches with more arches above them. The Great Mosque of Damascus (pages 114–15) is said to have been a model, but the overall compositional sense at Córdoba is quite different. Instead of the axial arrangement at Damascus, with a high nave flanked by lower aisles, there is in Córdoba the rhythm of a repetitive grid. The columns are narrow enough, and spaced sufficiently far apart not to seem intrusive in the prayer hall; rather, they resemble companions to the visitors and worshippers.

The mosque seems to stretch endlessly in all directions – rationally and without histrionics – like a forest. The ceilings in a space of this extent often seem low, but this is not the case at Córdoba, where the ceilings are obscured from view by the arches, and light filters down from four cupolas, giving good, even illumination. The idea of the basilica seems to have been superseded in this serene display of controlled magnificence, which made an apt setting for the ruling class at prayer as the city's influence, sophistication and cosmopolitanism steadily increased.

After 350 years there was another change of regime, when Ferdinand III of Castile captured the city in 1236, after a long siege. The mosque was immediately taken over for Christian worship and used as a cathedral for the following 300 years with only minor modifications (such as the introduction of small chapels around the perimeter).

In the sixteenth century, under Charles V, a soaring choir and chancel were added, interrupting the grid of columns. While this was undoubtedly an act of architectural barbarism, it makes for an arresting collision of styles, spaces and cultures. The relatively low space of the mosque makes a drama of the emergence into the much taller choir. Stylistically it follows a fairly conventional Renaissance pattern, making use of some old-fashioned Gothic motifs from the north, later overlaid with a profusion of heavy baroque ornament dating from the seventeenth century. It is not as finely conceived as the work in the mosque, but the hybrid building's violated fabric tells a compelling story about competing faiths and temporal power.

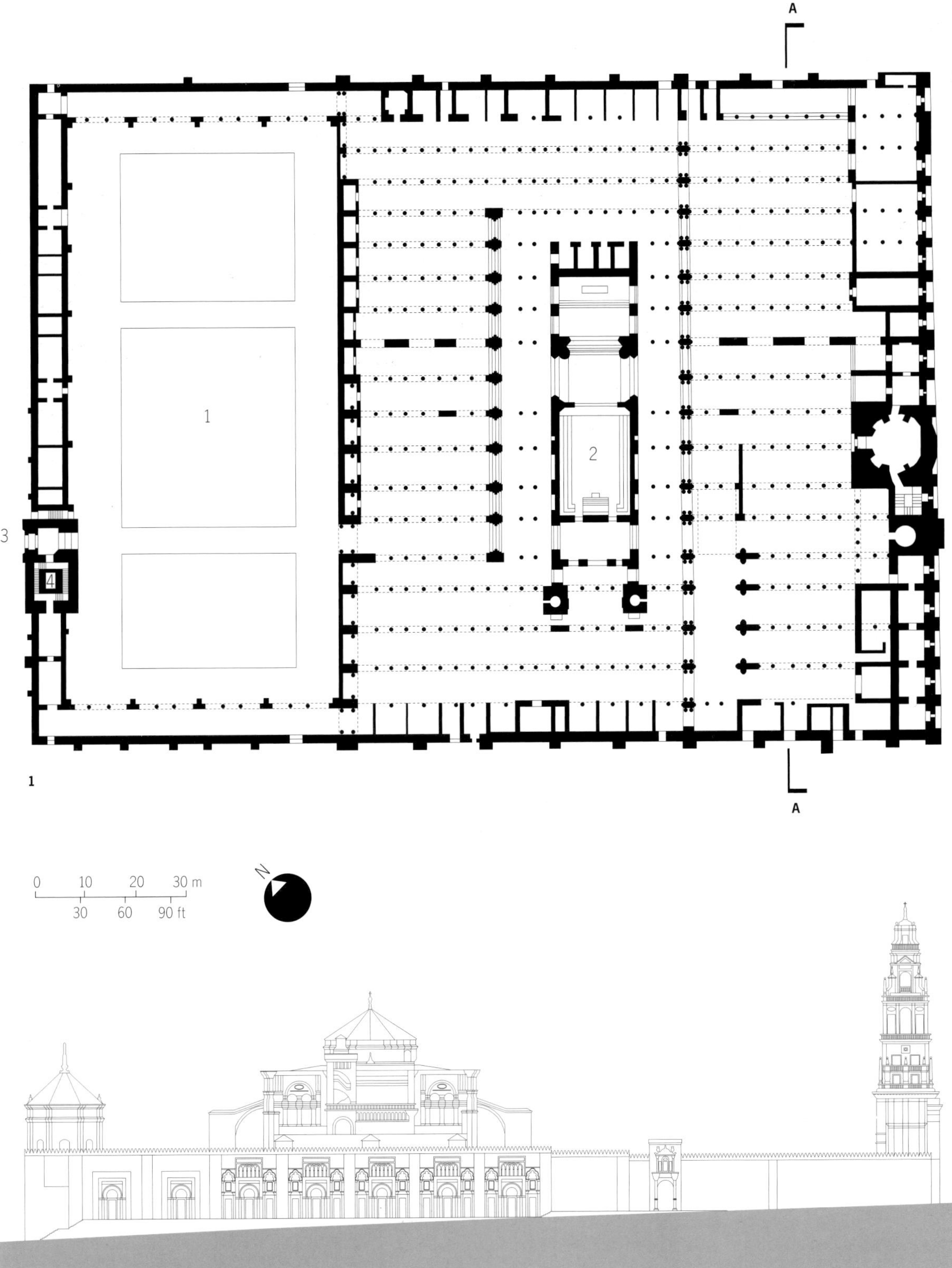

1

2

3

0 5 10 m
10 20 30 ft

1 Plan

1 Orange Tree Courtyard
2 Mosque Cathedral
3 Pardon door
4 Belfry

2 East Elevation

3 Section A-A

Borobudur Stupa

Gunadharma

Java, Indonesia, c.800

There are now some 160 million people living on Java, the most populated of the many islands that make up Indonesia. It is about 1,000 km (620 miles) long, with a spine of volcanic mountains running along its length.

In the past, the mountains made connections between different parts of Java difficult to maintain, and various traditions grew up in separate parts of the island. The local veneration of ancestors continued in some parts, but the monument called Borobudur (or Barabudur) has no part in that tradition. It is Indonesia's largest religious monument and it is dedicated to Buddhism.

Nothing is known about the circumstances of Borobudur's construction, although curiously an architect's name is associated with the place, albeit through oral tradition, which may be unreliable. There is no convincing etymology suggesting a meaning for the name Borobudur, but it might incorporate the name of a vanished village that was once nearby. It is 400 km (250 miles) from Jakarta, the island's main city, and on the other side of the mountains, but only about 40 km (25 miles) from Yogyakarta. The building's scale and sophistication suggests some sort of royal patronage for the project, and its sculptures carry echoes of Indian traditions. The style of the sculptural work gives the main clue to the building's date. The story is that the shrine fell out of use when the Islamic religion came to the island in the fourteenth century, and certainly it had long been neglected when it came to the attention of European colonial visitors in the early nineteenth century.

The shrine is an elaborate stupa, about 118 metres (387 feet) square. It was built on a mound of bedrock that rose from the surrounding plain – offering another instance of a natural landscape feature being claimed for human culture, this time by providing the foundations for a building. The structure takes the form of a *mandala*, which is a device for contemplation and meditation that is usually the size of a picture rather than a building. It embodies a Buddhist conception of the universe and the mind, and their different levels of reality and relevance to spiritual awakening.

The outer, lower reaches of Borobudur are more or less square, while the higher, inner levels are circular. The different levels, around which the pilgrims would have walked, are lined with sculpted stone panels (1,460 of them) that depict incidents from the life of the Buddha, a surprising number of which relate to the time before he was born and the period when he was known as Prince Siddhartha, predating his enlightenment. The monument's pinnacle is a large stone stupa, and it is surrounded by smaller versions – 72 of them, arranged in three concentric rings on the top three terraces, each with a statue of the Buddha inside it. In the ascent of Borobudur, the pilgrim is taken on a journey from the level of the world of desires, through the world of forms to the world of formlessness.

1 Plan

2 Section A-A

3 Elevation

A A

1

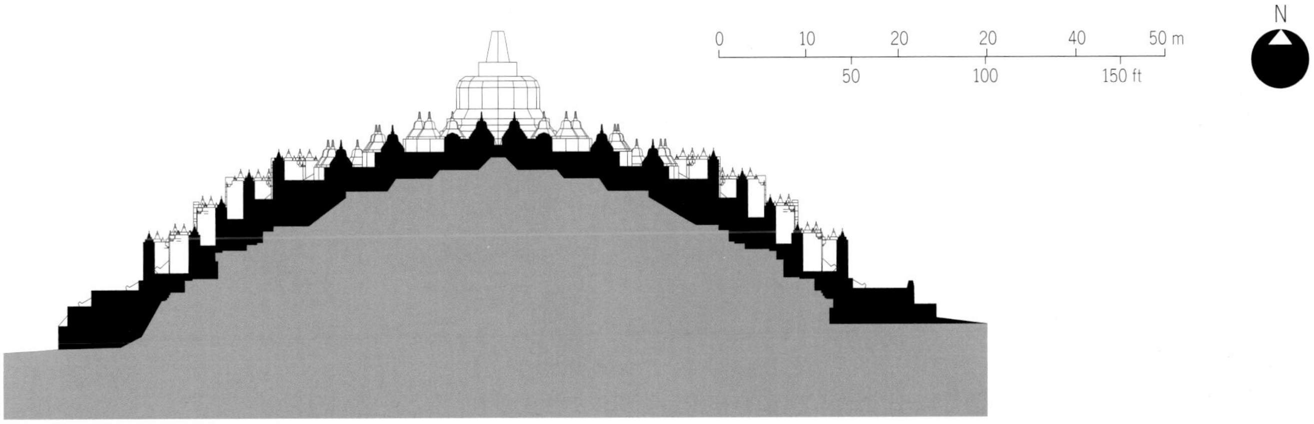

0 10 20 20 40 50 m

50 100 150 ft

N

2

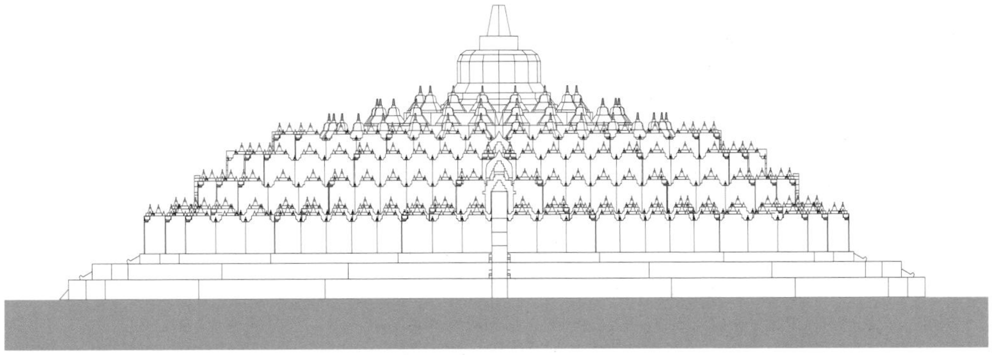

3

Lingaraj Temple

Bhubaneswar, Odisha, India; c.1080

Many traditions have been woven together to produce Hinduism, and they are not governed by a systematic orthodoxy, though some traditions do make claims to universality. The major Hindu gods make their appearance in the world by way of avatars, and gurus of different traditions argue between themselves about who among the most important gods is the avatar of whom.

The abundance of gods and the traditional belief that commissioning a temple is good for the commissioner's spiritual well-being have been combined to spectacular effect at Bhubaneswar, the capital of the east Indian state of Odisha (formerly Orissa). Bhubaneswar is known as 'the temple city' because of the number of temples there – more than 600 of them. The largest is Lingaraj, dedicated to the god Harihara, and set in a sanctuary with 130 smaller shrines around it. Even without the thousands of pilgrims that the site attracts at festival times, it has an atmosphere of teeming proliferation.

Harihara is a fusion of Vishnu and Shiva, bringing together two traditions that were at times in conflict, but are represented at Bhubaneswar as equal halves of one god (rather than either one as the avatar of the other). Lingaraj means 'king lingam' – the lingam being the phallus, normally identified with Shiva. The lingam is sometimes discussed as if it were an abstract symbol, but the iconography does not always support such an interpretation. In the Lingaraj the symbol is in place at the shrine, to receive offerings of flowers and libations of oil. It is also suggested in the tall space above the shrine, visible in the section through the building. The tower here rises to 35 metres (115 feet) externally, making it the tallest and most prominent of the city's temple structures.

Progression into the Lingaraj involves crossing four thresholds, each marking an intensification of sanctity. The earliest rock-cut temples seemed to mimic timber construction in their decoration, but the experience of entry into this temple is reminiscent of entering a cave, as daylight is left behind. The original temple had just two windowless inner rooms (*mandapas*); the other two were later additions that extended the route of approach.

The exterior of the temple is elaborately ornamental in a fairly abstract way. The surfaces of the tower's immensely thick walls are intricately developed in plan in a manner that seems to anticipate the self-similar pattern-making of fractal geometries, but in the elevations this is overlaid by bold horizontal striations. Lions sit on projecting corbels, and at the top of the tower there are more lions, who, along with seated deities, support an *amalka* (the bulbous ribbed form at the top of the tower) that carries an urn with a flag on top of it, signalling the presence of the god.

Repetition of forms at various scales around the tower (such as in the three small satellite shrines that flank it), in the original *mandapa* and the additions, and in other substantial shrines on the site, creates an extraordinarily powerful impression.

The numerous shrines, which have gradually accumulated over the years, are the work of many hands. People have come back to this place, and gone through similar moves from one generation to another, again and again. The individual stones have weathered and their surfaces patinated, so they now seem more like natural growths than the products of craft and artistry. But the proliferation of shrines, swarming with figures, starts to seem like a mania. One shrine was not enough, and the repeated feeling was that there was a need for one more. If the great pyramids leave the observer feeling overpowered by might, the effect here is different – more like being outnumbered.

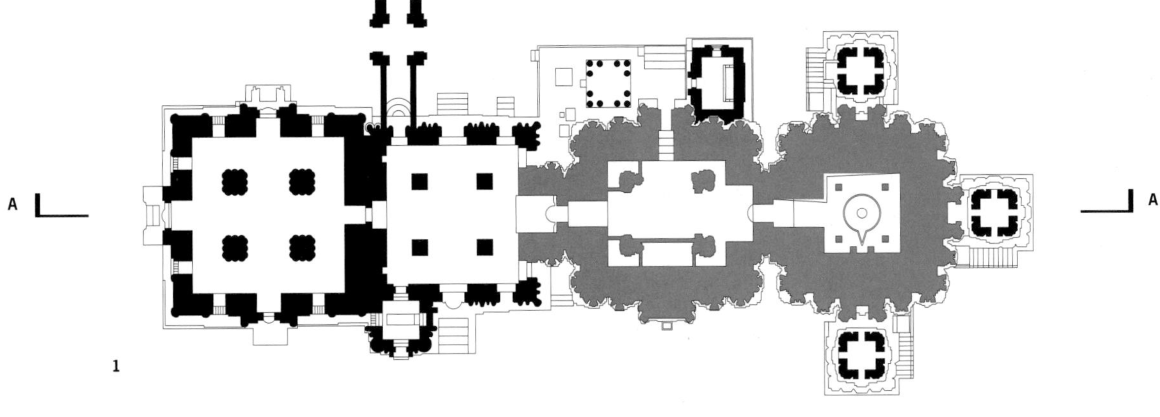

1

1 Plan

2 Section A-A

3 North Elevation

0 10 20 m
20 30 40 ft

2

3

Kandariya Mahadeva Temple

Khajuraho, Madhya Pradesh, India; c.1050

The temples at Khajuraho were built when the place was a capital city – the royal seat of the Chandela kings of Madhya Pradesh in central India. The Chandelas founded the city in the ninth century but had moved away by the fourteenth, and Khajuraho is now much depleted: a town with 10,000 inhabitants and India's finest collection of 1000-year-old monuments.

The Kandariya Mahadeva Temple is the culmination of a line of artistic development, and displays an astonishing level of formal control and sophistication, not to mention a huge amount of work lavished on a relatively small structure.

The plan shows how the building resolves into a sequence of four square blocks that merge with one another and are approached on axis by a flight of steps. In the lower parts, the blocks are carved with horizontal striations, and the openings in the walls align with one another horizontally, so there is a strong sense of cohesion. The roofs of the four main squares rise to different heights in an ordered sequence, culminating in the 33-metre (108-foot) tower over the inner sanctuary.

The sanctuary is separated from the exterior by a passageway that runs right round it, so it is set as a building within a building. Moreover, the way that the forms are elaborated externally suggests that there is a whole sequence of buildings occupying the same space, each one only partially visible, disappearing inside the next.

In plan, this is evident in the proliferation of corners – corners that are made more complex by being eaten away into statuary. At the roof level, though, these corners continue and turn into edges of the roof form, generating the impression of one building emerging from another. It can be seen most clearly in the window bays that project around the sanctuary. Each one is treated in the same way as the temple's porch, and has a roof over it that matches the roof over the porch, but is not quite as fully there because it is absorbed into the side of the tower. Nevertheless the visual effect is to present an echo of the porch, and the temple gives the impression of having been composed of a large number of square-plan buildings that interpenetrate.

It is astounding to consider the complexity of the challenge faced by the builders. The Kandariya Mahadeva Temple would have been an ambitious building project in any age, and the fact that it was built shows that there was not only a very highly developed masonry tradition in the area but also the patronage to sustain it across many generations.

The intricacy of the exterior is made even more complex by the sculptures that cover it. They include scenes of everyday life and some erotic scenes that look too acrobatic ever to have been commonplace. These finely worked sculptures fascinate tourists, but the most amazing thing about them is the way that they take their place as part of the building as an entirety, which organizes a vast amount of sometimes aberrant detail into a satisfying and thoroughly achieved whole.

1 Plan

2 Section A-A

3 South Elevation

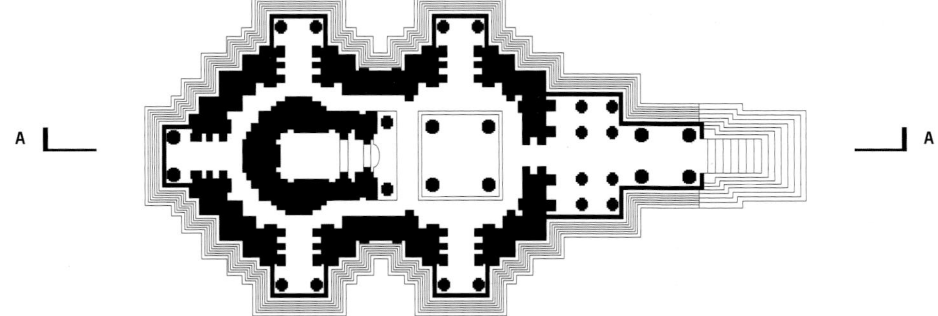

1

2

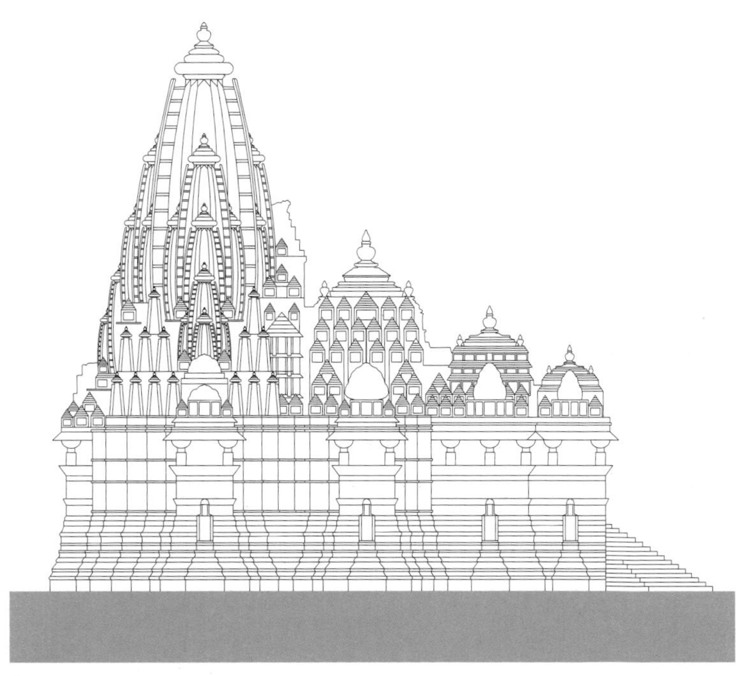

3

0 5 10 m
10 20 30 ft

N

Durham Cathedral

Durham, Co. Durham, UK; from 1096

The cathedral at Durham was an experimental structure that reached its present appearance after various initiatives that reshaped the building over several hundred years. It was the most monumental European cathedral of its time, taking up the challenge to rival the vaults left behind by the Romans. The original building had an apse at its east end, where the body of St Cuthbert – an inspirational local saint – was buried.

Its great monumentality was made possible by the great wealth available to its creators, deriving from the cult of Cuthbert and from Durham's military importance. From the time of the Norman invasion, as part of William the Conqueror's campaign to bring the kingdom under control, the site was fortified and established as the pre-eminent military base for the north of England. The Bishop of Durham was responsible for an army and had the status of a prince. The first appointed bishop was murdered. His replacement was William of Calais (or Carilef), who commissioned the cathedral.

The cathedral was built on a well-protected site, on a bend in the River Wear, which acts as a natural moat. The ground rises steeply from the river, and a castle was built to fortify the landward access to the city from the north. The top of the hill is the base for an assemblage of spiritual and temporal power, dominated by the cathedral. It was already established as a place of pilgrimage before the arrival of the Normans.

There were important remodellings that made the building look less old than it is. The Chapel of the Nine Altars was added from 1228 in a Gothic style influenced by the architecture of the cathedral at Salisbury in southern England. The towers were raised and given pinnacles, making them too look like Gothic structures of the thirteenth century or later. However, the building's greatest and most successful experiment was in the vaults above the aisles and, later, in those above the main space of the nave.

There had been earlier attempts to imitate Roman architectural style with 'groin vaults', where the curved surfaces of the vault meet as a simple fold. The innovation at Durham was the invention of the 'rib vault', where the meeting of surfaces is instead imagined as a diagonal arch, and built as such. At Durham this style can be seen most clearly in the vaults across the nave. The arches on the diagonal are the important ones: they are semi-circular Roman-style arches, while the arches that go straight across the width of the nave are pointed. This is because the diagonal is longer than the orthogonal side of a rectangle: if all the arches are to spring from the same level at the base and reach the same level at the apex, they cannot all be semi-circular. Either the diagonals have to stretch the semi-circle into something shallower, which weakens it, increasing the necessity for buttressing – or, alternatively, the orthogonal arches need to be steeper, making them more pointed and less in need of buttressing.

This method of building spread rapidly. It simplified the construction of vaults, making them easier to conceptualize and quicker to build. It was rapidly adopted and then used in increasingly elaborate ways for the rest of the Middle Ages, especially in connection with pointed arches.

1

2

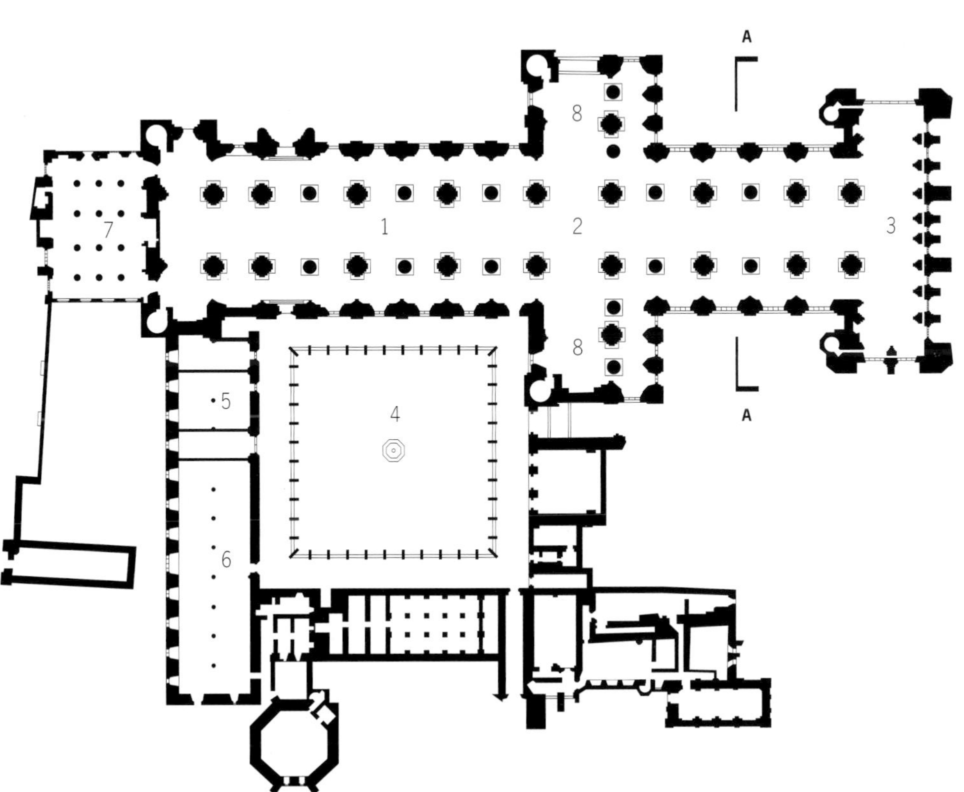

3

1 South Elevation

2 Section A-A

3 Plan

1 Nave
2 Crossing
3 Chapel of the Nine Altars
4 Cloisters
5 Monks' dormitory (above)
6 Treasures of St Cuthbert (below)
7 Galilee Chapel
8 Transept

0 5 10 m
15 30 ft

Temple of Kukulkan (Quetzalcoatl)

Chich'en Itzá, Yucatán, Mexico; eleventh to thirteenth centuries

The Yucatán Peninsula is now part of Mexico – a projection of land that separates the Gulf of Mexico from the Caribbean Sea. When Chich'en Itzá was built, it was inhabited by the Mayan people, whose civilization can be traced back to 2000 BCE and who occupied a sizeable terrain in Mesoamerica but had no capital city. This arrangement served them well when the Spanish conquistadores arrived in the sixteenth century, since no single stronghold could be stormed to gain control of the region, and the Mayans held out until the end of the seventeenth century, nearly 170 years after the Incas had succumbed. The temple at Chich'en Itzá is in the same tradition as that at Tik'al (pages 20–21), but from a different region and a later period. Precise dating is problematic.

Chich'en Itzá was a significant city with some impressive temples and, importantly, two large natural wells – vital in a region where the landscape is short of place-marking natural features. The city's name means 'mouth of the well of Itzá'. The land is flat, and its rivers flow underground. There are signs of settlement dating back to 8000 BCE, long before there was a recognizably Mayan culture. The city had a port and good contacts with the outside world, which account for the motifs from central Mexico that can be found in some of the buildings. The Temple of Kukulkan was at the heart of the city and evidently marked a place of cosmic significance. An earlier temple was found when it was excavated, buried inside the present one.

The number of steps on the temple's four sides add up to 365, the number of days in the year, and the north-east and south-west faces of the building align respectively with sunrise at the summer solstice and sunset at the winter solstice. Kukulkan was a winged serpent god, also revered by the Aztecs, who called him Quetzalcoatl. (Various kings were also called Kukulkan and are sometimes confused with one another and with the god.) The temple of Kukulkan was the god's principal shrine. Little is known about his attributes, but he seems to have been associated with prophecy, as was the great sacred well at Chich'en Itzá – a circular pool with a cliff around it – where sacrifices were made.

Displaying sophisticated knowledge about the movements of heavenly bodies, the monument is arranged with great precision. It was put in place by people who worked without metal tools or pulleys, and without the power of horses or oxen to help them move the stones. The stairs have giant serpents' heads carved each side at their base.

On the vertical wall at the edge of the steps, at daybreak on the days of the spring and autumn equinoxes, the sun casts a shadow of the corners of the pyramid's plateaux. It makes a bold wavy line of shadow, running right down the length of the stair, and connects to the fully modelled serpent's head. Tradition has it that the god comes down to Earth at that moment.

1 Plan

2 Section A-A

3 North Elevation

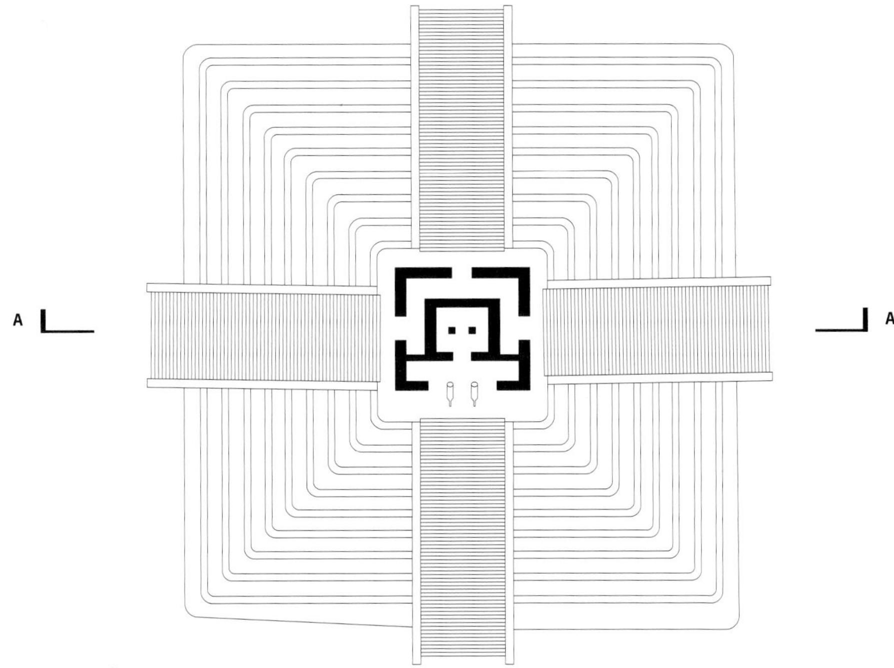

1

2

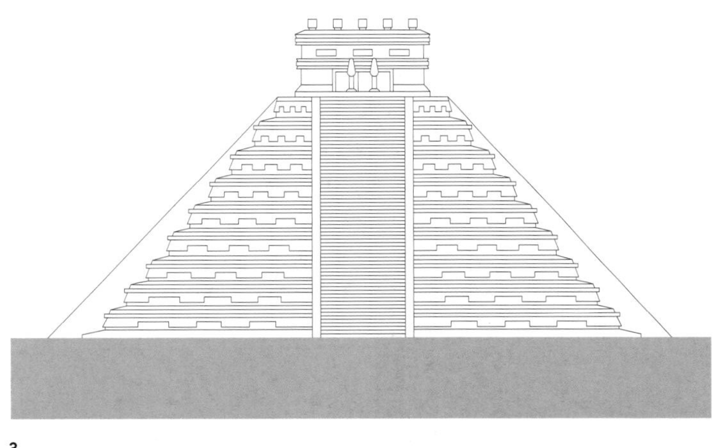

3

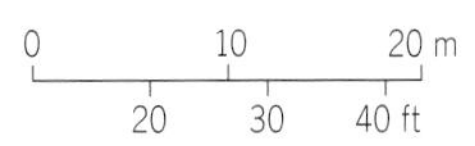

Basilica of the Madeleine

Vézelay, Burgundy, France; 1120–32

Although the Basilica of the Madeleine is the largest Romanesque church in France, it is located in a small village rather than a major city. Its building was financed by income from pilgrims who went there to venerate the relics of Mary Magdalene, one of Jesus Christ's friends and followers. It was a site of immense prestige that attracted the attention of kings and saints, but from 1280 rival claims undermined confidence in the relics and its influence waned.

Although constructed later than Durham Cathedral (pages 126–27), the Basilica of the Madeleine made use of the older-style groin vaults in between semi-circular arches spanning the nave. What makes it seem to anticipate later medieval buildings is its lightness. The choir is particularly light, but that was rebuilt after a fire in 1165 and is in the later Gothic style. In fact, it was remodelled again in the nineteenth century by Eugène Viollet-le-Duc during his great restoration project and was made lighter still at that time.

The main body of the church was built on the pattern of a Roman basilica and reflects the way in which a Roman building would have been decorated with columns and pilasters. Instead of using standard Corinthian capitals, the builders followed a tradition that was by then well established. The capitals at first look as if they might be Corinthian, but instead of stylized acanthus leaves they have a great variety of sculpted subject-matter, showing biblical scenes, allegories and mythical figures. It was far from being the first time that such capitals had been carved, but they were done exceptionally well at Vézelay.

There are also famously fine sculpted panels above the principal entrance doors in the narthex added between 1140 and 1150, which offered important protection. The corresponding sculptures on the building's exterior weathered badly and are not shown in Viollet-le-Duc's drawing of the original west front.

Viollet-le-Duc began his work at Vézelay in 1840 and transformed a neglected ruin into one of France's pre-eminent monuments. By today's standards he took liberties, but in doing so he made the building a model of coherence and charm that beguiled visitors into reappraising the Romanesque style. The building is highly expressive of Christian teachings in its sculptures, but it also makes connections with more primitive themes. Inside there can be seen a trick of light that suggests a cosmic alignment. At noon on the summer solstice, the sun streams in from the clerestory windows to make a perfect row of pools of light along the central axis of the nave.

The basilica is built on what is known locally as *la colline éternelle* (the eternal hill) because of its particular presence. Set amid rolling countryside, the village of Vézelay is most strikingly approached from the east, where at the brow of another hill, at a spot marked by a cross called la Croix Montjoie, the basilica comes into view in the middle distance – the summit of its hill appears to be at the same level as the horizon and as the observer, with sweeping valleys in between. Its hill rises more steeply than those around it, which seem to keep a respectful distance. The land-form suggests that this is a special place, and the inhabitants have responded to the suggestion.

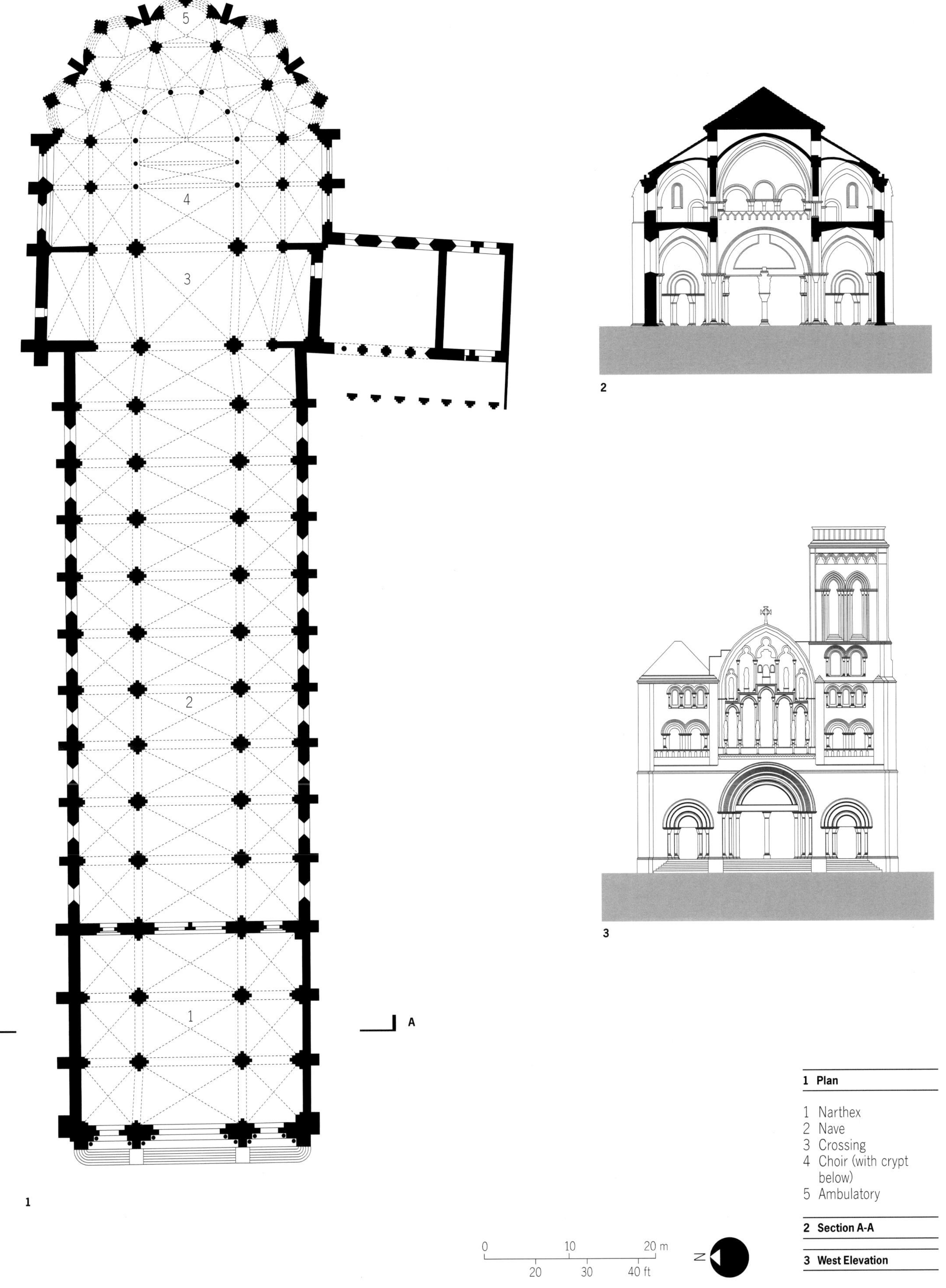

1 Plan

1 Narthex
2 Nave
3 Crossing
4 Choir (with crypt below)
5 Ambulatory

2 Section A-A

3 West Elevation

Angkor Wat

Angkor, Cambodia; 1113–50

History tells us time and again that ceremonial buildings are valued far more highly than functional ones. Angkor Wat (meaning 'city temple') was built as a temple to the Hindu god Vishnu with an associated royal palace and capital city. The local buildings that people used every day were made of timber and have disappeared, while the temple was made of intricately carved sandstone and survives as what is now a Buddhist shrine.

The city temple was built in the reign of the Khmer king Suryavarman, who until 1150 ruled an empire that included not only modern Cambodia but also Thailand, Laos and parts of Malaysia. Comparable in scale with Versailles, dominated by the towers which were inseparable from the dwelling of the god-king, it was built in under 40 years, and then sacked in 1177 – after which a new capital was established at Angkor Thom.

Angkor Wat became a backwater, but was never entirely abandoned. It amazed the Portuguese and French travellers who came across it in the sixteenth and nineteenth centuries, who thought it outdid anything that survived from Greece and Rome, but assumed that it must have belonged to some equally remote past.

Angkor Wat stands on flat ground, but the temple is the image of a mountain. It was made defensible by a broad moat that now separates the city from the jungle. At the height of its power, though, it was surrounded by urban sprawl that connected the various capitals that were eventually built, making Angkor the largest pre-industrial conurbation. The moat around Angkor Wat was crossed by a single causeway, placed on axis with the temple's dominating towers, which evoke the multiple peaks of Mount Meru, the dwelling place of the gods. The temple's precincts were set apart from the rest of the city by being placed on artificially raised plateaux, reached by very steep stairs that were supposed to remind the faithful of the strenuousness of spiritual discipline.

The inner part of the temple, 60 metres (197 feet) square, is an exercise in the elaboration of square geometries into towers, courtyards, corridors, galleries. Its central tower is 35 metres (115 feet) high, rising from its plateau which is already 20 metres (66 feet) higher than the surrounding natural ground level. The masonry buildings are covered in low-relief panels of narrative scenes, and some sections of wall have holes that might have held fixings for bronze panels looted in the distant past. The masonry was constructed without mortar – the blocks being finely ground together, so the joints are often invisible. The blocks were shaped so as to interlock, with mortice and tenon joints and dovetails, which are usually used in joinery. The consistency of style, coupled with the speed of building, makes it clear that thousands of people must have been at work there, all schooled in the same tradition. Their skills were still available in force for the construction of Angkor Thom a generation later. This level of non-utilitarian building activity persisted into the fifteenth century, when an attack in 1431 (by the Ayutthaya from the region now known as Thailand) saw the city looted and then abandoned in favour of Lovek (or Longvek).

Angkor Wat was the one part of Angkor that was not abandoned, surviving as an impossibly grandiose and underpopulated Buddhist foundation, which the monks themselves could never have commissioned. Its after-life continues as a significant generator of tourist income, since it still fills with wonder even the most jaded of travellers, and it remains a source of pride as the centrepiece of Cambodia's national flag.

1 Plan

1 Entrance
2 Terrace of Honour
3 Central sanctuary

2 Section A-A

3 West Elevation

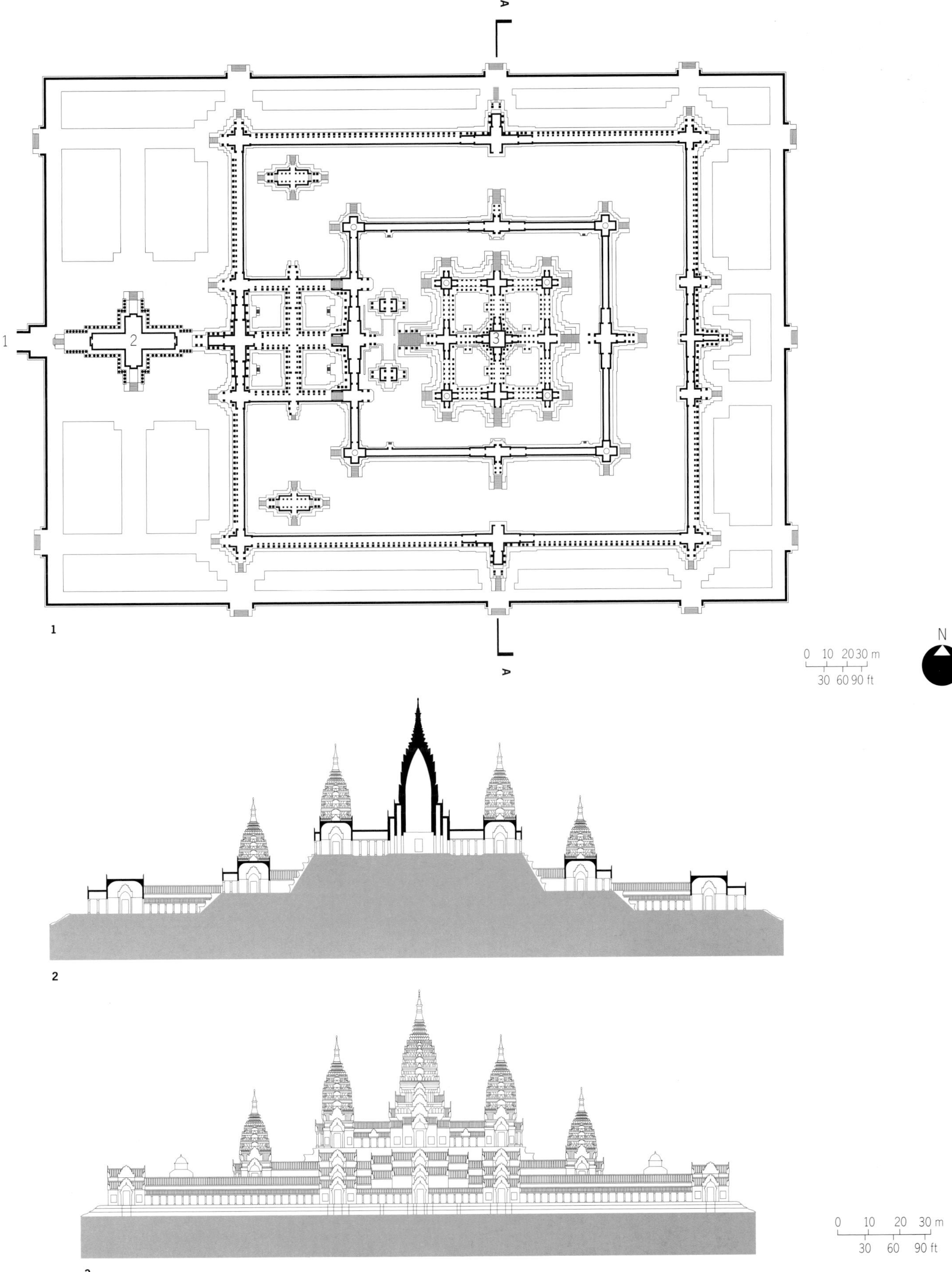

Stave Church

Urnes, Norway; 1130

The Norwegian people did not forsake the old Norse gods until the eleventh century, when King Olaf II (now known as St Olaf) succeeded in establishing Christianity in Norway. The tradition of building in timber goes back much further, and the methods used in church-building were developed in Viking mead-halls. Christianity was imported from England – with which the Vikings had powerful links, since there were numerous Viking settlements in the north of England.

The layout of the Urnes stave church derives from an extremely simple Anglo-Saxon type. There were timber churches in England too, but little trace of these remains except where the timber has rotted into undisturbed ground. They were often replaced by stone buildings, but even the small stone churches were usually upgraded in the fourteenth or fifteenth century, and the type is known from a few examples in stone: a rectangular nave with a narrower chancel.

By the time that the church at Urnes was built, the Romanesque style was well established in Norway, widely used in the churches erected by the Norman invaders. In Norway the timber church was once the normal thing, but very few of them survive – none is older than the church at Urnes.

This church is now in a remote location, but it clearly had significant patronage when it was built. From the outside its appearance is dominated by the steeply sloping roofs, which are replacements for the originals. The octagonal timber steeple is a later addition. There are few windows, and they are not large – just enough to illuminate the space, but hardly a feature of the architecture. The interior is clearly Romanesque, giving a clear impression of the basilica form, but without any clerestory windows above the aisles. A colonnade runs along the nave, supporting semi-circular Roman-style arches. Unusually this arcade is turned to run across the width of the nave at each end. The columns have capitals of a form familiar from Romanesque architecture with some carved decoration.

The remarkable thing about the interior is that it reproduces in timber an arrangement usually found in stone. The arches, for example, make no sense in timber construction – they are a useful way to span a large opening with small stones, but in a timber structure they are just decorative. The columns are narrower than they would have been in stone, but they could have been narrower still and have supported the roof. Their capitals are the same shape as stone capitals would have been.

The timber construction at the Urnes church dates from long before the time of power tools and sawmills. The columns would have been made from trees specially selected for the straightness of their trunks and then made regular by being hand-turned on a makeshift lathe. The planks for the walls and roof would have been sawn by hand – an extraordinarily laborious business. A few water-powered sawmills have been discovered from the ancient world, but none is known in Norway until the fourteenth century, despite the importance of forestry in this part of the world.

If the interior of the church seems to translate non-indigenous forms in a way designed to give the building an orthodox authority, the most interesting decorative work is a survival of an older tradition. There are panels around the 'north portal' that show intricately intertwining sinuous lines that look like the all-pervasive roots and growths of the Norse life-tree, Yggdrasil, which did not immediately vanish from the world of folk belief.

1 Plan

1 Altar
2 Nave

2 Section A-A

3 South Elevation

4 East Elevation

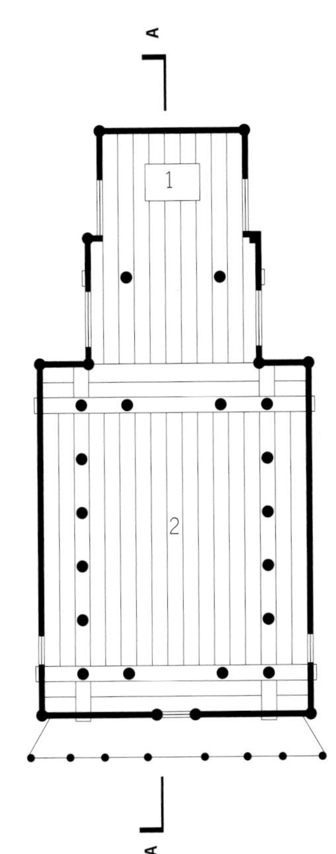

1

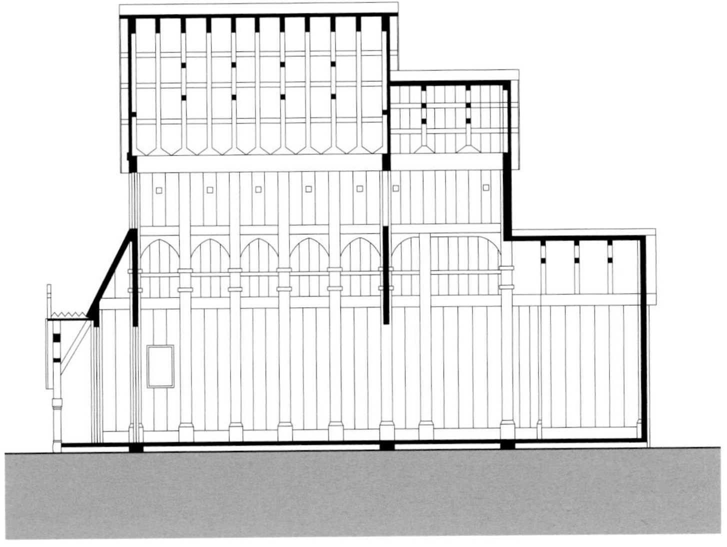

2

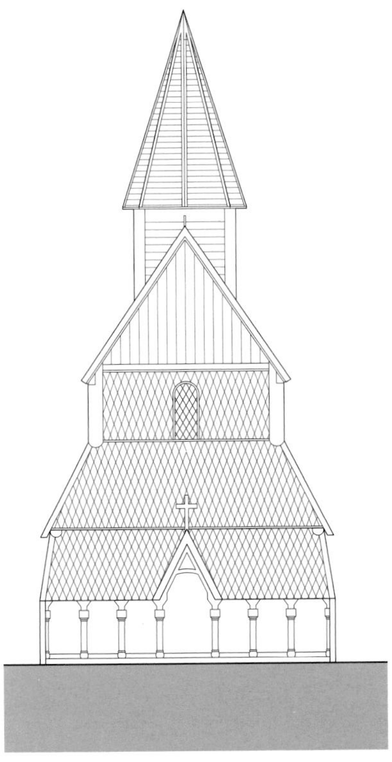

3

4

Bourges Cathedral

Bourges, Centre (central region), France; from 1200

A large Romanesque church such as Durham Cathedral (pages 126–27) is impressive because of the solidity of its masonry. During the twelfth century in France a new aesthetic developed, which impressed by making the masonry seem almost immaterial. This new style, which came to predominate in northern Europe until the beginning of the sixteenth century, is now called 'Gothic' – a term that was not used before the seventeenth century, and from then until the nineteenth century was used indiscriminately to mean anything not particularly classical in style.

The Goths were a Germanic tribe who were (among others) responsible for the fall of the western Roman Empire, and when it was originally applied the word 'Gothic' was pejorative, meaning 'barbaric'. The Vandals of North Africa had a similar reputation, which has never been redeemed.

Gothic architecture continued many of the Romanesque traditions but supplemented them with large windows, filled with stained glass in rich colours. Even plain glass was too expensive for ordinary households at the time, so the use of stained glass was extravagant. The church-builders freed up as much of the wall area as possible for windows, and they did this by propping up the tops of the walls with 'flying buttresses', which helped to stabilize the outward pressures from the stone vaults when the wall itself was too thin to be able to do that work by itself. The vaults made use of the innovations seen at Durham, such as diagonal ribs, and produced a harmonious effect by adding pointed arches everywhere – over windows and in arcades, not just where the vaulting made them expedient.

These architectural practices were begun c.1137 at the abbey church of St Denis, north of Paris, under the patronage of the abbot Suger, who had significant political influence. His church was already established as a burial place for kings of France and was very well endowed. His writings show him to have been fascinated by the mystical connotations of coloured light. The aim was not to produce a brightly lit interior but one where the subdued lighting allowed complete continuity between the richly painted wall surfaces and the richly coloured window glass.

The cathedral of St Etienne at Bourges shows this programme magnificently realized on a scale much larger than at St Denis and with breathtaking confidence. Two aisles run round the nave, the outer one being given over to chapels, and the nave is illuminated by windows in the wall (their sills above head height) and two sets of clerestory windows – one set above the inner aisle, the other immensely high up above the nave. The glass in the lower windows incorporates image sequences that, with cartoon-like clarity, tell stories of saints' lives and biblical episodes.

Internally the space seems to be a cage to support the coloured glass, with very tall slender columns soaring to great heights overhead and a vault that seems to float without effort. Externally it is a different story, because that is where all the hard work is being done: the outside of the building is scarcely visible behind the mass of diagonal stone props that shore it up like a permanent scaffolding.

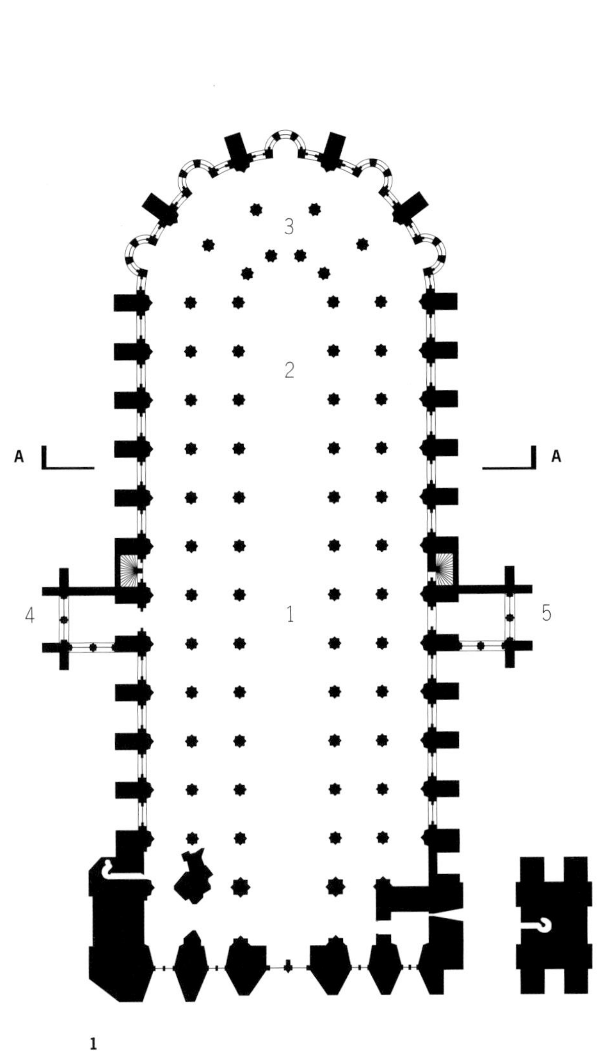

1

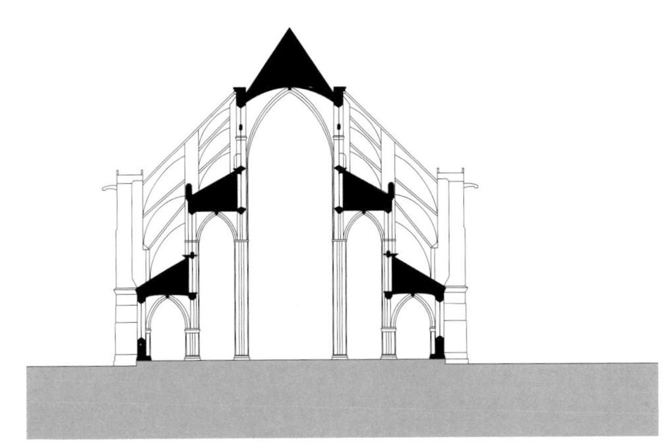

2

3

4

1 Plan

1 Nave
2 Choir
3 Ambulatory
4 North door
5 South door

2 Section A-A

3 West Elevation

4 South Elevation

0 20 40 m
40 80 120 ft

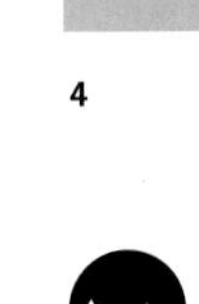

Cologne Cathedral

Cologne, North Rhine–Westphalia, Germany; from 1248

The Gothic style of architecture spread right across northern Europe and into Spain, developing local variations and sub-styles along the way and through the centuries. The German cathedrals followed quite closely the French pattern represented by the cathedral of St Etienne at Bourges (pages 136–37), but went further in developing the masonry's apparent lack of substance.

For example, at Strasbourg (a border city that has at various times been in France or in Germany), the solid masonry walls are often covered with an insubstantial screen of delicate stonework, including sculpture, which attracts attention, so that the structural walls become almost invisible in the background. Strasbourg induced rapture in the German writer Goethe, who published an essay about the cathedral in 1773 that would prove an important spur in reviving the appreciation of medieval building.

At Cologne the great spires of the cathedral dominate the city. They are sculpted with openings in the stonework through which daylight can be seen. The spires seem unfeasible, and the prospect of building them must have been daunting. They were actually constructed in the nineteenth century, when, with the Romantic appreciation of the Gothic style at its height, some medieval drawings showing the spires' design were found. It was decided to build them, and they were finished in 1880, reaching a height of 157 metres (515 feet) – which briefly made Cologne Cathedral the tallest building in the world, until it was overtaken by the Washington Monument in 1884.

The Cologne spires are the culmination of a long tradition of experimentation and attempts to outdo others. The first cathedral spires were built in the 1140s at Chartres in northern France, making a soaring monument that was visible across the plains of surrounding farmland. This was a translation into a gigantic scale of the pinnacle – a tall, steep pyramid of masonry that had an important structural role to play in flying buttresses, where it reinforced stability by applying a heavy load at a place where it was helpful to do so (usually more or less in line with the wall to which the lower part of the buttress attached). Spires were also used decoratively, to make a spiky silhouette.

Cologne's spires are harmoniously related to the rest of the cathedral, which is throughout an immensely daring and ambitious structure, plainly aiming to do significantly more than house the religious services that would be held there. The impetus to build them came from a realization by the citizens of Cologne and the Prussian state that this was a competition they could win. The spires were not only taller and later than anyone else's, they were also eye-wateringly expensive, and the open latticework of the stone recalls the bravura of an acrobatic performance.

As we now know, the Eiffel Tower (pages 36–37) – the ultimate in open latticework – was built only nine years later, and it is debatable whether all the effort at Cologne brought the city quite as much prestige as was anticipated. The spires are most impressive if they are seen as a very late medieval achievement.

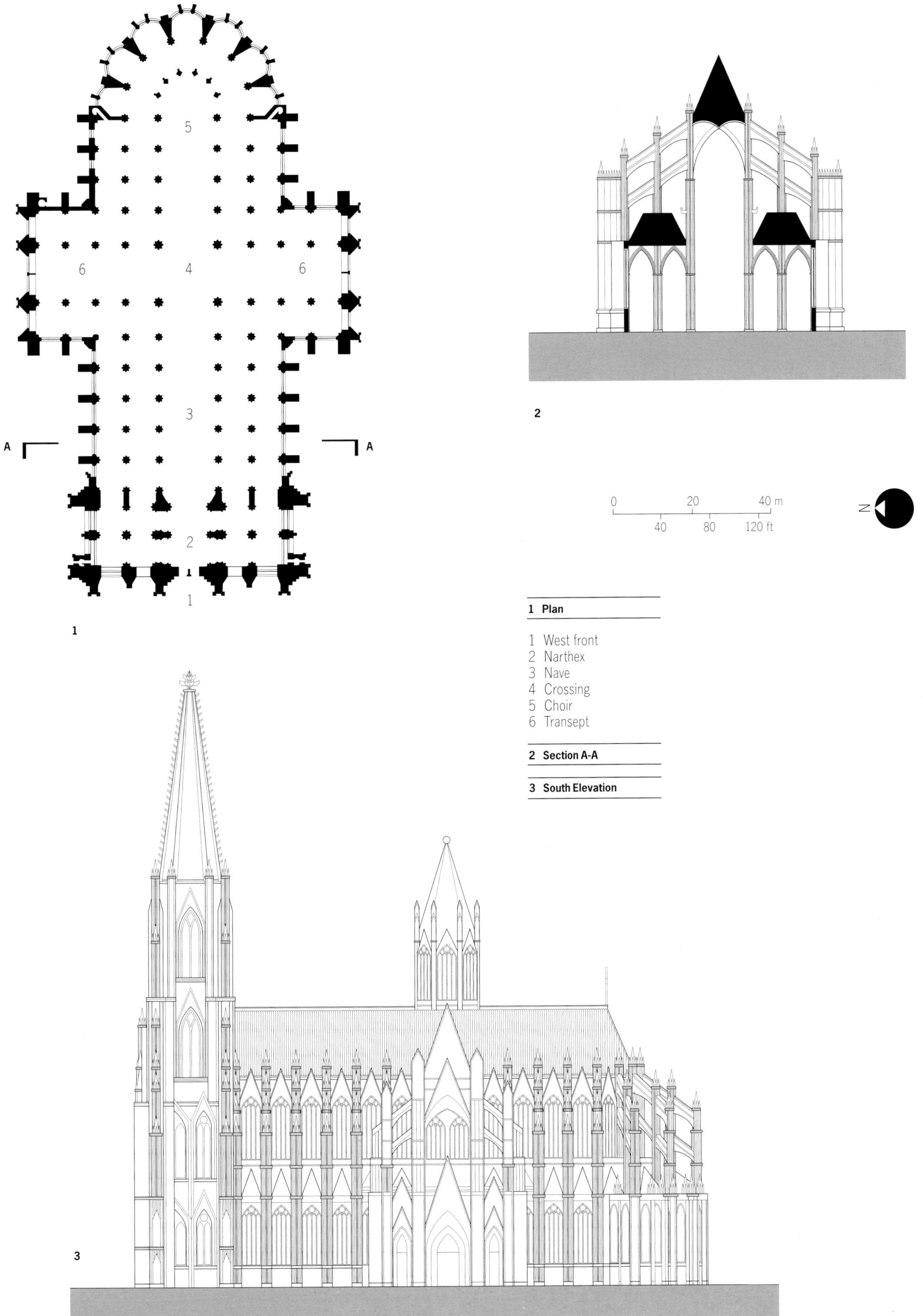

1 Plan

1 West front
2 Narthex
3 Nave
4 Crossing
5 Choir
6 Transept

2 Section A-A

3 South Elevation

Konark Sun Temple

Konark, Odisha, India; 1260

The temple at Konark in Odisha (formerly Orissa), sometimes known as the Black Pagoda, has at its gates a pair of monumental lions crushing elephants beneath them. The elephants in turn are crushing people. It is an ominous introduction. The temple is the ultimate manifestation of the type represented by Lingaraj (page 122–23). It was originally located beside the sea, but the shoreline has moved and the building is now 3 km (almost 2 miles) inland.

Dedicated to the sun god Surya, the temple was configured as a colossal chariot drawn by seven rearing horses (six of which survive) and rolling on 12 pairs of gigantic wheels – said to symbolize the hours of the day. The temple faced east to greet the rising sun. Its inner shrine and the huge tower that was above it have collapsed, but their podium is still in place and the outer chamber is standing.

The temple's abandonment and collapse has produced fanciful speculations, the most plausible of which alludes to the sixteenth-century adoption of Islam in the region, followed by the neglect and desecration of Hindu sites. The fact that this temple was commissioned by King Narasingha Deva (1238–64) to give thanks for a victory against Muslim opponents may have made it a target. The site was overtaken by jungle growth and drifting sand dunes, which were cleared in the late nineteenth century.

Royal patronage and victory in war made possible a building of outstanding quality. It was covered in exquisitely expressive sculptures, some of which are still in situ, while others have been removed to local museums or museums in Kolkata and New Delhi. Some of the sculptures are in sandstone; others, including panels in low relief, in green chlorite. The three little pavilions that look like associated minor shrines aligned with the sanctuary actually house chlorite panels depicting aspects of the life of Surya.

Konark Sun Temple is large. The *mandapa* – the audience chamber – is 38 metres (125 feet) high without its finial. The tower is thought to have been about 60 metres (200 feet) high and the tallest in India. The chariot wheels have a diameter of 3 metres (10 feet).

However, despite its mass, the monument is far from overbearing. It is rescued by the liveliness and humanity of its sculptures, which swarm everywhere. They depict a wide range of activity from public and private life, ascetic and indulgent, much of it joyful in mood, including many depictions of musicians and dancers. There are flocks and herds of birds and animals – including an estimated 2,000 elephants.

On axis with the temple, so that the god's penetrating vision would be able to see it, was a square pavilion for dancing. Its podium and columns survive but its roof has gone. Elsewhere in the temple's precincts were a refectory and a kitchen, as well as subsidiary shrines. Worship here must have been festive and pleasurable, and in modified form it continues on one day of the year, when devotees come to bathe in the sea to celebrate the sun's rebirth.

1 Plan

1 Inner shrine
2 Outer chamber
3 Pavilion

2 Section A-A

3 South Elevation

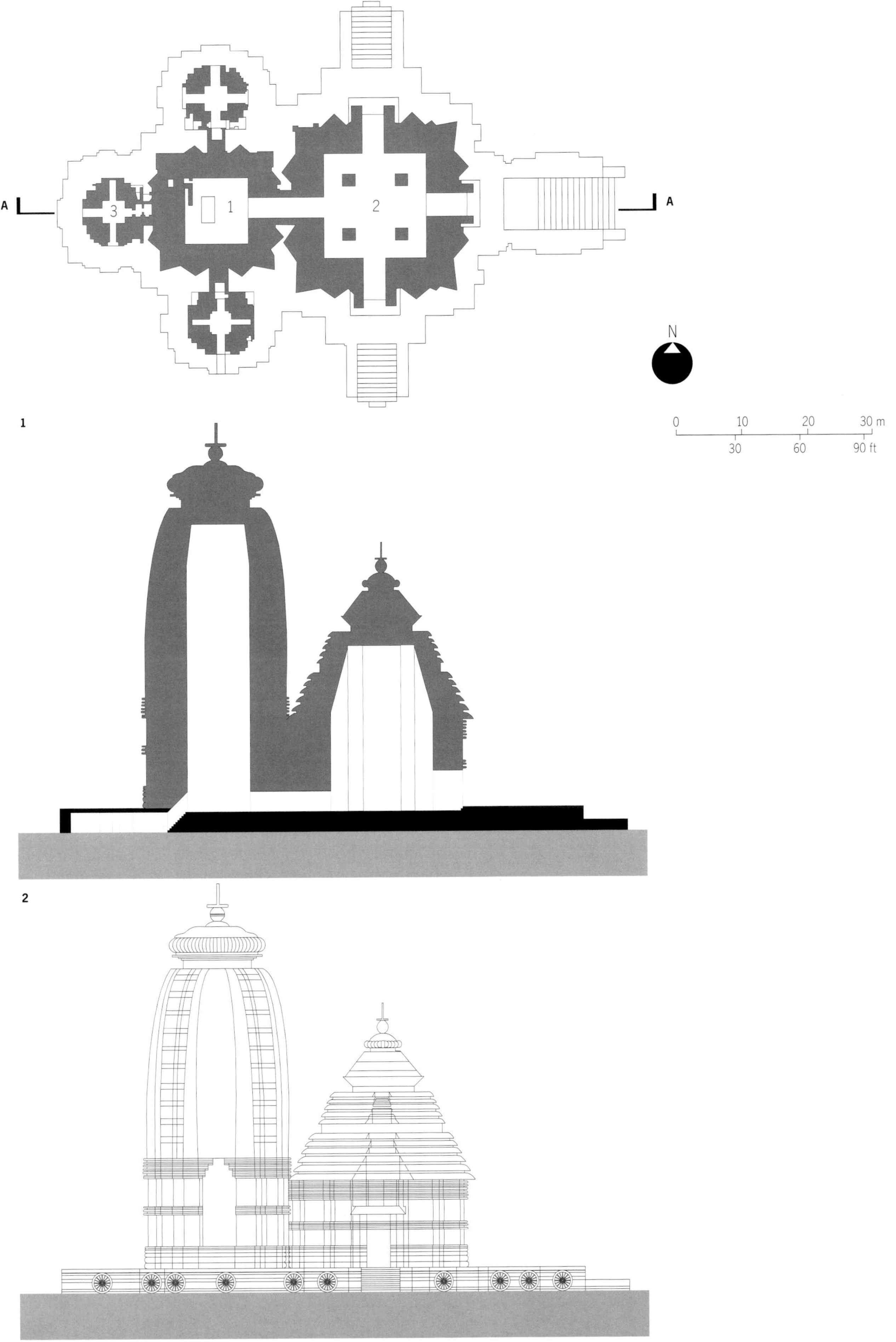

Golden Pavilion Temple

Muromachi, Kyoto, Japan; 1397

Muromachi is the name both of a district and of a period of Japanese history (from 1336 to 1573) when Japan was run by the Ashikaga shogunate. The emperor was the nominal head of state and an important symbolic figure – the head of the traditional Shinto religion – but in matters of practical politics the shogun was in charge. Originally, 'shogun' was a military title, but it became hereditary.

Ashikaga Takauji (1305–58), a samurai warrior descended from emperors, was the first of the Muromachi shoguns. The Golden Pavilion Temple, or Kinkaku-ji, was built by his grandson, Ashikaga Yoshimitsu (1358–1408) who became shogun at the age of 11, when his father died, in turn ceding the post to his own son in 1394.

Ashikaga Yoshimitsu's villa was his retirement project. He bought the land in 1397 and developed it as an impressive garden with pavilions. After his death, in accordance with his intentions, his son turned the largest pavilion into a Zen Buddhist temple, known as the Deer Garden Temple, or Rokuon-ji. Externally its two upper storeys are now, to spectacular effect, entirely covered in gold leaf.

Amid an atmosphere of quiet serenity, paths meander through woodland in which the various pavilions are screened from one another. Vistas open up across the lake, from one edge of which protrudes the Golden Pavilion, reflected in the water. Each of the pavilion's storeys has a projecting terrace running round it, covered by an overhanging roof; on the lower floors, the terraces are separated from the interior by panels that can be slid out of the way. On the top floor there are arched openings and hinged doors.

Each of the three floors was built in a different style. The ground floor evokes the architecture of the Imperial Palace in Kyoto (pages 248–49), establishing an aristocratic ambience with finely carved decorative embellishments. The first floor is in *buke-zukuri* style, suggesting the Ashikaga family's samurai warrior caste, and would have been more austere had it not been for the exterior gilding. The top floor is quite different: a Zen hall, Chinese in style, with arched openings rather than the exposed timber framework, and gilded inside and out. It includes a relic of some of the Buddha's ashes.

The site is still treated with reverence. The temple has burnt down and been replaced on more than one occasion – most recently in 1955, after an arson attack by one of the monks, so the building's fabric is not old. It is doubted whether in its initial incarnation the temple had as much gold leaf as it now has on the upper storeys. The firebird or phoenix was a mythical bird, with currency in many cultures, which was supposed to immolate itself and to be reborn from its own ashes. The sculpture of a gilded phoenix perching on the temple's roof may have been introduced after an early rebuilding, but sculpted phoenixes are to be found in other places (such as Kyoto's Phoenix Hall temple) where the symbolism is less piquant.

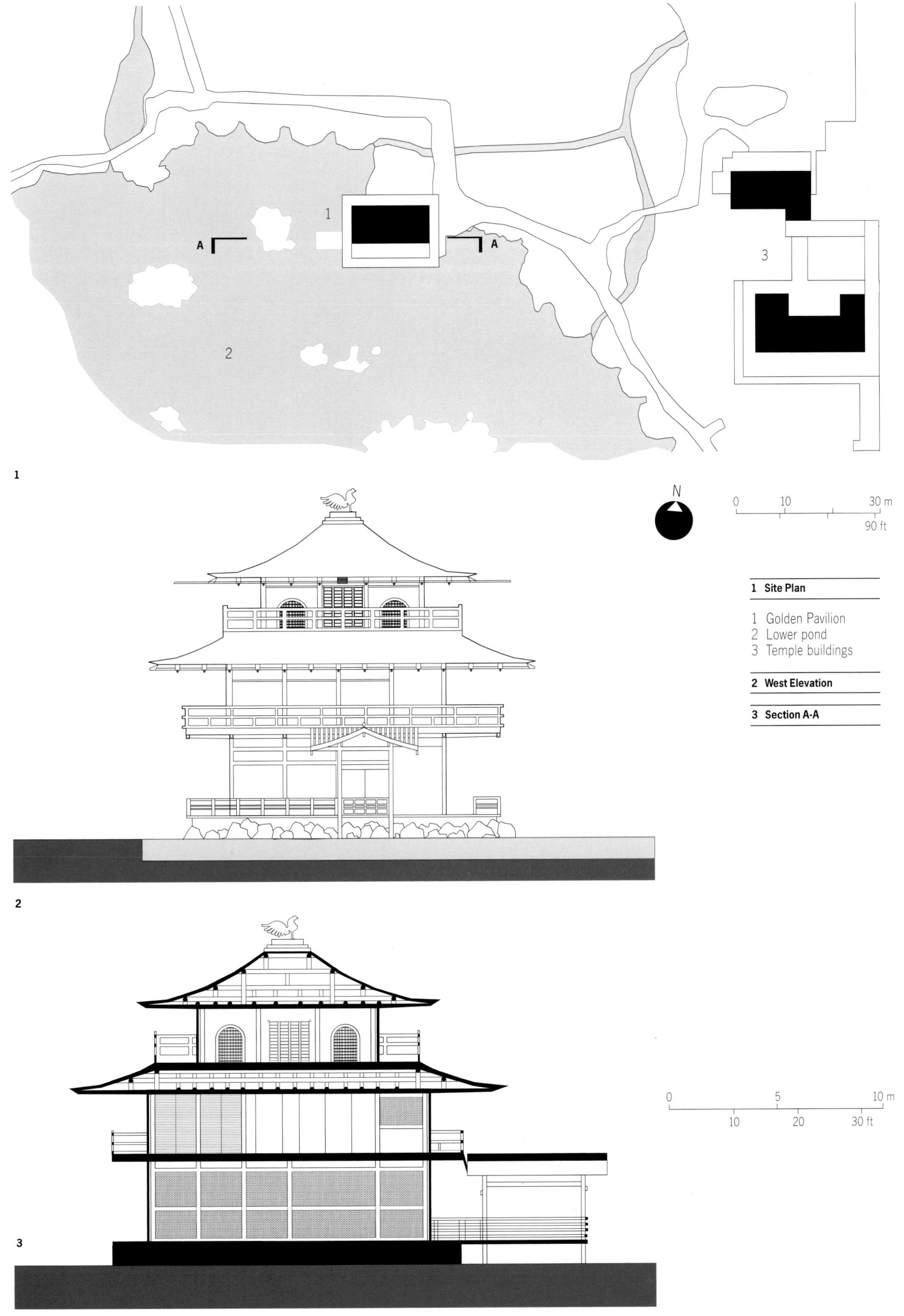

1 Site Plan

1 Golden Pavilion
2 Lower pond
3 Temple buildings

2 West Elevation

3 Section A-A

Goharshad Mosque

Qavam al-Din Shirazi, flourishing by 1410

Mashhad, Razavi Khorasan, Iran; 1418

After the killing of the holy man Imam Reza in 818, a mausoleum was established at Mashhad, whose name means 'the place of sacrifice'. It has been rebuilt and remodelled several times, and is now set beneath a spectacular golden dome, at the focus of the largest mosque in Iran, which is second in capacity only to the Great Mosque in Mecca. The Goharshad Mosque is incorporated in a larger complex, contributing one of seven courtyards to the overall scheme. It was built adjoining the mausoleum as a site of prayer that gave proper status to the sanctity of the place.

Razavi Khorasan is an eastern province of Iran, sharing borders with Turkmenistan and Afghanistan, but those borders were not in place in the fifteenth century. All these areas were part of the Timurid Empire, which had its roots further east, in Mongolia, with Genghis Khan and then Tamburlaine (Timur), who annexed Genghis Khan's empire and whose descendants assimilated Persian culture and religion.

Mashhad was adopted as a Timurid administrative centre and became an important city on the east–west trade route – the 'Silk Road' which made this part of the empire immensely rich. The dynasty later spread its influence to what came to be called Mughal India, so the Goharshad Mosque could be seen as a precursor of the Taj Mahal (pages 34–35). Some of the Taj Mahal's features were certainly rehearsed there; indeed, some of them, such as the portals, were brought from Samarkand.

The architect Qavam al-Din was responsible for designing other important buildings, including an earlier mosque in Herat, the Timurid capital (which is further east, in modern-day Afghanistan), but he was called 'Shirazi', which suggests an origin in south-west Iran. He, like his architecture, was cosmopolitan.

Domes, minarets and gateways are the most prominent features of the Goharshad Mosque. The whole building is exquisitely decorated with inscriptions and intricate patterns that often have a carpet-like quality to them. The decoration's dominant colours are white, blue and turquoise, and it is carefully modulated so as to enhance the play of the building's forms. The sanctuary faces Mecca, which is south-west of Mashhad.

The external dome is covered in a turquoise mosaic, and the sanctuary beneath it is approached through the tallest of the portals – a great screen that makes an impressive façade incorporating a minaret at each side. Beyond the screen is a pointed-arched recess, at the back of which a small door opens into the sanctuary. This vast recess is covered with fine decoration all in white.

The royal patronage that made the building possible came from Queen Goharshad, who married the youngest of Tamburlaine's sons and is supposed to have pioneered the adoption of Persian refinements. She is credited with moving the Timurid capital from Samarkand to Herat (where her mausoleum was built). After her husband's death, and the murder of her eldest son (by his son), Goharshad effectively ran the empire through her grandson. Even in her eighties, in 1457, she retained enough political power and vitality to provoke another of Tamburlaine's great-grandsons to bring about her execution.

1 Section A-A

2 Section B-B

3 Plan

1 Sanctuary
2 Minaret
3 Washing fountain
4 Courtyard

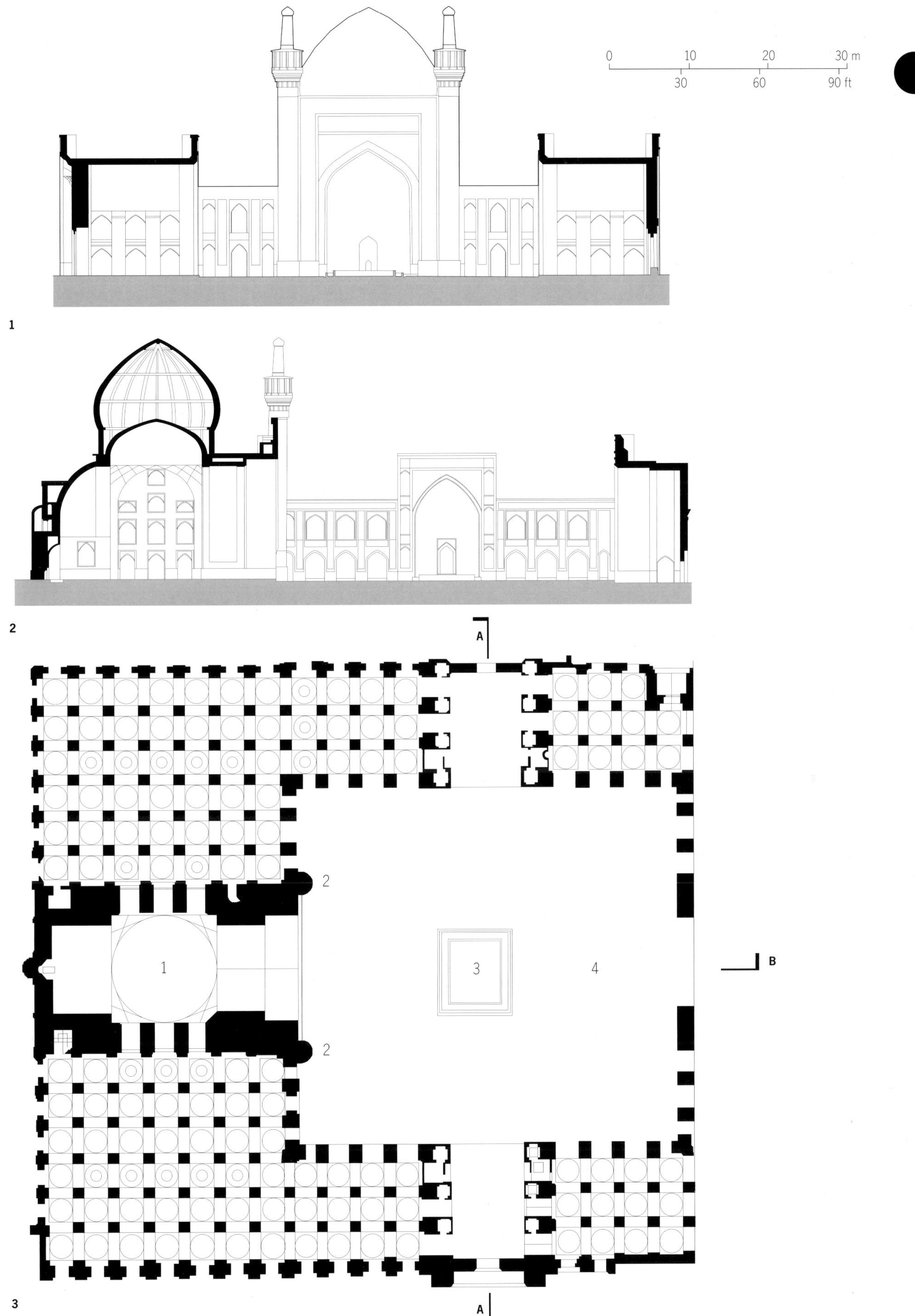

Santa Maria del Santo Spirito

Filippo Brunelleschi, 1377–1446

Florence, Italy; 1430–88

It is not always clear how ideas are transferred from one culture to another – and, when different cultures tell different stories about their development, it is sometimes easier to believe that an idea has been independently reinvented than to accept that it could have been copied.

The architect Brunelleschi was one of the leading lights of the Italian Renaissance, which is generally characterized as marking the end of the Middle Ages and the rebirth of Classical culture – and, indeed, there is nothing Gothic about the finely modelled basilica of Santa Maria del Santo Spirito.

There is no soaring verticality, no mysterious coloured light, but Gothic ideas had never taken root in Florence or Rome. The avowed models were early churches such as San Paolo fuori le Mura in Rome (dating from 395), but the layout is closer to later basilicas in the Romanesque tradition. The medieval tradition of using varied imagery in the capitals of columns is avoided, however, and all the columns are canonically Corinthian.

The most arresting development in the layout of Santa Maria del Santo Spirito is Brunelleschi's use of a squared grid for the positioning of the columns. It is accentuated by the church's floor pattern, which uses contrasting stones to mark out the grid. Renaissance paintings often show such a grid, turned into an evocation of architectural space. It can look like a diagram of geometric perspective – one of the crucial artistic discoveries of the age – but Santo Spirito has the real thing.

Domes were much more typical of churches belonging to the eastern orthodox tradition (which definitively went its own way after 1204, when western Crusaders sacked Constantinople). The gridded layout has precedents in the prayer halls of mosques – like those, for example, at Córdoba (pages 118–19) and Mashhad (pages 144–45), which also used a dome – but the grid at Santo Spirito is resolved around the basilica form, to give a taller central space, rather than being continued as an indefinitely spreading forest of columns as at the mosques, or as a dome over the cross-in-square plan that would have been characteristic of the orthodox tradition.

There is some reason to wonder whether Santo Spirito was affected by eastern influences. Constantinople was surrounded by Ottoman forces, who eventually took over the city in 1453. They would have managed to do so earlier had they not been fending off attacks from Timurids further east. Greek-speaking Christian scholars, apprehensive about their prospects in the eastern Mediterranean, moved to Italy when they could and made Greek texts accessible in a way they had not previously been, fuelling the passion for knowledge of antique culture that characterized the time.

Brunelleschi's layout for the building, which involves careful coordination of the repetitive units, seems predisposed to accept mechanical mass-production of arches, columns and semi-circular chapels, though such an idea was inconceivable at the time. The regular order of the interior space is very much the point of the building.

The arrestingly plain façade of Santa Maria del Santo Spirito is as it is because Brunelleschi's design for it was never executed – the interior is the part that matters. The building's orientation was also less ideal than the geometry of the interior. It follows the pre-established line of the street and incorporates the city-block accommodation for Augustinian nuns and their hospital. The liturgical 'west' end faces more nearly south, now presiding over a tree-lined piazza with cafés and a market, which is an important focus for everyday life.

1 Plan

1 Nave
2 Crossing
3 Choir
4 Aisle
5 Sacristy
6 Transept

2 Section A-A

3 North Elevation

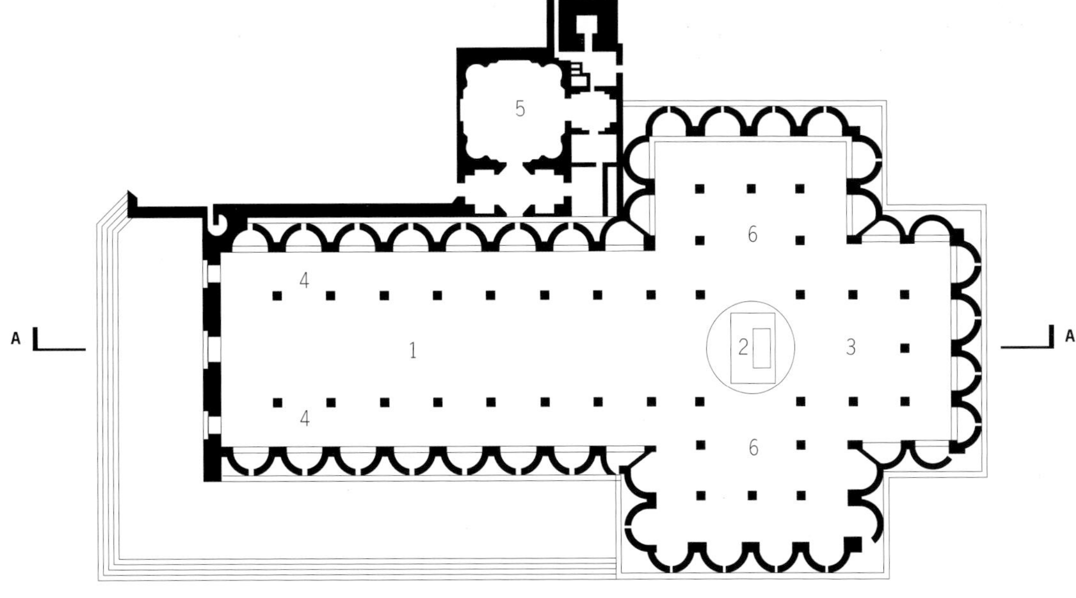

1

2

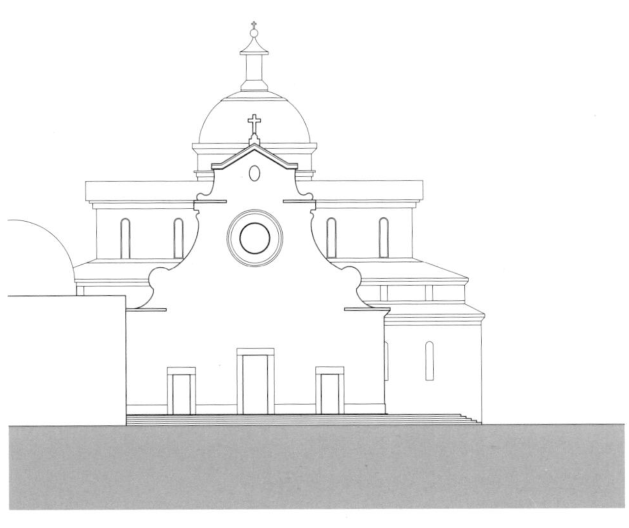

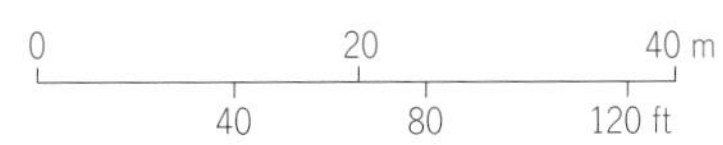

3

Sant'Andrea of Mantova

Leon Battista Alberti, 1404–72

Mantua (Mantova), Italy; 1470–82

Destined to become a prominent figure of the Renaissance, Leon Alberti was born into a rich family and had an excellent education. He wrote on a wide variety of subjects, including painting, horses, the family and architecture – and he did much to bring about the contemporary change in taste that led to a re-evaluation of ancient buildings.

Only one treatise on architecture has survived from ancient Rome: *De architettura* by Vitruvius, written in the first century BCE. Roman 'books' were scrolls, rather than having bound pages like modern volumes, and the ten books by Vitruvius had been rediscovered during Alberti's lifetime.

Alberti studied them, struggled to make sense of some of the specialized vocabulary, and brought the text up to date, so that it could act as a guide for modern patrons and builders. In doing so, he produced the first systematic study of buildings since ancient times, called *De re aedificatoria*; the title, which translates as *On building*, signals the author's concern with practical things. He wanted to put buildings on a sound footing, both literally, in terms of good foundations and structures, and figuratively – making architecture part of intellectual discourse and presenting good buildings as the embodiment of good principles. Early copies of Alberti's book were written out by hand in the way that books always had been. Gutenberg's printing press was invented around 1450, when Alberti was writing, and in 1485 *De re aedificatoria* became the first printed book on architecture.

The church of Sant'Andrea was built for the Marquis of Mantua, Ludovico Gonzaga (1412–78), to provide an impressive setting for its holy relic – a phial of Christ's blood (which had been found thanks to the miraculous intervention of Sant'Andrea).

Alberti called the building an 'Etruscan temple', thinking that it copied the form of a pre-Roman type, but actually it was modelled on the building now known as the basilica of Maxentius in Rome – a grand vaulted ruin close to the Forum. The basilica gave Alberti some cues for the interior of Sant'Andrea, but, as its façades had vanished, he had to look elsewhere for exterior inspiration.

For the west façade, he took as his model the Arch of Titus – a triumphal arch in the Forum – which he adapted to suit the form of the church, replacing its heavy superstructure with a shallow pediment. In the event, this façade became the most impressive part of the church. It is fully finished, with coffers and rosettes in its vaults, as there once were at the Pantheon (pages 108–109). The vault over the nave inside would have been treated similarly had the cost not been so huge. In the end, it was given a simple barrel vault and it was painted with trompe l'oeil coffers – an effect that works harmoniously with the baroque dome that was added later and completed in 1763.

The triumphal arch of the west façade presides over a small square on an important route through the city. The central arch evokes in miniature the vault on the other side of the wall. Like the Arch of Titus, the façade makes use of two different sizes of column – here flattened into pilasters – one starting at low level, and supporting the springing-point of the arch, the other larger and raised on a pedestal. These larger columns go up to the main cornice, and with Alberti's pediment they produce the effect of a temple-front.

So there are two different column-systems operating. They are given different capitals, and each supports its own cornice. The lower cornice is depicted as running behind the larger columns. But this is all decoration. In the Roman manner, the real work is being done by some very solid masonry, while the sophistications of the surface tell a compelling and beautifully resolved story about structure that is pure fiction.

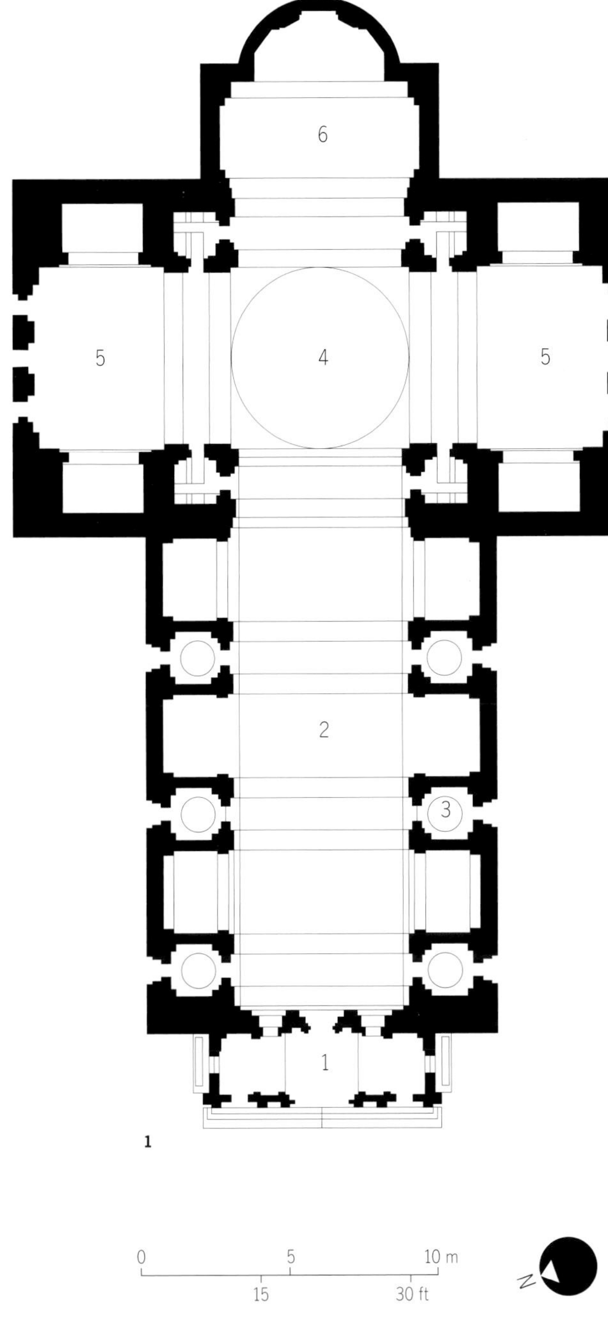

1

0 5 10 m
15 30 ft
N

2

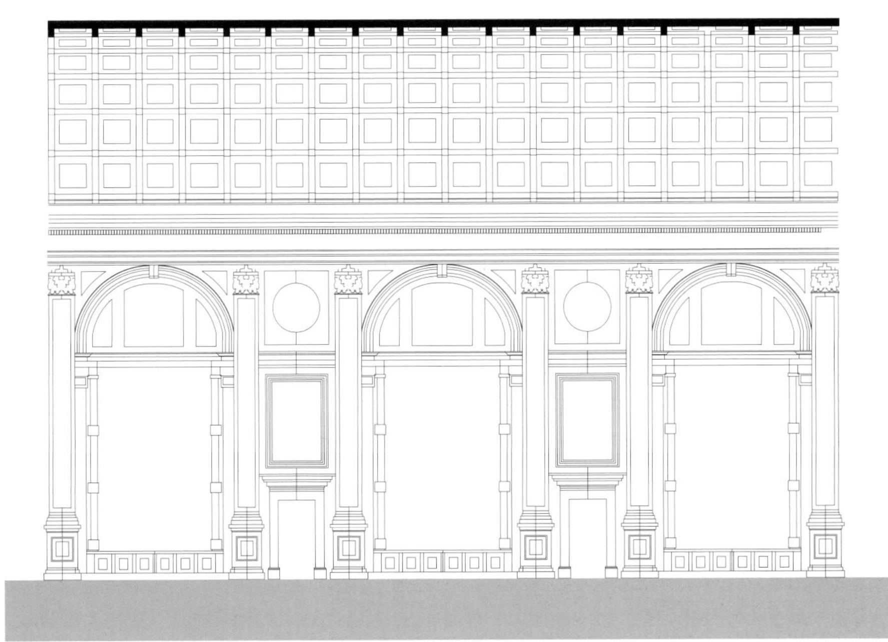

3

1 Plan

1 West portico
2 Nave
3 Stairs to crypt
4 Crossing
5 Transept
6 Chancel

2 North Elevation

3 Interior Elevation

Suleyman Mosque

Khoja Mimar Sinan Aga, 1498–1588

Istanbul, Turkey; 1551–58

In 1453, at the age of 21, Mehmed the Conqueror took control of Constantinople after a siege and turned the greatest church in Christendom into a mosque. The city was still an amazing place, even though its store of antiquities and holy relics had been savagely depleted between 1204 and 1261, when the city was treated like a gold mine by its Crusader rulers. The head of John the Baptist went to Amiens, where the cathedral developed into one of the largest and most beautifully decorated anywhere. The crown of thorns was sold to Louis IX of France, who built the jewel-like Sainte-Chapelle in Paris to receive it.

By contrast, after Mehmed invaded, he made Constantinople his capital and set about enriching it. In a place so overcrowded with monuments, it might have seemed that building new ones would not have been a priority, and the mosque of Hagia Sophia (pages 24–25) still had the power to stupefy. Nevertheless a tradition of imperial mosque-building took hold.

In the sixteenth century, the Ottoman Empire was rapidly expanding and its ruler, Suleyman the Magnificent, wanted to be able to show that not only his empire but also his reign was second to none. Having negotiated an agreement with Charles V, the Holy Roman Emperor (in return for withdrawing from Hungary), Suleyman styled himself Emperor of Rome, a title that would never be recognized in the west.

Hagia Sophia was by then a thousand years old and still unchallenged. The Suleyman Mosque was designed to surpass anything that had previously been built, Hagia Sophia included. The site was the top of the highest hill in the old part of the city, so, despite the fact that its dome is no larger than Hagia Sophia's, the Suleyman nonetheless has the dominant position and still makes an impact as the city's most important structure.

In its positioning, the building references the Dome of the Rock in Jerusalem, and invites a comparison between Suleyman and Solomon, just as Justinian did at Hagia Sophia ('Solomon, I have surpassed thee.').

One of Suleyman's most important reforms was his overhaul of the legal system. As a reflection of this, the mosque complex was established not only as a site of prayer but also as a place of the most advanced learning, where the scriptures would be studied and laws revised to bring them into accord with religious teaching. There was also a medical school. The schools are arranged as a sequence of buildings surrounding the mosque, with dozens of small domes on their roofs.

The mosque itself is modelled on Hagia Sophia, but the great masses of masonry needed to stabilize the structure are screened by lightweight galleries, so the straining mass of Hagia Sophia – cracked by earthquake, but still miraculously in place – is superseded by something that looks effortless. The pure geometries are undistorted by settlement and the ravages of time, the decoration is fine without being showy, and the building appears altogether impeccable. It is completely accomplished, and makes Hagia Sophia look like a hazardous but lucky experiment.

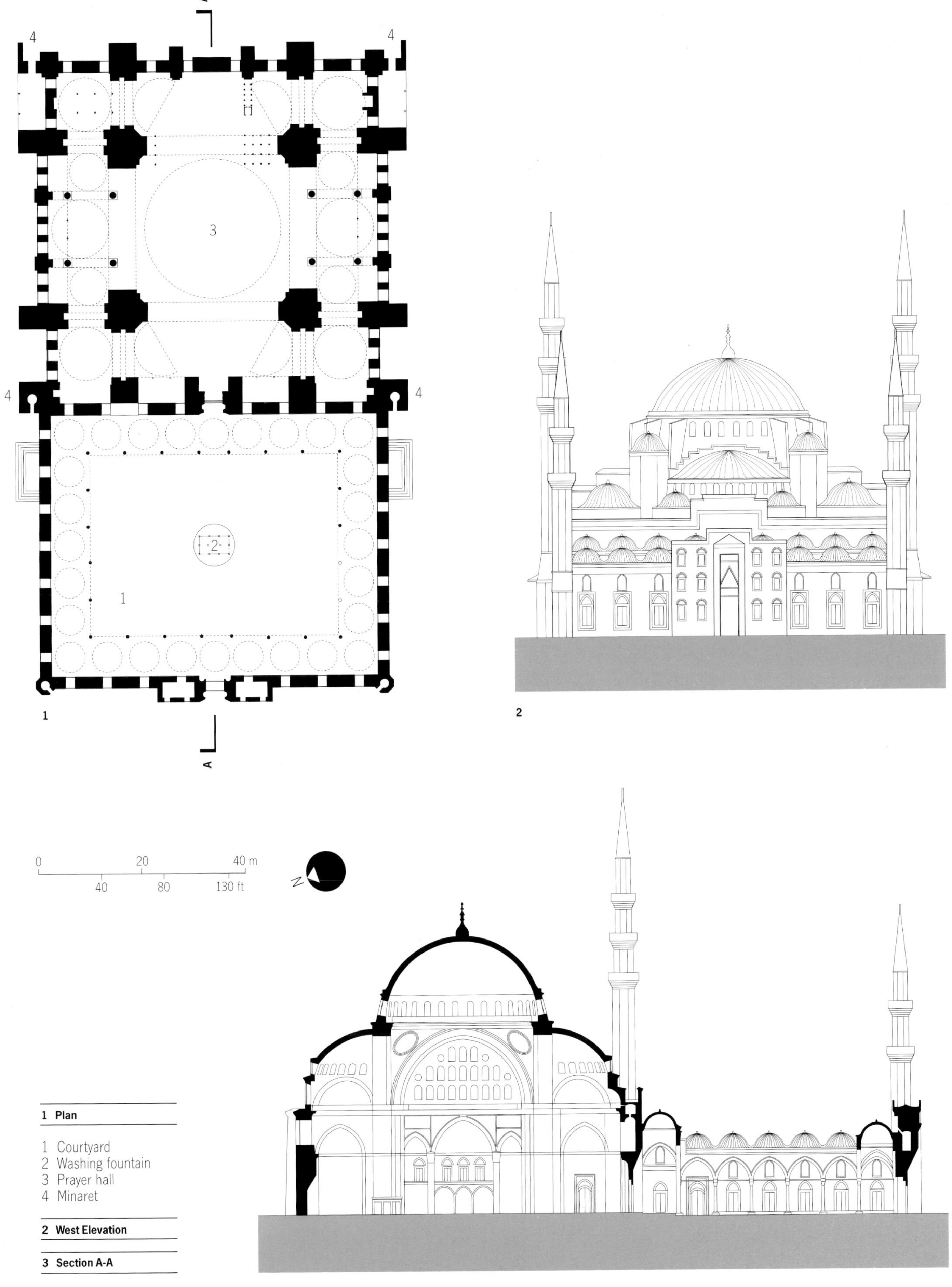

1 Plan

1 Courtyard
2 Washing fountain
3 Prayer hall
4 Minaret

2 West Elevation

3 Section A-A

St Basil's Cathedral

Postnik Yakovlev

Moscow, Russia; 1554

The Russian Orthodox Church used to be overseen from Constantinople but declared its independence just before Constantinople was taken over by Mehmed the Conqueror in 1453.

Russia's tradition of building domed and multi-domed churches developed from that link, but there were other influences. The external decoration and colour seem to have come from further east, along the Silk Road. St Basil's Cathedral in Moscow is the most famous Russian church, and there is nothing to match its exuberant display. It now seems to be in a permanent state of carnival, but it was not always so brightly coloured – the colouring was intensified in the 1840s. It is neither a proper cathedral nor dedicated to St Basil.

A 'cathedra' is a bishop's throne, and normally a cathedral is a church that has such a throne in it. The Russian Orthodox bishops were installed at the Cathedral of the Dormition, a five-domed church within the Kremlin, but there is a group of five churches there, around the Cathedral Square (Sobornaya Square) that are all styled 'cathedral' in recognition of their high status. St Basil's is a much more prominent building, being situated outside the Kremlin's high defence-wall. It is officially called the Cathedral of the Protection of Most Holy Theotokos on the Moat ('Theotokos' being a title of Mary meaning 'god-bearer' or 'mother of god'). But no one actually calls the church by that name, and few would recognize it. It was commissioned by Ivan IV (Ivan the Terrible) to give thanks for military victories in his campaign against troublesome Mongols in Kazan and Astrakhan.

The building is in fact a collection of one-room churches, huddled together around the principal structure at the centre: the Trinity Church. It has a roof of a type known in Russia as a 'tent roof' – an octagonal cone, rather like a western steeple, except that it covers the whole church rather than just a tower (or, to put it another way, it turns the whole church into a tower and steeple). This is a well-recognized Russian church-type. The other churches are analogous, but with domes instead of tent roofs. The arrangement is not designed to allow a large congregation to assemble inside the building. It is more like an unexpectedly autonomous gathering of chapels in search of a nave.

The positioning of St Basil's on the moat outside the walls of the royal stronghold clearly suggests a populist role for the building, quite different from that of the group of cathedrals sequestered within. Each of the churches was dedicated to mark a breakthrough in the war and was meant to engage the public in the state's victorious progress.

One element that is clearly an afterthought is the tenth chamber (top left on the plan) where the local saint, Basil, was buried.

During the 1680s a screen wall was built to bind the group of churches more cohesively together. They came to be seen as an image of a heavenly city, and in the public imagination seemed to be a representation of Jerusalem. Until 1651 on Palm Sunday the Tsar and the Patriarch re-enacted Christ's entry into Jerusalem on a donkey, by processing from the Cathedral Square to the new Jerusalem. On such occasions it becomes clear that the various cathedrals were all part of one organism that had the Jerusalem group as its sanctuary. The nave remained unbuilt, and the crowds of witnesses gathered in the open air.

1 Plan

1 Chapel
2 Trinity Church
3 Shrine of St Basil

2 West Elevation

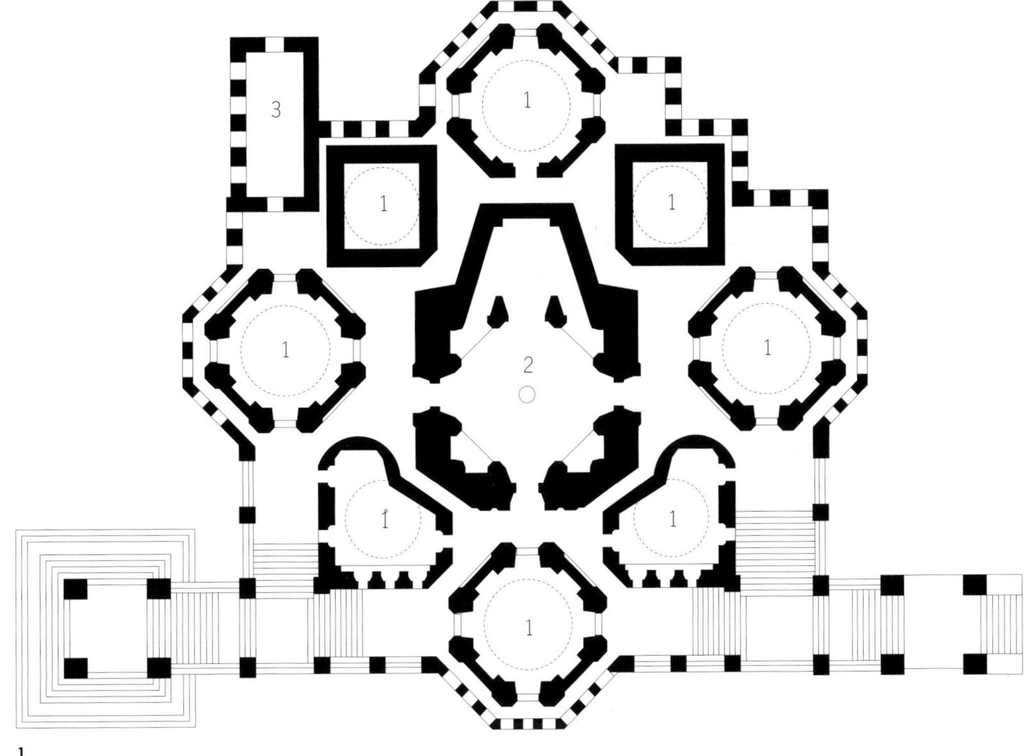

1

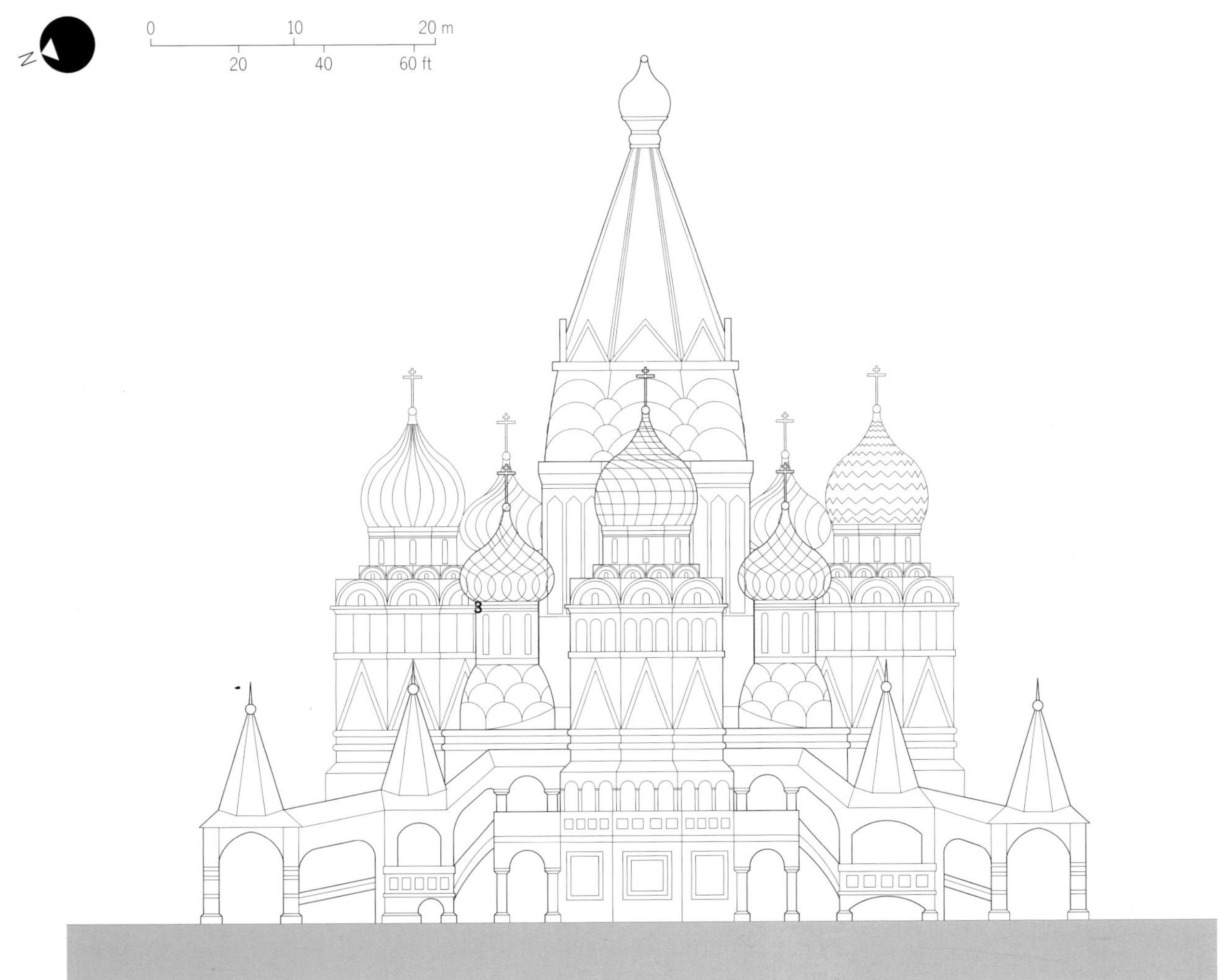

2

San Carlo alle Quattro Fontane

Francesco Borromini, 1599–1667

Rome, Italy; 1634–37

The Quirinal Hill, one of the seven hills inside the walls of ancient Rome, is now covered with a grid of streets in the city centre. A block away from the palace of the president of the modern Italian republic, San Carlo alle Quattro Fontane is almost lost on a long, very straight street that leads to Michelangelo's Porta Pia, on the corner of a block.

The building combines several different elements in a small space. Tucked away at the back of the site there is (on five floors) the residential accommodation for a small monastic community, reached by way of narrow stairs. It looks out on to a courtyard on the far side. Except on feast days, when the door from the street to the church might be open, the normal approach is through a shady courtyard. Its peristyle supports a little cloister above. From there a passage leads into the church, which is domed and very much taller than it is wide.

In the lower part of the church the forms are all sinuously distorted. The classical language of architecture is deployed there, but instead of its being organized by squares and circles, as in Brunelleschi's work, there is something much more complex and restless going on.

The plan gives an indication of the way in which the walls bulge and make concavities. The cornice lines snake their way along, and the various elements of the building are tilted to follow the curve. This is a building that confidently destabilizes any expectations based on knowledge of the earlier classical work to which it refers.

The church interior is lit from high up. There is a lantern right at the top, but most of the light enters through windows at the base of the dome, which are hidden behind a cornice that screens them from the view of anyone in the church. The light comes into the space by being reflected off the ceiling, which is consequently much the brightest part of the room – and what a ceiling it is.

The dome is not circular, but oval, supported on pendentives – curving triangles, which are normally used to resolve the transition between a square beneath and a circle above (as at Hagia Sophia, pages 24–25). At San Carlo, though, there is only the vaguest sense of an implied rectangle floating in the air, while the walls make shallow or tight curves and the lines of columns meander as on the façade.

Above the cornice, the composition resolves into a complex but harmonious set of coffers – octagonal, hexagonal and cruciform – which stack together neatly and diminish in size as the dome ascends. The setting-out of these coffers is a miracle of projective geometry – an art developed to a high pitch of perfection in the masonry of Gothic vaults, where the ribs could trace sinuous lines through the air. There is nothing stylistically Gothic about this vault, however. It is an image of incomprehensible geometric perfection to rival Islamic work, and it suggests an ideal that floats over people's heads while they engage with the more restless world beneath.

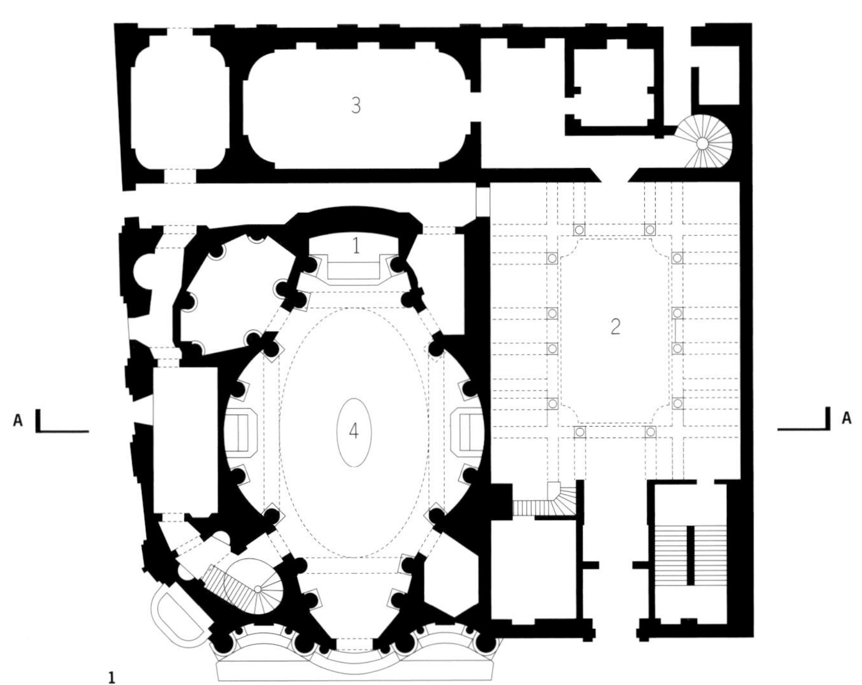

1

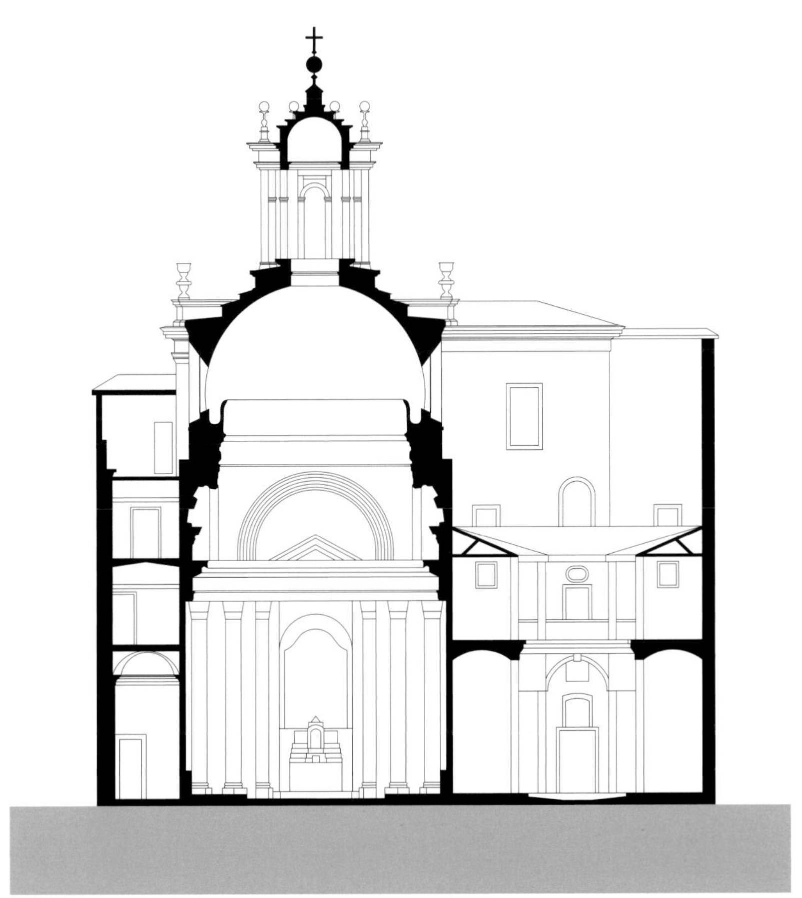

2

3

1 Plan

1 Altar
2 Cloister
3 Monks' accommodation
4 Body of church

2 Section A-A

3 Part North West Elevation

Vierzehnheiligen

Balthasar Neumann, 1687–1753

Bamberg, Bavaria, Germany; 1743–77

Vierzehnheiligen, or the Basilica of the Fourteen Holy Helpers, is a substantial eighteenth-century Bavarian church which attracted pilgrims because of its saints' reputations as healers of ailments ranging from headaches to bubonic plague.

Looking out across rolling countryside, it is the largest building for miles around, constructed in an extravagantly ornamental rococo style, reminiscent of the grandest contemporary palaces – and calculated to appeal to peasants' taste for all-out celestial glamour. It belongs to a Catholic movement known as the Counter-Reformation, in which the appealing aspects of ceremonial liturgy were given particular emphasis as a way to combat the drift towards Protestantism.

The elaboration of form represents the end of the line of development called baroque, which was just starting at the time San Carlo alle Quattro Fontane (pages 154–55) was built. Rococo is characterized by more intricate decoration and a lighter mood and colouring than baroque. The two styles share a basis in classical order, but in the case of rococo it is a classicism overlaid by a profusion of ornament and adapted to complex shapes.

The façade at Vierzehnheiligen is relatively conventional, merging a well-established classical façade with the silhouette of a Gothic cathedral's towers (the steeples being a regional variant). It was the interior that was groundbreaking. An idea of the basilica remains, with a central nave and side aisles, and chapels at the east end, but the spaces have been dissolved into one another. They are implied by curving lines of columns and the curves of domed plaster ceilings. The ceilings are painted illusionistically, so there is some ambiguity about just where they are – they dissolve away into clouds and sky, and their curvature helps with that illusion.

The structural work is hugely sophisticated. Enormous timber trusses span the considerable space. Arches that curve (in plan) as they leap from column to column would in isolation have tipped over backwards and had to be stabilized in some way with a counterbalance. Balthasar Neumann, the architect, had a background as a military engineer and took care of such matters without obvious fuss. There are no visible buttresses, but the domes do not actually float – they bear testimony to Neumann's ingenuity and daring.

The interior is as dematerialized as that of a Gothic cathedral, but the effect is achieved by different means. It is completely theatrical. Images and statues combine with the building to create a highly charged atmosphere. Lighting enters the space from concealed sources. Sculpted drapery seems to billow round scagliola columns which look like exotically coloured marble.

Near the main altar, statues of the 14 saints stand on pedestals and drape themselves round the complex, shell-like forms of a baldacchino, while some of the supporting cast look down, sitting attentively on high cornices. The figures seem to have wandered into this setting in much the same way as the pilgrims, and to be waiting around until they can be of help.

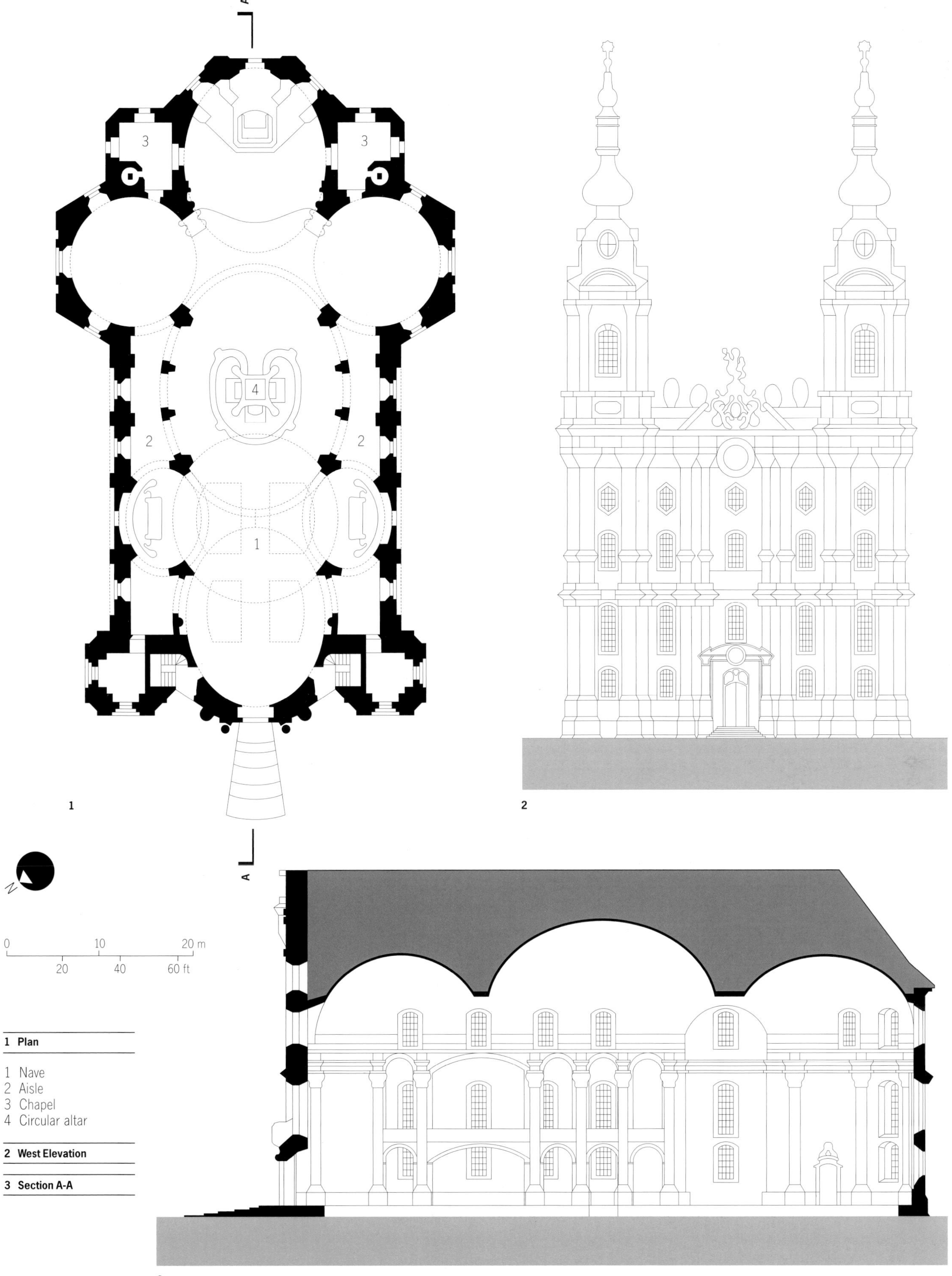

1 Plan

1 Nave
2 Aisle
3 Chapel
4 Circular altar

2 West Elevation

3 Section A-A

Sagrada Família

Antoni Gaudí, 1852–1926

Barcelona, Catalonia, Spain; from 1882

The Catalan architect Antoni Gaudí worked in Barcelona, where he tried to reinvent architecture by considering structural principles and analysing the forms produced by natural growth. Some of his European contemporaries tried to do comparable things (Victor Horta in Brussels, for example) and their efforts tend to be called Art Nouveau – signalling their simultaneous but individualistic attempts to escape from the historical styles that were used in mainstream nineteenth-century European architecture. The fact that they had little in common stylistically did not stop the single style-name being used to cover them all. Internationally, Gaudí's work is often labelled Art Nouveau, but in Barcelona the label for it is Modernismo.

Barcelona's medieval cathedral is in the Gothic Quarter, at the heart of the pre-industrial city, with an open space in front of it, but surrounded by narrow winding streets. Sagrada Família (the Church of the Holy Family), by contrast, is set in the square grid of streets laid out by Ildefons Cerdà (1815–76), which was used as the basis for the huge expansion of the city from 1859. It is in a modern cityscape.

The commission came from a bookseller, Josep María Boccabella, who started a religious foundation dedicated to his name-saint, St Joseph, whose status in the Holy Family is always somewhat provisional – as, in effect, the stepfather of God's son. Boccabella began to collect the money that enabled the church to be built. For the design he initially went to the Barcelona cathedral architect Francisco de Paula del Villar (1828–1901), for whom Gaudí had worked earlier in his career. Villar's design was in a conventional Gothic style, and work on building it began, but Villar resigned before the underground crypt was complete.

Gaudí's building is a reworking of Gothic forms, with pointed arches and pinnacles a-plenty, but everything has changed. How it has changed is clearest in the section drawing, which demonstrates how the columns lean towards one another, eliminating the need for external buttressing, and how they branch like trees, or form joints like bones.

Gaudí worked out the shape of his structures by modelling them upside down with hanging chains, from which he suspended weights that were proportional to the building's main loads. The chain would move into the position that most directly dealt with the various weights, and that gave Gaudí the line that the column or the vault should follow. This structural rationalism gives the building's forms their underlying rigour, which means that the building itself never seems merely whimsical – despite the mediocre quality of some of the sculptures that it now supports.

The limited flow of funds has made the rate of construction of Sagrada Família relatively slow, and it stopped altogether during the Spanish Civil War of the 1930s, not resuming until after World War II. Work is continuing, but the stones are being cut to their extraordinary shapes with the help of digital technology rather than chains, string and bags of sand.

From the outside, the building's appearance is dominated by the towers that become huge pinnacles. There should eventually be 18 of them, symbolizing the 12 apostles, four evangelists, Christ and Mary (Theotokos), but curiously, given the project's origins, not Joseph.

1

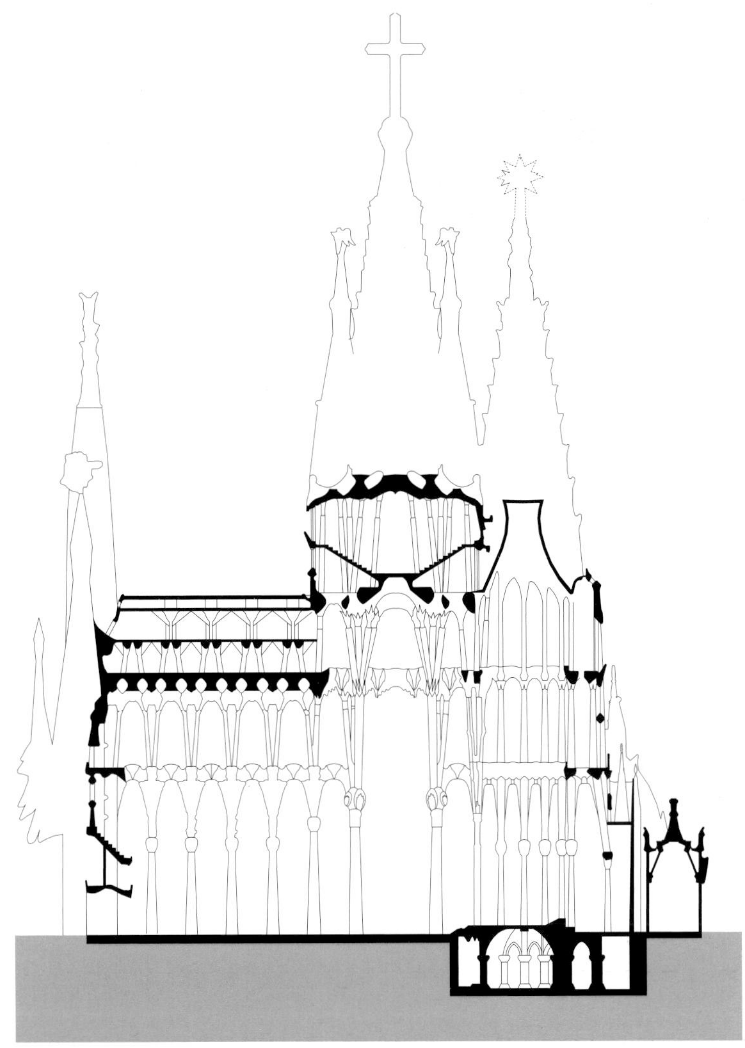

2

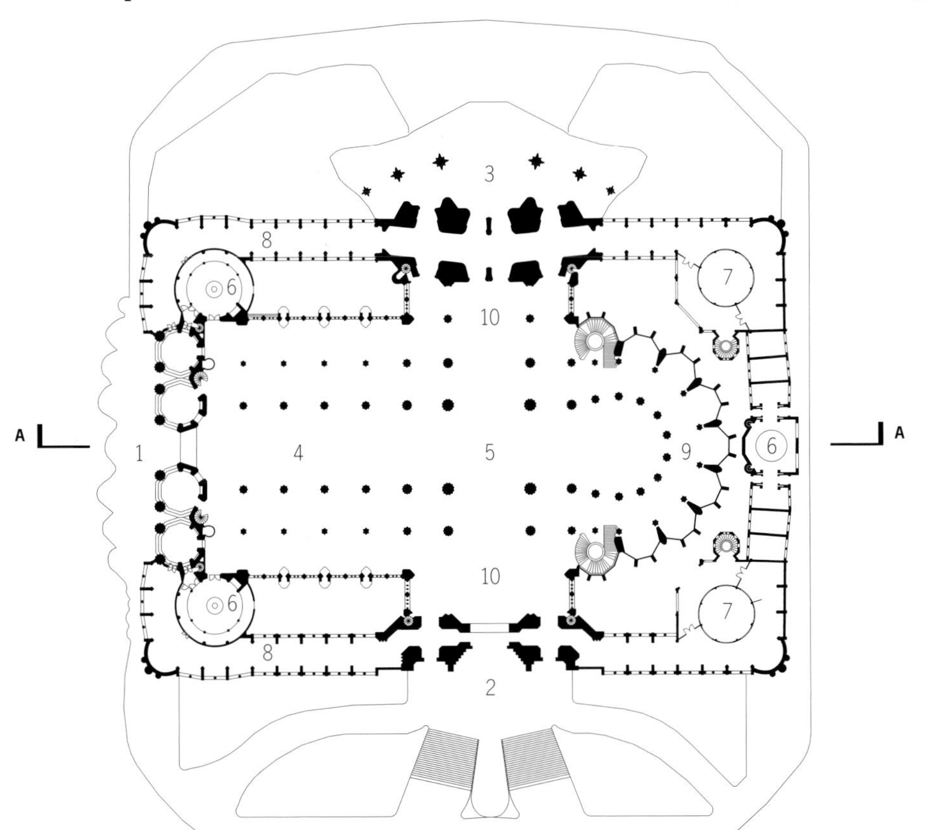

3

1 North Elevation

2 Section A-A

3 Plan

1 Glory façade
2 Nativity façade
3 Passion façade
4 Nave
5 Crossing
6 Chapel
7 Sacristy
8 Cloister
9 Ambulatory
10 Transept

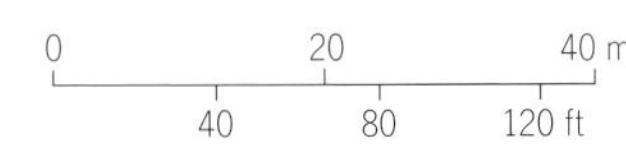

Westminster Cathedral

John Francis Bentley, 1839–1902

London, UK; 1895–1903

Religious and political upheavals in the sixteenth century left England's medieval churches in the hands of the Church of England, with the monarch and the archbishops of Canterbury and York at the top of its hierarchy. Roman Catholics were disenfranchised and barred from public office until 1829, when their legal status was restored. Pope Pius IX decreed a network of English Roman Catholic bishops in 1850, and there were early attempts to start work on a cathedral in London. A site was acquired, and the old prison that had been on it was demolished, but the funds for serious building work were not in place until the 1890s.

The most prominent Roman Catholic architect in England had been Augustus Pugin (1812–52), whose passionate advocacy of 'pointed or Christian architecture' had found expression in the new Palace of Westminster (pages 256–57) and various churches. His ideas were widely taken up by others, and nineteenth-century English church architecture was dominated by the Gothic Revival. Gothic would have been the most obvious choice of style for this building, just as it had been for the Sagrada Família before Gaudí took over (pages 158–59).

John Bentley's choice of Byzantine style for the building made reference to the early years of the Church, and to Rome. He visited St Mark's in Venice, and would have gone on to Istanbul to see Hagia Sophia (pages 24–25), had not the news of cholera reached him, making the journey imprudent.

Parts of the cathedral are decorated with Byzantine-style mosaics, with gold backgrounds, as in Venice and some of the older Roman churches, but the cathedral was funded by a minority group, not the general population, and the money was not available to make it possible to cover every surface. So the main vaults over the nave and aisles were left bare, looking like the majestic ruins of the Basilica of Constantine in the Forum in Rome.

The building made manifest its connection with a heritage that was not only Christian but also very specifically Roman. It was this link that gave the Roman Catholic community its identity, and made it problematic for the country's Protestant mainstream.

From a modern viewpoint, the bareness of the vaults looks principled. We can see the real materials from which the building was constructed, both inside and outside, where brick and stone create striated bands, which are decorative but made from the structural materials. There is no coating of applied decorative finish such as marble or mosaic, which the Romans would certainly have deployed on a building of such importance.

Despite the building's powerfully monumental qualities, it lacks the 'presence' in London's fabric that it would seem to merit. Had it been the cathedral of the ruling establishment since the late-Roman era – the era that it evokes – then without doubt street patterns would have formed around it that would have given it much greater prominence. The Church would have been able to secure a site at the heart of the city, rather than have to settle for this one, stranded in a backwater near Victoria Station. If that had been the case, then this building would have had a prominence to match St Paul's Cathedral – at the top of Ludgate Hill in the City of London, with a major road leading up to it.

In the event, Westminster Cathedral is less prominent than Westminster Abbey – a smaller building, but one with a much longer history that connects it with the life of the nation and with royal patronage. Westminster Cathedral embodies in monumental form the aspirations of a significant group, but its location is a reminder that this group is no more than a significant minority.

1 **South East Front Elevation**

2 **Section A-A**

3 **Plan**

1 Entrance
2 Nave
3 Sanctuary

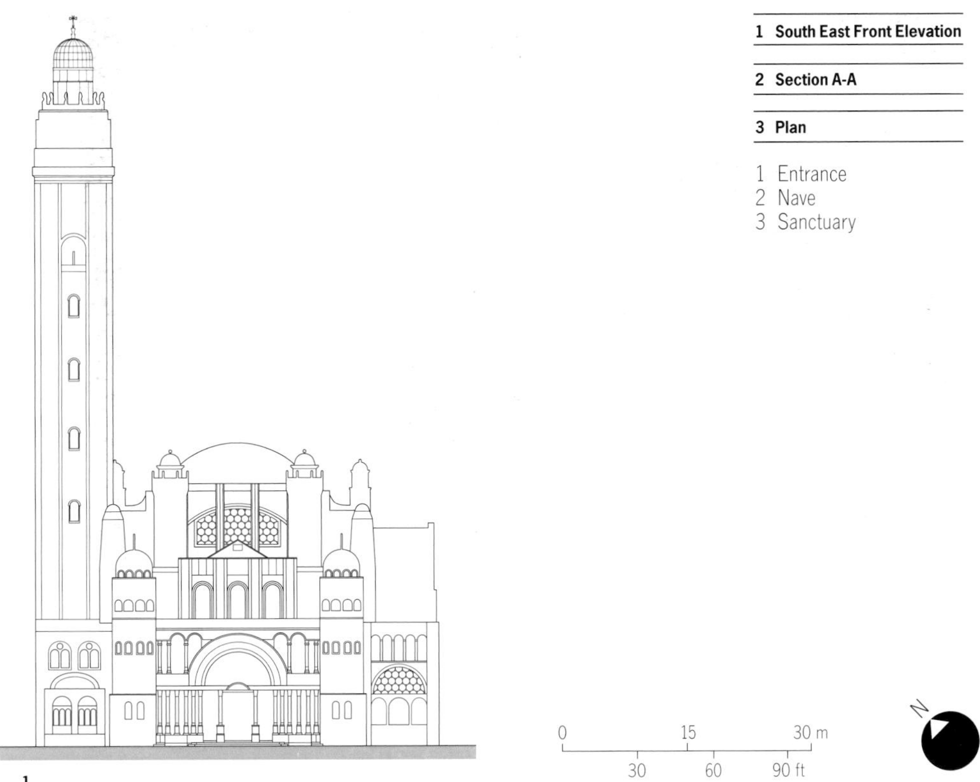

1

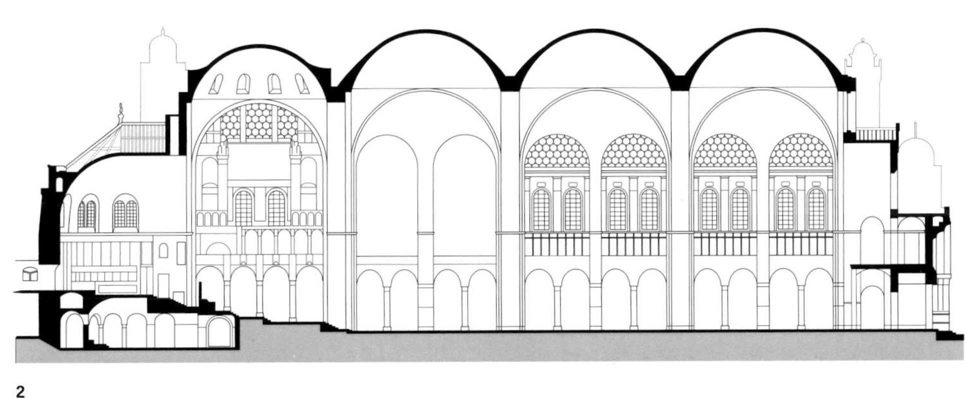

2

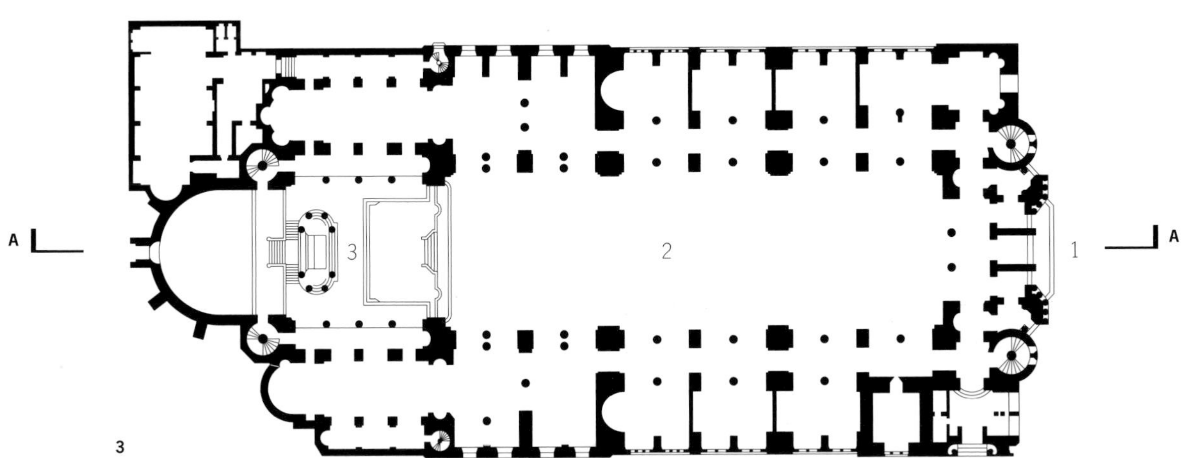

3

Great Mosque of Djenné

Djenné, Mali; 1907

Just south of the Sahara Desert, the River Niger – one of Africa's great rivers – meets an important tributary, the Bani. The ground here is fairly flat, and for most of the year the area is arid, but the volume of water in the rivers builds up so that they flood across a great plain between July and November, making the land fertile. It was here, at the Niger's inland delta, that the city of Djenné grew up. It was closely linked with Timbuktu – a further staging post on the trade route that carried salt, gold, ivory and slaves across the Sahara from the thirteenth to the beginning of the seventeenth century. After that, Timbuktu declined, having been completely dependent on its links with the world outside, and it has since become proverbially remote – an emblem of a place at the ends of the Earth.

Djenné had a more sustainable local economy and continued to thrive. It is vulnerable to the vagaries of the rivers, which do not bring as much water as they used to, and efforts are now being made to dam them, in order to be able to control the flooding and irrigate more land more effectively. The city is still left as an island during the months of flood, and the great mosque that dominates the urban fabric is a monument made of the mud that brings the community its life.

There has been a mosque at Djenné since the thirteenth century, when the city was probably part of the Mali Empire. It subsequently came under the control of the Songhai Empire, which flourished during the fifteenth and sixteenth centuries. It was controlled by Morocco during the seventeenth century and changed hands several more times before being annexed by the French in 1893.

The first European known to have visited Djenne, in 1829, was René Caillié, who found the old mosque still in use and impressive to see, but unpleasant to enter. He said that its courtyards were a preferable place for prayer because of the foul smell of the interior. During the 1830s the old mosque was knocked down and replaced with another one by Seku Amadu, an imam intent on reform. When the French took over in the 1890s, they rebuilt the old mosque, based on its remains, Caillié's account of it and local memory.

The building's form is regulated by the structural capability of mud, which can be moulded into high façades and towers as long as the walls are enormously thick. The structure is stabilized by the use of tree trunks as reinforcement – their regular projecting ends create the 'spikes' that are distinctive in the large monuments of this region. The dwellings here use a similar constructional method, but since they are smaller the mud comes under less strain. Nevertheless every householder knows how necessary it is to reapply a fresh layer of mud to the walls and roof every other year. In the case of the mosque it happens every year. The local people are aware that they have a remarkable monument on their hands, and when the flood is rising and the clay is ready, they cooperate by rallying in huge numbers to resurface it.

Even so, parts of the building have collapsed after exceptional heavy rain. This is a fragile architecture, which depends for its survival on the commitment of the community that sustains it. Internally it is sound and dry, and can accumulate the trappings of a settled place of worship, but externally the treatment is rigorously unornamented and very directly expresses the means of construction and the continuing care of many hands.

1 Plan

1 Prayer hall
2 Open-air prayer hall/ courtyard
3 Quibla/prayer wall facing Mecca
4 Main entrance

2 East Elevation

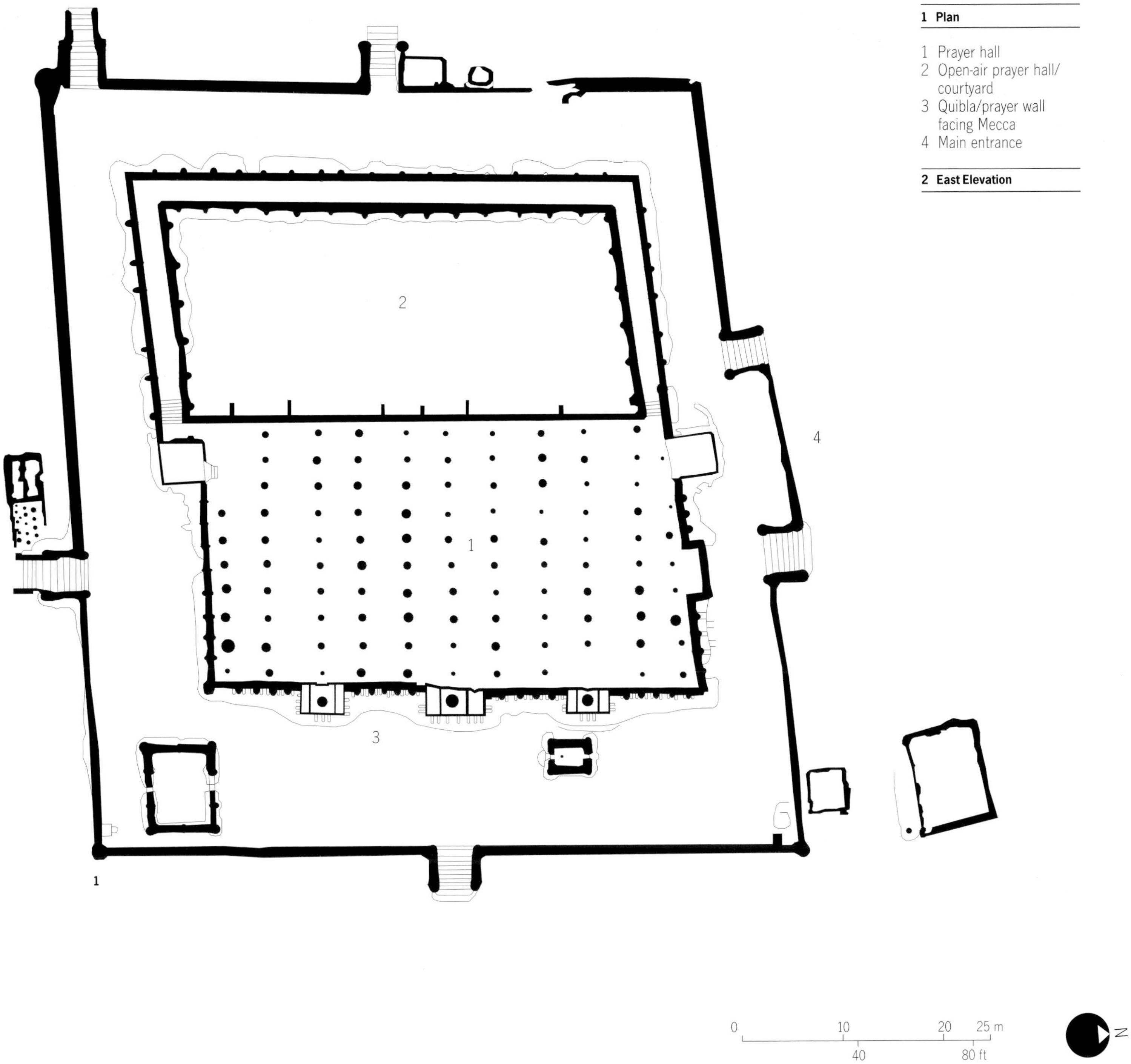

1

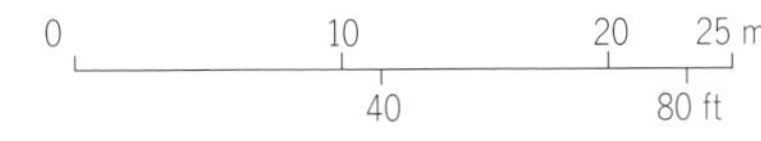

2

Crystal Cathedral

Johnson Burgee

Garden Grove, California, USA, 1978–80

Film-making developed in southern California because the region had regular bright sunlight and the early film-stock needed powerful light for it to work well. Now digital cameras make much less exacting demands on the cinematographer. In the 1970s television cameras still needed bright lights, and the Crystal Cathedral was built with television in mind. It was set up for the ministry of Robert H. Schuller, a televangelist, who had been broadcasting since 1970; before that Schuller had set up and run a drive-in church, commissioned in 1961 from Richard Neutra (1892–1970).

The Crystal Cathedral's name refers to the building from which the principal idea derives: the Crystal Palace of 1851. (Technically it is not a cathedral, but then nor was the Crystal Palace a palace, and nor was it crystal. To make too much of this would be to miss the point, which was to choose an evocative name.)

Structurally the building is a lattice of fine steel members which distribute the loads so that there is no intense build-up of forces that would need an intrusively large beam or column. The building's prismatic shape suggests that it might be made of solid glass. Its design was driven by similar impulses to those that guided the designers of the nave at Bourges (pages 136–37) – making a cage of light-filled space – but at Garden Grove the late twentieth-century technology allows the idea to be taken further. It is a dazzling technical achievement, which could easily be overlooked because it so nearly disappears.

The main space can seat 2,800 people, with raked seating directing attention towards a stage on which the pastor is joined by a choir arranged in front of two towers of organ pipes. The congregation in the building however is outnumbered by those who watch the broadcast version of the service, *The Hour of Power*, which reaches more than two million viewers, being syndicated on 165 television stations. In these circumstances, the building's location becomes insignificant. Its place in the city matters very much less than its place in the listings, so its location in the suburbs of Los Angeles (not far from Disneyland) is no disadvantage.

In 1978, when the church was being built, the architect, Philip Johnson, appeared on the cover of *Time* magazine holding a model of another large project: a Manhattan skyscraper with some classical detailing – especially a big broken pediment held against the sky. It made him the most famous architect in the world at the time, causing a sensation, in part because he had introduced the modernism of Mies van der Rohe to the USA in the 1930s, and had written persuasively in its praise. Johnson's switch to a more historical style seemed to many to be a form of betrayal. However, Johnson did not change his principles. He was already learning from historic buildings, learning from Mies's example, or, in the church here, learning from the Crystal Palace. It was a change of allusion, not a change of method.

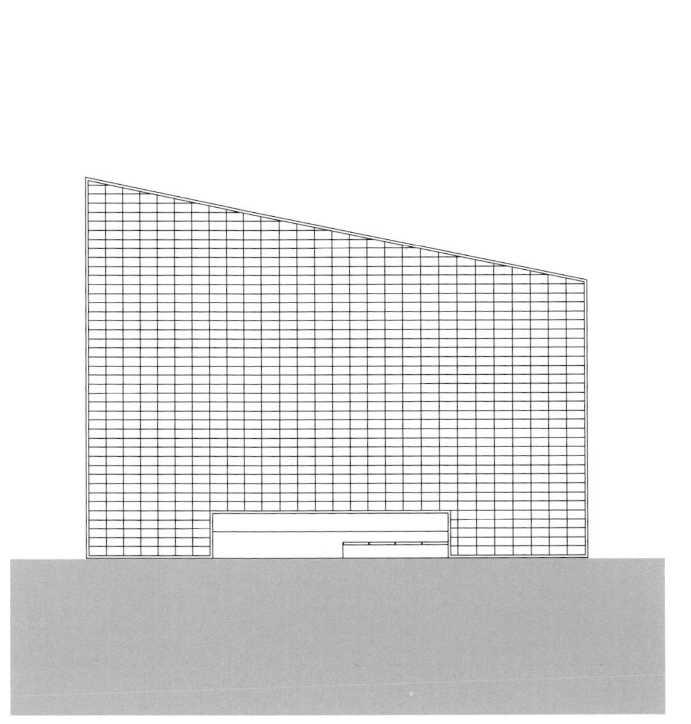

1

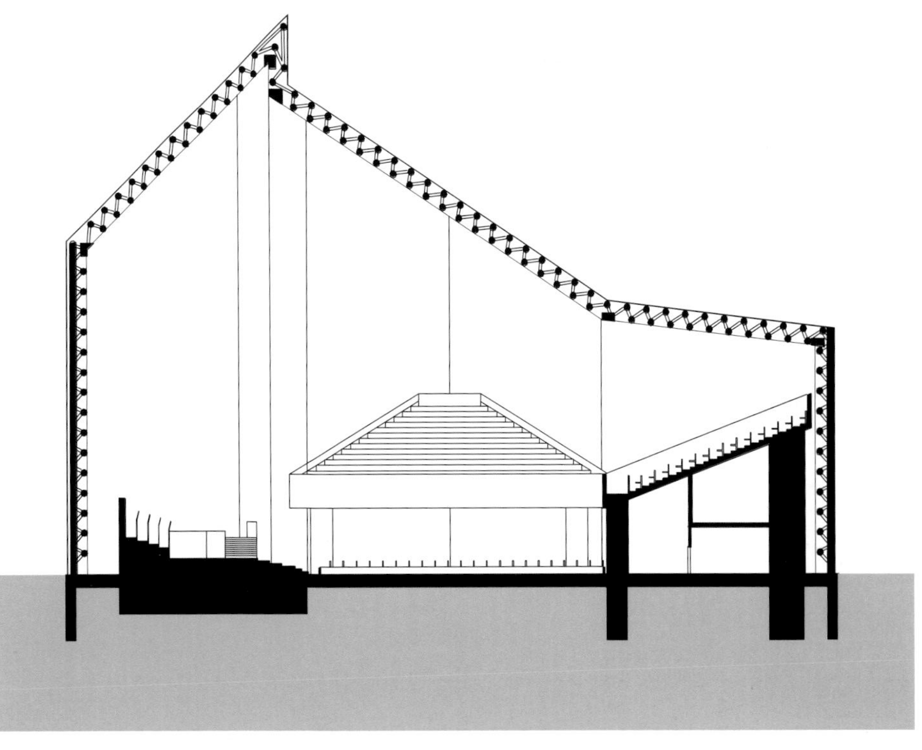

2

A

3

A

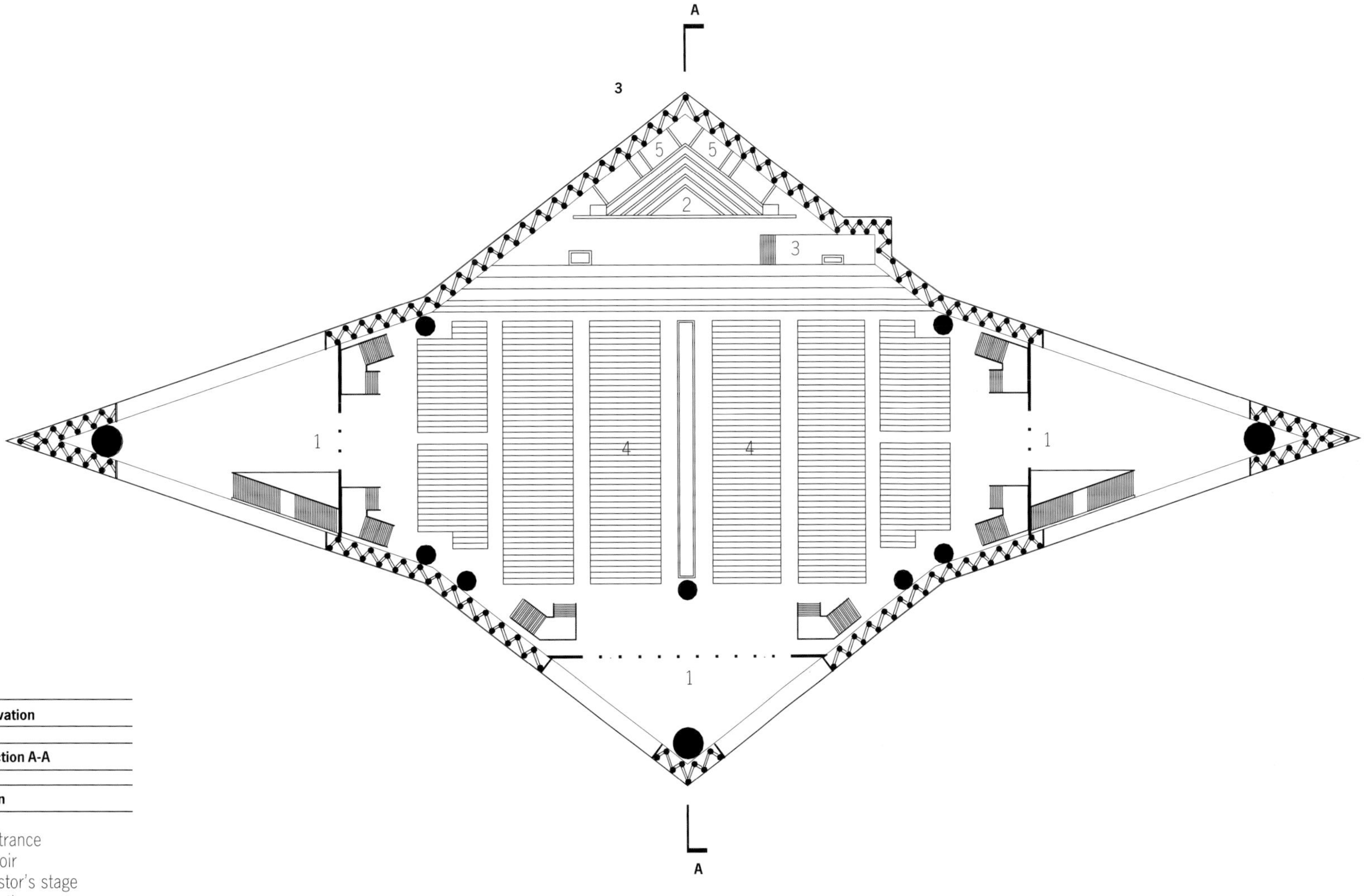

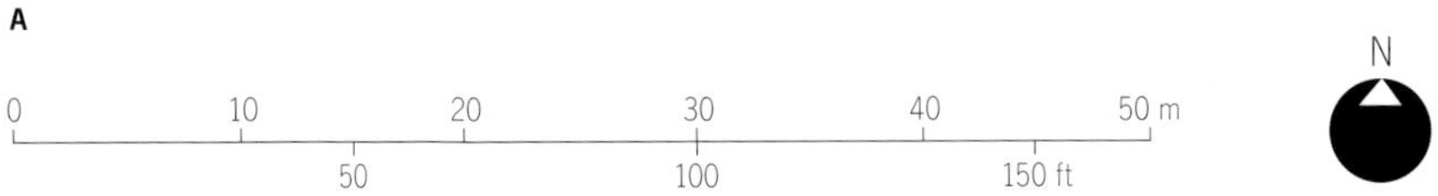

1 Elevation
2 Section A-A
3 Plan

1 Entrance
2 Choir
3 Pastor's stage
4 Seating
5 Organ pipes

0 10 20 30 40 50 m

50 100 150 ft

N

Bridges and Defences

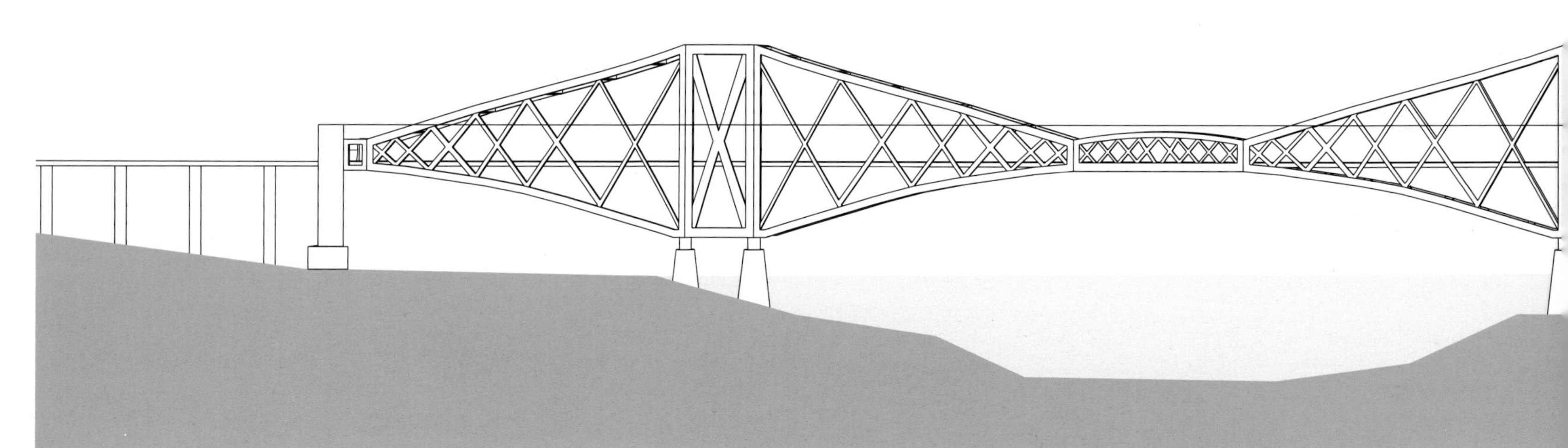

In principle, bridges and defences are utilitarian structures, but they have ways of taking on symbolic roles. Defences are barriers that protect and obstruct or control. Bridges make connections across rivers or chasms that might otherwise be defences. In time of war, of course, they both have military significance, but, even when their intended use is in abeyance, they have a cultural role that is usually more familiar.

The defensive walls of Carcassonne and Neuf-Brisach, for example, have not come under attack for generations, but they continue to give their towns a well-defined edge and a sense of identity. Carcassonne, in particular, has inspired visitors to come and daydream about the Middle Ages and siege warfare – which would have been squalid and grim when it happened centuries ago, but with enough historical distance can seem ingenious and even romantic.

Carthage's naval harbour was lethal in its day – a base for launching surprise attacks on enemy ships that was well concealed, disguised by the neighbouring commercial port. Himeji and the Athenian Acropolis were both citadels from which attacking forces could be sent out. The raised plateau of the Acropolis was later transformed into a religious sanctuary, but it reverted to military use under the Turks, who used the Parthenon as a store for gunpowder. The temple remained substantially intact until 1687, when a Venetian shell scored a direct hit and the whole store of explosives went up.

The Great Wall of China and the Roman frontiers, including Hadrian's Wall, were built to protect the citizens in their respective empires from outside attack. The Berlin Wall was built to keep out the influences of the west, and actually worked by keeping the East Berliners in.

All these walls were once militarized areas, but their cultural role is more enduring. They established the idea of zones of civilization and barbarism, safety and danger – danger that might combine fear of physical attack with a sense of moral panic.

The symbolic role of bridges in the Roman mind is recalled in the title *pontifex* – meaning, literally, 'bridge-builder' – which was given to the people who regulated the state religion. The emperor assumed the title *pontifex maximus* (chief bridge-builder) that was later used by popes. Had the city of Nîmes ever come under siege, its aqueduct, the Pont du Gard, would certainly have been destroyed by enemy action, to restrict the city's water supply. The Mostar Bridge actually was destroyed when Yugoslavia tore itself apart in 1993.

The imposing bridges of the modern age can take transport systems improbable distances across terrain that would otherwise be a barrier to speedy progress. The delicate cable supports of suspension bridges can carry roadways between continents and across wide estuaries with a grace that looks effortless.

High-speed-transport bridges are represented in this chapter by an old and heroic example: the Forth Rail Bridge in Scotland. Its tubular steel sections do not look as if they are working hard, but they still do the job of taking trains from Edinburgh to the north of the country.

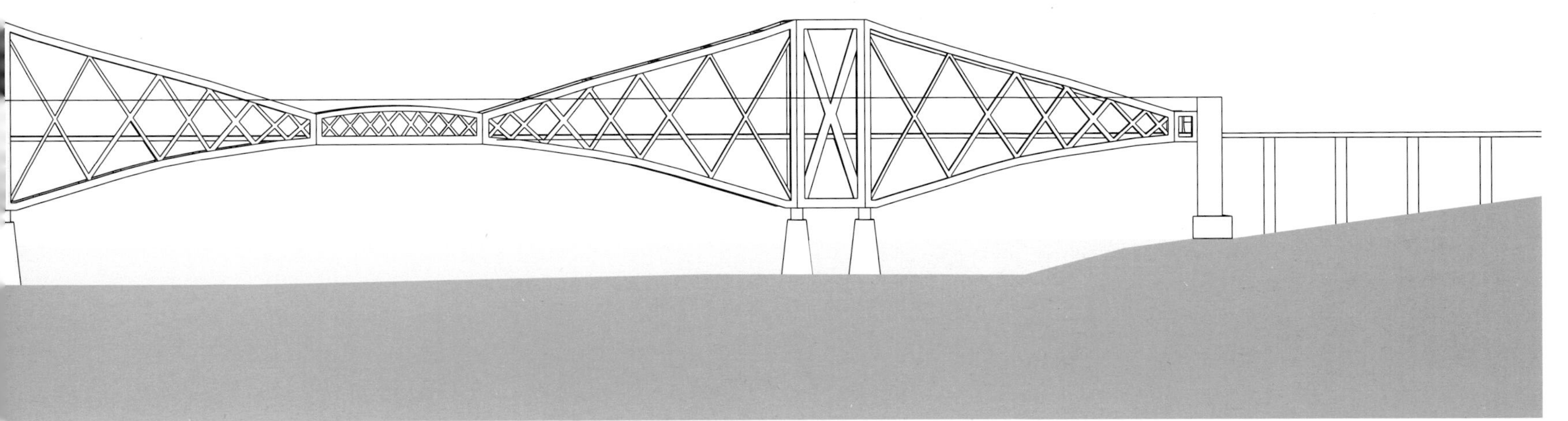

Acropolis of Athens

Athens, Greece; from c.1500 BCE

Used to designate a 'high city', acropolis actually means 'high part of a city'. There are many examples in Greece, but the most famous is in Athens, because that is where the spectacular monuments were built in the fifth century BCE. It is these monuments more than any others that have acted in modern times as ambassadors for ancient Greek culture. They have been admired and copied across the western world from the eighteenth century onwards. They were measured and documented by travellers from north-western Europe when Athens was still a small provincial town in the Ottoman Empire.

The civilization responsible for creating these monuments – principally the Parthenon (pages 16–17), the Erechtheion and the Propyleion – emerged over the course of about 300 years, preceded by an era that has traditionally been called the Greek Dark Age because hardly anything seemed to have survived from then. It is looking less dark than it used to, and one day there may be a coherent story to tell about what happened then.

What we can say is that, earlier still, there was a civilization in this region that produced monuments, statues and inscriptions, and that it died out about 1250 BCE – perhaps as the result of an invasion. Belonging to the Greek Bronze Age, that civilization is called Mycenean, after Mycenae, the first settlement of that era to be excavated. Between the end of the Bronze Age and the dawn of classical civilization, the culture went through a convulsion and came out of it reordered but with some cultural memory intact. Homer's epic poems about Troy and Odysseus are very old, maybe from the eighth century BCE, and are thought to include folk memories of real events in the Bronze Age, transmitted in an oral tradition before being written down. The kings and princes from the Bronze Age city-states, brought together to fight in Troy, become the mythic heroes of the Classical Age.

Something similar happened in the case of the architecture. A natural outcrop in a broad basin of land, bounded by mountains and clearly defensible, the Athenian Acropolis used to be a Mycenean citadel. Later – during the Classical Age – it became a sanctuary: the dwelling-place of the city's gods. This was far from unique. Classical sanctuaries had often been Mycenean settlements in an earlier era.

Athens's walls mark out different stages of its development. The Acropolis was extended in order to enlarge the sanctuary, but the inhabited part of the classical city was outside its cliffs and walls, on land that was protected by an encircling wall. Pericles, the great ruler of the fifth century BCE, who commissioned the Parthenon and much else besides, was responsible for the augmentation of the city's defences with walls that gave Athens a protected zone linking the city with its port, Piraeus, 10 km (6 miles) away.

Most of the space within the walls would have looked rather rural by modern standards. Monumental architecture was reserved for the public realm, concentrated around the Agora (pages 306–307) and on the Acropolis. Even the richest households kept the exteriors of their houses modest. There was plenty of open space, so that in time of war the surrounding populations and their herds could be brought in for safety. In Pericles' time, Sparta laid siege to Athens. The city became overcrowded and plague broke out, taking Pericles' sons before killing him. The walls could act as a trap as well as a defence.

1 Site Map

1 Piraeus
2 Long walls
3 Acropolis

2 Site Plan

1 Parthenon
2 Site of older temple
3 Erechtheion
4 Propyleion

3 Section A-A

1
2
3
N
0
1
2
3 km
1
2 miles

1

A
1
2
3
4
A
0
30
60
90 m
60
120
180
240 ft

2

0
30
60
90 m
60
120
180
240 ft

3

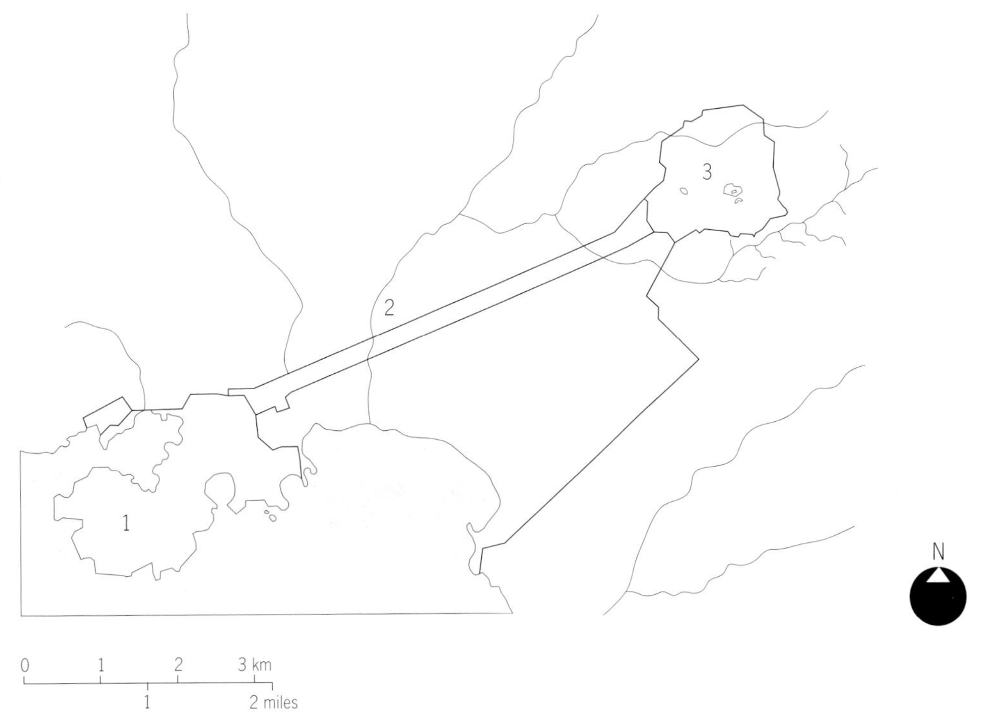

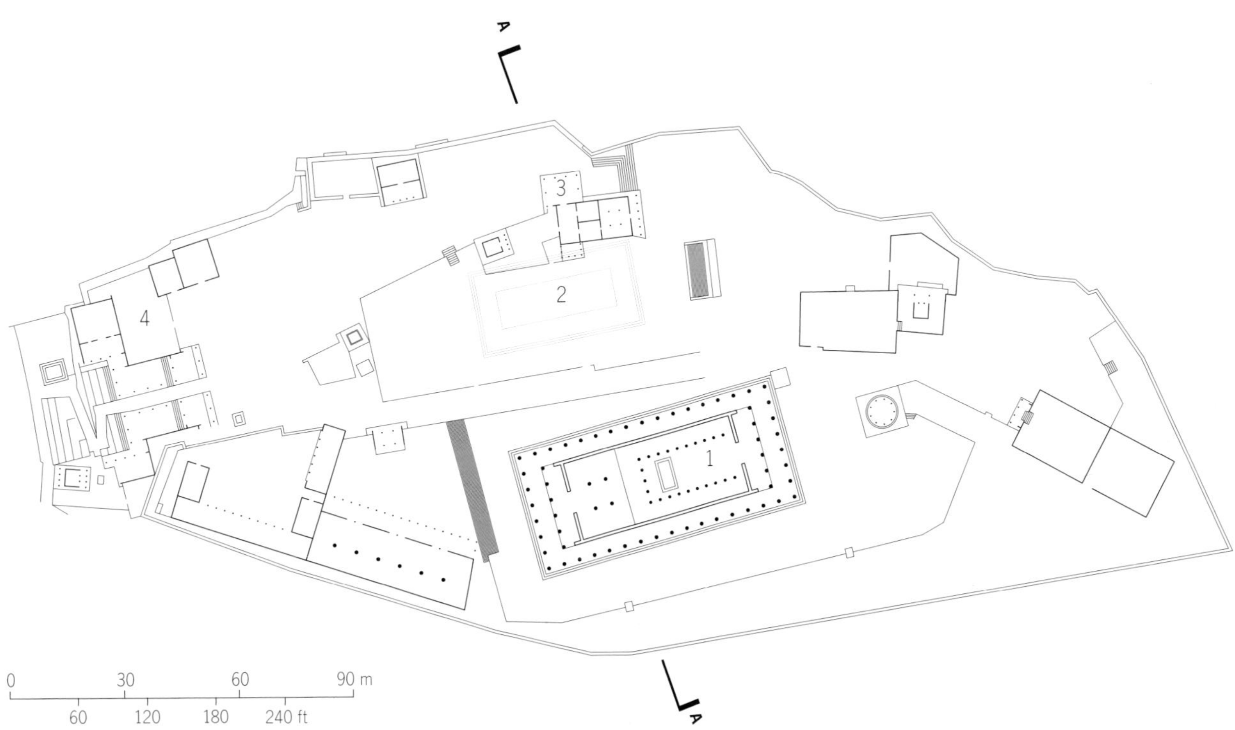

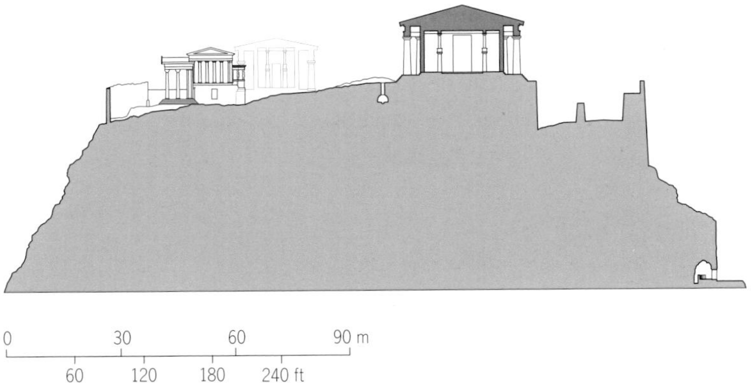

Carthage Harbour and Naval Base

Carthage, Tunisia

Carthage was the ancient rival of Rome for a while. Alluding to the Carthaginians' Phoenician heritage, the Romans used the word Punic to describe them, and the antagonism between the two peoples developed through the Punic Wars.

Carthage is located on the north African coast at a point where the Mediterranean is quite narrow, and Sicily and Italy are not far away. There is desert to the south – so, for a state that had territorial ambitions to equal Rome's, the annexation of Sicily was an obvious first step.

During the period of the first Punic War (264–61 BCE), Carthage had a superior navy but the Romans learned to outwit it. They were later humiliated in a famous attack by the Carthaginian general Hannibal, but exacted revenge by destroying the city of Carthage in 146 BCE, burning it to the ground and building a Roman temple on its most sacred site, as well as filling the naval port with rubble to make it inoperable.

The Romans' complete destruction of the earlier city makes it difficult to retrieve an image of pre-Roman Carthage and it is best known as a mythical idea from Virgil's treatment in the *Aeneid*. Virgil's poem, a Roman epic to rival Homer's *Odyssey*, tells the story of Aeneas, a Trojan who left the city when it was defeated by the Greeks, taking with him his household gods, which went with him to Italy. By Virgil's time, these tokens from Troy were to be found in the temple of Vesta in Rome, helping to give Rome its special sense of destiny and a link to one of the great cities of the past. The other great city in the story is Carthage, where Aeneas is described as romantically involved with the city's founder, Dido, of whom there is no historical record. Virgil is symbolically suggesting in their dalliance, and in Aeneas' desertion of Dido, that there was a time when the special destiny might have come to rest in Carthage, but (to Carthage's despair) it found its way to Rome.

Despite the competition, Carthage did annex Spain before ceding to Rome, and even for the Romans the battles were no pushover. Their use of crucifixion as a punishment was learnt from the equally ruthless Carthaginians.

Carthage's international power emanated from its navy, based in a harbour that survives – or has been reclaimed – in outline. There was a round pool with a circular island in the middle of it, reached by a narrow causeway. On the island and around the edge, the Punic battleships could be kept, battle-ready, in dry dock on stone-block slipways. At very short notice, 222 ships could be launched and set on their way. The naval base was hidden and could only be approached by way of a much larger commercial port, which made it difficult for an enemy to find the base to attack it.

The Roman city is also long gone, but the ancient sacred hill still remains, looking down on the basin. There is no sign of the Roman temple that was once here, but the neglected baroque Cathedral of St Louis, with which the French declared their claim on the place in 1884, still stands.

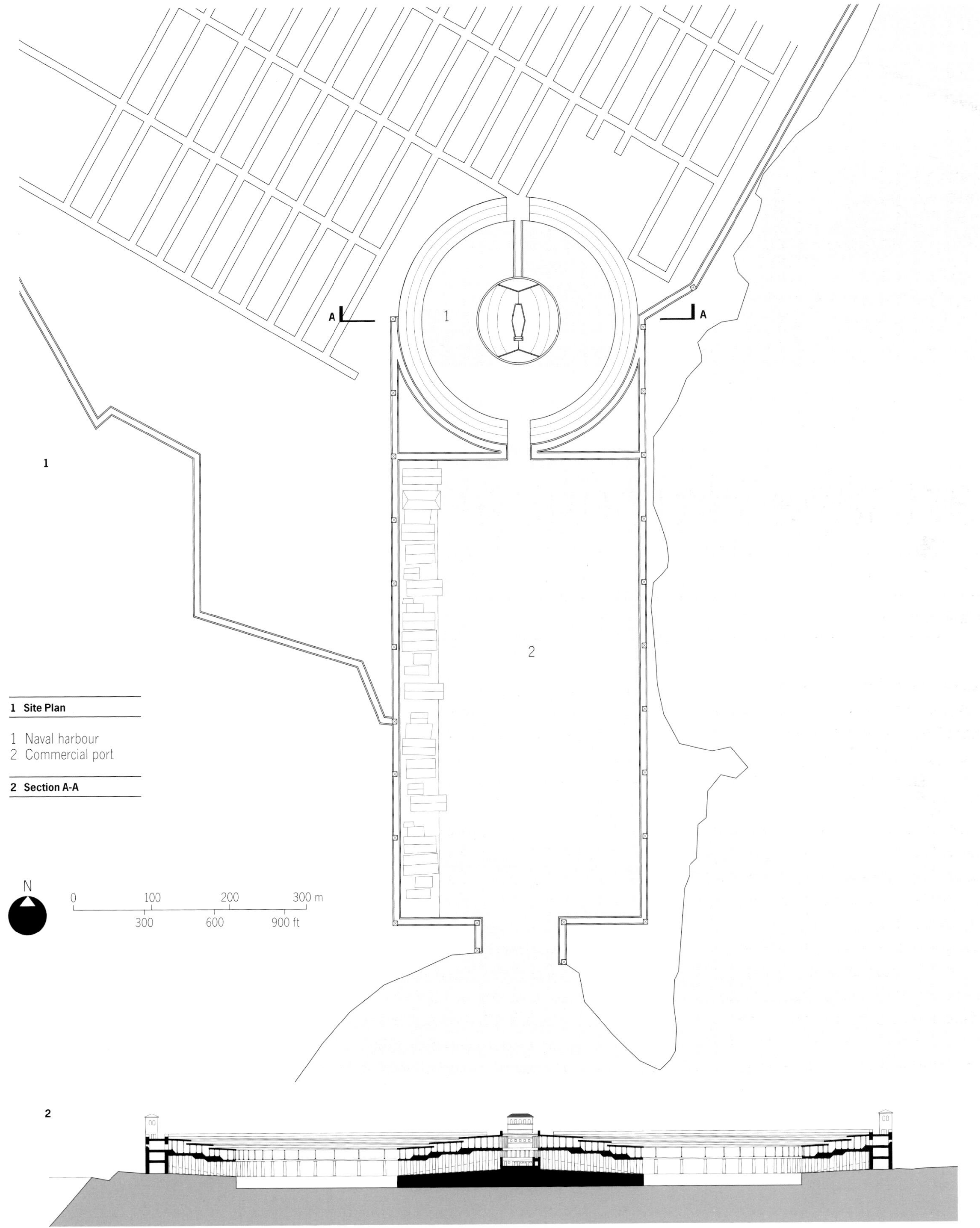

1 Site Plan

1 Naval harbour
2 Commercial port

2 Section A-A

Pont du Gard

Nîmes, France; c.20 BCE

The Romans brought urbanism to places that had never experienced it before. Before the advent of motorized transport and mass production, people in rural districts would have done for themselves everything necessary for their own sustenance. In a city it is possible to develop a specialism – to make shoes, do joinery or make fine pottery. With enough people around to make use of the specialized work, a business can thrive. The larger the city, the more specialized the trades are likely to become. And the more specialized the business, the more efficiently and skilfully the goods can be produced, and the more refined they can be. There are distinct advantages for a society that has a network of cities.

Across the Roman Empire, roads made it possible to maintain links between cities and between the provinces and the supreme powers in Rome, which consumed a steady supply of the world's most luxurious goods. Provincial cities were lower down the command structure, but a regional administrative centre such as Nîmes plainly enjoyed a form of life that was very sophisticated compared with that of the countryside.

The Pont du Gard, as it is now called, was part of Nîmes's infrastructure. The city consumed crops and minerals from the surrounding rural areas, and also water. Some of its water supply reached the city by way of the Pont du Gard, which was built to carry a stream of water across a steep valley (with another river at the bottom of it).

The bridge's purpose lies in the channel that runs across the top, closed in from the sky with stone slabs, and the rest of the bridge was built to hold that channel in place. Its position is exact. The water was brought almost 50 km (30 miles), and along that distance it dropped only about 17 metres (56 feet), so the watercourse was almost flat – but not quite. Water cannot be persuaded to flow uphill, and had the engineering been less precise – if the watercourse had wandered up and down even a little – the water supply would not have flowed at all. In fact, it flowed well, and continued in use for some 800 years, until sustained neglect meant that the watercourse silted up and stopped working.

In spite of the fact that the bridge is an impressive monument, it was not built as a monument. The construction is in blocks of stone that were neither decorated nor trimmed to an even surface. To make the arches, stone blocks were put in position on timber formwork, which held them in place until there was a complete arch that could support itself. Then the temporary timber structure was taken away and moved to the next arch that was being built. These timbers were large because they had for a while to support very heavy masonry. They rested on projecting stone corbels – blocks that were longer than the blocks above them – and, if the building had been intended for public view, these projections would have been chiselled off. But at the Pont du Gard they are still in place. The aqueduct, which is now one of the most visited monuments in France, was built as a self-effacing part of the city's infrastructure, lost in the countryside.

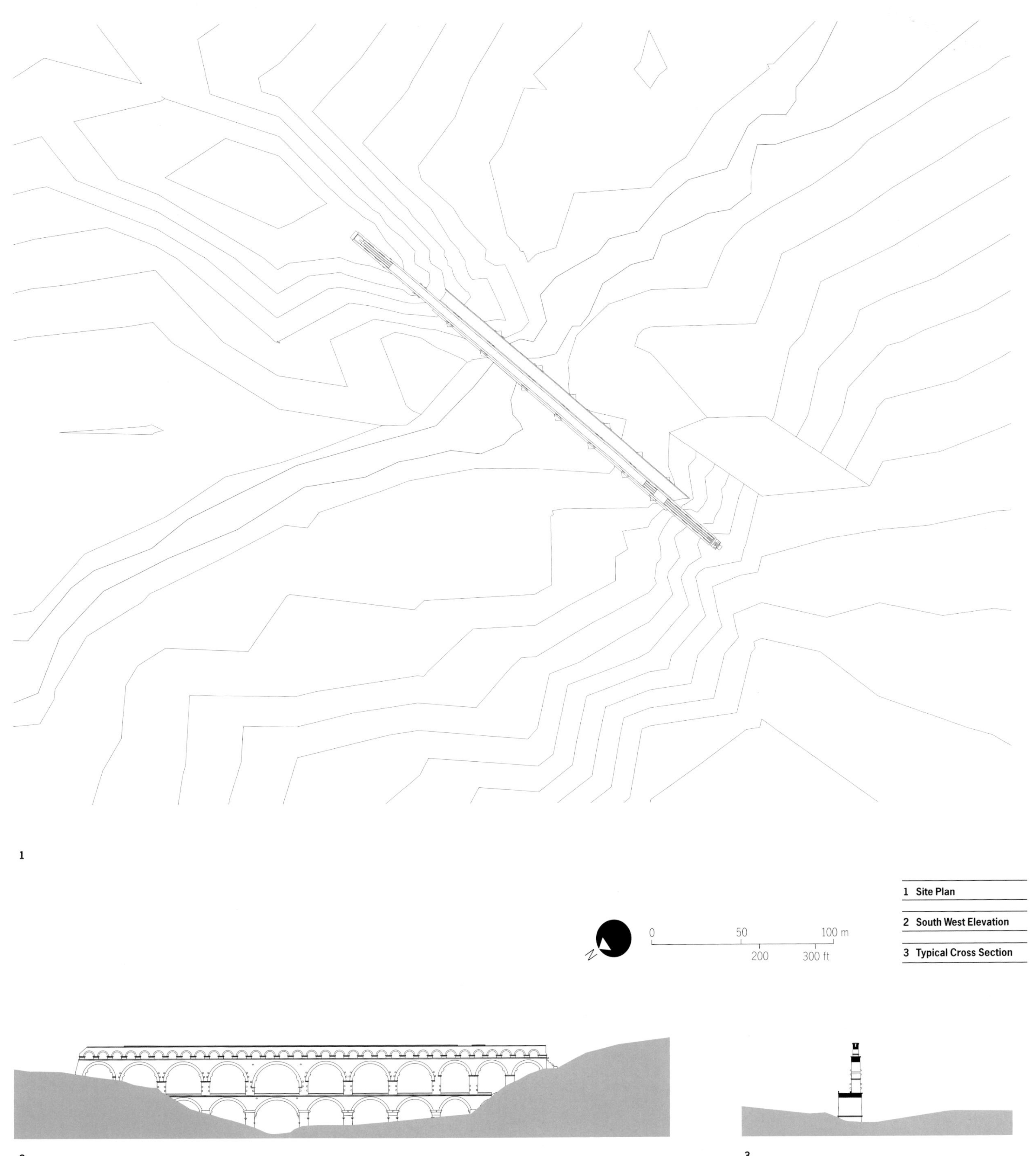

1 Site Plan

2 South West Elevation

3 Typical Cross Section

Frontiers of the Roman Empire

Rhaetian Wall; from c.73 | Hadrian's Wall; from c.122 | Antonine Wall; 142–54

The Roman Empire established the Roman way of life across a vast territory that encircled the Mediterranean, taking in land on three continents – Europe, Africa and Asia – as well as some further-flung places such as the island of Britannia.

The border between the zone of civilization and the surrounding barbarian territories was called the *limes*, or limit. There were places where natural boundaries meant that the *limes* did not need definition – where a range of mountains or a body of water separated the populations on each side. A long stretch of the Rhaetian Wall, for example, ran along the bank of the River Danube.

People at the edges of the empire had to put up with disadvantages such as having to pay taxes to Rome and the fact that a foreign law was enforced by foreign soldiers. But there were also advantages, such as protection against the depredations of rival tribes and links to a system of patronage that could boost the career of a man with ambition, especially if he were prepared to travel. Roman law was enforced by Roman citizens who came from all over the empire, not only from Rome.

There were places where the boundaries had to be defined, in order to prevent illicit traffic across them. A well-managed farm in the empire might be producing valuable crops and livestock, and it was believed that the benefits from it should flow to the local community and to Rome, not to the warlords of Arabia, Germania or Caledonia. The boundaries covered a total of some 5,000 km (3,100 miles); in places they were fortified, and some fortifications survive – a length of wall here, a reconstructed fort there. The best-preserved stretches are parts of the Limes Tripolitanus in north Africa, the Limes Germanicus–Rhaetia in modern Switzerland and Germany, which was 500 km (310 miles) long with 900 watchtowers and 120 forts, and the Limes Britannicus in England – known as Hadrian's Wall (shown above) – which ran across the island at a narrow point, 120 km (75 miles) wide, with the same frequency and the same patterns for the towers and forts as was used in Germany.

The borders shifted when new territories were annexed, but sometimes these territories were more trouble than they were worth. Hadrian's Wall was superseded for a while by the Antonine Wall further north – 63 km (40 miles) long and made mainly of turf mounds, and therefore less monumental and less well preserved, but effective in its day. It was abandoned after 20 years, and Hadrian's Wall resumed its role as the frontier.

When they took the form of structures, the boundaries were defensive, allowing traffic to pass through at fortified gates. The Roman army, recruited from around the empire, was mostly deployed at the borders, with relatively little presence elsewhere.

Except when required to make a territorial advance, Roman troops were not supposed to cross into the untamed territories, which were seen as synonymous with barbarism and savagery – more from superstition than on the basis of direct contact. In the mind of a Roman citizen, the *limes* represented the ultimate extremity of civilized life.

1 Map Showing Wall Routes

2 Plan of Saalburg Fort, Germany

3 Elevation of Saalburg Fort

4 Plan of Turret on Germanic Limes

5 Section of Germanic Limes

6 Section of Hadrian's Wall Turret

7 Section of Hadrian's Wall

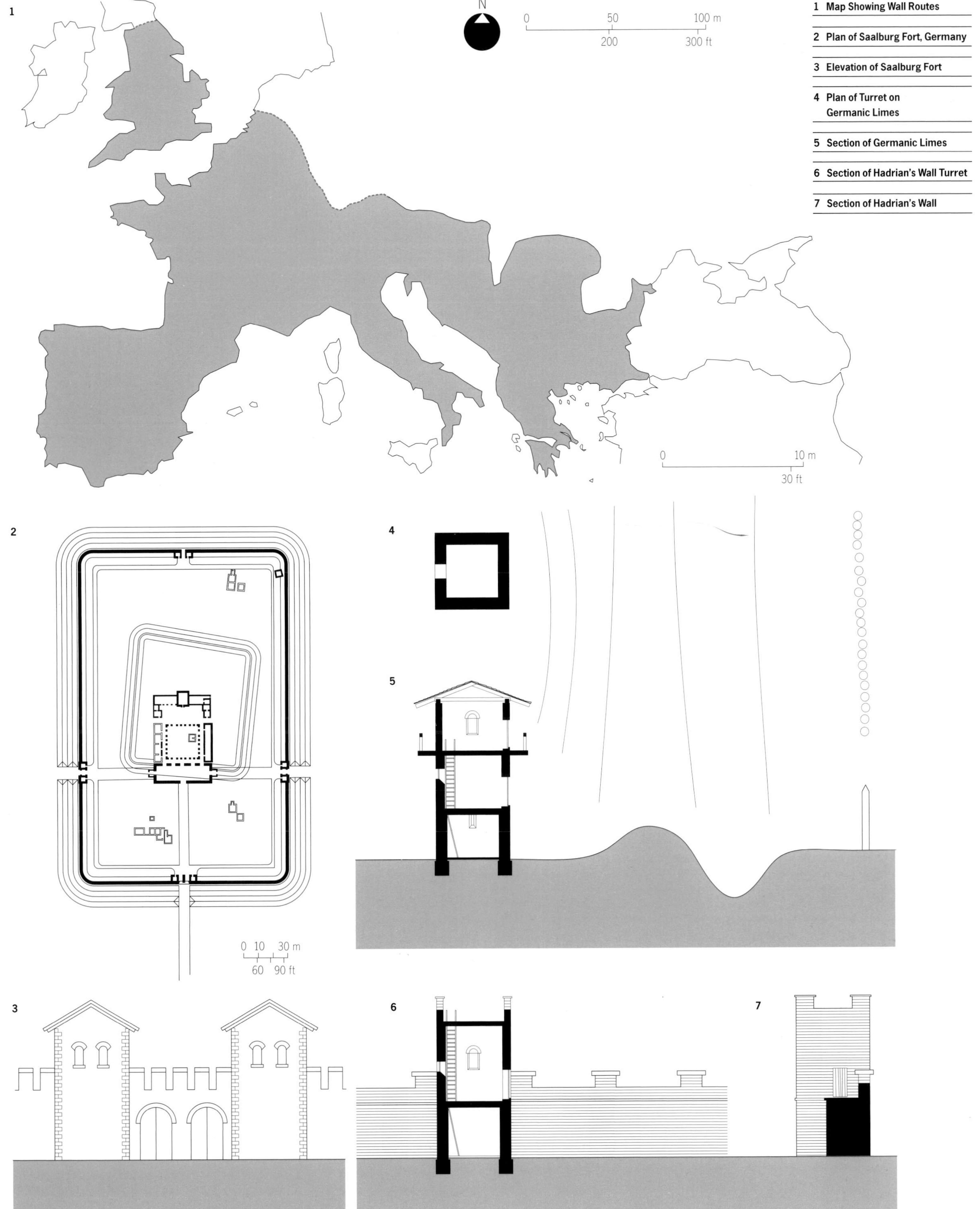

Himeji Castle

Himeji, Kansai, Honshu, Japan; founded 1333

Himeji Castle's history is long, complex and well documented but, since its various extensions involved the demolition of earlier work, its present manifestation is a hilltop fortification of the early seventeenth century, when the Lord of Himeji was Honda Tadamasa (1575–1631) – a daimyo, answerable only to the shogun. Many castles from this period were destroyed during the nineteenth century, so Himeji has rarity value. It is the best preserved of the samurai castles, and the largest, with dozens of minor buildings inside its walls.

With an estimated 25 million man-days devoted to its construction, Himeji has always been special. The territory over which the castle presided was a vast estate, 650 km (400 miles) west of Tokyo, producing enough to feed 150,000 people, and it was never successfully attacked. Over the years, the main threat to the castle's preservation turned out to be the high cost of its upkeep after the old feudal system had passed away and there was no longer a military role for its commanders.

The tallest part of the castle is its keep, with seven floors and sloping roofs that give it a pagoda-like silhouette. It has few openings to the outside on its exposed façade but it is lit and ventilated from the side that overlooks a protected courtyard. The lower reaches are mainly built very solidly in masonry, but the walls to the upper floors are timber, which is covered in a thick layer of plaster as protection against fire.

On the topmost floor there was an altar, and one of the courtyards was designated as the proper place for ritual suicide if occasion demanded it. The keep's white-plastered walls and its position on high ground overlooking the surrounding plain made people think of it as a bird preparing to fly – and it is sometimes called the 'white egret castle' or 'white heron castle'.

Guarded by a system of defensive walls and moats up to 20 metres (65 feet) wide, the keep was the most strongly protected part of the castle. There were three moats, and the walls overlooking them had small apertures to allow the firing of arrows or muskets, and projections that made it possible to drop rocks and boiling water on attackers.

The tortuous routes of paths through these outer defences were designed to disorientate people who were unfamiliar with the place. Similar defensive strategies could be found elsewhere, but at no other place were they more highly developed. The outer reaches of the castle encompassed more than a kilometre in each direction. Much of this has now been landscaped as parkland, so it seems unconnected with the idea of fortification, but the wandering paths that guide visitors through gateways and gardens on the approach to the castle are still as confusing as they were designed to be.

1 Site Plan

1 Castle keep
2 Moat
3 Fortification

2 Elevation

3 Section A-A

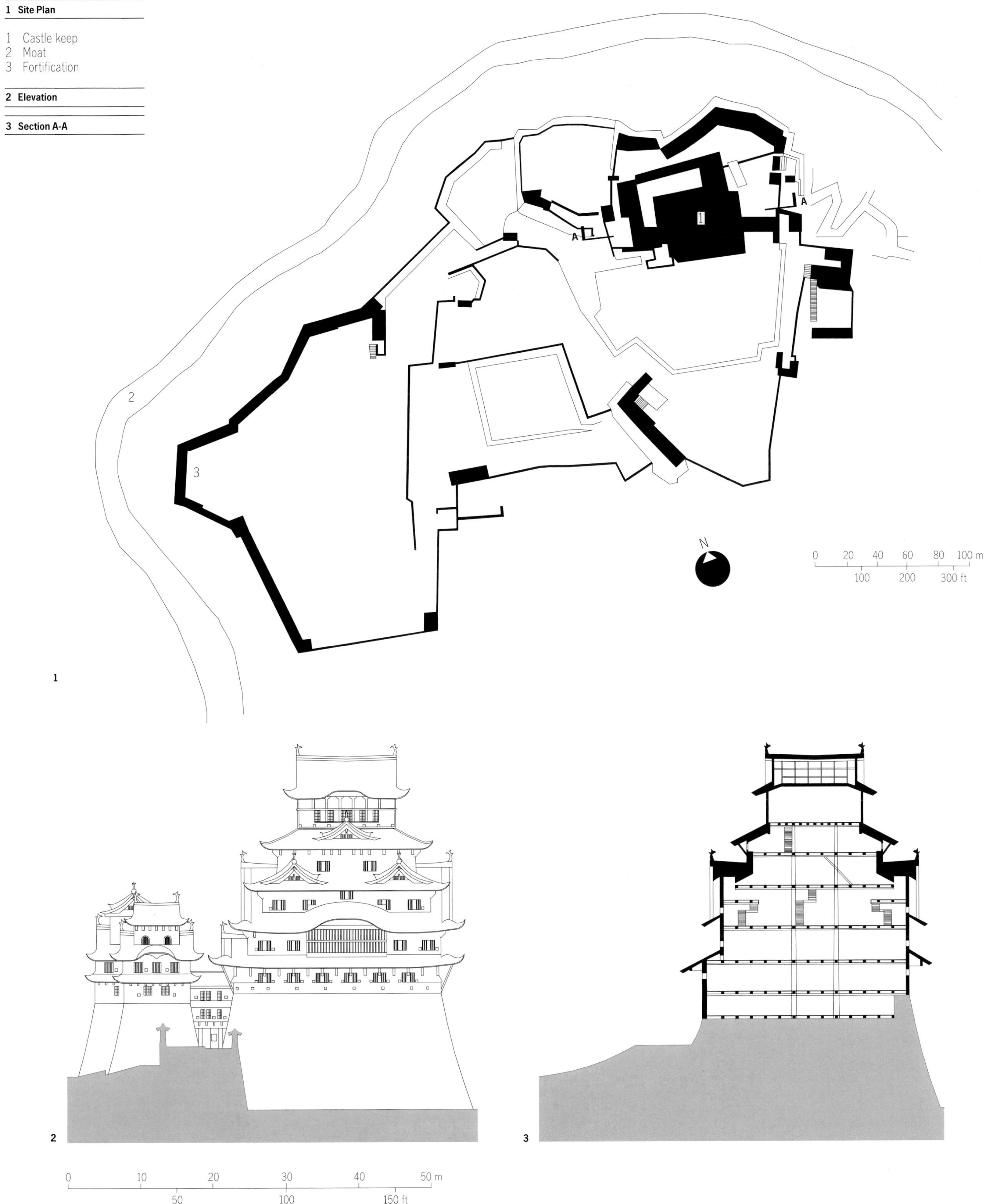

Great Wall of China

China; from 1449

Nomadic warrior tribes from Mongolia established a great empire under their leader Genghis Khan (1206–27). It stretched from eastern Europe across the north of India into China – the Mongols destroyed Beijing – and as far north as anyone wanted to live. Genghis's grandson Kublai Khan (1215–94) took control of China as the founder of the Yuan Dynasty.

Traditionally, the achievements of civilizations such as the Mongols have been marginalized by architectural historians. Being nomadic, they built no monuments, but they clearly had the upper hand. The Mongols' great invention was the stirrup, and their skill at horsemanship was admired, but above all their sedentary neighbours feared their savagery. If a town resisted but fell to them, the captured townsfolk would be executed en masse. If there was any doubt about a conflict's outcome – and their fighting skills and determination were legendary – it was prudent to welcome the Mongols in, let them take as much treasure and provisions as they wanted, and allow them be on their way. At least then there was some possibility of recovery.

The Great Wall of China is a less unified project than at first it seems, with various attempts at building extensive defences against the Mongol hordes and their predecessors, but the wall as we know it was constructed during the Ming Dynasty (1368–1644). The earlier walls, mainly of rammed earth, had been insufficient to protect China against its predatory northern neighbours, and when the idea of a wall was revived it was made more solid than ever, using fired bricks and stone.

The Yuan emperors had taken little interest in administration and, by the time the dynasty foundered, the country was at war with itself and being preyed upon by bands of wild horsemen that the government could not control. By contrast, the emperors of the Ming Dynasty were bureaucratic and effective governors of a sedentary state. They conceived the Great Wall as a way of keeping the Mongols at bay.

Begun in 1449, the wall eventually stretched across more than 6,000 km (3,700 miles) – or 8,000 km (5,000 miles) if the natural features along the way that acted as an equivalent barrier are included. It is an extraordinary feat of organization – a measure of how much the Mongol hordes were feared – and the millions of working lives that were used up in its construction were guided by enough common purpose to achieve a coherent result. The wall was well maintained and remained as an effective protection into the seventeenth century. It has become emblematic of the power of collective effort.

The story that the Great Wall can be seen from the Moon is a fabrication – but it is a potent myth that continues to circulate, even though it has been repudiated by astronauts. It seems to have originated in a speculation by William Stukeley (1687–1785). Not only was Stukeley in no position to know, but he had a reputation as a fantastist, having invented the modern idea of the ancient British Druid (on the basis of very little evidence).

The Great Wall was a straightforward idea, based on the practical desire to keep people safe in their homes. For an individual devoting a life to the project, it must have felt much like any other building project, but the vast scale of the common effort, the ingenuity with which it deals with the varied conditions along the way, and the accidentally picturesque effects of the wall ascending through mountainous scenery, have made it a thing that stirs the imagination and takes it completely outside the realm of ordinary experience.

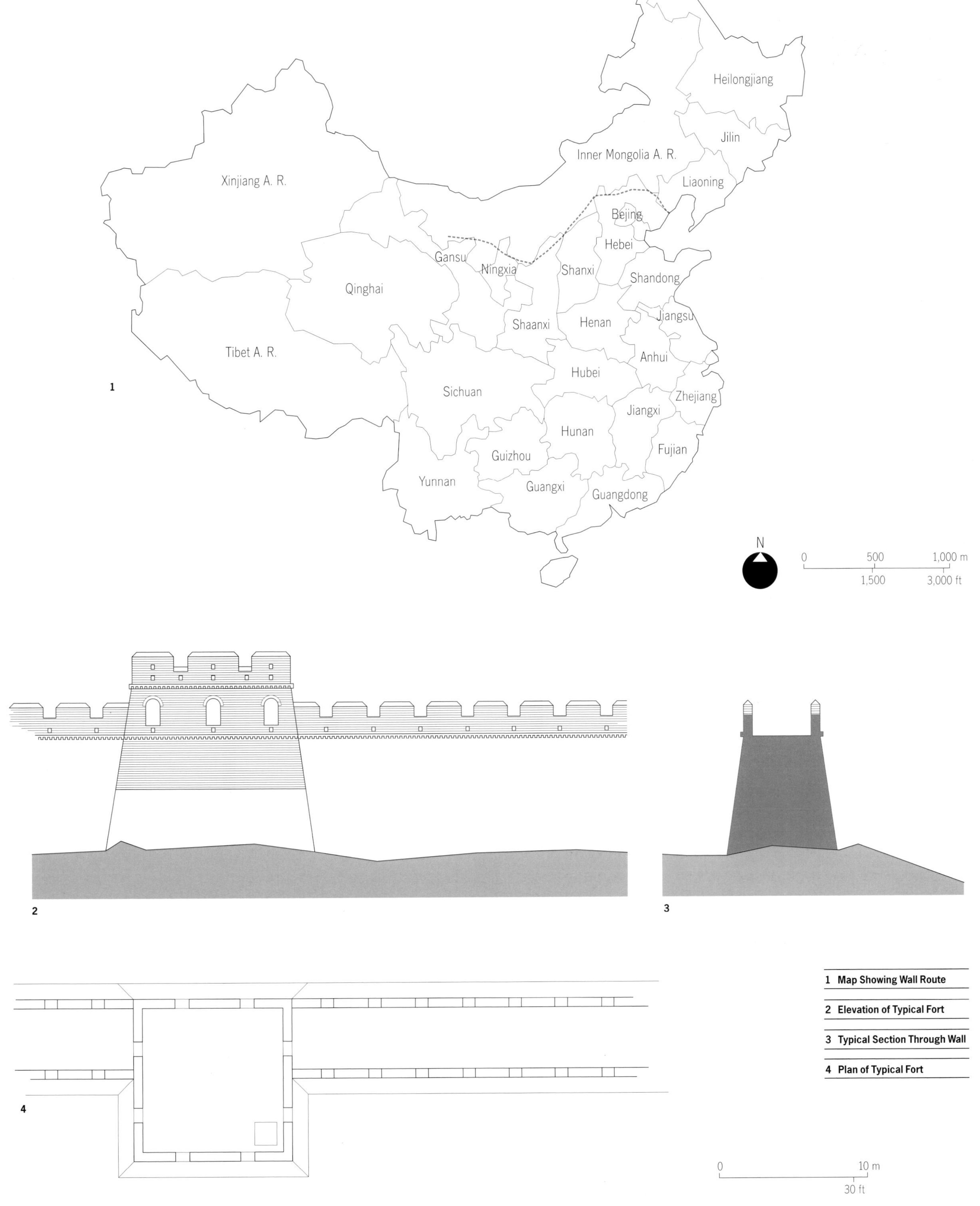

1 **Map Showing Wall Route**

2 **Elevation of Typical Fort**

3 **Typical Section Through Wall**

4 **Plan of Typical Fort**

Mostar Bridge

Mimar Hayrüddin

Bosnia and Herzegovina; 1557–66

Taking its names from the Balkan Mountains, the Balkan peninsula is the most easterly of the three main peninsulas of Europe – the others being Iberia (Spain and Portugal) and Italy. It has been governed as a part of several empires. Slavs settled there, followed by mobile populations connected with the Holy Roman Empire, run from Vienna; the Byzantine Empire, run from Constantinople; and the Ottoman Empire, run from Istanbul (as Constantinople had become).

Differences in local histories and loyalties have produced a mixed population that includes various ethnic groups of different faiths: Catholic and Orthodox Christians, and Muslims. With the dissolution of the empires, national boundaries have been drawn and redrawn, identities discovered and asserted, and populations have moved to territories where they feel safer.

When Mostar Bridge was built in the mid-sixteenth century, it was in the Ottoman Empire, and the ruling class was a cosmopolitan elite. The architect, Mimar Hayrüddin, had been a marble-cutter but had been elevated to the corps of royal architects and worked for Sinan, the architect of the Suleyman Mosque (pages 150–51), initially as an assistant but then with more autonomy. One of Sinan's key achievements was to organize the implementation of building designs in a way that ensured consistency, reliability and a recognizable style across the empire. While buildings were adapted to suit local circumstances, they tended to incorporate standard elements, which made their production quicker, and the team of people that Sinan assembled perpetuated their methods across several generations. It is likely that Hayrüddin was also responsible for Karagöz Mehmed Beg Mosque in Mostar, which is a hundred metres away from the bridge and is sometimes attributed to Sinan.

Mostar was made by its bridge: *mostar* means 'bridge keepers'. There was a fort here, and a timber bridge was built in the fifteenth century, when the place was known as Pons (the Latin for 'bridge'). It came under Ottoman control in 1468 and was known as Köprühisar ('fortress at the bridge'). It was developed as the centre for administration in the Herzegovina region and was organized with commercial activity on one side of the river and a residential area on the other.

The bridge was rebuilt in stone from 1557 on the orders of Suleyman the Magnificent. It is protected by a small fort at each end, showing its continuing strategic importance as a part of a route for the transport of minerals that links inland mines with the Adriatic coast – but the main engineering achievement is the arch, spanning the river in a single graceful curve. The span was made possible by the cliffs on each side of the river at this point, which are immobile and can resist the strong outward pressures made by the arch. If the arch had been shallower, a level road might have been built across the top of the bridge, but the engineer's prudence kept it high, and the upper surface is stepped and slopes quite steeply.

The Ottoman Empire dissolved during World War I, and the region was incorporated in the new kingdom of Yugoslavia in 1918. The bridge was much appreciated for its picturesque qualities when tourism developed there in the later twentieth century, but the town's complex history made it a contested site during the war that saw the break-up of the former Yugoslavia, replaced in this area by Bosnia and Herzegovina. During that war, in 1993, the old bridge was destroyed. It was subsequently rebuilt, and in 2005 it was inscribed as a UNESCO World Heritage Site, partly for its historic value, but also more significantly for its symbolic value, as an emblem of hoped-for reconciliation and harmony in a multicultural population.

1 Site Plan

2 Elevation

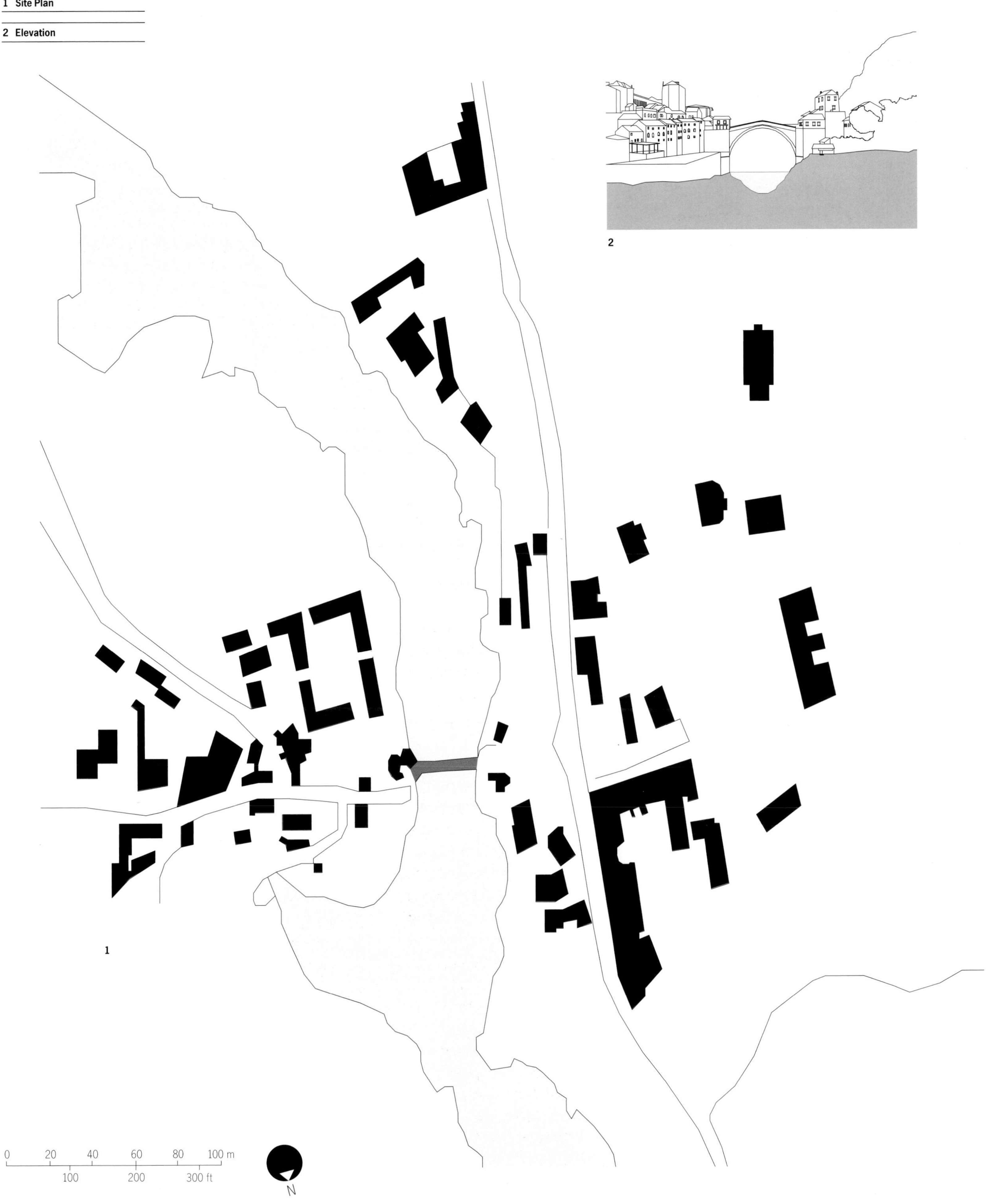

Neuf-Brisach

Sébastien Le Prestre, Marquis de Vauban, 1633–1707

Alsace, France; 1698–1712

Vauban was Louis XIV's principal military engineer, and he was responsible for fortifications around the perimeter of France, consolidating the sense of the nation as a stronghold. His base was the chateau at Bazoches in Burgundy, from which he had a distant view of the Basilica of the Madeleine at Vézelay (pages 130–31), and from this central location he sent out instructions to the borders in every direction. He was buried in the little church at Bazoches, but Napoleon found him such an inspiration that he had his corpse exhumed. Vauban's heart is now in a lead casket, reburied, near Napoleon himself, under the dome at Les Invalides (pages 298–99).

Some of Vauban's fortifications were based on established medieval strongholds that took advantage of natural features, but the building at Brisach is of particular interest because it is on flat ground and is therefore the example of Vauban's work that comes closest to his models of the ideal fortified town, enclosed in regular geometric figures.

Neuf-Brisach (French) or Neu Breisach (German) is situated 4 km (2.5 miles) from the River Rhine, on land that changed hands between French and German rulers both before and after its construction. It replaced an earlier town on the other side of the river, which was extended with a fortified settlement on an island, but both had to be surrendered to the Prussians under a treaty of 1697 and were razed to the ground.

Vauban saw the land immediately next to the river as vulnerable to attack, so he established a new settlement a short distance away – beyond the reach of cannon firing from Prussian territory. But a town was needed here, to protect a bridge – the only one across the Rhine on the major route between Basel and Strasbourg.

Neuf-Brisach consists of a squared grid of streets and a large central public space, enclosed within a system of multiple fortified walls and bastions designed to withstand attack from cannon and artillery. In comparison with the protected inner district, the spread of the fortifications is vast – significantly greater in area than that of the inhabited part of the town.

The walls are basically octagonal in plan, but with projections that make it possible for guns to be turned on any attackers who might reach the walls. There were multiple obstacles to prevent such an eventuality, however. The outer ramparts could take artillery emplacements, but they also acted as impassable barriers, with narrow routes between them that would channel an approaching hostile force into slim columns, making the men vulnerable. Barracks were built immediately. A church on the central square, dedicated to St Louis, the royal saint, was consecrated in 1831.

The costly fortifications were funded by decree of the king because of the settlement's strategic importance. However, Neuf-Brisach's position on an important route meant that it survived as a town. It was more than just a military post, and is still inhabited. Vauban worried that it was too close to Colmar on the French side and old Breisach on the German side to be able to flourish, and it never sustained the population of 4,000 that he thought necessary (the number of inhabitants stabilized at 1,500). Vauban's last project, it was a success in military terms, remaining inviolate until 1870, when it fell during the Franco-Prussian War.

1 Site Plan

1 Church
2 Arsenal
3 Town hall

2 Section A-A

3 Elevation of Gateway

A
A
1
2
3
0
50
100
150
200
250 m
250
500
750 ft
N

1

2

0
10
20 m
50 ft

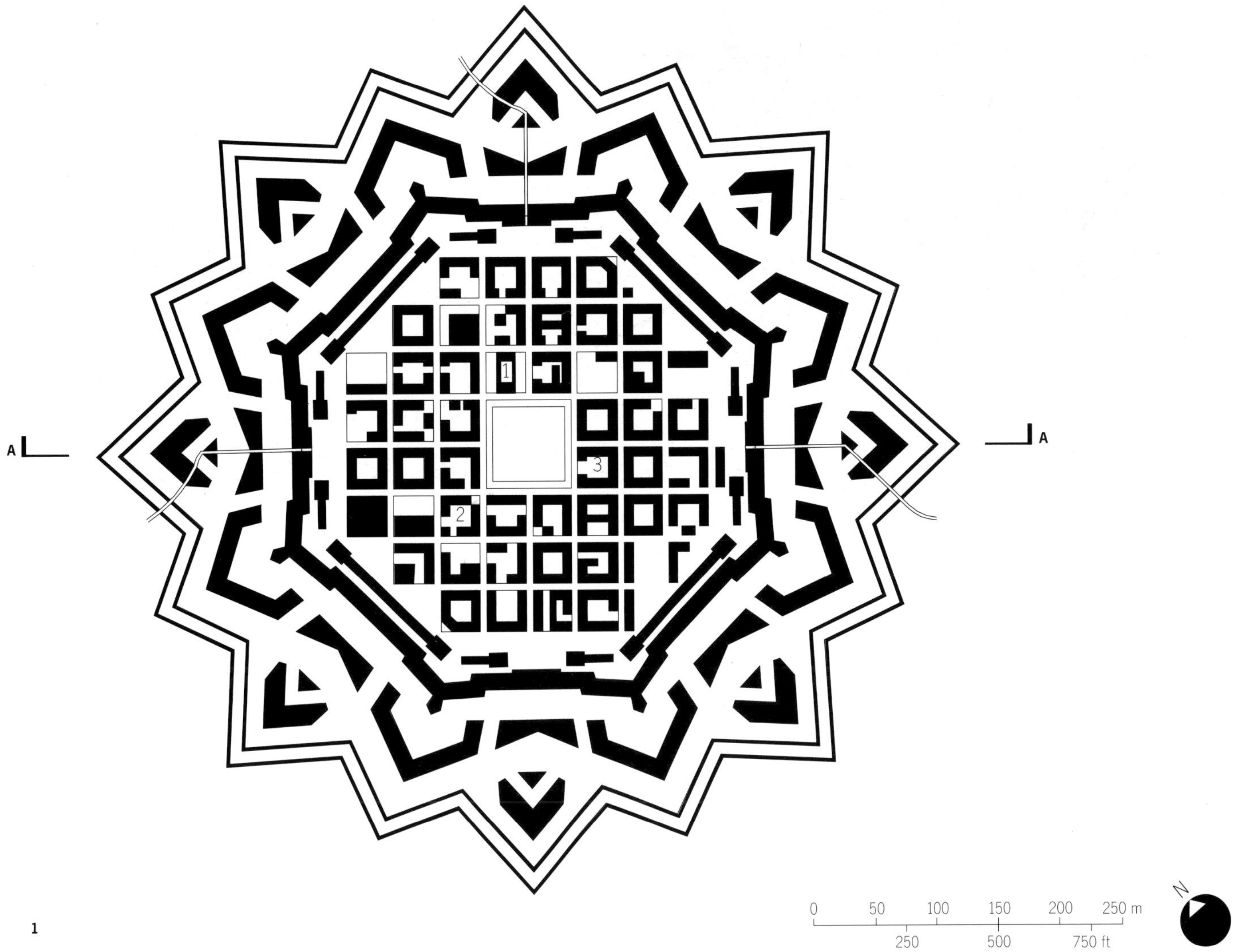

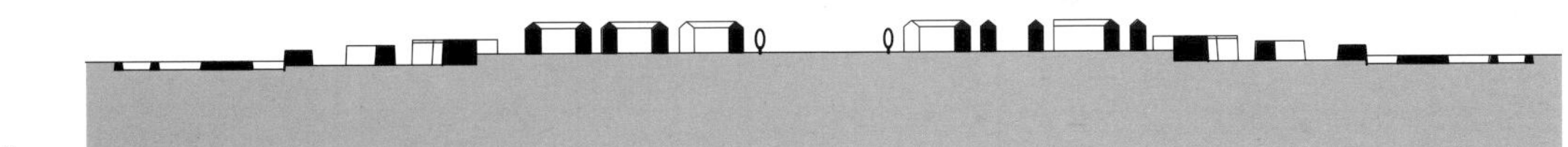

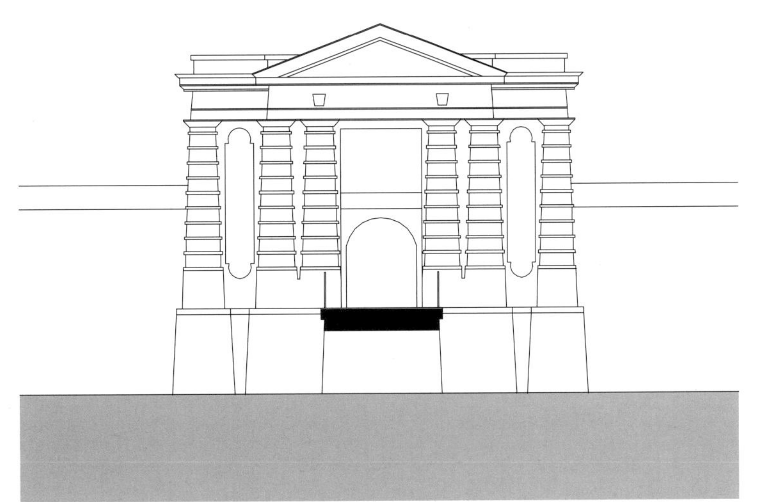

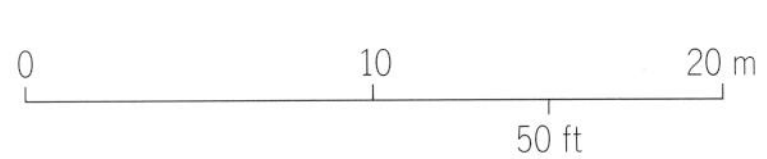

3

Carcassonne

Eugène Viollet-le-Duc, 1814–79

Carcassonne, Languedoc-Roussillon, France; restored from 1853

In common with a surprising number of France's medieval strongholds, the defences at Carcassonne were maintained by the French army until the middle of the nineteenth century, when they were reclassified as historic monuments and restored for their heritage value.

It is difficult to believe that the Carcassonne defences had any residual military value, but, according to the French body responsible for historic monuments, a generation earlier they could not have been reclassified in that way – or, at least, such a reclassification would have had no practical effect. It was realized that such monuments required formal protection, not least from the people in charge of them, who might be more concerned about a building's utility than its beauty or historical significance.

A commission on historical monuments was set up in 1837, with Prosper Merimée as its secretary. Merimée is best remembered as the author of the novel *Carmen*, but he achieved wider influence through his tireless campaign to raise awareness about ancient and medieval monuments and their fragility in the face of neglect or commercial development. He assembled a team of architects, archaeologists and politicians to advise and carry out works, and many French monuments are appreciated today only because of work that was done during the nineteenth century.

Eugène Viollet-le-Duc was the least self-effacing of Merimée's restoration architects. He published his ideas about architectural principles as well as his historical research. He was undoubtedly brilliant, and Merimée was so impressed with him that he put him in charge of the restoration of the Basilica of the Madeleine at Vézelay (pages 130–31) when Viollet-le-Duc was only 25. He went on to restore other prominent monuments such as Notre-Dame in Paris and the Sainte-Chapelle. At Carcassonne he transformed the ruins into the perfect image of a medieval fortified town, and it is a moot point whether the result belongs more to the Middle Ages or to the nineteenth century.

It was Viollet-le-Duc's peculiar achievement that he not only grasped intuitively what the medieval engineers had been trying to do but also persuaded others to believe in the re-creation of that vision and, more surprisingly, to pay for it. Incredibly, having signed over the fortifications to be restored as historic monuments, it was the army that paid for the restoration. The extent of the work was considerable. The towers were given tall conical roofs, with projections from which objects could be dropped on people attacking the walls below; the ramparts were stabilized and cleared – and it was agreed that the land around the town would be kept clear of future development because the open space had had a military use and would need to be seen for the ramparts' use to be understood.

Carcassonne is now the perfect embodiment of a dream of the Middle Ages and, since it is in the south of France, where so many people take holidays, it has become a picturesque tourist-trap. Some of its towers are Roman, however, and the fortress controlled the only valley that runs between the Mediterranean and the Atlantic, just north of the Pyrenees. For nearly 2,000 years the site was a serious military establishment with strategic significance.

1

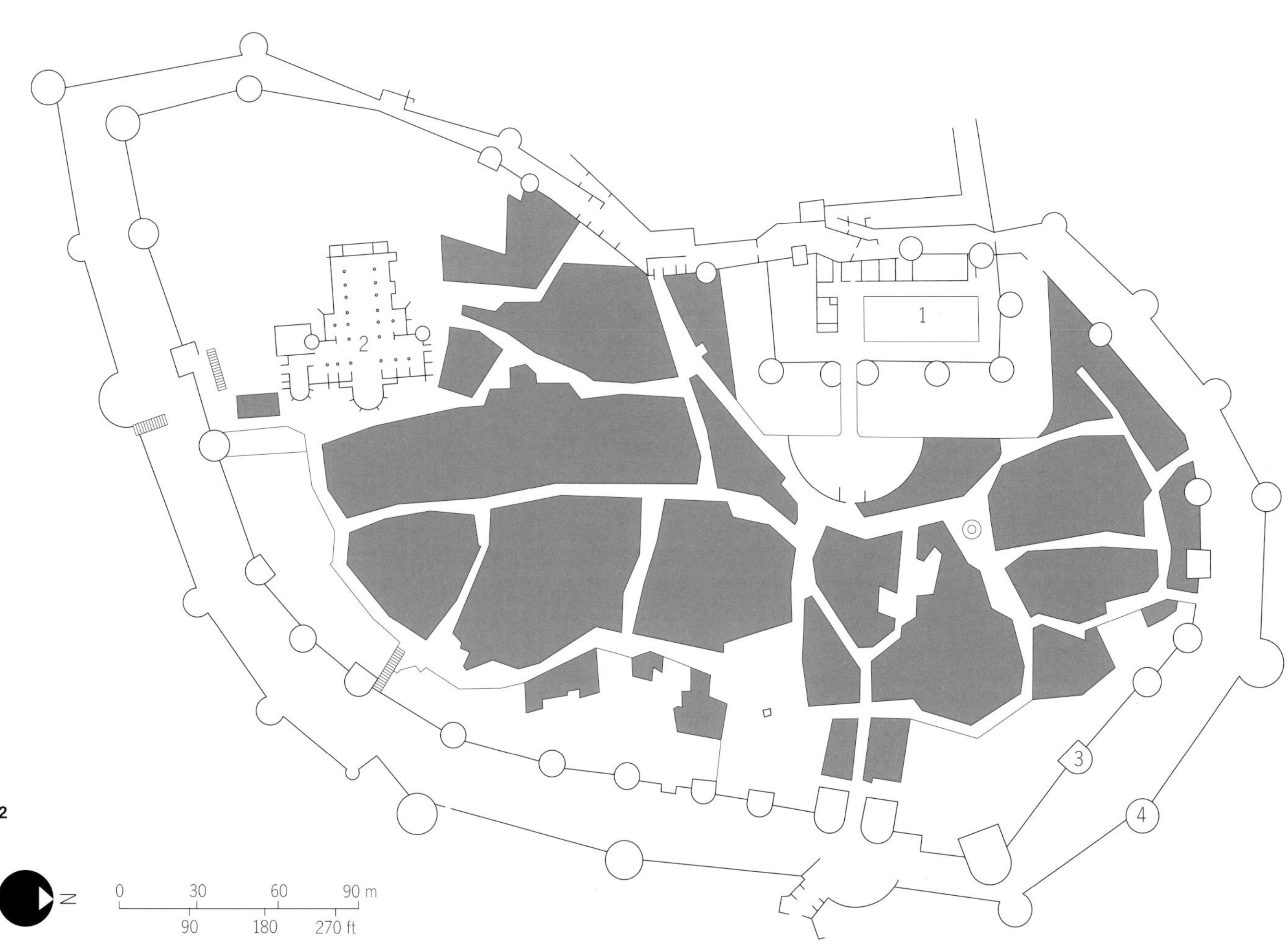

2

1 Typical Tower Section

2 Site Plan

1 Castle
2 Basilica of St Nazaire
3 Inner ramparts
4 Outer ramparts

Forth Bridge

John Fowler, 1817–98, and Benjamin Baker, 1840–1907

Edinburgh, UK; 1883–90

Trains leaving Edinburgh for the north of Scotland, taking passengers up the east coast to Dundee, Aberdeen or Inverness, cross the Forth estuary by a bridge with an arresting appearance. It was Britain's first steel bridge, using hollow steel tubes for its main structure, and has two main spans of 521.3 metres (1,710 feet) each, carrying the railway tracks 46 metres (151 feet) above high tide.

The nineteenth century was a heroic age of bridge-building, with spectacular structures such as Telford's Menai Bridge of 1819–26 (a suspension bridge made in iron) leading the way. Later feats included the Brooklyn Bridge (1869–83), the first suspension bridge in New York, and Gustave Eiffel's Viaduc de Garabit (1880–84), a wrought-iron structure, with an enormous open-latticework arch taking a railway line of extraordinary delicacy across a steep river valley.

However, the Forth Bridge's development was influenced by the disastrous collapse in 1879 of the Tay Bridge, built to the designs of Thomas Bouch to take trains into Dundee across the Tay estuary, and completed only the previous year. The effects of side-winds had not been properly appreciated at the time, and on the night of the collapse there was a fierce gale. It would have been less of a public sensation had a passenger train not been crossing at the time; 75 people lost their lives in the accident and thousands of potential rail travellers were left feeling vulnerable.

Bouch's design for a suspension bridge across the River Forth was already under construction at the time of the Tay Bridge disaster, but work on it was stopped, his reputation in ruins. It was necessary not only to redesign the bridge but also to restore public confidence in its safety.

To that end, the new engineers, John Fowler and Benjamin Baker, gave a demonstration, which was photographed, and the image (reconstructed above) was widely circulated. Two men sit in chairs, their arms outstretched, holding timber props that support their arms; the lower end of each prop rests on the chair. A third person sits on a board supported by the left hand of one man in a chair and the right hand of the other. The reason that this manoeuvre can be achieved without apparent effort is that the two supporters are each holding in their other hands a counterweight (on a rope) that balances the weight of the person in the middle.

So, rather than being designed as an arch – in which every element would be pressed together to make it work – the Forth Bridge depends on a system of cantilevers. The upper members (the arms) are being stretched, and the lower ones (the struts) are being compressed.

The construction of the bridge was a heroic effort that cost dozens of lives (the official number was 57, but revisionist history has raised that number to 98). Its maintenance demands a different kind of heroism. The ancient Greeks had the myth of Sisyphus, who was punished by the gods by having endlessly to roll a boulder uphill – only to find when he reached the summit that it rolled down to the bottom and he had to start again. It is an image of futility. An idea took hold that the Forth Bridge needed constant repainting to protect the steel from rusting. It was supposed to take so long to paint the bridge that, by the time it was finished, the paint at the beginning was ready for renewal. It is not clear that this claim was ever valid, and is certainly not valid now that paint technology has improved, but 'painting the Forth Bridge' has become a metaphorical expression for a task that seems endless – though not necessarily futile.

1 Site Plan

2 Typical Section

3 Elevation

1

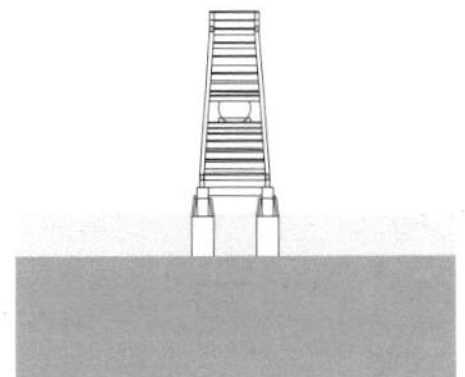

2

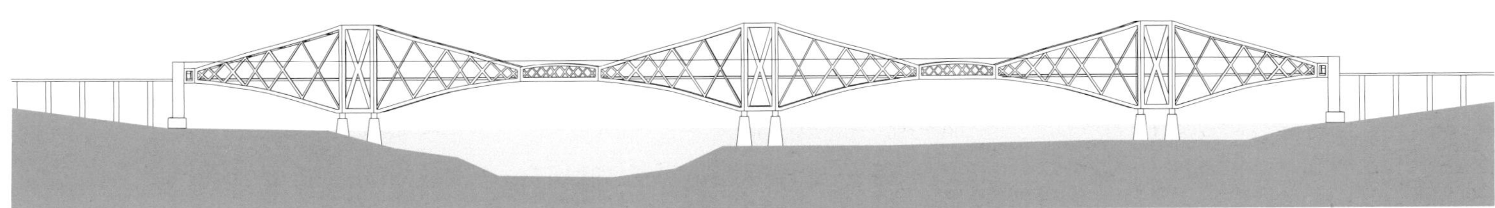

3

Berlin Wall

Berlin, Germany; 1961

The Berlin Wall is not much to look at, but it became an extraordinarily potent symbol of the division between east and west – which at the time meant the division between free-market capitalism and communism. Although it was not a great engineering achievement, the wall was the concrete embodiment of mounting political tensions.

Berlin was the old capital of Prussia, and from 1871 to 1918 it was the capital of the German Empire, which unified most of the German-speaking states and left the city with a legacy of grandiose buildings. After 1918 the capital moved to Weimar, returning to Berlin on Hitler's accession in 1933. Hitler's plans for the further aggrandizement of the city got out of hand and, following the defeat of Germany in World War II, the whole country was divided up between four occupying forces (the USA, the Soviet Union, Britain and France). The eastern part of the state, in which Berlin lay, was to be overseen by the Soviet Union, led by Joseph Stalin, but the city itself had too much symbolic importance to be ceded to Soviet control – so it, in turn, was also divided into four.

The USA, Britain and France were resolved to cooperate and administer their sectors in a unified way, but the Soviet vision for Europe was fundamentally different. So the nation was split in two, with the German Federal Republic (West Germany) run from Bonn, and the German Democratic Republic (East Germany) run from Berlin – but with an outpost of West Germany in West Berlin, which was surrounded by East German territory and supplied by a rail link to the west.

The disparities between East and West Germany became pronounced, and it was in Berlin that they were most visible and most acutely felt, with the values of Moscow rubbing up against those of New York. There were many defections from East to West Germany of people lured by the bright lights of capitalism. In order to put a stop to the defections – or perhaps to protect the citizens of East Berlin from capitalist propaganda – the East German authorities built the Berlin Wall.

The wall appeared overnight, in the early hours of Sunday, 13 August 1961, as a line of tangled barbed wire combined with a blockade of streets running east–west; it was consolidated in concrete over the following weeks. To the east, there was an area of open land that could be surveyed from watchtowers and strafed by gunfire. Its western side was approachable and came to be covered in graffiti. The East Germans said that the wall was put in place to keep western influence out, but the way it was arranged strongly suggests that it was to keep the easterners in.

In 1989 the politics had changed and the wall came down. First it was breached, and then systematically dismantled, except for a short stretch that was kept as a relic. Germany was reunified the following year. In retrospect, it seems incredible that the city could have been divided in such a way, blocking access to national cultural institutions such as galleries, libraries and museums, as well as separating families, while some of the monuments on the other side remained visible and part of the cultural landscape. The fragment of wall that remains helps modern visitors to understand that the division of the city was once a concrete reality, not just an urban myth.

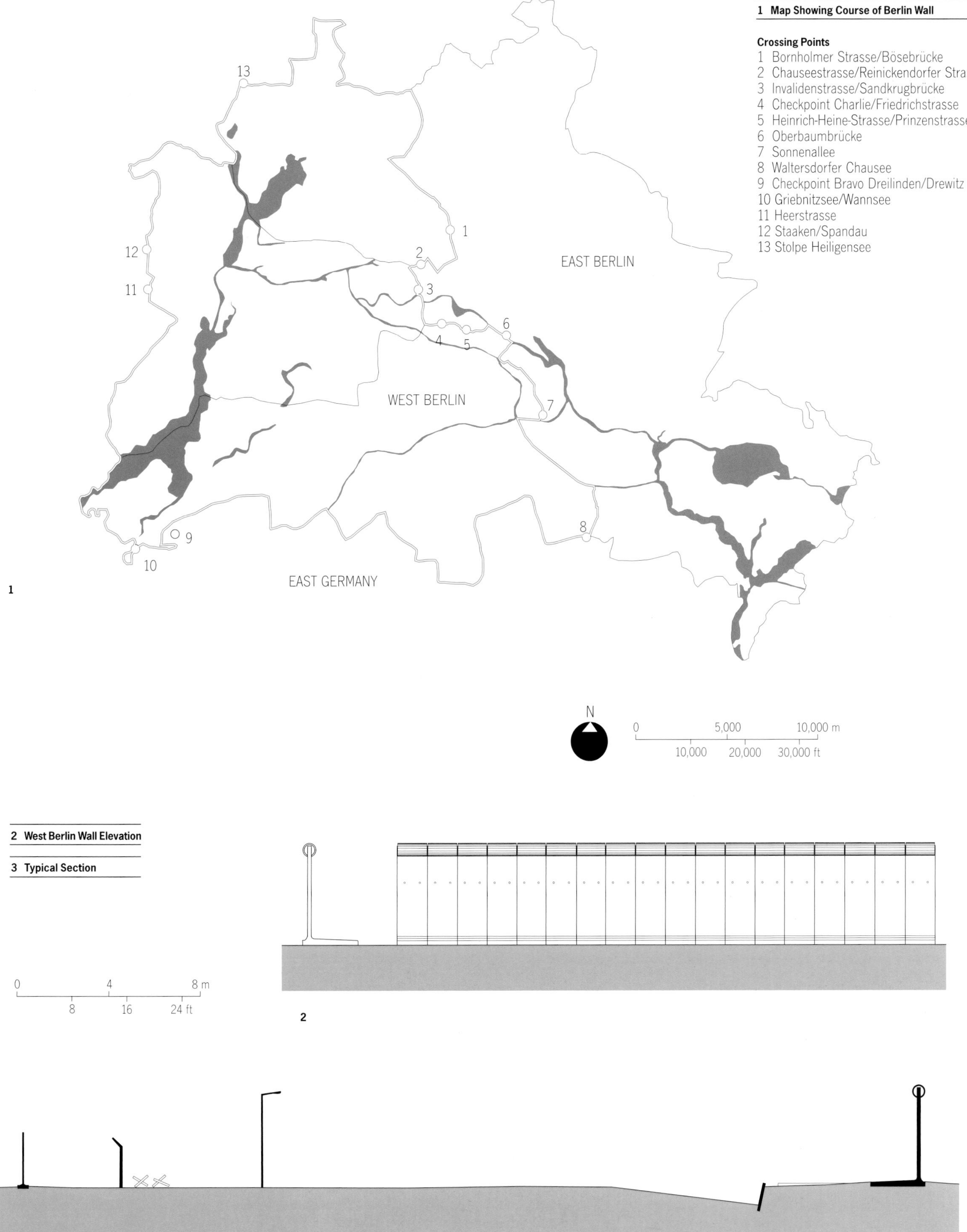

1 **Map Showing Course of Berlin Wall**

Crossing Points
1 Bornholmer Strasse/Bösebrücke
2 Chauseestrasse/Reinickendorfer Strasse
3 Invalidenstrasse/Sandkrugbrücke
4 Checkpoint Charlie/Friedrichstrasse
5 Heinrich-Heine-Strasse/Prinzenstrasse
6 Oberbaumbrücke
7 Sonnenallee
8 Waltersdorfer Chausee
9 Checkpoint Bravo Dreilinden/Drewitz
10 Griebnitzsee/Wannsee
11 Heerstrasse
12 Staaken/Spandau
13 Stolpe Heiligensee

2 **West Berlin Wall Elevation**

3 **Typical Section**

Production, Trade and Education

Most of the really useful buildings in any civilization have no great merit beyond their usefulness. They are part of the background fabric of the city and the countryside. They are built as simply as possible, used until they collapse or until the need for them goes away, and then they are ploughed into the ground or built over. In such buildings, the activity that is accommodated is more important than the fabric of the building.

Growth of towns is usually based on a growth in commerce. At Neuf-Brisach, on the borders of France and Germany, there was a priority to establish a defensive outpost, but the military engineer was keen to see the town made viable by its ability to attract trade. Such activity can be accommodated quite effectively in temporary market stalls that come and go with the traders – structures that are absent most of the time and leave no trace when they have gone. The modern equivalent is the trader in rural communities who sells provisions from a van. This dynamic arrangement limits the range of goods that can be sold, and it takes effort to set up and dismantle the stalls – so, if the settlement is large enough to sustain them, it becomes preferable to put up buildings. In large cities, the buildings can become an important part of the public realm.

The Medina at Fes represents a relatively modest but highly developed market quarter, while the Galleria Vittorio Emmanuele II in Milan houses essentially the same activity but incorporates it in a route that makes a display of civic monumentality.

There is a parallel development in office buildings. The activities that take place in them were once conducted in the home or in the marketplace, but they moved into special buildings. In 1560, Giorgio Vasari designed the offices for the city of Florence's officials – now the Uffizi Gallery. He was working for Cosimo de' Medici, whose family's business was conducted from the Palazzo Medici, a place of work that was also a dwelling. While offices can be the blandest of buildings, there is commercial value in making them eye-catching so as to promote the company that is housed in them. The Fuji Broadcasting Centre, the Seagram Building and the Petronas Towers all demonstrate in their different ways how high visibility can be turned into a commercial asset.

Buildings concerned with education and transport are often utilitarian, but such buildings can for various reasons become spectacular. With the construction of the nineteenth-century railway stations there was a desire to add an element of glamour to inter-city travel, and the stations draw on the history of monumental buildings to achieve their effects.

The libraries included in this chapter are far more than stores for books. They glorify their collections, and in doing so make a statement about the cultural value of books and reading. Similarly, the dignified treatment of the Lawn at the University of Virginia makes a declaration that the state, and indeed the USA, will belong to an international culture of intelligence and sophistication – a declaration that was by no means to be taken for granted at the time it was made.

Stoa of Attalos

Athens, Greece; c.140 BCE

A stoa is a covered porch that has been constructed as an independent building. It developed in ancient Greece, from obscure origins, and the known examples are monumental, but earlier versions may have vanished without trace. The typical stoa is a long narrow building, with a solid wall along one of the long sides and an open colonnade along the other. If it were part of a house, it would be called a loggia, or maybe a verandah, but a stoa is a public building rather than a domestic space.

The Stoa of Attalos is the best-known example of this building-type because of its prominence in central Athens, giving a defined edge to the Agora (pages 306–307). It is a reconstruction dating from the 1950s – a meticulous piecing together of the archaeological remains.

The original stoa was a gift from Attalos, King of Pergamon. (Now in Turkey, Pergamon was then an independent, Greek-speaking city-state.) Attalos had gone to Athens for his education, and the gift to the city brought him cultural standing – in the same way that, in the twentieth century, payment for the reconstruction gave added lustre to the name of Rockefeller. The structure was meant to be as magnificent as possible. It was an unusually elaborate stoa, having two storeys, each with a row of rooms leading off it. In the original design these rooms might have been shops. In the rebuilt stoa they are used as a museum. During the heat of the summer, the shady space is comfortable and a good place to linger.

Stoas can often be found in sanctuary sites, where the rooms would have been public dining rooms. In a dining room, the diners would recline on litters placed around the walls and support themselves on the left elbow, leaving the right hand free to deal with the food. However many people the room was designed to accommodate, the arrangement only worked if people were reclined head-to-toe around the room, with somebody's feet tucked into each corner – to find one's head and shoulders in the corner would be unsatisfactory. Slaves would circulate with the food, bringing it to the diners. The entrance to such rooms was usually off-centre; indeed, when nothing of a stoa survives above skirting level, it is possible to infer from its off-centre doorways that the building housed dining rooms.

The Stoa of the Athenians at Delphi was a display case for treasures looted in battle. But the most famous stoa was the Stoa Poikile – the Painted Stoa – which was a public place in the corner of the Agora, used as a school of philosophy. Its site was not discovered until after the Agora's archaeological site had been defined, and it is now cut off from the Stoa of Attalos by a railway track. The philosophers in the Stoa Poikile taught logic and ethics, and are particularly associated with a set of beliefs that advocates being in control of, rather than a victim of, one's emotions. Their attitudes are still characterized as 'stoical'.

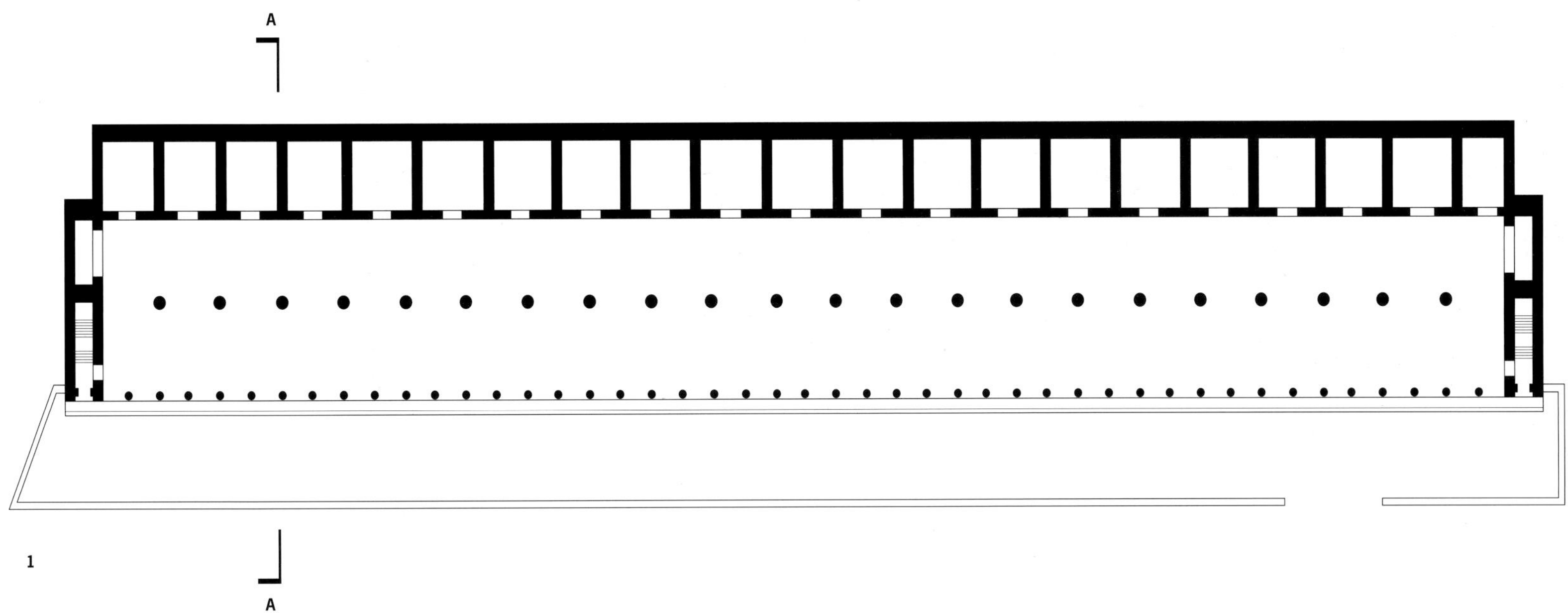

1

1 Plan

2 Section A-A

3 West Elevation

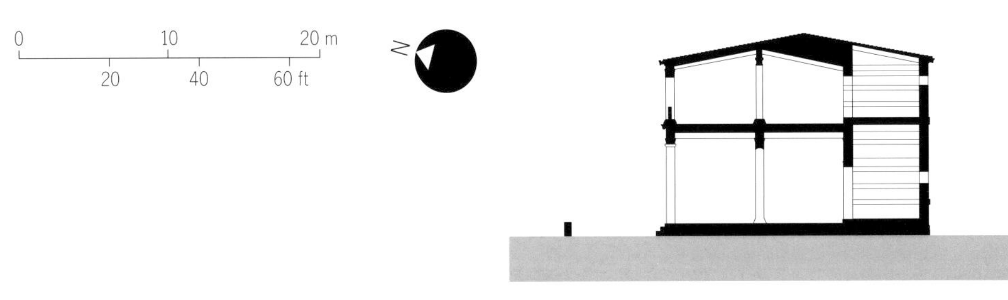

2

3

Trajan's Markets

Apollodorus of Damascus

Rome, Italy; c.100–c.110

Commerce is a necessary part of any settlement that has the feel of a town. It does not require monumental buildings for it to happen. Many a thriving country town has flourished with traders bringing their goods to sell from the back of a cart or a tray set out on the ground.

The activity is important not only for the town but also for the countryside, where some of the money goes, helping to sustain the population as it grows the next crop, scrapes salt off rocks by the sea or lands the next catch of fish.

Commerce can be very well developed without leaving any trace. In such a case, archaeologists would have to infer that the activity once took place because it must have taken place – and because of the existence in the town of an unbuilt area that looks as if it would have been a market place.

If an economy depends on small producers coming into town to sell their goods, then, given the costs involved, it is unlikely that any of these traders would be in a position to build a monument, not even as a collective effort. It is rare to find survivals from the ancient world of buildings that can securely be identified as shops. Shops tend to perish along with the domestic buildings, while the more sturdily built public monuments remain.

Trajan's Markets were an exception. They were part of a huge monumental complex including a triumphal arch, a basilica, the largest forum in Rome, a smaller forum with a monumental column in it, and a temple that presented the Roman emperor Trajan himself as a god. The scale and ambition of the project was clear. Other emperors would try to outdo him later, and Constantine, who converted to Christianity, started to dismantle the monuments in the fourth century, reusing sculpture from Trajan's buildings in his own triumphal arch.

The complex was funded by Trajan's conquest of Dacia (territory which is now in Romania and Hungary) – and it was on the Dacian campaign that Trajan met his architect, a cosmopolitan Greek, who devised a timber bridge on stone piers that enabled the Roman armies to cross the Danube. The bridge is depicted in one of the scenes on Trajan's Column (pages 292–93).

The markets were built in excavated ground on the Quirinal Hill, with the form of the main building marking a transition between the grand formality of the forum on one side and the grain of the commercial city on the other. The plan shows the semi-circular exedra – an outdoor apse – that acted as an adjunct to the forum and extended the monumental realm. The other side of the building seems formless, but it presumably meshed with the street pattern, subsequently redefined by sixteenth-century and later buildings.

Facilities included some spaces with fine finishes, such as a library, but the markets' prevailing atmosphere must have been recognizably similar to that of a bustling shopping mall.

1 Site Plan

1 Exedra
2 Trajan's forum

2 Section A-A

3 West Elevation

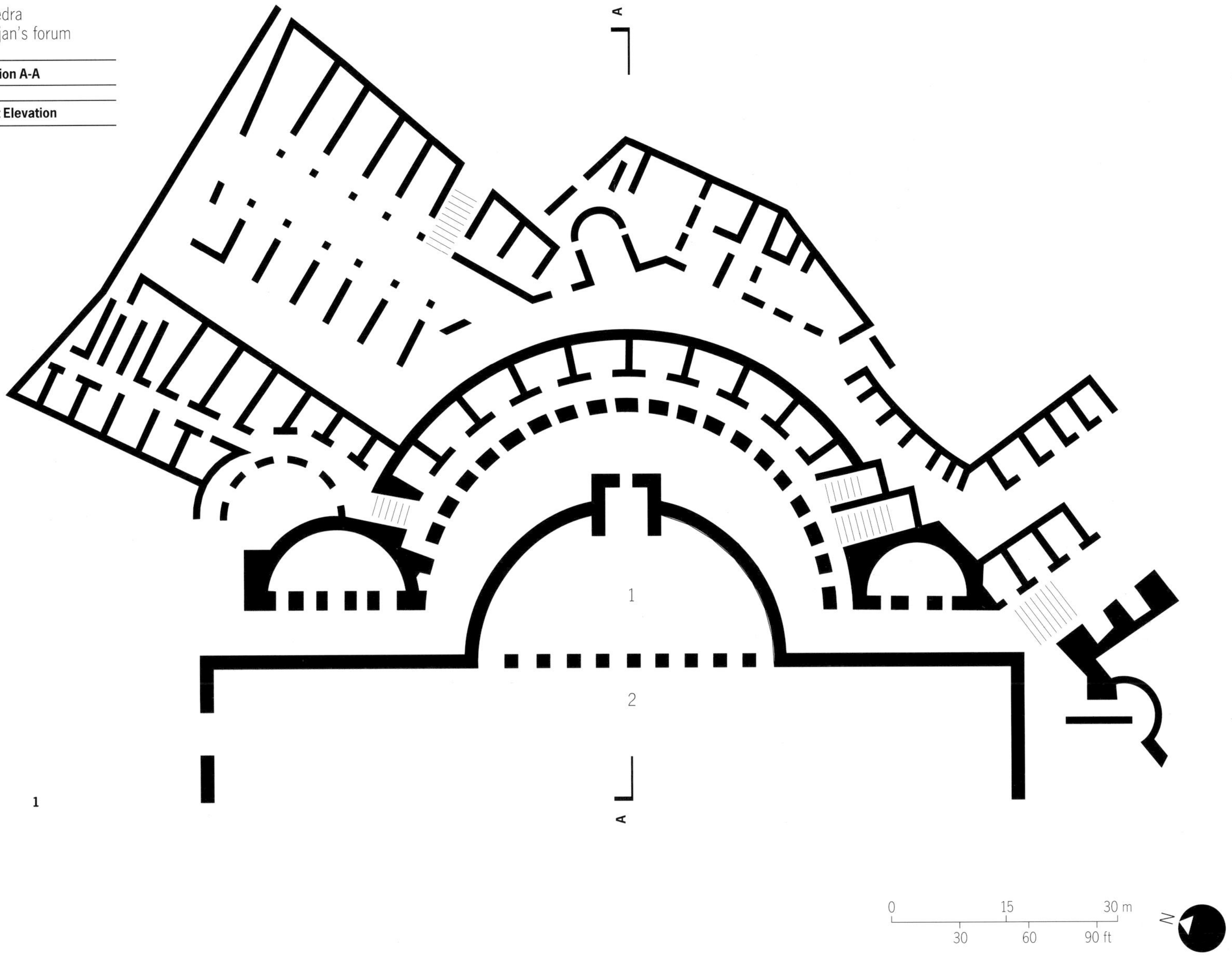

A

1

2

A

1

0 15 30 m
30 60 90 ft

N

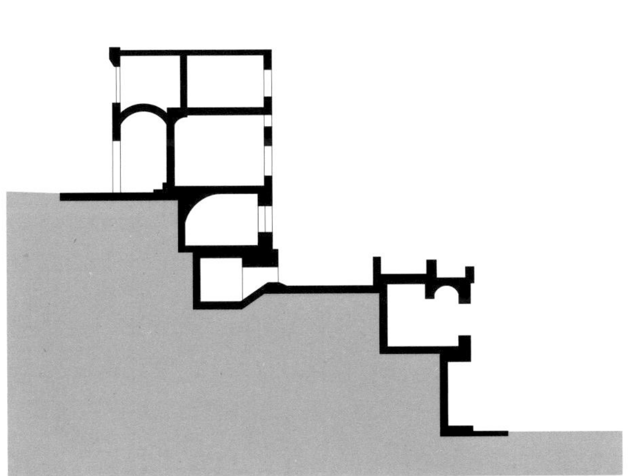

2

3

Medina at Fes

Fes, Morocco; c.1100

Fes was the capital city of Morocco until 1813, when the new French administration found it to be more or less ungovernable and moved the Moroccan capital to Rabat.

The heart of the old city, the Medina, is medieval, and it is easy to see how the narrow interconnecting passageways would have seemed troublesome to French troops. There were many urban places with similar environments, not only in Africa, but also in northern Europe and Asia – places where people of modest means lived close to one another, running businesses of one sort or another, some of them growing prosperous in the process and extending their space by buying neighbours' property.

Fes is unusual in having preserved its medieval urban fabric into the modern age. The city was founded in 789 and, although no buildings of that antiquity survive, it is said to be unchanged since the twelfth century. This is an exaggeration, but the changes have been limited, absorbing new elements such as glazed windows and electricity into the traditional framework.

The streets are very narrow and typically lined with two- and three-storey buildings. Where there are shops at ground level, the shop front is wholly open, the upper storeys supported on the cross-walls, so the goods can be readily displayed, with the proprietor in attendance, drawing attention to them and safeguarding them. Especially where there are projecting awnings, sometimes thrown across at roof level, the street may resemble an indoor aisle – a souk.

At the back of the shops, stairs lead to the upper rooms, which sometimes interconnect, and to flat roofs, which are too hot to be comfortable in the heat of the summer but can be used for drying produce, such as herbs, olives and flax, or sometimes for sleeping. In summer, the streets' narrowness is an advantage in keeping out the sun. They are doused with water in the early hours of each morning, to clean them and also for the cooling effect of the evaporating water.

The pattern of settlement here is derived from incremental growth – the unselfconscious production of small individual decisions that have aggregated over a long time. It is quite different from the imposed geometry of Neuf-Brisach (pages 182–83), for example, or the monumental side of Trajan's Markets (pages 194–95).

Instead of an orthogonal grid, there is a more fluid sense of a community that has development through adjustment to circumstances, an arrangement that makes sense to someone familiar with the locality – the idiosyncrasies of one's own home, the approach through familiar alleyways and so on – but would be utterly baffling to a stranger. Foreigners trying to rule the city, and suspecting the local population of trying to outwit them, might wonder, if someone went upstairs, whether he would ever be seen again or would leave by another route.

This warren of alleyways and bewildering intersections was not just a den of possible insurrection, however; it was the beating heart of a great city – in Morocco, only Casablanca is larger. Fes's university, Al-Karaouine, founded in 859, is the oldest continuously functioning university in the world. There is a fine-grained order here that escapes the militaristic rigidity of geometric form and means that the Medina is better understood as an organism than as a monument.

1 Plan

2 Typical Street Elevation

3 Typical Section

Trinity College Library

Christopher Wren, 1632–1723

Cambridge, UK; 1676–95

The library is the finest architectural element of Trinity College, Cambridge, outdoing its chapel as a place of splendid veneration. Its utilitarian function was to store books and make them accessible to scholars, but it would have been possible to make an arrangement of low-ceilinged corridors to accomplish that objective much more cheaply. Trinity Library is a temple of learning, which elevates the contents of printed books – ideas – to the highest cultural level, and gives the books and scholars a room that could be part of a royal palace.

Isaac Barrow was appointed Master of Trinity College by King Charles II in 1673. He was a mathematician (who had spent some time in Istanbul) and had known Christopher Wren as an astronomer before he took up architecture. By 1676, Wren was already working on St Paul's Cathedral in London, his major work, but Barrow persuaded him to design the library for his college, which Wren did without charge.

Barrow managed to raise some money for the library, but he then contracted a fever, died, and was buried in Westminster Abbey – Britain's traditional way of acknowledging a great life. The library's magnificence is due partly to the feeling that such splendour was appropriate for the building's function, and partly to the fact that both the architect and his client had excellent connections at court.

The composition of the façade is based on Roman models – an arched structure making the openings, but decorated with an idea of classical columns and beams. The ground floor is open on one side, taking the form of a stoa, which is entirely apt for this location. However, the arrangement is continued around three sides of a courtyard, so it has an even closer resemblance to a monastic cloister – actually a very similar building-type, but arranged around a square rather than running in a straight line.

The main part of the library occupies the upper floor and the space below it is lower than might be expected. The treatment of the façade indicates that the interior consists of two equal storeys, with the floor level suggested from the exterior by the cornice line that runs across the top of the lower colonnade. In fact, the floor is set lower, at the height of the springing of the arches. This arrangement means that the storey-height windows that seem to belong comfortably to the upper floor are set at an unusual but appropriate height above the level of the bookshelves. So the space inside is magnificently high and very well lit, while the proportions of the façades look decorously conventional.

There is a point of principle at stake here: it could be said that Wren was deceiving the viewer by sleight of hand. It is clear, though, that Wren did not feel that there was a violation of any principle that mattered. The interior works well, the exterior is well composed, and the two are brought into reasonable harmony. He thought in the same way about the dome of St Paul's, where the real dome (seen on the interior) supports a framework of timbers that create a scenic 'dome' that makes a dramatic impact when seen from outside. For Wren, architecture was theatrical and the important thing was to make the right impression.

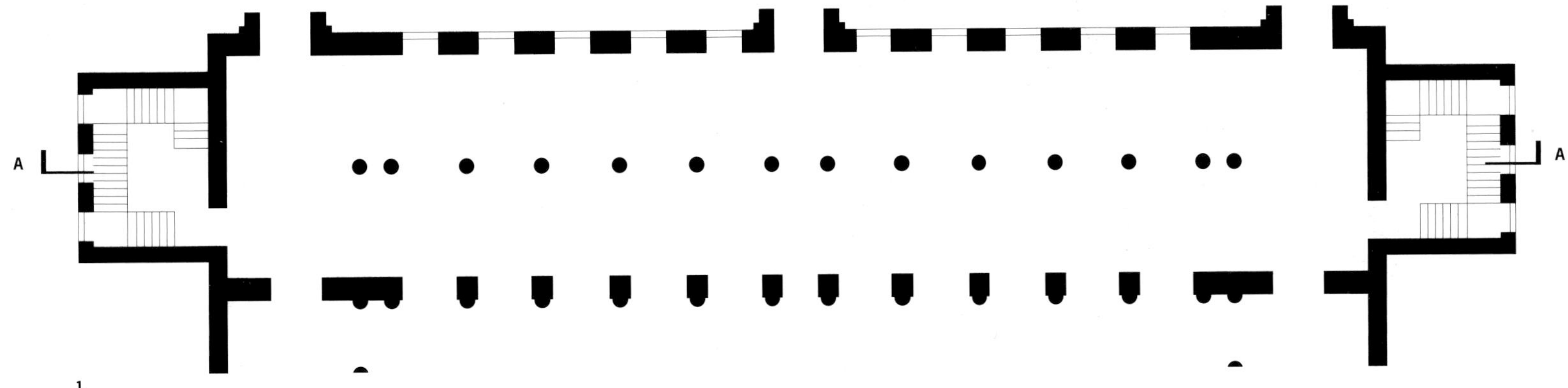

1 Plan

2 West Elevation

3 Section A-A

0 8 16 m
15 30 45 ft
N

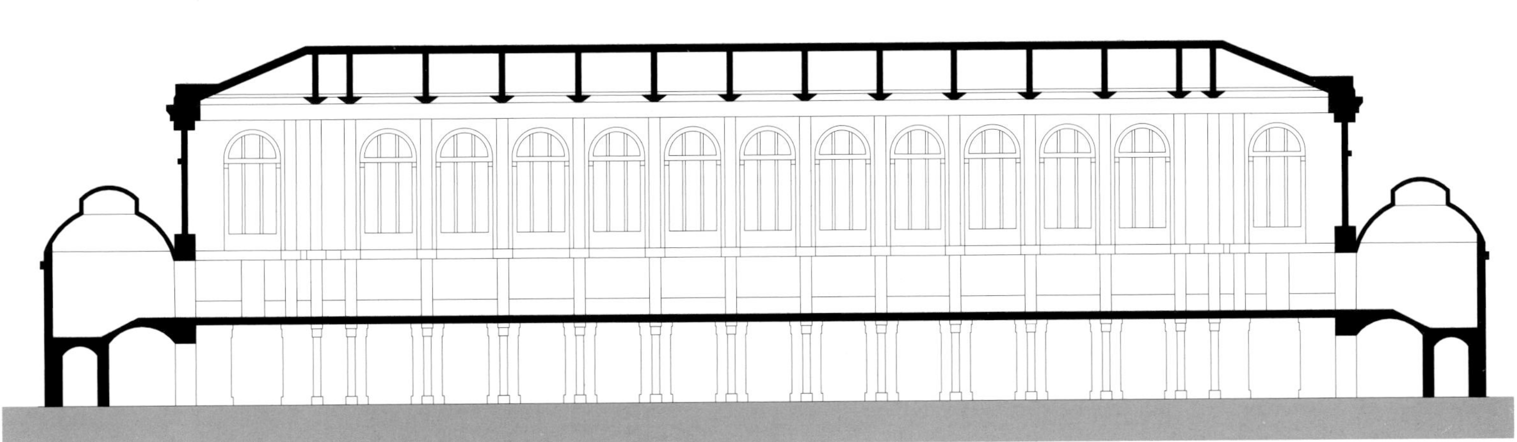

Royal Saltworks

Claude Nicolas Ledoux, 1736–1806

Arc-et-Senans, Franche-Comté, France; 1774–79

Salt is now plentiful and can be cheap. Humans are regularly told to beware of consuming too much of it, but in traces it is an essential mineral for health, and it used to be expensive. In France, the production of salt was controlled by the king and it was heavily taxed. Around the coasts, especially where the sun shone, it could be produced by evaporating water from the sea. Inland there were salt mines.

Arc-et-Senans, 500 km (300 miles) from the coast, was a major site for salt production. The salt came from Salins-les-Bains, some 16 km (10 miles) away. It was extracted from the ground by dissolving it in water, which was then piped to Arc-et-Senans, where it was heated to evaporate the water and leave a deposit of salt crystals. The area round Arc-et-Senans was forested, and it was more economical to transport the salt solution than the timber that was burned to make the heat for the process.

The saltworks was given an astonishingly monumental treatment by Claude Ledoux, who designed buildings of precisely cut stone. There is a prismatic geometry running through the shaping of the blocks which is to be found in all Ledoux's work. Classical details were used, but without the delicate ornament that would have been usual for courtly work at this time. This was a robust kind of classicism, and Ledoux was trying to reinvent architecture from first principles, looking to the geometric origin of forms.

The buildings at Arc-et-Senans are laid out in a vast semi-circle. The director's house has a portico with six columns, which are given a treatment that goes beyond rustication. They seem to be composed of blocks that alternate between the elegant tapering cylinder of a Doric column and the rectangular block from which it was hewn.

At the entrance to the complex is a gateway with another Doric portico, but in the shadows behind it, instead of the expected doorway, there is a rocky cave, modelled to evoke the place where the salt came from – and the principal decoration on the severe boundary walls is a repeated motif resembling the end of a pipe from which salt-water has been running, leaving stalactites dripping beneath it. Ledoux called this his *architecture parlante* (speaking architecture), making direct allusion to the function of the building, rather than using iconography from classical literature.

Ledoux was also responsible for a series of gatehouses around Paris. People bringing produce to sell at Parisian markets had to pay a duty, which was levied at these *barrières*. Fifty of them were constructed to his designs between 1785 and 1788. The tax was seen as unfair and the buildings were hated because of their association with it.

In 1789 there was a revolution. Ledoux, aged 53, was firmly associated with the old regime and never worked again. He was lucky to escape with his life. He carried on designing – increasingly fantastical designs, for an ideal town that he called Chaux, which had a circular saltworks at its centre, and monuments in prismatic stone to serve as dwellings for woodcutters and herdsmen in a world turned upside down.

1 Window Detail

2 Section through Propyleion

3 Elevation of Propyleion

4 Plan

1 Propyleion
2 Director's house
3 Evaporation boilers
4 Forge

1

2

3

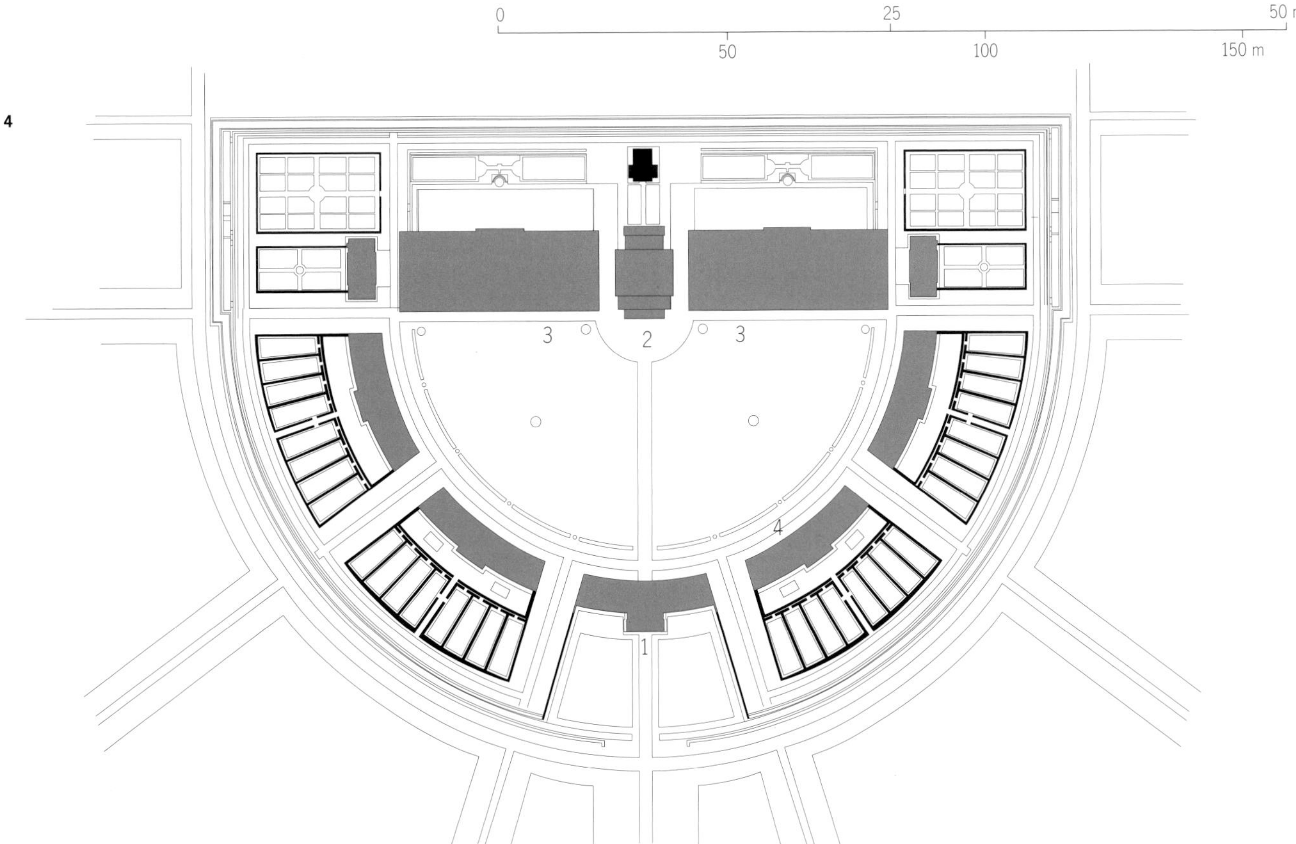

4

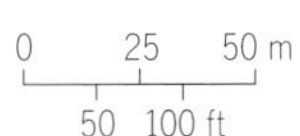

Engelsberg Ironworks

Per Larsson Gyllenhöök, 1645–1706

Ängelsberg, Västmanland, Sweden; 1681–1919

Steel is the structural material that holds up most twenty-first-century buildings. It is not necessary to use steel in dwellings with small windows and rooms that are not too wide, but for everything else – including industrial and agricultural buildings – it is ubiquitous.

The cost of steel production came down in the mid-nineteenth century, when Henry Bessemer's process was introduced. Patented in 1855, the Bessemer process soon began to be employed on a industrial scale. It involved passing air through molten iron as a way of removing impurities and regulating the carbon content. Steel is an alloy of iron and, usually, carbon. The presence of the carbon makes the steel stronger and harder but less ductile. Wrought iron is purer and softer than steel. Cast iron has a higher carbon content and is more rigid but brittle.

Before the invention of Bessemer's process, steel was produced by taking very pure wrought iron and adding carbon to it. It was recognized that the purest wrought iron came from Sweden, where it was manufactured in relatively small-scale works such as Engelsberg and exported to the technologically advancing places that needed this specialized product.

Iron smelting in the seventeenth century entailed the burning of large quantities of charcoal – made by the controlled part-burning of timber – and in Sweden the ironworks were typically found on forested aristocratic estates, as at Engelsberg. They harnessed water power for machinery that crushed ore and hammered the cooling iron. Engelsberg's blast furnaces were upgraded in 1778–79, when the forge was at the peak of its prosperity, but the old process could not compete with the larger-scale Bessemer production, and the forge limped to closure in 1919.

The buildings around the Engelsberg Ironworks are simple, low-cost coverings to protect the important, sophisticated and more solid constructions within. Timber is the principal building and cladding material, but there is some variety among the 50 or so structures on the site. They include dwellings for ironworkers, buildings to accommodate the estate's agricultural operations and a brewery. The manor house has a roof made of iron plates. Corrugated iron – which later became an important low-cost roofing material – is not in evidence. (It was invented by Henry Palmer in the 1820s.) 'Slag', the crushed rock left over after the iron has been extracted from iron ore, would normally be thrown away as waste, but some of the smaller buildings were made from concrete blocks that used slag as the aggregate material. Some experimentation is evident in the architecture, but aesthetic aims were not paramount and the dwellings reflect conventional Gustavian decorum.

Such an installation was once characteristic of the Swedish countryside, but now this site is conserved as a unique historic place. The wooded setting and the eighteenth-century taste that informs the more prominent buildings makes the Engelsberg Ironworks look composed and serene, but when it was in action this would have been a noisy place – the idyll shattered by the pounding of mechanical hammers. Traffic bringing in charcoal and ore and taking away iron ingots and slag would have added to the din. Paintings of the forge, hanging in the manor house, show that the owner was proud of this important source of his prosperity.

1 Plan

1 Water wheel
2 Blower
3 Blast furnace
4 Anvil

2 Section A-A

3 East Elevation

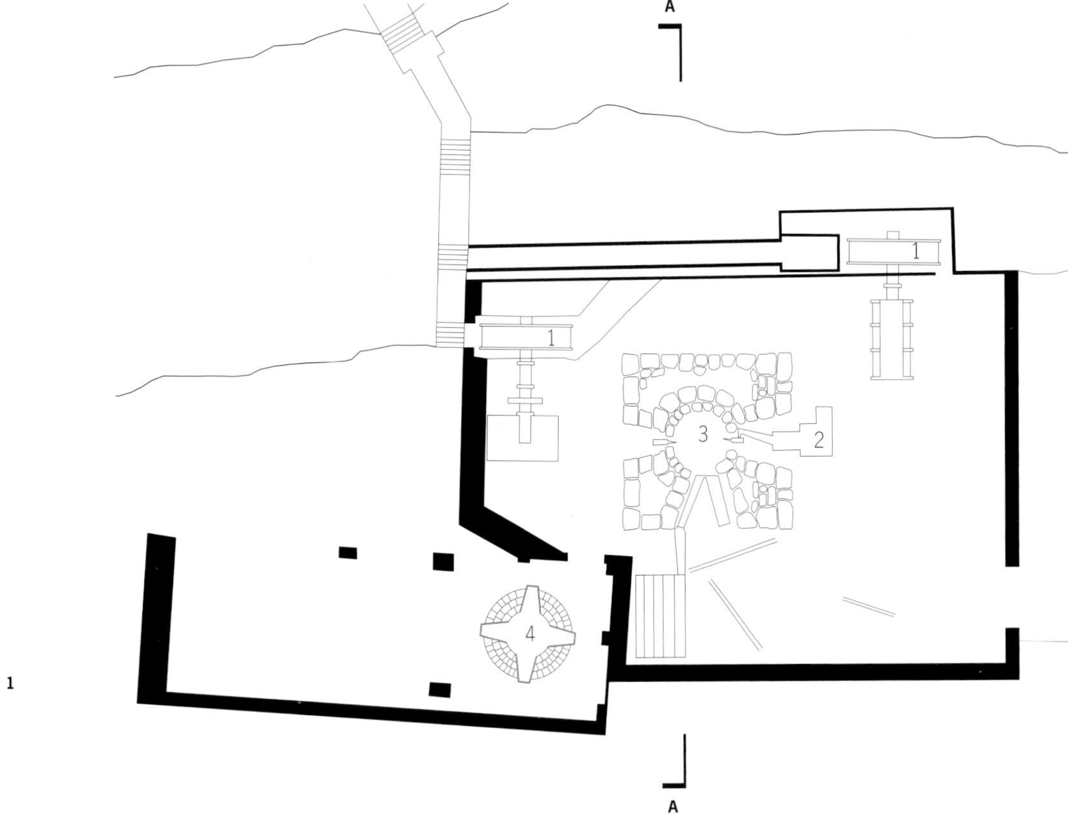

1

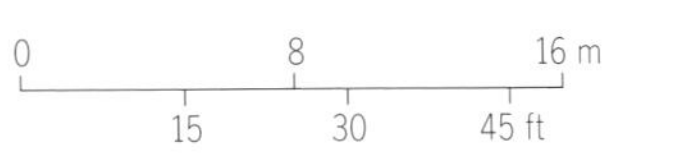

2

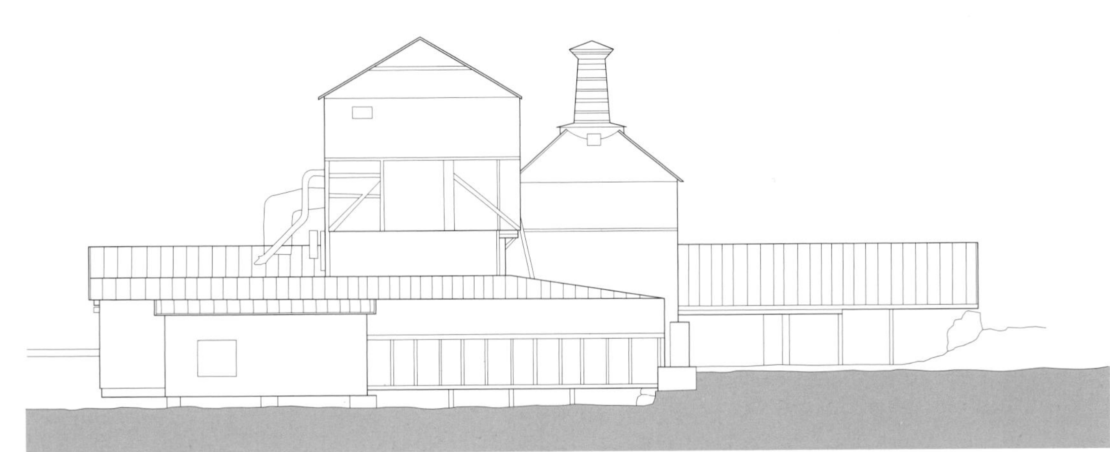

3

The Lawn, University of Virginia

Thomas Jefferson, 1743–1826

Charlottesville, Virginia, USA; 1819–25

When Thomas Jefferson founded the University of Virginia in 1819, there were few other such educational establishments around. Harvard (1636) was the oldest university foundation in the USA and by 1776 the country had ten universities – a remarkable number, given that there were still only two in the UK. Like the medieval European universities, they were all religious institutions, and none was further south than Philadelphia.

Opened in 1825, the University of Virginia was among the first not to require its students and staff to have a particular religious affiliation. It was to be funded by the state, making it accessible to a broad range of people – mainly to white men, in its early days, but not only white men from rich families like the other universities. Jefferson did not want Virginia to award degrees, seeing them as unnecessary embellishments, but encouraged people to attend university for the purpose of intellectual exploration, to develop their ideas about what to know and how to live by talking to other people, as well as through reading.

The buildings that Jefferson designed to promote this vision were grouped around an open space, or lawn, which would act as a focus for the community. Colonnaded walks ran down its edges, connecting the ten professors' houses, which had teaching rooms in them, and the students' rooms in between. He sought to avoid setting up the university in a single institutional building, which he feared would turn out to be ugly, unhealthy and inflexible. This university was envisaged as an 'academical village'. The south end of the lawn remained open to a view of distant mountains. The north end was closed by the largest building, modelled on a half-size Pantheon (pages 108–109), with the library given pride of place on its upper floor, under the dome.

Some diversity was introduced within the symmetrical set-up. The students' rooms are identical and the walkway colonnade is modestly scaled. Each of the professors' pavilions, though, is individual. These are two-storey buildings, in some of which the columns extend through the building's full height; others engage with the colonnade in different ways. All the pavilions incorporate a different column-type taken from an authoritative source, such as Palladio (1508–80), so they could be used as the basis for an architectural education.

For example, Pavilion VIII drew on the work of Fréart de Chambray (1606–76), Palladio's first French translator and a theorist in his own right. His representation of the Corinthian order, as seen in the Baths of Diocletian in Rome, was the basis for the pavilion's two-storey columns, which are used in antis (between walls). There are two full columns in the centre, and a half-column on each side – implying that the other half of the column is lost inside the projecting wall. In this pavilion, the lower colonnade of student columns marches past the pavilion without breaking its rhythm, and more or less hiding the taller columns from view. In such ways, the group of buildings sets up regular arrangements, but allows quirkiness and individuality to offset any danger of architectural pomposity.

1 Plan

1 Library
2 Lawn
3 Pavilions
4 Gardens

2 South Elevation of Library

3 Section A-A

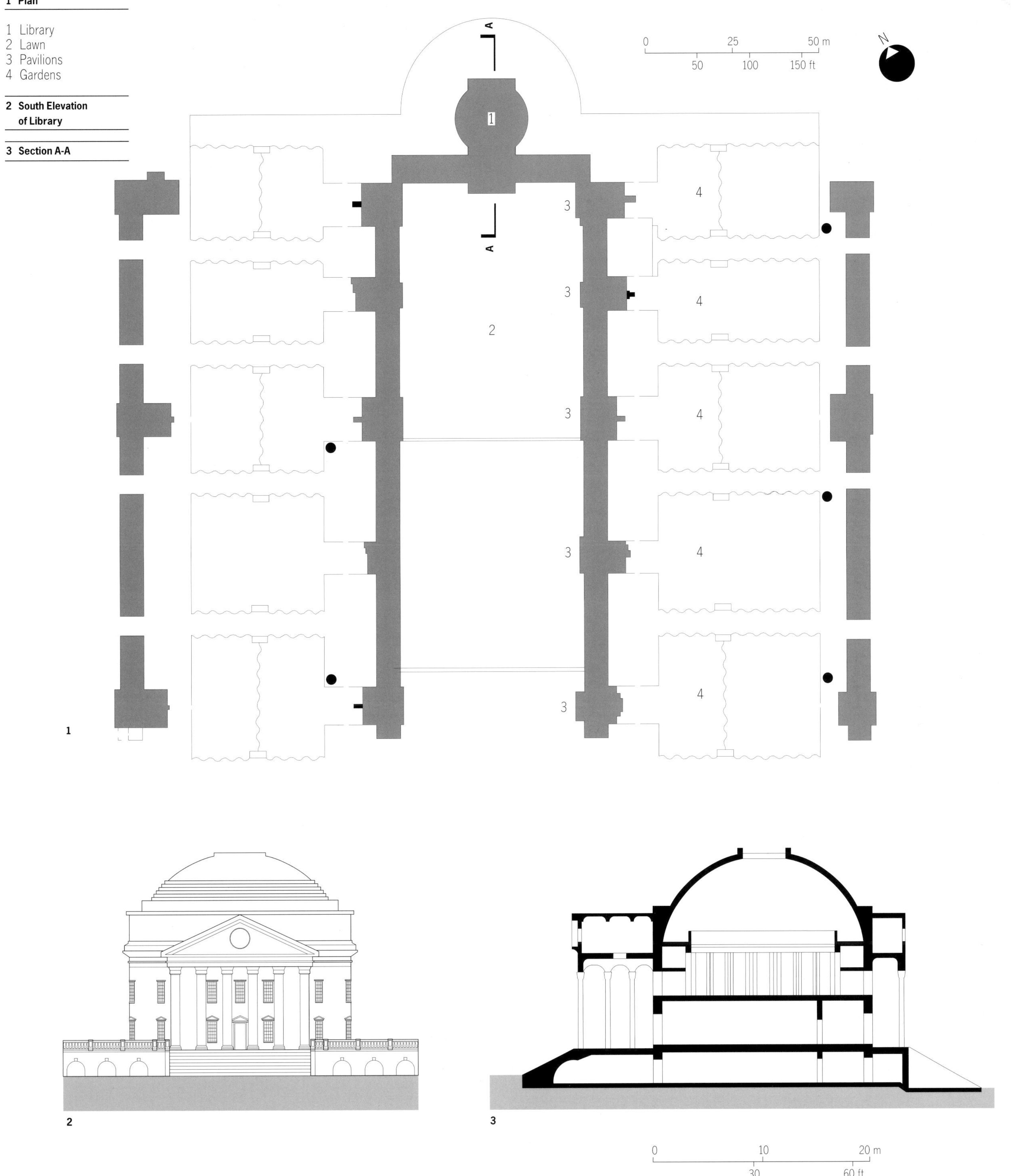

Albert Dock

Jesse Hartley, 1780–1860, and Philip Hardwick, 1792–1870

Liverpool, UK; 1839–46

Liverpool is on the north-west coast of England, connected to the Atlantic by way of a slight detour around the north of Ireland. Its growing prosperity during the eighteenth and nineteenth centuries emanated from its port. Ships brought in many goods, including cotton from America for the Lancashire textile mills, and until 1807 took slaves from Africa to work on the American cotton and tobacco plantations.

For the transport of heavy goods over long distances, water was overwhelmingly the most efficient means of transport everywhere, until the advent of the railways in the mid-nineteenth century, and Liverpool's port continued to flourish.

The Albert Dock was conceived as an advanced installation, designed by Jesse Hartley, who specialized in dock design in Liverpool – he already had six Liverpool docks to his name before the Albert Dock, and went on to do another ten.

Philip Hardwick was brought in from London to add polish to the project. He had studied architecture at the Royal Academy, then in France and Italy, and made a name for himself with buildings for the railways, most famously as the designer of the Euston Arch of 1837 – not really an arch at all, but a Doric propylon that was a prominent landmark in London, and an entrance for Euston, London's first railway station, from where trains went up the west coast. The 'arch' was demolished in 1961.

The dock was opened amid popular clamour by Prince Albert in 1846. It allowed sailing ships to moor alongside warehouses and unload directly into them from their decks. The heroic scale of the buildings derived from the need to allow the ships and their attendant machinery enough room to manoeuvre in the central basin. Lock gates trapped water in the dock, so that the ships could be moved about at any time, but they could enter or leave it only at high tide.

Major engineering work was carried out below water level, to make the water deep enough and to keep it in, and the warehouses were equally grandly conceived, with arches (accommodating cranes) supported on and punctuating the rhythm of a run of cast-iron Tuscan columns 5 metres (16 feet) high. The warehouses were five storeys high, with cast-iron and masonry construction.

The use of iron as a building material had been pioneered in the iron bridge at Coalbrookdale of 1779 and in the Derwent Valley, near Derby, where William Strutt built a 'fireproof' warehouse in 1793 and subsequent mills that avoided use of timber in their construction but which had multi-storey iron frames to support floors made of hollow terracotta pots. At the Albert Dock these technical developments were put to use on a much grander scale. Sadly, the scale was not grand enough, and the dock was unable to deal with the ships when sails became old-fashioned. Larger steam-powered vessels took over. Some of Hartley's docks have suffered the unedifying fate of becoming landfill sites, but the Albert Dock's aesthetic quality has saved it for culture and leisure.

1 Site Plan

2 Section A-A

3 Section B-B

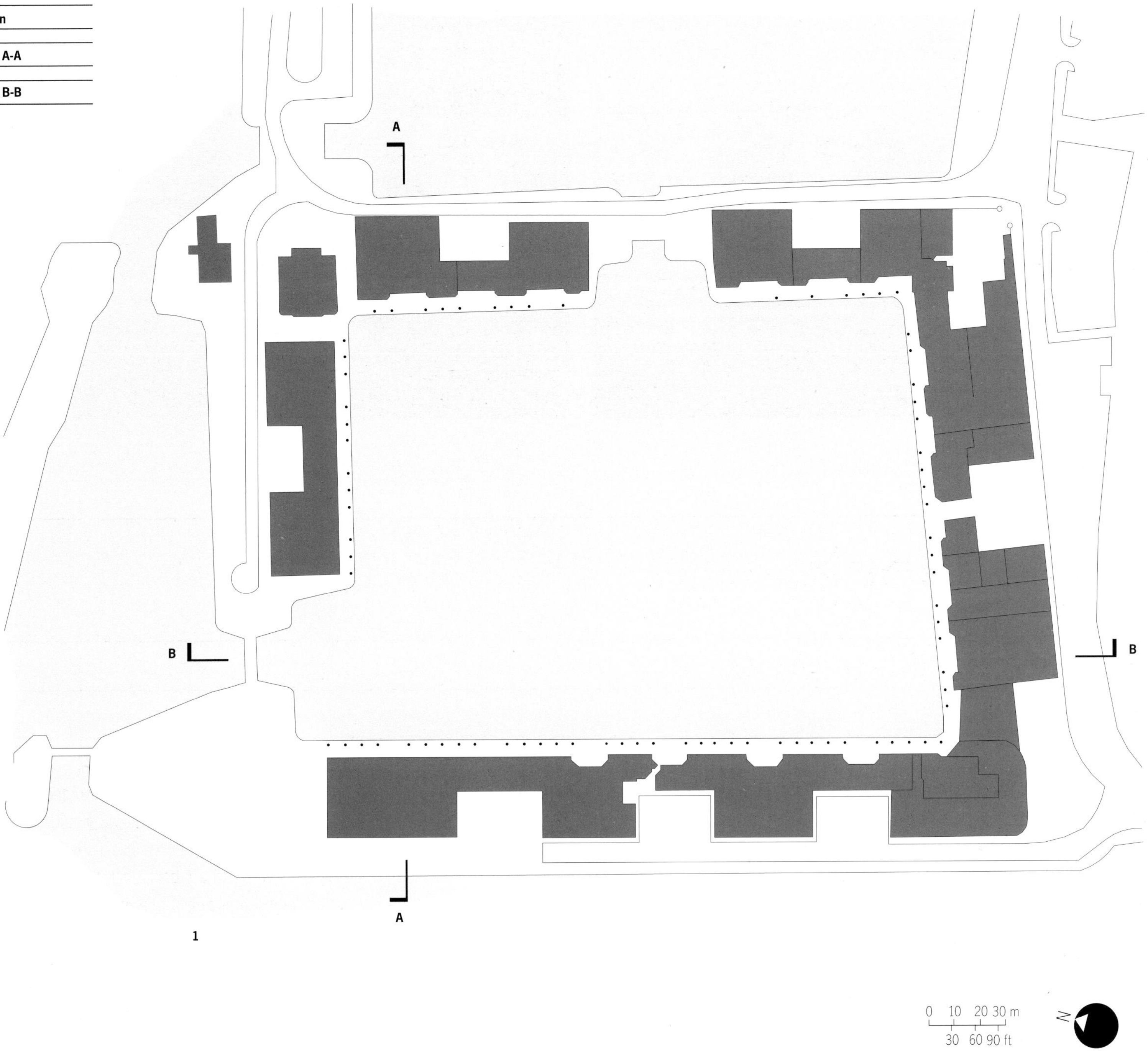

A

B

B

A

1

0 10 20 30 m
30 60 90 ft

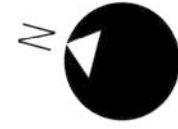

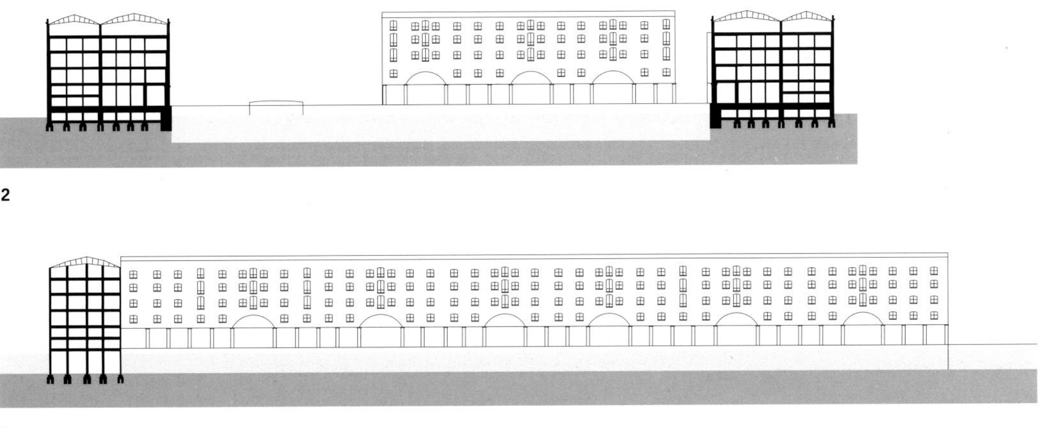

2

3

Saltaire

Titus Salt, 1803–76

Saltaire, West Yorkshire, UK; 1853

Mechanized industrial production was pioneered in textile mills in the north of England and it eventually changed the whole rhythm of life. The old agricultural calendar had its seasons: a time to sow, a time to reap, times when the earth was fallow, times when animals were being born. A machine, by contrast, could be active for as long as there was someone to tend it, at any time of the year, at any hour of the day or night.

Richard Arkwright is credited with the invention during the 1770s of shift-working, at his mill at Cromford in the Derwent Valley, Derbyshire, as a way to keep his expensive machines running continuously. His mills were water-powered, which meant that they needed a fast-moving watercourse.

The switch to steam power meant that mills could be sited anywhere that a workforce could be induced to go. Where it was convenient to use water, many continued to do so, but steam engines gradually took over. They worked by heating water until it turned to steam and using the built-up pressure to drive a piston or (later) a turbine. Steam production needs a water supply. Production of heat entails burning a fuel, typically coal.

Titus Salt made fine woollen cloth. Most remarkably, he invented alpaca fabric. The alpaca is a llama-like creature from Peru with a long, fine fleece. There had been earlier attempts to use the fibre, but it was Salt who worked out how to do it, and he became immensely rich as a result. Alpaca cloth is fine with a lustrous sheen. It fetches a high price, and Salt became the world's leading supplier. He also became mayor of Bradford, where his business was based – and not only his.

Dismayed by the pollution from the town's factory chimneys, and having failed in his attempts to do something about it, Salt moved his own operation out of Bradford and set up a new community by the River Aire, just beyond the edge of town – a move that anticipated Ebenezer Howard's advocacy in 1898 of 'garden cities', or small, sub-urban planned towns.

There are two impressive monuments in Saltaire: the unusually splendid Congregational Chapel, which Salt paid for, and Salt's Mill, the enormous building where the fabrics were produced, and which continued in use until 1986. The rest of the settlement is made up of a grid of streets, including housing for Salt's three or four thousand employees and excellent community facilities, planned from the outset, that demonstrate the founder's benevolent paternalism.

Salt's Mill itself covers a vast area, using the fireproof building methods that were by then well established. Its principal façade is composed symmetrically, with two towers and serried ranks of windows. Its method of construction was no longer absolutely innovative but it surpassed all previous limits. An immensely tall chimney, reminiscent of an Italian campanile, took the smoke from the steam engines' boilers way up into the sky. This would have done nothing to prevent global warming, but it was an efficient way of dispersing soot so that it did not diminish the air quality of Saltaire.

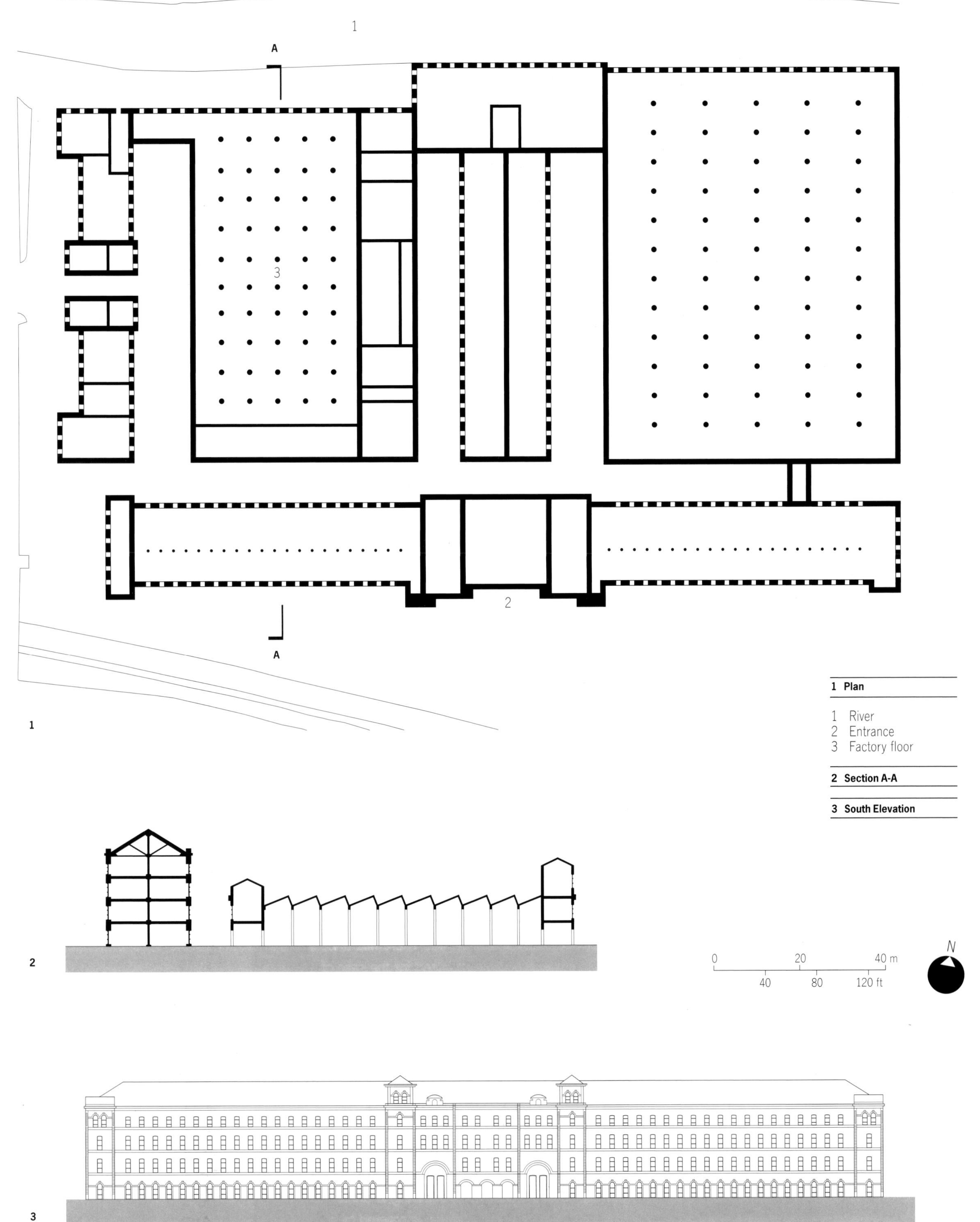

1 Plan

1 River
2 Entrance
3 Factory floor

2 Section A-A

3 South Elevation

Bibliothèque Nationale

Henri Labrouste, 1801–75

Paris, France; 1860–67

Henri Labrouste spent six years studying in Rome, where he was impressed by the ingenuity of Roman constructional methods, and his drawings were more like engineering studies than the scenographic drawings of most of his near-contemporaries. When he returned to Paris, he set up an atelier, taking on his own students and coaching them in what he called a 'rationalist' manner, dealing with practical problems in building and giving proper expression to their parts.

His first significant commission was the Bibliothèque Sainte-Geneviève (1840–48), an academic library next to the Panthéon in Paris, which resembles a rationalist reworking of Wren's Trinity College Library in Cambridge (pages 198–99) with the floors correctly legible from outside. What is unexpected in the interior is its breathtaking lightness. Within the traditional masonry shell, the structure is iron, and the iron is most visible in the library's main space, which had shelves around the walls and high windows above them. The ceiling over this high space consists of two shallow barrel vaults, supported by delicate wrought-iron beams and a central row of thrillingly thin cast-iron columns. It was the first time that structural iron had been put on show in a high-status interior.

As it turned out, Sainte-Geneviève was a rehearsal for Labrouste's greatest commission: the Bibliothèque Nationale in the rue de Richelieu. The external wall of the Bibliothèque Nationale is traditional masonry and unremarkable except in its relentlessness. Entrance is through a *cour d'honneur* – a formal courtyard, off the street – which preserves the fine façade of an earlier building as the entrance to the new library.

Inside, on axis, there is the reading room, with the book stacks beyond. The stacks were always out of reach of the public, but they are in an amazing space containing five storeys of books, with an iron structure throughout. There was once a glass roof over the whole (changed for the sake of book conservation). The stacks are grouped around a central atrium, which was flooded with daylight and crossed by delicate bridges. All the floors and stairs are in perforated cast-iron panels that allow daylight to penetrate to the lower depths.

A large window separates this space from the reading room, so that readers can see into the central atrium. The reading room itself is more polite, but scarcely less daring. Sixteen slender cast-iron columns mark out a square grid (three bays by three), each bay of which is covered by a lightweight dome of white glazed terracotta panels. The top of each dome has an open oculus, letting in light. There is glazing above them, to keep out the rain, but that does not show from the inside. The edges of each dome are supported on a curved iron arch with an open lattice of wrought iron, and these are gathered together at the top of the columns, most sensationally in the central bay, where the descending corners of four domes taper away to nothing, apparently to pirouette on the impossible-looking columns.

Around the edges of the room, the walls beneath the domes' arches are glazed where they can be, but in most bays above the bookcases there is a panel of wall, painted with an illusionistic mural suggesting leafy trees set against a perfect summer sky. It was in this room that the philosopher and social commentator Walter Benjamin (1892–1940) began to think about his never-completed 'arcades project', working and dreaming 'under an open sky of cloudless blue that arched above the foliage'.

1 Plan

1 Court of Honour
2 Reading room
3 Garden
4 Courtyard (staff)
5 Book stacks (administration)

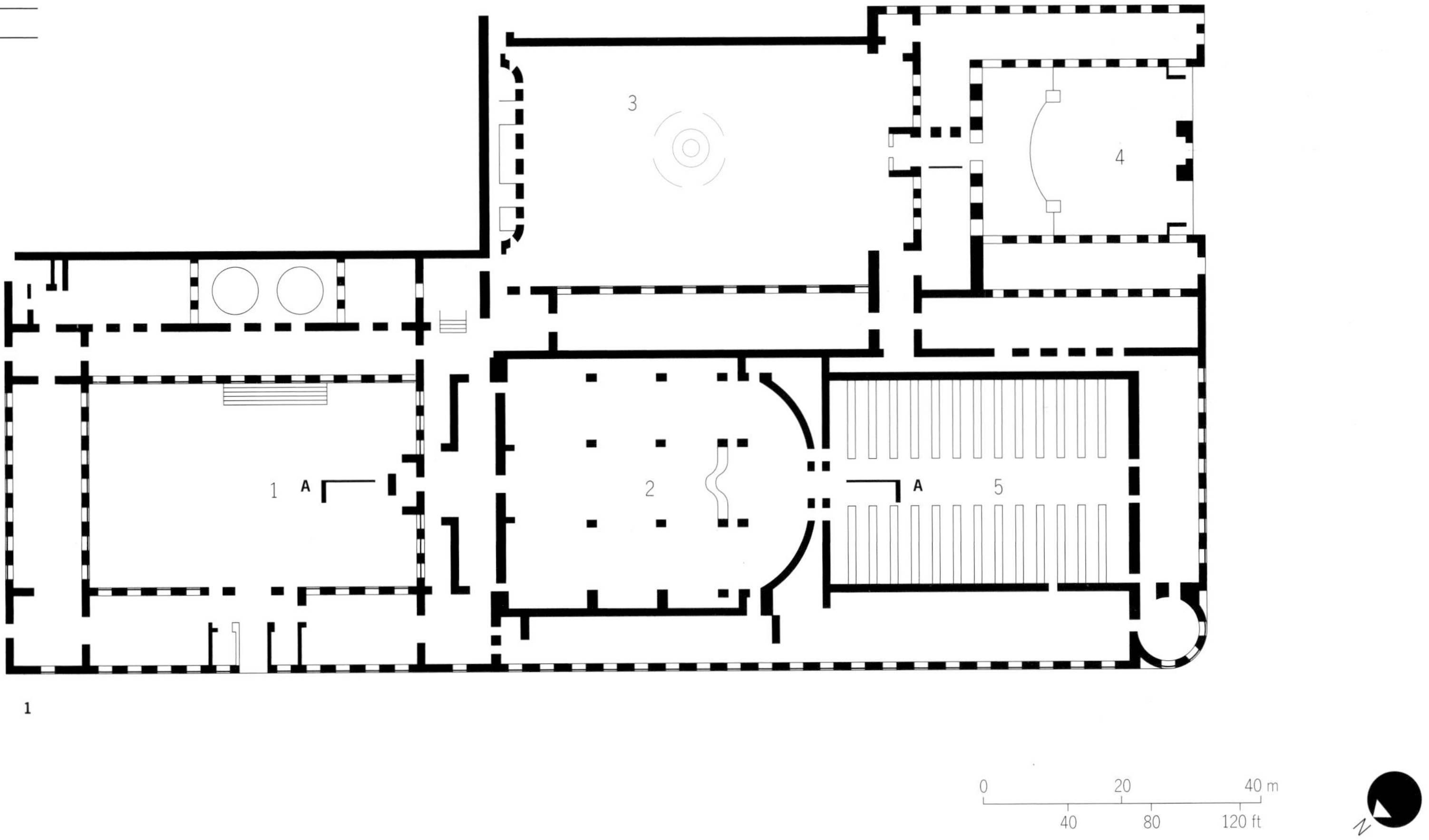

3
4
A
1
2
5
A
0
20
40 m
40
80
120 ft
N

1

2

0
20
40 m
40
80
120 ft

3

2 West Elevation

3 Section A-A

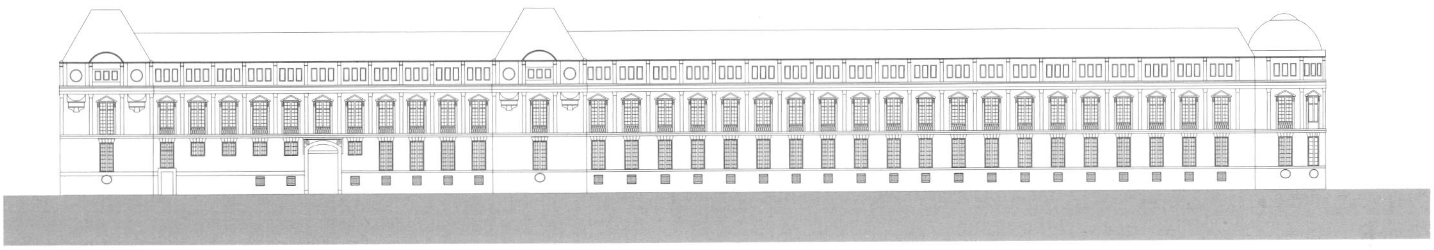

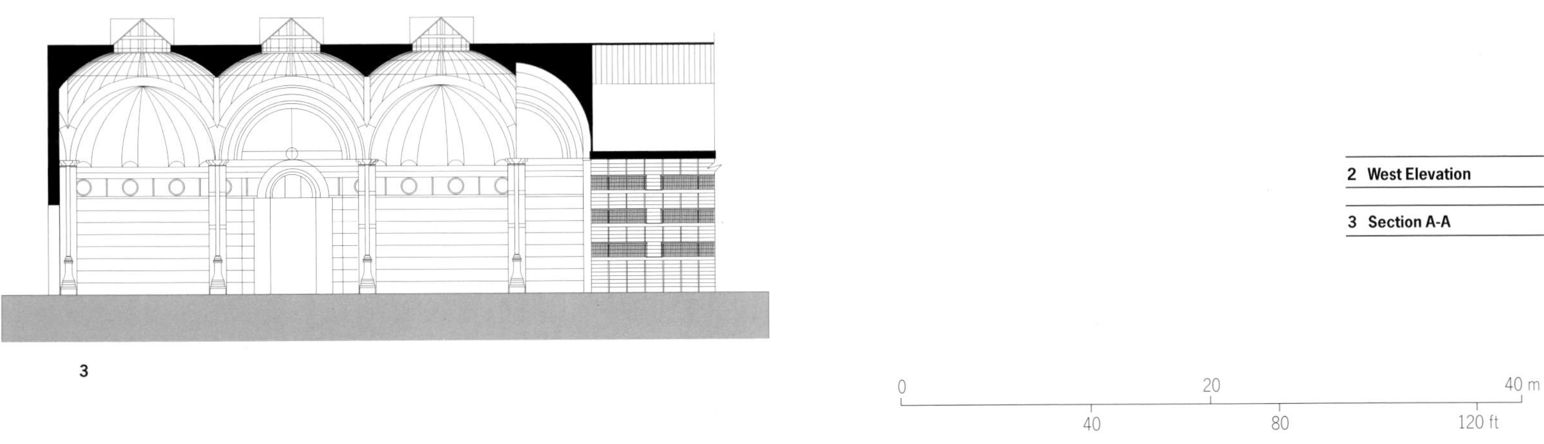

Galleria Vittorio Emmanuele II

Giuseppe Mengoni, 1829–77

Milan, Italy; designed 1861, constructed 1867–78

The arcades of Paris, which so preoccupied the philosopher Walter Benjamin, were the precursors of the department store and the shopping mall. There were dozens of them, each typically linking one side of an urban block with the other by a covered passage with a glazed roof to let in daylight. Some were smarter than others, but by Benjamin's day (the 1930s) they were run down and being demolished – seeming to belong to the world of the unconscious, lurking just out of sight of the official streets, forming their network of hidden routes, and displaying faded goods or consigning a low-rent home to a dubious activity. Many of the arcades that have survived have been refurbished and are now treasured.

Although it had a similar starting point, the Galleria Vittorio Emmanuele II in Milan could hardly be further in mood from the spaces that Benjamin knew. Its scale is vast, its location prominent and perennially fashionable, and it is in effect a national monument.

Italy after the fall of the Roman Empire had been a shifting assemblage of different powers. There were separate kingdoms in Sardinia and Naples, a republic with its own empire operating from Venice, various places under foreign control (Spain, Austria, France under Napoleon) and a powerful duchy with its capital in Milan. Almost all the regions of the Italian peninsula were brought together as a unified country in 1861, with Vittorio Emmanuele II as king. (Vittorio Emmanuele I had been king only of Sardinia.) The rest followed soon afterwards. It was at that point that the grand Galleria in Milan was conceived.

The arcade connects the piazzas in front of Milan's two most important buildings: the cathedral and the theatre – both internationally celebrated. The cathedral is a spectacular Gothic monument; as well as being the largest of Italy's cathedrals, it is the only genuinely Gothic masterpiece among them. The theatre is La Scala, best known globally for its operatic productions.

The main passage, which is fully the width of a street, is lined with five-storey buildings and paved with gleaming terrazzo and mosaics. At the middle point there is a crossing, which picks up the line of a side street of the same size; where they meet is an octagon in plan roofed by a glass dome. The glass vaults over the passages are supported by curved wrought-iron lattice beams that come to rest behind the line of the masonry parapet, so the supports are tucked away out of sight. Behind the traditional (neo-baroque) façades, the building is stiffened by a structural iron frame.

The design's triumphalism is underscored by the triumphal-arch façade that was added to the entrance near the cathedral, reawakening memories of imperial Rome – and by the fact that Vittorio Emmanuele II himself came to open it, on 1 January 1878. The architect, Giuseppe Mengoni, missed the ceremony. On 30 December 1877, he had fallen from the glass dome to his death on the terrazzo below.

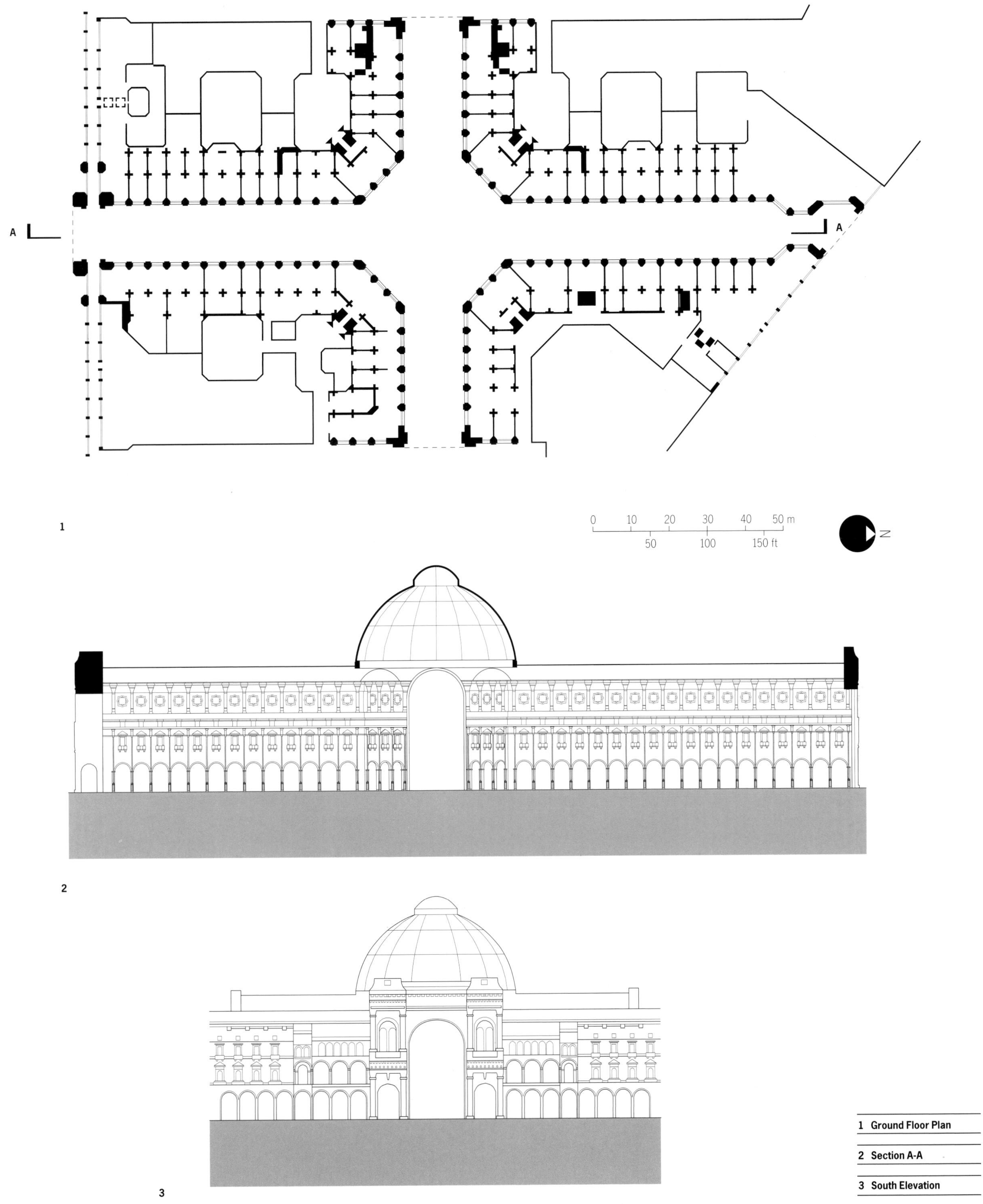

1 Ground Floor Plan

2 Section A-A

3 South Elevation

St Pancras Railway Station

George Gilbert Scott, 1811–78, and William Henry Barlow, 1812–1902

London, UK; 1864–68

In the early years of the nineteenth century, there were experiments to harness steam power for transport, and the idea turned out to be one of the great transformative inventions of the century. By 1830 in the UK, 158 km (98 miles) of track had been laid. By 1860 the figure was closer to 16,800 km (10,440 miles). Investors saw that they could make a fortune by investing in railways, and many of them did. Competition was intense and victory was richly rewarded.

The first passenger trains to bring people to a London station travelled on the line from Birmingham to Euston, built in 1835 in a classical style, with a Doric propylon (the Euston Arch) by Philip Hardwick (1792–1870). It was redeveloped and expanded in the 1840s, when Hardwick's son, Philip Charles Hardwick, designed a magnificent neoclassical hall that gave a glamorous sense of occasion to the business of arriving and departing. It was originally built to serve the London and Birmingham Railway Company, but it was used by others, including the Midland Railway Company.

As traffic intensified, the line coming into London became congested, and the Midland Railway Company decided that it would need its own line and its own London terminus.

The purchase of the station site was only a small part of the logistical nightmare of bringing a new railway line into London, but the company managed it. To the east was King's Cross Station by Lewis Cubitt (1799–1883), a cleanly elegant design which had been in operation since 1852, bringing in trains from the north by the east-coast route, while Euston's trains took travellers to the north-west. Paddington had opened in 1838, bringing trains from Bristol and the west; in 1854 it had been turned into a great iron cathedral by Isambard Kingdom Brunel (1806–59), whose train shed had transepts and a clear span of 30 metres (98 feet). The Midland Railway set out to upstage them all.

Steam engines produced huge quantities of smoke. When a steam train pulled into a covered station, it would fill the air with choking soot, unless the volume of the space were sufficiently large to allow the soot to remain high up and disperse. There was a functional imperative behind the building of the great train sheds. At St Pancras, William Henry Barlow engineered a train shed with a clear span of 74 metres (243 feet), rising to a height of 30 metres (98 feet). Amazingly, rather than being given absolute prominence, this achievement was completely screened from external view.

The Midland Hotel by George Gilbert Scott included the arrivals hall as well as luxurious facilities for the traveller visiting London. The Gothic Revival was at its height, and the hotel's fantastical silhouette hid the shed and suggested that rail travel was the stuff of dreams. Its positioning on the site shows it jockeying for position with nearby buildings. Had it been set 100 metres further back, it would have saved on a little track and made a great public square with the two stations presiding over it. In its actual position, it blocks the view of King's Cross, which looks out obliquely at the side of St Pancras, definitely in the inferior position.

1 Plan

2 Section A-A

3 East Elevation

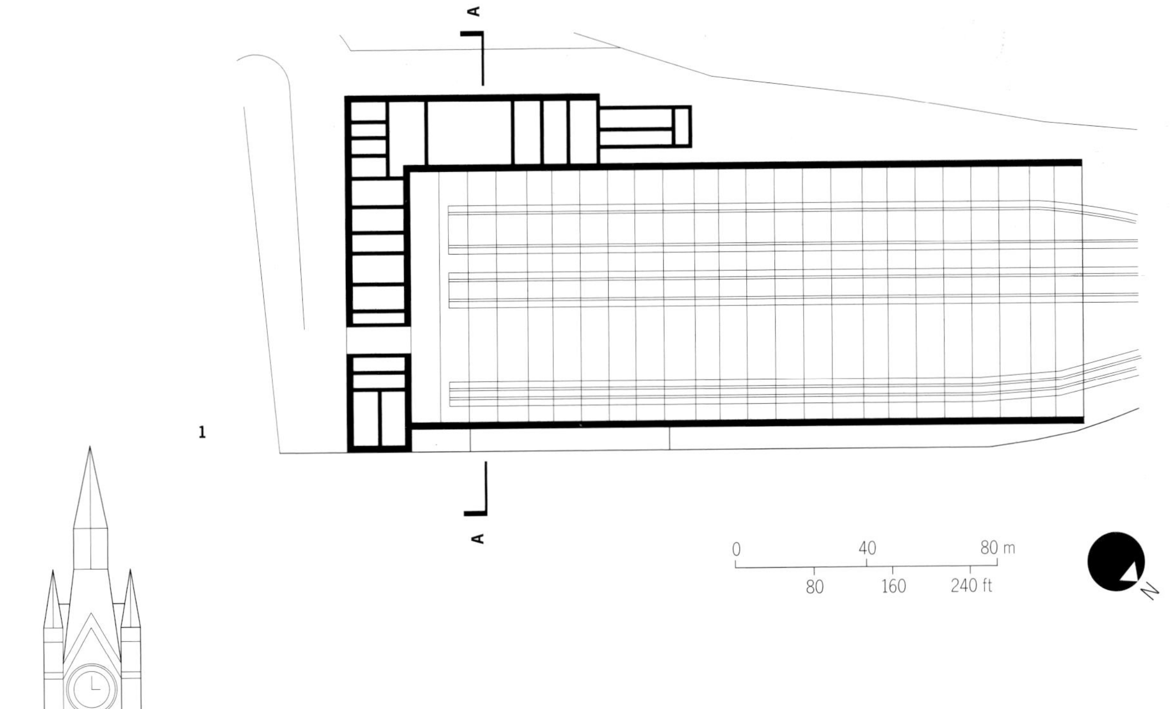

1

2

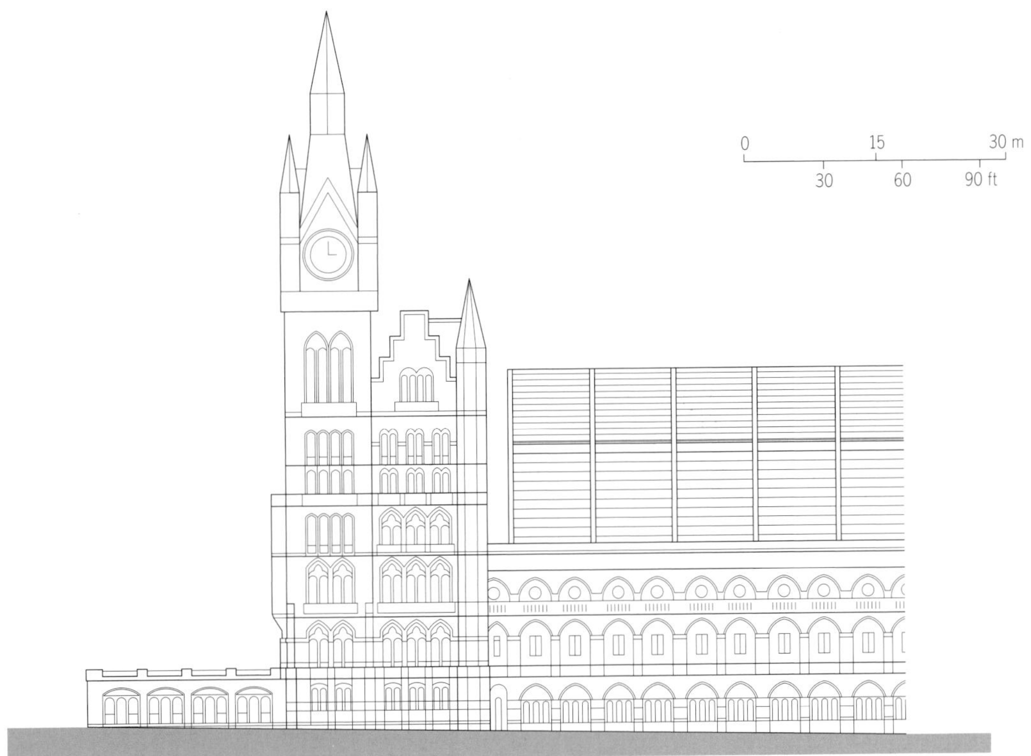

3

Keretapi Railway Station

Arthur Benison Hubback, 1871–1948

Kuala Lumpur, Malaysia; 1910

The coming of the railway transformed life in ways that its inventors could not have imagined. It became possible to travel in scarcely an hour a distance that would have taken a day on a horse, and the speeds increased all the time. The spread of railway systems allowed cities to sprawl, and the effects of industrialization in Europe drew people in from the countryside to work in factories. Those who could afford it then sought better living conditions away from the factory chimneys and travelled to work by train.

In the vast spaces of India, the idea of rapid travel was highly appealing, and investment in railways was encouraged and started to produce results in the 1840s and 1850s. The network of rail tracks in India grew to be immense and came to have an important role in bonding the various parts of the country together.

In Malaysia, the first railway lines were built a little later, starting in 1885 with a prosaic 13-km (8-mile) line connecting the tin mines at Taiping with Kuala Sepetang (known at the time as Port Weld). This was followed in 1886 by a 31-km (19-mile) line between Kuala Lumpur and Klang, in Selangor – the old capital, where the sultan's palace was located. By the time that Keretapi Station was built, Kuala Lumpur was the capital of the Federated Malay States, founded in 1895. The British were responsible for foreign affairs and defence, while domestic affairs were left to the sultan, acting on the 'advice' of a British resident appointed by the monarch, who took an interest in the mainly British commercial interests in the region.

Keret api means railway, but Keretapi is also the proper name of this station. It was designed to be an appropriate point of entry for a capital city, and its general strategy closely follows that of St Pancras (pages 214–15), but without the sense of straining to overachieve. The structural spans across the tracks are about 20 metres (66 feet), and the hotel facilities are less tall, but they are similarly positioned to mask the trains behind.

This was not a terminal station – the trains run to the coast in one direction and deeper into Malaysia in the other – so the hotel building is placed to one side of the tracks. When drawn at small scale, its rationality is very apparent. The building is disciplined mainly by the need to accommodate the railway tracks and give access to them. The trains are accommodated beneath ironwork, while human values take over in the more comfortable masonry buildings. These are composed on a regular grid, which is evident in the elevation, but for the visitor the effect is broken up by the projecting bays and decorative pinnacles, and especially by the arresting domes, supported on fine pillars, that seem to float above the corners of the building to give a pronounced oriental mood to the whole.

Colonial architects thought about the appropriateness of style and debated whether it was better to impose a traditional European style or to adopt a more local architecture. Arthur Hubback, the architect of Keratapi, did both. He was responsible for a classical station at Ipoh, and in Kuala Lumpur for both the Tudoresque building that housed the Royal Selangor Club and for what was then the main central mosque (the Jamek mosque) a short walk away from it. Rather than imitate traditional local architecture, which was built in timber and seemed ill adapted to large institutional and monumental buildings, he imported his sense of an appropriate regional architecture from Mughal India and Moorish north Africa.

1 Plan

2 Section A-A

3 West Elevation

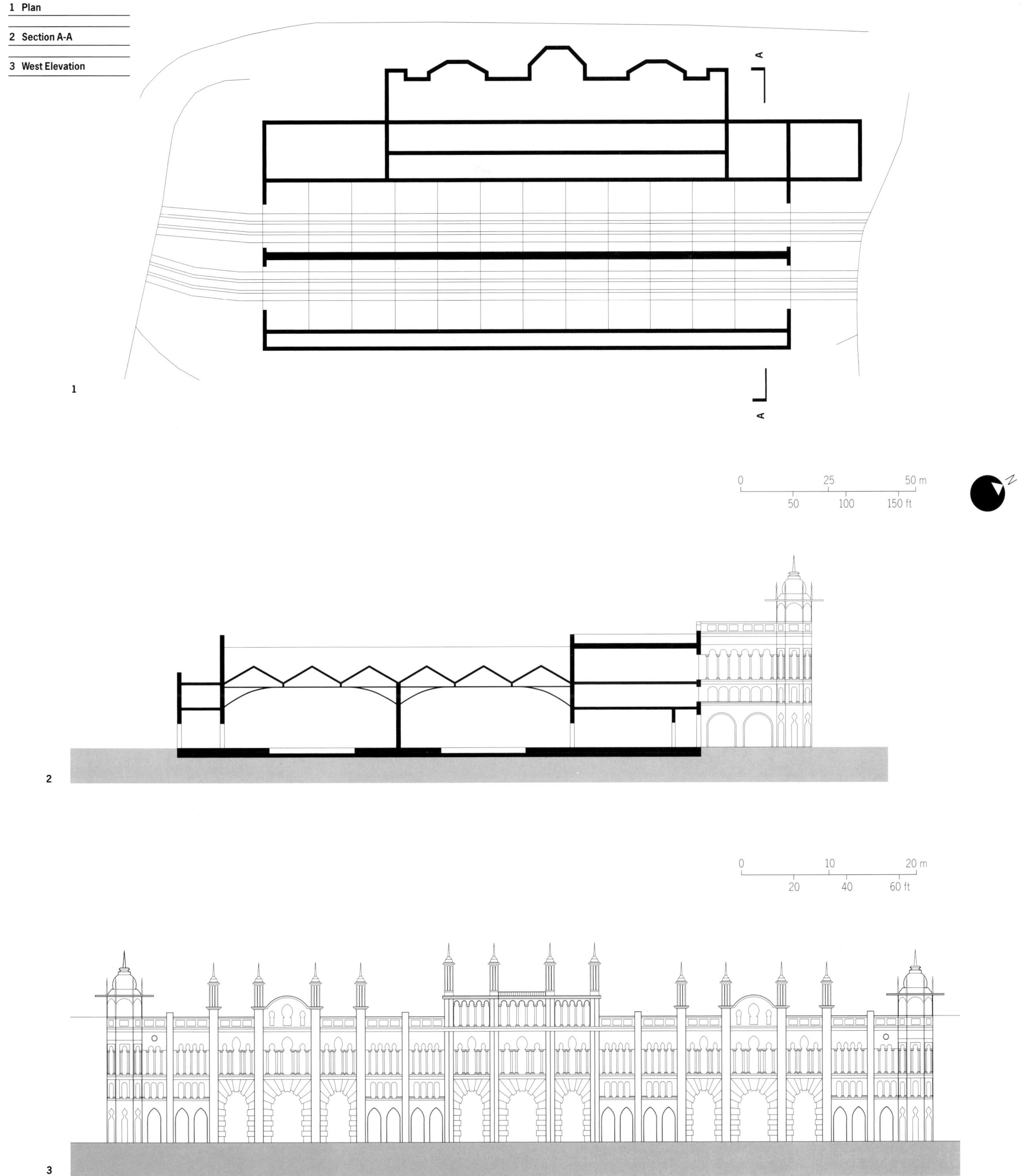

1

2

3

Grand Central Terminal

Reed and Stern, Warren and Wetmore

New York City, New York, USA; 1913

Manhattan's two major railway stations were, and still are, Pennsylvania Station and the Grand Central Terminal. Pennsylvania Station, commonly known as Penn, was designed in 1910 by the architects McKim, Mead and White in an imposing neoclassical style, with a peristyle of Doric columns, a huge central hall the size of St Peter's in Rome (pages 32–33), modelled on the vaulted central hall of the Baths of Caracalla (pages 270–71). Charles McKim had studied at the Ecole des Beaux-Arts in Paris and absorbed its methods of composition.

The original Penn was a very sober building, looking like a large museum. The rail platforms and tracks were below street level. Glazed roofs supported by iron frames covered the platforms and trains – but the whole superstructure was demolished in 1964, to make way for the development of a sports arena, Madison Square Garden, while the trains continued to operate below. Having been electrified, the engines no longer produced smoke and could make their arrival in a more confined space.

The Grand Central Terminal was arranged in a similar way and might have met a similar fate, had the demolition of Penn Station not caused such an outcry. Development at Grand Central means that the tracks are no longer daylit, but the main hall still stands and has acquired the status of a national treasure.

Two firms of architects were involved: Reed and Stern to organize and manage the work, and Warren and Wetmore to elevate its style. A cousin of the Vanderbilts, who commissioned the Grand Central Terminal, Whitney Warren (1864–1943) was the key figure in determining the building's appearance. He had spent ten years studying at the Ecole des Beaux-Arts, and the building looks much more specifically French than Penn Station did. It is in the neo-baroque style of the Opéra Garnier (pages 282–83), and like that building is animated by old-fashioned but very fine statues that obliquely express the building's character by allusion to classical gods.

The terminal's main façade is topped off with a sculptural group of heroic size, with Hermes about 10 metres (33 feet) tall as the central figure. He was the messenger of the gods. At Grand Central, Hermes is flanked by Minerva and Hercules, representing wisdom and strength. Known collectively as the Glory of Commerce, the figures were sculpted by Jules-Félix Coutan, who worked in Paris, teaching at the Ecole des Beaux-Arts from 1900. They are the icing on the cake.

Reed and Stern won the commission by presenting design proposals that matched Cornelius Vanderbilt's ideas about how the building should function, connecting different rail networks. There had been a bad fire on this spot, at an earlier station, when two steam engines had collided, and Vanderbilt consequently pioneered electric-powered rolling-stock (using Edison's direct current, rather than Tesla's alternating current, which would eventually catch on more widely). That enabled the introduction of two underground platform levels and the surface development of land previously open above the rail tracks (now Park Avenue North).

The great hall references Roman baths, but what would have been a concrete vault in the ancient world is here supported by a steel frame, hidden from view by a plaster ceiling. The thousands of people who use the place every day do so because it works, without quite knowing how it does so. Their attention is more likely to be engaged by the painted stars on the plaster vault or by the glorious sculpture than by the ingenious underground interconnections.

1 Ground Floor Plan

1 Entrance
2 Waiting room
3 Main concourse
4 Taxi rank

2 Section A-A

A A
4 3
2
1

1

0 10 20 30 40 50 m
50 100 150 ft
N

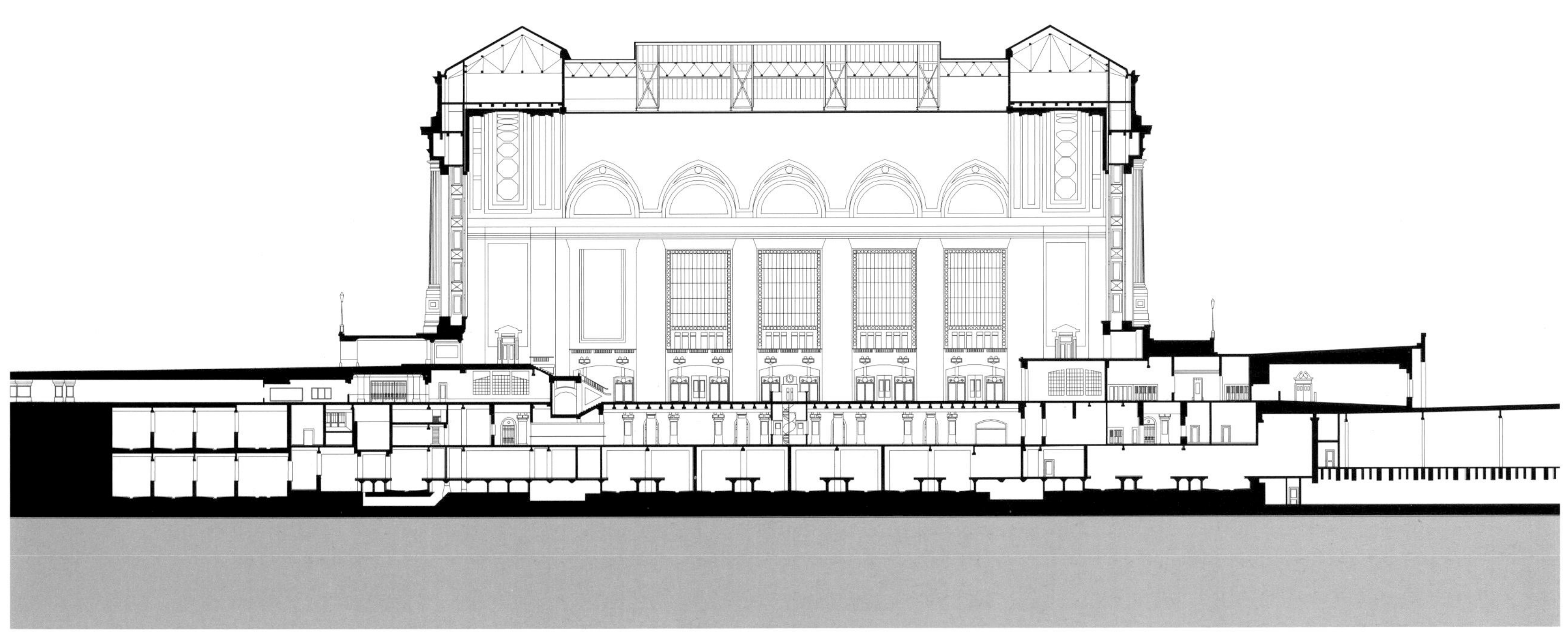

2

AEG Turbine Factory

Peter Behrens, 1868–1940

Berlin, Germany; 1910

In 1883 a German entrepreneur called Emil Moritz Rathenau formed the German Edison Society for Applied Electricity, which evolved a few years later into the General Electricity Company, the Allgemeine Elektricitäts-Gesellschaft (AEG). In 1907 the architect Peter Behrens was engaged as a consultant; he designed not only buildings for the company but also products and advertising. The stylistic coherence Behrens shaped out of this disparate activity is generally seen to be the beginning of the idea of 'corporate identity'. His student assistants included Mies van der Rohe, Le Corbusier and Walter Gropius. The atelier was one of the key places where the ideas of twentieth-century architecture took shape.

Before Behrens moved to Berlin, he lived at Darmstadt and made a name for himself as an artist and graphic designer, so he was taken into the artists' colony established by the Grand Duke of Hesse. The idea of the colony was to champion design and innovative living, and Behrens's house at Darmstadt was one of eight to be exhibited in 1901, everything in it designed by Behrens. The house survives, at least in its external appearance, and looks extremely odd – like a gloomy expressionist version of Tudoresque.

From 1907 Behrens was involved with the Deutscher Werkbund, which sought to promote good design in everyday objects and was influenced by the values of William Morris and the Arts and Crafts Movement. However, Morris had anathematized machines, whereas the Werkbund enthusiastically embraced them as the harbingers of a new world.

The AEG Turbine Factory is Behrens's best-known building. It shows him designing like a mid-century modernist; but this was an industrial building, and Behrens's sense of decorum led him to adopt, for example, a stripped-down classical style when he was awarded the commission to design the German Embassy in St Petersburg in 1911. The AEG building was envisaged as a model of rectitude and sobriety. Its steel frame is clearly evident most of the time, with large areas of glazing slightly set back to make the columns fully visible.

To give the building a certain monumental dignity, Behrens made the corners look solid by using concrete panels. Younger architects criticized him for this. Ludwig Hilberseimer, who was working in his office, saw Behrens, with his independent means, as an oppressor, accusing him of 'being led astray by imperialistic power consciousness'. When the Nazis took control in Germany in the 1930s, they identified Hilberseimer as a potential troublemaker. He left for America. But Hitler's chief architect, Albert Speer, admired Behrens's St Petersburg Embassy, and employed him.

An associate of Behrens while the turbine factory was under construction was Walter Gropius, later better known as the director of the Bauhaus and Professor of Architecture at Harvard. Gropius's first building came his way through Behrens's influence – Fagus Factory, for the production of shoe-lasts. It followed Behrens's example in using a steel frame and glass walls, but Gropius pointedly used glass, rather than concrete, to turn the corners, in order to make the non-traditional construction method more obvious. Moreover, the beams at the corners were cantilevered, so when they met at a corner they did so without a column there to support them. Everything that used to be solid had melted into the air.

1

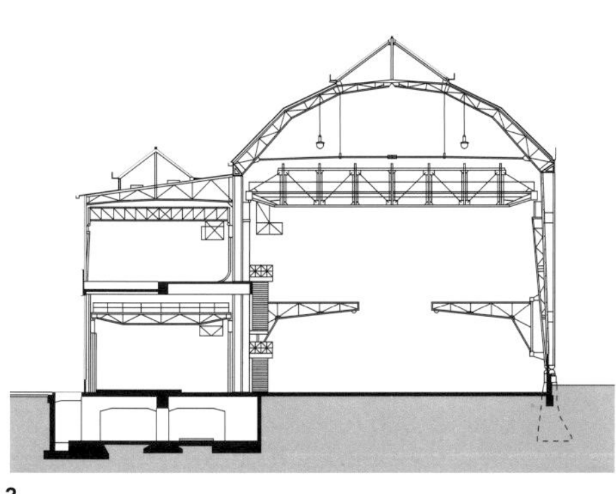

2

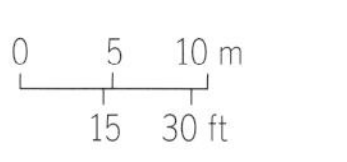

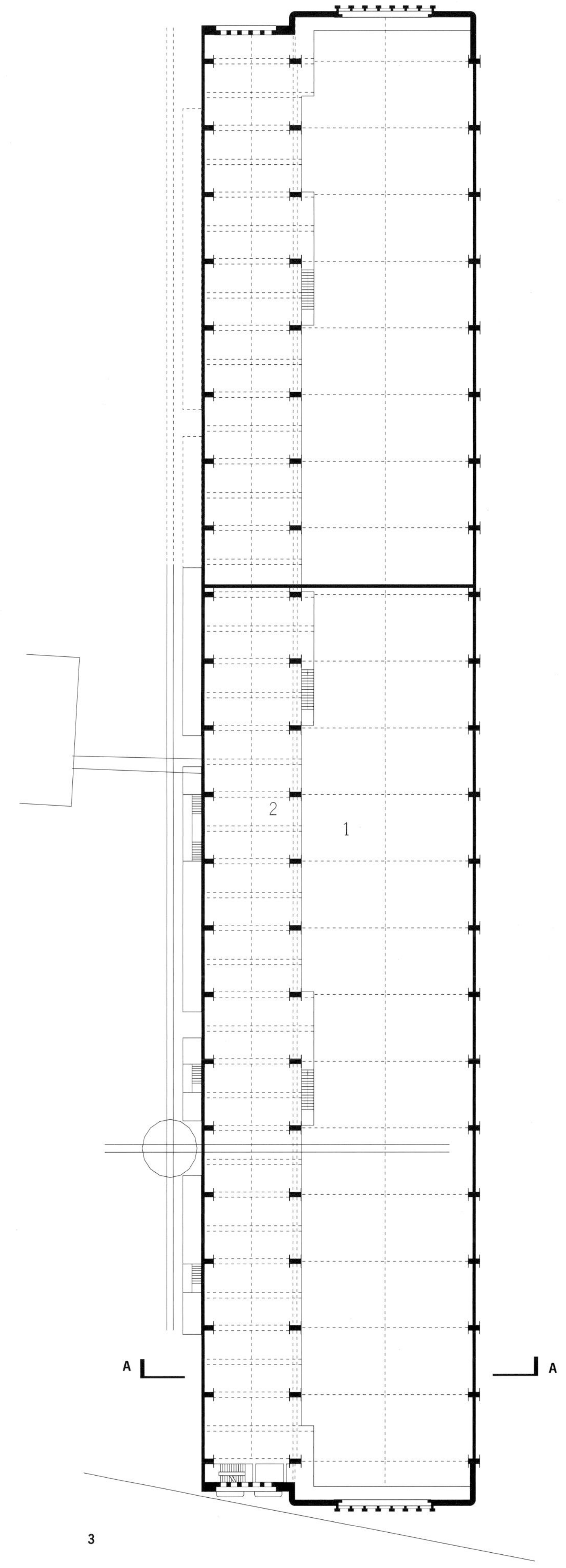

3

1 North Elevation

2 Section A-A

3 Plan

1 Main hall
2 Side hall

Seagram Building

Ludwig Mies van der Rohe, 1886–1969

New York City, New York, USA; 1954–58

Mies van der Rohe's minimalism was often invested with a sense of luxury that does not always come across in photographs. When everything has been refined to the simplest of forms, the things that matter most about a building are its materials and its size. Neither of these aspects is reliably conveyed by the camera. A painted vista looks as spacious as an open view; a panel of plasterboard and a sheer stone wall can look equally solid – but if our foot falls close to them, we have a sense of the difference, whether from the acoustic or the way we feel the air on our face. Similarly, in a photograph, something small and close can be interchangeable with something large and far away. We cannot tell how tall film actors are, or whether a film-set has been built at nine-tenths life size or with an accelerated perspective.

So although the appeal of the Seagram Building may not be apparent from a photograph, it certainly does have appeal. It was intended to be the New York headquarters of the Seagram distillers company but, following a series of corporate takeovers, that company no longer exists, and the building's tenants pay some of the highest rents on Manhattan. It is a building that very rich people want to be in. Why? Because it is the absolute embodiment of probity, quality and distinction in a culture where things can go badly wrong if one trusts the wrong person or acts on the wrong advice. Most of the present tenants are involved in providing financial services.

The Seagram Building stands on Park Avenue, with the Vanderbilts' trains running underground. In order that a decent level of daylight comes into the Manhattan streets, local bylaws insist that buildings above a certain height are set progressively further back from the road. For this reason, some of the very tall buildings, such as the Empire State Building (pages 38–39), which have an impressive presence in the city when seen from a distance, seem surprisingly self-effacing when encountered close up. The Empire State Building's towering parts disappear from view behind the parapet of a lower block just a few storeys high. Extraordinarily, the Seagram Building gives over about a third of its site to a public plaza. This means that its tower is brought visibly down to ground level, and the impact of all its 38 storeys is felt in the street.

Fire-protection rules meant that the Seagram Building's real structure could not be exposed in its façades. Instead, something that looks like structure is attached to the outside. The 'I'-section elements that run up the outside of the building are more or less the shape of industrial steel stanchions, but they are refined and cast in bronze – the traditional material for monumental sculpture. They give the façade some depth and complexity, as the flat outer flange seems to float in front of the bronze-tinted plate glass in the floor-to-ceiling windows. The bronze glass was a new material when it was used in the Seagram Building. The bronze mullions were an extravagance; 1,500 tons of bronze was used in them, and they are oiled twice a year to prevent deterioration.

The ground floor is given over to a tall, empty lobby glazed from floor to ceiling. The four lift-shafts are lined in travertine; a Picasso tapestry hangs next to the entrance to the Four Seasons restaurant, famously patronized by power-brokers. The opulence is understated but real. Everything is a little larger and more solid than normal. Public spaces have high ceilings and feel generously sized – in a city where space has a high price. When it opened in 1958, the Seagram Building was the world's most expensive skyscraper. Minimalism does not come cheap.

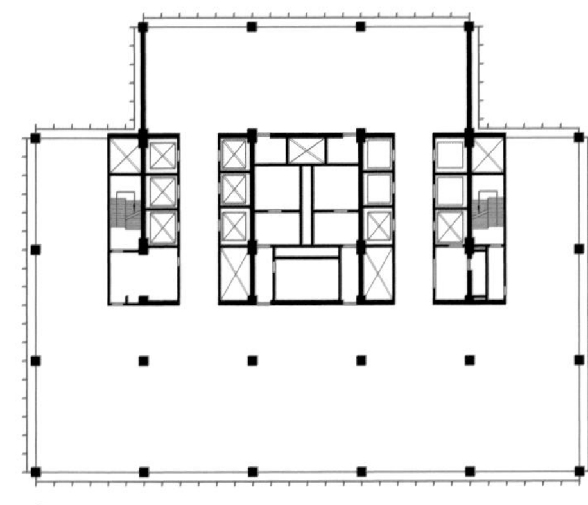
1

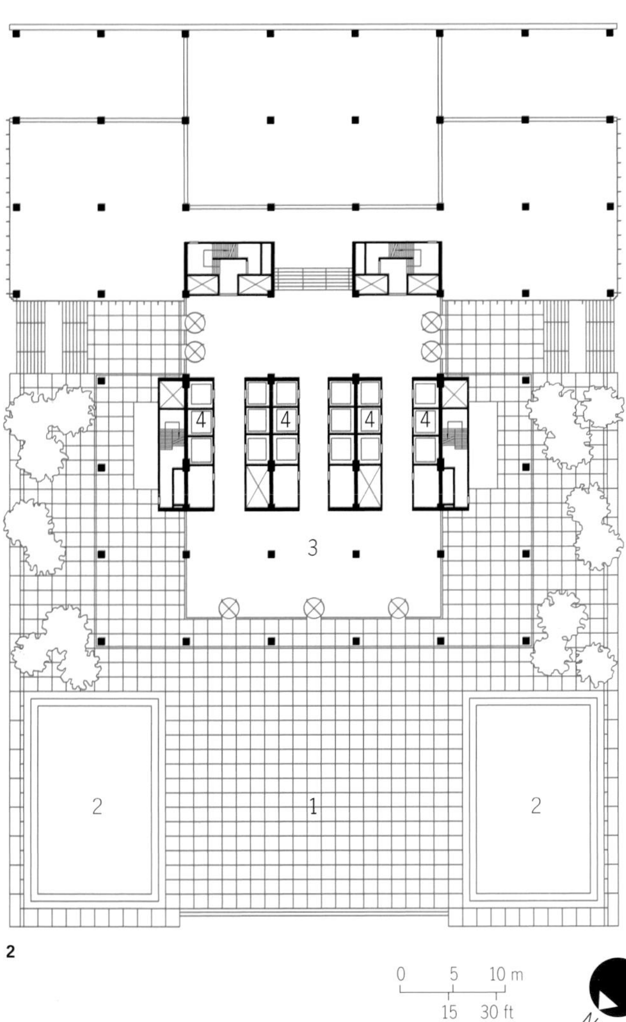

2

1 Upper Floor Plan

2 Ground Floor Plan

1 Plaza
2 Reflective pool
3 Lobby
4 Lift shaft

3 North West Elevation

3

Dulles Airport

Eero Saarinen, 1910–61

Washington DC, USA; 1958–62

Air travel used to be more glamorous when only the rich could afford it, but it was not necessarily any more comfortable then. The oldest airports claim to date from before World War I, but their buildings have changed beyond recognition.

The Empire State Building's finial mast was designed for the tethering of airships, which went out of service after the disastrous arrival of the *Hindenberg* in New Jersey in 1937. Aeroplanes were much faster than airships, but they needed runways. As planes have increased in size, runways need to be longer. As the passenger numbers have increased, so has the size of terminal buildings. Their function remains essentially the same as it ever was – keeping people comfortably sheltered while they wait to board a plane – but there has been a growing need to find expression in the buildings. Passport and security checks and baggage-reclaim procedures have now become part of the ritual of air travel that need to be properly accommodated.

The terminal that Eero Saarinen designed for Dulles Airport dates from the early days of mass air travel. The main hall has modest practical functions. There are places to sit, take refreshments and buy newspapers and gifts. The security checks happen on the lower floor. The passports of the relatively few people taking international flights are checked later, at the subsidiary international terminal. The main issue at stake in the building's design was not so much the provision of facilities, which could be done unobtrusively with little fuss, but instilling a sense of occasion in the journey.

Dulles Airport has its precedents in the great halls of Euston and Grand Central Terminal (pages 218–19) and is designed to make the business of arrival and departure feel significant. Dulles is the entrance hall to Washington DC, the USA's capital city, but, being an airport, it is miles away from the urban centre and there is nothing else there that would impress the visitor. Saarinen's building rises to the occasion.

The dramatically wide span of the roof is held up on columns that lean outwards, the better to resist the inward pull of the mass of concrete that they support. The roof's swooping shape follows a catenary curve – the shape that a hanging chain would take up if it were supported at the ends. This means that the roof does not need nearly as much stiffening in it as it would if it had been straight. It does not require beams, which would have added more mass and made the columns wider.

Saarinen also designed one of the terminals at J. F. Kennedy Airport in New York – the TWA Terminal (1956–62), where his client was the billionaire Howard Hughes, who wanted a building that would upstage all other airports. The result was astonishing, with complex curves intersecting in self-consciously sculptural ways. It looked wonderful and attracted attention, but it never worked well and the increase in the size of passenger planes made it completely unworkable. Its intricate roof forms were difficult to keep watertight. Security arrangements could be fitted in only clumsily, and the seating areas designed for 1950s planes could not handle the numbers waiting for jumbo jets.

The Dulles terminal is much larger and had a more modest budget, but it has proved far more flexible and adaptable. It has been extended by the addition of new bays and it keeps planes at a distance, taking passengers out to them in an idiosyncratic truck (which feels like a cross between an elevator and a bus) with mechanisms that can adjust the height of the passenger car to meet the door of a plane. The plan opposite shows the building in its original state, but the elevation shows it after it was extended in 1996, making it 380 metres (1,240 feet) long.

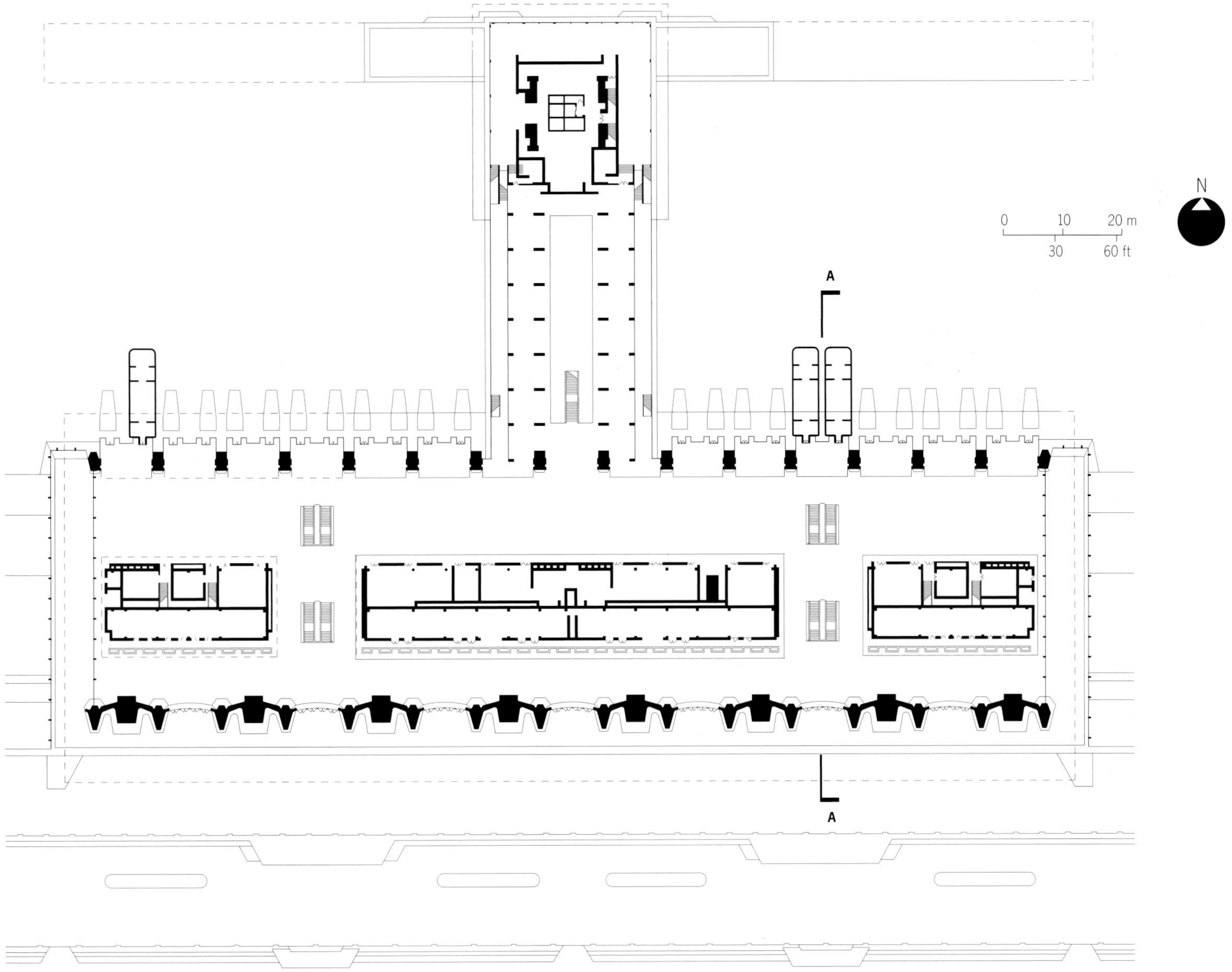

N

0 10 20 m
30 60 ft

A

A

1

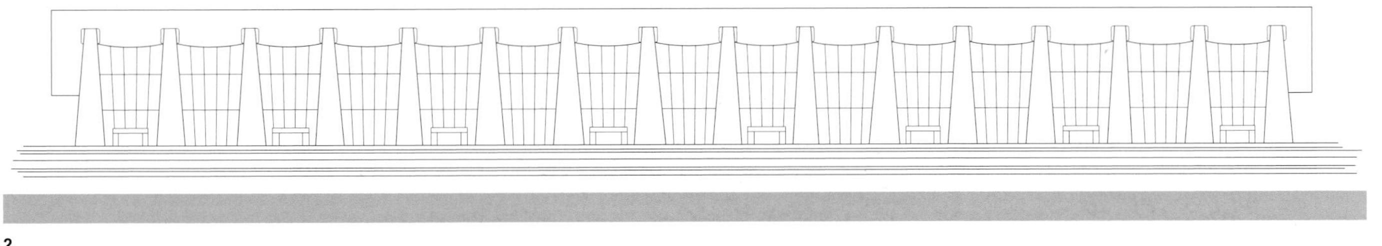

2

0 10 20 m
30 60 ft

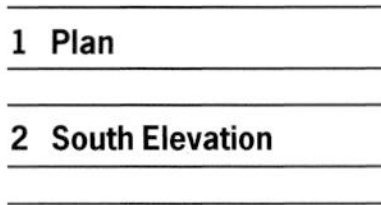

1 Plan

2 South Elevation

3 Section A-A

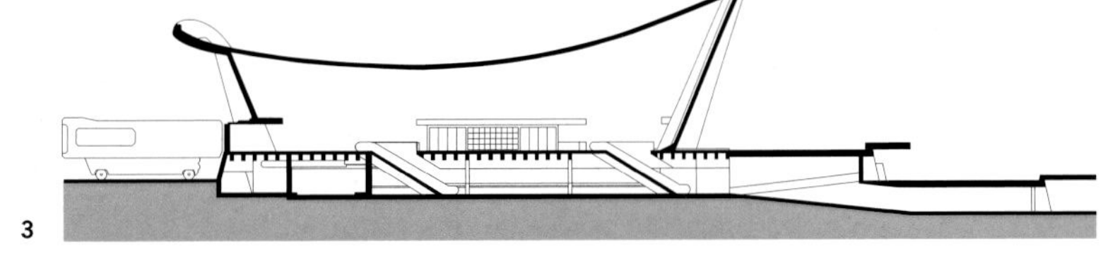

3

Fuji TV Headquarters Building

Kenzo Tange, 1913–2005

Odaiba, Tokyo, Japan; 1993–96

Kenzo Tange was Japan's best-known modern architect, both in his own country and overseas. He studied architecture and urban design, and made his reputation in Japan before securing major commissions around the world. He is particularly associated with megastructures that combine different functions in one large-scale building, for which there was ample scope in the reconstruction of Tokyo and Hiroshima after the end of World War II. Tange's large projects are best understood with reference to his understanding of urban design. They are treated like small towns, with 'public' spaces that seem superfluous to the obvious requirements but which make the buildings work.

The headquarters building for the Fuji Television Network, for example, seems crazily extravagant. It is a bravura display for one of the world's leading companies, and was commissioned when the Japanese economy was still relatively buoyant, though the economic climate was more austere by the time it was completed. The building is highly visible, located on Odaiba, a large island of reclaimed land in Tokyo Bay. From the city centre it can be approached by the Rainbow Bridge, a suspension bridge 570 metres (1,870 feet) long and high enough for shipping to pass beneath it.

The Fuji TV Headquarters Building is designed to have an impact when seen across the water and from the bridge. At night it forms part of a sparkling scene that includes an enormous Ferris wheel, with the harbour full of small boats in the foreground.

The Fuji complex is made up mainly of offices and studios, which are grouped into two perfectly sensible towers, one at each end of the site. The towers are supported by steel columns that are clad in such a way as to resemble lattices that run from the ground to the roof – four on the main façade of one tower, six on the other. In some parts of the building these lattices are real. There is open space around them and they support the accommodation on the floors above. They are evident, for example, when approaching the building's west end, where there is a broad flight of steps.

Between the two towers is the most arresting part of the building, where the lattices are fully exposed and arranged to make a super-lattice in three dimensions, at five times the size of the other ones. There is no particular need for these lattices; they seem to be supporting nothing but themselves. Corridors are included in the horizontal ones, but it is difficult to believe that these have an important functional purpose. The horizontal structures span a great distance and are stiffened by vertical shafts that have the same dimensions but which are simply openwork. The effect is like some of the drawings of the twentieth-century Dutch artist Maurits Escher, where people who seem to be in the same space are under the influence of impossible gravity that pulls them in one of three different directions. This game of gravity-defiance culminates in a shiny silver sphere that seems to have lodged weightlessly in the grid structure. It is 32 metres (105 feet) in diameter and weighs 1,300 tons. Somehow that lattice of corridors is taking quite a strain.

Inside the sphere is a viewing platform, which is open to the public. Its floor is on the sphere's horizontal meridian, and there is a ring of windows running round. To the north is a view of the city of Tokyo, spread out as a spectacle. To the west, on a clear day, it is possible to see Mount Fuji. The silver sphere has a role similar to that of the Ferris wheel, drawing people across the water to explore the island and to see what wonders it enfolds.

1 Plan

2 South Elevation

3 Section A-A

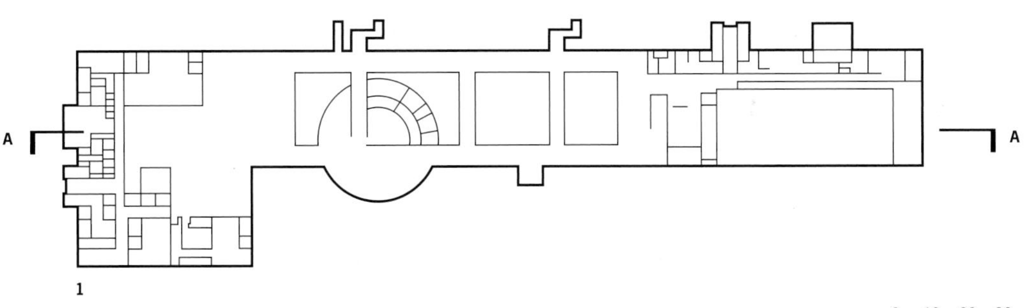

1

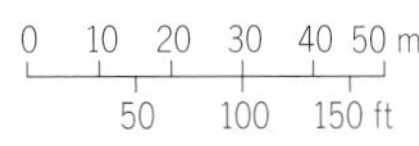

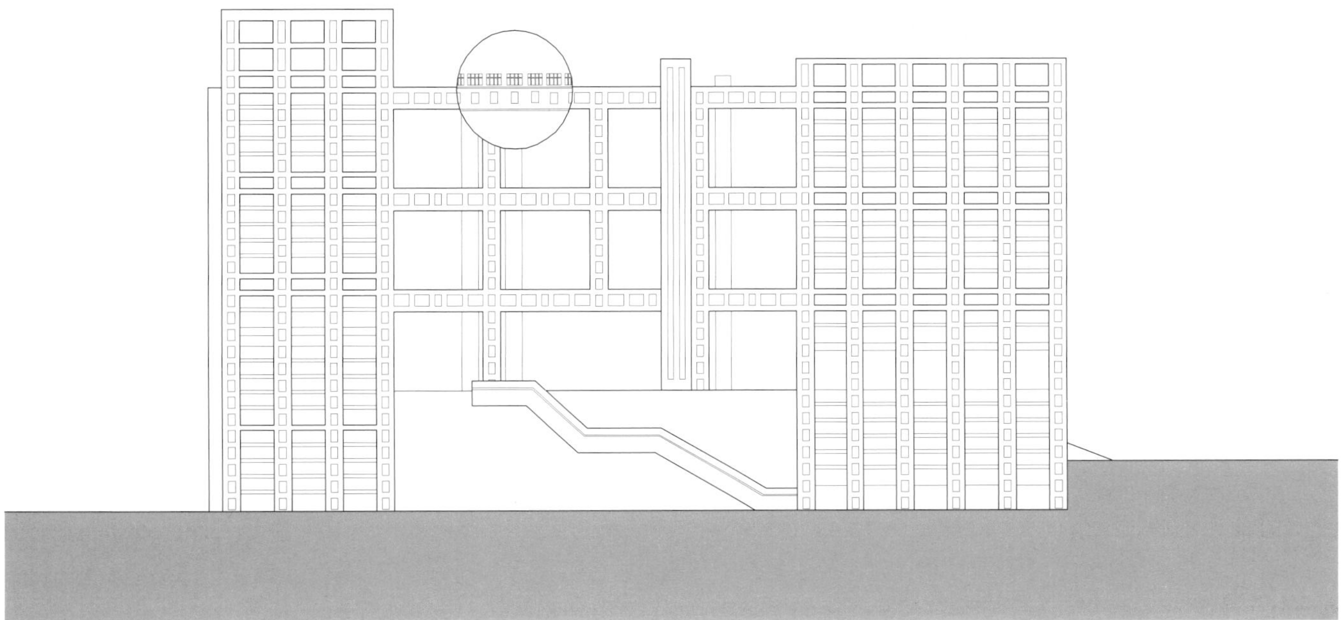

2

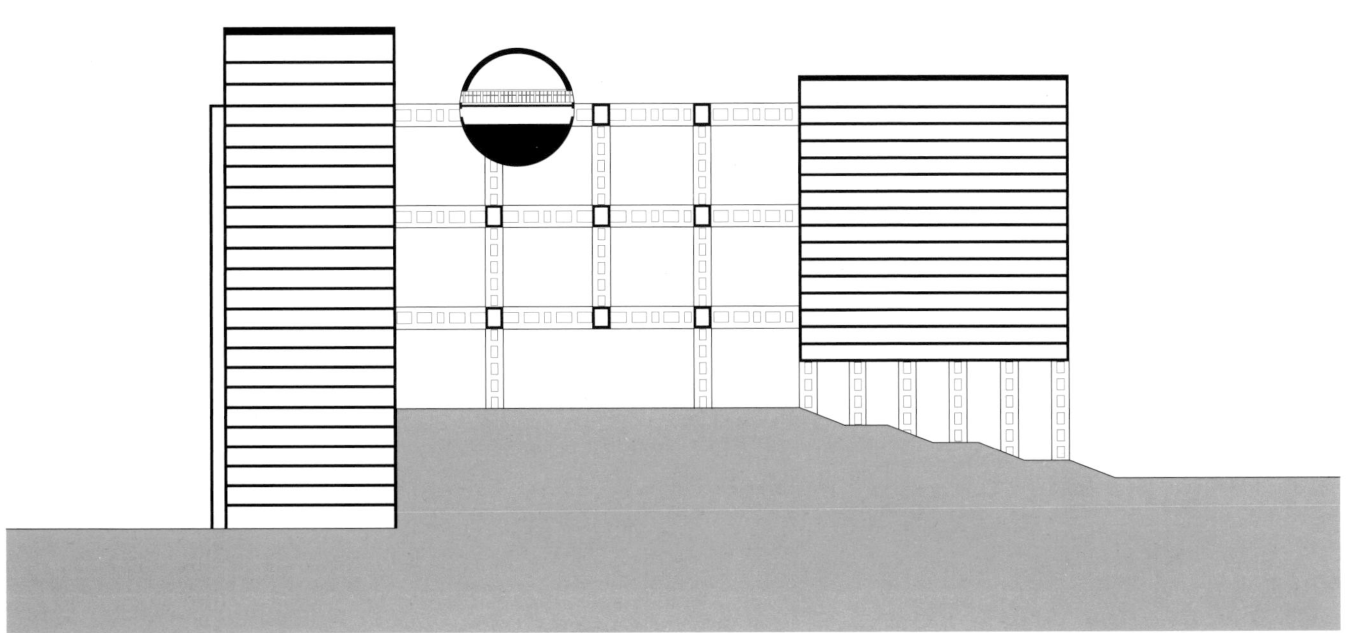

3

Petronas Towers

César Pelli, 1926–

Kuala Lumpur, Malaysia; 1992–98

Petronas is the national petroleum company of Malaysia, controlled by the state. It owns all the country's oil and gas reserves and is responsible for generating an income from them. Petronas is among the world's largest and most profitable companies, so, if it decides to build the tallest office tower in the world, there will be no problem about providing the resources to do so – and the achievement will be a matter of national pride.

The architect was César Pelli, who was born and trained in Argentina but has practised mostly in the USA. Pelli has had a distinguished academic career and his practice has been responsible for a wide variety of buildings, including the 88-storey International Finance Centre in Hong Kong (Hong Kong's tallest building), One Canada Square at Canary Wharf (the tallest building in London until 2012) and the Bloomberg Tower on Lexington Avenue in New York.

Petronas Towers have been overtaken in height, but for six years they were the tallest buildings in the world. Such an ambitious project was plainly undertaken for symbolic reasons, rather than simply to meet a practical need, and it succeeded in drawing the world's attention to the prosperity of the region, marking its emergence from the shadow of colonialism. There was a desire to give the towers a form that would be modern but specifically South-east Asian. To that end, the shiny steel and glass façades envelop a plan that is an elaboration of the Rub el Hizb – a Muslim symbol, made of two squares, overlapping on the diagonal to make an eight-pointed star. In the plan these eight points turn into eight projected pointed bays, which alternate with similarly sized curved bays.

Each of the two towers was built by a different contractor, in reinforced concrete rather than steel for the core structure. It was necessary to import the steel for the buildings, and the cost would have escalated even higher had steel been used for the whole of the structure.

About halfway up, a bridge connects the towers, and this provides a viewing platform for visitors who do not suffer from vertigo. In Kuala Lumpur's hot and humid climate the atmosphere is often steamy, so the views are less extensive than might be anticipated, as neighbouring towers become pale silhouettes and the distance is masked by warm luminous mist.

The accessible space that is much more important for the towers' vitality and engagement with the public is the multi-storey shopping mall, partly below ground, that spreads out around their base. There is a wide range of activity here, in a part of the world where the cooler air of shopping malls makes them more appealing than the streets as places to linger. There are luxury goods here at internationally sky-high prices, and smart restaurants, but also normal high-street shops, a noisy and lively food court and a philharmonic concert hall. The towers' reach is plainly global and competitive, but the city's people have been welcomed in to enjoy the success.

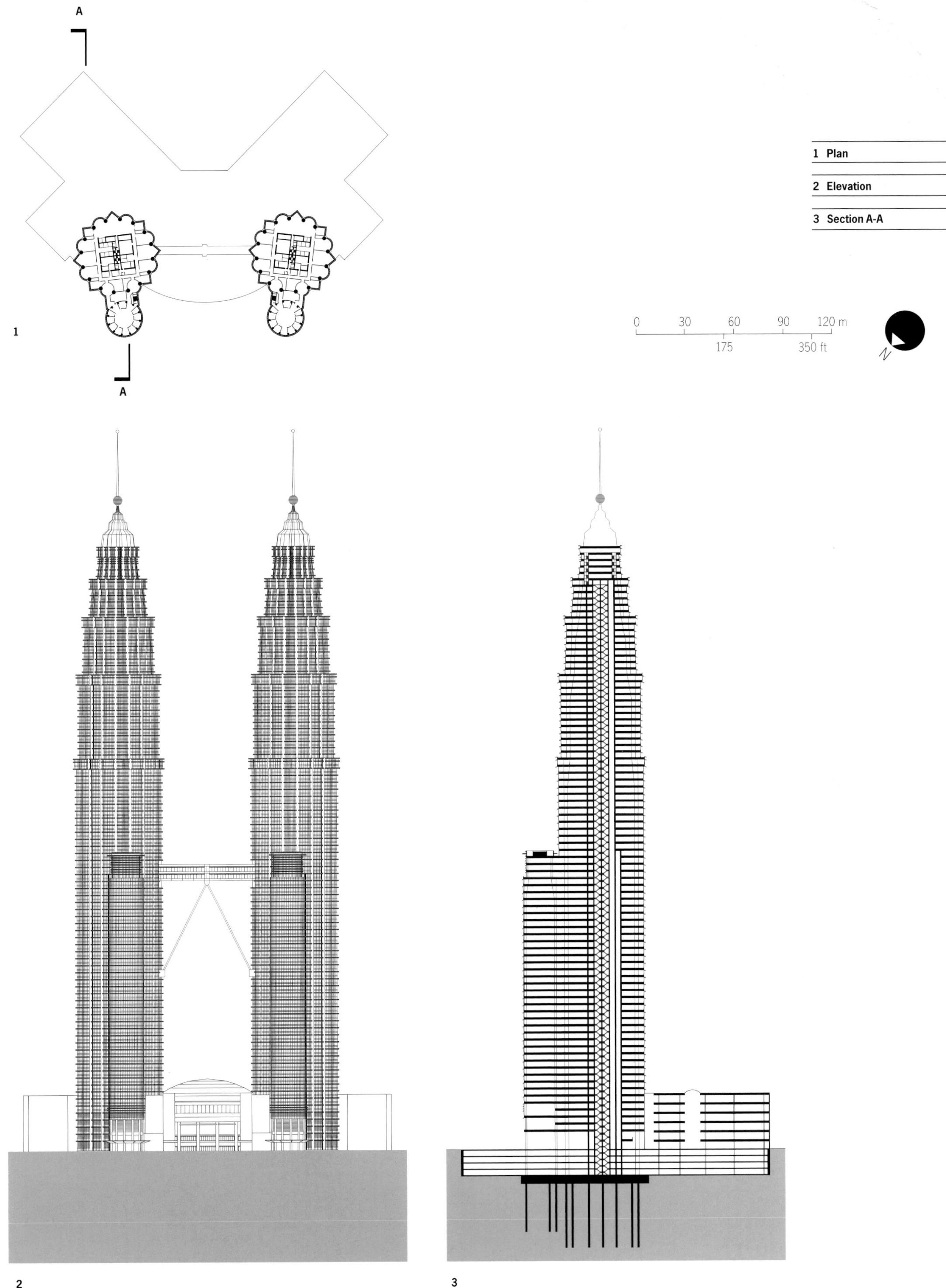

1 Plan

2 Elevation

3 Section A-A

China Central TV Headquarters

Office for Metropolitan Architecture (OMA)

Beijing, China; 2004–08

The Office for Metropolitan Architecture (OMA) was founded in 1975 by Rem Koolhaas (1944–) and others. In 2000 Koolhas was awarded the Pritzker Prize, an important international award (Kenzo Tange won it in 1987), as much for his writing and ideas as for his built work. At that time, the practice's largest commission was the redevelopment of an area of Lille in France, including the station for the rail-link under construction between London, Paris and Brussels, which gave Lille new prominence.

The practice announced to the wider world its preoccupation with 'bigness' in 2002, with the publication of a sprawling compendium that is part scrapbook, part manifesto, entitled *s, m, l, xl* – like the sizes in a range of clothing (the projects are organized by size rather than chronologically or alphabetically). Since then, its work has included some striking commissions, including a public library in Seattle, USA (2004) and a concert hall in Porto, Portugal (2007).

OMA's work is characterized by very careful analysis in advance of the design, and then by conceptual audacity and flamboyance in its development. Traditional architectural values (such as quality) are often bypassed along the way, making the projects seem more like experimental mash-ups than perfectly honed and finished pieces.

China Central Television's headquarters is big – but, even so, it was in danger of being lost in its surroundings, where 300 skyscrapers are projected to be built in the next few years. The accommodation includes offices and studios, but that is far from obvious on the exterior. Internal spaces do what they have to do. It is impossible to tell from the outside how many floors there are, since the steel frame is clad in reflective glass with an irregular grid of diagonal lines breaking it up. There are 55 storeys.

Designed neither as a tower nor as a straightforward arch, the building is configured as a loop that works its way round six of the edges of a slightly tapering cube. The top slopes slightly, so the number of storeys bridging at the top is not constant, but about a dozen storeys take the leap from one near-vertical shaft to the other, the bridges hanging unnervingly in space as they turn a right-angled corner on their way.

The lowest floor of this overhang is given over to a viewing platform, including some views through glass panels in the floor, as part of a route that takes visitors around the building's loop, so the sculptural form brings with it the opportunity for sensational engagement as well as high visibility. Construction costs were very high because the building's form was not generated by the logic of the structural frame. Spatial and imagistic logic took priority, and the structure was organized so as to make possible the breathtaking shape.

There is a huge amount of steel in the frame, which is arranged as a diagonal lattice and made visible in the glazing grid. Where there is a build-up of stress in the steel frame, there are more steel members and more glazing bars, so it is possible to read from outside where the structure is having to work hardest. Significantly more steel was used than would have been the case if the accommodation were organized as a single vertical tower, but China is the world's largest producer of steel, and evidently the cost was not too great for the television company to pay, though the project may not have found favour with its accountants.

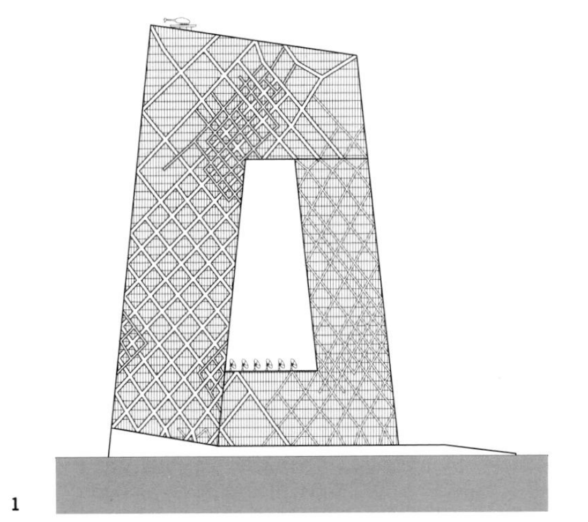

1

2

1 **West Elevation**

2 **Section A-A**

3 **Site Plan**

1 Television cultural centre
2 Hotel
3 Production (lower floors)
4 Administration (upper floors)
5 News and broadcasting (lower floors)

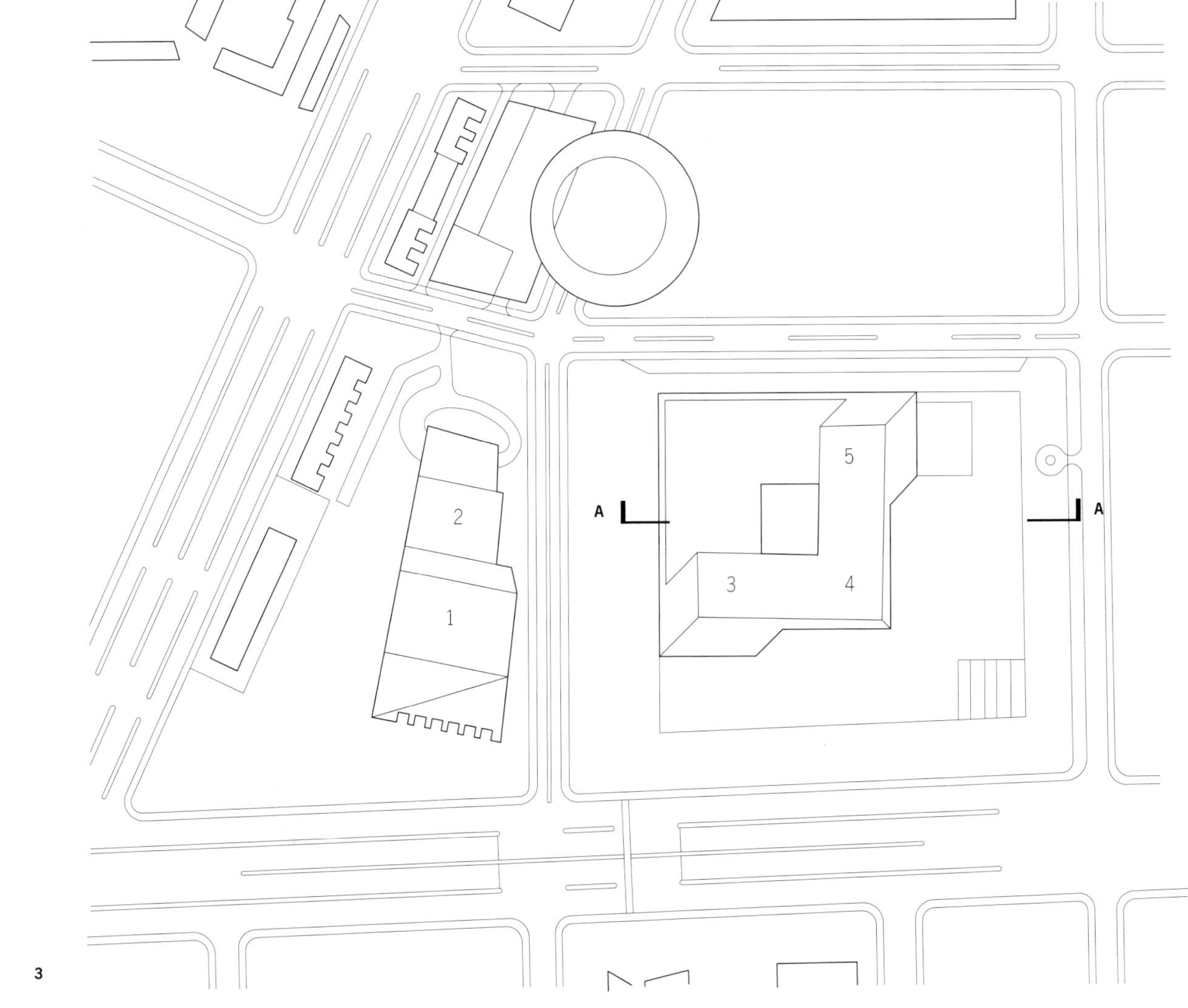

3

Government Administration

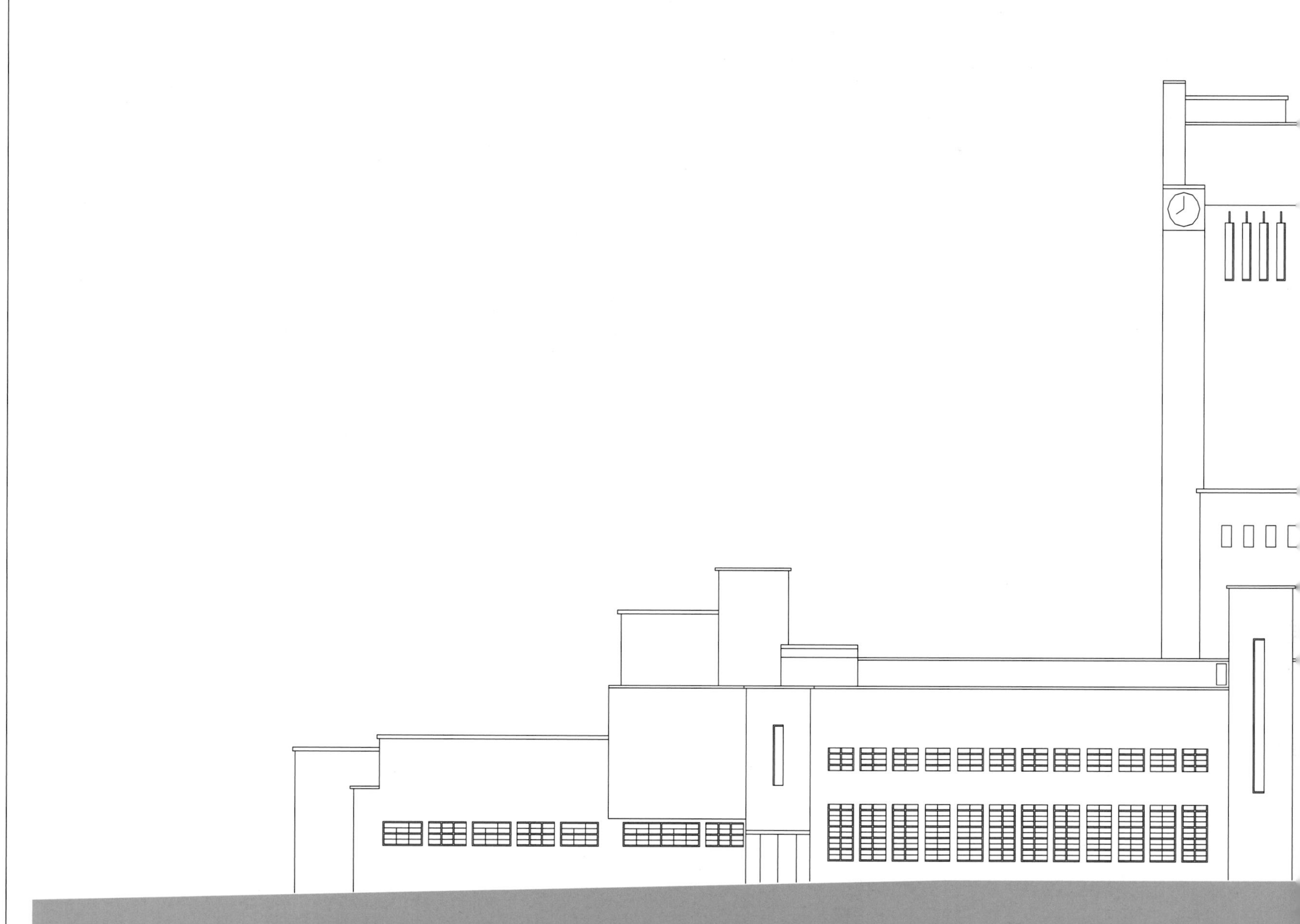

Buildings for government administration are often no more than anonymous offices, but those featured in this chapter all have a strong presence in the societies that they had, or have, a role in administering. In most cases, the administration in question was strongly connected with the character of the ruler, and the personal domain of the palace was extended to accommodate the activities of the people who increased that ruler's influence.

This is shown most clearly in palaces such as Versailles and the Topkapi in Istanbul, where the public role was played out in rooms of great splendour immediately adjacent to more personal realms, which may have been equally magnificent, but to which access would have been much more restricted. The personal and the political became inseparable, and the ruler's wives and mistresses were integrated into the machinery of government, since they could influence the way in which the ruler was thinking.

Sometimes the rulers were considered to be divine or semi-divine. Stories about the ancient Minoan palace of Knossos associate the place with gods and heroes, and the location of Machu Picchu, high above everyday life among mountain peaks, underscored the sense of divinity that made the Incas the legitimate rulers in Peru. There is a strong connection between religion and government in the prince-bishops' palace at Würzburg in Bavaria, where the church was in charge of governing the region and where its incumbents decided that a magnificent palace would make the appropriate setting for the exercise of their authority.

The plan of the nineteenth-century new Palace of Westminster makes it clear that the government of the UK was seen to be a balance between the 'three estates' – the House of Commons, the House of Lords and the monarch (Queen Victoria when the building opened). Victoria was head of the Church of England and Empress of India, and was given as much space in the building as were all the elected members of Parliament put together, since she had equal authority in the constitutional arrangements at that time.

Now that the practice of democracy is widespread, it is difficult to recapture the sense of how strange the idea seemed when it was devised in the ancient world. The Pnyx in Athens was the first structure built to facilitate the functioning of a democratic government. This process was much more onerous than simply being called out to vote from time to time: it was government by the citizens themselves, not by their elected representatives, so the whole of the citizenry had to be assembled to hear speeches that would inform their decisions.

By contrast, the Roman Senate was a small assembly, which took decisions that had a far wider reach, affecting the whole empire. The Senate, though, was always answerable to the emperor, who was sometimes officially recognized as a god – and more often expected to be treated like one.

The organization of buildings for local government reflects the need to accommodate public meeting spaces alongside chambers where a community's elected representatives could discuss and decide on courses of action. The best examples, such as the capitol building in Richmond, Virginia, and the town halls at Hilversum and Säynatsälo, combine the dual role of providing public accessibility to the process of government and investing the process with an appropriate level of sobriety and official presence.

Megaron of Pylos

Pylos, Greece; c.1500 BCE

The civilization on mainland Greece during the Bronze Age before 1250 BCE is called Mycenean – a name deriving from a once-oral tradition that transmitted stories down through the generations. Although these stories are now generally regarded as fantastical myths, there may be elements of historical truth embedded in them. The two ancient epic poems by Homer, the *Iliad* and the *Odyssey*, are usually imagined as dating from the eighth century BCE, making them the oldest works of western literature, but they seem to be written versions of an older oral tradition, recounting events that would date from the early twelfth century BCE.

The most famous excavator of Bronze Age Greece was Heinrich Schliemann (1822–90), who was guided by Homer in his search for ancient sites. There are doubts about Schliemann's methods, but he did find things. At the place that he thought was Troy, in Turkey, he found a hoard of gold objects that he called 'Priam's treasure', supposing it to have belonged to the king of Troy. Schliemann's wife was photographed wearing 'Helen's jewels'. In Greece, he excavated at Mycenae and found a gold burial mask that he declared to be 'the face of Agamemnon' – who figured in the *Iliad* as the king of 'Mycenae rich in gold'.

While these identifications are certainly incorrect, the places where they were found were real enough, and those places were inhabited at the time of the Trojan War. So the kings and heroes whose deeds we hear about would have lived in buildings such as those whose remains have been found. Even if the people and events were fictional, the imaginary people's dwellings would have been like these. Mycenae was an important settlement.

Agamemnon rallied the forces to go and lay siege to Troy, and Homer listed them all in the 'catalogue of the ships' in the *Iliad*. They came from many city-states that were not answerable to one another – Achilles was particularly reluctant to take orders from Agamemnon, but eventually played a decisive role in the war. This assembly of disparate people was an important event in establishing a sense of common purpose among the Greek-speakers, long before there was a sense of a Greek nation.

There are striking monuments at Mycenae (such as the Cyclopean walls around the citadel, and the so-called 'Treasury of Atreus' – actually a spectacular vaulted burial chamber), but the most important legacy is traceable from a building now in ruins: the megaron. It is a royal presence-chamber, or throne room. It was arranged with a level of formality umatched elsewhere on the site. The ground there has fallen away, leaving even the ground plan incomplete, but the pattern is repeated in other city-states on the Greek mainland. The best preserved Mycenean megaron is at Pylos, excavated from 1939 onwards by the American Carl Blegen (1887–1971), which is used as the basis for the drawings opposite. On axis with the entrance, there was an arrangement of four timber columns on stone bases, grouped around a central hearth. Everything above the floor level is speculative, but there was a porch with columns.

In many instances a place that was a Mycenean (Bronze Age) settlement became a religious sanctuary in the classical era, and the megaron seems to be the precursor of the classical temple, not least because there is some plausibility in the idea that it would be appropriate to house a god in a monumental version of the dwelling of a king. The idea is repeated in the 'basilica', which is now most often a large church building, but which was originally the Greek name for a royal presence-chamber.

1 South East Elevation

2 Section A-A

3 Plan

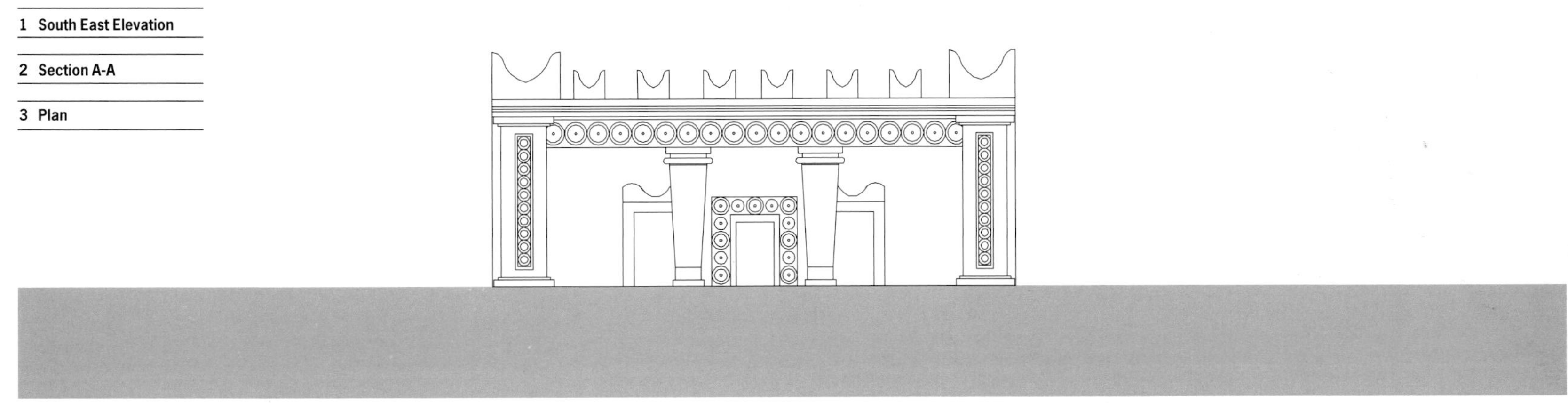

1

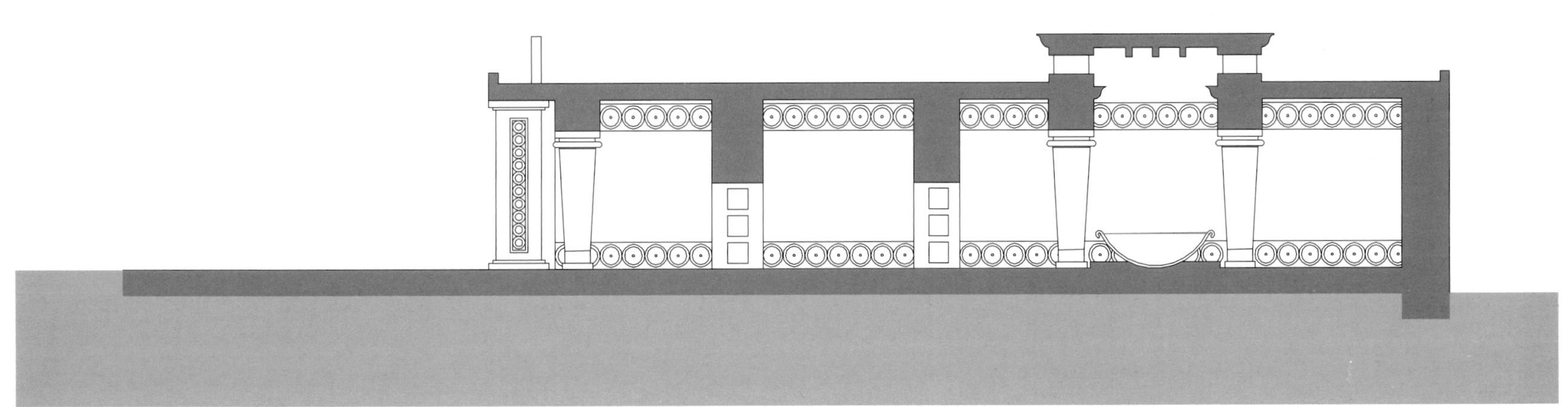

2

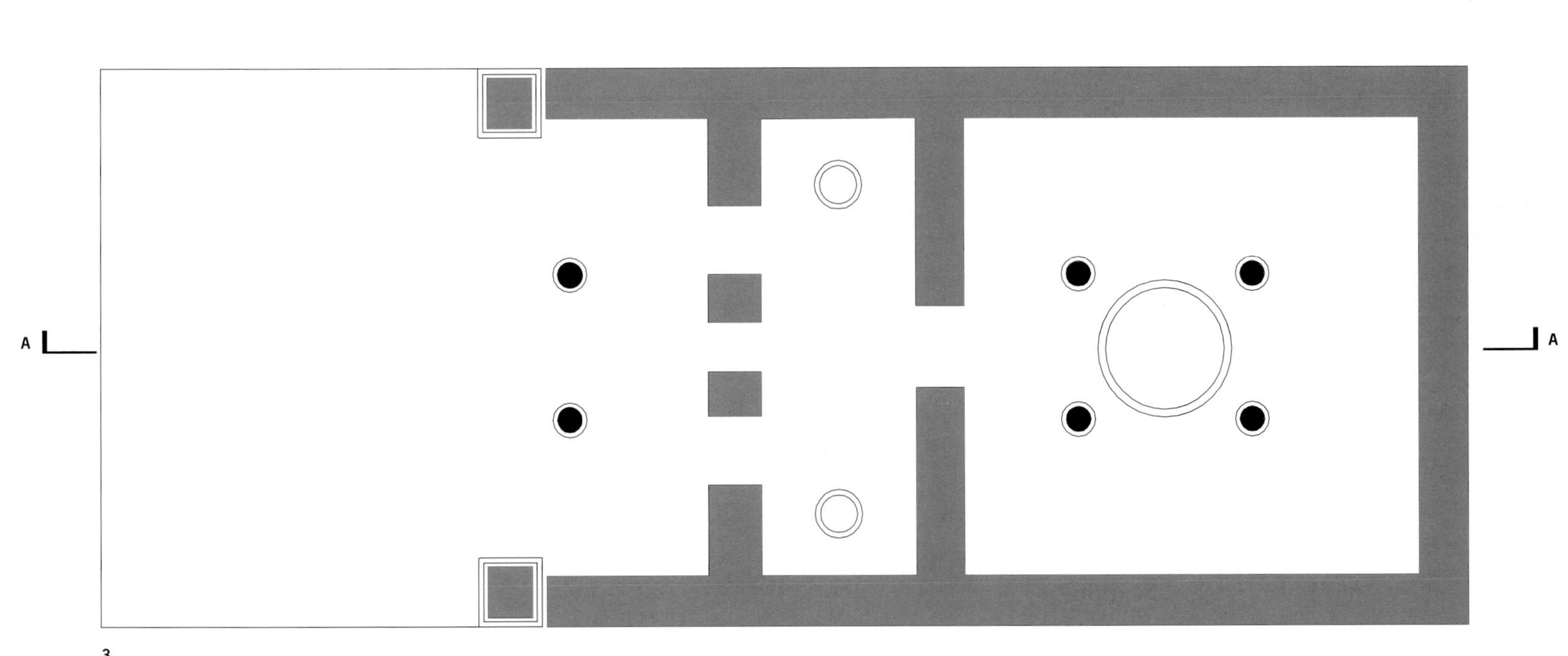

3

Pnyx

Athens, Greece; 508 BCE

The Pnyx is a hill outside Athens that came into use when Kleisthenes introduced democracy in 508 BCE. He had been within reach of political office earlier in his life, but was forced into exile by his main rival, Isagoras, who announced that Kleisthenes was cursed and would bring ruin to the city. Installed as archon (ruler), Isagoras continued to expel people from the city – hundreds of them – in a way seen as unjust. He provoked a popular uprising when he tried to close down the council that was there to advise him. At that point, Kleisthenes took over as leader and reformed Athens's institutions to introduce what we would call democracy, but which he called *isonomia* – equality before the law.

There were rivalries between different tribal groups in Athens, which had led to the tensions that had caused Kleisthenes' original expulsion. He invited the different factions put their cases to one another at meetings on the Pnyx – the name of which implies a crowded place. It would have been symbolically significant that the Pnyx was outside the city, suggesting that this was a fresh start. The hill offers one of the best views of the Acropolis (pages 168–69), which at that time had on it none of the buildings now known, but there were temples there and it was the city's most sacred site.

Another hill, the Areopagos, stands between the Pnyx and the Acropolis. It was the place where legal trials took place, and the modern Greek high court still uses this name. The Areopagus was associated with the old aristocratic law that would be called into question by Kleisthenes' reforms. It was unsuitable as a place for the new form of political debate, both because of its associations and because it was too small for the purpose.

By the time of Pericles (495–429 BCE), the Pnyx was a valued institution. Pericles was ancient Athens's most famous politician, responsible for the building of the main monuments on the Acropolis. He extended the franchise to include men from the lower classes which increased the need for space on the Pnyx. He also rebuilt the city's walls, moving them so that the Pnyx was included within them.

The gathering-place was developed over the time it was in use, which continued until at least 322 BCE, though at some undefined point the Theatre of Dionysus on the lower slopes of the Acropolis began to be used for political discussion. From 146 BCE, following the Roman occupation, the city's autonomy was limited.

The original, ad hoc arrangements were formalized by flattening an area at the top of the Pnyx to ease the assembly of the crowd. An orator's platform was carved out of the rock, from where the speaker could see the Acropolis and be reminded of his responsibilities to the city. Taking part in the meetings was regarded a sacred duty, preceded by the sacrifice of young pigs, a few drops of whose blood was sprinkled on the seats of the officals. The Athenian police force – the Scythian Archers – would round up stragglers and ensure their attendance.

The assembly area was extended twice, with the introduction of one retaining wall and then another, larger one. Instead of following the slope of the ground and positioning people so that they looked down at the speaker, it was decided to retain the relationship between the speaker and the Acropolis. So the gentle slope of the assembly area of the Pnyx goes against the main slope of the hill, held in place by a colossal rampart. The rampart has collapsed but remains visible on the hillside, and the area that once resonated to Pericles' stirring speeches still commands a wonderful view.

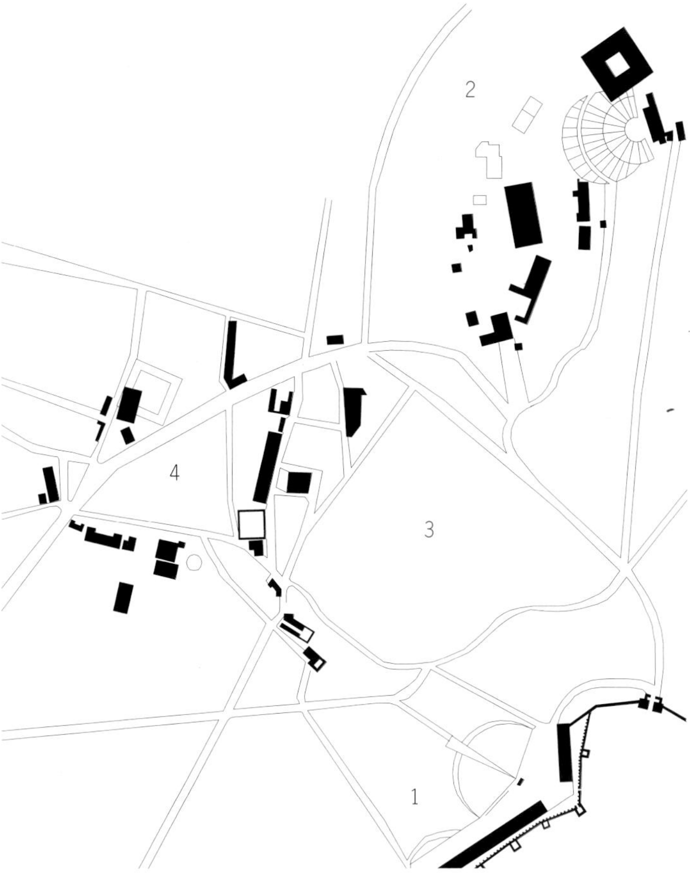

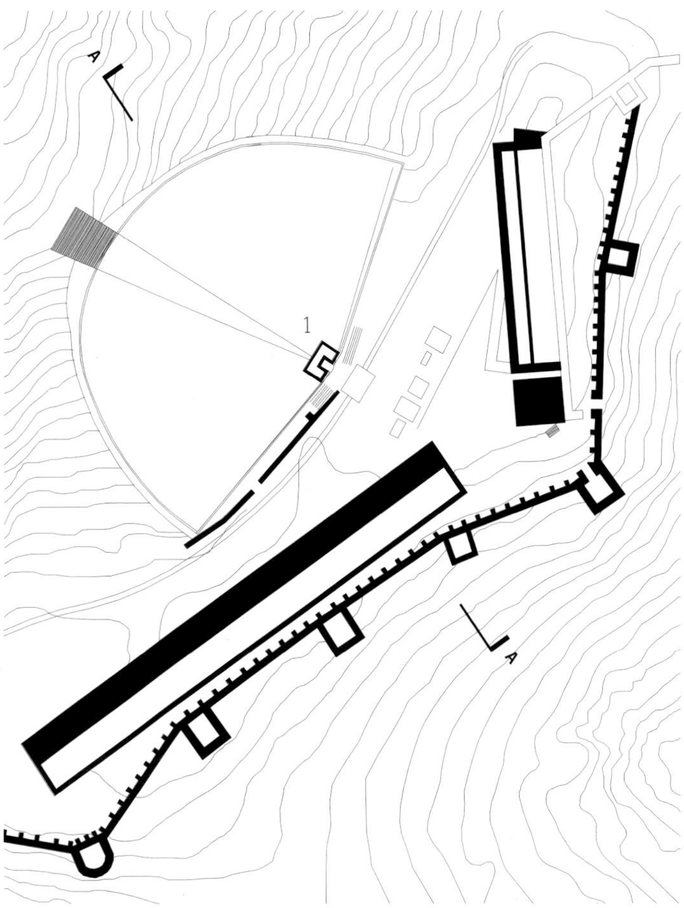

1

2

0 20 40 60 80 100 m
100 200 300 ft

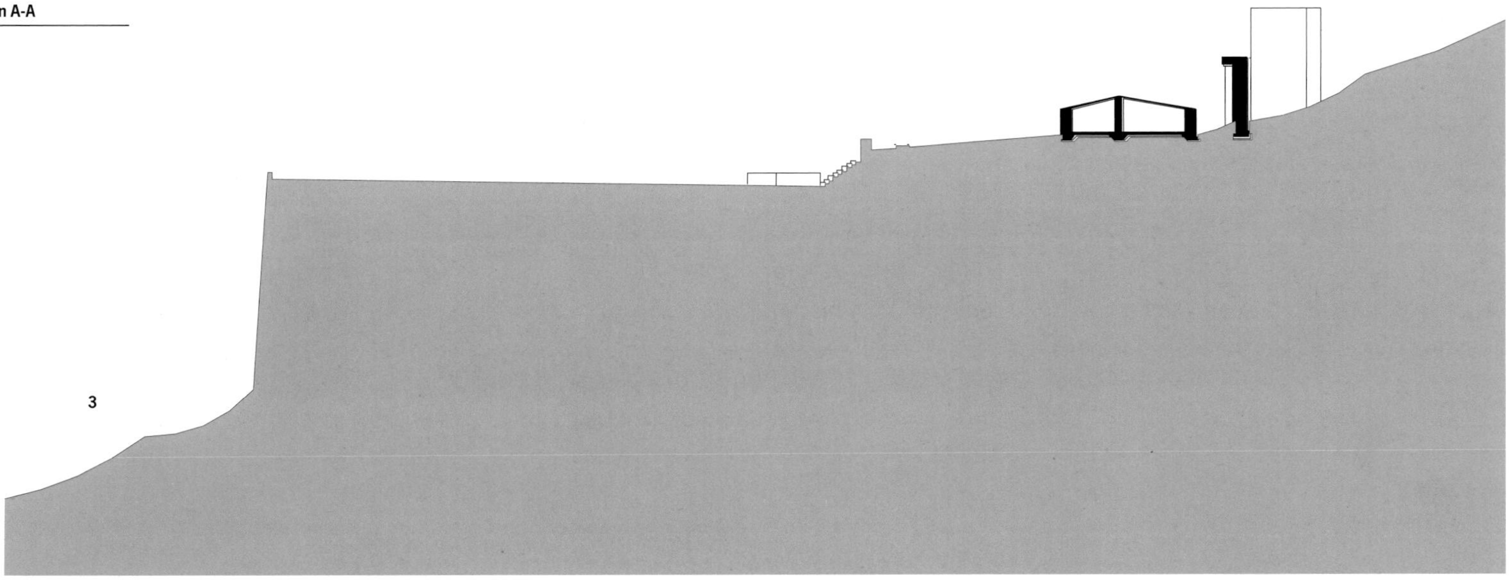

0 80 160 240 320 400 m
400 800 1,200 ft

1 Site Plan

1 Pnyx
2 Acropolis
3 Aeropagos
4 Agora

2 Pnyx Plan

1 Speaker's podium

3 Section A-A

3

Curia Julia

Rome, Italy; 44–29 BCE

The Senate was Rome's governing body, composed of influential citizens who could command the support of parts of the population, whether through persuasive rhetoric or bribery. In the imperial period, there was sometimes a tense relationship between the Senate and the emperor. According to Suetonius, whose account was not impartial, and may not have been accurate, the emperor Caligula tried to make his horse Incitatus a senator, which Suetonius saw as a symptom of insanity. Ordinary senators, though, were drawn from the Roman elite. They were fabulously rich by any standards, and as well as their own employees and slaves they would have a network of independently wealthy clients, keen to do favours for them in the hope of patronage, promotion and public glory.

The Senate was one of Rome's oldest and most enduring institutions, and it went through changes. It met in several buildings, called *curiae*, the most important of which, now known as the Curia Julia, was in the Forum (pages 306–307). This building had various incarnations, having once been an Etruscan temple, but it retained its air of sanctity, with its deliberations presided over by a shrine to Victoria, the Roman personification of victory. It was reconstructed by Julius Caesar, finished by Augustus and later rebuilt again by Diocletian. It was monumental in scale, as was symbolically appropriate given its importance, but small enough to be roofed.

The Curia Julia is still standing, in surprisingly good condition, but the brick-faced concrete was just the building's structural core. The finishes used to be much finer. Marble lined the lower parts of the walls, with stucco above; the floor was covered in a visually sumptuous layer of intricately worked green and purple marbles. It later became a church. The bronze doors with which the emperor Domitian refurbished the Curia Julia in the first century were removed in 1660 to the church of St John Lateran (the Lateran Basilica), where they survive.

The Roman Senate was a very different kind of assembly from the Athenian crowd that met at the Pnyx (pages 236–37). The Senate was more like a parliamentary assembly, with representatives arguing for and against a course of action until a decision was taken, but the 'representative' could inherit the post rather than be elected to it. At Athens there were no representatives, but the whole citizenry gathered together.

The root of the word democracy is *demos*, the Greek word for 'pebble'. When the moment came for voting after speeches at the Pnyx, votes would be cast by placing pebbles in the appropriate rack. So democracy originally meant 'government by pebble', which does not match the dignity of *isonomia* (equality before the law). At Athens, in principle, all the eligible citizens were required to be at the Pnyx, listening to political speeches, whenever there was a decision to be taken. And in principle anyone could make a speech, though in practice most speeches were by people with education – an advantage that only the rich had access to.

By contrast, the Roman Senate was protected and sequestered. In the early days of the Roman Republic, there were meant to be 100 senators, all from the patrician class. By the time that the Curia Julia was built, they were supposed to come from a wider range of backgrounds, and their number had risen to 900, but Augustus reduced this to 600, and they would not all have been in the building at the same time.

It is estimated that there were between 100 and 200 active senators, and the Curia Julia has space for no more than 300. The senators might strenuously argue against one another but, unlike what happened at Athens, their speeches were not subjected to regular heckling by the hoi polloi.

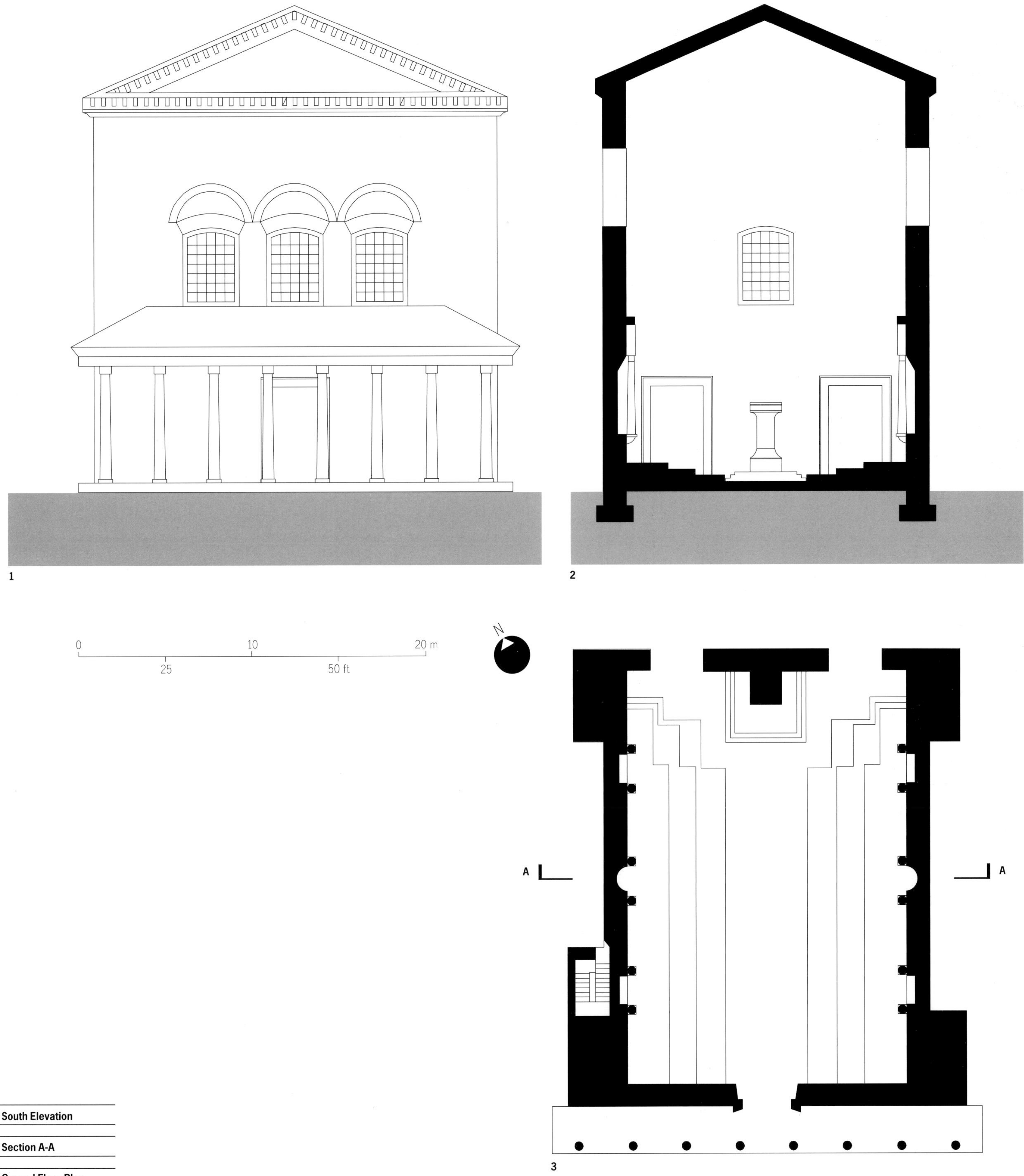

1 South Elevation

2 Section A-A

3 Ground Floor Plan

Alhambra

Granada, Andalusia, Spain; 1338–90

At the heart of the Alhambra is a carpet of water – a reflecting pool, with a row of myrtle trees on each side. The stillness and coolness of the place were a preparation for entry to the throne room of the Nasrids, the last Muslim dynasty to rule al-Andalus (Andalusia). This part of Spain was under Muslim control from 715 until 1492, when it was conquered by Isabella of Castile and Ferdinand of Aragon.

In the sixteenth century, the emperor Charles V (known as Carlos V in Spain), the grandson of Isabella and Ferdinand, built his own palace next to the Nasrid palace in Granada's citadel. It appears on the plan as a perfectly square block with a perfectly circular courtyard. Its octagonal chapel was in close proximity to the earlier courtyards, which the new palace connected and annexed.

Granada was once contained within its citadel and the Nasrid palace had other buildings surrounding it. There were five palaces grouped together in a 'royal quarter' but designed and used as separate entities until after 1492, so the progression from one courtyard (*patio* in Spanish) to another sometimes seems haphazard.

The throne room, known as the Hall of the Ambassadors, is a square vaulted space, lodged in a tower in the ramparts. Its timber vault and tiled walls are intricately decorated with abstract patterns, observing the Islamic avoidance of figuration. Light enters, as if by stealth, through high windows with patterned grilles and coloured glass. The subdued lighting, especially as it contrasts with sunlight in the court outside, evokes the atmosphere of a dream. Walls and ceilings feel insubstantial, and there are no windows to make a visual connection with the world outside. It is an enclosed, protected realm – the watery garden an image of paradise, the Hall of the Ambassadors a place of absolute splendour that, given the effect of the low lighting, seems understated.

Similar magic can be found in the Court of the Lions, which also uses water, but not in such great quantity. The centre of the courtyard is marked by a circular stone basin supported by 12 marble lions. Breaking the ban on figuration, the lions' presence in this place has provoked speculation. Presumably, the craftsmen who made them were not Muslim; if the clients followed the Islamic faith, they must have been tolerant. This was a more private space than the Court of the Myrtles, which had a role in high-level public relations, and where there would have been an effort to avoid an impression of laxity.

The Court of Lions looks like a place of display, but the display may have been reserved for family members and trusted allies. The courtyard was originally planted, making it a lush and shady space, and the lions spouted water from their mouths to feed four rivulets running in narrow channels on each axis, each finishing in a small circular pool in an indoor space.

Spaces around the courtyard are covered with 'stalactite vaults', carved with incredible elaboration and illuminated only by reflected light that picks up some of the colour of the stone or the shimmer of water; these would in the past have had a greenish hue from the light penetrating the garden's leaves.

The reflected light, which makes everything seem to tremble on the edge of reality, is enhanced by the extreme delicacy of the workmanship and the structure. Columns proliferate around the courtyard and, because there are so many of them, each one can be very slender. So the dozens of columns look decorative rather than structural, and there is a sense of continuity from the paradise-garden space to the shady interiors, emphasizing the promise of glorious respite from the scorching summer heat.

1 Site Plan

1 Court of the Myrtles
2 Court of the Lions
3 Palace of Carlos V

2 Plan

1 Court of the Myrtles
2 Hall of the Ambassadors
3 Court of the Lions

3 Section A-A

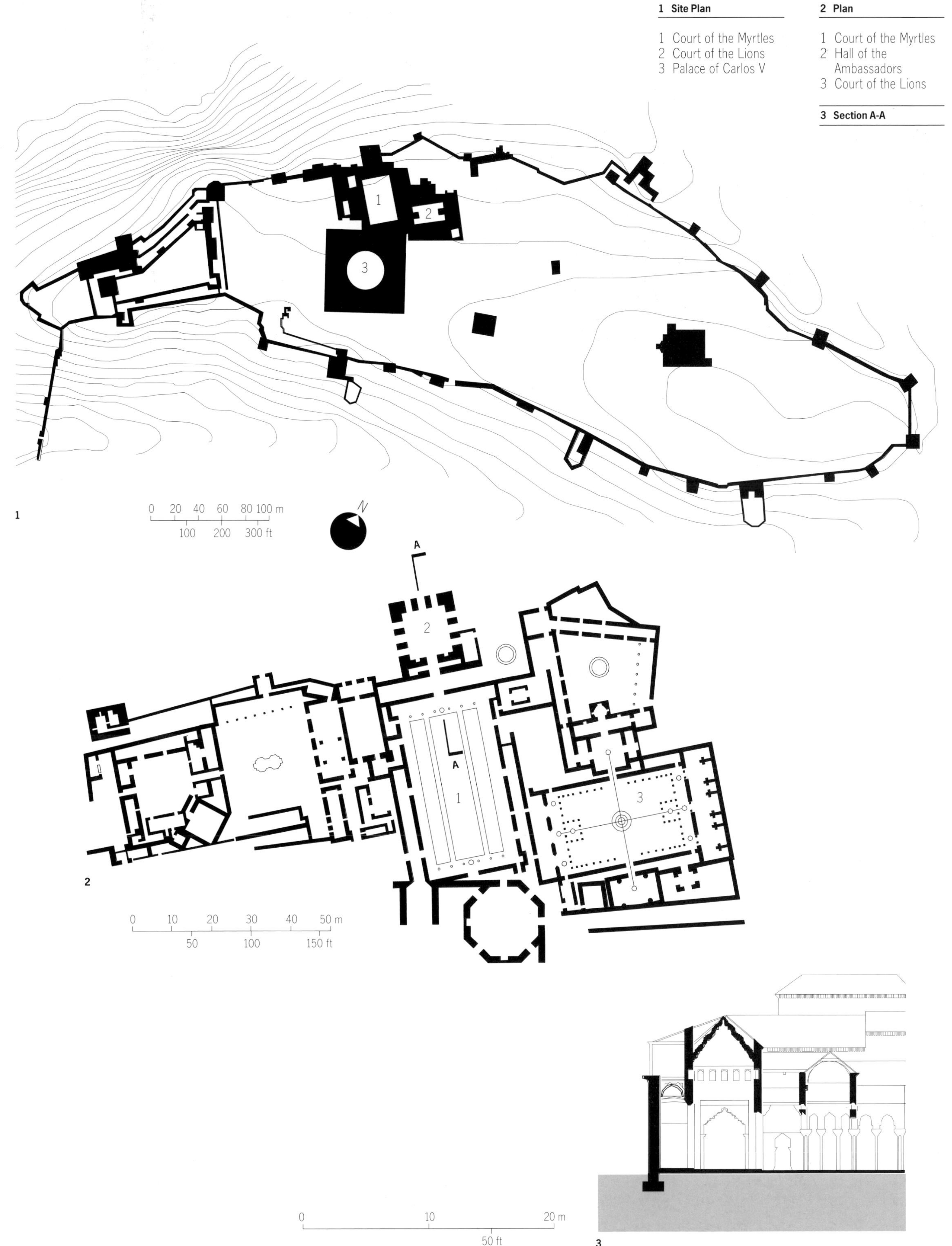

Forbidden City

Beijing, China; 1406–20

It seems implausible that a building complex as large as the Forbidden City took only 15 years to construct, without the help of industrial machinery and earth-moving equipment – until it becomes clear that about one million people were involved in the enterprise. It is also hard to imagine how it was possible to unite a million workers to produce a set of buildings reflecting a unified vision. Evidently it was done, as the structures themselves bear witness. China's great power rests in its ability to harness a collective will in order to accomplish things that would be unimaginable for an individual and beyond the dreams of ordinary kings.

The Forbidden City is not only the product of a collective will; it also held in place the organizing system, or collective organism, that ran China for 500 years and only stopped operating as intended with the revolution of 1949, when the communists took over. (The emperor was part of the super-organism, but only part, and without the rest of it in place he would not have had any significant power.) It was established by Zhu Ti (1360–1424), the third emperor of the Ming Dynasty, who was also known as the Yongle Emperor (*yongle* means 'endless happiness'). Zhu Ti's systematizing mental approach is also evident in the *Yongle Encyclopedia*, a great scholarly project in which he aimed to bring together everything that was known. It ran to about 1,200 handwritten volumes. Duplicate copies were made, but most of them perished by fire in 1900, and the original vanished long ago.

Lying at the heart of Beijing, the Forbidden City is isolated by a broad moat 52 metres (171 feet) wide and 6 metres (20 feet) deep with four causeways across it, one on each side of the rectangular plan. There is a tower at each corner, with multiple sloping roofs, and massively thick walls, built with a core of rammed earth and faced with layers of fired bricks. Within the defensive wall, obscured from public view, are a thousand buildings that once housed the innermost machinery of state.

The largest buildings are placed on axis on a shared podium, approached by flights of steps. (The section drawing opposite is taken through the podium.) These were the buildings where the Ming emperors held court and where ceremonials took place. The largest of them, the Hall of Supreme Harmony, has been rebuilt many times.

Dating from the late seventeenth century, the current hall is thought to be about half the size of the original. It is nevertheless the largest timber building to survive from the days of imperial China. The Imperial Dragon Throne was there, surrounded by carved and gilded dragons. The slightly smaller hall to the north (on the left of the section drawing) was the Hall of Preserving Harmony, used for rehearsing the ceremonies that would be enacted in the Hall of Supreme Harmony. Between them was a hall where the emperor could rest.

North of these large ceremonial halls, the buildings are on a smaller scale. The next group of three structures on axis, surrounded by a wall that creates a courtyard, was the emperor's domestic domain, including the Palace of Heavenly Purity and other palace buildings. This was the innermost part of the empire, with many layers of walls around it, protecting the emperor, who had the title Son of Heaven, from contact with the mundane world. It was a life of the highest imaginable privilege, but there was little freedom. Each rank of servant had its own system of rules and codes of behaviour, as did the emperor himself. The emperor had the ultimate power at the heart of this great machine, which kept him safe, but which was also the most comfortable of prisons.

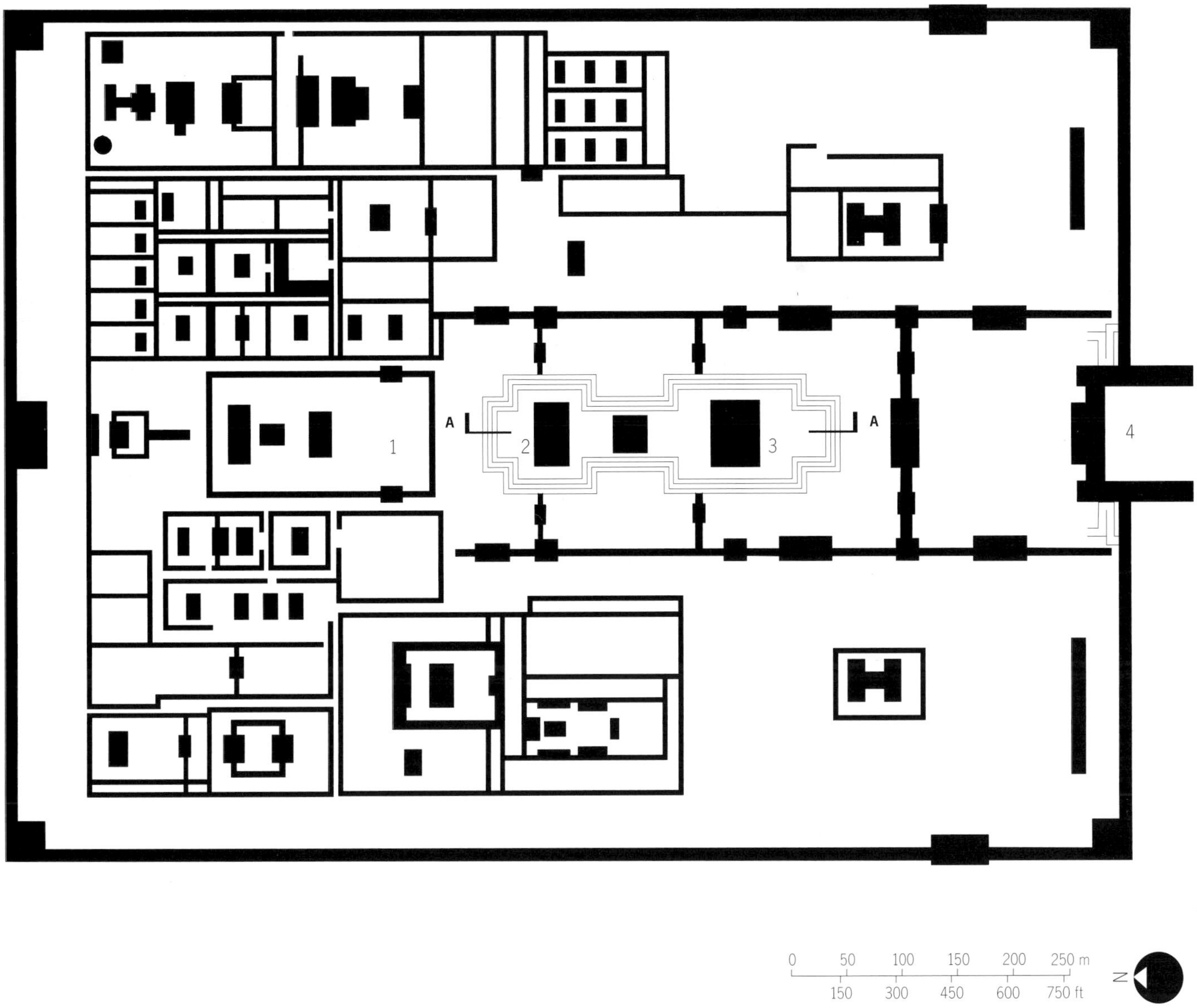

A A 1 2 3 4

1

2

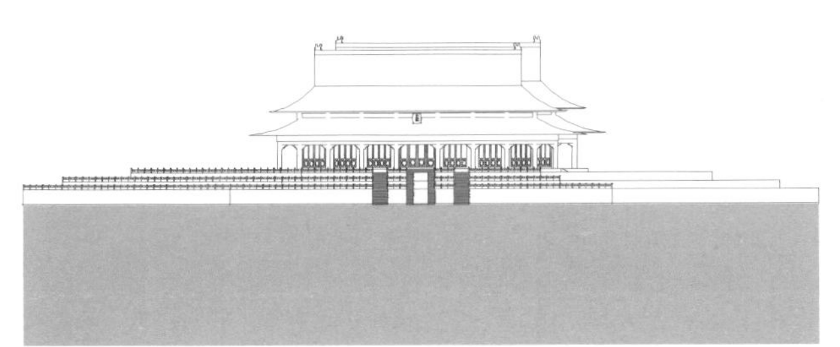

3

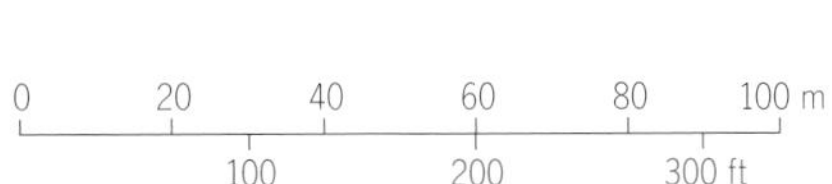

1 Site Plan

1 Palace of Heavenly Purity
2 Hall of Preserving Harmony
3 Hall of Supreme Harmony
4 Tiananmen Gate

2 Section A-A

3 Elevation

Machu Picchu

Peru; 1450–1572

Cusi Inca Yupanqui (1438–71) lived at Cuzco. His father was king and his elder brother was crown prince. But, when Cuzco came under attack, it was Cusi who rallied the defence and routed the enemy, earning for himself the name Pachacuti, meaning 'the earth-shaker'.

Pachacuti not only took over the throne but also went on to make conquests and strike alliances that would give rise over three generations of the Inca family to the most extensive empire that South America had ever seen. Everything changed after 1532, however, with the arrival of the Spanish conquistadors, who brought with them their own imperial ambitions and gunpowder.

The Inca settlement at Machu Picchu was more a palace than a city. Cuzco remained the capital of the kingdom, but Pachacuti removed himself to a palace-estate above the clouds. The architecture of Machu Picchu is almost entirely in its site. The grandiose gestures are natural rock formations, while the buildings are relatively low-key. They are finely constructed in strikingly large stones, fitted together with amazing precision.

Machu Picchu means 'old peak', and the settlement is built on a ridge between the so-called old peak and a younger one, Huayna Picchu. It is a highly defensible site with commanding views and sheer cliffs plunging 450 metres (1,480 feet) to the Urubamba River below.

There are regular earth tremors in the region, and the drystone masonry technique that was used for the main buildings seems to have been adopted because of its resilience. The Inca builders did know about mortar, but a wall bonded by mortar would be effectively monolithic along its whole length – so, when the Earth shook, it would be likely to crack somewhere and crumble. Laboriously shaping the stones to fit together without mortar was worthwhile because the stones would all shift slightly during tremors and then settle back into place. Some of the stones are enormous, but unobtrusively so. It is possible to walk down a stair thinking that it is concrete and realize only when looking at it from the side that the steps were all cut from a single, intact block of granite.

Much of the site is given over to terraced land, which would have been farmed to provide food for the palace. There was a water supply. Machu Picchu would have been able to withstand a prolonged siege. Inca bridges cross spectacular ravines and could in an emergency have been destroyed to protect the place. But its remoteness meant that the Spanish never found Machu Picchu. As it happened, they had no need to find it because the Incas had withdrawn from their palace in anticipation of attack; they did not treat it as their ultimate stronghold.

Around the settlement are many sacred sites, including an artificial platform at the top of the high peak, and sacred stones. One stone points directly up at the sun: at noon on the summer and winter equinox, the sun casts no shadow. Another stone, with a flat front 3 metres (10 feet) high, is shaped to match the outline of the Machu Picchu peak when seen from this point. In making this place his home, the earth-shaker Pachacuti was moving in with the gods.

1 Site Plan

1 City gate
2 Main plaza
3 Inca trail
4 Cultivation terraces
5 Cemetery
6 Sacred rock
7 Temple of Three Windows

2 Section A-A

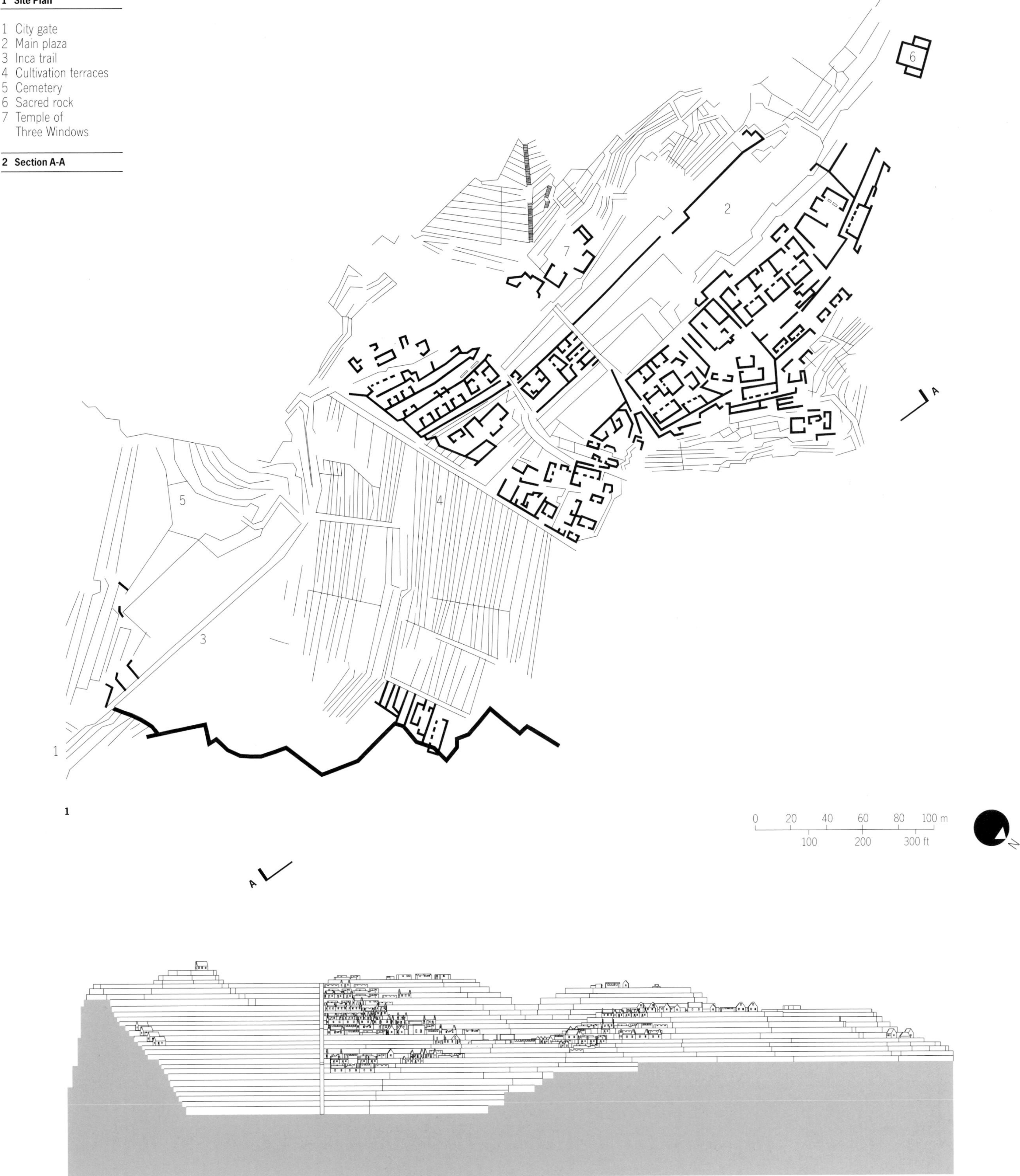

1

2

Topkapi Palace

Istanbul, Turkey; from 1459

Mehmed II began work on the Topkapi Palace soon after he took control of Constantinople in 1453. It was used and enhanced by his successors until 1921, but by then it was no longer really a palace, since in 1856 the Ottoman sultans had moved their court to the Dolmabahçe Palace.

Topkapi takes its name from a gate, Cannon Gate, now vanished. It was built on a prominent headland, protected by defensive sea walls, looking out across water: the Bosphorous to the east and the Golden Horn to the north. This had been the site of the main fortification of the Byzantine emperors, who had moved out of the Great Palace that was connected with the hippodrome (the arena for sports and entertainment) and Hagia Sophia (pages 24–25). The last Byzantine emperors, the Palaiologoi, built the Blachernae Palace, just inside the ancient defence known as the Theodosian Land Walls. Mehmed's decision relocated the sultan's palace to a more commanding military position and to the innermost core of the old city.

The Topkapi Palace incorporated extensive grounds and large courtyards. Its buildings are not tall – most of them no more than two storeys – but some individual rooms are lofty. Visitors would have been impressed by the wide open spaces at the disposal of the sultan in the crowded city of Constantinople. Foreign ambassadors were received in the throne room, a sturdy pavilion, not particularly large, set in a courtyard. Its roof overhangs the walls on all sides, so they are shaded and kept cool, and the ceiling is quite high, to allow warm air to rise up out of the way and be vented through high-level openings under the eaves. The throne would originally have been a sofa – a raised platform covered with carpets and cushions. (The Ottoman reputation for decadent luxury seems to have been based on foreigners' envy of their soft furnishings.)

The relative intimacy of the throne room contrasted with the great expanse of courtyard that had to be crossed to reach it. It was also the room where the sultan's council, the divan, would report to him. None of their deliberations was conclusive until they had been approved here.

The council met in a chamber called the Court of the Divan off the north side of the courtyard. Next to it were the smaller rooms of the harem, linked to the sultan's apartments and open terraces overlooking the Golden Horn. (In any system of government where the office of head of state is hereditary, a clear separation between personal and official life is impossible.) The harem was the women's quarters; it housed powerful sultanas as well as widows of close relatives who needed somewhere to live and who would be classed as 'wives'. There were sometimes intense rivalries, as well as alliances. For some women, the living conditions were luxurious; for others, they were not. Royal marriages were arranged to reinforce an existing alliance or to establish an alliance with a neighbour who could cause trouble. The presence of a king's daughter in the palace could inhibit her father from attacking the state. There are times when a royal woman's position of privilege looks remarkably like that of someone who has been taken hostage.

1 Throne Room Plan

2 Throne Room East Elevation

3 Palace Complex Plan

1 First courtyard
2 Second courtyard
3 Throne room
4 Third courtyard
5 Fourth courtyard
6 Harem (shaded area)
7 Divan
8 Second throne room

1

0
15
30 m
30
60
90 ft

2

1
2
3
4
5
6
7
8
0
100
200
300 m
300
600
900 ft

3

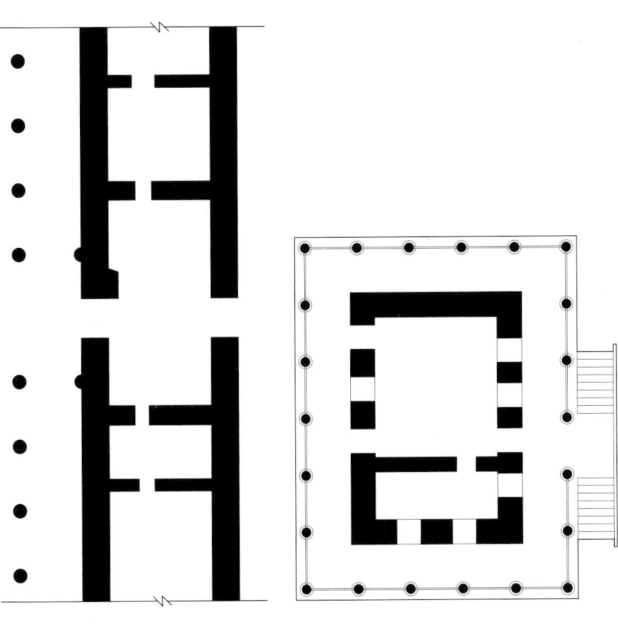

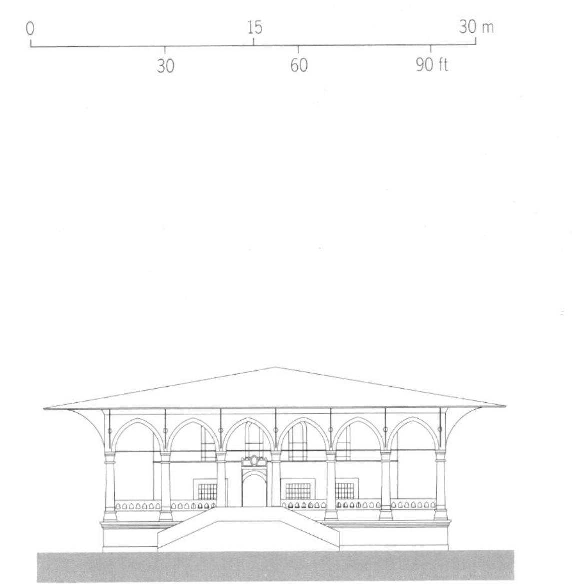

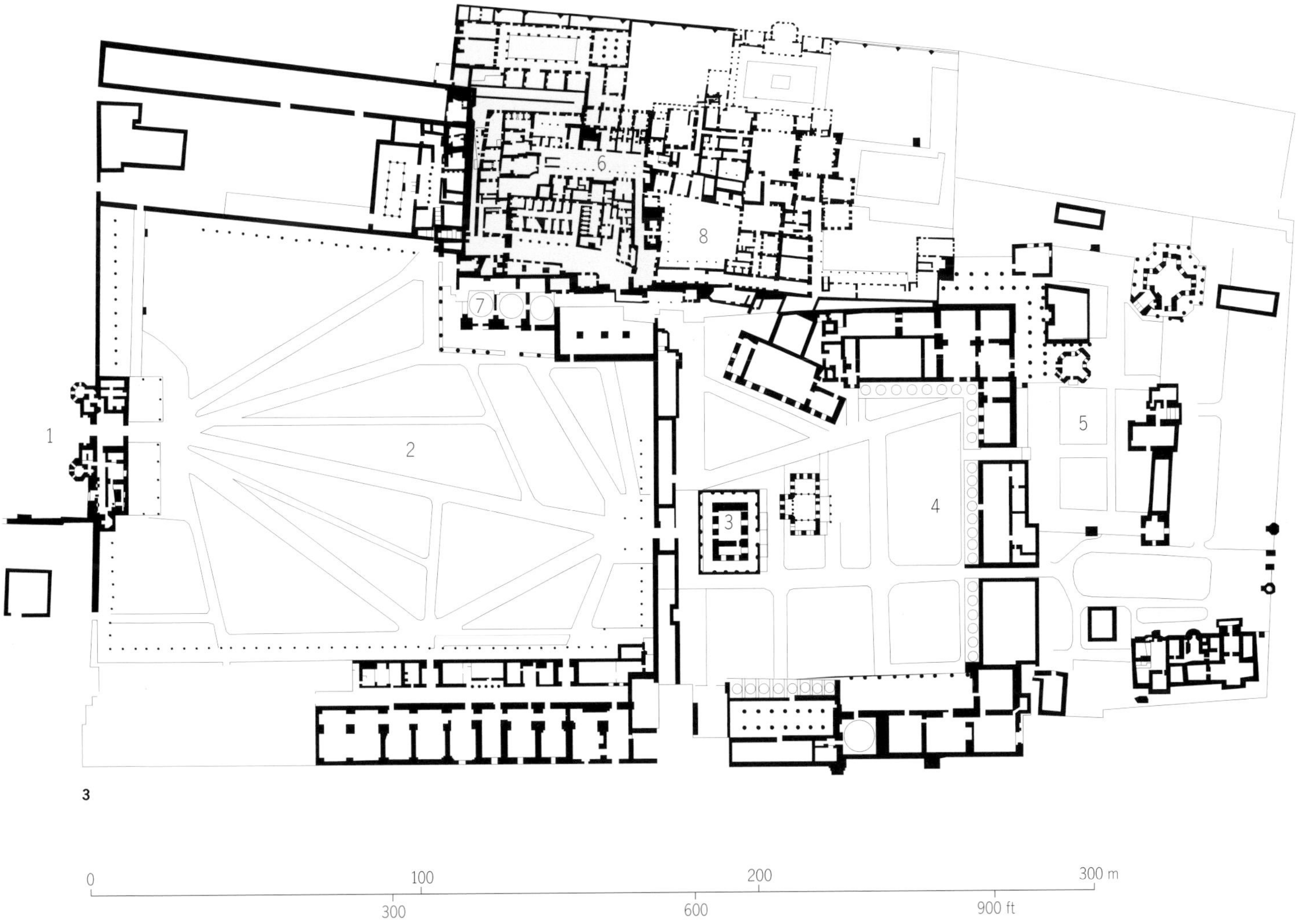

Imperial Palace of Kyoto

Kyoto, Japan; 794–1855

The Imperial Palace was part of the city of Kyoto when it was laid out in 794. Over its history it has burnt down at least eight times, so it has been through a process of renewal like that of the Ise Jingu shrine (pages 26–27), but rather less systematic. The current structural fabric dates from 1855, but the traditions it embodies were very well established by the time it was built, so it was probably successful in its aim to reproduce the buildings of the Heian period (794–1185), when the palace was founded.

The Heian era took its name from the place. Heian-kyo, meaning 'tranquillity and peace capital', is the old name for Kyoto, which was adopted as the capital city of Japan at that time in succession to Nagaoka-kyo, where it had moved – disastrously as it turned out – only nine years earlier. Kyoto was a more successful choice, remaining as capital until 1868.

Kyoto's development began with the building of the palace and the main road leading up to it, and the rest followed. The palace stands on a rectangular plot edged by a high wall. The road leads to a gateway, with a courtyard and an imposing block on axis, but the rest of the palace is made up of pavilions placed in parkland or aligned with the boundary wall. Outside the palace, enclosed by another wall, used to be the villas and gardens of very high-ranking officials. Sometimes the emperor himself was found to be living in one of these villas rather than in his official palace. The villas have now gone, along with the wall, leaving an area of public parkland.

The main hall, called Shishinden, measures 37.5 by 23 metres (123 by 75 feet) in area and 20.5 metres (67 feet) in height. Facing on to an entrance courtyard covered in white gravel, it was used for important state ceremonies such as enthronements. The thrones for the emperor and empress, which stood on a raised platform, are elaborately enclosed and draped, resembling festive tents with pennants sticking out at the corners.

Domestic quarters for the emperor were in a building placed orthogonally – as all the buildings on the site are – but off-axis, at the side of a courtyard beyond Shishinden.

The remainder of the site breaks with the rigid symmetry of the entrance court, making a sophisticated play of carefully adjusted rectangular shapes set in an apparently quasi-natural landscape, which is in fact artfully contrived. There is a prevailing mood of philosophical contemplation and spareness. Each activity seems to have been given the time and space it deserves, plus a little more. The buildings are made from simple-looking elements that mostly run in straight lines. They are dark or lacquered bright red, with white flat panels between. At ground level, sliding panels are a common feature – translucent or opaque, some of them painted with figures, creatures or landscapes. Sometimes doors or gracefully curved barge boards are enriched with ornament in sheet metal.

This is the world of *The Tale of Genji*, where an emperor can have a study called Ogakumonjo with a terrace overlooking a pool. He can read about politics there and entertain guests who are able to recite 31-syllable verses to one another.

1 Shishinden South Elevation

2 Shishinden Section A-A

3 Site Plan

1 Ogakumonjo
2 Shishinden
3 Imperial domestic buildings
4 Service court and servants' quarters

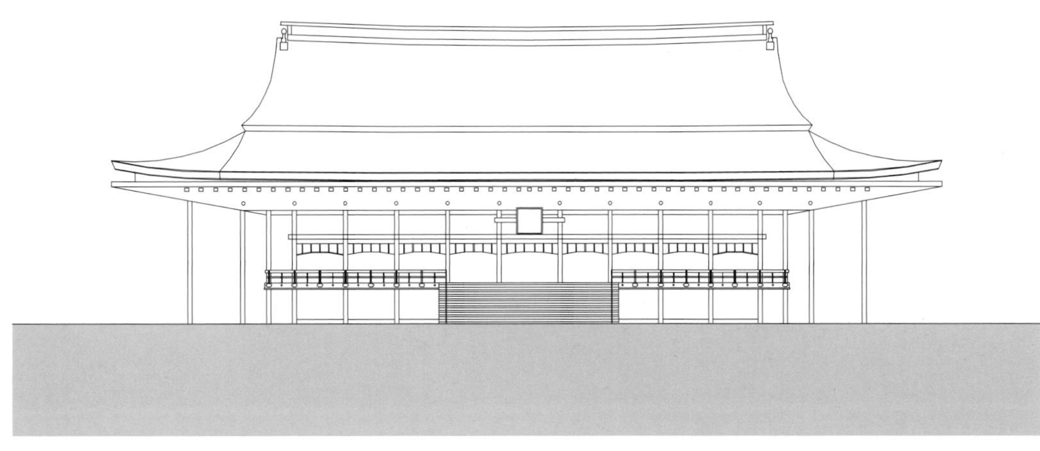

1

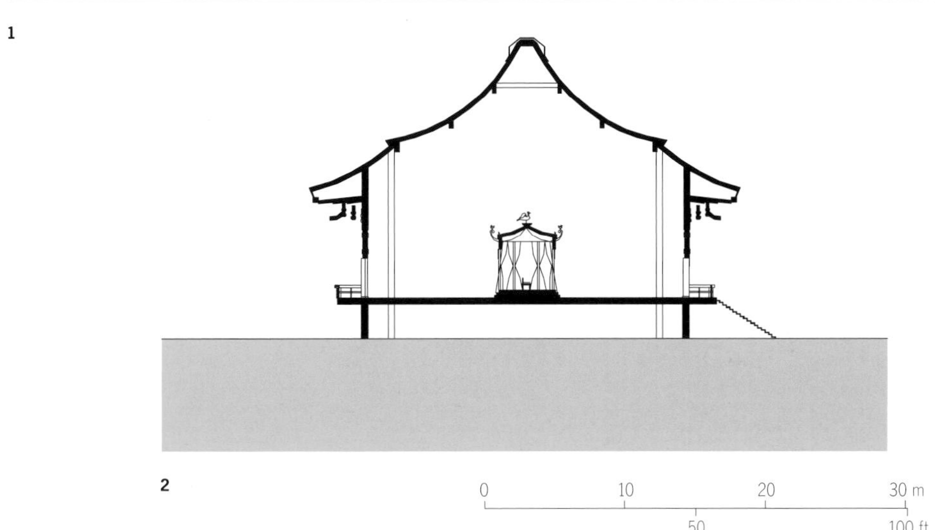

2

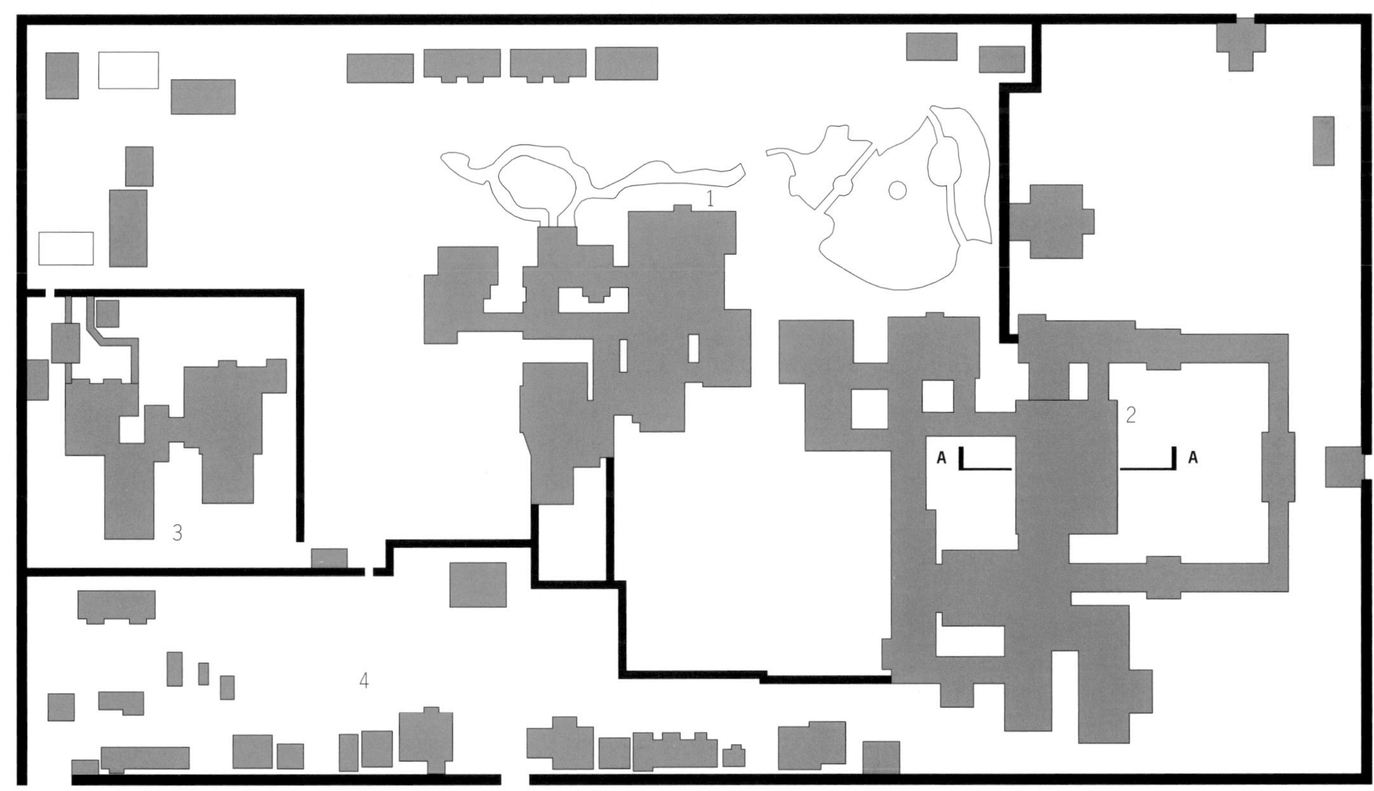

3

Palace of Versailles

Louis Le Vau, 1612–70, André Le Nôtre, 1613–1700, Charles Le Brun, 1619–90, and Jules Hardouin-Mansart, 1646–1708

Versailles, Île de France, France; 1678–84

Louis XIV of France (1638–1715), known as the Sun King, is Europe's most potent emblem of absolute monarchy. He came to the throne at the age of four, on the death of his father, but took up the reins of power at 15, when he was crowned. His mother had been a Hapsburg princess, born in Spain but known as Anne of Austria, and in 1660 Louis married one of her relatives, Maria Theresa of Spain. He went on to outlive his expected heirs, so it was his great-grandson who succeeded him as Louis XV.

The old feudal order, which had seen the king of France brokering power between dukes who were sometimes richer and more powerful than he was, had already been supplanted by something closer to a modern nation-state. The French nobility opposed this reduction in their powers, however, and between 1648 and 1653 there was a rumbling of dissent called La Fronde, which was quashed – but which signalled the kind of problem that the Palace of Versailles was designed to defuse.

The noble families had *hôtels particuliers* (their own palaces) in Paris as well as the landed estates that produced their wealth. To maintain influence when the court moved to Versailles, they had to rent apartments in the palace. They were required to be in residence for part of each year and, while there, to act deferentially towards the king. On their estates they might be lords, but at Versailles they were the king's servants.

A hunting lodge once belonging to Louis XIII had been vastly extended to create the Palace of Versailles. Court ritual even penetrated the elegant gardens that spread out as far as the eye could see. There were broad avenues and planes of water, populated with statuary and animated by fountains, all bearing witness to the king's magnificence and his position at the centre of the things.

Inside the palace, the state rooms included the Galerie des Glaces (Hall of Mirrors), which ran the whole length of the garden façade of the central block. Now that large mirrors are relatively commonplace, it is difficult to imagine the astonishing impact this room made when it was unveiled. The epitome of glamour and opulence, it was used for celebrations and the reception of ambassadors, and each day the king walked through it on his way to chapel, hearing requests from courtiers as he went.

Extraordinary rituals were associated with the king's bedchamber, where the most trusted courtiers (who sometimes paid for the privilege) would put the king to bed and ensure that, wherever he had actually slept, he was in the same bed in the morning to be woken for the ceremonial levée. In addition to his 'private apartment', which included this rather public bedchamber, there was a 'small apartment' where Louis could be genuinely off-stage, with his own books and collections of medals and curiosities. It included a billiards room, Louis's wardrobe and his wig room.

The sophistication and sumptuousness of the buildings' appearance – gilded decoration, silver furniture that was melted down to help pay for battles – and the courtliness of the ritual was undermined by the indignities meted out to the nobility by the complete lack of sanitation. Standards were different in those days but, even so, Versailles's provision fell below what might have been expected. This cannot have been an oversight. Versailles operated as a political machine par excellence, and such an expedient reminded everyone that they were not at home and, while in the palace, were not in charge of even the most basic aspects of their life.

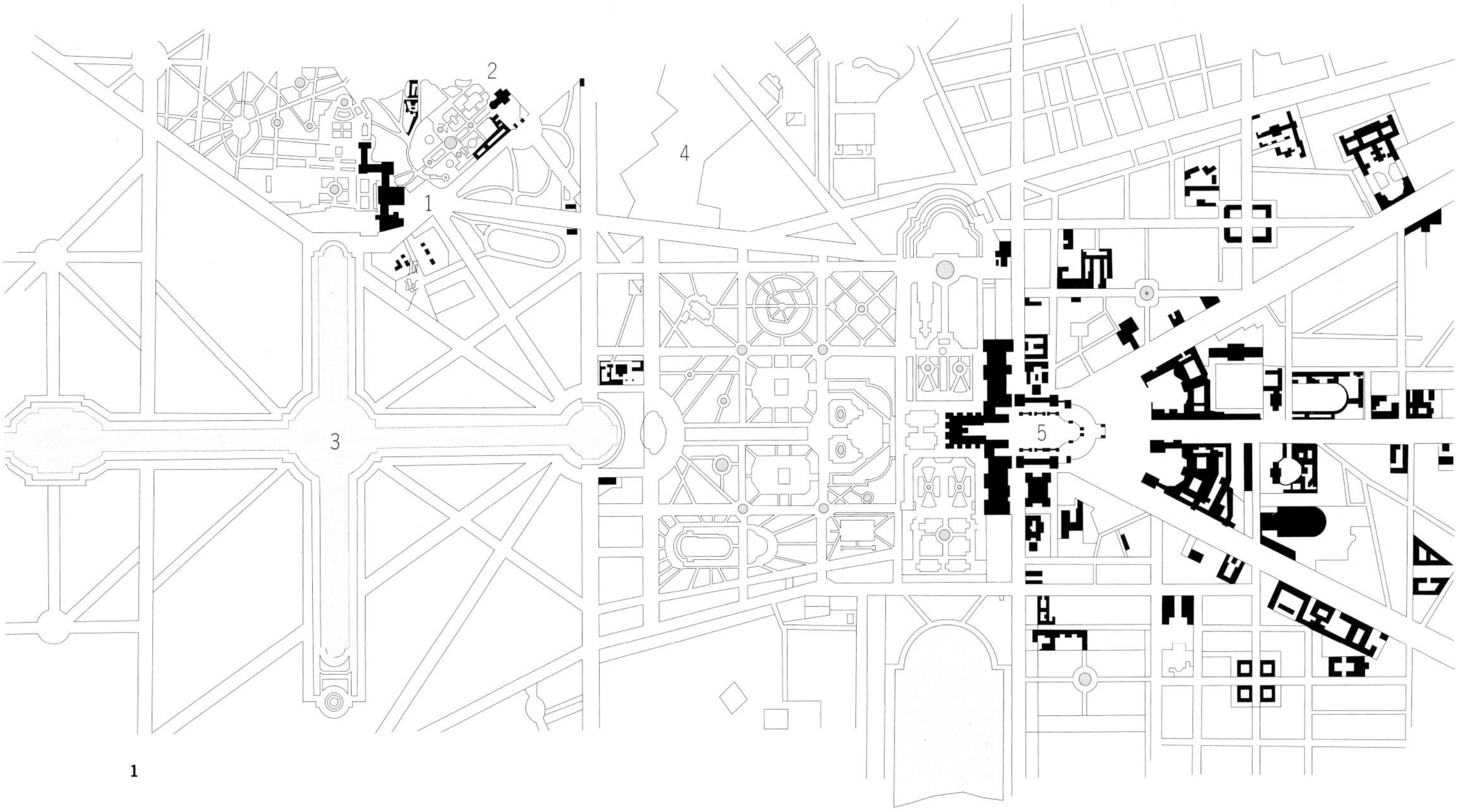

1

0 60 m
200 ft

1 Site Plan

1 Trianon
2 Queen's House
3 Grand Canal
4 Plaine Saint Antoine
5 Royal Court

2 First Floor Plan

1 Peace Salon
2 Hall of Mirrors
3 War Salon
4 King's chamber
5 King's salon
6 Court of honour
7 Royal chapel
8 King's private rooms

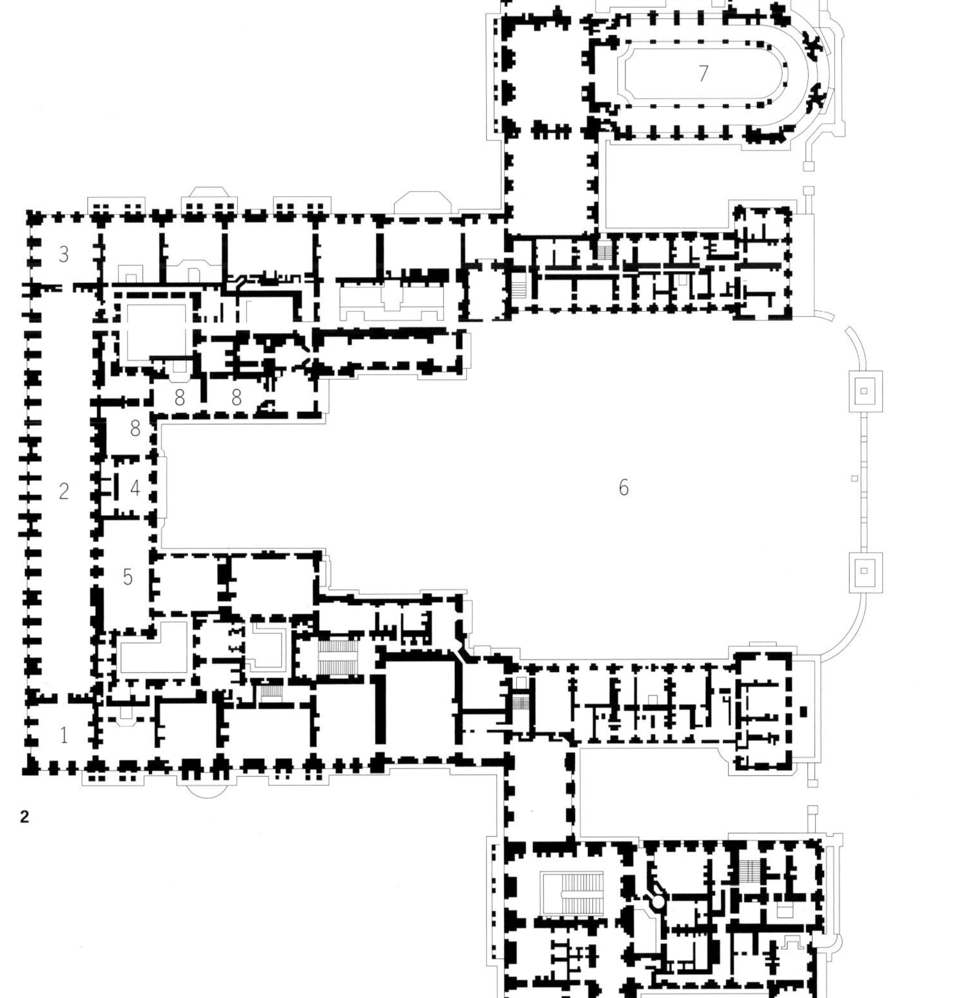

2

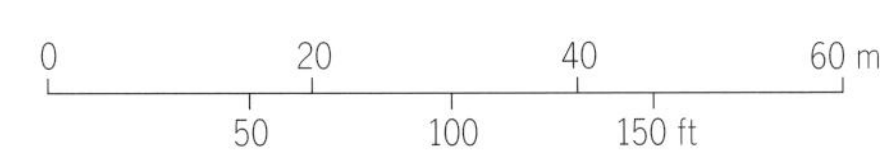

Residenz at Würzburg

Balthasar Neumann, 1687–1753

Würzburg, Bavaria, Germany; 1720–44

When the Residenz was built, the prince-bishops of Würzburg ran Franconia as a fairly independent country, answerable directly to the Holy Roman Emperor Charles VI in Vienna. Franconia later became part of Bavaria, and later still Bavaria became part of Germany, so Würzburg is now a provincial German town with some monuments that bear witness to its more prominent past. The bishops' palace, the Residenz, was built in the eighteenth century, with Balthasar Neumann as court architect. He went on to design Vierzehnheiligen in Bamberg (pages 156–57).

The Residenz was one of the most splendid palaces in Europe, outshining many a royal edifice. It is particularly associated with Johann Philipp Franz von Schönborn (1673–1724), who began it, and his brother Prince Bishop Friedrich Carl von Schönborn (1674–1746), who almost completed it (he was bishop of Würzburg and Bamberg, and is the link with Vierzehnheiligen).

It was not a 'family' building in the style of a royal palace. However public and official the spaces might be, a royal palace would usually pass by inheritance to another member of the same family. That was never the case with palaces belonging to the church. Such buildings passed to new bishops as they were appointed; for a celibate clergy, inheritance was out of the question. It is remarkable that two brothers should have been appointed to the same post – Johann Philipp held office between 1719 and 1724, Friedrich Carl from 1729 to 1746. They poured money into the project, some of it their own, but the incumbent who held office between them stopped as much of the work as he sensibly could.

The von Schönborns approached the building of the Residenz as if they were absolute monarchs rather than clergymen, achieving a dazzling display of cosmopolitan sophistication that would impress the uneducated as well as ambassadors who had been to Versailles and Vienna.

The most important room is the Imperial Hall, a tall vaulted space with three ceiling panels by Giambattista Tiepolo integrated into an elaborate scheme of gold rococo ornament that enlivens the classical columns and vaults. In spite of the prismatic glitter of its chandeliers, this well-lit space with its light colour scheme seems church-like. The hall is located in the projecting bay of the garden façade, and its tall principal windows overlook the garden, while the vault is illuminated from the oval windows of the clerestory above. It is part of an enfilade of stately rooms stretching along the garden front, all decorated to a similar level of opulence. Perhaps the most unexpected of them, in a bishop's palace, is the Spiegelkabinett – one of the smaller spaces, it is lined almost entirely in mirror glass, some panels of which incorporate decoration in gold and paint applied to the back surface of the glass before silvering.

This whole ensemble of rooms is approached by a grand staircase, the building's most sublime achievement. The vault over it is significantly larger than that of the Imperial Hall, but it is hardly noticeable, because it disappears behind the special effects of the painted ceiling.

Tiepolo's masterpiece, this is the most famous ceiling in the world after the Sistine Chapel's – which is smaller. Tiepolo was brought here from Venice to paint it, and put the whole world into it, with representative figures from the different continents gathered around Europe and the Arts. Around the coved edge, the real architecture of the staircase hall is completed with a parapet in the painting. Painted figures seem to be standing on the shelf of the real cornice, leaning precariously over the void, while others are borne aloft in a rush of cloud and drapery, floating in illusionistic space.

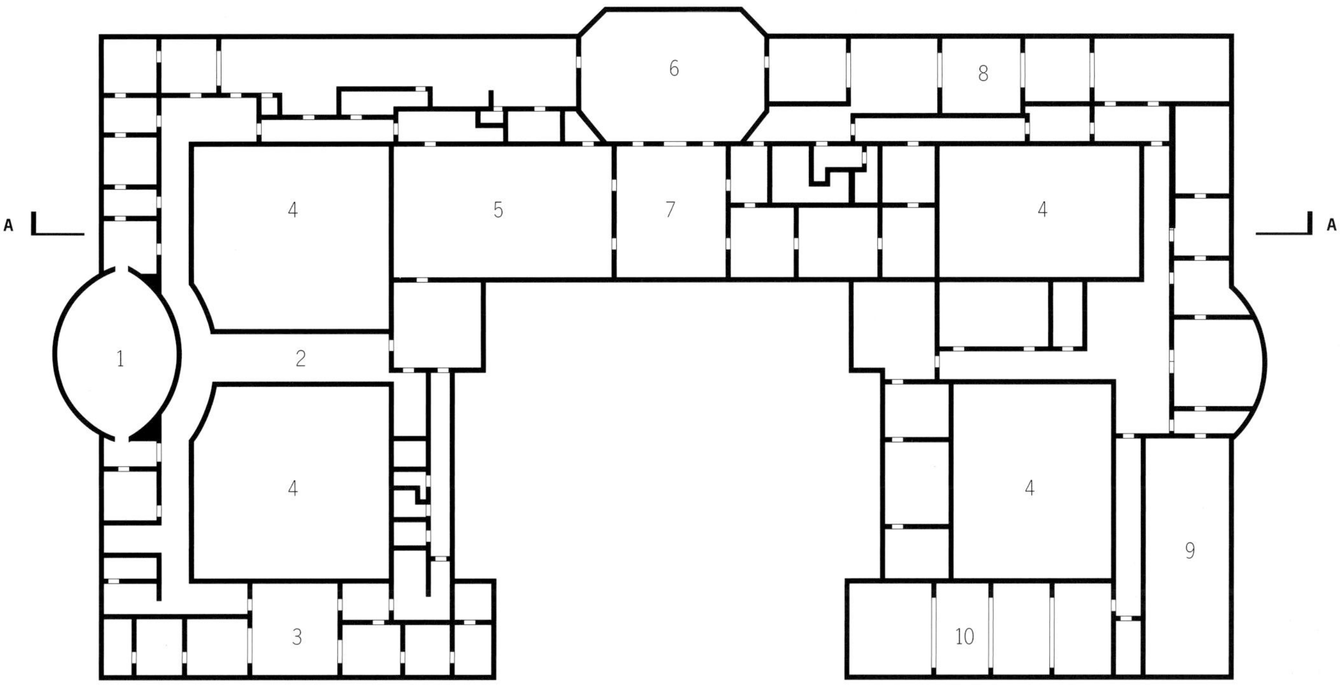

A A

6 8 4 5 7 4 1 2 4 4 9 3 10

1

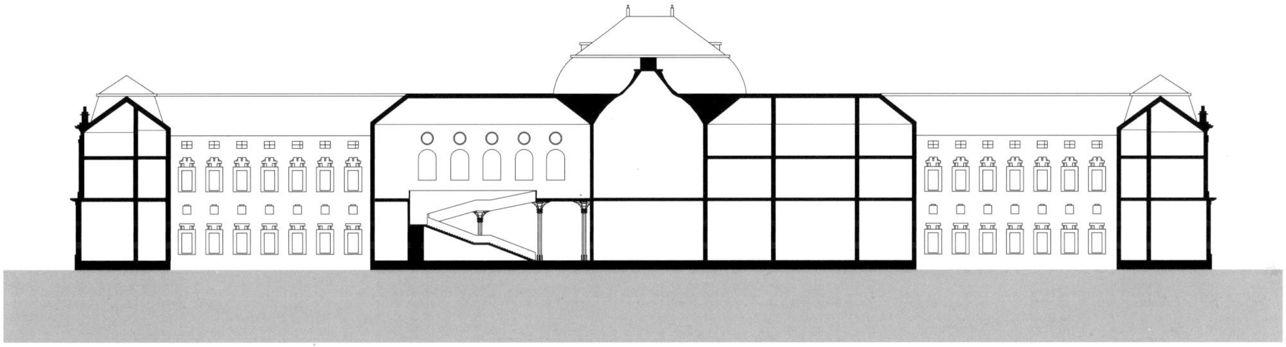

2

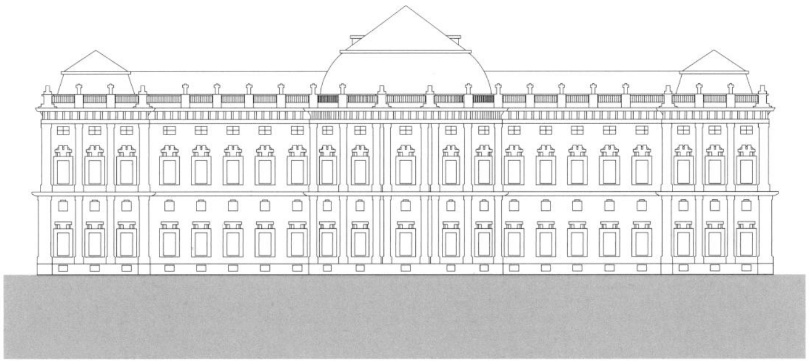

3

1 Plan

1 State gallery
2 Princes' Hall
3 Audience room
4 Courtyard
5 Staircase
6 Imperial Hall
7 White Hall vestibule (below)
8 Mirror cabinet
9 Chapel
10 Museum

2 Section A-A

3 North Elevation

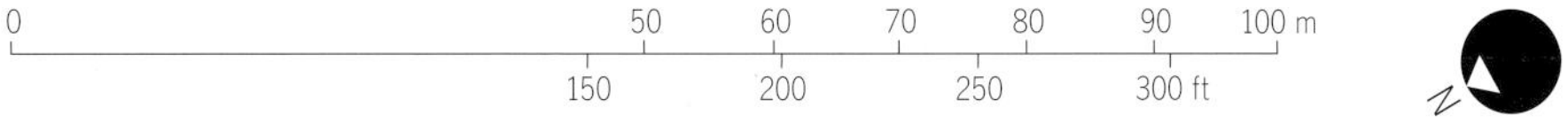

0 50 60 70 80 90 100 m
150 200 250 300 ft

Richmond Capitol

Thomas Jefferson, 1743–1826, and Charles-Louis Clérisseau, 1721–1820

Richmond, Virginia, USA; 1789

The Capitol is in Richmond because of the influence of Thomas Jefferson, who was anxious to move the seat of government away from Williamsburg, the colonial capital (which the British would attack in 1799). Richmond was seen as safer, and the transfer was made in 1780. The Capitol building took shape over the next few years, and was completed in 1789 – the year of the French Revolution.

Jefferson had been the American ambassador to France before the revolution, and while he was there he visited Nîmes, where he fell in love with the Maison Carrée (pages 106–107). He spent hours contemplating it and was convinced that the locals thought he was on the point of suicide because he appeared to be consumed by melancholic meditation. This was no doubt valuable to him as an aesthetic experience, but it was not particularly effective as historical research. He came away convinced that the building dated from the time of the Roman Republic (which would make it older than it actually is) and that it would therefore be an ideal model for the Virginia Capitol.

In Paris he sought out Charles-Louis Clérisseau, who had spent about 20 years in Rome. In 1778 he had published meticulous studies of the Maison Carrée. Clérisseau is now best remembered for his drawings and gouaches – fantasy illustrations of ancient buildings in ruins, which were collected by Catherine the Great of Russia, who invited him to St Petersburg to design for her. He was also the architect of the Palais de Justice at Metz (1776) and could usefully have discussed with Jefferson the practicalities involved in adapting the form of the Maison Carrée into a capitol building.

Clérisseau drafted the drawings that Jefferson sent back to Virginia, where they were interpreted by Samuel Dobie, the builder, who made some significant modifications as construction progressed.

The adoption of a classical model gave the building an air of principle and authority. In comparison with a palace such as the Residenz at Würzburg (pages 252–53) – the seat of an absolute ruler – it is also very austere. It is dignified, but there is nothing lavish or luxurious about it. The central space under a dome (which might have been one of Dobie's modifications) was a two-storey 'conference room' with a mezzanine gallery that could be used for public gatherings. The other main rooms – a debating chamber for the people's representatives and the state's high court – were reached from this space. This arrangement put the building's main entrances on its long sides. The portico did not mark the entrance. That changed in 1906, when additional wings were added, along with the flight of steps to the portico, and the internal accommodation was entirely rearranged.

As a building to adapt, the Maison Carrée is an interesting choice, because even in its original form it was an adaptation. It took as its model the Greek temple and modified it by putting a solid wall between the peripteral columns. At Richmond, windows are introduced into this wall, making it significantly less monumental in character than the Maison Carrée – although the building itself is quite a bit larger – but the windows did make the structure much more useful as an administrative building.

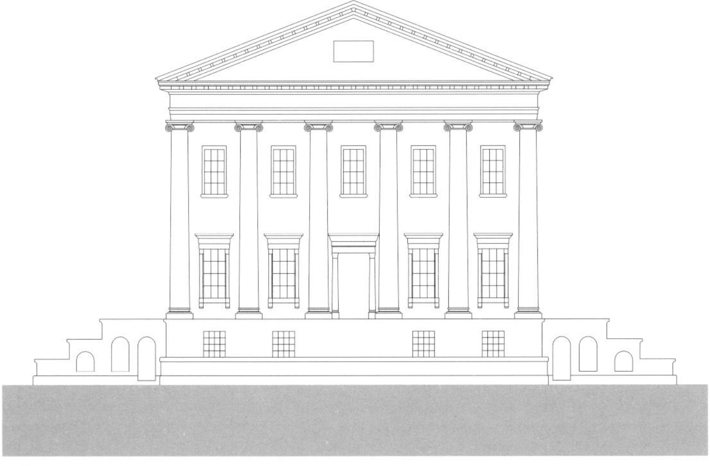

1

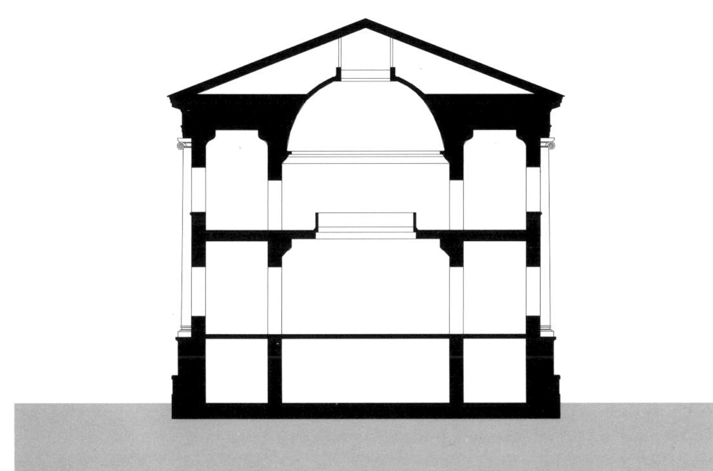

2

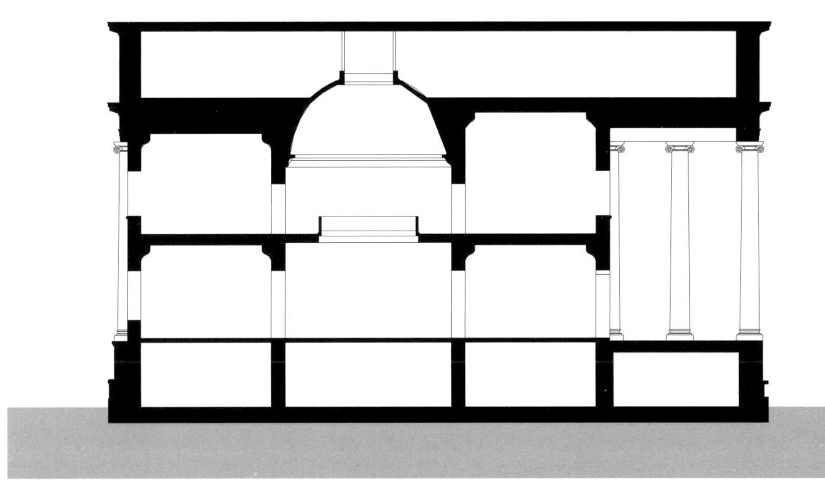

3

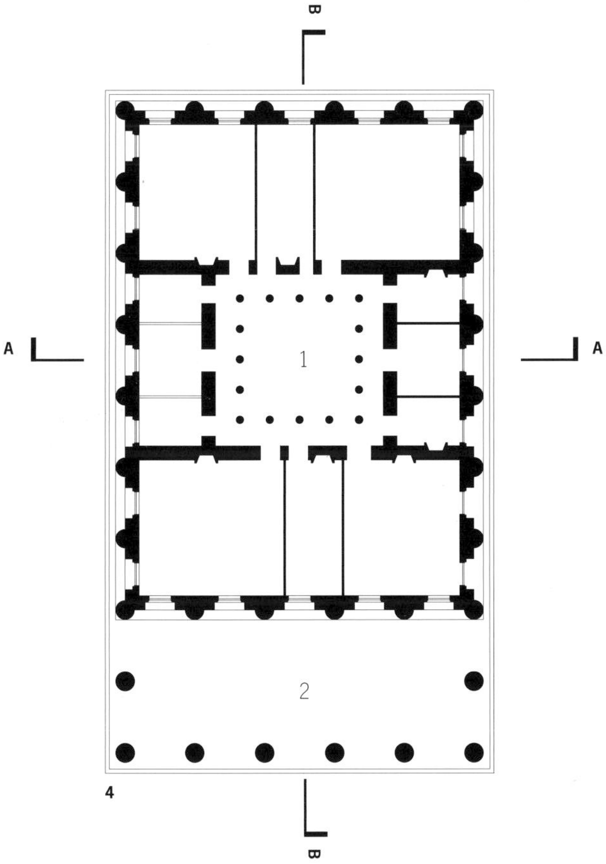

B

A 1 A

2

4

B

1 South Elevation

2 Section A-A

3 Section B-B

4 Floor Plan

1 Rotunda
2 Portico

0 10 20 m
20 40 60 ft

Palace of Westminster

Charles Barry, 1795–1860, and Augustus Pugin, 1812–52

London, UK; 1836–68

In 1834 the old Palace of Westminster burnt down and there was a contest to replace it, calling for entries in Gothic or Elizabethan style, for nationalistic reasons. Charles Barry's design won because it proposed a rational organization of the main elements and reconciled this with surviving elements of the old building, such as the medieval Westminster Hall, which had powerful symbolic value. Barry adopted a style known as Perpendicular Gothic, taking its cue from Henry VII's extension of Westminster Abbey, across the road from the main public entrance to the new building.

Once Barry had won the competition, he invited Augustus Pugin, the most fanatical Gothic Revivalist of the time, to develop the decorative detail. The decoration makes a strong impression, and Pugin's wallpaper designs are particularly well known, but in the plan it is the clarity of the organization that makes the most impact.

The building was arranged around a series of courts, whose purpose was to bring light and ventilation to nearby rooms. This was essential at the time, long before electric light and air conditioning made it possible to inhabit deep-plan offices. Bigger rooms also had to be high if they were to be satisfactorily lit and ventilated. Barry proved adept at managing light and heating systems for large country houses and buildings such as the Reform Club in London's Pall Mall (completed in 1841).

Barry's plan for the Palace of Westminster enshrines the system of government as it was understood in 1836. House of Commons membership had just been reformed to increase representation from the industrial cities, but eligibility to vote still depended on being male and owning property of a certain value, so many people were excluded from the process. The long central spine of the building links three large spaces: the House of Commons, the House of Lords and the Royal Gallery. The octagonal central hall (above right), lit by windows high overhead in the side of the central tower, is a soaring Gothic space, and the point of arrival for members of the public.

Visitors who walk north from the central hall go along a corridor to a square lobby and from there into the House of Commons. Those who head south go along a corridor to a square lobby and then into the House of Lords, which in the 1830s was populated exclusively by men with hereditary posts and was seen as the more important chamber. People who walk east find themselves in an enormously long corridor with doors off it leading into libraries and committee rooms. At the north end of this corridor is a suite of rooms for the Speaker, who is responsible for the management of the House of Commons, and at the south end a corresponding suite for the Lord Chancellor, who performs a similar role for the Lords.

The UK is governed by three 'estates' that were thought to hold each others' powers in check. The first of these is the monarch; the others are the two Houses of Parliament. The Victoria Tower, at the south-west corner of the building, marks the monarch's entrance to what is still officially designated a royal palace. No one else uses this entrance. A flight of steps leads up to the Royal Gallery, which is the same size as the House of Lords and somewhat larger than the House of Commons. The size is symbolic, rather than practically necessary.

The entrance and the rooms to which it leads are used when the monarch opens each new Parliament. The members of the Commons process through the corridor to the House of Lords, where the monarch addresses the assembly from a gilded throne and reminds it who is in charge.

1 Ground Floor Plan

1 Central Lobby
2 St Stephen's Hall
3 Peers' Lobby
4 House of Lords Chamber
5 Prince's Chamber
6 Royal Gallery
7 Royal Robing Room
8 Members' Lobby
9 Westminster Hall
10 House of Commons Chamber
11 Royal Court
12 Peers' Court
13 Speaker's Court

2 East Elevation

9
2
7
6
5
4
3
1
8
10
11
12
13

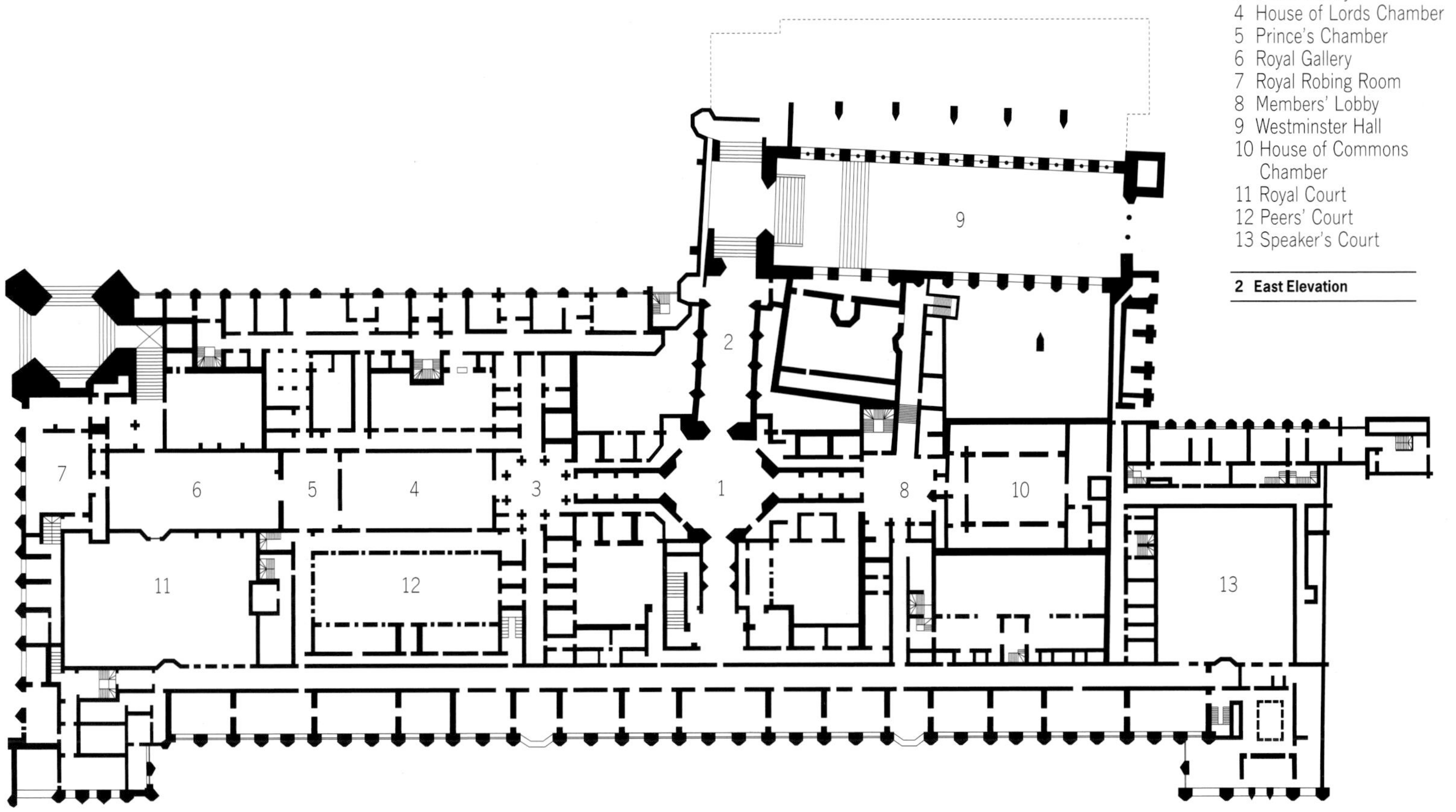

1

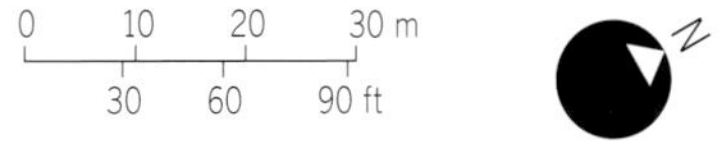

0 10 20 30 m
30 60 90 ft
N

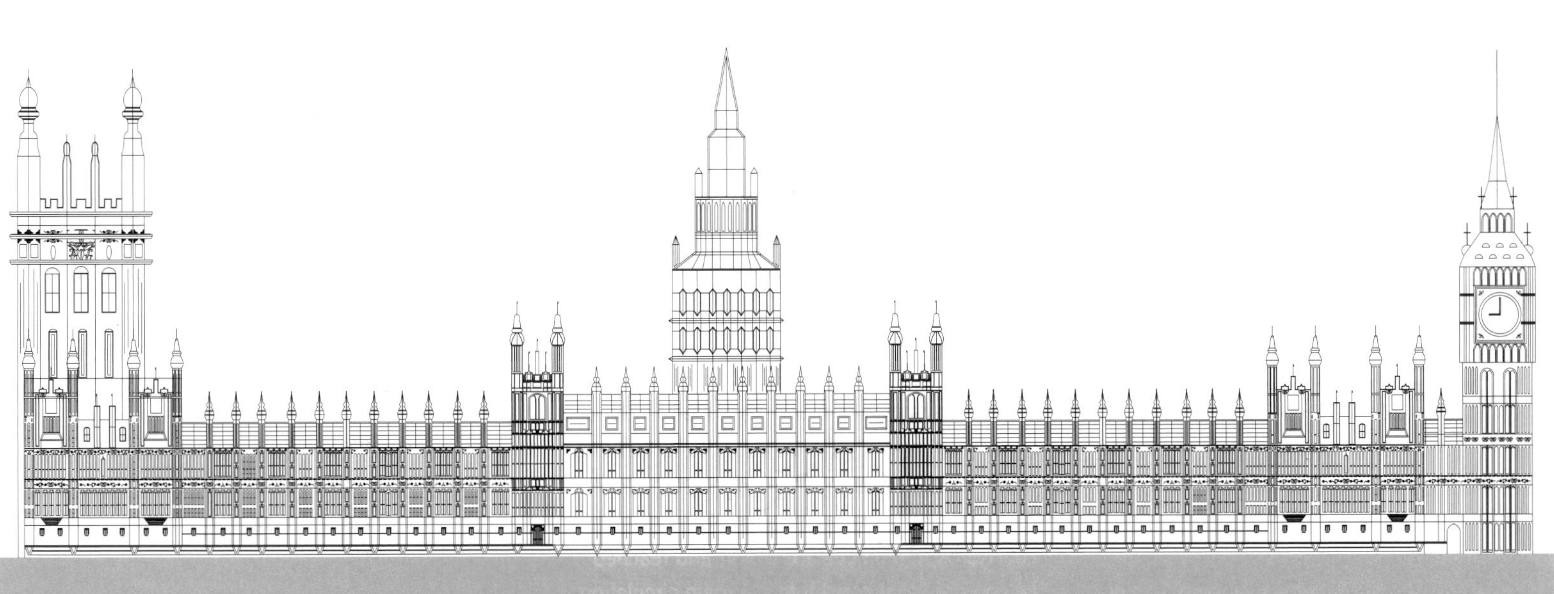

2

Hilversum Town Hall

Willem Dudok, 1884–1974

Hilversum, Netherlands; 1928–31

Brick has a long history in the Netherlands. Much of the country was once below sea level, and land has been reclaimed by allowing the build-up of fine clay silt from river estuaries, but substantial areas of the natural land also are clay. Fired clay can be as strong as stone, and it is typically made into bricks that can be lifted with one hand, so a skilled bricklayer can make surprisingly rapid progress with construction.

Before the advent of the railways, bricks were expensive to transport, so they were made locally – often with a temporary kiln on a building site. They did sometimes travel as ballast in ships, which is why Dutch bricks were used for seventeenth-century buildings in Hull, an English port on the other side of the North Sea from Amsterdam.

The streets and canals of Amsterdam itself are lined with brick buildings, and many of the streets are paved in brick. Brick was the material used by the modernist Amsterdam School and has generally been seen as a rational building material, suitable for modern work.

In 1928 Willem Dudok was appointed city architect of Hilversum. (Officially, the settlement is not a city but a large village, which currently has 84,000 inhabitants.) A broadcasting company is based there, and it is close enough to Amsterdam to be home to some prosperous commuters, but it is limited in size by a nature reserve that surrounds it – an arrangement negotiated by Dudok.

Dudok engaged with international modernism but, at a time when concrete and steel were the fashionable materials, he continued to use brick as the surface material for his buildings. In doing so, he produced buildings that made modernism look mainstream rather than edgily avant garde. His work weathered well and was widely admired by architects in other countries. Dudok was awarded the British Royal Gold Medal for Architecture in 1935, and the American Institute of Architects' Gold Medal in 1955.

Hilversum Town Hall or Raadhuis – also on occasion called Hilversum City Hall or Village Hall – was his masterpiece. It houses the civic offices, a council chamber and a hall for public meetings and weddings. The principal rooms are double-height spaces on the upper floor. Arranged around courtyards, the offices are well lit and reached by corridors that constitute the main circulation. This is all very straightforward. The building faces Dudok Park, but between the road and the town hall there is a large rectangular pool, longer than the building's central block. An approach along the edge of this pool leads to a covered walkway. The main entrance is at the foot of the tower, which makes a very effective marker. Public circulation up to the next floor is located at the base of the tower, where there is a lobby giving access to the council chamber and the Citizens' Hall.

The building's asymmetrical composition in cuboid blocks is well balanced and gives the building a presence and poise beyond its relatively modest circumstances. Hilversum Town Hall is admirable for its sanity and restraint.

1 Ground Floor Plan

1 Council chamber
2 Citizens' Hall
3 Clock tower

2 Section A-A

3 West Elevation

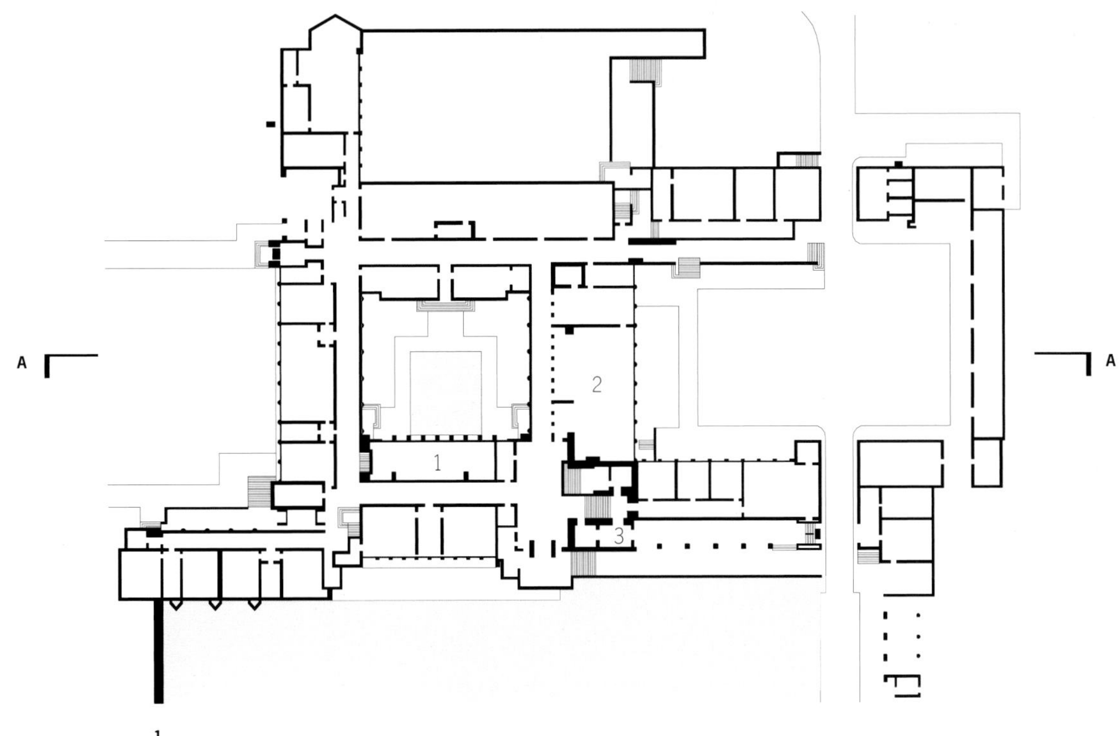

1

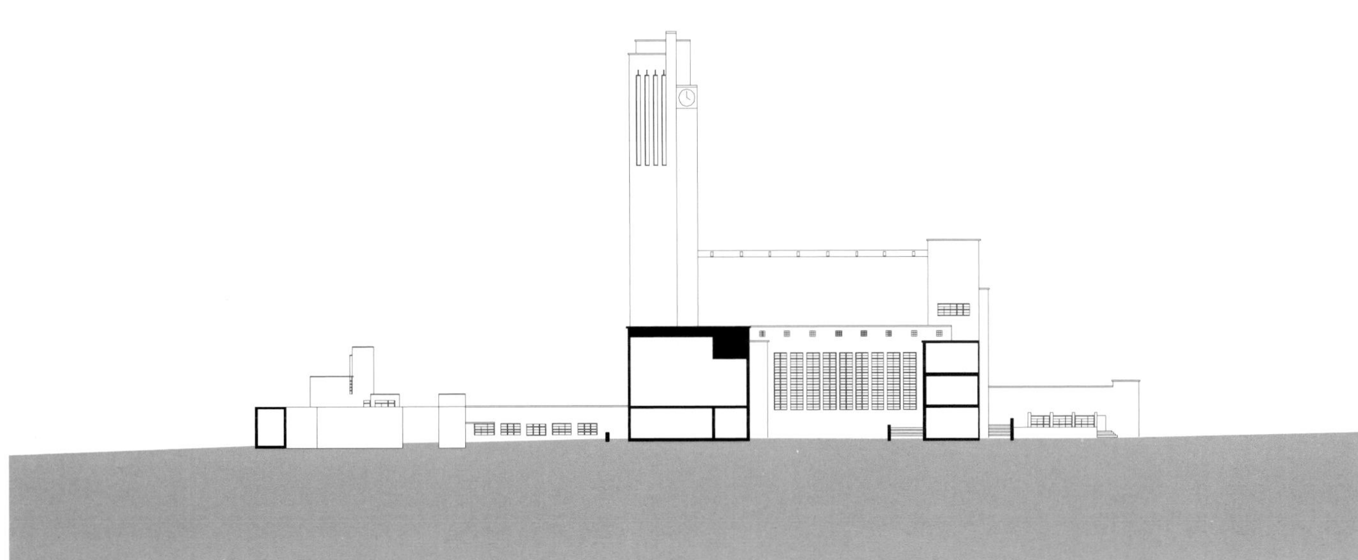

2

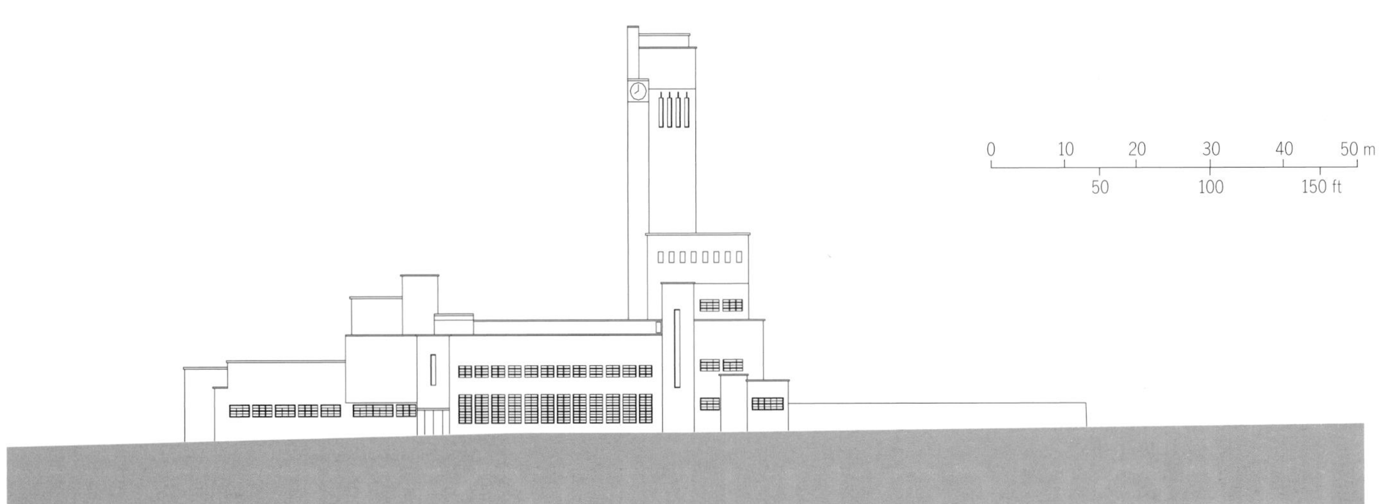

3

Säynatsälo Town Hall

Alvar Aalto, 1898–1976

Säynatsälo, Finland; 1949–52

Säynatsälo is an island in central Finland reached by bridges on a lake. This is not a well-populated region – even now, it is estimated that only 14,000 people live within 7 km (4 miles) of the island – so the town hall is modest in size. What is more surprising is that it was commissioned from an architect of such distinction.

Ten years earlier, Alvar Aalto had designed the Finnish national pavilion for the World's Fair in New York; he had a permanent building to his name in the USA (Baker House at MIT in Cambridge, Massachusetts, 1948) and his reputation was growing. Säynatsälo was home territory for Aalto, who had grown up in Jyväskylä and started his first office there. Jyväskylä grew rapidly and in 1993 it officially absorbed Säynatsälo.

Finland is a modern nation, which has had problematic relations with its stronger neighbours, Sweden and Russia, but it has a strong sense of deep-rooted cultural identity that comes from the language, the national poem *Kalevala* (a nineteenth-century epic based on oral traditions) and a romantic attachment to the forest.

The area around Säynatsälo is forested, and the largest local employer is the Enzo–Gutzeit timber company, for which Aalto had already designed a company town (1944) and would go on to design a prominent office building overlooking Helsinki's harbour (1959–62).

Säynatsälo Town Hall is a low-density development, which tries to achieve a sense of an urban civic presence while expressing contact with nature and the forest. It is approached through trees, and its principal building materials are brick and timber. The functions of the town hall itself would have made a building no larger than some of the nearby houses. The building's bulk was increased by the inclusion of a public library and some domestic accommodation; a bank and a shop were also included, but these subsequently closed for want of custom. These elements account for the lower storey and two sides of the courtyard around which the building is arranged.

The town hall is approached by a flight of steps that brings the visitor up to a grassy courtyard. There is an entrance to the civic offices, and from the lobby a shallow stair leads through an enclosed passage lit by a high-level clerestory. It turns two corners before reaching the council chamber – a tall, fairly dark space, whose most arresting feature is the pair of timber trusses that support the roof. The trusses do their job effectively, and in their splayed radiating timbers there is a deft improvised quality that lends some panache to the room. Externally, the courtyard reconnects with the countryside by means of an irregularly shaped flight of grassy stairs.

The presence of Säynatsälo Town Hall does more than anything else in the locality to convince people that they are in a town while remaining aware that the Finnish forest is never far away.

1 Section

2 South West Elevation

3 Council Chamber Level Plan

1 Council chamber
2 Attic store

4 Courtyard Level Plan

1 Entrance hall
2 Children's library
3 Librarian's desk
4 Adults' library
5 Newspaper and magazine reading room
6 Living room
7 Study
8 Bedroom
9 Kitchen
10 Guest room
11 One-room apartment
12 Staff coffee room
13 Welfare office
14 Local government/council meeting room
15 Municipal tax office
16 Municipal treasurer's office
17 Municipal principal's office
18 Council offices (information services)
19 Cloakroom

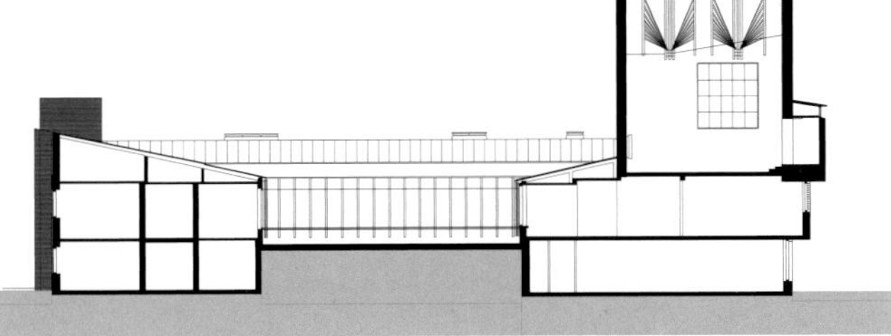

1

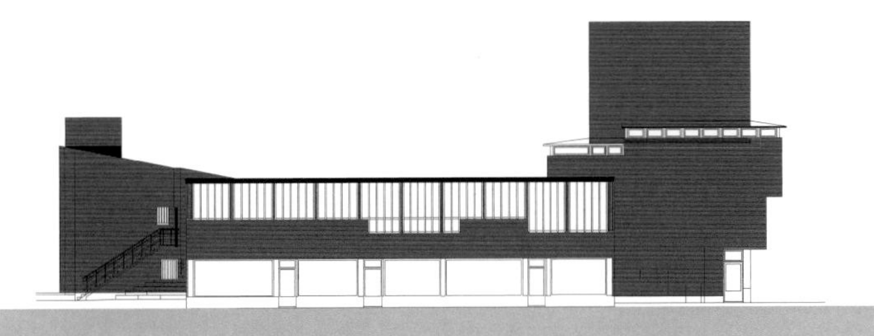

2

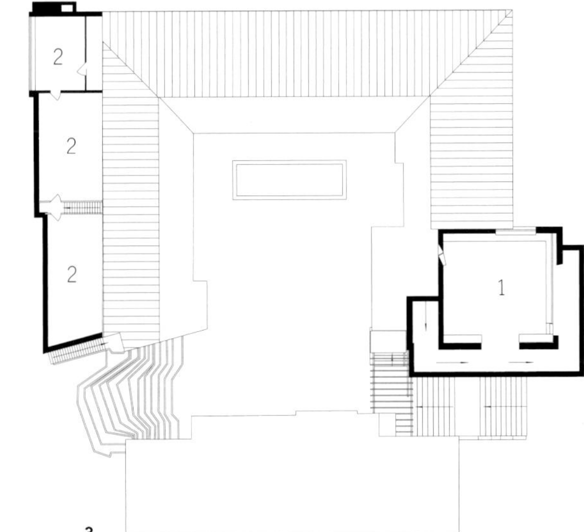

3

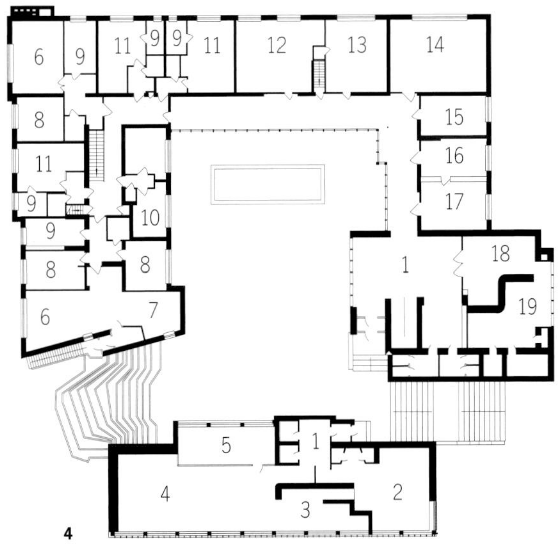

4

0 5 10 m
15ft 30 ft

Culture and Entertainment

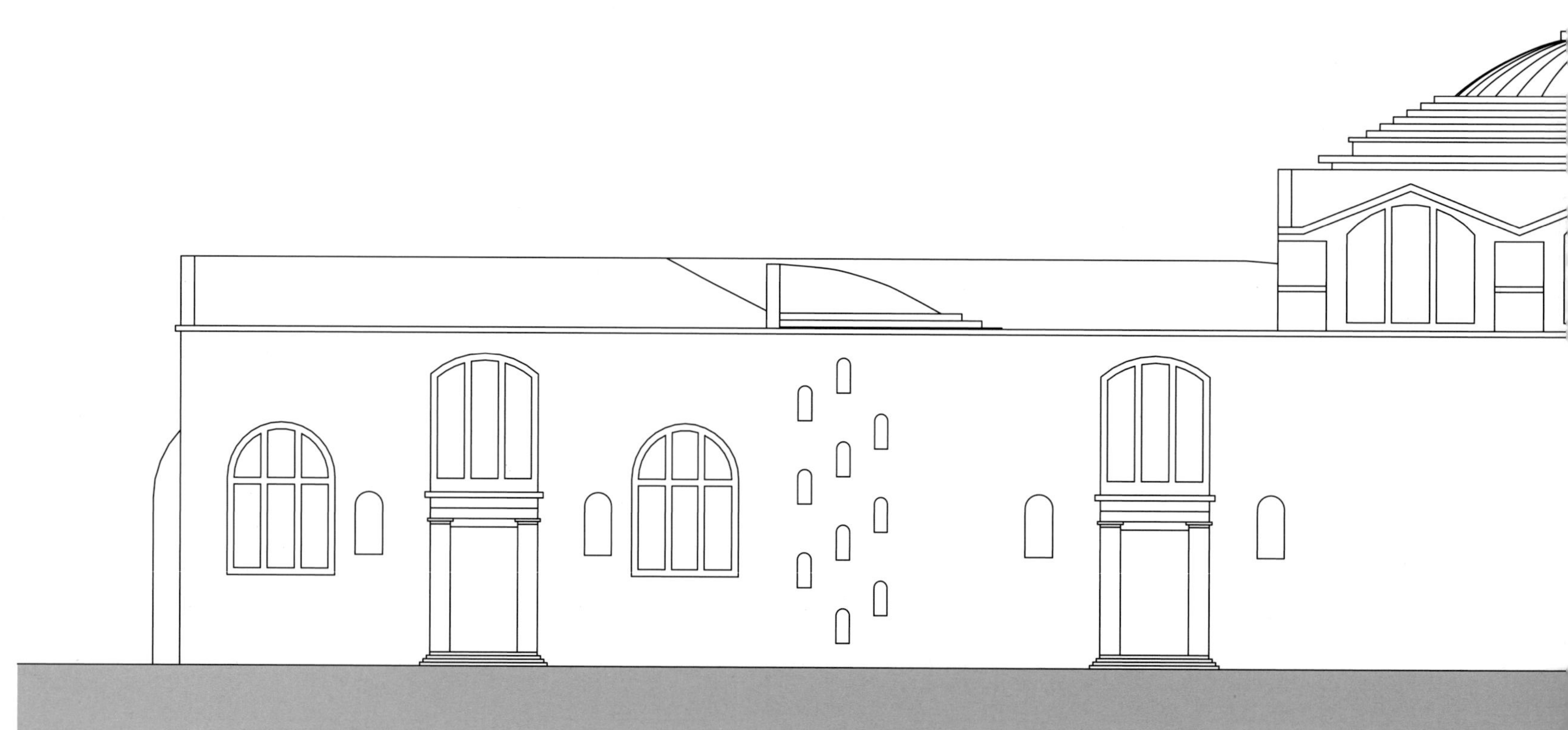

The range of buildings linked to cultural spectacles is absolutely vast, indefinable and ever-changing. Processional routes often include an element of theatre and can have declared intentions or unannounced overtones that give them a role in religion or government. In the modern world, there is so much entertainment in the home that the future for live theatre and music looks uncertain. The buildings featured in this chapter are all permanent versions of structures that could have been smaller and simpler but which turned into something noteworthy.

The Great Bath at Mohenjo-Daro in Pakistan might have had a religious function, but it is impossible to be sure about this. Its early date makes it a very remarkable building indeed, whatever its precise use. The Baths of Caracalla in Rome represent the most monumental development of a bathing establishment, which did far more than simply enabling people to keep clean. The gift of the baths to the city, from the emperor Caracalla, had a political purpose in allowing the emperor to ingratiate himself with the citizenry, and would have been a place to enjoy and to be seen. The pools and gardens, libraries and statuary represented the last word in imperial luxury and artistic achievement and were accessible to ordinary citizens, who would have felt themselves privileged to be there.

Theatres and stadiums are organized so as to bring as many people as possible within reach of the event. The principle is much the same whether the event is a speech or a football game, but the size of the venue where it takes place can be very different. Speech travels only a limited distance, and that distance limits the size of a theatre for drama, but music and dance can make the effects of a drama carry further, and might have made tolerable a seat near the back where most of the words had little power to move the audience.

A chariot race or fights to the death with wild animals could reach a far larger audience and could fill the Colosseum, where a word-based drama would be lost to the winds. The Globe Theatre in London held the audience as close to the actors as possible, so that the words could be heard, and it is comparatively tiny, but there the words were critically important. The concert hall is a more recent and more specialized development, where the quality of the sound is of prime importance, and where a larger space can be suitable as long as it is possible to increase also the size of the orchestra.

Regardless of the category in which it is put, the Crystal Palace is an anomaly. It caused a sensation when it was built in the mid-nineteenth century, but it was imitated more in the twentieth century than in its own. It was an exhibition building, to house a great international exhibition, and the concept of putting on a show of what the nations of the world could produce and sell to one another caught on immediately. The idea that a large greenhouse could be more than a temporary and expedient stand-in for a public building took much longer to take hold, but is deliberately referenced in the Crystal Cathedral in Los Angeles.

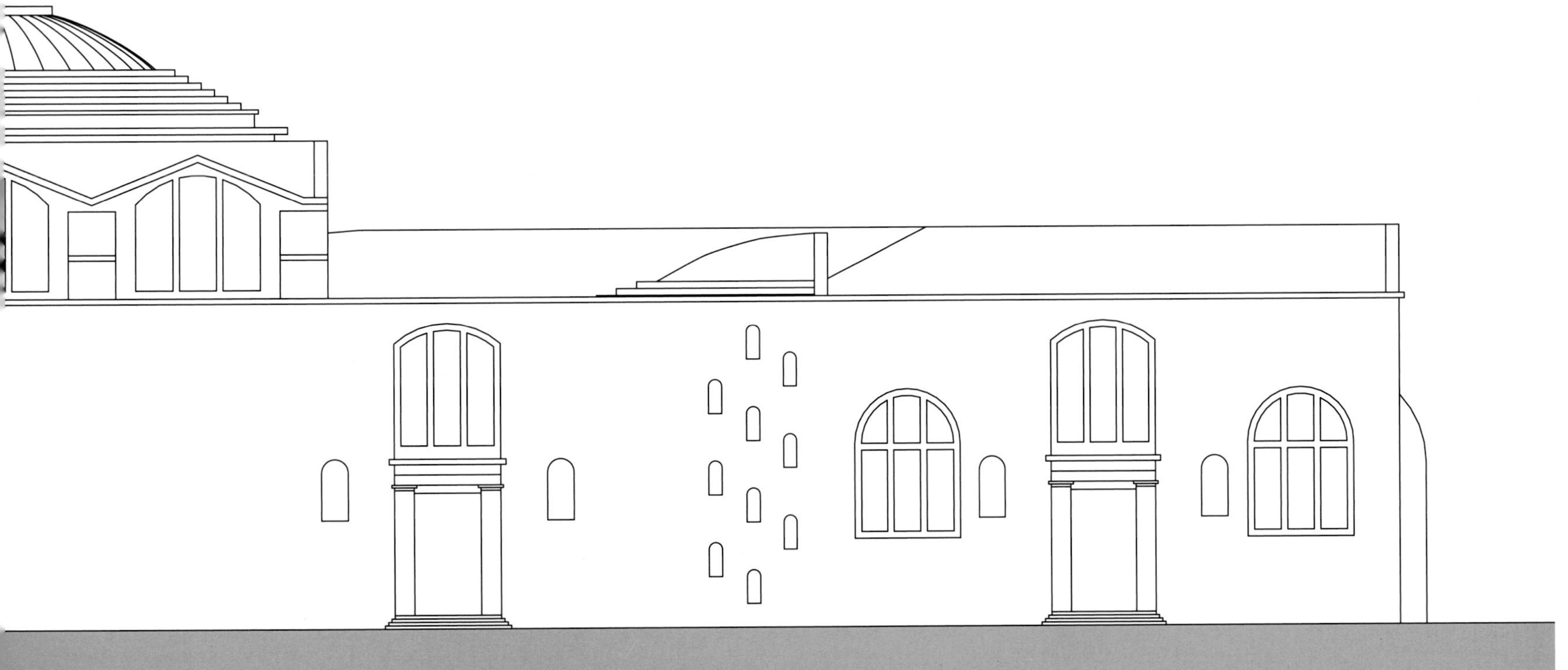

Great Bath at Mohenjo-Daro

Mohenjo-Daro, Pakistan; 2500 BCE

The early civilizations of the Indus Valley left no written records to help us to understand how they saw the world and how they tried to organize it. There are the remains of great cities, but no one knows what to make of them.

Mohenjo-Daro might have had 40,000 inhabitants in 2500 BCE. Most of the city was built in the river valley, which was sometimes flooded, so there was also a citadel at a higher level with what could be granaries for food storage. The houses in the valley were laid out on a grid, giving the impression there was someone in control to decree the grid, but there is no sign of a palace structure, nor of temples.

Mohenjo-Daro appears to have been an egalitarian society without great differences in rank and access to resources. It is conceivable that its people could have agreed collectively to set out a city on a grid, and then abided by the decision, but study of more recent civilizations makes that seem unlikely. Maybe this was a place where the everyday structures were more substantial and robust than the religious structures, but such an approach to building is not found elsewhere. Perhaps the religious devotees venerated trees or boulders, or lit great fires, as the Parthians did.

What, then, can be made of the Great Bath? It looks for all the world like a swimming pool, 12 by 7 metres (39 by 23 feet) in area and 2.4 metres (8 feet) deep. It is well built, and would probably have been watertight even without the layer of bitumen that seals it and confirms that its purpose was to hold water.

Clearly an important institution, the Great Bath has a formality that suggests a ritual interpretation. Its location on the high ground might mean that it was functionally connected with the granaries, or that it was thought worthy of an honorific place above the level of everyday life. The houses mostly had drained washing areas, so it might have been a place for ritual or religious cleansing rather than practical hygiene.

The plan drawn opposite is accurate enough but, since the walls do not survive above skirting level, the section above the pool is conjectural. The actual use of the buildings habitually called 'granaries' has also been called into question. No traces of anything like grain, nor any storage vessels, have turned up in the excavation. The 'granaries' shared a foundation that runs for 50 metres (164 feet), divided by passageways and supporting timber columns. This was a building with many rooms. If it were in fact an administrative area for what was originally a palace, the nearby pool might have been used in conjunction with it, perhaps as a luxurious amenity for an elite group.

The lesson of places such as Mohenjo-Daro is that, when there is very limited evidence to back up the speculation, assumptions about what looks plausible and what does not reveal more about the person speculating than about what has actually been found.

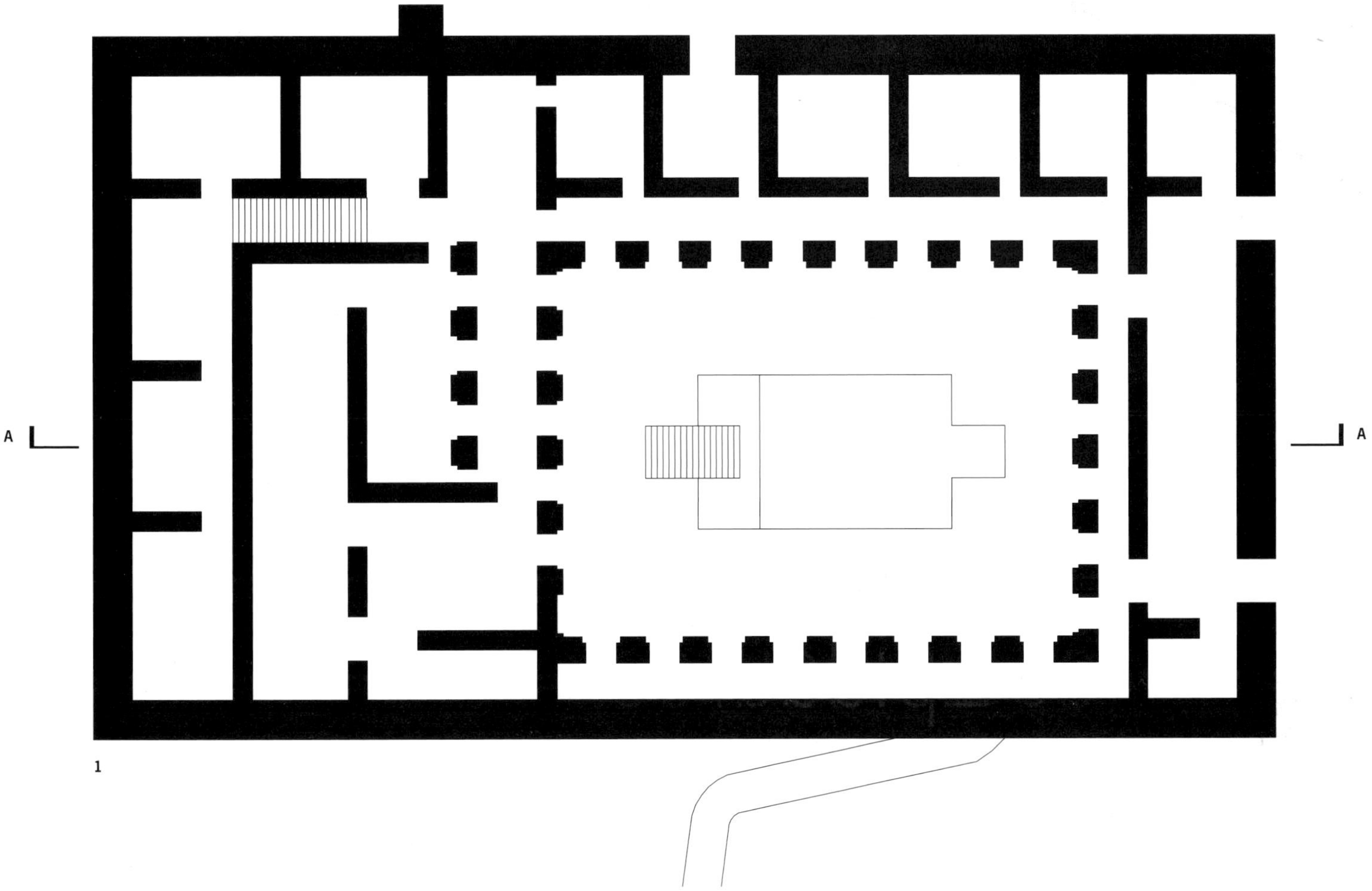

A

A

1

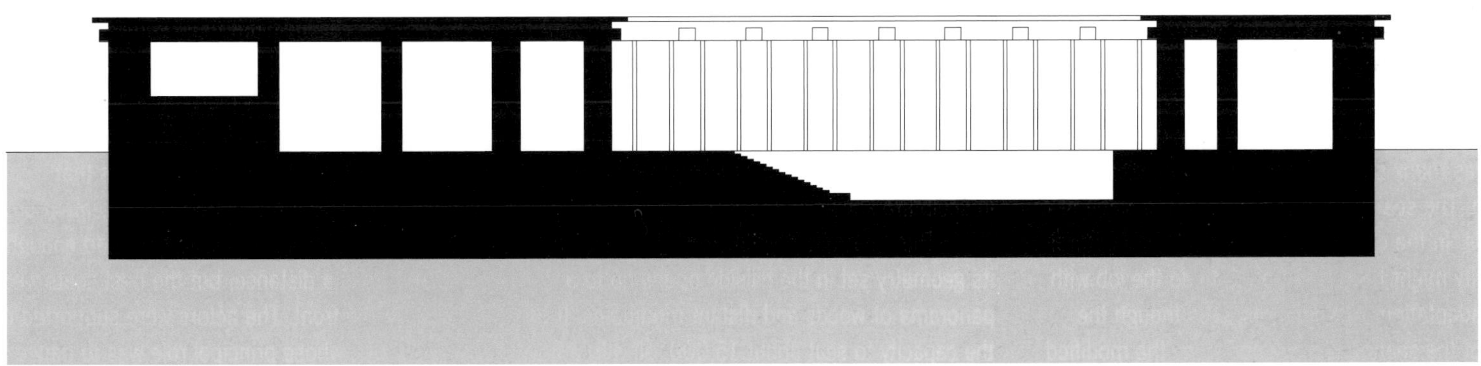

2

3

1 Plan

2 Section A-A

3 South Elevation

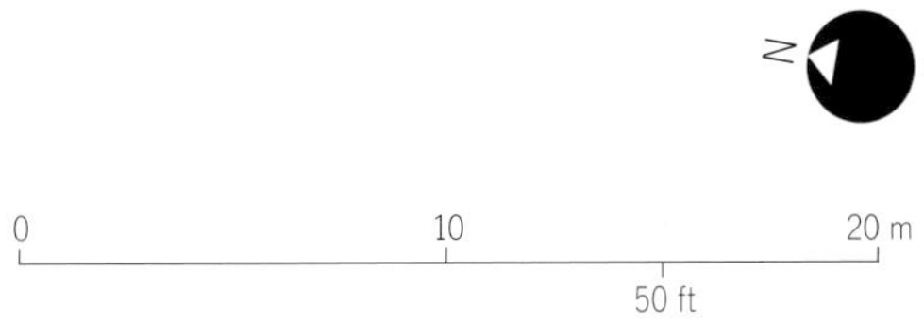

N

0 10 20 m

50 ft

Theatre at Epidauros

Polykleitos the Younger

Epidauros, Greece; 350 BCE

The great theatre at Epidauros is the largest surviving ancient Greek theatre. Based on a simple idea, it turned into something spectacular through the rigour of its large-scale execution.

At the heart of the theatre is an acting area, the orchestra, which is more or less circular and virtually surrounded by raked seating designed to allow as many people as possible to be close to the action. The seats were supported by the slope of a hillside. In the case of a smaller theatre, a natural declivity might have been found to do the job with little adaptation. At Epidauros, even though the rake of the seating was supported by the modified slope, major work was involved.

Selection of the site was an important part of the design. This theatre was located not in a city but in the main sanctuary of Asklepios, the god of medicine and healing. People travelled there for treatment and recuperation – a process that involved some hit-and-miss elements as well as relaxation and entertainment. The diagnosis, for example, was made by getting the patient to sleep in a particular building so that the god could reveal the problem in a dream.

The attribution of the theatre at Epidauros to Polykleitos the Younger is uncertain, but he worked on an elaborately decorated circular building (a *tholos*) in the sanctuary, making early use of the Corinthian order. In his day, Polykleitos was recognized for sculpting figures of athletes, but he was always less well known than his father, whose bronze sculptures were famous and were copied in marble. Some of those copies survive. Polykleitos the Elder was the author of a treatise on proportion in sculpture known as the *Kanon*.

The theatre is magnificent. The sweep of its geometry set in the hillside opens up to a panorama of woods and distant mountains. It has the capacity to seat about 15,000, all with a good view of the stage, though for some it is distant. The acoustics are reported to be miraculous and, when the auditorium is empty, sounds produced on the stage can be heard with surprising clarity. However, since bodies absorb sound, amplification is used when performances are given today in front of an audience.

The most noticeable difference between Epidauros and a modern auditorium arranged on similar lines is in the circulation. The stairs are long and without a place to pause, with the result that thousands of people are obliged to pass through very few exits – which can be problematic, causing crowding and impatience if everyone wants to leave at the same time. Order is maintained by positioning an armed policeman at the end of each stair. A similar measure must surely have been in place in earlier eras.

In ancient times there were no electronic gadgets to help the performers, but they worked with caricatural costumes and masks that sometimes had a megaphone arrangement around the mouth. The acting had to be broad enough to carry across a distance, but the best seats were close to the front. The actors were supported by the chorus, whose principal role was to dance – the modern word choreography derives from directing the movements of such a chorus.

In modern productions the stage lighting is a great advantage, and the theatre comes into its own after dusk, but in ancient times this would have been out of the question; the setting of the sun would, so to speak, have brought the curtain down.

1 Plan

1 Orchestra
2 Proscenium
3 Scene

2 Section A-A

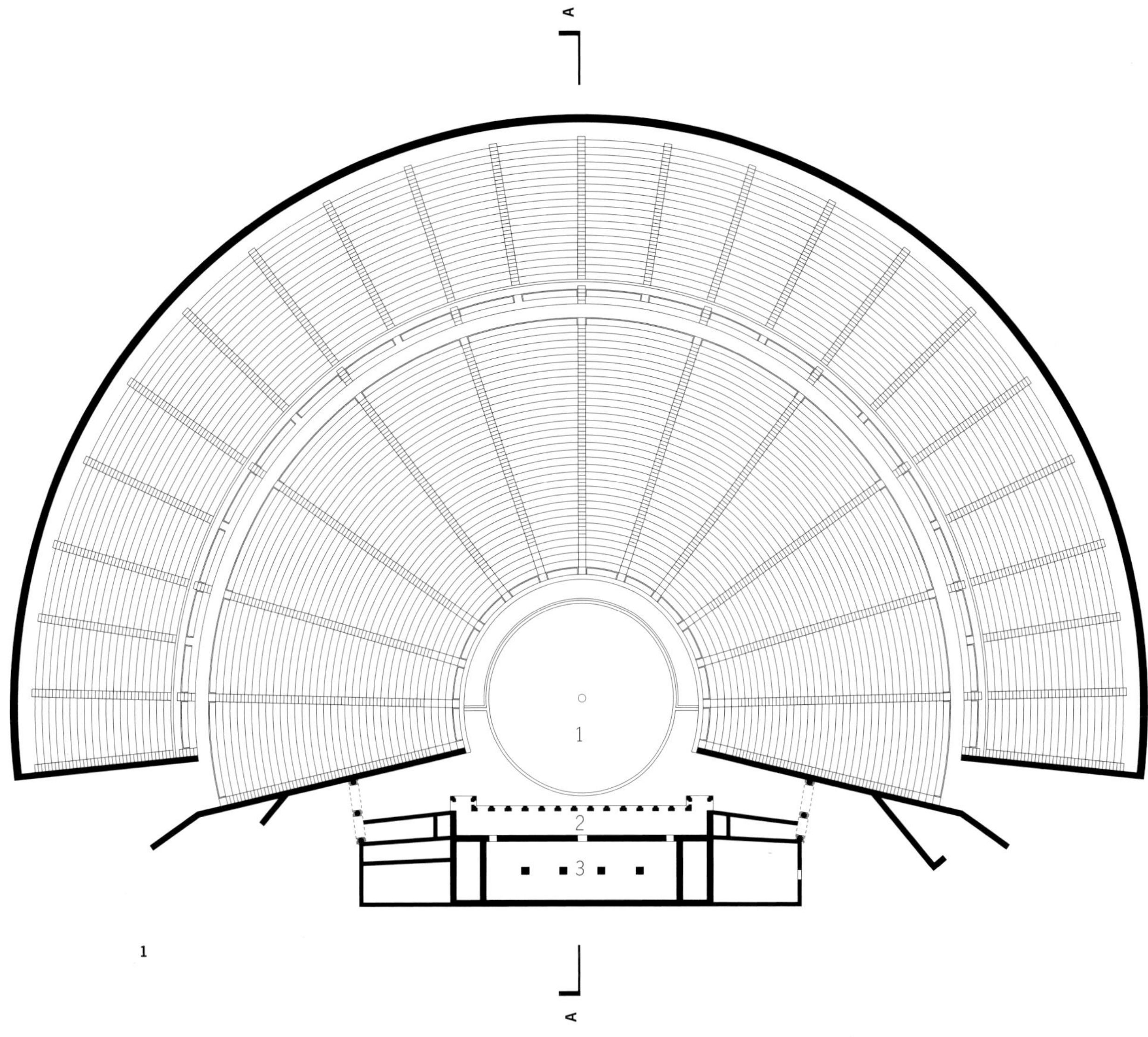

1

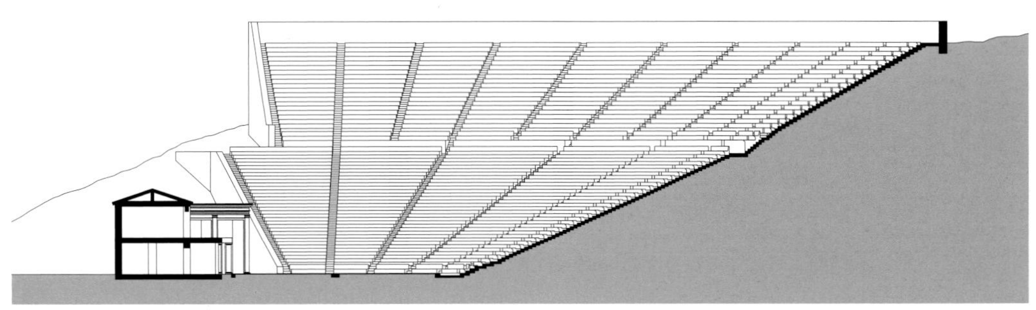

2

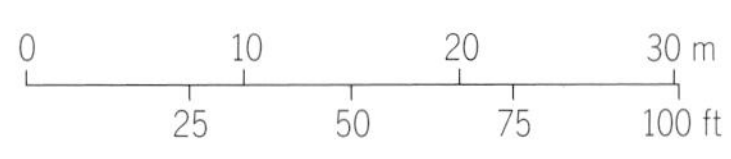

Theatre of Marcellus

Rome, Italy; 13 BCE

Audience and actors in a Roman theatre were arranged in the same way as in a Greek one, but the structure holding the audience was completely different. Whereas the Greeks sought out sloping ground to make the rake for theatre seating, the Romans could build a theatre anywhere. Roman theatres were typically located in city centres, while Greek ones were more often associated with sanctuaries such as Epidauros (pages 266–67) and Delphi (pages 102–103). Even in Athens, the Theatre of Dionysos was on the slopes of the Acropolis (pages 168–69) rather than in the Agora (pages 306–307). By contrast, in the days of the Roman Empire, there was a theatre in every city – one of the benefits of submission to Roman rule. There was no need for the theatre-builders to look for sloping ground since the raked seating was supported by a concrete substructure.

The first theatre built on the Roman pattern was the Theatre of Pompey, which resembled an integrated forum of the kind that would become characteristic of Rome under the emperors. It included a new temple to Venus and a row of four older temples behind it, all of which were incorporated into a composition with a new curia, known as the Curia Pompeii – which had acquired notoriety as the meeting place for the Senate to which Julius Caesar was progressing on the ides of March in 44 BCE, when he was murdered. The Theatre of Pompey had a seating capacity of about 20,000 and remained the largest theatre in Rome. (It does not survive.) The Theatre of Marcellus was built close by, at the initial instigation of Pompey's rival, Julius Caesar, who organized the demolition of two temples to clear the site, but was stopped in his tracks before building could begin.

The project came to fruition under Augustus (63 BCE–14 CE), who named it after his nephew and son-in-law Marcus Marcellus, whose promising career had been cut short by his early death. Enough of the Theatre of Marcellus survives to enable a reliable reconstruction. Part of it was demolished, part was converted into apartments during the Middle Ages, and subsequent renovations have kept it habitable.

The Greek theatres had incorporated a relatively small built space behind the acting area from which actors could make their entrances. The audience could see beyond it to the outside world. In the Roman theatre, stage-building became much more developed. A multi-storey wall housed backstage facilities behind an architectural display facing the audience. This permanent scenery rose to the height of the back row of seats, shutting out the exterior or maybe (as in the Theatre of Marcellus) allowing some views out between columns. The arrangements for reaching the seats were far superior to those in the Greek theatres. The audience approached from below and found their way up through the building by following a multitude of stairs and passages, which led past vomitoria to the ranks of seating. There were far more exits, and since the audience dispersed by making a general move away from the stage – rather than initially having to move towards it to reach the exit level – there was no bottleneck of the type experienced at Epidauros.

The external façade of the Theatre of Marcellus was much admired. It was there that the different styles of columns were superposed: Doric below, Ionic above and, presumably, Corinthian on the now-missing third storey – an arrangement that was imitated at a larger scale in the Colosseum (pages 18–19). In the fifteenth century, it was imitated by Alberti in the façade of the Rucellai Palace in Florence, but that is another story.

1 Plan

2 Elevation

3 Section A-A

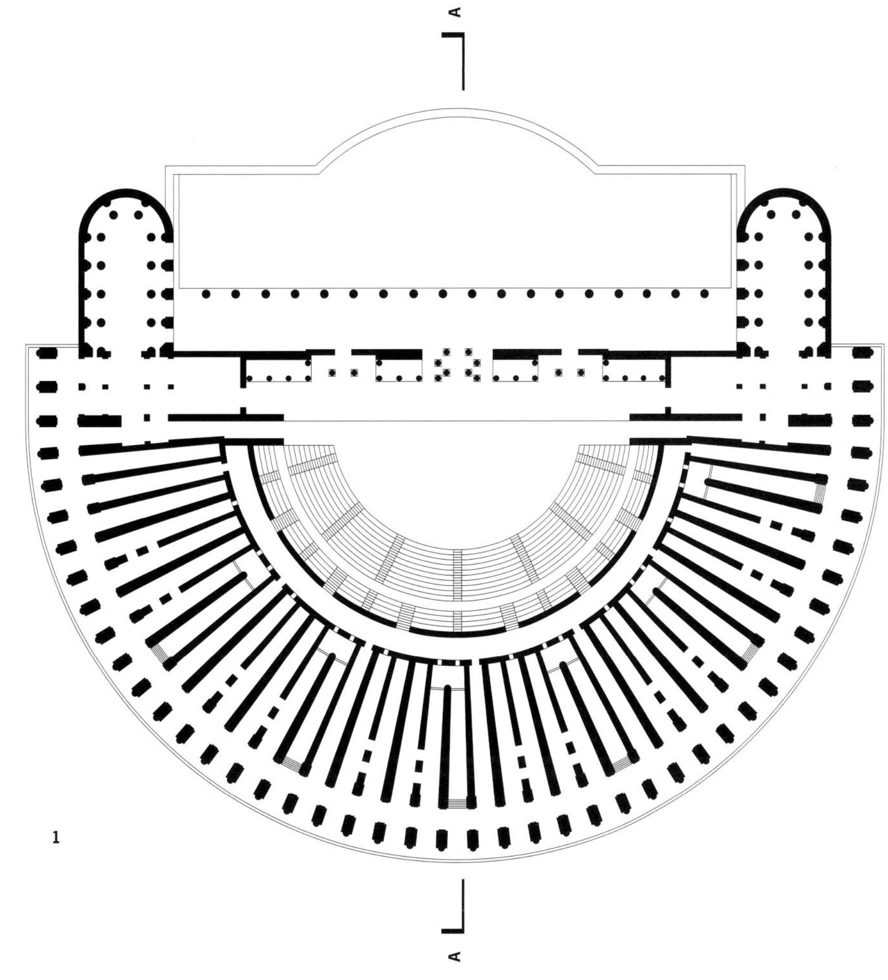

1

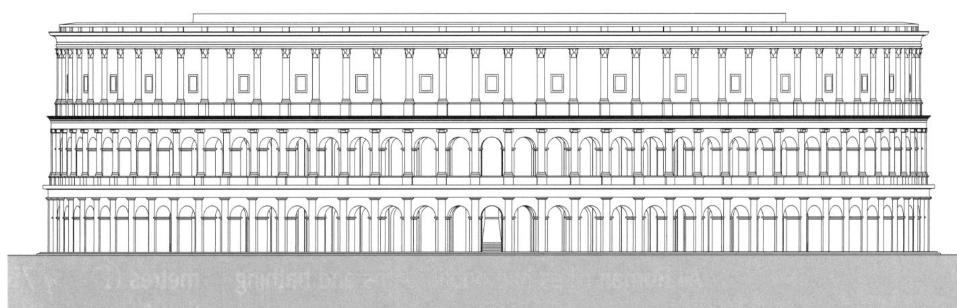

2

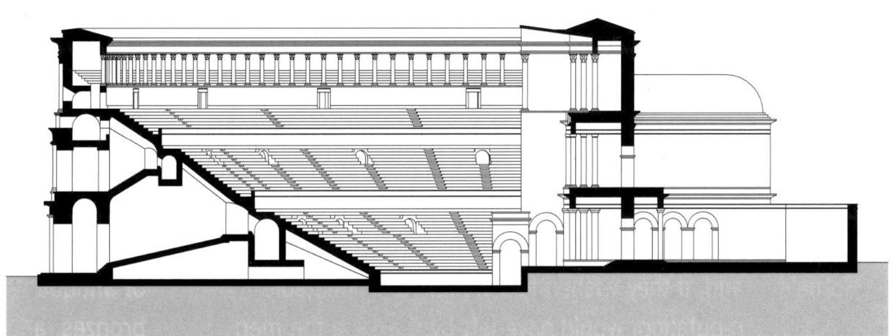

3

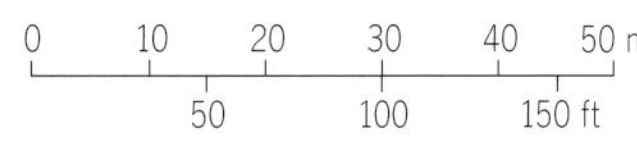

Baths of Caracalla

Rome, Italy; 212–16

Caracalla (188–217) was the most thuggish of Roman emperors. He had his brother murdered in 211 rather than share the empire with him, but made the excuse that he had acted in self-defence. In Alexandria a satirical play mocked this excuse, and the play became popular. Caracalla sent his soldiers to ransack the city and – according to Cassius Dio, who may have been exaggerating – 20,000 Alexandrians were killed. Caracalla's portrait shows him not as a serene philosopher, as earlier emperors had presented themselves, but as an impassioned soldier. He was murdered by one of his bodyguards while urinating at the side of the road. Caracalla ruled alone for only six years and, had it not been for his *thermae*, it is unlikely that he would be remembered any more clearly than his immediate successors, who had brief and sometimes equally lurid lives.

Caracalla's grand populist gesture – the public bathing complex that bears his name – was so magnificent that even in ruins it is one of Rome's most visited sites. It was one of the last large buildings built in Rome before the focus of attention shifted to Constantinople (founded in 324). For ordinary citizens, Rome had become a difficult place to live in. By the third century, the central area was crowded with monuments that gave the population a sense of privilege and destiny, but the citizen's private dwelling was likely to be flimsy, cramped and squalid. Rather than reform basic provisions, various emperors had built monumental public baths, which allowed ordinary people to feel that they were part of a privileged elite.

All Roman cities had public baths and bathing was seen as a pleasurable activity. The process involved warming and then overheating the body to produce sweat, oiling and scraping the skin, and then cooling off with a cold plunge or a swim. In the Roman imperial baths – built by the emperors Titus, Trajan, Diocletian and Caracalla – the room for each part of this process was given monumental treatment, but the same elements would be found in private baths. In public baths, women and men were separated, sometimes in different buildings; more often, they used the same baths at different times of day. Women would bathe in the mornings and, if they wished to maintain a respectable reputation, would have left by the time the men arrived in the afternoon, after the working day.

In the Baths of Caracalla, the caldarium, or hot room, was the pivot of the composition: a domed space 35 metres (115 feet) in diameter. This was kept hot by furnaces underneath and a hypocaust system that passed hot air beneath the floor and through channels in the walls – the floor and walls being covered in fine mosaics. On its axis was the much smaller tepidarium, which was warm, a huge vaulted central hall – the frigidarium, or cool room – and a swimming pool measuring 54 by 23 metres (177 by 75 feet), which was unroofed but had fine architectural decoration round its tall walls.

In the central block (shown in the plan) there were subsidiary spaces for changing and for exercise – the palaestra courts at each end were for gymnastics and boxing. The central block was set in a much larger precinct covering 400 square metres (more than 4,300 square feet) and raised up 6 metres (20 feet) above the surrounding street level. This included shops, a library and a grove of trees.

The perimeter buildings also were lavishly treated. From these precincts and those of other *thermae* came some of the most valuable finds of antique statues, often copies of admired Greek bronzes, and many of them now in the Vatican museums. The Baths of Caracalla yielded a statue of Asklepios 4 metres (13 feet) high and the Farnese Hercules – both appropriate guardians to watch over a place of health and physical culture.

1 Plan

1 Caldarium
2 Tepidarium
3 Frigidarium
4 Palaestra
5 Natatio

2 Section A-A

3 South Elevation

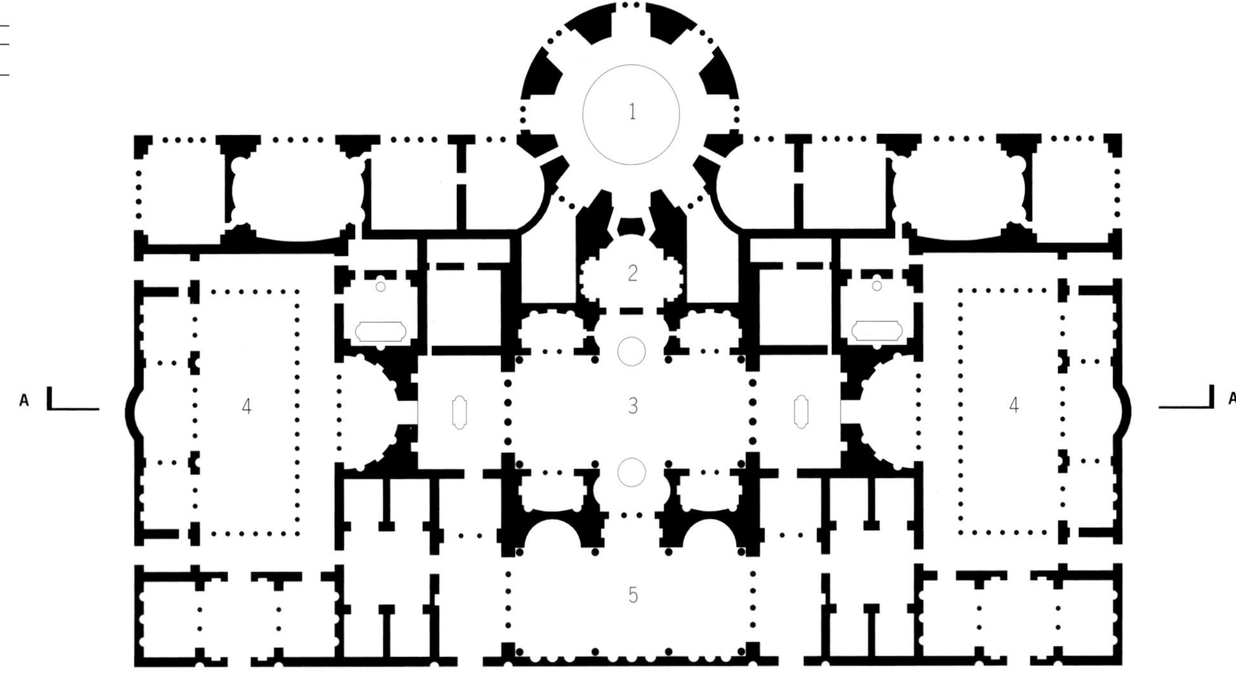

1

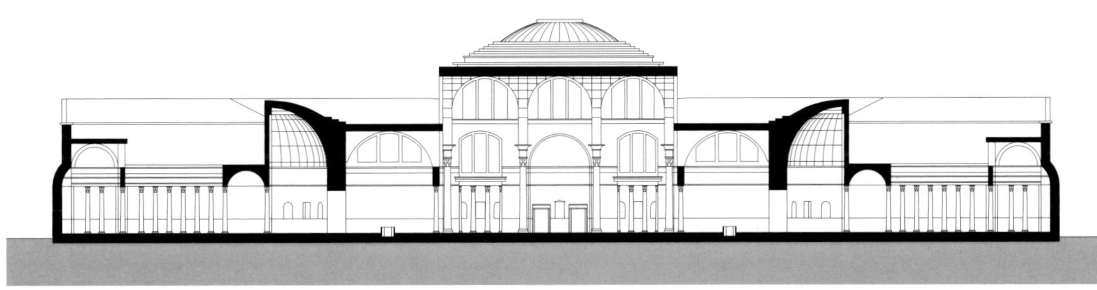

2

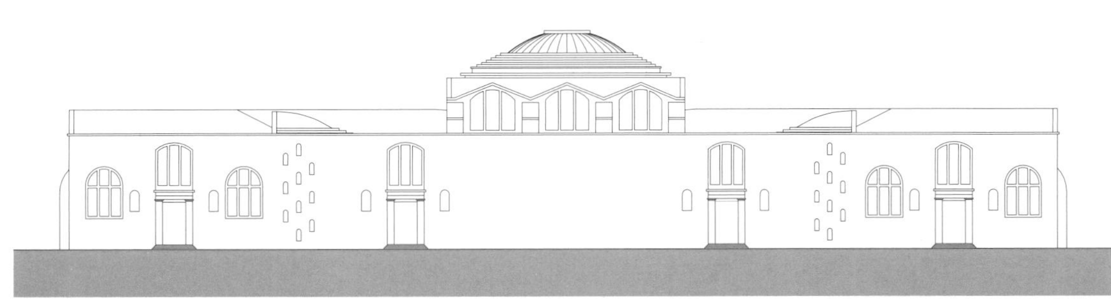

3

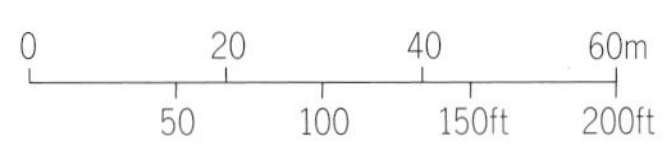

Teatro Olimpico

Andrea Palladio, 1508–80, and Vincenzo Scamozzi, 1548–1616

Vicenza, Italy; 1580–85

The Olympic Academy in Vicenza was made up of a mixed group of people, some of whom had money, others only a passion for learning. Andrea Palladio was one of its founder members, introduced by his patron Count Giangiorgio Trissino. It was Trissino who had given his protégé the name Palladio. He wrote an ambitious and successful play, *Sofonisba* (1524), and his grand vision for Vicenza fused theatre with architecture, seeing architectural design as the art of making settings suitable for the events that would unfold there. He believed that dignified buildings would ennoble lives.

When the academy wished to stage performances of dramatic works, Palladio would design temporary structures for the purpose. The project for a permanent theatre came into focus only at the end of Palladio's life, but he was very well prepared for the commission, having read what the Roman architectural theorist Vitruvius had to say in the first century BCE about the layout of theatres, and having studied the remains of several ancient theatres, including one in Vicenza itself and another to the south, at Pola, which he drew.

The building that the Olympic Academy acquired for the theatre was a former medieval fortress that had more recently been used as a prison. Palladio had to work within the envelope of the existing structure, which involved making some changes to the ideal design. Most obviously, he squeezed the shape of the seating area from what had been a semi-circle into half an ellipse. The row of Corinthian columns running round the back of the seating was pressed against the back wall in the central section, but was far enough away from the corners of the room to allow staircases to be installed there.

The Teatro Olimpico is the first known permanent indoor theatre, but the ceiling is painted with clouds and blue sky, recalling the open air, illuminated by a clerestory above the cornice line.

Palladio died before construction had finished and his assistant Vincenzo Scamozzi took over. Scamozzi made self-effacing decisions that saw the building completed, but his main work there was the scenery for the theatre's first production (*Oedipus Rex* by Sophocles), which has remained in place ever since. It depicts serious monumental buildings, suitable for the expression of high-flown emotion in a tragedy, and shows streets leading away from openings in the wall at the back of the stage. Scamozzi developed the Renaissance obsession with perspective by constructing these streets in an accelerated perspective – the buildings diminish sharply in size as they recede from the openings. This produces an illusion of much greater depth than could really be achieved in the confined space, but the 'streets' are not viable performance spaces; if an actor were to walk away up one of them, he would seem to grow alarmingly.

In a Roman theatre, the statues might have depicted gods or emperors – muses or patrons. In the Teatro Olimpico, the lively figures that stand around on the cornice above the Corinthian columns, and who pose in the niches and on top of columns on the stage wall, are portraits of the academicians.

The theatre was little used after its initial success, and now stands as a rare survivor, permanently populated by a significant number of the members of its first audience.

1 Section A-A

2 Section B-B

3 Plan

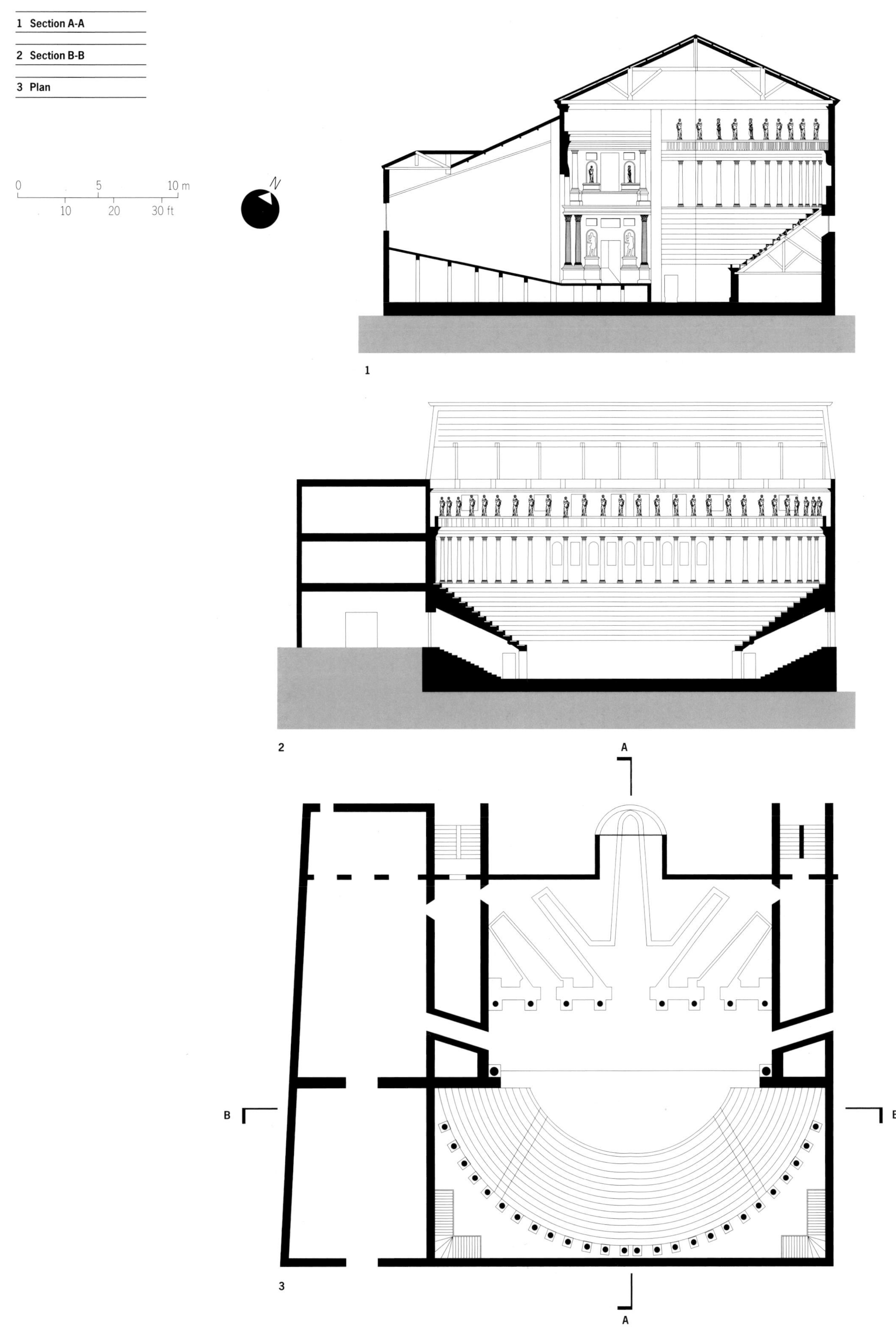

Globe Theatre

London, UK; 1598

William Shakespeare's play *Henry V* (1599) opens with a prologue that explains what he expects of the audience. The action of the play to follow will revolve around the Battle of Agincourt: a confrontation between the armies of England and France. Is there room in the theatre to assemble the armies of two great nations and have them fight a battle?

> *Can this cockpit hold*
> *The vasty fields of France? or may we cram*
> *Within this wooden O the very casques*
> *That did affright the air at Agincourt?*

The answer is no. For the drama to work as intended, the audience must use its imagination. The 'wooden O' is the theatre, round and open to the sky, where the play was first performed: the Globe Theatre in London. It is famous principally because it was where Shakepeare's plays first saw the light of day. The original building disappeared long ago, so the drawings opposite represent a reconstruction.

There is also a 'real' reconstruction of the Globe (shown in the photographs above) – a working theatre on the south bank of the Thames near where the original is known to have stood.

The Globe is almost exactly contemporary with Palladio's Teatro Olympico (pages 272–73), but the two buildings belong to different traditions. In the Globe, there is less scope for dancing and spectacle, but more chance of everyone hearing all the words. The characters could come on to the stage from the back; in unusual situations, they might descend from the canopy over the stage or come up through a trap door, but there was no scope for illusionistic scenery.

The picture-making was in the audience's minds, and Shakespeare's dialogue gives the necessary place descriptions as it goes along. His plays have many more words in them than a 'naturalistic' twenty-first-century film – which might show an image accompanied by music or ambient sound to establish location and mood, at which point a character might utter a short phrase or simply gaze at the scene, saying nothing. In Shakespeare, it is the words that do the work.

Someone watching the staging of a play at the Globe would have seen a place crowded with people – standing in galleries overlooking the central space, filling the courtyard, even sitting on the stage. Shakespeare called the theatre a 'scaffold' – and it does look like a series of props that are barely strong enough to hold the audience in position, too frail a thing to sustain such an elevating vision as the words and actions of the drama would evoke. The building fabric is neither elaborate nor showy. The sturdy timber-framed structure could have been found in manor houses all over the country. To an audience at the turn of the seventeenth century, it would have looked relatively ordinary, and the sense of mounting anticipation would develop from the assembling throng rather than from the look of the building.

In England, the baroque style was slow to take root and was then dispensed with fairly quickly, as Andrea Palladio – rather than Balthasar Neumann or Jules-Hardouin Mansart – became the dominant influence on British architecture after Christopher Wren. Strikingly, the word 'theatrical' is commonly used to describe the effects of early baroque architecture, while the theatre of the day actually had no recourse to what are now called theatrical effects; they would develop later, in indoor theatres that used artificial light.

1 Plan

1 Stage
2 Backstage

2 North Elevation

3 Section A-A

0 5 10 m
10 20 30 ft

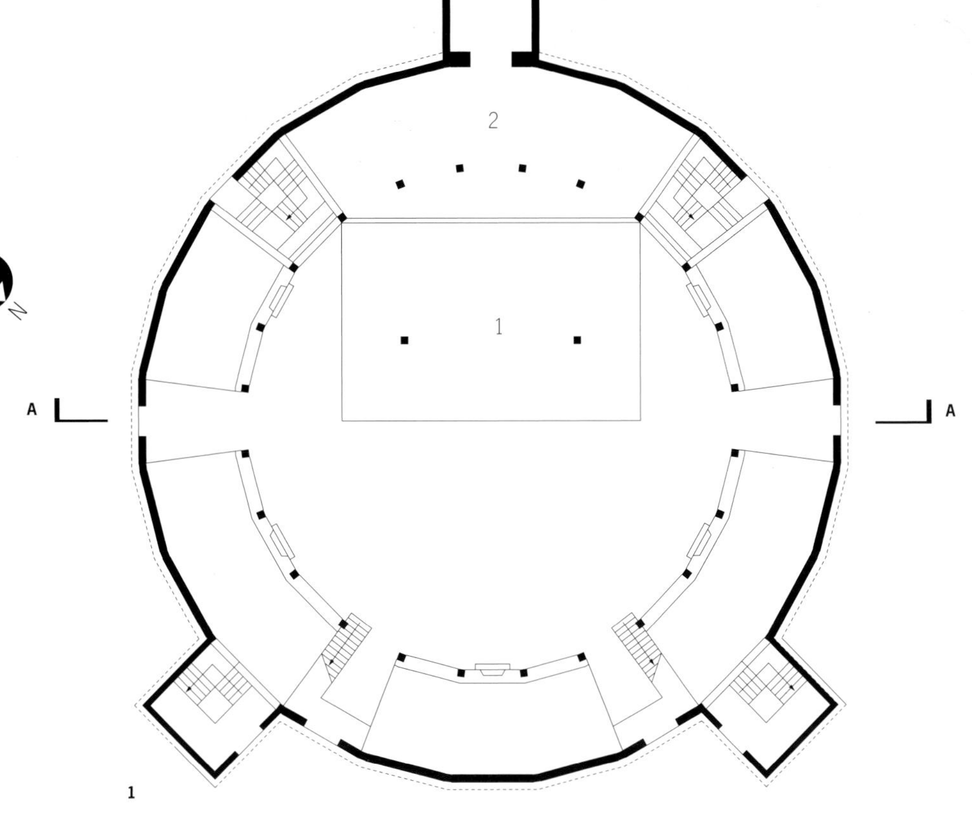

1

2

3

Louvre

Pierre Lescot, 1515–78, Claude Perrault, 1613–88, Ludovico (Louis) Visconti, 1791–1853, and others

Paris, France; c.1190–1989

Long straight lines slice their way across Paris, establishing vistas with monuments sited squarely at the end of them. The vistas can be far-reaching, but the monuments are big enough to register from a distance, and the city is bound together by these lines, which offer views of familiar orientation-points.

The longest line runs along the Champs-Elysées, to stop at the Louvre – or, rather, it seems to start at the Louvre and work its way west, through the Tuileries gardens to the gold-topped Obelisk, the Arc de Triomphe and, far in the distance, the Grande Arche de la Défense. Viewed from Bernini's equestrian statue of Louis XIV in front of the Louvre, in the Cour Napoléon, they all fall perfectly into line. The Louvre is not just an edifice; it is a major event in the city.

Originally a twelfth-century fortification, the building was adopted by royalty in the fourteenth century, since it offered much more scope for development than had their previous palace site on the Île de la Cité. Part of the current Jardin des Tuileries was established as a garden when Catherine de Médici commissioned the Tuileries Palace from Philibert de l'Orme (1510–70). It was outside the city, and faced the city wall, which at this point on its circuit was a bastion of the Louvre.

Between 1590 and 1605, Henri IV built the Grande Galérie, which stretched some 400 metres (more than 1,300 feet) along the bank of the Seine, linking the Louvre with the Tuileries Palace. Its lower floors provided dwellings and workshops for hundreds of artists and craftsmen.

The square court at the east of the present Louvre was consolidated (but left unfinished) by Louis XIV, before the royal court moved to Versailles in 1682. It included the building now known as the Pavillon Sully, designed by Jacques Lemercier (1585–1654), which set the style and scale for subsequent developments. Later works removed the city wall and (as late as 1883) the remains of the Tuileries Palace. It was only then that the Louvre's commanding position could be fully recognized. By then its use as a museum was already established.

After the move to Versailles, Louis XIV had a display of antique sculptures set up at the Louvre and let the Académie Française use the palace. From 1699, painters of the Académie Royale de Peinture et de Sculpture held an annual show there. After the 1789 revolution, the museum and gallery functions were consolidated and Napoleon's conquests gave access to artistic treasures that enhanced the collections. The institution's size was increased enormously by Napoleon III's addition of wings with internal courtyards (completed 1857) stretching west towards, and linking with, the end pavilions of the Tuileries Palace. One of these, the Pavillon de Flore, survives in its original form; the other was rebuilt to match it after the demolition of the rest of the palace.

The ensemble makes a grand urban gesture – not matched by an internal coherence until the buildings were reorganized in the 1980s by the Chinese American architect I. M. Pei (1917–). He designed a huge undercroft beneath the Cour Napoléon, making a circulation space linking the north, east and south wings and including facilities that a modern visitor would expect. Reached through a glass pyramid at street level, this space is now the point of entry for the museums.

It is clear from looking at a plan of Paris, from the layout of the roads and parks, that the Louvre is the most important building in the city. It is no surprise to learn that it was once the residence of a head of state – a place that combined political power with cultural prestige. But the political element disappeared with the demise of the Tuileries Palace. It is now an embodiment of cultural prestige for its own sake.

1 Site Plan

1 Pyramid (main entrance)
2 Arc de Triomphe du Carrousel
3 Courtyard

2 Section A-A

3 Section B-B

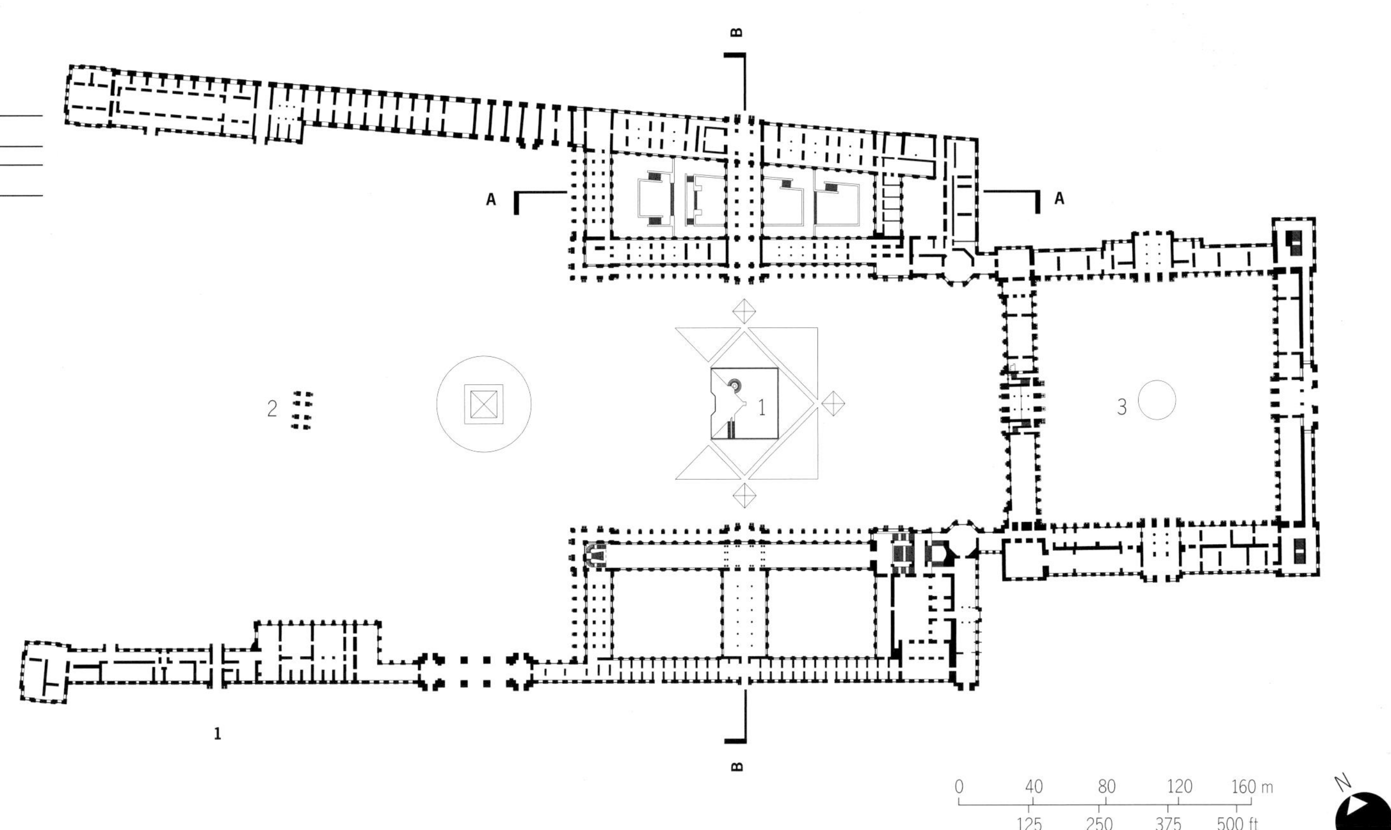

1

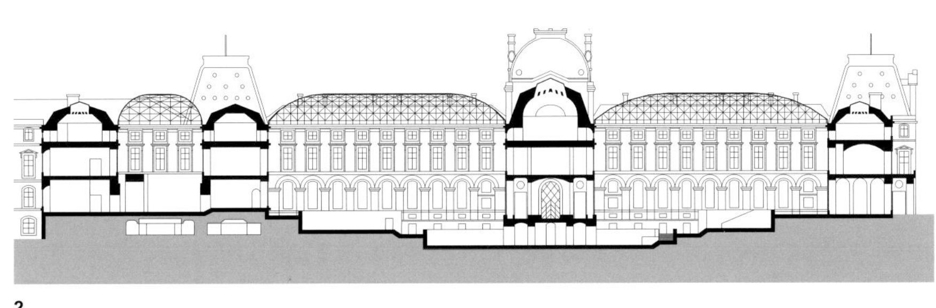

2

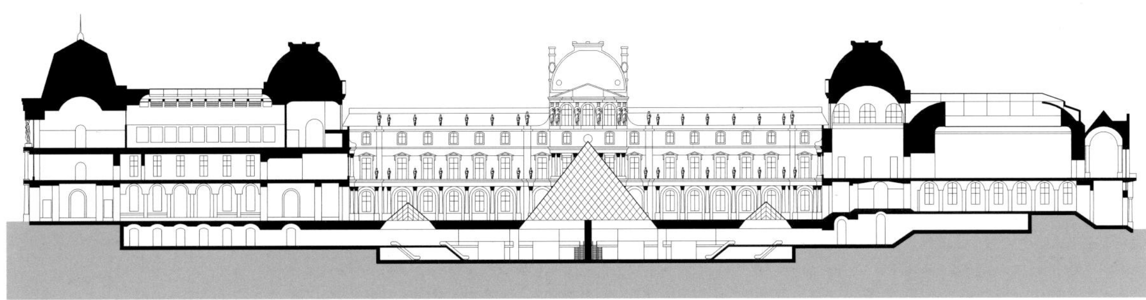

3

0 20 40 60 80 m
50 100 150 200 250 ft

Altes Museum

Karl Friedrich Schinkel, 1781–1841

Berlin, Germany; 1823–30

One of Karl Friedrich Schinkel's late fantasies was revealed in a series of disturbingly plausible drawings for a royal palace on the Acropolis of Athens (pages 168–69). Such a building would have destroyed a great deal of archaeological evidence, but would have made a fine place for Otto Wittelsbach, the Bavarian king of newly independent Greece, to receive foreign visitors.

Ancient Greek culture had a hold on the minds of many educated people across western Europe, not least in Scotland. The Scottish National Monument, begun in 1826 on Calton Hill overlooking Edinburgh, was a reproduction of the Parthenon (pages 16–17). Ludwig I of Bavaria built another such reproduction – his Valhalla – at Regensburg in 1830, which might have been part of a campaign to see his son Otto on the Greek throne. (Ludwig's grandson, Ludwig II, built Neuschwanstein, pages 84–85.)

In the 1820s the philosopher Georg Hegel, a professor at the University of Berlin, argued that the spirit that had made the Greeks great in ancient times had now come to rest in German culture. A century earlier, Johann Joachim Winckelmann had communicated an enthusiasm for Greek art that influenced everyone who read him. In Winckelmann's view, what had made Greek culture great was the ready contact between artistic and physical activity, which gave vigour and beauty of expression to every waking thought and deed.

Art was seen to have a cultural value that would be good for society as a whole. The Louvre (pages 276–77) had made ancient sculpture accessible to the public from 1699. The British National Gallery was founded in 1824 and opened its doors in 1838. In Berlin, Friedrich Wilhelm III of Prussia made his art collection available for public display and commissioned the Königliches Museum in 1823. It would be completed to Schinkel's design by 1830, changing its name to Altes Museum (Old Museum) in 1845, when the Neues Museum (New Museum) was under construction.

Schinkel's design drew on classical precedents. Its central space was a reproduction of the Pantheon in Rome (pages 108–109), creating an aura reminiscent of a temple of art. The dome was hidden from view by being placed in the middle of the block and edged with a high parapet. (Schinkel thought it wise to avoid direct competition with the baroque domed cathedral next door.) When seen from outside, the building's form is that of an Ionic stoa, but a stoa more monumental than any known examples from ancient Greece. Its columns are fully two storeys high – the same scale as those in a large temple. They stand on a tall plinth, reached by a broad central square, and run the whole length of the building. There is a shallow porch behind them, deeper in the central five bays, around the entrance, where there is a double row of columns. Around the perimeter on each of two floors is an enfilade of rooms, providing display spaces for most of the exhibits.

Schinkel's buildings have a lightness of touch that prevents even the most authoritative of them from seeming overbearing. One surprise for visitors to the Altes Museum is the revelation of the great central space. Another occurs on the half-landing of the staircase, which is actually outdoors, allowing a view of the portico columns from behind (though this sense of surprise has been substantially undermined by the decision in the 1960s to close off the space with plate glass).

Outside on the cornice is a row of stone eagles – one sitting above each column, looking slightly predatory – which revitalizes the traditional ornament. And at the top of the building, against the sky, in the position of acroteria, are statues of naked handlers taming fiery horses.

1 Plan

1 Rotunda
2 Courtyard
3 Portico
4 West hall
5 North hall
6 East hall

2 South Elevation

3 Section A-A

A
5
1
4
2
2
6
3
A
0
10
20
30
40
50 m
50
100
150 ft
N

1

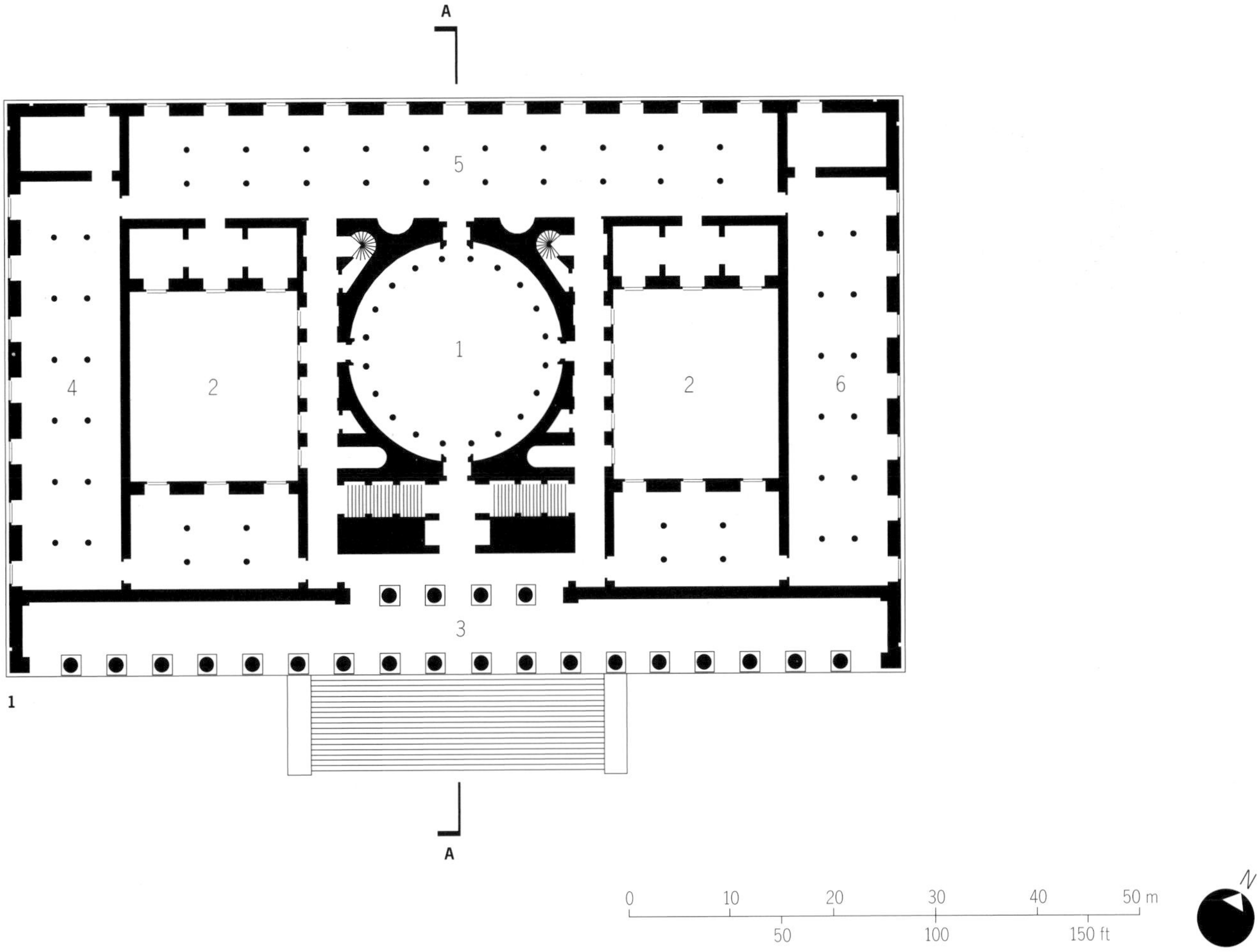

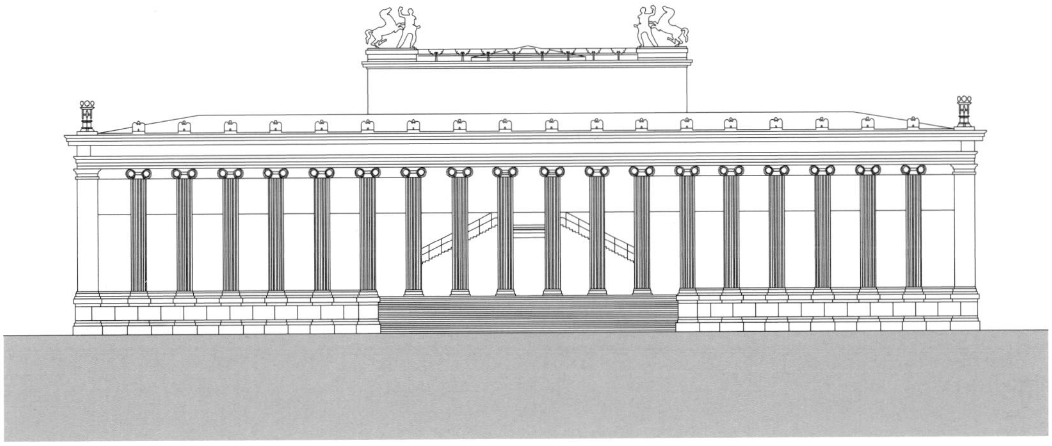

2

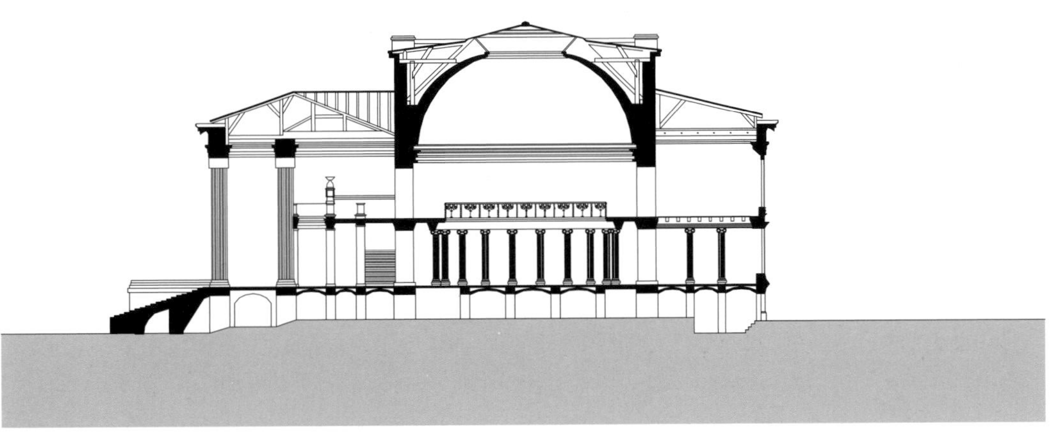

3

Crystal Palace

Joseph Paxton, 1803–65

London, UK; 1851

Prince Albert of Saxe-Coburg and Gotha, who married Victoria, Queen of the United Kingdom, was not allowed to rule as king, but he did much behind the scenes to help Victoria and further the causes in which he believed. He took charge of a royal commission to oversee the decoration of the new Palace of Westminster (pages 256–57), where he was instrumental in choosing artists and deciding what themes from British history they would depict in their work. And he took an interest in the work of the Society for the Encouragement of Arts, Manufactures and Commerce, founded in 1774 and granted a Royal Charter in 1847. (It still exists and is usually known as the Royal Society of Arts.)

An annual exhibition organized by the Society of Arts was the inspiration for a Great Exhibition of the Works of Industry of All Nations. A royal commission was set up in 1850 with the Prince Consort as its president and Henry Cole as its chief administrator. Working with other members of the society, they organized an international architectural competition to design a building to house the exhibition in London's Hyde Park, but it produced no viable results. The building had to be huge, needed to be constructed quickly, and had to be removable after the event.

Joseph Paxton became involved by chance. He was the head gardener at Chatsworth House in Derbyshire, and had built a conservatory there for its owner, the Duke of Devonshire. He was also a director of the Midland Railway, which brought him into contact with one of the royal commission's advisors. Paxton realized that his conservatory design could be extended to cover a vast area, using industrial production methods to manufacture its components – iron structural members that incorporated gutters, supporting the largest sheets of glass yet made. Its assembly could be much quicker than would have been possible with traditional building methods. During a Midland Railway board meeting, he produced a small sketch on blotting paper explaining the basis of the idea. Eight months later, the building was complete.

The Great Exhibition was highly successful. It displayed technological marvels, including industrial machinery, alongside just about anything else: silks, furniture, paintings, cutlery, minerals – including the world's largest known diamond, the Koh-i-Noor. The multitude of paying visitors generated an income that covered the exhibitions costs and paid for the purchase of land south of Hyde Park that later came to be known as 'Albertopolis'. It was there that educational buildings were developed to consolidate the prospects of British manufacturing and design: the Imperial Institute (now Imperial College), the Victoria and Albert Museum, the Natural History Museum, the Science Museum, the Royal College of Art, and the Royal Albert Hall of Arts and Sciences. Originally to be called the Central Hall of Arts and Sciences, the Royal Albert Hall was renamed by Victoria after her late husband when it opened in 1871, confirming its link with the Albert Memorial, placed on the hall's axis, across the road in Hyde Park.

The building itself provoked strong reactions. Some saw it as a new sort of architecture; others saw it as not architecture at all. Paxton's design was amazingly free from ideas of 'style' and was very much the product of pragmatic thinking. Even the transept had a pragmatic basis – it was designed in such a way that there was no need to cut down any trees. It was scarcely more than scaffolding, holding in place a waterproof covering that protected the exhibits and the visitors, and it almost disappeared from view. But the Crystal Palace caught the imagination of the world as an image of modernity, and sparked the development of a tradition of international expositions, or world fairs.

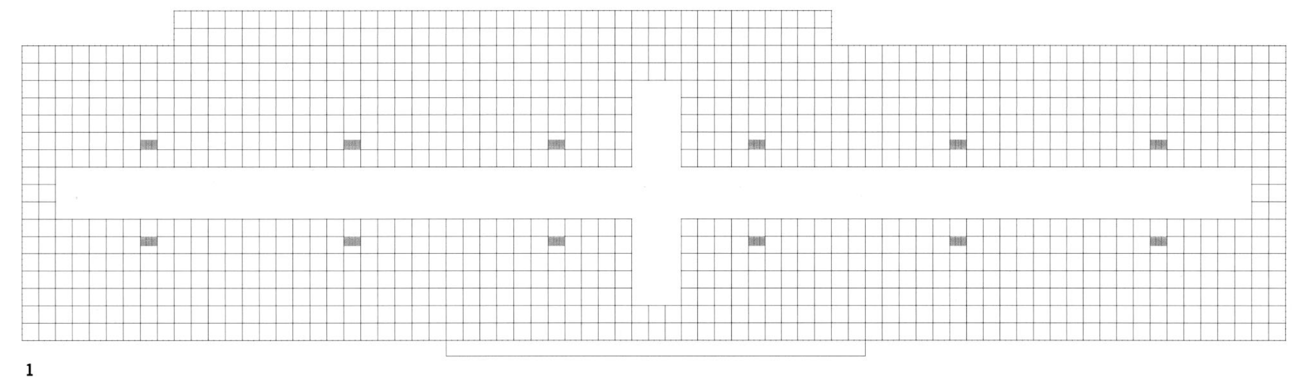

1

2

3

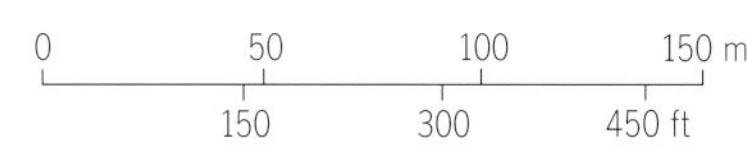

1 Plan

2 East Elevation

3 South Elevation

4 Detail

4

0 50 m
150 ft

Opéra Garnier

Charles Garnier, 1825–98

Paris, France; 1862–75

In the centre of Paris, around the corner from the Louvre (pages 276–77), is one end of a boulevard that is terminated by the Opéra Garnier – a building that has been renamed to distinguish it from a newer, larger opera house in the Place de la Bastille. It is significant that the opera house has been called after its architect rather than its patron or a composer of operas: the architecture makes an impact that cannot be ignored.

Like the Louvre, the Opéra Garnier is a monumental presence in the city, but in this case the building forms, particularly its sculptural details, are lively and exuberant. The style, known as Second Empire, is neo-baroque, adopted after a wave of severe neoclassicism and – with nineteenth-century money and production methods behind it – made even more sumptuous than eighteenth-century baroque had been.

It is in the interiors that the building comes into its own and where its real purpose becomes apparent. A comparison between a section of the Opéra and one of the Globe (pages 274–75) shows how far the theatre had developed as a type in 250 years. At the Globe, the auditorium takes up nearly the whole volume. At the Opéra, it is almost lost, buried deep within the building; it is central to the plan and section, but there is far more to the structure. First, the stage is a colossal apparatus of platforms and cables that makes it possible to change illusionistic scenery in moments. A great hall of a palace can be winched out of the way to be replaced by a forest, a grotto or an artist's garret.

Behind the stage there are facilities for the performers – small rooms on many floors. The musicians are hidden from view while performing, in an orchestra pit half concealed by the front edge of the stage.

From the theatre's inception, the lighting would have been entirely artificial – generally gas burners, but with spotlights burning lime trained on the principal performers. Above the auditorium's ceiling would have been a great gas burner, to heat the air in the roof space and make it rise up through the vented cupola. The air escaping at the top would have lowered the pressure below and drawn fresh air into the lower levels of the auditorium.

The stage and backstage facilities occupy about half the theatre's footprint. The other half is devoted to the audience, including the auditorium, which takes up maybe a quarter of the remaining area. Most of the rest is given over to a series of spaces for circulation and entertainment, which have a regal appearance. They are grouped around a staircase of the most bewitching theatricality, where ornamentation and cut-glass details are piled up and draped to create a finely judged effect of lavish glamour. This is the heart of the Opéra – the real theatre, where the aristocracy and bourgeoisie of the Second Empire would have gone to impress one another and claim their position in fashionable society.

It is not surprising that these things were done, but the architecture of the building makes it possible to imagine exactly how absorbing such occasions would have been – to the point where the performances on stage must have been regarded as a mere adjunct to the main proceedings.

1 South Elevation

2 Section A-A

3 Ground Floor Plan

1 Rehearsal room
2 Stage
3 Auditorium
4 Principal staircase
5 Entrance lobby

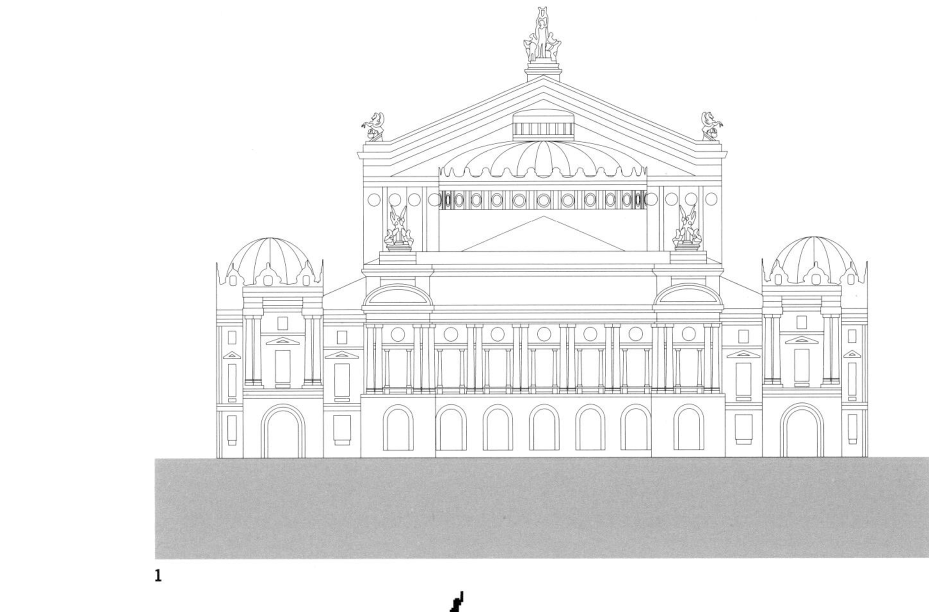

1

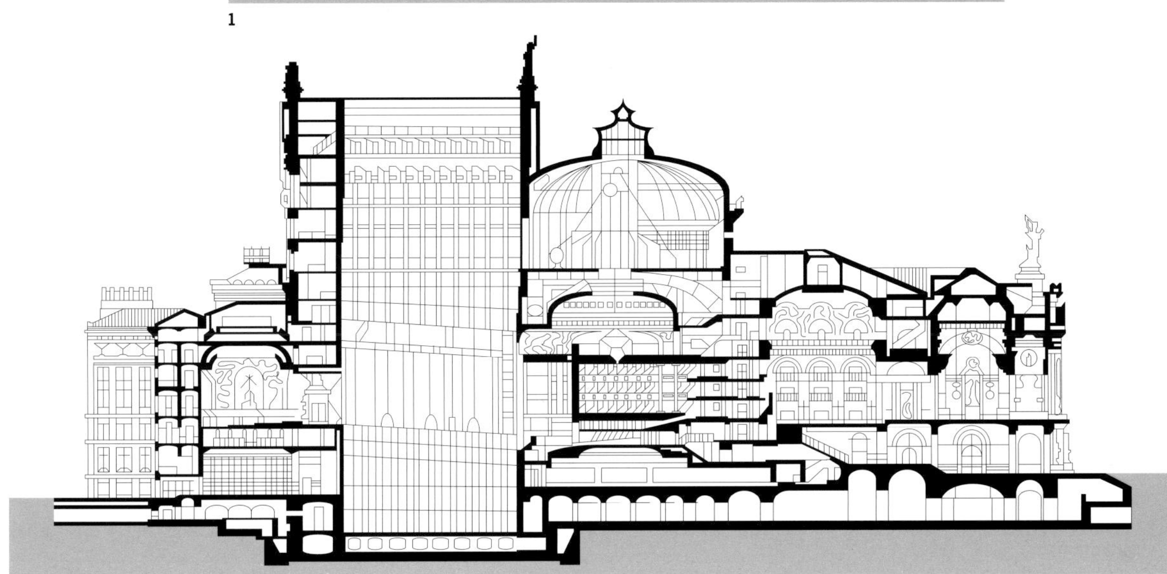

2

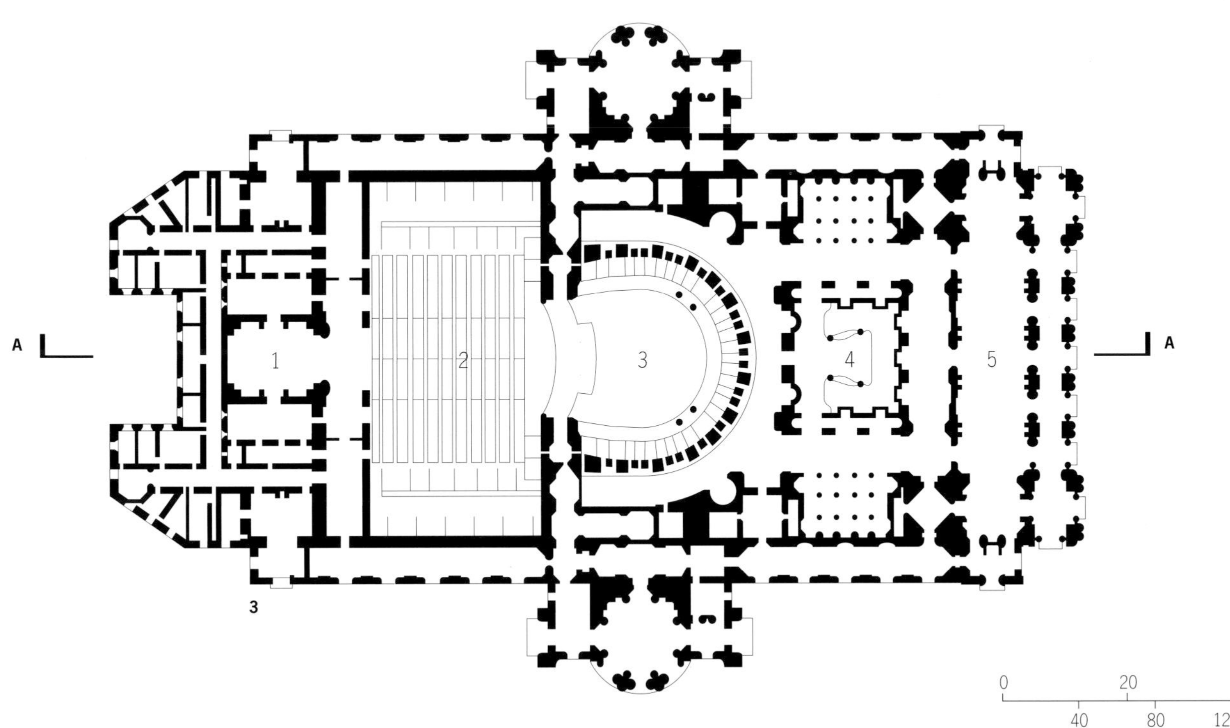

3

Philharmonie

Hans Scharoun, 1893–72

Berlin, Germany; 1956–63

The symphony orchestra is one of the great cultural developments of western civilization, producing a range of sounds that can stir profound emotions and bring a sense of serenity. In the twenty-first century, the music of symphony orchestras is most often heard in recorded form, perhaps on personal headphones – in the home, in shops or while travelling. Music was not always so pervasive.

Before the nineteenth century, classical music was heard most frequently in churches or in aristocratic households where musicians were employed. Music would be performed in salons and ballrooms, but there were no purpose-built halls for public performances. The Musikverein in Vienna opened in 1870, the Concertgebouw in Amsterdam in 1888, and Boston Symphony Hall in 1900, but most purpose-built concert halls are twentieth-century buildings.

There are two organizing principles at work in a concert hall, one concerning the acoustics, the other the positioning of the audience. They pull in different directions. It is important that the acoustic properties of the place work to enhance the music. If they are wrong, the music can sound muffled, even if the musicians are performing wonderfully well. A certain volume of air is needed to produce enough resonance. The ceiling must be high. But also the sound must be reflected back to the audience – otherwise it will seem dead and strangely quiet. As concert halls developed, the size of the orchestra increased significantly in order to produce enough sound.

Like a Roman amphitheatre, the Royal Albert Hall in London is excellently arranged to give a large audience a good view of an event in the central arena. The hall's curved walls have the effect of focusing sounds, however, and its shortcomings became apparent during the opening concert in 1871, when a distinct echo could be heard. (A means to correct it was eventually devised in 1969.) A good acoustic depends on sound being dispersed rather than focused. In ornate buildings, the irregular surfaces can have a dispersing effect. In a modern building incorporating planar surfaces, other means must be found to achieve it.

The strategy used by Hans Scharoun at the Philharmonie in Berlin was to set up non-parallel walls that reflect the sound in different directions. The roof's curves are convex from the underside, so they too help the process of dispersal. The gathering of the audience around the orchestra is an acknowledgment that some positions in the concert hall are better than others – there is not an even distribution of sound in all directions. Most of the audience sits in front of the orchestra, looking in the same direction as the conductor, but there are also some seats behind it, because it is preferable to sit there and be close to the orchestra than to listen to the music from a great distance.

Audience seating is also grouped into blocks, so that each block of 100 or so people is about the same size as the orchestra. The hall is raised off the ground and can be reached through large foyers in which the stairs are angled to the direction of anticipated travel.

The plan of the Philharmonie looks complex and is said to have dismayed the builders when they first saw it, but, now that everything is in place, it works intuitively for the audience and is renowned among performers for its excellence. The sound is fine, and people in the audience do not feel as if they are being treated like a massed mob.

1 Section A-A

2 Lower Level Plan

3 Upper Level Plan

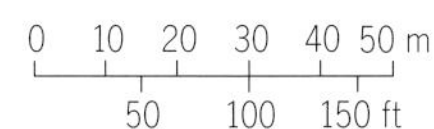

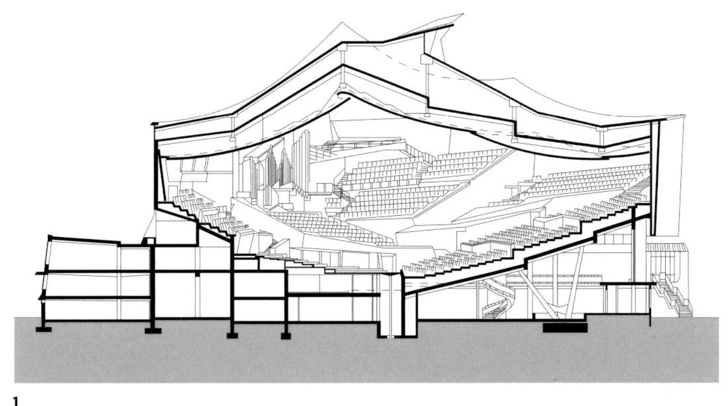

1

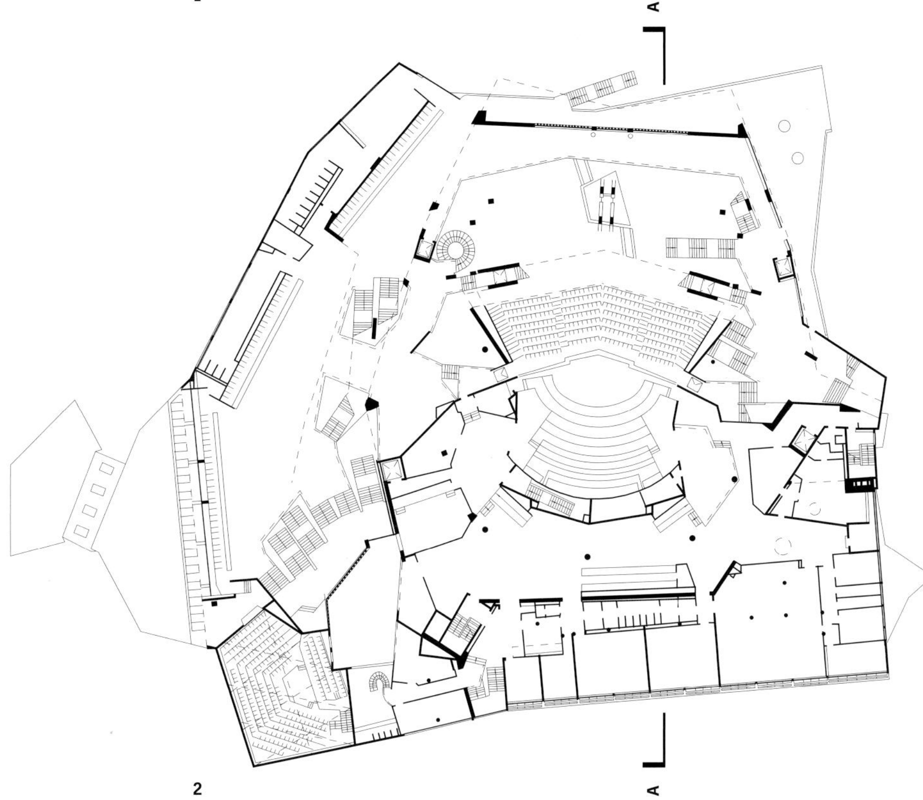

2

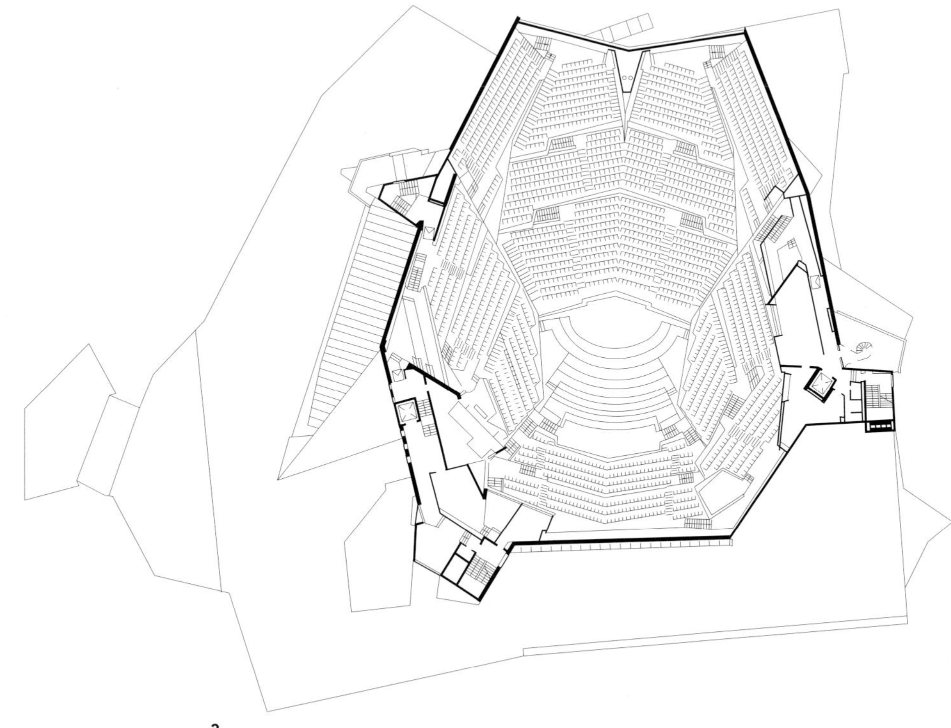

3

Memorials

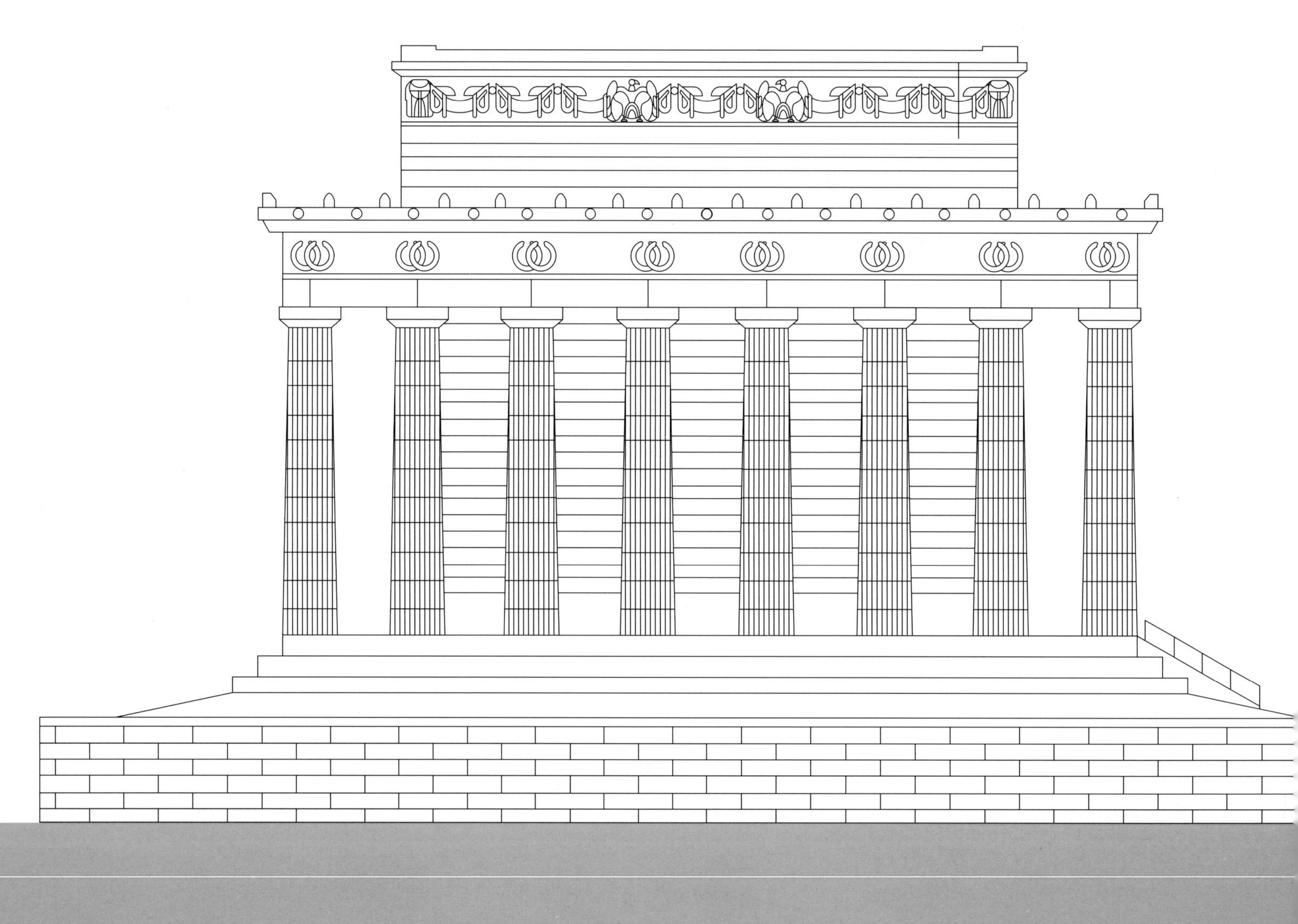

Memories can be awakened by the most fleeting sensations – the smell of an attic, a stray image of a childhood friend – but those who seek to secure a lasting reputation for themselves or others have often done so through buildings. The memorial built for Mausolus at Halicarnassus outdid all others and became one of the wonders of the world. It did not so much awaken memories as plant them in the minds of those who came to wonder. The best sculptors and architects were employed, and the building was huge. Grandiose mausoleums have gone out of fashion in the modern age, but there seems to be no upper limit to the scale of these monuments, except the limits of what power and money can bring to bear on a project.

Some burial places have more metaphysical aims. Apparently thinking that the ruler's reputation was imperishable, the builders of the Great Pyramid and the tomb of the first emperor of China with his terracotta warriors took steps to see that death would be overcome and that the ruler would be well provided for in the afterlife. The idea that the bodies of saintly people do not decompose was particularly firmly held in the Russian Orthodox tradition, and carried over into the secular mausoleum built for Lenin in Red Square, where his embalmed body was put on display. That was the intention originally at Sun Yat-sen's Mausoleum in Nanjing, but complications with the body led to a change of plan. The mausoleum is enormous. Its antechamber echoes the Lincoln Memorial in Washington DC, with a seated statue looking out along the axis of the approach, while the placing of the sarcophagus evokes the arrangement of Napoleon's tomb at Les Invalides in Paris.

The Romans not only built great mausoleums for the emperors but also commemorated great events, such as the accession of new territories to the empire. The triumphal arches would be built hastily as temporary structures for the day of the great procession, when the hero-emperor would ceremonially arrive in the forum to the acclaim of the populace, and then be rebuilt as permanent monuments with fine statuary evoking the achievement. This idea was developed further in Trajan's Column, where the monument was elegantly elemental but bore a continuous frieze that spiralled all the way up, to tell in low-relief marble the high points of Trajan's adventures in the conquest of Dacia.

Memorials are nearly always solemn in mood and old-fashioned in style. The design of the dome of Les Invalides was already 150 years old by the time that Napoleon was installed there in 1861, and architectural fashion had changed from its exuberant baroque to the severe lines of neoclassicism that are evident in his actual tomb – and again in the Lincoln Memorial in the following century. Napoleon was buried with the French generals, not at St Denis with the kings, though that was considered. In the event, he took his place in Paris, that most monumental of cities, much more visibly than they did.

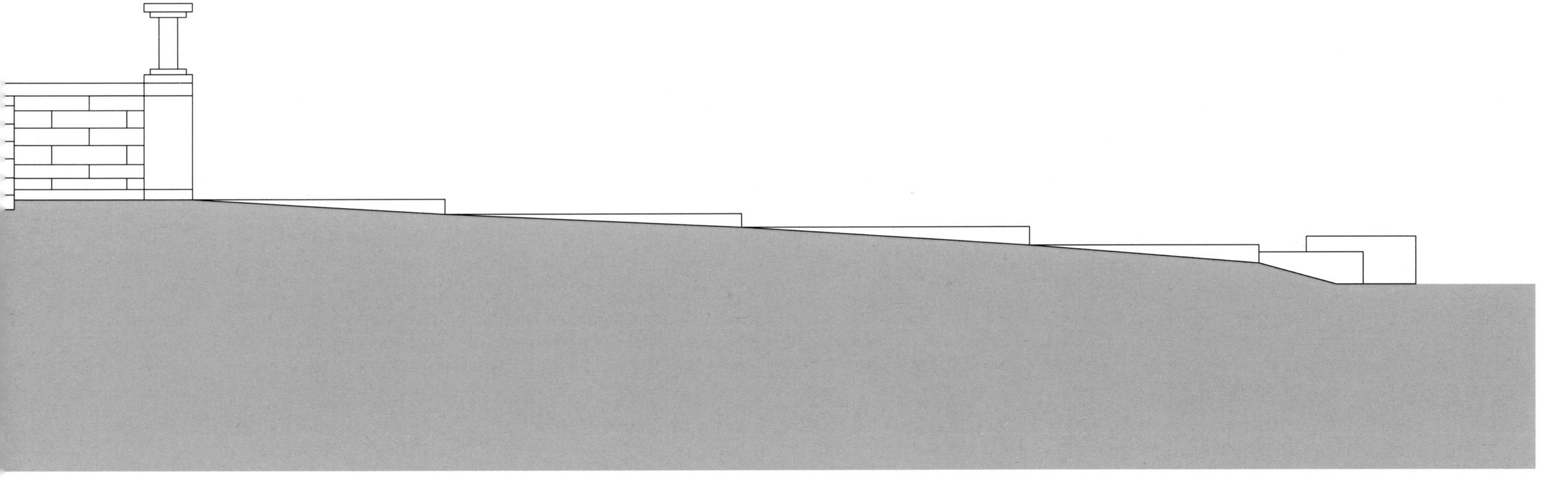

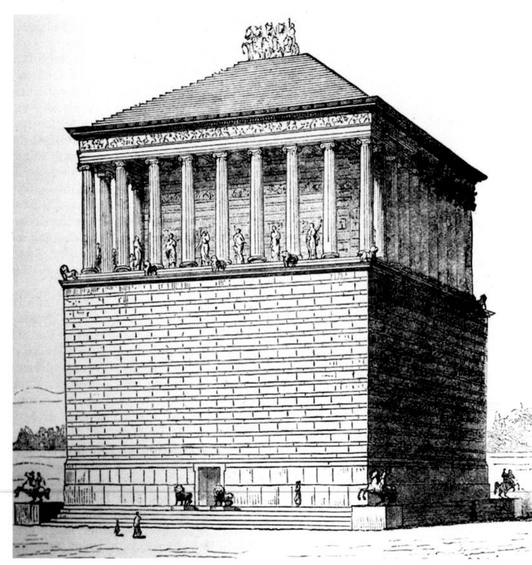

Tomb of Mausolus

Satyros and Pythis

Halicarnassus (Bodrum), Turkey; 353–350 BCE

Mausolus died in 353 BCE. His sister Artemisia had also been his wife, which was not an unusual arrangement among the ruling class of the Persian Empire. Such was her devotion to him that she drank his ashes, so that she could become his living tomb, and she did not stop there. She commissioned a funerary monument so extravagant that it became known as one of the world's wonders: the Mausoleion (Latinized to Mausoleum), which began as the tomb of Mausolus and later became the general name for a monumental tomb.

Halicarnassus was part of the Persian Empire, and Mausolus' official title was satrap rather than king. He was a state official, answerable to the emperor in Babylon, but he acted with almost total autonomy. His father had ruled before him, but Mausolus extended his territories on the Anatolian mainland and annexed some islands. He moved his capital city from Mylasa to Halicarnassus. He improved the harbour and commissioned Greek-style buildings, including a theatre and a temple that was dedicated to Ares, the Greek god of war. The artists who worked on the Mausoleum were brought by Artemisia from Greece. So, although the region, called Caria, was under Persian control, it was strongly philhellene in its culture.

Satyros and Pythis are known mainly for this building, which cannot have been their first. Pythis went on to design the temple of Athene at Priene, completed in 323 BCE, for Alexander of Macedon (Alexander the Great). Pythis also sculpted the colossal marble chariot pulled by four horses (the quadriga) that surmounted the Mausoleum's stepped pyramidal roof. Other sculptors who worked there included Scopas of Paros, Bryaxis and Timotheus, who were all famous in their day.

The chance consequences of survival and identification mean that Leochares' work is better known to the modern world. He was the sculptor of two of the most famous statues of antiquity, of Diana and Apollo, which are now known from Roman copies at Versailles and the Vatican respectively (the Diana of Versailles and the Apollo Belvedere). The architectural and sculptural work at the Mausoleum was undoubtedly of the highest imaginable quality, and the story is that the artists contributed their work without payment, for the glory of their art.

Nothing remains on the site of the Mausoleum above foundation level. Some of the sculptures from it – weathered marble figures of Mausolus and Artemisia and a marble lion – are lodged in the British Museum. The majestic building survived substantially intact until it was brought low by a series of earthquakes in the years around 1400, and after that the heap of stones became a convenient quarry for other buildings. Some of the marble slabs can still be seen in the walls of Bodrum Castle, built soon after the collapse by Christians involved in the Crusades, the Knights Hospitaller of Jerusalem.

When Artemisia died, the satrapy was taken over by her younger brother and sister (another married couple), Idrieus and Ada. Idrieus died in 340 BCE; Ada ruled briefly but another brother, Pixodarus, wrested control from her. When he died, the rule passed to his son-in-law Orontobates, who was in charge in 334 BCE when Alexander the Great conquered the region, laying siege to the city and leaving it devastated. Alexander restored Ada to her former position, and left as her adopted son, ready to inherit her title. In the event, Alexander took over the whole Persian Empire with the surrender of Babylon in 331 BCE. Halicarnassus never fully recovered, but it did become fully Greek.

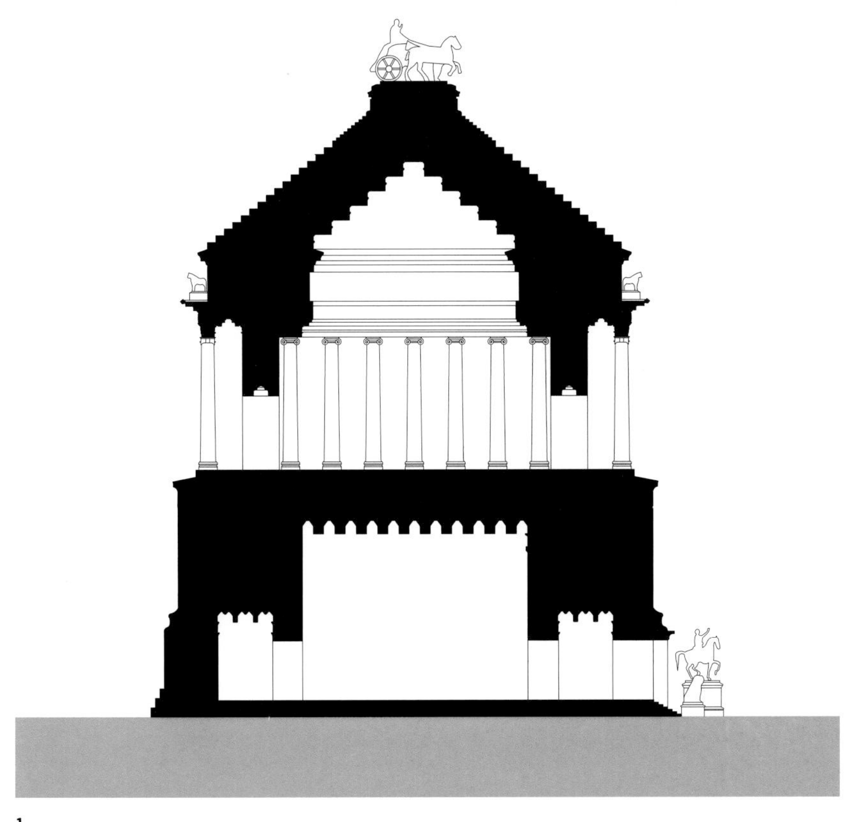

1

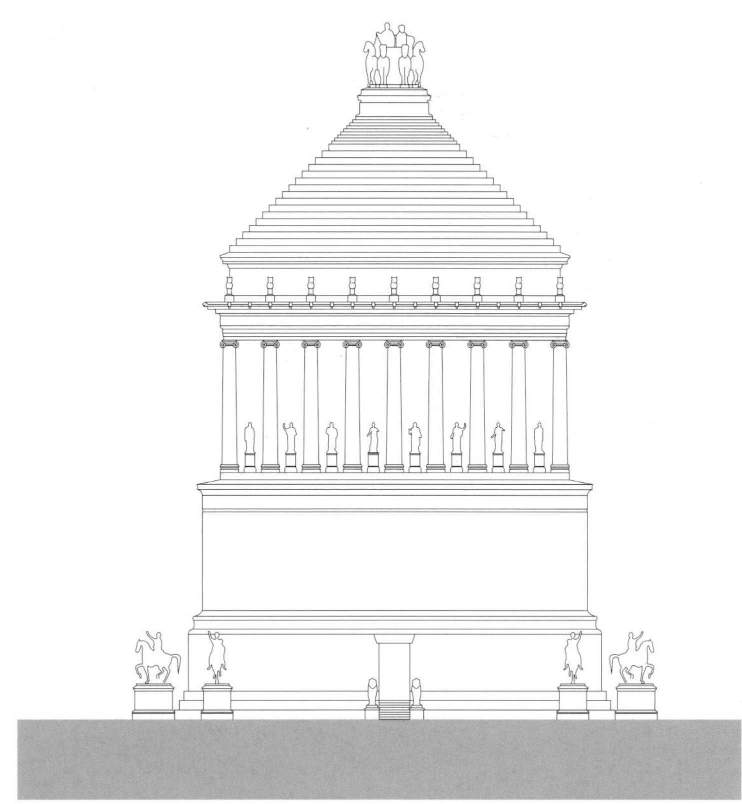

2

A A

3

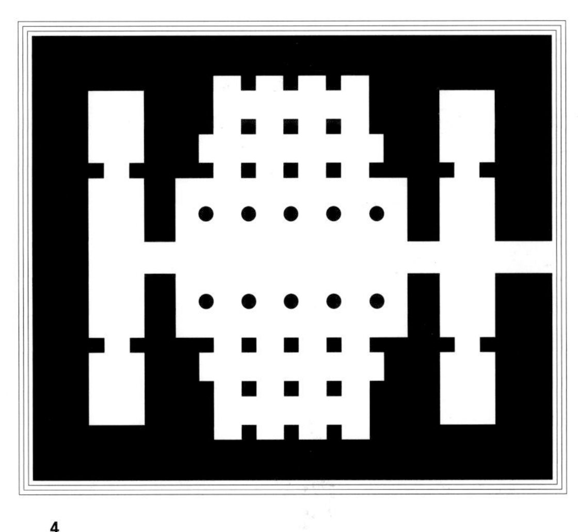

4

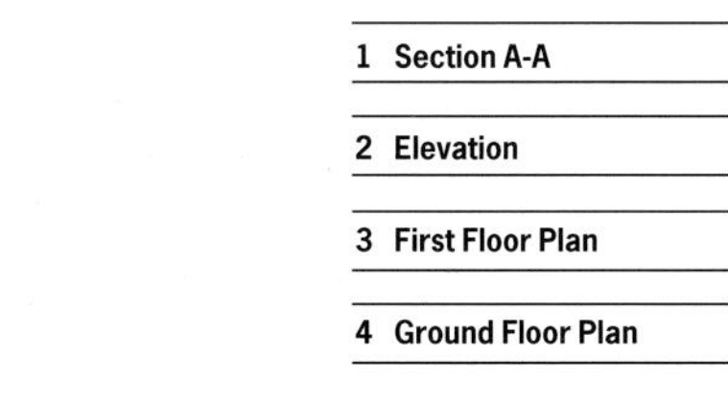

1 Section A-A

2 Elevation

3 First Floor Plan

4 Ground Floor Plan

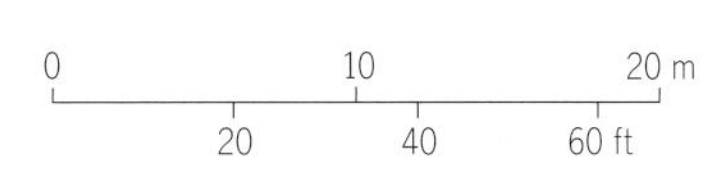

Qin Shi Huang Imperial Necropolis

Shaanxi, China; 246–207 BCE

In Hollywood films, archaeologists seem regularly to get themselves into scrapes that involve lethal mechanisms associated with ancient tombs. When treasures are buried with the dead, it makes sense for robbers to violate the tomb. Nevertheless most tombs have relied for their protection on their sheer solidity and the presence of guards, rather than resorting to elaborate booby-traps designed to kill intruders.

The Imperial Necropolis at Shaanxi is an exception. According to ancient texts, there were crossbows in its underground passages, primed to shoot a bolt into the head of anyone who disturbed the place. It is inconceivable that these mechanisms would still be in working order, but the site remains substantially unexcavated.

The Imperial Necropolis was the burial place of Qin Shi Huang (259–210 BCE), the first emperor of China. He inherited a throne at the age of 13 and started building his tomb. The scale of the works increased when Shi Huang unified China and became immensely powerful, able to command great works. He began a road-building programme and was responsible for the first attempt to build a great wall in the north of the country. He was keen to prolong his life, and sent expeditions out to find the elixir of life, but – knowing that, if they returned empty-handed, they faced certain death – none of them came back.

According to the possibly defamatory official record, Shi Huang ordered the burning of books that entertained ideas incompatible with official teaching, and he buried alive hundreds of scholars. He apparently hoped to discover any who had found practical means of overcoming death, but was disappointed. On the advice of his doctors he took mercury pills, as a way of securing immortality, but they poisoned him, and he died at the age of 49.

The report that 700,000 workers toiled for 39 years to build Shi Huang's necropolis is certainly exaggerated – and maybe it is also untrue that the emperor's tomb is surrounded by 100 rivers of mercury. It was, however, a vast undertaking, covering an area the size of a city, and all of it was underground.

Most of the site is unexcavated, but what has been excavated is amazing. Four pits have been discovered in which life-size terracotta figures were meant to stand. In the event, on the fall of the short-lived Qin Dynasty, the work was abandoned, by which time only three of the pits had been filled, with an estimated 8,000 figures – a whole army, with chariots and horses. The pits have rammed-earth walls and brick-paved floors. The figures were made from cast basic parts, which were individualized with hand-modelled finishing touches in the facial features and expressions. They were coloured, but the colour has deteriorated.

Twenty families were installed to act as guardians for the tomb, which – in contrast to the Tomb of Mausolus (pages 288–89) – seems not to have been intended to broadcast its occupant's eternal fame. Its accomplishments were hidden from view and must have been intended to have a practical but occult effect, preserving Qin Shi Huang's capacity to rule in a kingdom believed to exist on the other side of death. Meanwhile, his terracotta army, its patience inexhaustible, continues to wait.

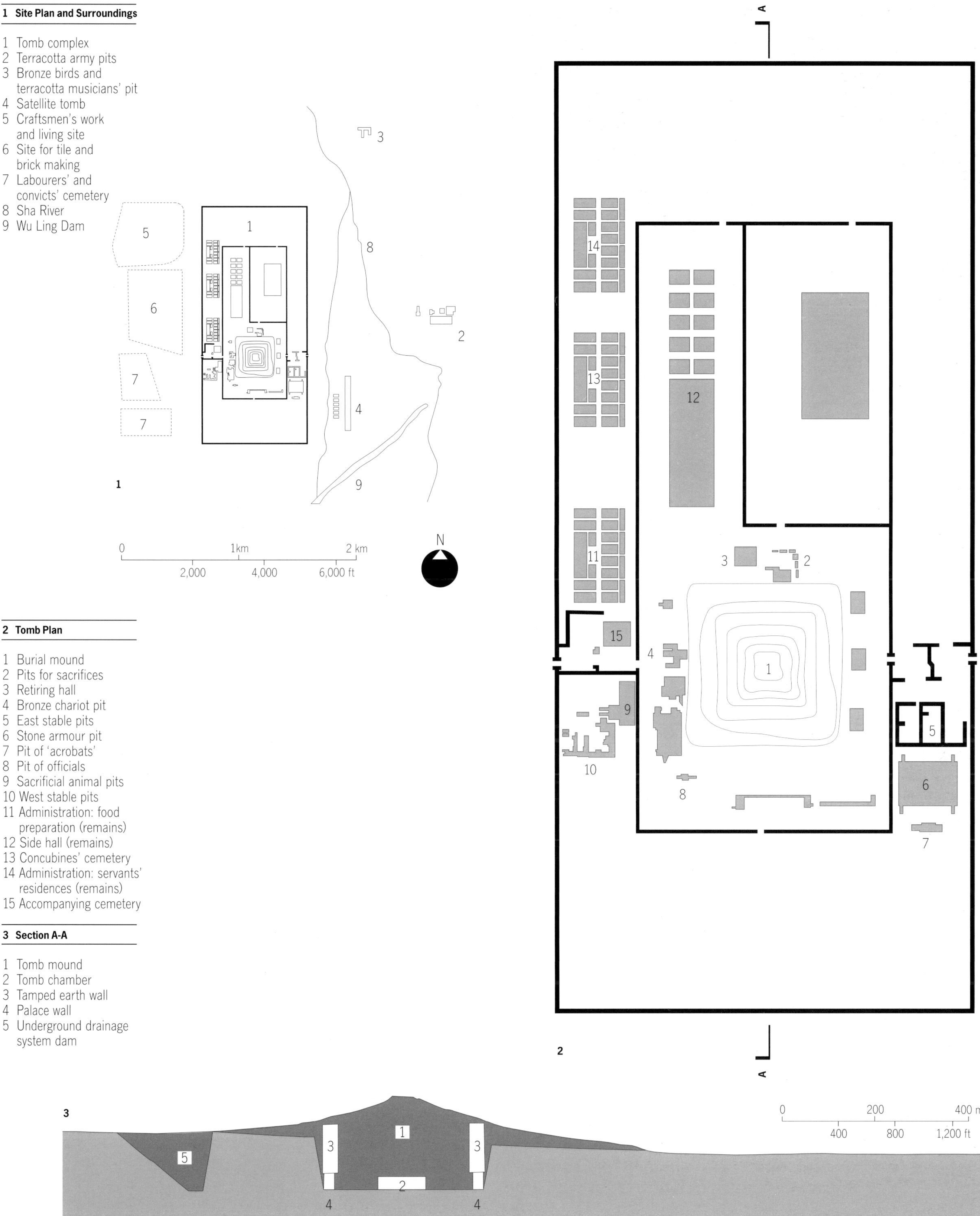

1 Site Plan and Surroundings

1 Tomb complex
2 Terracotta army pits
3 Bronze birds and terracotta musicians' pit
4 Satellite tomb
5 Craftsmen's work and living site
6 Site for tile and brick making
7 Labourers' and convicts' cemetery
8 Sha River
9 Wu Ling Dam

2 Tomb Plan

1 Burial mound
2 Pits for sacrifices
3 Retiring hall
4 Bronze chariot pit
5 East stable pits
6 Stone armour pit
7 Pit of 'acrobats'
8 Pit of officials
9 Sacrificial animal pits
10 West stable pits
11 Administration: food preparation (remains)
12 Side hall (remains)
13 Concubines' cemetery
14 Administration: servants' residences (remains)
15 Accompanying cemetery

3 Section A-A

1 Tomb mound
2 Tomb chamber
3 Tamped earth wall
4 Palace wall
5 Underground drainage system dam

Memorial Columns

Trajan's Column, Rome; 106–13 | Column of Marcus Aurelius, Rome; 193 | Colonne Vendôme, Paris; 1806–10 | Nelson's Column, London; 1843

Emperor Trajan commissioned a great complex of buildings in Rome that included a forum, a temple, a basilica, libraries and markets. The only part of it still standing and performing something like its original function is a monumental column, which once supported a statue of a great eagle – replaced after Trajan's death by a larger-than-life-sized statue of the emperor himself (above left). The column is about 30 metres (100 feet) high, and is made up of 20 drums about 3.7 metres (12 feet) in diameter, carved from solid Carrara marble. Each drum was hollowed out to accommodate a spiral stair (carved integrally from the drum, not fitted in as a separate construction) that leads to a railed platform above the column's simple Doric capital. The stair is illuminated by narrow window slots piercing the walls of the drum, invisible from the outside because they are lost in the shaft's decoration.

The column's shaft is carved with images of Trajan's conquest of Dacia (land now in Romania and Hungary). These are arranged in a frieze that spirals up the column, gradually increasing in height from about 60 cm (24 inches) at the base to about 120 cm (47 inches) at the top, but it is impossible to see the detail of the higher parts with the naked eye. When the column was built, it was in a small forum and surrounded by several tiers of galleries outside the libraries that flanked it, so upper parts of the frieze would have been more visible than they are today, and salient details would have been picked out in gilding and coloured paint.

The column of Marcus Aurelius follows the same architectural pattern, and the two columns were restored as a pair by Pope Sixtus V in 1589. The ground level around Marcus Aurelius' column had risen by about 3 metres (10 feet) and the base was raised to the new ground level. A new statue of St Paul replaced Marcus Aurelius, while a statue of St Peter supplanted Trajan. The detail of the frieze on the Marcus Aurelius column is more caricatural – no doubt intended to make an impact from a greater distance. Changing the statues from emperors to saints made a connection with some of the early Byzantine saints, notably Simeon Stylites, who decided to live on top of columns as an ascetic practice.

The column in the Place Vendôme was set up by Napoleon to proclaim his victory at Austerlitz in 1805 (above right). The square had been built in 1702 by Louis XIV on land formerly occupied by the palace of the duc de Vendôme. The new square was called the Place des Conquêtes and had as its centrepiece a bronze equestrian statue of Louis XIV that was destroyed by revolutionaries in 1792. Napoleon's adventures at Austerlitz, defeating the combined might of the Holy Roman Empire and Russia, are detailed in bronze panels that spiral up the column in imitation of Trajan's. This site was already associated with victories, and the column with a statue of Napoleon in Roman dress standing on it was resonant because of comparisons with Roman imperial forbears; the statue has been replaced several times. The whole column was pulled down by revolutionaries of the Paris Commune in 1871 and subsequently rebuilt.

The same form was chosen when it came to erecting a monument in London to honour the admiral Lord Nelson, who defeated Napoleon's naval forces on several occasions, but most momentously in 1805 at Trafalgar, where he died a hero's death. The column was erected in 1840–43 on land previously covered by a warren of small buildings, which was cleared and called Trafalgar Square. It has bronze relief panels round its base, where they can be clearly seen. Its shaft is made of granite, and is fluted, while the capital is Corinthian and cast in bronze. The granite statue of Nelson looks out over the most popular public gathering-place in London.

1 Trajan's Column, Rome

2 Column of Marcus Aurelius, Rome

3 Colonne Vendôme, Paris

4 Nelson's Column, London

Pazzi Chapel

Filippo Brunelleschi, 1377–1446, and Giuliano da Maiano, c.1432–90, or Michelozzo di Bartolomeo, 1396–1472

Florence, Italy; 1440–60

The Basilica of Santa Croce in Florence is one of the oldest and largest churches associated with Franciscan friars – the order founded by Giovanni Francesco di Bernardone (1181–1226), St Francis of Assisi. The church building there was begun in 1294, and it came to be a burial place for some of Florence's most illustrious citizens, including Michelangelo, Galileo and Machiavelli.

The Pazzi family was prominent in the city, with an aristocratic lineage linking them with a Crusader who had brought back a stone from the basilica of the Holy Sepulchre in Jerusalem. Florence's Easter festival of Christ's resurrection was celebrated by extinguishing all the fires burning in the city and then relighting them by carrying torches lit from a new fire started at the cathedral. That new fire was lit by a spark struck from the stone brought from Jerusalem, and it was struck each year by a descendant of the Crusader.

The Pazzi family was not as rich as the Medici family but richer than everyone else. Several of its members were caught in a rivalry that erupted in 1478 in the attempted double murder in the cathedral, at high mass, of the brothers Giuliano and Lorenzo de' Medici. What came to be called the Pazzi Conspiracy has overshadowed the family's reputation ever since. The conspirators were hanged, and for a while the family was exiled from Florence. They are mentioned in Dante's *Inferno* as residents of hell.

Dating from a time when the Pazzi still had ambitions to displace the Medici and rule the city, the Pazzi Chapel is a family mausoleum and also a building with a practical use. It was built as the chapter house of Santa Croce, and is sited exactly where one would expect a chapter house to be: in the cloister on the south side of the church. (This was the meeting place for the chapter, the church's administrative body.) The cloister is irregularly shaped and does not function as a complete circuit round the central open space.

The chapel porch looks as if it is part of the cloister circuit, but the change of floor level between it on the cloister's east side and the covered walk along the north side is too great for them ever to have been connected.

Open to the outside, the porch has six Corinthian columns, which support an entablature with a decorated frieze. There is a break in the entablature for the wider central bay, which has an arch. Wall surfaces are relatively plain, decorated with pilasters that match the fully formed columns, but above the entablature line the treatment is very richly sculpted. There is a coffered barrel vault with rosettes carved in the coffers, and in the central bay, behind the arch, is a small dome similarly encrusted and brightly coloured in blue and yellow. The curved triangular shapes (pendentives) that are generated beneath the dome when it is placed over a square plan are carved into scallop shells.

A large dome covers the main interior space and internally the surfaces of the vaults are smooth. They are set out with a geometric precision where lines of circles and squares are marked out in *pietra serena* – an unusual dark limestone that accepts fine decorative carving and is used in Florence's main monuments. Blue and white roundels in fired ceramics by Luca della Robbia (1400–82) adorn the upper parts of the walls with figures of saints. The effect is austere, as would be seen as fitting by the Franciscans, but nevertheless magnificent in a manner appropriate to a socially ambitious family.

This is one of the most serene interiors of the Renaissance, gracefully resolving the tensions that are inevitably set up in making an assemblage of domes and cubes.

1 **Plan**

2 **Section A-A**

3 **West Elevation**

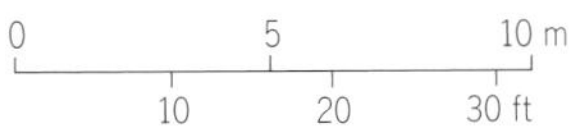

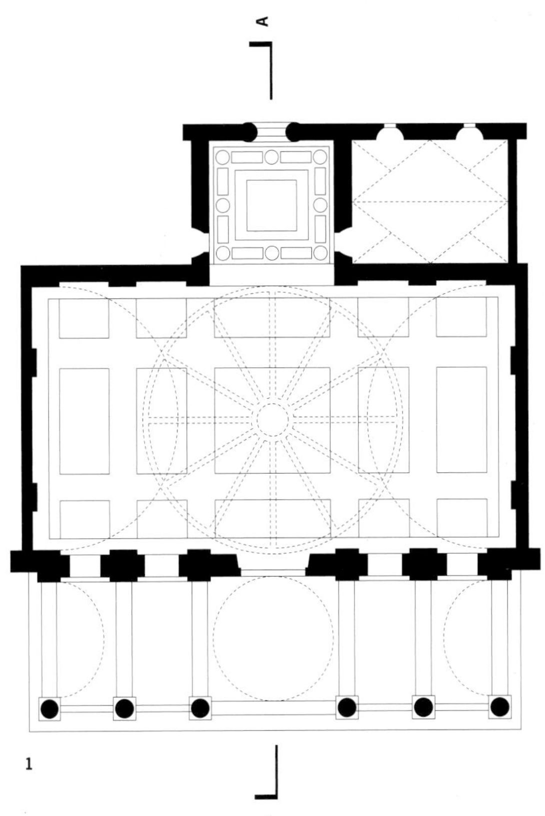

1

2

3

Tempietto, San Pietro in Montorio

Donato Bramante, 1444–1514

Rome, Italy; 1508–11

In 1506 Bramante started work on the great domed Basilica of St Peter in Rome (pages 32–33). An enormous undertaking, it was not finished until long after his death, by when the design had been modified by many hands and no longer looked like Bramante's work. In contrast, the little shrine that he designed for San Pietro in Montorio had an importance much greater than its size would suggest, as an authoritative example of Bramante's considered idea about what architecture should be. Serlio and Palladio in their books about architecture published illustrations of the Tempietto alongside reconstructions of ancient Roman buildings. It was presented as a model from which to learn.

Tradition has it that St Peter was crucified head down in 64, after the emperor Nero blamed Christians for the fires that had destroyed parts of Rome, and the Tempietto marks the supposed spot of his martyrdom. The Circus of Caligula and Nero, where the crucifixion is said to have taken place, was on the site where St Peter's Basilica was subsequently developed. Although the historical accuracy of this account is in doubt, the myth is important in understanding Bramante's building. It is set up as if it were a mausoleum, but the saint's body was never supposed to be here. The domed upper space has an altar in it but is too small for a congregation. A circular grille in the middle of the room gives a view down into the crypt, where there is another altar, this one incorporating a foundation stone that records the patronage of Ferdinand and Isabella of Castile. The building stands in the cloister of the church of San Pietro in Montorio, a repository for some spectacular works of art.

In Serlio's presentation of the Tempietto, it is shown surrounded by the circular peristyle of an ideal cloister that was never built (but which is shown in the plan opposite). It would have integrated the Tempietto with the larger building. As it is, the shrine is treated like an ornament – a building of much greater intensity than the main church, which reserves its treasures for the interior and presents an unadorned face to the world.

Tucked away in a courtyard, the Tempietto is elaborate inside and out, but the detail is fastidious rather than exuberant, and the effect is of sobriety and rectitude. The columns are of the plainest (Tuscan) type and unfluted (in the Roman manner), with a modelled base and a simple capital. They carry an entablature with a Doric frieze that alternates – as a Doric frieze must – triglyphs and metopes. Triglyphs are rectangular panels divided into three, which might represent the covers for the end of beams and should line up with the columns below.

Metopes in the Greek Doric temples, such as the Parthenon (pages 16–17) and Apollo's temple at Bassae (pages 104–105), were square sculpted panels showing fighting figures. In the Tempietto they show elements of the church liturgy – chalices, thurifers, candlesticks. They also manage to avoid one of the perennial problems faced by the builders of rectangular temples: each time a Doric frieze approached a corner, the metopes had to change proportion to achieve the correct alignment (and avoid an awkward half-metope at the corner). Bramante sidestepped the problem by using the frieze on a circular building that has no corners.

There is the same sort of enrichment as in the Pazzi Chapel (pages 294–95), with coffering, carved stone rosettes and scallop shells (here making the semi-domes in the top of niches). It is all conceived and executed with precision, and was therefore a more perfect example of Bramante's architectural vision than the larger project that took up so much more of his time.

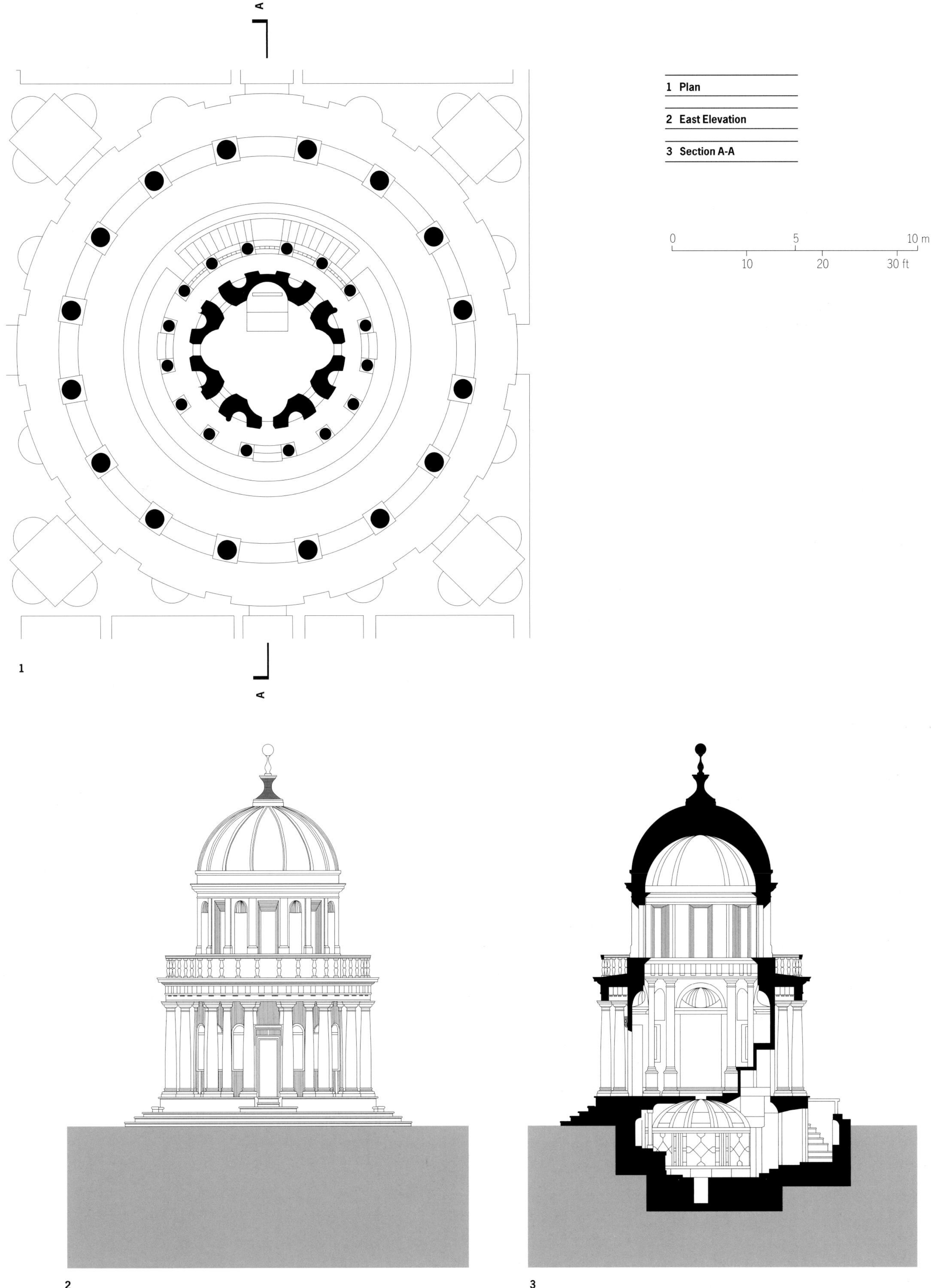

1 Plan

2 East Elevation

3 Section A-A

L'Église du Dôme, Les Invalides

Jules Hardouin-Mansart, 1646–1708

Paris, France; 1680–1708

L'Église du Dôme was built as a royal chapel for Les Invalides, the military hospital and retirement home where the elderly and disabled former members of the French military services could live on condition that they attended church once a day. Its dome is closer in scale to that of St Peter's (pages 32–33) than of the Tempietto (pages 296–97), but the chapel has striking similarities with both buildings.

The accommodation at Les Invalides, designed by Libéral Bruant (c.1635–97), was organized around 14 quadrangles flanking a larger central court dominated by the servicemen's church, dedicated to St Louis. The whole ensemble was arranged to make a grand axis through a park planted with blocks of trees at the same scale as the blocks of accommodation. The axis started at the Champs Élysées, crossed the river by a bridge and came up the Esplanade des Invalides to the chapel, which was completed in 1679.

Jules Hardouin-Mansart worked with Bruant and supervised the completion of his church design before stepping into the limelight with his design for the domed chapel that became the great centrepiece of the composition. Louis XIV seems to have intended it as a burial place for himself and his successors, but in the event he was entombed at St Denis, along with most of the other kings of France, and the chapel was used for burials and monuments to military heroes. From 1830, the tomb of Napoleon, directly beneath the dome, occupied centre stage: a red quartzite sarcophagus standing on a granite catafalque, set apart in a circular pit excavated beneath the dome to make an open crypt.

From the moment it was built, the dome of Les Invalides was a prominent sight in the city, and even now, despite strong competition from more recent monuments, its majestic profile holds its own, helped by regilding and floodlighting. This is no accident, since the building's main purpose has always been scenographic.

Its interior was made as tall as it plausibly could be, but the exterior dome, lacquered and gilded, was raised much higher again, with an immense roof void of timbers to support the outer covering. Christopher Wren contemporaneously, and for the same reason, made a similar arrangement at St Paul's Cathedral in London.

The plan is curiously close to that of the Taj Mahal (pages 34–35) – a new building when Les Invalides was being built, whose reputation had certainly not reached Paris or London. The thick walls of the lowest storey have fairly small openings, to make them as strong as possible, while the upper walls are made thinner to keep them light.

At Les Invalides the baroque sense of theatre and extravagance is in full play. There are in fact three domes, the outer of which makes a glittering impact in the city. The lowest, which springs from a cornice, is expressed as an arrangement of gilded coffered ribs that stops well short of the centre of the space. This leaves a large oculus that gives a view of the third dome – a smooth curved surface illuminated by small windows tucked out of sight, and painted with a view of sky, clouds and cavorting figures. Everything is gauged for effect – and the effect is absolutely glorious.

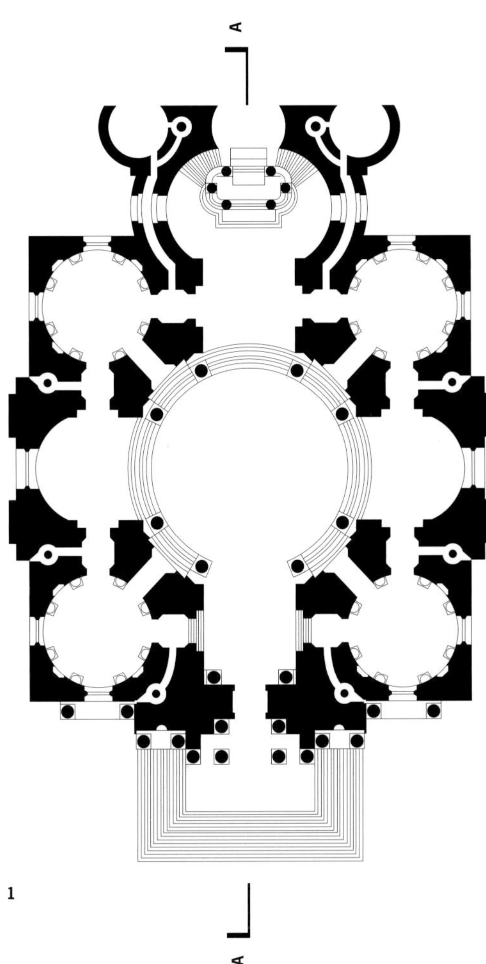

1

1 Plan

2 South Elevation

3 Section A-A

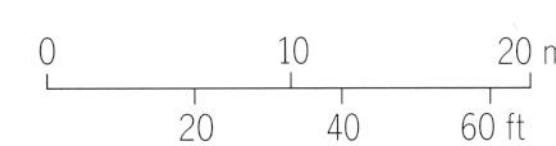

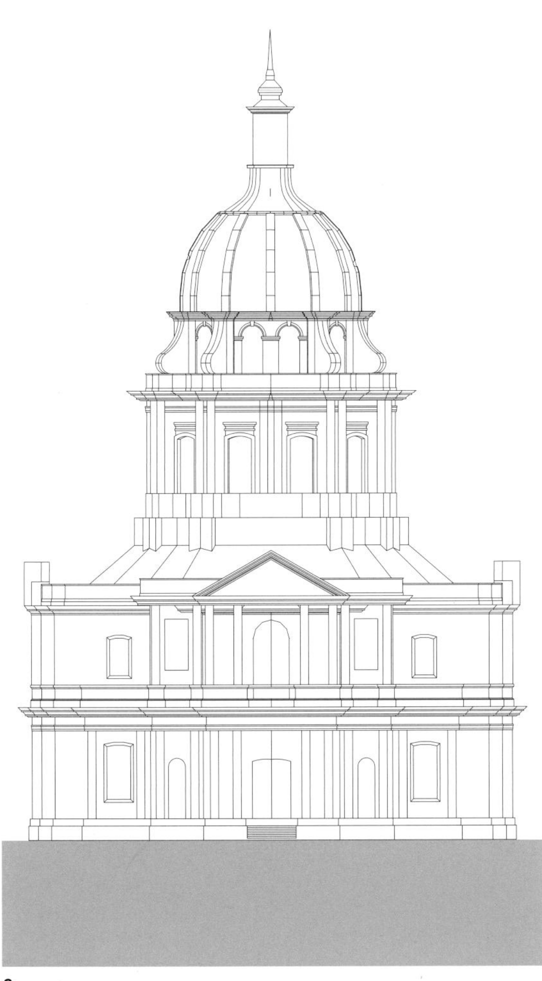

2

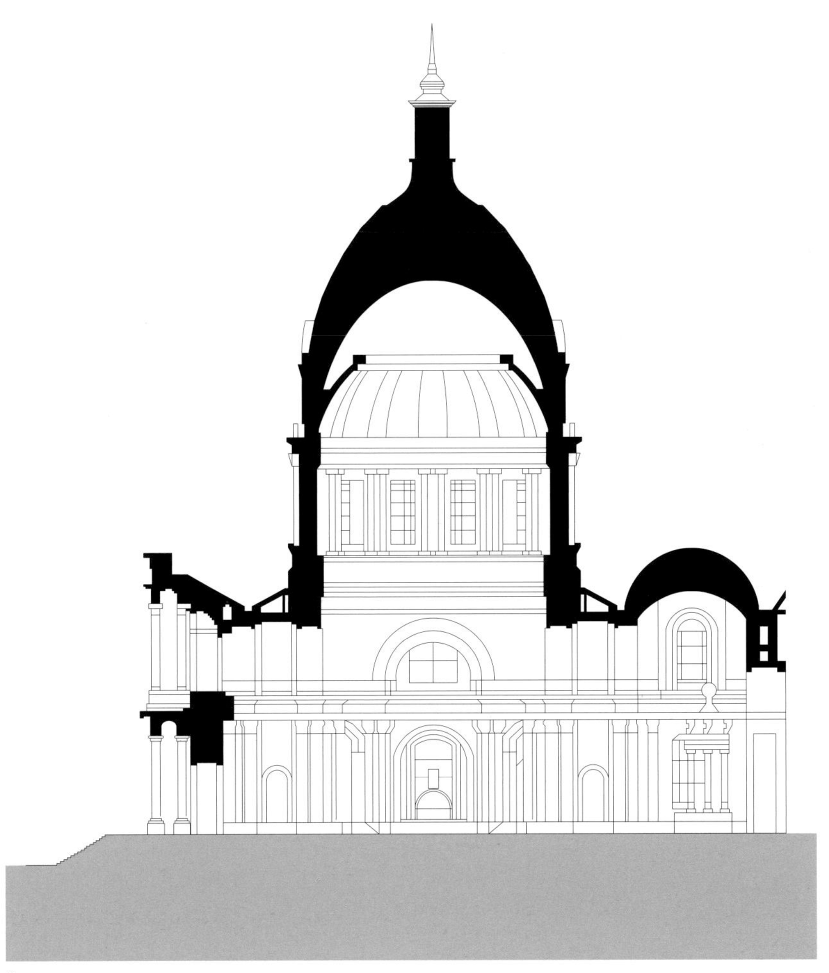

3

Lincoln Memorial

Henry Bacon, 1866–1924

Washington DC, USA; 1912–22

The grand baroque vistas of Versailles and Paris were brought to Washington DC by Pierre Charles L'Enfant (1754–1825), who laid out its first streets in 1791, envisaging a broad central mall for national monuments. He tried to control too closely the designs that developed, and was soon dismissed, but the idea of the National Mall survived: a broad swathe of green with clear views from the domed capitol building at the east end to the Lincoln Memorial 3 km (2 miles) away at the west end, built on reclaimed swampland that doubled the mall's original length.

Abraham Lincoln was president of the USA from 1861 until his assassination in 1865. His administration saw the outbreak and conclusion of the Civil War and, in 1863, the abolition of slavery. He was not one of the original founding fathers of the nation, but he certainly had a hand in forming it, and he remains one of the most recognized and admired of American presidents.

There were early campaigns for a memorial to be erected, but none found sufficient support in Congress until 1910. When the support came, it produced the stateliest of monuments. The Lincoln Memorial looks like a Greek temple, which is appropriate because of the associations with democratic Athens. A colossal statue of Lincoln sits facing out in the entrance in the manner of Michelangelo's Moses, or the giant statue of Constantine that presided over his basilica in Rome, or Pheidias' enthroned Zeus at the temple of Olympia. It looks up the mall towards the Capitol, along the 618-metre (2,028-foot) length of a pool reflecting the image of the giant obelisk that is the Washington Monument.

On closer inspection, the Lincoln Memorial starts to look less like a temple. It does not have pediments at the ends but a flat roof all the way round, the enclosed cella rising up higher than the surrounding peristyle of fluted Doric columns.

The entrance is in the centre of the long side of the building, not in the short end as would be expected. So the arrangement takes on overtones of the stoa, as at the Altes Museum in Berlin (pages 278–79). The detail of the external decoration involves eagles – American eagles – along with swags, wreaths, lions heads and the names of the states in the union that Lincoln held together.

In the interior, the space is divided into three by rows of columns, and the side spaces have severely blank walls, except for a frieze of paintings of symbolic figures in subdued colours high on the wall and a large stone slab engraved with some of Lincoln's inspiring words, given in this way the authority of tablets of law. (On one side is a quotation from the Gettysberg Address and on the other an extract from his second inaugural speech.)

The space is illuminated by light penetrating a translucent ceiling of fine marble slabs supported on bronze beams – cast with a delicate decoration of oak leaves and flowers. Since the white marble statue of Lincoln was felt to be under-lit, concealed electrical floodlights were installed at an early stage in the building's history – and early in the history of electrical floodlights.

This is a twentieth-century building, commemorating a courageous social reformer, an 'everyman' figure whose image has here been given the authority of an emperor and a prophet. The steps of the monument have become a rallying point for populist political gatherings, including celebrations when presidents are inaugurated. The building's rhetoric was harnessed deliberately and effectively in Martin Luther King's 'I have a dream' speech, which was delivered from its podium.

1 East Elevation

2 South Elevation

3 Plan

1

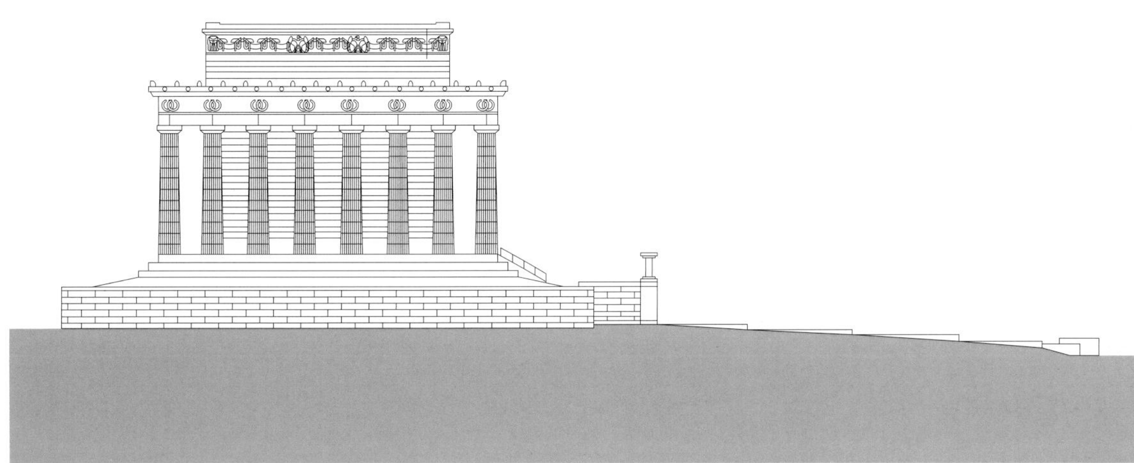

2

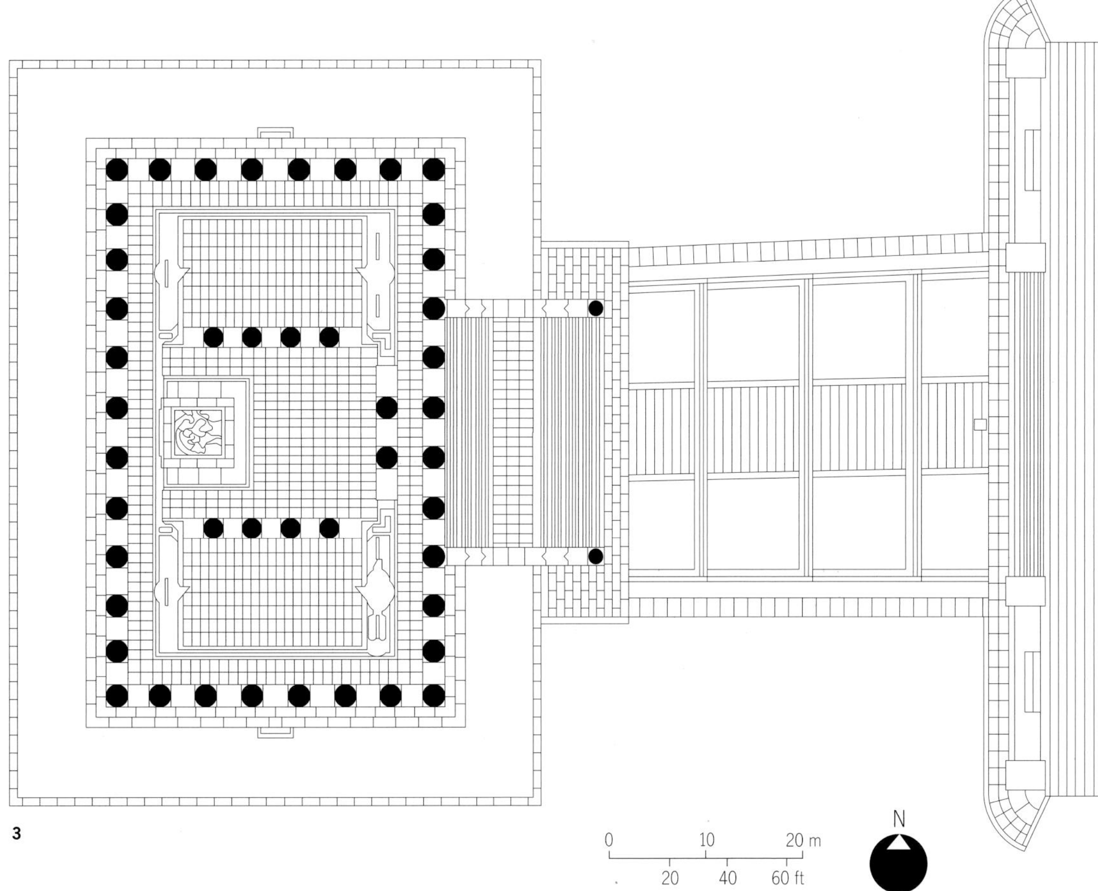

3

Sun Yat-sen Mausoleum

Lu Yanzhi, 1894–1929

Nanjing, Jiangsu, China; 1925–31

Sun Yat-sen (1866–1925) was the first President of the Republic of China, taking office in 1912, following the overthrow of the Qing Dynasty, which brought to an end about 3,000 years of dynastic rule. Although he held the post of president for only 44 days, Sun Yat-sen continued to influence events until his death through his inspirational writings and his continuing political engagement. He co-founded the Kuomintang, the Chinese National People's Party and became its first leader.

The importance of Sun Yat-sen's role in the modernization of China was recognized by sympathetic revolutionaries who held a competition to design an appropriate memorial in accordance with his expressed wish that his body be preserved like Lenin's. The winning design, by Lu Yanzhi, was (as the competition demanded) in classical Chinese style – but part of the building's importance is that the 'classical Chinese style' was not at all well defined at the time of the competition, and the winning design helped to establish its outlines.

The location was on the Purple Mountain at Nanjing, where Sun Yat-sen had wanted to establish the capital of modern China. The architect of the winning design was Chinese but had spent formative years in Europe and the USA, and the design incorporates gestures such as a sunken crypt that allows visitors to circulate round the sarcophagus – in an arrangement reminiscent of that at Napoleon's tomb at Les Invalides, (pages 298–99). And, as at the Lincoln Memorial in Washington DC (pages 300–301), the mausoleum contains a monumental seated statue that is visible from the outside.

Modern construction methods were used, and the aim was to make the building in a simple manner rather than magnificently – so, despite its grandiose scale, it has the atmosphere of a civic building rather than an imperial palace and the effect is not overbearing. While the building's roof forms drew on ancient Chinese precedents, the imagery of sculpture avoided anything that was associated with the more recent imperial past, such as the dragons that often found their way into the decoration of imperial roofs.

The scale is immense. The steps in front of the mausoleum building are arranged in eight broad flights and can accommodate 50,000 people at a time. It was the layout of these steps that proved to have the most important symbolic significance, because in plan their retaining walls give the site the shape of a bell.

The mausoleum was intended to announce the start of a new beginning for China, sounding a bell that would be heard around the world. The bell form, while hardly perceptible to a visitor, and apparently unintended by the architect, was seen as symbolically powerful by the assessors when they were looking at the plan, and it was decisive in the design's competitive success.

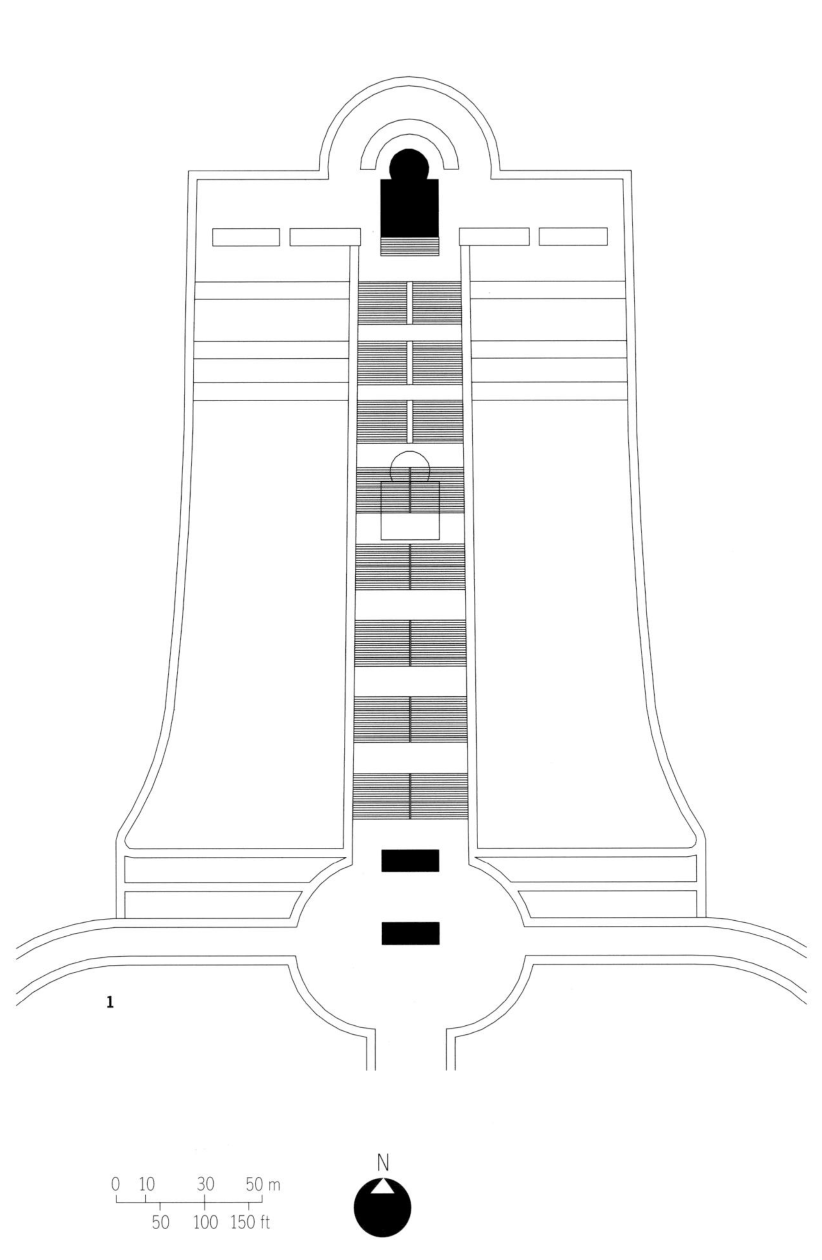

1

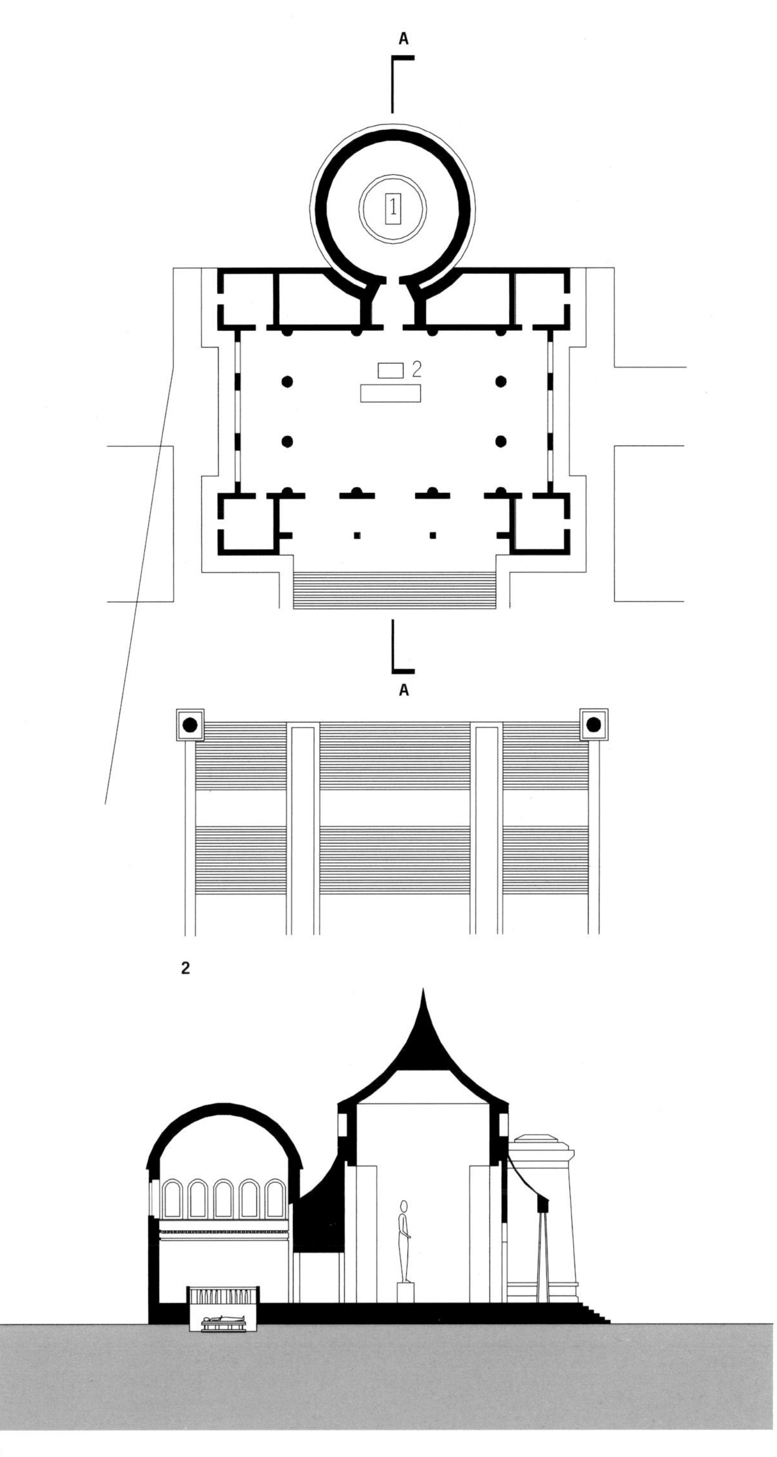

2

3

4

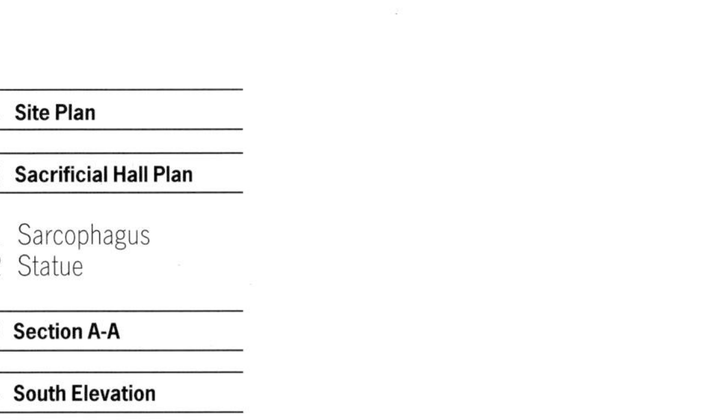

1 Site Plan

2 Sacrificial Hall Plan

1 Sarcophagus
2 Statue

3 Section A-A

4 South Elevation

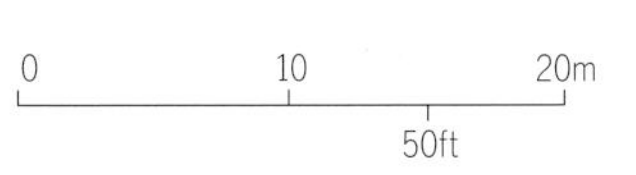

Public Spaces

In a small village the people who meet in the street are quite likely to know each another, but in a city people encounter a multitude of strangers who are likely to be quite different from one another – much more varied in their range of appearance than the inhabitants of the village.

The stimulation and challenge of living in a city stems from the fact that people meet others who are not like themselves. The bigger the city, the more scope there is for brushing past someone from another world: someone with an unexpected sense of what to wear, or maybe a celebrity who quietly passes by and is suddenly familiar after the event – or someone with an exceptional sense of how to comport themselves, such as a woman in Paris making stately progress with a large bottle of water confidently balanced on her head.

Some public places are famous for being beautiful, others are known as sites of official spectacle, and others again attract crowds through their distinctive vitality, which animates the city. It is not always easy to analyse what has made a place successful, and sometimes the success seems to have taken even the city's designers by surprise. The Place des Vosges is acknowledged as a beautiful square and a delightful retreat, but another of Henri IV's building projects, the Pont Neuf, emerged as the lively place that became identified as the central point in Paris.

Red Square in Moscow has a distinctly 'official' character. The citadel (the Kremlin) that runs along one side of the square protected the palaces and cathedrals of the Tsars, except for St Basil's Cathedral, which Ivan the Terrible built outside, and the square took shape around it. Over the years, the square has accumulated monuments, most notably Lenin's tomb, whose severe abstract geometry contrasts with the playful patchwork of St Basil's. During the Soviet era, the square was the site for solemn processions on May Day, to display the army's might.

However, on all the days that are not special occasions Red Square's character is animated more by the immense 'department store' GUM – actually a shopping mall with 200 shops in it on several levels in an arrangement that invites comparison with the Galleria Vittorio Emmanuele II in Milan. The rather forbidding fortifications on one side of Red Square are tempered by activity on the other.

For sheer vitality, the reputation of Nevsky Prospekt in St Petersburg is hard to beat. The city was laid out with a strong sense of abstract geometry, and Nevsky Prospekt is not the street that would be picked out on the city plan as the most prominent thoroughfare, but that is how it has developed. It is a broad street that runs in a straight line, between palaces at one end of it and docks at the other. Every rank of society can be found at some point along the street, and it promotes the frissons of near-encounter that make a city buzz. The same characteristics are repeated on other long, diagonal streets that cut across an established grid, such as Broadway in New York and the Ramblas in Barcelona. In the final analysis, it is this vitality that matters more than the beauty of a place. In Times Square, Piccadilly Circus or Potsdamer Platz, one has the sense of being in a city that is fully alive, despite the lack of perfect resolution of the architectural form.

Agora of Athens | Forum of Rome

Athens, Greece | Rome, Italy

Ancient Athens was much less built-up than the modern city. Nevertheless it had a designated open space – the Agora – that was set apart as a sanctuary and had an important role in civic life. Indeed, it was the principal instrument in engendering civic life. It brought people together, sometimes casually by chance, sometimes in order to participate in events. In its early days, it was nothing more than an open space, with a temple presiding over it (the Hephaisteion – dedicated to Athena and her half-brother, Hephaistos, a blacksmith). The Athenians liked their activities to have architectural settings, and over the years they gave definition to the Agora by building stoas along its edges. The defined space gradually accumulated monuments within it.

One of the important official roles of the Agora was as a place for political speeches and decision-making. These activities were once conducted in the open air, but came to be housed in the Bouleuterion, a building in the Agora where the governing council (*boule*) met. Its role was partly superseded by the building of the Pnyx (pages 236–37). Other government buildings included the mint, where the Athenian coinage was produced. There were shops, and presumably a large amount of market trading took place in the streets, both before the shops were built and as an adjunct to them.

The Monument of the Eponymous Heroes was a high plinth, running in a straight line, that carried a row of statues of the ten mythical figures who founded the ten tribes of Athenian citizens. Official notices – decisions from the council and other public news – were posted on the vertical surfaces of the plinth. The spreading of information through the citizenry was important, and at Athens it was done by the use of a monument.

The ancient Roman Forum (above) also started as an open space, and it too gradually became overwhelmed by monuments as it developed over several centuries.

Aeneas, whose father was a Trojan prince and whose mother was the goddess Venus, had left Troy when it was sacked by the Greeks, and came to Rome, bringing with him his household gods – the Lares and Penates – and giving Rome its special destiny. Aeneas' statues were housed in the Temple of Vesta, the most sacred place in the Forum, dedicated to the goddess of the hearth. Every household had its little gods, associated with the hearth, where a flame would be maintained, and there was a superstitious belief that if it went out there would be a death in the family. The Temple of Vesta was the hearth of the city and the empire. It was maintained by a body of priestesses; if its sacred flame went out, they were put to death.

The Forum's original mixed character was overtaken by religious and ceremonial functions. Its north side came to be defined by the Basilica Aemilia, built by Marcus Aemilius Lepidus, who died in 152 BCE. (Clearing the site to build it involved demolishing butchers' shops.) The south side was formalized with the building of the slightly larger Basilica Julia by Julius Caesar (100–44 BCE), who also rebuilt the Senate House or Curia Julia (pages 238–39) adjacent to the Basilica Aemilia.

Julius Caesar claimed to be descended from Venus. In addition to establishing a prominent presence in the old Forum, he also built, just to the north, a new Temple of Venus, placed axially in its own rectangular precinct. This established the pattern for the later imperial forum, as in Trajan's Forum and the Forum of Augustus, dominated by the overbearing Temple of Mars Ultor, which was a declaration of vengeance on Julius Caesar's assassins. The forum was a place where public rhetoric was turned into stone.

1 Ground Plan, Agora

1 Royal Stoa
2 Arsenal (weapons store)
3 Stoa of Zeus
4 Altar of Twelve Gods
5 Hephaisteion (temple)
6 Temple of Apollo Patroos
7 Bouleuterion (council chamber)
8 Monument of the Eponymous Heroes
9 Middle Stoa
10 Fountain House
11 South Stoa
12 East Stoa
13 Mint
14 Stoa of Attalos
15 Speaker's platform
16 Stoa Poikile

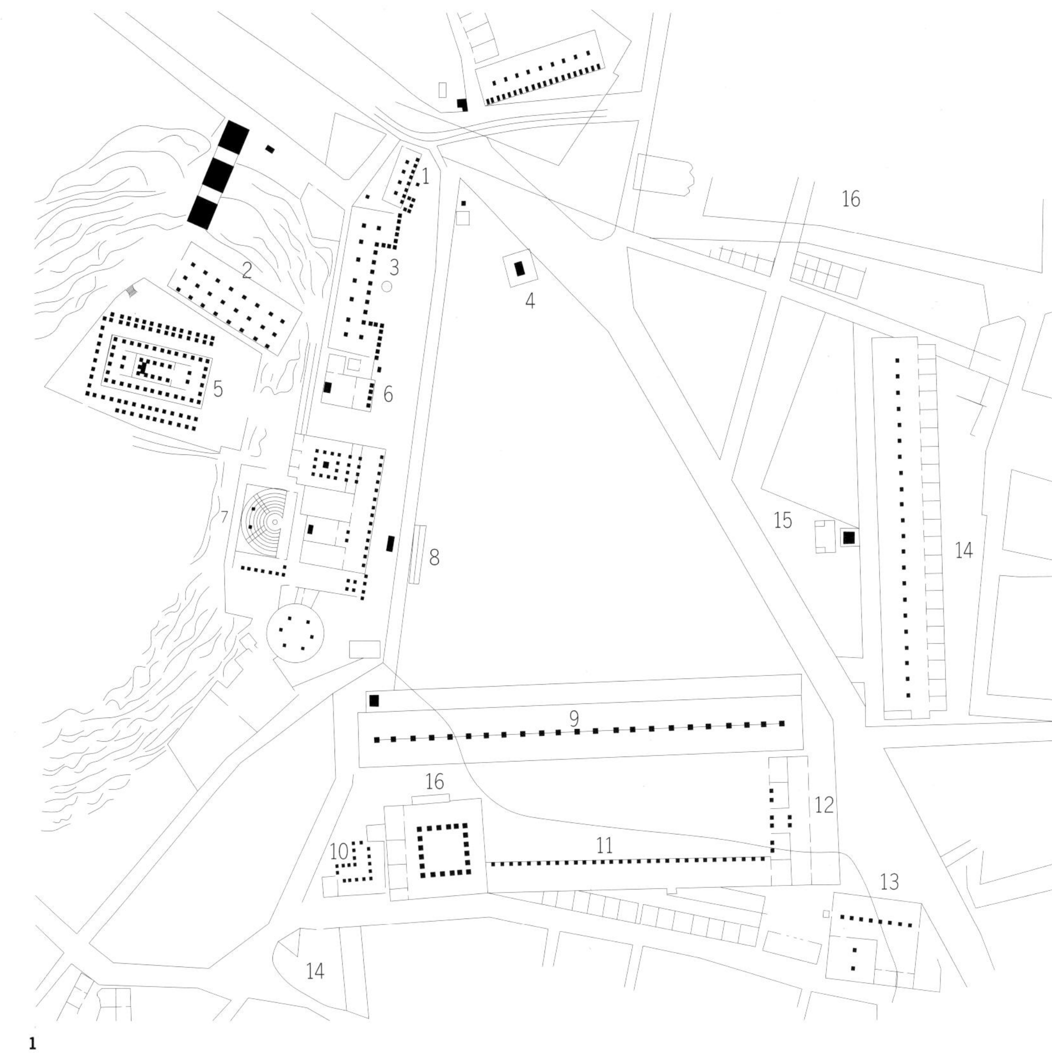

1

2

2 Ground Plan, Forum

1 Prison
2 Temple of Concord
3 Arch of Severus
4 Temple of Vespasian
5 Navel of Rome
6 Golden Milestone
7 Portico of the Twelve Gods
8 Temple of Saturn
9 Basilica Julia
10 Arch of Tiberius
11 New Rostra
12 Column of Phocas
13 Equestrian Statue of Domitian
14 Equestrian Statue of Constantine
15 Vestibule of Domitian's Palace
16 Guards' House
17 Temple of Castor and Pollux
18 Spring of Juturna
19 Temple of Vesta
20 House of Vestals
21 Arch of Augustus
22 Temple of Caesar
23 Temple of Antonius and Faustina
24 Basilica Aemilia
25 Senate House

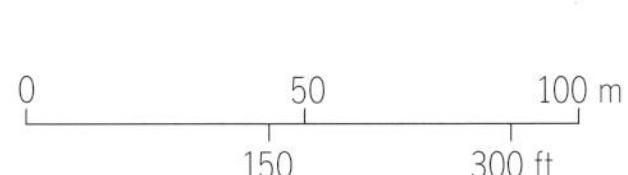

Piazza del Campo | Piazza Navona

Siena, Italy | Rome, Italy

The Piazza del Campo in Siena (above left) took shape in the early fourteenth century, making an appropriate civic setting for activities that must already have been taking place. It is an open space, which used to be in between three settlements on neighbouring hills. The settlements grew together but retained separate identities as neighbourhoods in the larger city. Twice a year these districts maintain an old tradition by competing against one another in a horse race that is run round the edges of the piazza – a colourful spectacle that draws a tightly packed crowd into the middle of the space.

The piazza is dominated by the city hall – the Palazzo Pubblico – which was begun in 1297. It is an imposing building, decorated with frescoes inside and signalling its importance with a huge brick tower. Siena was once a rival to Florence, but plague killed off a large proportion of its inhabitants in 1349 and it never caught up. Siena's cathedral was going to be the world's largest, but after the plague the project was cut back, and the transept of the original design (which had been built) was turned into the nave, while the intended nave still stands incomplete. For a long time, the city's built fabric was greater than the resident population needed, so the medieval buildings there did not face the redevelopment that occurred in more prosperous places and the medieval city centre remains harmoniously intact.

The piazza is approached by shady cavernous streets too narrow for modern traffic. They converge from all parts of Siena, and anyone crossing the city is bound to cross the piazza unless there is a deliberate decision to avoid it.

For anyone stepping from the confines of an approaching street into the large open space, which slopes down to the Palazzo Pubblico, there is a sudden awareness of contrast. The space is bounded by a continuous run of domestic buildings, mostly five or six storeys high, broken only by narrow interruptions for the roads. There is a low rectangular fountain at the top of the slope, with finely sculpted panels round three of its four sides. The piazza's brick paving is laid out with radiating lines that focus at the Palazzo Pubblico. The piazza is the work of many hands and many designers, but their aims were in harmony.

In any city, the lines of streets and squares tell stories that go deeper than those of individual buildings. An individual owner can rebuild a single structure, but it takes a more significant power to change the route of a built-up road or to establish a new open space. The Piazza Navona in Rome (above right) would seem to be a baroque development because of the fountains and buildings that give it its architectural character. The most prominent of these are the church of Sant'Agnese in Agone by Francesco Borromini (1599–1667), the Palazzo Pamphili by Girolamo Rainaldi (1570–1655) for Pope Innocent X, and the Fountain of the Four Rivers by Gianlorenzo Bernini (1598–1680) – a lively writhing base supporting a trophy obelisk, brought to Rome from Egypt in ancient times.

Despite the powerful patronage involved, the general lines of the piazza remained unchanged, conserving the outline of an ancient stadium, the Stadium of Domitian or Circus Agonalis, dedicated in 86. It is this site of competitions (*agones*) from which the church takes its name. The stadium was built for athletic events, and long ago there was a monumental structure there, supporting raked seating in the same way as at the Colosseum (pages 18–19) but on a smaller scale. Every part of that structure has gone, with many of its components having been reused in the surrounding buildings, but the general line of it survives.

1 Ground Plan, Piazza del Campo

1 Palazzo Pubblico
2 Fountain
3 Market hall

0 50 m
150 ft

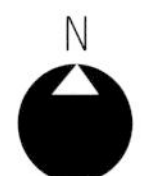

1

2 Ground Plan, Piazza Navona

1 S. Agnese
2 Fountain of the Four Rivers
3 Palazzo Pamphilj
4 S. Giacomo degli Spagnoli

0 30 m
100 ft

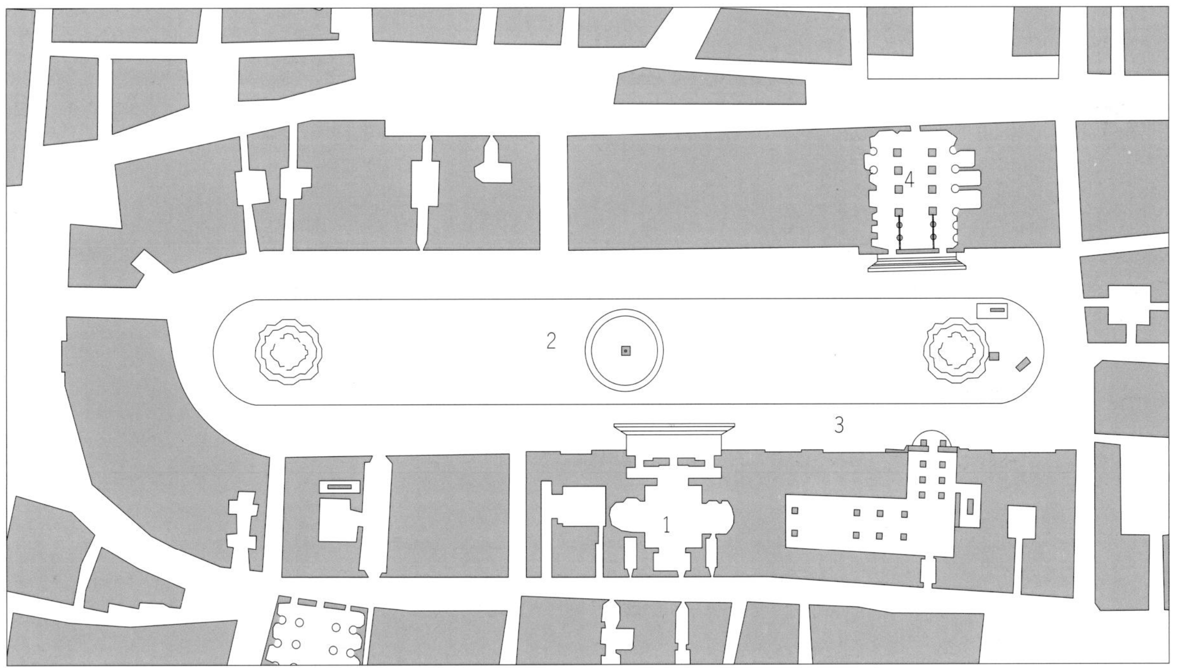

2

Place des Vosges | Tiananmen Square

Paris, France; 1605–12 | Beijing, China; from 1651

The Place des Vosges (above left) was the public square in Paris to be built to a unified design – and the first one anywhere in Europe since the forums of imperial Rome.

Commissioned by Henri IV in the first decade of the seventeenth century, it was built on the site of a medieval royal palace, the Hôtel Tourelle, and was known until 1800 as the Place Royale. In 1559 Henri II had died there, from injuries sustained while jousting in the grounds, and his widow, Catherine de' Medici, sold most of the vast estate to pay for the Tuileries Palace.

In addition to the Place Royale, Henri IV changed the face of Paris by constructing the Grande Galérie of the Louvre, and extending the Île de la Cité by building up the land on which the Place Dauphine was built, creating a bridge to that island from each bank of the Seine in the shape of the Pont Neuf. The Place Dauphine was laid out in 1609, while the Place Royale was under construction, but none of the original buildings survives. The Place Royale (Place des Vosges) is substantially intact.

The central pavilions in the north and south sides of the Place des Vosges are gateways, slightly taller than the buildings round the central open space, which is laid out as a perfect geometric square. These pavilions sit on a vaulted structure that allows a road and two pavements to enter the square. The brick vaults continue round the perimeter, beneath the front part of the aristocratic dwellings above.

Bound together by the identical façades of the houses and the clear geometry of its design, the Place des Vosges seems much closer to a palace courtyard than a medieval marketplace. Early residents included many for whom the Louvre would have been accessible, most famously Cardinal Richelieu (1585–1642). The central area was originally paved, but it is now a garden with fountains and clipped trees, and makes a serene oasis among the little streets around it.

Tiananmen Square in Beijing (above right) is similarly associated with heads of state. It takes its name from the Tiananmen (Gate of Heaven's Pacification) of the Forbidden City, which stands centrally on the square's north side. A square was originally set out here in 1651, making a space in between the palace and ceremonial gate, which came to be known as the Gate of China. This gate was demolished in the 1960s, when Mao Zedong extended the space to make it the largest urban square in the world, capable of accommodating up to 500,000 people. It ran all the way to one of Beijing's historic city gates – Zhengyangmen (Gate of the Zenith Sun) – a distance of about one kilometre.

The west side of the square is defined by the Great Hall of the Chinese People, and the east by the National Museum of China. Monuments within the square include the Chairman Mao Memorial Hall and the Monument to the People's Heroes, which is 38 metres (125 feet) high.

The scale of Tiananmen Square is so vast that human individuals seem infinitesimally small, and the place comes into its own when crowds of people gather there to give displays of coordinated and synchronized movement. The governmental character of the place, which comes from the uses of the surrounding buildings, makes it a site for official parades and for popular protest.

1 Ground Plan, Place des Vosges

1 Pavillon du Roy
2 Pavillon de la Reine
3 Statue of Louis XIII

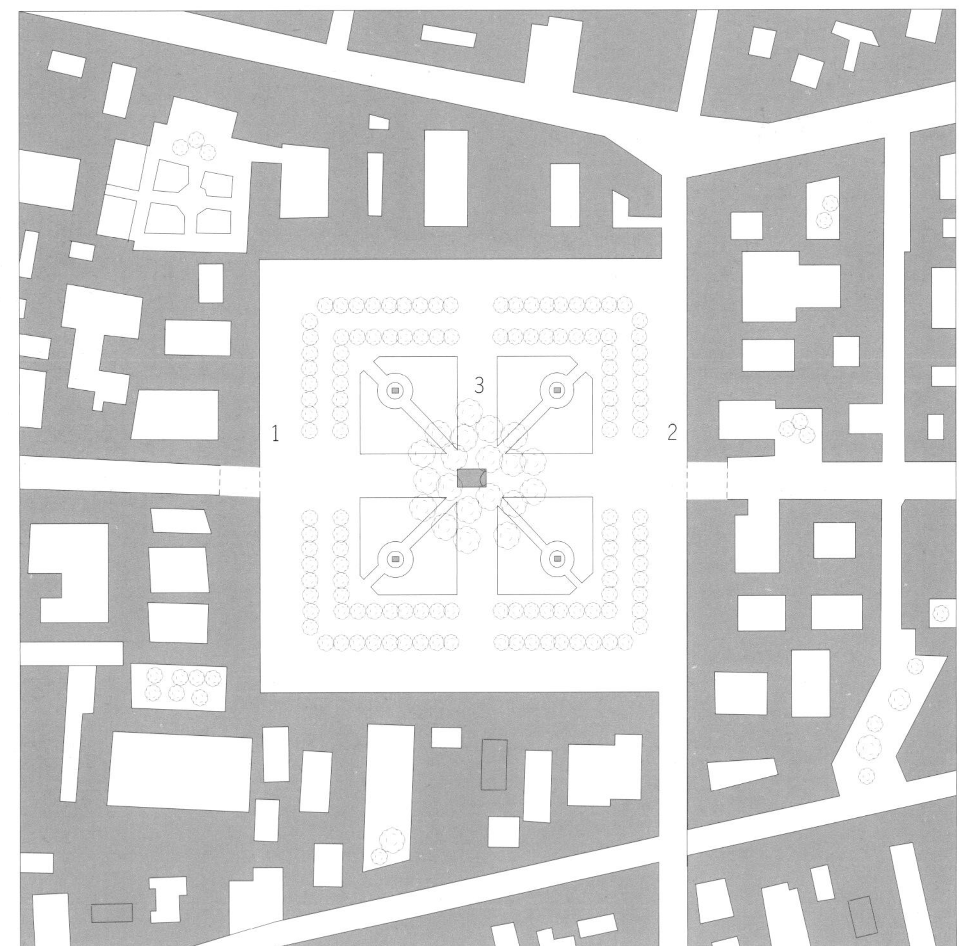

1

2 Ground Plan, Tiananmen Square

1 Tiananmen Gate (to the Forbidden City)
2 Great Hall of the People
3 Monument to the People's Heroes
4 Chinese National Museum
5 Chairman Mao Memorial Hall

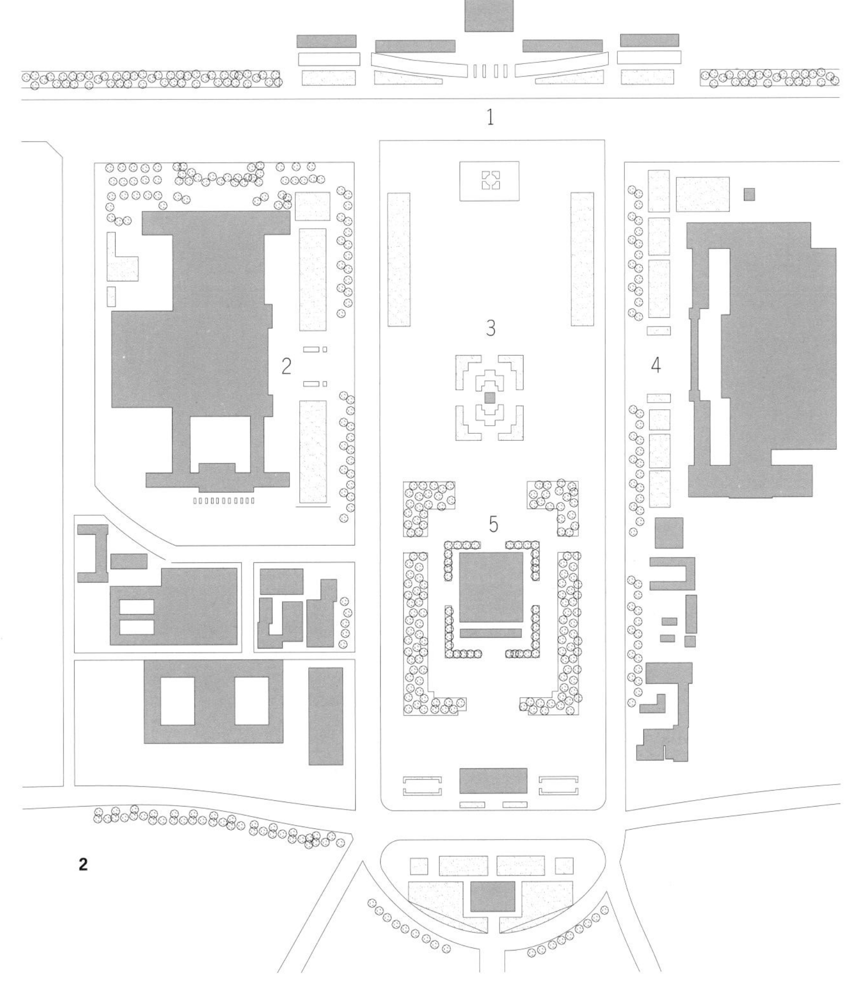

2

Piazza San Marco | Potsdamer Platz

Venice, Italy | Berlin, Germany

In a place like Venice, where land is in short supply, it may seem profligate to devote as large an area as the Piazza San Marco to open space, and yet the vast piazza seems essential to the vitality of the city (above left). The canal and the lagoon open up spectacular views that are unequalled anywhere, but the glancing encounters and human exchanges that make a city live are not much more likely to occur on a waterway than they do on a motorway.

The streets and alleys of Venice seem to lead pedestrians back to the piazza, whether or not it was their intention to go there. The Grand Canal may be the place for display, but the Piazza San Marco conveys a sense of having arrived in the city, and is the place to meet people.

The east end of the piazza is defined by the west front of the cathedral, dedicated to St Mark. It is a Byzantine building, but enlivened by the Gothic spikiness in its many finials. It puts on a fine show, with its gilding, mosaics and statuary, including some looted from Constantinople during the fourth Crusade (1204), such as the predecessors of the famous Roman horses that preside over the square.

Piazza San Marco developed over several centuries but was given façades that harmonized. The two main buildings, which face one another, running along the north and south sides of the square, were built in the sixteenth and seventeenth centuries, with an open arcade at their base. For reasons lost to history, but no doubt partly to show that he was in charge following his conquest of 1797, Napoleon demolished the buildings that closed off the west end of the square, including a church, and commissioned a new building in a more severe neoclassical manner. It did nothing to impair the coherence of the whole, but made him no friends in Venice – nor did the fact that he took the Roman horses to Paris. They returned to their loggia in the Piazza San Marco soon after the Battle of Waterloo in 1815, but in the 1980s they were replaced by replicas. The originals are conserved in museum conditions inside the basilica.

Potzdamer Platz in Berlin (above right) underwent more severe trauma. It developed as a traffic junction at the edge of the city, rather than a public square, and it was adjacent to the classically composed Leipziger Platz – a planned octagonal form. But roads and tramlines converged from all directions to bring a multitude of people to Potsdamer Platz, which acquired a distinct identity. Karl Friedrich Schinkel (1781–1841) formalized the arrangement with the Potsdam Gate – a pair of Doric pavilions facing one another to make an entrance to Leipziger Platz and the city, but Berlin's subsequent growth meant that Potsdamer Platz came to be seen as the lively commercial centre of Berlin and its cosmopolitan nightlife. It was one of the earliest places in the world where circulation was regulated by a traffic light.

The buildings in both Potsdamer Platz and Leipziger Platz suffered significant bomb damage during World War II, and in 1961, when Berlin was partitioned by the Berlin Wall (pages 188–89), the squares' buildings were demolished completely. The wall ran across both spaces. Since Potsdamer Platz in particular had been seen as the focus of the city's vitality, its division and eradication acquired symbolic importance. It was there more than anywhere that the building of the wall seemed to will the death of the city.

After the reunification of Germany in 1989–90, the redevelopment of Potsdamer Platz became both symbolically important and commercially very attractive. The new buildings assert the importance of the place, without giving a particularly composed form to the public square. Nevertheless the area's commercial vitality is thoroughly restored, and the capital once again has a beating heart.

1 Ground Plan, Piazza San Marco

1 Piazza
2 Campanile
3 Basilica San Marco
4 Piazzetta
5 Doge's Palace

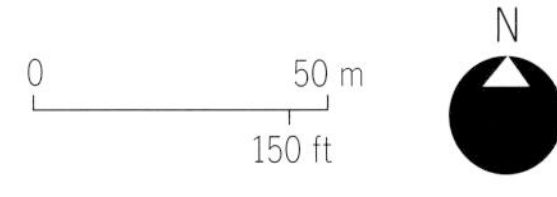

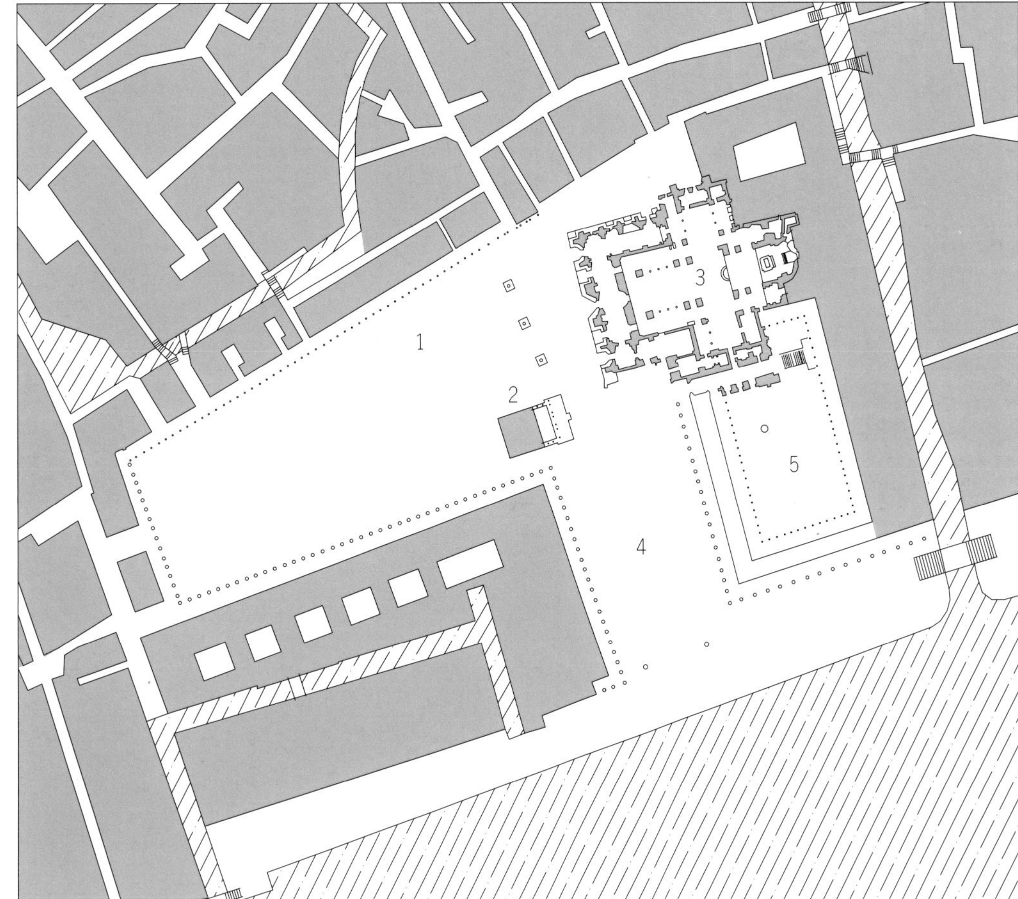

1

1 Ground Plan, Potsdamer Platz

1 Potsdamer Platz
2 Leipziger Platz

0 50 m
150 ft

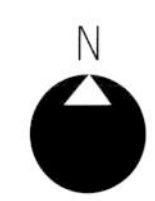

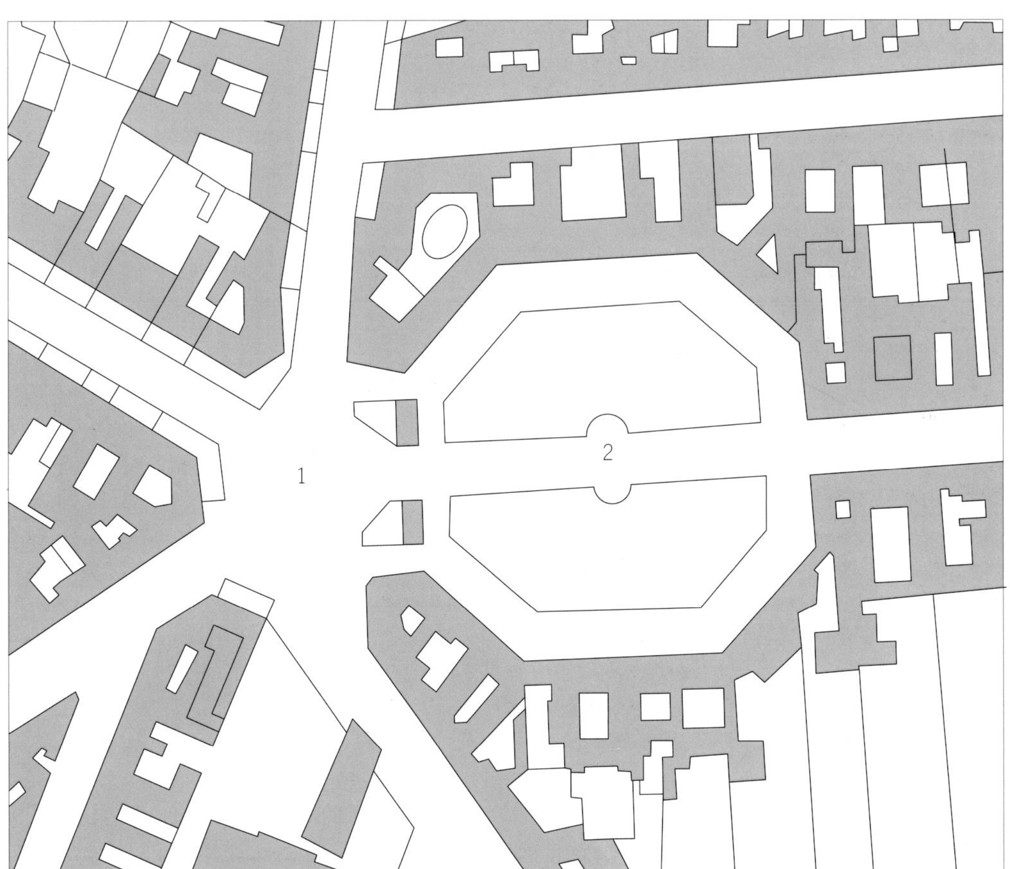

2

Further Reading

Suggestions for further reading are limited to books with a wide range. Many of the individual buildings and architects featured in *Key Historical Buildings* have entire books dedicated to them, but no book with that level of detail is included here. Many of the books listed have their own suggestions for further reading, which, if pursued, could proliferate into a lifetime's reading for anyone who has the inclination. Some of the books are bigger than others. Europe has more detailed coverage than the other continents, partly because the buildings there have been more studied and written about.

Modern architecture is part of an international culture, with many leading architects designing buildings outside their country of residence. The Sydney Opera House was designed by a Danish architect, and its design is more closely linked with Scandinavian tradition than with Australian, even though it has become emblematic of Australia. Similarly, Mies van der Rohe's buildings in New York and Chicago derive from the German building culture of the 1920s, even though they seem to be such a prominent part of the mid-twentieth-century American scene. So the list includes some books about international modern architecture and goes on to categorize books about earlier periods by region.

General

Dan Cruickshank (ed.), *Sir Banister Fletcher's A History of Architecture, 20th Edition* (Oxford: Architectural Press, 1996)
The 'classic' reference work in architectural history for architects. It first appeared in 1896, but none of the original text survives in recent editions.

Michael Fazio, Marian Moffat and Lawrence Wodehouse, *A World History of Architecture* (London: Laurence King, 2008)
Offers a good orientation in world architecture.

Paul Oliver (ed.), *Encyclopedia of Vernacular Architecture of the World*, 3 vols. (Cambridge, UK: Cambridge University Press, 1997)
A monumental work that catalogues varieties of ordinary buildings from around the globe.

International modern architecture

Alan Colquhoun, *Modern Architecture* (Oxford: Oxford University Press, 2002)

Kenneth Frampton, *Modern Architecture: A Critical History* (London: Thames and Hudson, 1980, revised 2007)

Africa

Dieter Arnold, *The Encyclopaedia of Ancient Egyptian Architecture* (London: I.B. Tauris, 2003)

N. Elleh, *African Architecture: Evolution and Transformation* (New York: McGraw Hill, 1996)

Peter Garlake, *Early Art and Architecture of Africa* (Oxford: Oxford University Press, 2002)

America: North

David P. Handlin, *American Architecture* (London: Thames and Hudson, 1997)

Tom Martinson, *The Atlas of American Architecture* (New York: Rizzoli, 2009)

Dell Upton, *Architecture of the United States* (Oxford: Oxford University Press, 1998)

America: Central and South

Adriana Von Hagen and Craig Morris, *The Cities of the Ancient Andes* (London: Thames and Hudson, 1998)

Michael E. Moseley, *The Incas and their Ancestors: The Archaeology of Peru* (London: Thames and Hudson, 2001).

Charles Phillips, *The Art and Architecture of the Aztec and Maya: An Illustrated Encyclopedia of the Buildings, Sculptures and Art of the Peoples of Mesoamerica* (New York: Lorenz, 2004)

Henri Stierlin, *Living Architecture: Ancient Mexico* (New York: Grosset and Dunlap, 1968)

Asia

Gaudenz Domenig, Peter J. M. Nas and Reimar Schefold (eds.), *Indonesian Houses: Tradition and Transformation in Vernacular Architecture* (Jakarta: Kitlv Press, 2004)

J. C. Harle, *The Art and Architecture of the Indian Sub-Continent* (London: Penguin, 1986)

E. B. Havel, *Encyclopaedia of Architecture in the Indian Subcontinent* (New Delhi: Aryan Books, 2002)

Alexander Soper, *The Art and Architecture of China*, revised by Laurence Sickman (London: Penguin, 1979)

Liang Ssu-Ch'eng, *Chinese Architecture: A Pictorial History* (Cambridge, MA: MIT Press, 1984)

Nancy S. Steinhardt (ed.), *A History of Chinese Architecture* (New Haven, CT: Yale University Press, 2003)

Roxana Waterson, *The Living House: An Anthropology of Architecture in South-East Asia* (New York: Watson-Guptill, 1998)

Australia

Patrick Bingham-Hall, *Austral Eden: 200 Years of Australian Architecture* (Boorowa, NSW: Watermark Press, 2000)

Charles Pearcy Mountford, *Ayers Rock: Its People, Their Beliefs and Their Art* (Sydney: Angus and Robertson, 1965)

Europe

Barry Bergdoll, *European Architecture 1750–1890* (Oxford: Oxford University Press, 2000)

Axel Boethius, *Etruscan and Early Roman Architecture* (London: Penguin, 1970)

William C. Brumfield, *A History of Russian Architecture* (Seattle: University of Washington Press, 2003)

Nicola Coldstream, *Medieval Architecture* (Oxford: Oxford University Press, 2002)

Kenneth John Conant, *Carolingian and Romanesque Architecture 800–1200* (London: Penguin, 1974)

Mark Wilson Jones, *Principles of Roman Architecture* (New Haven, CT: Yale University Press, 2003)

Richard Krautheimer, *Early Christian and Byzantine Architecture* (London: Penguin, 1965)

Arnold Walter Lawrence, *Greek Architecture*, revised by Richard Tomlinson (New Haven, CT: Yale University Press, 1996)

Nikolaus Pevsner, *An Outline of European Architecture*, (London: Thames and Hudson, 2009)

Lyn Rodley, *Byzantine Art and Architecture: An Introduction* (Cambridge, UK: Cambridge University Press, 1994)

Roger Stalley, *Early Medieval Architecture* (Oxford: Oxford University Press, 1999)

John Travlos, *Pictorial Dictionary of Ancient Athens* (New York: Hacker Art Books, 1981)

John Bryan Ward-Perkins, *Roman Imperial Architecture* (London: Penguin, 1981)

David Watkin, *A History of Western Architecture*, 5th edition (London: Laurence King, 2011)

Middle East

Richard Ettinghausen and Oleg Grabar, *The Art and Architecture of Islam 650–1250* (London: Penguin, 1987)

Index

Page numbers in **bold** denote main entries.

Picture Credits

All photos © ALAMY apart from the following:

14 © Paul M.R. Maeyaert
16 Craig & Marie Mauzy, Athens
26 *left* Corbis © Gideon Mendel; *right* Corbis © Werner Forman
36 *left* © Paul M.R. Maeyaert; *right* Andrew Ballantyne
40 *both* © Corbis
42 *both* Richard Weston
48 *left* Corbis © Yann Arthus-Bertrand; *right* Laurence King Publishing
54 *left* Corbis © Mimmo Jodice; *right* © Fotografica Foglia, Naples
56 *right* Andrew Ballantyne
58 *right* Corbis © Paul Almasy
66 © Paul M.R. Maeyaert
68 Corbis © Bob Krist
72 *left* Corbis © Richard Bryant/Arcaid
76 *both* The Art Archive/Gianni Dagli Orti
78 akg-images/A.F. Kersting
80 *both* Andrew Ballantyne
86 *left* © DACS 2011; *right* akg-images/Erich Lessing © DACS 2011
88 *both* Paul Koslowski © FLC/ADAGP, Paris and DACS, London 2011
90 *left* Corbis © G. E. Kidder Smith © DACS 2011; *right* Corbis © Underwood & Underwood © DACS 2011
92 *both* Richard Weston © DACS 2011
98 *right* Laurence King Publishing
104 *right* Andrew Ballantyne
108 *both* © Vincenzo Pirozzi, Rome
110 *right* Fotolia © bulldognoi
112 *right* Fotolia © Paul Fisher
130 *right* © Paul M.R. Maeyaert
138 *left* Corbis © Werner Dieterich/Westend61
140 *right* Fotolia © Ashwin
148 *left* Alinari Archives/Seat Archive; *right* © 2011 Photo Scala, Florence, courtesy of Diocesi di Mantova
158 © Inigo Bujedo Aguirre, London
160 *right* Corbis © Pawel Libera
162 *right* Corbis © Remi Benali
168 *right* Henrietta Heald
170 *right* The Art Archive/Museum of Carthage/Gianni Dagli Orti
172 *left* © Paul M.R. Maeyaert; *right* Andrew Ballantyne
180 *right* Thinkstock/Hemera
182 *left* TopFoto/Roger-Viollet; *right* © Norbert Blau
186 *right* Peter Silver and Will McLean
200 *both* Andrew Ballantyne
220 *left* akg-images; *right* akg-images/Florian Profitlich
222 © DACS 2011
224 Corbis © Angelo Hornak
226 *right* Corbis © Michael S. Yamashita
230 *right* Corbis © Imaginechina; *both* © OMA/DACS 2011
236 *right* Getty Images/Time & Life Pictures
240 © Paul M.R. Maeyaert
246 *left* Corbis © Yann Arthus-Bertrand
248 Corbis © Carl & Ann Purcell
250 *left* © Paul M.R. Maeyaert
256 *left* © Peter Ashworth, London; *right* Corbis © Hulton-Deutsch Collection
258 Arie den Dikken
260 Richard Weston © DACS 2011
264 Getty Images/Robert Harding World Imagery/Luca Tettoni
268 © Vincenzo Pirozzi, Rome
280 *left* Corbis © Historical Picture Archive
284 © DACS 2011
290 *right* Corbis © Bob Krist
292 *left* © Vincenzo Pirozzi, Rome; *right* © Paul M.R. Maeyaert
294 *right* © Quattrone, Florence
296 © Vincenzo Pirozzi, Rome
310 *right* Corbis © Diego Azubel/epa

Drawings of works by Alvar Aalto are © DACS 2011
Drawings of works by Le Corbusier are © FLC/ADAGP, Paris and DACS, London 2011
Drawings of works by Victor Horta are © DACS 2011
Drawings of works by OMA are © OMA/DACS 2011
Drawings of works by Gerrit Rietveld are © DACS 2011
Drawings of works by Ludwig Mies van der Rohe are © DACS 2011
Drawings of works by Hans Scharoun are © DACS 2011

Drawing Credits

Carolyn Fahey, Sally Anne Atkinson and Giles Shorter deserve special mention for their roles in co-ordinating the production of drawings and in completing and amending the work when information was sometimes difficult to find.

Individual drawings were made by:

Sally Anne Atkinson
Christopher Beale
Rebecca Berry
Joanna Doherty
Carolyn Fahey
Seun Idowu Gbolade
Sarah Louise Gibbons
Tanya Haslehurst
James Harrington
Ruth Heyes
Dominic Lamb
Ceri Lewis
Jo Meyer
Edward Perera
Rachel Phillips
Alexander Price
Glenn Robinson
Nicholas Simpson

About the CD

The attached CD-ROM can be read on both Windows and Macintosh computers. All the material on the CD-ROM is copyright protected and is for private use only.

All drawings in the book and on the CD-ROM were specially created for this publication and are based on the architects' original drawings held in archives or supplied by the architects, or on previously published material either in professional journals or in books. Every effort has been made to ensure accuracy in the drawings.

The CD-ROM includes files for all the plans, sections and elevations featured in the case studies of the book. The drawings for each building are contained in a numbered folder as listed below. They are supplied in two versions: the files with the suffix '.eps' are vector Illustrator EPS files but can be opened using other graphics programs such as Acrobat and Photoshop; all the files with the suffix '.dwg' are generic CAD format files and can be opened in a variety of CAD programs.

The generic '.dwg' file format does not support 'solid fill' utilized by many architectural CAD programs. All the information is embedded within the file and can be reinstated within supporting CAD programs. Select the polygon required and change the 'Attributes' to 'Solid'; the colour information should automatically be retrieved. To reinstate the 'Walls', select all objects within the 'Walls' layer/class and amend their 'Attributes' to 'Solid'.

The numbered folders correspond to the following buildings:

01. Uluru
02. Great Pyramid of Khufu
03. Parthenon
04. Colosseum
05. Temple 1, Tik'al
06. Great Stupa of Sanchi
07. Hagia Sophia
08. Ise Grand Shrine
09. Great Enclosure, Great Zimbabwe
10. Twin Pagodas
11. St Peter's Basilica
12. Taj Mahal
13. Eiffel Tower
14. Empire State Building
15. Cathedral of Light
16. Sydney Opera House
17. Judge Harry Pregerson Interchange
18. Houses at Catal Huyuk and Troy
19. Houses at Nagano and Skara Brae
20. Igloo, Tipi and Bedouin Tent
21. Villa of the Mysteries
22. Houses in Burkina Faso and Kythera
23. Karo Batak Houses
24. Le Thoronet Abbey
25. Dürer House
26. Palazzo Medici
27. Chateau of Chambord
28. Chateau of Ancy-le-Franc
29. Villa Capra
30. Hardwick Hall
31. Tea Houses, Katsura Imperial Villa
32. Chateau of Maisons-Laffitte
33. Berrington Hall
34. Queen's Hamlet, Versailles
35. Monticello
36. Neuschwanstein
37. Horta House
38. Unité d'Habitation
39. Lake Shore Drive Apartments
40. Schröder House
41. Megalithic Temples
42. Great Ziggurat of Ur
43. Great Temple of Amon-Ra
44. Temple of Apollo, Delphi
45. Temple of Apollo Epikourios
46. Maison Carrée
47. Pantheon
48. Mahabodhi Temple
49. Dome of the Rock
50. Great Mosque, Damascus
51. Shore Temple
52. Mosque Cathedral, Córdoba
53. Borobudur Stupa
54. Lingaraj Temple
55. Kandariya Mahadeva Temple
56. Durham Cathedral
57. Temple of Kukulkan
58. Basilica of the Madeleine
59. Angkor Wat
60. Stave Church
61. Bourges Cathedral
62. Cologne Cathedral
63. Konark Sun Temple
64. Golden Pavilion Temple
65. Goharshad Mosque
66. Santa Maria del Santo Spirito
67. Sant'Andrea of Mantova
68. Suleyman Mosque
69. St Basil's Cathedral
70. San Carlo alle Quattro Fontane
71. Vierzehnheiligen
72. Sagrada Família
73. Westminster Cathedral
74. Great Mosque of Djenné
75. Crystal Cathedral
76. Acropolis
77. Carthage Harbour and Naval Base
78. Pont du Gard
79. Frontiers of the Roman Empire
80. Himeji Castle
81. Great Wall of China
82. Mostar Bridge
83. Neuf-Brisach
84. Carcassonne
85. Forth Bridge
86. Berlin Wall
87. Stoa of Attalos
88. Trajan's Markets
89. Medina, Fes
90. Trinity College Library
91. Royal Saltworks
92. Engelsberg Ironworks
93. The Lawn
94. Albert Dock
95. Saltaire
96. Bibliothèque Nationale
97. Galleria Vittorio Emmanuele II
98. St Pancras Railway Station
99. Keretapi Railway Station
100. Grand Central Terminal
101. AEG Turbine Factory
102. Seagram Building
103. Dulles Airport
104. Fuji TV Headquarters Building
105. Petronas Towers
106. China Central TV Headquarters
107. Megaron of Pylos
108. Pnyx
109. Curia Julia
110. Alhambra
111. Forbidden City
112. Machu Picchu
113. Topkapi Palace
114. Imperial Palace of Kyoto
115. Palace of Versailles
116. Residenz, Würzburg
117. Richmond Capitol
118. Palace of Westminster
119. Hilversum Town Hall
120. Säynatsälo Town Hall
121. Great Bath, Mohenjo-Daro
122. Theatre, Epidauros
123. Theatre of Marcellus
124. Baths of Caracalla
125. Teatro Olimpico
126. Globe Theatre
127. Louvre
128. Altes Museum
129. Crystal Palace
130. Opéra Garnier
131. Philharmonie
132. Tomb of Mausolus
133. Qin Shi Huang Imperial Necropolis
134. Memorial Columns
135. Pazzi Chapel
136. Tempietto
137. L'Église du Dôme
138. Lincoln Memorial
139. Sun Yat-sen Mausoleum
140. Agora of Athens/Forum of Rome
141. Piazza del Campo/Piazza Navona
142. Place des Vosges/Tiananmen Square
143. Piazza San Marco/Potsdamer Platz

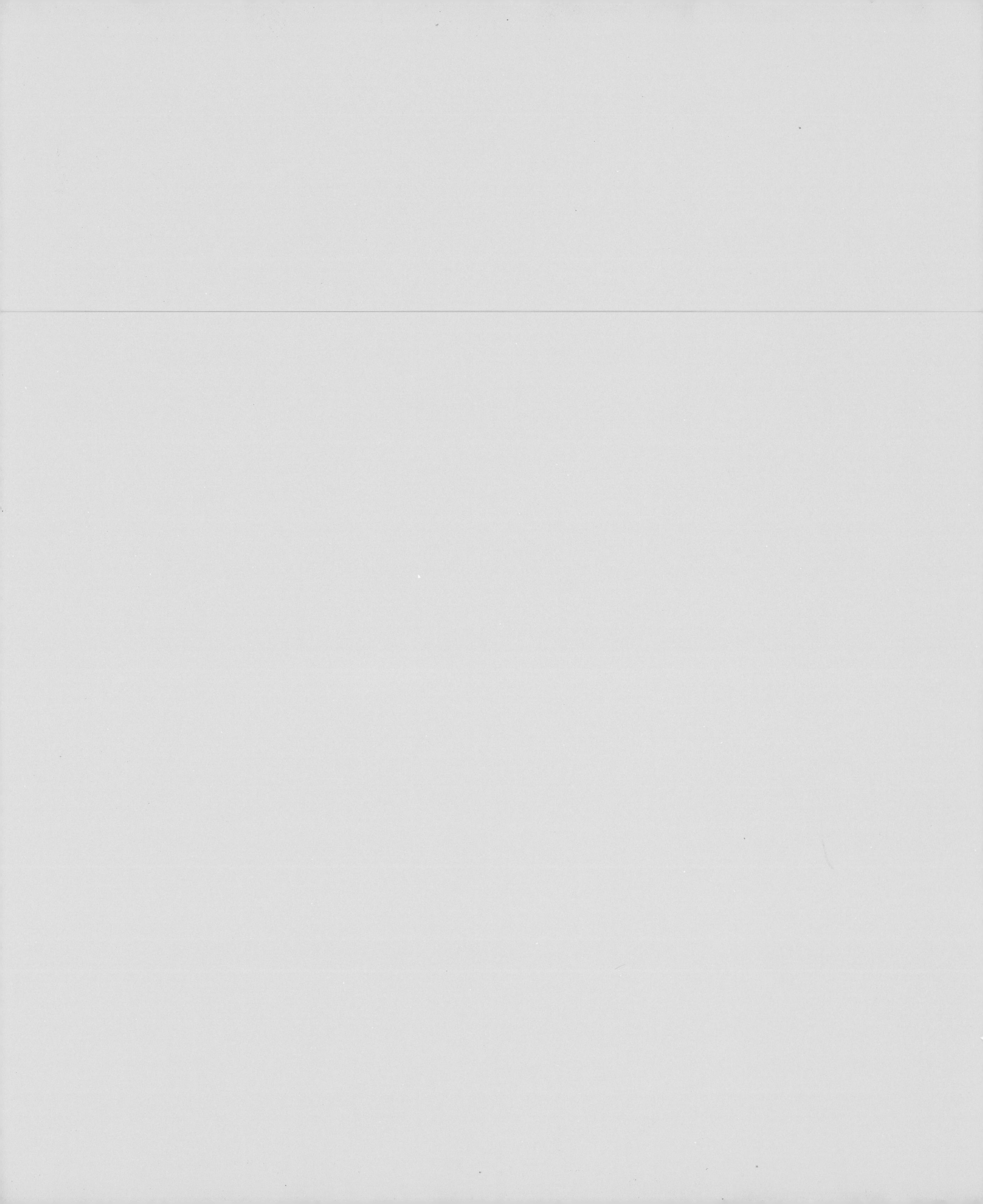